The Handbook of the History

Blackwell Handbooks in Linguistics

This outstanding multi-volume series covers all the major subdisciplines within linguistics today and, when complete, will offer a comprehensive survey of linguistics as a whole.

Already published:

The Handbook of Child Language
Edited by Paul Fletcher and Brian MacWhinney

The Handbook of Phonological Theory
Edited by John A. Goldsmith

The Handbook of Contemporary Semantic Theory
Edited by Shalom Lappin

The Handbook of Sociolinguistics
Edited by Florian Coulmas

The Handbook of Phonetic Sciences
Edited by William J. Hardcastle and John Laver

The Handbook of Morphology
Edited by Andrew Spencer and Arnold Zwicky

The Handbook of Japanese Linguistics
Edited by Natsuko Tsujimura

The Handbook of Linguistics
Edited by Mark Aronoff and Janie Rees-Miller

The Handbook of Contemporary Syntactic Theory
Edited by Mark Baltin and Chris Collins

The Handbook of Discourse Analysis
Edited by Deborah Schiffrin, Deborah Tannen, and Heidi E. Hamilton

The Handbook of Language Variation and Change
Edited by J. K. Chambers, Peter Trudgill, and Natalie Schilling-Estes

The Handbook of Historical Linguistics
Edited by Brian D. Joseph and Richard D. Janda

The Handbook of Language and Gender
Edited by Janet Holmes and Miriam Meyerhoff

The Handbook of Second Language Acquisition
Edited by Catherine J. Doughty and Michael H. Long

The Handbook of Bilingualism
Edited by Tej K. Bhatia and William C. Ritchie

The Handbook of Pragmatics
Edited by Laurence R. Horn and Gregory Ward

The Handbook of Applied Linguistics
Edited by Alan Davies and Catherine Elder

The Handbook of Speech Perception
Edited by David B. Pisoni and Robert E. Remez

The Blackwell Companion to Syntax, Volumes I–V
Edited by Martin Everaert and Henk van Riemsdijk

The Handbook of the History of English
Edited by Ans van Kemenade and Bettelou Los

The Handbook of English Linguistics
Edited by Bas Aarts and April McMahon

The Handbook of World Englishes
Edited by Braj B. Kachru; Yamuna Kachru, and Cecil L. Nelson

The Handbook of Educational Linguistics
Edited by Bernard Spolsky and Francis M. Hult

The Handbook of Clinical Linguistics
Edited by Martin J. Ball, Michael R. Perkins, Nicole Müller, and Sara Howard

The Handbook of the History of English

Edited by

Ans van Kemenade
and Bettelou Los

A John Wiley & Sons, Ltd., Publication

Dedicated to the memory of Richard M. Hogg (1944–2007)

This paperback edition first published 2009

Edition history: Blackwell Publishing Ltd (hardback, 2006)

Blackwell Publishing was acquired by John Wiley & Sons in February 2007. Blackwell's publishing program has been merged with Wiley's global Scientific, Technical, and Medical business to form Wiley-Blackwell.

Registered Office
John Wiley & Sons Ltd, The Atrium, Southern Gate, Chichester, West Sussex, PO19 8SQ, United Kingdom

Editorial Offices
350 Main Street, Malden, MA 02148-5020, USA
9600 Garsington Road, Oxford, OX4 2DQ, UK
The Atrium, Southern Gate, Chichester, West Sussex, PO19 8SQ, UK

For details of our global editorial offices, for customer services, and for information about how to apply for permission to reuse the copyright material in this book please see our website at www.wiley.com/wiley-blackwell.

Library of Congress Cataloging-in-Publication Data
The handbook of the history of English / edited by Ans van Kemenade and Bettelou Los.
p. cm. — (Blackwell handbooks in linguistics)
Includes bibliographical references and index.
ISBN: 978-0-631-23344-2 (hardcover : alk. paper) — ISBN: 978-1-4051-8786-2 (pbk : alk. paper)
1. English language—History. I. Kemenade, Ans van, 1954– II. Los, Bettelou. III. Series.

PE1075.H335 2006
420.9—dc22

2005033628

A catalogue record for this book is available from the British Library.

Set in 10/12 Palatino by Graphicraft Ltd, Hong Kong
Printed and bound in Malaysia by KHL Printing Co Sdn Bhd

1 2009

Contents

Editors' Introduction

The format of this Handbook is not a traditional one, as will immediately be clear from the Contents list. Its chapters are not arranged chronologically, moving from Old to Middle to Modern English, or linguistically, moving from phonology to morphology to syntax. We realized from the start that it was going to be impossible to achieve any degree of exhaustiveness in the choice of topics in the format of a single volume, especially in the case of a language whose history is as well studied as that of English – a fact borne out by the existence of the *Cambridge History of the English Language* (CHEL), which requires six volumes with virtually book-length chapters to give comprehensive survey treatment of the work done on relevant aspects of the English language. We decided to concentrate instead on other typical handbook functions: those of providing shortcuts to current thinking for readers who want to become familiar with subjects that are outside their own areas of interest, and of providing a "state of the art" overview of current research. This led us to concentrate on the kind of work which is grounded in philological expertise and care but which is also informed by recent theoretical advances and issues in the study of English historical linguistics and of historical linguistics and language change more generally. The term "theoretical advances" should be taken in a broad sense here, including theoretical models of linguistic competence and language use, the theory and methodology of social and regional variation in language, quantitative corpus-driven work and corpus-making, or a combination of any of the above. Given this chosen slant of the Handbook, we also specifically requested a number of our contributors to go beyond the survey approach that is so readily associated with handbooks, and to try as much as possible to present chapters in which the work for which they are best known is argued and illustrated, while also presenting new material and suggesting new avenues of research. This has led to a fairly unorthodox chapter division.

The first part presents a discussion of four very different approaches to the study of the history of language change in the context of the English language.

They all represent ways of researching language change that have become part of the research agenda relatively recently: April McMahon evaluates the viability of Optimality Theory for historical work in English phonology. David W. Lightfoot presents the case for approaching syntactic change from the perspective of the language learner, and highlights the role of grammatical cues in the acquisition of the grammatical rule system by new generations of learners. Anthony Warner presents a theoretically informed variationist approach which casts new light on the classical problem of the diffusion of a new syntactic feature, in this case that of periphrastic *do* in early Modern English. Finally, William Croft discusses evolutionary models in combination with functional-typological theories as they apply to the phenomenon of language change.

The second part presents historical work done at the level of the word. The chapters by Donka Minkova, and Paula Fikkert, Elan B. Dresher, and Aditi Lahiri present work done in prosody, an exciting area of research which brings together changes in phonology and morphology. The chapters by Dieter Kastovsky and Laurie Bauer provide overviews of historical word formation.

The chapters in Part III, by Cynthia L. Allen, Ans van Kemenade and Bettelou Los, Susan Pintzuk and Ann Taylor, and David Denison, are concerned with various aspects of word order change, with the perennial problem of the interaction between inflectional change and syntactic change, and with the problem of how to model this interaction. They also illustrate the value of corpus work in historical syntax. The use of corpora in English diachronic syntax is an excellent, and possibly unique, example of how formal theories and performance data can be brought together to provide us with a better understanding of the syntax of early English and the phenomenon of syntactic change.

In Part IV, "Pragmatics," the chapters by Laurel Brinton and Elizabeth Closs Traugott represent approaches that focus on how word-meanings may change in non-arbitrary ways. Particularly interesting is the development of degree adverbs, focus modifiers and pragmatic markers, which have acquired these special functions via pragmatic implicatures and inferences that can be deduced from the uses of lexemes in specific constructions. Elena Seoane's chapter discusses the interaction of syntax and information structure that is evident in the changing role of the passive construction in the history of English.

The chapters in Part V, "Pre- and Post-colonial Varieties," discuss regional variation and the origin of varieties of English and, conversely, how historical change is reflected in present-day dialects. The fine-grained philological concerns of Old and Middle English dialectology and the construction of corpora suited for such research, as presented in the chapters by Richard Hogg, and Margaret Laing and Roger Lass, are complemented by the detailed arguments emerging from recent exciting work on the British dialectal origins of African American English in the chapter by Shana Poplack, the spin-offs of older regional dialects in present-day language features in the chapter by Sali A. Tagliamonte, and the development of Celtic Englishes in the chapter by Markku Filppula.

Finally, Part VI contains three chapters that have as their common denominator various types of external influence on the language: a chapter on the impact of eighteenth-century prescriptivism by Ingrid Tieken-Boon van Ostade, one on sociolinguistic influences as brought to light by careful corpus work in the chapter by Terttu Nevalainen, and one on the development of English as a world language, by Suzanne Romaine.

Although we have been much concerned with putting together a book with work that attempts to give new and theoretically informed answers to old questions, we have been reluctant to make divisions in terms of theoretical issues. The most important reason for this is that we were worried that any theoretical division would construct as much as reflect theoretical ideologies. Not only was this never our concern, we also feel that it would have been entirely inappropriate as an approach toward a handbook on a field that is as empirical as "the history of English." This attitude is also reflected in the chapters by our contributors, who on the whole seemed a good deal more concerned with presenting theoretically informed work that resolves puzzles in their various empirical domains than with engaging in polemics with each other. The division of the book into parts has, in the end, been guided by the empirical domains in which theoretical progress of various kinds has been made since the mid-1990s, as reflected in detailed case studies. There is a good deal of emphasis overall on language variation of various kinds, and this chimes well with the recent general booming in the field of sociolinguistics and language variation. The strength of the book lies, we hope, in applying recent insights to old problems.

We wish to conclude with a work of thanks to most of our contributors for their prompt delivery, and for their willingness to engage in a dialogue on their chapters, and to exchange views with each other. Many thanks are also due to Sarah Coleman at Blackwell for her cheerful and practical guidance of the whole project.

Ans van Kemenade and Bettelou Los
May 2005

Notes on Contributors

Cynthia L. Allen

Cynthia L. Allen is a Reader in the School of Language Studies at the Australian National University and the Director of ANU's Centre for Research on Language Change. She is a Fellow of the Australian Academy of the Humanities. She specializes in history of English morphosyntax and her publications include *Case Marking and Reanalysis: Grammatical Relations from Old to Early Modern English* (1995) and *Genitives in Early English: Typology and Evidence* (2008).
cindy.allen@anu.edu.au

Laurie Bauer

Laurie Bauer holds a personal chair in Linguistics at Victoria University of Wellington, New Zealand. He is the author of a number of works on morphology and English word-formation, including, most recently, in collaboration with Rodney Huddleston, the chapter on English word-formation for the *Cambridge Grammar of the English Language* (eds. R. Huddleston and G. Pullum, 2002). He also writes on international varieties of English.
laurie.bauer@vuw.ac.nz

Laurel Brinton

Laurel Brinton is Professor of English at the University of British Columbia, Canada, specializing in the history and structure of the English language. Her research areas include verbal aspect, grammaticalization, lexicalization, and historical pragmatics, with particular attention to the development of pragmatic markers. Most recently, she has co-authored *Lexicalization and Language Change* (with Elizabeth Closs Traugott, 2005) and *The History of English: A Linguistic Introduction* (with Leslie Arnovick, 2005). She has a forthcoming book *The Comment Clause in English: Syntactic Origins and Pragmatic Development* (2008).
brinton@interchange.ubc.ca

William Croft

William Croft is Professor of Linguistics at the University of New Mexico (USA). His main areas of specialization are typology, including grammaticalization;

evolutionary models of language change; construction grammar; and cognitive linguistics. His books include *Explaining Language Change: An Evolutionary Approach* (2000), *Radical Construction Grammar: Syntactic Theory in Typological Perspective* (2001), *Typology and Universals* (2nd edition, 2003), and *Cognitive Linguistics* (with D. Alan Cruse, 2004).
wcroft@unm.edu

David Denison
David Denison is Professor of English Linguistics at the University of Manchester, one of the founding editors of the journal *English Language and Linguistics*, author of *English Historical Syntax* (1993) and of the "Syntax" chapter in vol. 4 of *The Cambridge History of the English Language* (1998), one of the editors of *Fuzzy Grammar* (2004), and joint editor (with Richard Hogg) of a *History of the English Language* (2006, CUP).
david.denison@manchester.ac.uk

B. Elan Dresher
Elan B. Dresher is Professor of Linguistics at the University of Toronto. He has published on a wide variety of topics, including Hebrew phonology and morphology, historical linguistics, and learnability. His work on historical linguistics includes Old English and the theory of phonology and joint work with Aditi Lahiri on historical West-Germanic. He is also well known for his work on learnability, published in major journals. His current research interest concerns the role of contrast in phonological theory. He has been a columnist for *Glot International*.
Dresher@chass.utoronto.ca

Paula Fikkert
Paula Fikkert is Professor of First Language Aquisition and Phonology at the Radboud University of Nijmegen. She received her PhD in 1994 at Leiden University, and from 1994 to 1999 she was a researcher at the University of Konstanz, returning to the Netherlands as a research fellow of the Royal Dutch Academy of Science. Recent publications include "Acquisition of Phonology," in *The First Glot International State-of-the-Article Book* (2000); (with N. Schiller and C. Levelt) "Stress priming in picture naming: an SOA study," in *Brain and Language* (2004); and (editor with H. Jacobs) *Development in Prosodic Systems* (2003).
p.fikkert@let.ru.nl

Markku Filppula
Markku Filppula is Professor of English at the University of Joensuu, and Docent in English Philology at the University of Helsinki. He is also currently Director of *LANGNET*, the Finnish Graduate School in Language Studies. He was awarded his PhD by the National University of Ireland (Dublin) in 1986, and has published widely on Hiberno-English, other "Celtic Englishes" and language contacts in general. He is the author of *The Grammar of Irish English: Language in Hibernian Style* (1999), *English and Celtic in Contact* (with Juhani Klemola and Heli Pitkänen, forthcoming), and he wrote the chapter on Irish

English morphology and syntax for *A Handbook of Varieties of English*, vol. 2: *Morphology and Syntax* (eds. B. Kortmann *et al.*, 2004). He was also one of the editors (with Klemola and Pitkänen) of *The Celtic Roots of English* (2002).
markku.filppula@joensuu.fi

Richard Hogg
Richard Hogg was Smith Professor of English Language and Medieval Literature at Manchester between 1980 and 2007. His doctorate was awarded by the University of Edinburgh, and he held further appointments in Amsterdam and Lancaster. His research interests were English historical linguistics, particularly in dialectology and Old English phonology and morphology. His publications include *Old English Grammar* (1992). He is General Editor of *The Cambridge History of the English Language*, the fifth and final volume of which was completed in 2001. He edited volume 1 (*The Beginnings to 1066*), and wrote the chapter on phonology and morphology for that volume. Other publications include *An Introduction to Old English Language* and *A History of the English Language* (2006, CUP) with David Denison. Richard Hogg died on 6 September 2007. This book is dedicated to his memory.

Dieter Kastovsky
Dieter Kastovsky is Professor of English Language and Translation Studies at the University of Vienna. His doctorate is from the University of Tuebingen and he has held a further appoint at Wuppertal, and guest professorships at Stockholm, Cape Town, Georgetown and Lublin (Poland). His major research interest is in early English word formation, and he has published widely on this and related topics, including his contribution on Old English word formation to Volume I of the *Cambridge History of the English Language* (1992).
Dieter.Kastovsky@univie.ac.at

Ans van Kemenade
Ans van Kemenade is Professor of English Language and Linguistics at the Radboud University of Nijmegen. After her doctorate in 1987 at the University of Utrecht, she held posts at the University of Leiden and the Vrije Universiteit Amsterdam. Her main research interests are in historical syntax and in syntactic variation and change. She has published *Syntactic Case and Morphological Case in the History of English*. She has edited special issues of *Lingua* (1993, vol. 89/1–2 with Aafke Hulk), *Linguistics* (1999, vol. 37.6) and the *Yearbook of Morphology 2003* (with Geert Booij), and, with Nigel Vincent, *Parameters of Morphosyntactic Change* (1997). She has published numerous articles, mainly on Old and Middle English syntax.
a.v.kemenade@let.ru.nl

Aditi Lahiri
Aditi Lahiri is Professor of Linguistics and Fellow of Somerville College, University of Oxford. She has taught at University of California at Los Angeles and Santa Cruz, has been a research scientist at the Max-Planck-Institute for Psycholinguistics in the Netherlands and Professor of General Linguistics at the

University of Konstanz in Germany. Her research interests include phonology and morphology (synchronic and diachronic), phonetics, experimental psycholinguistics, and neurolinguistics. Recent publications on Germanic include *Analogy, Leveling, Markedness: Principles of Change in Phonology and Morphology* (editor, 2000), as well as papers in *Language 75* (1999; with Elan B. Dresher), *English Language and Linguistics 3* (1999; with Paula Fikkert), and *Transactions of the Philological Society 102* (2004; with Astrid Kraehenmann).
aditi.lahiri@uni-konstanz.de

Margaret Laing

Margaret Laing is Research Fellow in the Institute for Historical Dialectology, English Language, University of Edinburgh. She contributed to the production of *A Linguistic Atlas of Late Mediaeval English* (1986). Since then she has been engaged in research towards the creation of a Linguistic Atlas of Early Middle English (LAEME) in collaboration (from 2002) with Roger Lass. She has published extensively on early Middle English, including *A Catalogue of Sources for a Linguistic Atlas of Early Medieval English* (1993) and many articles arising out of the investigation of early Middle English dialects and scribal systems.
M.Laing@ed.ac.uk

Roger Lass

Roger Lass is Professor Emeritus of Linguistics and Honorary Research Fellow in English at the University of Cape Town. He has published numerous books and technical papers in the fields of theoretical and historical linguistics and the history of English. His most recent books are *Historical Linguistics and Language Change* (1997) and volume 3 of the *Cambridge History of the English Language* (1999), which he both edited and contributed a major chapter to. Most of his current research is dedicated to the LAEME project for which, among other things, he is responsible for the etymological corpus.
lass@iafrica.com

David W. Lightfoot

David Lightfoot works on language acquisition, change, and syntax. His major appointments have been at McGill University, the University of Utrecht, the University of Maryland, where he established a new department of linguistics, and at Georgetown University, where he was Dean of the Graduate School of Arts and Sciences. He is now Assistant Director of the National Science Foundation. He is the author of ten books, including *The Language Lottery: Toward a Biology of Grammars* (1982), *How to Set Parameters: Arguments from Language Change* (1991), and (with Stephen R. Anderson) *The Language Organ: Linguistics as Cognitive Physiology* (2002), and most recently *How New Languages Emerge* (2005).
lightd@georgetown.edu

Bettelou Los

Bettelou Los is a Senior Lecturer in English at the Radboud University of Nijmegen. She graduated from the University of Amsterdam in 1986 and has since held teaching and research positions at the University of Amsterdam, the

Vrije Universiteit Amsterdam (where she obtained her doctorate in 2000), the University of Nijmegen, the University of Leuven and other colleges of higher education. She contributes, with Wim van der Wurff, to the morphology and syntax section of *The Year's Work in English Studies*. She has published *The Rise of the* to-*infinitive* (2005) and many articles on diachronic syntax.
blj.los@let.vu.nl

April McMahon
April McMahon is Forbes Professor of English Language at the University of Edinburgh. She previously worked in the Department of Linguistics at the University of Cambridge and held a Chair in English Language and Linguistics at the University of Sheffield. Her research interests involve the interaction between phonological theory and historical evidence, as well as issues of language comparison and classification. Her books include *Understanding Language Change* (1994), *Lexical Phonology and the History of English* (2000), *Change, Chance, and Optimality* (2000), and *Language Classification by Numbers* (with Robert McMahon, forthcoming). She is currently the President of the Linguistics Association of Great Britain.
April.McMahon@ed.ac.uk

Donka Minkova
Donka Minkova is Professor of English at University of California, Los Angeles. She has published widely in the areas of English historical phono-logy, meter, dialectology, and syntax. She is the author of *The History of Final Vowels in English* (1991), *English Words: History and Structure* (with Robert Stockwell, 2001), and *Alliteration and Sound Change in Early English* (2003). She has co-edited *Studies in the History of the English Language: A Millennial Perspective* (with Robert Stockwell, 2002) and *Chaucer and the Challenges of Medievalism* (with Theresa Tinkle, 2003).
minkova@humnet.ucla.edu

Terttu Nevalainen
Terttu Nevalainen is Professor of English Philology at the Department of English, University of Helsinki, Finland, and the Director of the Research Unit for Variation and Change in English, co-funded by the Academy of Finland and the University of Helsinki. She is the leader of the project "Sociolinguistics and Language History," which has produced the *Corpus of Early English Correspondence* (CEEC) and a number of publications on the topic, including *Historical Sociolinguistics: Language Change in Tudor and Stuart England* (co-author with Raumolin-Brunberg, 2003). Her other research interests include phonetics and historical lexicology.
Terttu.Nevalainen@Helsinki.Fi

Susan Pintzuk
Susan Pintzuk is Professor of English Language and Linguistics at the University of York (UK). Her research interests include syntactic variation and change, particularly in the history of English and other Germanic languages; statistical models of language change; and corpus linguistics. She has

participated in the construction of corpora in the English Parsed Corpora series (the York–Toronto–Helsinki Parsed Corpus of Old English Prose, with Ann Taylor, Anthony Warner, and Frank Beths; the York–Helsinki Parsed Corpus of Old English Poetry, with Leendert Plug; a parsed version of the Corpus of Early English Correspondence, with Taylor and Warner, in collaboration with the Research Unit for Variation and Change in English, Helsinki) and the Brooklyn–Geneva–Amsterdam–Helsinki Parsed Corpus of Old English, with Eric Haeberli, Ans van Kemenade, Willem Koopman, and Frank Beths.
sp20@york.ac.uk

Shana Poplack
Shana Poplack is Distinguished University Professor and Canada Research Chair in Linguistics at the University of Ottawa, where she also directs the Sociolinguistics Laboratory. An expert in linguistic variation theory and its application to diverse areas of language contact, she has published widely on code-switching, Hispanic linguistics, English as well as Canadian French and numerous aspects of African American Vernacular English.
spoplack@uottawa.ca

Suzanne Romaine
Suzanne Romaine has been Merton Professor of English Language at the University of Oxford since 1984. Her research interests lie primarily in historical linguistics and sociolinguistics, especially in problems of societal multilingualism, linguistic diversity, language change, language acquisition, and language contact in the broadest sense. She edited volume IV (*1776 to 1997*) of *The Cambridge History of the English Language* (1998).
suzanne.romaine@ling-phil.ox.ac.uk

Elena Seoane
Elena Seoane is Associate Professor of English in the Department of English at the University of Santiago de Compostela, and a member of the research project "Variation and Linguistic Change," directed by Professor Teresa Fanego. In 1996 she received her PhD in English historical linguistics from the University of Santiago. Her main areas of specialization are syntactic change in the history of English, historical pragmatics, and grammaticalization theory. She has co-edited *Theoretical and Empirical Issues on Grammaticalization* and *Rethinking Grammaticalization: New Perspectives* (with M. José López-Couso, 2008).
iaelena@usc.es

Sali A. Tagliamonte
Sali A. Tagliamonte is Professor of Linguistics and Director of the Sociolinguistics Laboratory at the University of Toronto, Canada. Her expertise is language variation and change in synchronic corpora. She has published on African American English, British and Irish dialects, teen language and television. Ongoing research focuses on morph-syntactic developments in English through cross-variety and apparent time comparisons.
sali.tagliamonte@utoronto.ca

Ann Taylor

Ann Taylor is a Research Fellow at the University of York (UK). Her research interests include syntactic variation and change, particularly in Old and Middle English. She is co-creator with Anthony Kroch of the Penn–Helsinki Parsed Corpus of Middle English; with Anthony Warner, Susan Pintzuk, and Frank Beths, of the York–Toronto–Helsinki Parsed Corpus of Old English Prose; and is currently producing a parsed version of the Corpus of Early English Correspondence with Warner and Pintzuk, in collaboration with the Research Unit for Variation and Change in English, Helsinki.
at9@york.ac.uk

Ingrid Tieken-Boon van Ostade

Ingrid Tieken-Boon van Ostade holds a Personal Chair in the Department of English at the University of Leiden. She specializes in the field of historical sociolinguistics (social network analysis), has published on periphrastic *do* and multiple negation, and has recently obtained a major research grant for her project "The Codifiers and the English Language." The aim of this project is to trace the origins of the norm of standard English as well as to study the influence of prescriptivism on actual usage.
i.m.tieken@let.leidenuniv.nl

Elizabeth Closs Traugott

Elizabeth Closs Traugott is Professor Emeritus of Linguistics and English at Stanford University, California. Early work included research in historical syntax, socio-historical linguistics, and linguistics and literature. In the last two decades her prime research focus has been on grammaticalization, lexicalization, and semanticization of conversational inferences and subjectification, and she is currently studying the syntax–pragmatics interface in Old English. Her publications include *A History of English Syntax* (1972); *Linguistics for Students of Literature* (with Mary L. Pratt, 1980); *On Conditionals* (1986; co-edited with Alice ter Meulen, Judith Snitzer Reilly, and Charles A. Ferguson); *Grammaticalization* (with Paul Hopper, 1993, 2nd much revised edn. 2003); and *Lexicalization and Language Change* (with L. Brinton, 2005). She has been a Guggenheim Fellow, a Fellow at the Center for Advanced Study in the Behavioral Sciences, and is a Fellow of the American Association for the Advancement of Science.
traugott@csli.stanford.edu

Anthony Warner

Anthony Warner is Professor of English Linguistics at the University of York (UK). He has written on the history of English syntax and on monostratal syntax. His interests include the study of variation and the creation and use of electronic parsed corpora, both seen as major components of a historical syntactician's tool kit.
aw2@york.ac.uk

I Approaches and Issues

1 Change for the Better? Optimality Theory versus History

APRIL McMAHON

Change is not made without inconvenience, even from worse to better.
Dr Johnson, quoting Richard Hooker

1.1 Introduction

Optimality Theory (OT) may have been described by Archangeli (1997: 1) as "THE Linguistic Theory of the 1990s," but it is clearly making a bid, at least in phonology, for continuation of that favored status into the twenty-first century. OT analyses have now been developed for a vast range of phonological phenomena in the languages of the world; and as the architecture of OT has changed, and the edifice has grown, so competing possibilities have been proposed. The OT phonological community has also reached a point of generally acknowledging the strengths of the model (mainly in prosody, in the enlightening modeling of the interaction of competing motivations, and in the integration of typological evidence into phonology), and also its weaknesses (mainly the handling of opacity, specifically in morphophonological alternations; and in some areas of persistent inclarity about central tenets of the theory, notably the role of GEN, the shape of the input, and whether constraints are universal).

In this chapter, I shall try to highlight some of these issues as they affect the OT analysis of sound change. Historical linguists, who may well begin from a situation of relative theoretical neutrality, will be persuaded to make use of a particular formal model only if they are convinced that it offers the possibility of providing more enlightening analyses of change than would be possible in the absence of the model. It is therefore important to show what OT claims to be able to say about change, and how the OT approach has changed during the (relatively short) life of the theory.

This chapter consequently has two goals, though their development will be interwoven rather than sequential. On the one hand, I shall show that the OT approach to sound change has altered considerably since the first applications of the model to diachronic questions. Early OT accounts tended to assume that change was, in some sense, for the better, notably in the analysis of emergence of unmarked effects; and these analyses tended also to be presented as a change for the better over other possible accounts in different models, in providing direct explanations of change. However, more recently, some of these claims have been diluted, so that not all historical linguists now working in OT necessarily expect or attempt explanations of change, but rather a neat method of modeling conflicting factors and motivations. In a sense, this means the OT approach to change is now less concerned with the details of, and the impulses behind individual changes, and more involved with a global view: hence, Bermúdez-Otero and Hogg (2003) focus on OT modeling of the "life-cycle" of phonological processes, while Minkova and Stockwell (2003) demonstrate that various rankings of four constraints give rise to different, though perhaps related, types of change.

This concentration on macroanalysis of language history might itself be seen as a change for the better; however, in the second theme of this chapter, I shall show that some of the areas of inclarity in the current formulation of OT are of particular relevance and concern for analyses of change. For instance, the well-known question over the acceptability of different constraints and constraint types means it can be hard to evaluate alternative accounts of the same change, and this overlaps with the unresolved question of the universality of constraints. Perhaps even more seriously, recent questions over the possible phonetic grounding of phonological constraints are of particular relevance to sound change, if we accept that changes often have their inception in phonologizations of automatic, phonetically motivated processes. Many of these points can be made with reference to alternative OT analyses of a single, central change, namely the Great Vowel Shift, which will therefore be the focus of much of the discussion below.

1.2 Optimality Theory and Sound Change: The Basic Ingredients

For the benefit of those readers who have not yet acquainted themselves with the (sometimes slightly arcane) paraphernalia and impedimenta of OT, a very brief outline of the model might be helpful (and see also Further Reading, below). OT is based around the idea of a set of constraints, Con: initially, and still in some current versions, these constraints are seen as universal and innate, but crucially violable. For each input, or mental lexicon form postulated on the basis of primary linguistic data, all possible parses, or outputs, are generated by a mechanism called Gen. These alternative, competing parses are then evaluated by the ranked set of constraints; the parse which violates fewest high-ranking constraints will win and be produced. However, although the constraints are universal, their ranking is not, and differences between languages therefore result from a different prioritization of the same constraints.

We might as historical linguists be faced with two sister languages, one of which has an onset in every syllable, while the other often has onsets, but not in absolutely every case. These onset consonants routinely match; but where the second language has no onset consonant, the first consistently has a glottal stop. In OT terms, we conclude that in the first language (1a), the universal constraint Onset (which requires all syllables to have onsets) is ranked so high that it will always be obeyed on the surface. If there is no onset in the common ancestral form, or in a borrowed form, an onset is inserted *ex nihilo* in the form of a glottal stop. In the second sister (1b), although the same constraint is inherited by children, it is less important than another constraint (normally stated as Dep-io in current versions of OT), which requires the output to be faithful to (that is, essentially the same as) the input, and which specifically forbids the insertion of segments. So, in this case, onsets are welcomed wherever they are already available in the input, but the higher ranking of Dep-io as compared to Onset means it is more important to keep the one-to-one relationship between input and output than to resort to epenthesis and satisfy the requirement for an onset consonant. In the first language, the priorities are the other way around.

(1) a.

/atel/	Onset	Dep-io
[ʔatel] ☜		*
[atel]	*!	

b.

/atel/	Dep-io	Onset
[ʔatel]	*!	
[atel] ☜		*

The very great advantage of this constraint-ranking approach is its resolution of a venerable problem in linguistics, namely the existence of universal pressures which do not always create absolutely universal results. We can say that languages typically prefer to have filled onsets; but there is a continuum from those languages (like Arabic) that absolutely require them, through those where onsets will be allowed, although speakers do not go out of their way to produce them in every case. The status of universal tendencies of this kind was unclear in earlier models, but they are a straightforward and predictable part of OT, where the violability and rankability of constraints create different outputs depending on language-specific priorities. We can also model the range of results provided by all possible rankings of a set of constraints, and should ideally find that each ranking provides an attested output: we shall return below to an illustration of this so-called factorial typology from Minkova and Stockwell (2003).

Given that different rankings will produce different outputs, a neat and straightforward means of modeling change presents itself, and it is not surprising that OT phonologists seized on this relatively early in the development of the theory: "Under OT, the formal characterization of language change through time is that constraints are reranked" (Archangeli 1997: 31). That is, taking our "toy" example of the onset-requiring language, and its sister which can take onsets or leave them, we might assume that the latter represents the historical situation, and that the first sister has subsequently undergone a reranking whereby ONSET is now more highly ranked than DEP-IO. In other words, at some point a discontinuity arose between generations, such that parents arguably had a grammar with one ranking, and their children instead acquired an alternative grammar with the two relevant constraints ranked the other way round. Although this is undoubtedly a pleasing analysis, and has the added advantage of following very directly from the OT account of synchronic, typological variation, it does raise the problem of explanation; and this is a key issue to be explored in the next section. Armed with a very basic outline of the architecture of OT, and the consequent model of change, we now turn to a more complex change and some alternative means of modeling it in constraint-based terms.

1.3 Optimality Theory and the Great Vowel Shift

1.3.1 The Great Vowel Shift: one thing after another, or just one thing?

A diagram bearing at least a close resemblance to (2) below is almost an expected ingredient of survey courses on the history of English, and the Great Vowel Shift, which it portrays, is highly likely to figure on the average top ten list of sound changes in English, or indeed Germanic.

(2)

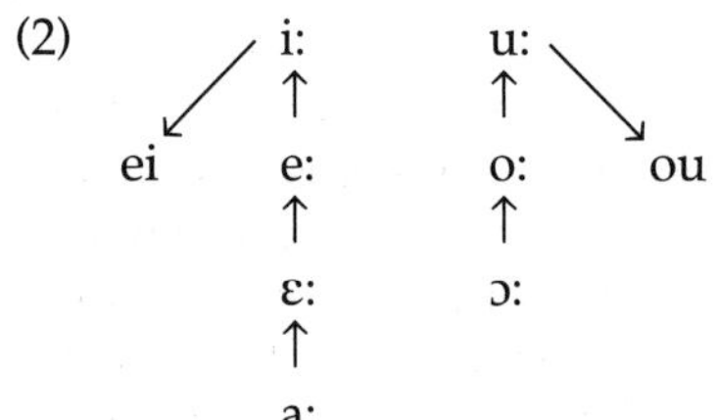

As presented, this change involves the diphthongization of the high vowels (which subsequently continue to lower to their present-day values of /aɪ/ and /aʊ/, and the stepwise raising of the long monophthongs. Later changes obscure aspects of this pattern, since Middle English (ME) /a:/ does not remain at /ɛ:/, but continues to raise to /e:/ (now often diphthongal [eɪ], as in *name*), while ME /ɛ:/ itself raised two steps to /i:/ in most cases (*sea, beat*; exceptions are *great, steak*), merging therefore with ME /e:/ (*green, sleep*) which had itself raised by one step to /iː/. Other changes following the Great Vowel Shift seem to fit into the same pattern – so, as ME /uː/, having diphthongized in the early stages of the Shift, continued to lower to [aʊ], earlier /au/ raised and monophthongized in words like *law*, filling the low mid slot vacated by /ɔː/ when it earlier raised to /oː/ (*boat, coat*).

As this brief description has already shown, it is very hard to write about the Great Vowel Shift (GVS), or indeed any chain shift, without thinking in terms of systems containing specific slots. From these slots some elements will shift, leaving space for others to move in (the classical description of a drag chain); alternatively, elements already moving may put pressure on others, which are forced into a consequent shift away to avoid merger (giving rise to the traditionally termed push chain). Either way, the core of the GVS seen in this way is "a particular kind of chain shift, in which segments in a given phonological subspace play musical chairs and don't go anywhere" (Lass 1988: 397). Indeed, Lass (1976) used the GVS specifically to argue for the inclusion and recognition of systems and inventories in phonological theory. Intriguingly, he also proposed a series of metarules and output conditions to analyze large-scale shifts of this kind; a "metarule" which effectively says vowels should raise seems presciently close to the "vowels are high" type of OT constraint.

Lass notes that "probably the majority of historians of English . . . have come to accept the GVS as something that can be talked about, on a par with other reifications of diachronic correspondence-sets like Grimm's, Verner's, Grassman's Laws, the High German obstruent shift, and the like" (1988: 396); elsewhere, and indulging in a little reification himself, he characterizes such "major sound changes" as having "left the languages they affected very different from what they were before, either in inventory (Grimm's Law, the High German Consonant Shift), or in morphophonemic complexity (the Great Vowel Shift)" (1976: 52). But although this acceptance of the unity of the GVS might be fairly general, it is not uncontested. Indeed, a slightly unorthodox but closely fought game of academic tennis has been going on over this point for the last 20 years: on one side of the net is Lass (1976, 1988, 1992, 1999), who argues for the unity of at least part of the conventionally described GVS, and on the other are Stockwell and Minkova (Stockwell 1975; Stockwell and Minkova 1988a, 1988b, 1990, 1997, 1999; Minkova 1999), who believe that the "GVS" is a misleading label for a series of changes which are essentially unconnected except in being examples of the kind of changes that routinely happen in the history of English, because English is the sort of language where that kind of change routinely happens.

Obviously, a challenge of this kind to the integrity of the GVS is a major issue (not least for this chapter, where I propose to discuss several accounts of a possibly non-existent change): as Lass (1992: 145) puts it: "For nearly a century the exegesis of the GVS has been one of our major cottage industries," but "Certainly questions about the causes, beginnings, and structure of something that did not happen are rather thin stuff for serious scholars to be spending their time on." In this context, it is reassuring to note that Stockwell and

Minkova do not deny the individual changes often grouped together as the GVS: "The facts, indeed, seem quite clear; the question is how to make sense out of them" (Stockwell 1975: 333). In other words, all parties to the discussion would agree that the changes in (3) can reasonably be postulated for the history of English; the difference is that Lass would also accept the geometrical representation in (2), which shows (some of) the same individual changes as linked.

(3)	ME		EModE		ModE
	i:	→	ei	→	aɪ
	e:	→	i:	→	i:
	ɛ:	→	e: ⟶	↗	
	a:	→	ɛ: → e:	→	eɪ
	u:	→	ou	→	aʊ
	o:	→	u:	→	u:
	ɔ:	→	o:	→	oʊ

In such an extensive series of arguments and counterarguments, there are of course further detailed points of disagreement, some of them fundamental to the analysis of the individual changes. For instance, while both Stockwell and Minkova and Lass agree that the original ME high vowels diphthongized to some intermediate form before lowering to /aɪ aʊ/, they propose different intermediate forms. Furthermore, Lass (following Luick's original suggestion) argues that the first step in the GVS was raising of the high mid vowels /e:/ and /o:/, and provides dialectal data in evidence: wherever /o:/ had already moved out of the back vowel system through a northern change of /o:/-Fronting, leaving an "empty space" in the back column, /u:/ failed to diphthongize, giving Scots *hoose, moose* rather than *house, mouse.* Lass and Luick take the line that, since there is no parallel disparity with the front vowels, and no sound change which specifically targeted /e:/, the fronting of /o:/ and the failure of /u:/ to diphthongize must be connected. In other words, the GVS began as a push chain, as the raising high mid vowels put pressure on the high ones, which consequently diphthongized: in cases where no pressure was applied from below, the diphthongization did not happen. Stockwell and Minkova, on the other hand, argue that the change of diphthongization (which for them is a much lower-level process, a merger of possibly pre-existing diphthongal variants of the high vowels with pre-existing diphthongs from other sources) came first. It is also possible to detect a degree of rapprochement in later contributions to the debate, with Lass (1992: 149) maintaining that the "top half" of the traditional GVS (that is, the combination of high vowel diphthongization and high mid vowel raising) shows an inner cohesion and unity, but accepting that the "bottom half" might well be a series of independent vowel raisings which should be referred to as "pseudo-GVS" or "Post-GVS Raising" rather than Phase II of the GVS proper (a term he reintroduces, however, in Lass 1999). But the core of the disagreement remains the same now as in the earliest contributions. On one view, either part or all of the GVS is a unified series of events, which "can be and has been shown to have what Luick . . . called an 'innere Zusammenhang' " (Lass 1992: 148). On the other, there are several relatively minor and self-contained changes, which are due to the same underlying motivations of maximizing the perceptual optimality of diphthongs, or maintaining contrast; but these take place over too long a period to be recognized as forming a unitary shift, and the generally accepted GVS pattern is simply a "linguist's creation through hindsight" (Stockwell and Minkova 1988a: 376). In that case, "the massive GVS becomes a classic example of structuralist overgeneralization more suited for a history of linguistics than for a history of the English language" (Minkova 1999: 84).

It would be presumptuous to assume that I could reach any definite conclusion on this debate, and more so in the space available here. On the other hand, a contested change, or series of changes, of this kind does provide an excellent focus for a discussion of the OT approach to change. As we shall see, there are several alternative analyses of the GVS in the literature, and it might be instructive to see whether modeling these change(s) in OT terms helps us reach a view on their relatedness. That is, we shall be concerned below with the efficacy of OT in modeling sound change; the several different approaches to the GVS each highlight a number of key issues on this matter. However, we shall also consider what might justify a selection of OT over other possible models in the analysis of sound change, and a relevant issue here is whether or not OT might help us decide on the most reasonable view of the "GVS."

1.3.2 *Miglio (1998)*

Miglio (1998), like most early attempts to apply OT to sound change, is engaged with explanations: "Optimality Theory . . . can be . . . an important means to explain language change" (1998: 1). A typical early analysis of sound change in OT, simplifying for the sake of argument (see, further, McMahon 2000a, 2000b, 2002), might model the loss of a relatively marked segment via a markedness or well-formedness constraint disfavoring that segment . At Stage I, this constraint is ranked low, and speakers do not attend to it; they get by pronouncing the difficult segment somehow. But at Stage II, the markedness constraint has been reranked higher, and the difficult segment is no longer pronounced. Sound change therefore involves a gradual prioritization of markedness constraints over time, and its consequence is a shift towards less marked pronunciations (though changes may have effects elsewhere in the grammar which let other cases of markedness in). As Minkova and Stockwell (2003: 169) put it:

> Optimality Theory is the ultimate capitalist economy. It conceives not just of change but of all phonetic realizations as the result of competition. The basic competition for change that has been envisaged is competition between markedness constraints and faithfulness constraints. The scenario is, the faithfulness constraints are

> constantly battered by the markedness constraints; the latter are constantly climbing the corporate ladder and dislodging the entrenched corporate management.

The most significant difficulty for such early OT accounts of sound change involves the nature of reranking, the process of advancement of markedness constraints up the ladder in the quote above, and crucially whether this mechanism can be seen as explanatory: this is the chicken and egg problem of McMahon (2000a: 126–7). Why, for instance, did the loss of [k] in [kn-] clusters (*know, knee, knight*) happen? Does reranking happen in response mode, allowing children to build the simplest grammar, since they (and quite possibly their parents) were already not pronouncing [k]? Or is the reranking causal? Does it take place first, for whatever reason, so that the next generation has no choice but to produce [n-], even where they hear [kn-] in their primary linguistic data? From the point of view of language acquisition and what we know about the sociolinguistic input to language change, the latter is, of course, much less plausible than the former: the causal account of reranking might be appealing since it allows phonological theory to explain change, rather than having to rely on factors outside the grammar itself, but what it gains in this respect it loses very decisively in its reliance on mystical grammatical determinism. This seems to be the consensus in current OT treatments of change: better to see reranking as *post hoc* grammar tidying and as an effect of acquisition, however prosaic this might seem, than claim reranking is explanatory where this really only pushes the real explanation one step back.

Miglio (1998) attempts to extend analyses of this kind to the GVS, which in itself is a tricky proposition: chain shifts are a notorious locus of opacity, a major difficulty for OT accounts of synchronic phonology, and as changes they are logically impossible to deal with using only markedness, since by definition disfavoring a particular vowel, which might therefore be encouraged to raise or diphthongize, would lead us to expect that vowel to remain disfavored – not for the same slot to be refilled by another vowel shifting in from somewhere else. Miglio's solution (without going into full details on this or the other accounts below, for reasons of space) is to identify "weak spots" in the system as probable triggers of change; "weakness" here might equate to markedness or to perceptual difficulty. In the case of the GVS, Miglio identifies /ɛ: ɔ:/ as the "weak spots," because long lax mid vowels are typologically rare, and therefore highly marked. In fact, these vowels had been in the system for some time, but Miglio argues that they became more frequent and therefore more noticeable as outputs of the preceding sound change of Middle English Open Syllable Lengthening. The higher frequency of these vowels then triggered a constraint reranking promoting the constraint *[–ATR]mm, which disfavors long lax vowels (ATR, or Advanced Tongue Root, is here used to signify the lax–tense opposition). One might expect this to have caused vowel mergers; but the constraint DISTANCE, which is also quite high-ranked, favors the maintenance of contrasts.

Miglio's identification of the long lax low mid vowels as "weak spots," which consequently shift, and her invocation of constraints discouraging mergers, account for the raisings from low mid to high mid, and high mid to high, and for the diphthongization of the ME high vowels. However, Miglio also includes /a:/ > /ɛ:/ as part of the shift – although /ɛ:/ is one of the disfavored vowels which started the whole process. Here, Miglio must assume a further re-reranking, demoting *[–ATR]mm, and promoting a local conjunction of faithfulness constraints for [ATR] and height (we return to the issue of local conjunction in the next section); /a:/ then raises to low mid.

This is potentially an interesting result: after all, Stockwell and Minkova see the "GVS" as composed of a series of independent changes, and Miglio's inability to model the whole sequence without further reranking might square with their position. However, Stockwell and Minkova, and Lass, agree that the elements of the traditional Shift which are most likely to show unity are those involving the high and high mid vowels: neither suggests that diphthongization plus the raisings of both mid vowel series qualify as part of a unitary change, without the raising of /a:/, yet this is what Miglio's model would suggest. It is worth noting here that Ahn (2002) provides a closely parallel account to Miglio's, proposing that "the overall chain shift could have been initiated by the raising of lax vowels for phonetic reasons. Then, the subsequent raising and diphthongisation were consequences of Maintain Contrast requiring that the input vowel contrast be maintained in the output" (Ahn 2002: 153). Ahn also divides the Great Vowel Shift into two shifts, each stage characterized by a different constraint ranking; again, the second stage involves the raising of /a:/, and this time also the further lowering of the diphthongs from ME /i: u:/, to [aɪ aʊ].

There are several difficulties with Miglio's account. First, seeking the motivation for the GVS in the output of Middle English Open Syllable Lengthening (MEOSL), which, Miglio asserts, produced a superfluity of long lax low mid vowels, is potentially problematic given that MEOSL preceded the GVS by approximately 300 years – one of Stockwell and Minkova's objections to the GVS as a unitary change involves the more than 150 years between the top and bottom halves. Reranking also seems to be used fortuitously, and in particular there seems little motivation for the temporary rehabilitation of /ɛ:/, which has to be seen as less marked purely so low /a:/ can shift to it; though since, of course, there was a further step later, post-GVS, which raised this new /ɛ:/ to high mid /e:/, Miglio is going to have to re-re-rerank the constraints again. It is hard to see reranking as in any sense explanatory under these circumstances. Finally, if /ɛ: ɔ:/ are the weak points in the system which motivate the change, we must ask why only the front one is lost through the GVS, while its highly marked back congener continues into the present-day system. Further issues, involving novel mechanisms like local conjunction, and the "grounded" nature of general constraints like DISTANCE, will be pursued below.

1.3.3 Miglio and Morén (2003)

Miglio and Morén (2003) carries over two main issues from Miglio's earlier analysis of the GVS. Miglio and Morén also deal only with the diphthongizations of the high vowels, and the single-step raisings from low mid to high mid and high mid to high. They do not include the raising of /a:/; but as with Miglio's account, this seems to produce a strange split on either the Lass or Stockwell and Minkova view: if we attempt to model only Phase I or the "top half" of the traditional GVS as a unitary change, then the shifts of low mid /ɛ: ɔ/ should not be included; but if we include those later raisings, as Miglio and Morén do, there seems no good reason not to include the raising of /a:/ too.

Miglio and Morén argue that the English vowel system, leading up to the GVS, developed complete predictability of vowel length for all but the long mid vowels, which had developed a tense/lax distinction. Like Miglio (1998), though proposing different constraints, they ascribe the vowel shift to the disfavoring of long lax mid vowels, and an avoidance of merger. Essentially, Miglio and Morén see the GVS as both a lengthening and a raising change. Contextual lengthening takes place in certain environments, including open monosyllables (unfortunately, Miglio and Morén decline to discuss the rationale for this predisposing change: "The motivation for lengthening is not important here and is not shown" (2003: 206)). For the most part, this lengthening only involves tense vowels; but there is also "a combination of constraints forcing some mid vowels to be long" (2003: 206), so that both lax and tense mid vowels will undergo conditioned lengthening. Miglio and Morén then invoke a family DEPLINK-MORA of moraic faithfulness constraints, which spell out what happens when a segment of a particular type is forced to carry an extra mora, as in the coerced lengthening ("motivation . . . not important") of lax mid vowels. Assuming that DEPLINK-MORA [RTR, HIGH, LOW] (where RTR is Retracted Tongue Root) outranks DEPLINK-MORA [HIGH, LOW], "it is worse to add a mora to a surface lax mid vowel than it is to add a mora to a surface tense mid vowel" (2003: 209). Consequently, lengthened /ɛ/ must also tense to /e:/, raising perceptually. In turn, the pre-existing /e/, when lengthened, has to raise to /i:/ – this time because it is worse to add a mora to any mid vowel than to add a mora to a high vowel, as DEPLINK-MORA [HIGH, LOW] outranks DEPLINK-MORA [HIGH]. Raising rather than lowering is guaranteed because IDENT [HIGH] outranks IDENT [LOW] among the faithfulness constraints.

There is one final piece of the puzzle, which is the fact that /ɛ/ becomes /e:/, rather than raising all the way to high – the usual chain shift paradox. Miglio and Morén assume a Local Conjunction of (IDENT [RTR] & IDENT [LOW]). As Kager (1999: 392) puts it, "Under *Local Conjunction*, two constraints are conjoined as a single constraint which is violated if and only if both of its components are violated in the same domain." This conjoined constraint universally outranks its component constraints. In a chain shift, a double raising will violate more faithfulness constraints, like the IDENT ones considered here, than a single-step shift. In the present case, (IDENT [RTR] & IDENT [LOW]) says "it is worse to change both [RTR] and [LOW] at the same time than it is to change only one or the other" (Miglio and Morén 2003: 212), allowing a one-step but not a two-step shift.

Miglio and Morén see the constraint interactions set out above as applicable to their Stage II, the active stage of the GVS, which "consists of a re-ranking of constraints to (i) disfavor long lax mid vowels, and (ii) cause the rest of the non-low vowels to raise or break (diphthongize) to avoid merging them. This causes a complex correspondence between input and output vowels that bear little resemblance to each other" (2003: 203). This second stage is emphatically not a change for the better, then, and marks a departure from the earlier close connection of change with decreasing markedness. On the contrary, local pressures and constraint interactions produce a highly opaque relationship between input and output, and this is then subject to a later restructuring of the input on the basis of the new output forms.

There are several difficulties with Miglio and Morén's account, in addition to the undeveloped motivation for lengthening in the initial stages of the change noted above, and the problem that the aspects of the traditional GVS they model seem to correspond neither to the widely accepted "top half" of the chain or to the conventional Phases I and II. Staying with historical issues for the moment, Miglio and Morén discuss the relative chronology of the traditional GVS in some detail early in their paper, and clearly do not accept the Jespersen/Stockwell and Minkova position that diphthongization of ME /i: u:/ was the first step. However, they are equally uncomfortable with the Luick/Dobson/Lass argument that the high mid vowels initiated the overall Shift; they do not mention the pervasive (and persuasive) dialect evidence showing that, in northern areas where /o:/ had fronted earlier, /u:/ failed to diphthongize. Since their account of the GVS relies centrally on the assumption that the low mid vowels raised as the first step in the Shift, their solution is to argue that:

> the overlap between the quality changes of the various vowels, as provided by direct (orthographic) and indirect (reconstructed) evidence, does not allow for a strict sequence of events whereby some vowels changed before others. We believe that the relevant changes of the GVS (long mid lax vowels becoming tense, long mid tense vowels becoming high, and high vowels diphthongizing) are best modelled phonologically by a unique grammar that depicts this part of the GVS as a synchronic chain shift. (2003: 195)

From the perspective of a historical linguist, it is disappointing that Miglio and Morén's proposed OT account, and its limitations, should apparently override the very clear orthoepic-evidence for the considerable chronological priority of the changes of ME /i: u:/ and /e: o:/ over those of the low mid vowels (see Lass 1999). It would appear that sound change is productive ground for OT, unless the historical sequence of events is at odds with the preferred OT analysis; in which case, collapsing the lot into a single synchronic grammar (regardless of the several generations between the stages in real-time terms) is taken as solving the problem.

If the GVS is a synchronic chain shift, we must ask whether Miglio and Morén are presenting an analysis of sound change at all. Miglio and Morén themselves, to judge from their abstract, do consider themselves to be dealing with change: they tell us that their paper involves "a discussion of how language change can be dealt with in OT. . . . The paper addresses the question of language change in general and of chain shifts specifically" (2003: 191). One could argue, of course, about just what they mean by "change" here: is it the reranking that moves from their Stage I (before the GVS), to Stage II (when the GVS is "active")? Is it the input reanalysis that leads from the opaque input–output relationships at the end of Stage II, to the more transparent situation in Stage III? For historical phonologists, just as important as either of these would be the various steps contained within Stage II, the interlocking, or not so interlocking, stages of the GVS itself; but as we have seen, Miglio and Morén, though they appear to see the subshift of the long low mid vowels as representing the start of the mechanism, regard the whole of Stage II as essentially a synchronic chain shift, so this ambiguity is hard to resolve. Even if we accept that Miglio and Morén's proposals are intended to apply to change, there is a final question of explanation. Throughout the paper, their emphasis is squarely on the ability of OT to "model" changes, though they do also claim to be "motivating the GVS changes by means of a combination of established lengthening phenomena and markedness considerations" (2003: 191). Motivating a change, as it turns out, is not the same as explaining it; and indeed, Miglio and Morén (2003: 227 fn.10) state explicitly that they "believe that formal phonology should explain how phenomena happen and not necessarily why: in this case a coherent model of the GVS is as close to an explanation as we want to get. The psychological and sociolinguistic factors pertaining to 'why' the change happened have no place in an OT model of the GVS."

It seems entirely plausible that, in the early stages of development of a new model, proponents of OT should have claimed that its application to sound change might provide direct explanations: Miglio and Morén are now expressing a principled retreat from this position, towards a more limited, descriptive application of OT. This might seem also to correspond to a careful limitation of the types of constraints permissible in the grammar: Miglio and Morén are at pains to point out (2003: 227, fn.10) that the most important issue here is "the constraints' claim to universality, given the make-up of the theory. . . . Where we ourselves had doubts as to the universality of the constraint, we have stated it openly." This applies, for instance, to "*SHORT[TENSE] – Tense vowels must be bimoraic" (2003: 201), which Miglio and Morén describe as a " 'dummy constraint' " which "may or may not be a contender for universal status" (2003: 201). It does not seem entirely clear, however, what the difference is between a constraint like *SHORT[TENSE], which Miglio and Morén accept may be problematic, but nonetheless employ in their analysis, and DISTANCE or MINDIST, as used by Miglio (1998). Indeed, if the main criterion in adopting a constraint is whether it is likely to be universal, one might expect the latter to be better candidates for innateness, since avoiding wholesale mergers might be in the language user's interests. It may be that Miglio and Morén reject constraints like DISTANCE because these can be seen as encoding some idea of motivation, which goes against their view that explanation is not to be aimed at: "the factors that influence a linguistic community towards merger of lexical categories or chain shifting are not intrinsic to the grammar of the languages, but sociolinguistic and unpredictable in nature" (2003: 224). But is a constraint like INTEGRITY (2003: 213), which disfavors breaking or diphthongization, really much different from one like DISTANCE, which disfavors mergers? In any case, if the whole goal is simply coherent description and not explanation, how important is the inventory of constraints? If we are not to try to explain anything, should we not at least attempt to describe everything we can?

This problem of determining the constraint inventory, in terms of both constraint types and tokens, is an important and recurring one in the literature on OT, in both its synchronic and diachronic applications. It is difficult, in the absence of any clear prioritization of constraint types, to argue for one analysis over another. If we allow only universal constraints, what arguments are we to use for their universality? And how much leeway should we allow over the types of constraints we accept? For instance, although Miglio and Morén reject "functional" constraints like MINDIST, they accept Local Conjunction, although allowing combinations of constraints contributes to the problem of limiting the constraint inventory in such a way as to make it plausibly innate (or indeed, realistically learnable). On the other hand, if we accept (see Haspelmath 1999) that constraints should be language-specific and learnable rather than innate, the issue of change becomes potentially more difficult and less restrictive, since relationships between grammars other than simple reranking become possible. That is, if constraints could be added or removed between the grammars of different generations, as children learn a grammar which is essentially independent in constraint inventory as well as ranking, the modeling of change follows much less clearly from the architecture of OT, and the possible advantages of using that model become less clear.

1.3.4 Minkova and Stockwell (2003)

The last account to be considered here does not have the problem of Local Conjunction, or of language-specific constraints, but does share with Miglio (1998) the adoption of constraints against merger, and for the maintenance of contrast. We have seen already that Stockwell and Minkova, in a series of papers, argue against the unity of the traditional GVS: instead, they suggest that in languages like English, with both long vowels and diphthongs, "the two constant tendencies are for diphthongs to dissimilate and, having dissimilated maximally, to reassimilate" (1988a: 373). If monophthongs regularly gain diphthongal variants, then those may develop in two ways: either the elements of diphthongs become more different from one another, to "develop a healthier diphthongal form" (Stockwell and Minkova 1988a: 368); or they move back towards a monophthongal representation and merge with other monophthongs in the system. Such changes may, of course, be sequential and cyclic.

Minkova and Stockwell (2003) grows out of these earlier papers; and it is perhaps misleading to categorize it as an account of the GVS in OT terms, since as we have seen, the GVS is not something Minkova and Stockwell are inclined to believe in. It does, however, deal with chain shifts, along with three other change types, namely nucleus-glide dissimilation, nucleus-glide assimilation, and merger. This is a fascinating paper, partly because it does exactly what OT is meant to be extremely good at: that is, it takes a relatively small inventory of possible constraints, and shows that differential ranking produces different changes. Minkova and Stockwell (2003) exploit the idea of the factorial typology to show how the same motivating factors, differently prioritized, can give rise to these four types of change – which "can be independent of each other and should not be classified as the same unified historical phenomenon loosely referred to as shifts" (2003: 169).

Minkova and Stockwell isolate four factors which "jointly determine the behavior of English long vowels in processes commonly labelled chain shifts, or vowel shifts" (2003: 170): these appear in (4).

(4) "(a) Diphthong optimization in perceptual terms
(b) Diphthong optimization in articulatory terms
(c) Optimal spacing of adjacent entities – merger avoidance
(d) Vowel mergers and input–output faithfulness"
(Minkova and Stockwell 2003: 170)

In turn, these factors relate to four OT constraints. First, perceptual optimality in diphthongs depends on there being considerable distance between the two elements; this auditory distance follows from the constraint Hear Clear: "Maximize the auditory distance between the nuclear vowel and the following glide (measured in formant frequency" (Minkova and Stockwell 2003: 173). The best diphthongs will have endpoints that are easily perceived as different, while those with perceptually close endpoints are likely to be avoided.

The second constraint is *Effort, which prioritizes articulations requiring less effort. Whereas Hear Clear favored diphthongs with maximally distinct endpoints, "with respect to this constraint 'the best diphthong is a long vowel' " (Minkova and Stockwell 2003: 180). If a diphthong is to be maintained, then Hear Clear will be ranked above *Effort, whereas monophthongization will correspond to a higher ranking of *Effort relative to Hear Clear.

The other two crucial constraints involve the shapes of segment inventories, and the interplay of elements within them. Minimal Distance encodes an instruction to "Maximize the auditory distinctiveness of contrasts" (Minkova and Stockwell 2003: 182); the overlapping but distinct Ident io (Contrast) "Preserve categorical contrasts" (2003: 184) disfavors mergers and splits. It might initially seem odd that Minkova and Stockwell adopt these constraints, in view of their earlier claim (Stockwell and Minkova 1988a: 378) that

> psychological and perceptual principles and explanations based on them, such as optimal intuitive organisation of the vowel space, or the discouragement of homophony, or displacement to avoid merger, are irrelevant. . . . The only principle that might be relevant is that the vowel space shouldn't be too crammed, that overcrowding results in mergers. But we don't think even *that* putative principle is worth trying to salvage. Such principles probably explain nothing in language change.

However, a closer reading reveals that their position has not changed: Minkova and Stockwell (2003: 183) also argue that Minimal Distance and Ident io (Contrast) are "unlike the Hear Clear and *Effort constraints, which we see as genuine *triggers* of change, based on universal phonetic properties"; further, "In the murky waters of historical data, appealing to phonetic properties as an 'explanation' can be justified, but an appeal to the well-formedness of the entire inventory as a trigger is not justified."

Minkova and Stockwell argue strongly for a distinction between phonetic functional factors on the one hand, and systemic issues such as preservation of contrast on the other. They also argue that tracing these factors to distinct constraints allows them to be differently prioritized, giving a classic OT factorial typology as shown in (5).

(5) Nucleus-glide dissimilation:
Ident io (Contrast) >> Hear Clear >> Minimal Distance >> *Effort
Nucleus-glide assimilation:
Ident io (Contrast) >> *Effort >> Minimal Distance >> Hear Clear
Chain shift:
Ident io (Contrast), Minimal Distance >> Hear Clear, *Effort
Merger:
*Effort >> Ident io (Contrast), Minimal Distance >> Hear Clear

Four different rankings of these four key constraints provide four different outcomes in terms of the observable resulting changes. If it is most important to avoid splits and mergers, for instance, either dissimilation or assimilation within diphthongs may follow, depending on whether Hear Clear or *Effort ranks higher – depending, that is, on the relative prioritization of what is good for the speaker versus what is good for the hearer. Merger will take place where the most important factor of all is ease of articulation; and chain shifts, like the putative GVS (or at least, perhaps, the "top half") will arise when avoiding mergers and keeping contrasting units maximally distinct, are higher priorities than the convenience of either speaker or hearer.

Some of the issues which arise from this very neat demonstration of typological modeling overlap with those raised in relation to Miglio and Morén, above. There is, for instance, arguably the same ambivalence over the explanatory power of OT with respect to change; Minkova and Stockwell (2003: 190 fn.28) themselves ask:

> what was the motivation for the different constraint rankings that are invoked to account for the different historical results? This is the breaking point of any account, and the challenge that OT meets here is no worse than the challenge met by previous theories. . . . The re-ranking of constraints, like the application of a rule, is effected by individuals and their speech community over time, information unrecoverable by definition.

On the other hand, we have already seen that Minkova and Stockwell see the relative prioritization of the hearer's and the speaker's needs, via HEAR CLEAR and *EFFORT, as "genuine *triggers* of change" (2003: 183), while they are less comfortable with factors relating to the system rather than directly to the language user, describing MINIMAL DISTANCE as "a useful OT translation of 'preservation of contrast' which is only epiphenomenal in the description of chain shifts" (2003: 183), and IDENT IO (CONTRAST) as "a shortcut . . . naively, a cover term for the intuition that lexical contrasts should be respected, an injunction against mergers" (2003: 184). The same issues as discussed in section 1.3.3 therefore arise over whether these constraints, albeit expressing universal motivations, should really be part of the inventory.

Perhaps the most pressing concern is the nature of the two constraints Minkova and Stockwell support most strongly, HEAR CLEAR and *EFFORT, which on any definition are irreducibly phonetically grounded. One of the most controversial issues within OT at present is the very question of whether constraints should be phonetically grounded or not – and this is a matter of more general debate in phonology, since it has very serious implications for the relationship between phonology and phonetics, the relationship of phonology to Universal Grammar (UG), and hence the definition of phonology. Radically different approaches to this question can be found in Hale and Reiss (2000a, 2000b) and Carr (2000).

Hale and Reiss argue on grounds of principle that "[p]honology is not and should not be grounded in phonetics, since the facts that phonetic grounding is meant to explain can be derived without reference to *phonology*. Duplication of the principles of acoustics and acquisition inside the grammar constitutes a violation of Occam's Razor and thus must be avoided" (2000a: 167). They are keen for phonology to be neutral between modalities, for instance between speaking and signing, and are also concerned by the trend to extrapolate phonetic measurements directly into phonological units and arguments – they argue that this is seriously inadvisable, since we do not currently have a clear enough idea of how individual cues combine to produce percepts, so there is an uneasy relationship between actual measurements and our conclusions in terms of "difficulty" or "salience." Since phonology and phonetics are seen as necessarily distinct, phonological arguments cannot coherently be stated in phonetic terms: attempts to do so are (rather cleverly) described as "substance abuse."

Furthermore, Hale and Reiss argue explicitly that functional constraints like LAZY (= Minkova and Stockwell's *EFFORT) and MINIMAL DISTANCE should not be permitted because "functional principles can be replaced by their opposites, which we will call 'dysfunctional' principles, with no significant change in the set of grammars predicted to exist" (2000a: 180). Hence, these constraints could be replaced by "OBFUSCATE: merge constrasts, use a small inventory of distinctive sounds . . . ," and "NO PAIN – NO GAIN: maintain contrasts, use a large inventory, generate allomorphy . . ." (2000a: 180), with no significant difference in results. The formulations we typically choose depend on our view of human nature, not on anything phonological.

Carr (2000), on the other hand, argues that "[t]here is only one sustainable conception of UG, one that takes it to be *radically internal*, in the sense that it is an innate endowment that does not consist of perceptual capacities, behavioural dispositions, general cognitive capacities, or capacities that are not species specific" (2000: 87). If we accept this, then "phonological knowledge does indeed fall outside UG" (2000: 89). Carr accepts that, at least at first sight, some OT constraints might seem to be reasonable candidates for inclusion in UG, but argues that any which make reference to phonetics, or which are functionally inclined, will have to be excluded. This is the case, for example, for any constraint referring to relative perceptual salience: "the relation 'perceptually more salient than' is general-cognitive: it is the figure–ground relation. That relation cannot be said to constitute part of UG, since UG, by definition, excludes general cognitive capacities" (2000: 91).

This leaves OT with something of a difficulty. Hale and Reiss see phonology as part of Universal Grammar, and therefore as not plausibly phonetically grounded. Carr argues that phonology is phonetically grounded, and therefore cannot be part of UG. We therefore have a rather striking result: either way, innate and universal constraints based on phonetics are not viable. It appears that we must either choose innate phonological constraints, which cannot be grounded; or grounded constraints, which cannot be innate. This brings the issue of language specific-constraints, learnability, and the implications for the OT account of change, firmly into the foreground.

1.4 Change in the Making?

One of the most significant issues to arise from our discussion of OT and sound change, then, involves the phonetic grounding of constraints. This is important primarily because it throws into sharp relief a whole range of other, connected questions, which urgently need answers before historical linguists can feel confident about the use of OT to resolve historical problems (and which are all being debated, as we have seen, in the OT literature). The question of grounding is obviously related to that of innateness. As a general rule, the more functionally inclined a linguist is, the more likely s/he is to see OT constraints as grounded but learned: thus, Haspelmath (1999: 204) argues that "the grammatical constraints are not innate, and are not part of Universal Grammar. They arise from general constraints on language use, which for the most part are in no way specific to language." But if the constraints are grounded in phonetics, perception, or some other universal but not phonological capabilities, just what is OT contributing? If OT allows clear modeling and hierarchization of a series of priorities (for instance, the convenience of the speaker versus the hearer), but those are not themselves phonological, what does OT become a theory of? As Hale and Reiss note, if we build in "a sufficiently rich and explicit theory of the human personality . . . and the human articulatory and perceptual systems . . . , phonology itself will turn out to be epiphenomenal" (2000b: 167). Alternatively, if we excise issues of phonetic motivation from our constraints, we lose many of the advantages OT offered in the cases considered above, by modeling the interaction of familiar preferences, like the constant struggle between speaker and hearer. There is a further paradox: if grounded constraints are based on universal factors, but are learned, new generations might acquire novel constraints, and hence our model of change becomes less restricted since reranking is no longer the only available means of grammar differentiation. However, if we reject grounding and opt for innate and specifically phonological constraints, how are we to limit the explosion of constraints and constraint types which has recently bedeviled the theory?

The issue of grounding is also helpful because it highlights further difficulties in establishing the basic ingredients of OT; the nature of the input, for instance, is currently quite unclear, undermining the development of learning theory (Hale and Reiss 1998; McMahon 2002). Hale (2000) points out that we do not seem to be very clear on the nature of the output either: does it mean "bodily output," actual phonetics, or is it an intermediate representation, the end of the phonological grammar? As for Gen, Haspelmath (1999: 204) holds that it "has been largely ignored, apparently because of the implicit presumption that it is not very interesting. However, from an innatist perspective it is the most interesting part of the theory, because it is the part that is the most likely to be innate." Here again, we find a strong connection with grounding, since its interpretation is unclear if we do not understand the level of representation to which constraint evaluation applies: "To advocate the inclusion in an OT grammar of constraints which make reference to issues such as the 'auditory consequence of gestural timing' without explicitly discussing the nature of a Gen component that would generate representations of the type that would allow for the evaluation of such constraints is not responsible science" (Hale 2000: 250).

Finally, these doubts and inclarities highlight the uneasy relationship between change and formal theory. It is intuitively tempting to see change as functionally motivated, and yet we find linguists who believe phonology is and must be part of UG (Hale and Reiss 2000a, 2000b), and those who argue it cannot be (Carr 2000), agreeing that it is incoherent to hypothesize innate, grounded constraints. This might mean that Miglio and Morén (2003), or Minkova and Stockwell (2003), are prescient in their arguments that formal theories should not be expected to provide "causal explanations," only at best "proximate mechanisms" (Minkova 1999). Whether OT can offer any actual explanations will depend, of course, on whether it is part of a theory of UG or not; and here we find another, perhaps surprising, twist in the argument.

Hale (2000) visualizes a continuum of phonological processes, with absolute universals at one end, impossibilities at the other, and a range of more or less likely phenomena in between. Hale argues that UG can be invoked to account for the absolute universals and perhaps for the unattested cases (though note here McMahon 2002, where it is argued that OT, in the absence of any restriction on the number and type of constraints permitted, can model impossible changes just as readily as rule-based models). However, he believes that "the middle portion of the continuum can be coherently accounted for without reference to the synchronic phonological system at all," since "[t]he relative rarity of a given phonological process, cross-linguistically, is a simple function of how likely the misperception . . . required for the coming into being of that process is" (Hale 2000: 254). Hale's radical proposal is to exclude markedness considerations from phonology, and to seek explanations of synchronic systems through understanding diachronic processes. It would appear that historical linguists can look forward to their domain of enquiry coming conclusively back into the limelight – but in the service of synchronic linguistics, rather than the other way around. If historical factors explain synchronic systems, then surely we cannot look to synchronic models, like OT, to explain language change – or perhaps even to model it. Will that be a change for the better?

REFERENCES

Ahn, Sang-Cheol (2002). An Optimality approach to the Great Vowel Shift. *Korean Journal of Linguistics* 27: 153–70.

Archangeli, Diana (1997). Optimality Theory: an introduction to linguistics in the 1990s. In Diana Archangeli and D. Terence Langendoen (eds.), *Optimality Theory: An Overview* (pp. 1–32). Oxford: Blackwell.

Bermúdez-Otero, Ricardo and Richard Hogg (2003). The actuation problem in Optimality Theory: phonologization, rule inversion, and rule loss. In D. Eric Holt (ed.), *Optimality Theory and Language Change* (pp. 91–119). Amsterdam: Kluwer.

Carr, Philip (2000). Scientific realism, sociophonetic variation, and innate endowments in phonology. In Noel Burton-Roberts, Philip Carr, and Gerard Docherty (eds.), *Phonological Knowledge: Conceptual and Empirical Issues* (pp. 67–104). Oxford: Oxford University Press.

Hale, Mark (2000). Marshallese phonology, the phonetics–phonology interface and historical linguistics. *The Linguistic Review* 17: 241–57.

Hale, Mark and Charles Reiss (2000a). Phonology as cognition. In Noel Burton-Roberts, Philip Carr, and Gerard Docherty (eds.), *Phonological Knowledge: Conceptual and Empirical Issues* (pp. 161–84). Oxford: Oxford University Press.

Hale, Mark and Charles Reiss (2000b). "Substance abuse" and "dysfunctionalism": current trends in phonology. *Linguistic Inquiry* 31: 157–69.

Haspelmath, Martin (1999). Optimality and diachronic adaptation. *Zeitschrift für SprachWissenschaft* 18: 180–205.

Kager, René (1999). *Optimality Theory*. Cambridge: Cambridge University Press.

Lass, Roger (1976). *English Phonology and Phonological Theory*. Cambridge: Cambridge University Press.

Lass, Roger (1988). Vowel shifts, great and otherwise: remarks on Stockwell and Minkova. In Dieter Kastovsky and Gero Bauer (eds.), *Luick Revisited* (pp. 395–410). Tübingen: Gunter Narr Verlag.

Lass, Roger (1992). What, if anything, was the Great Vowel Shift? In Matti Rissanen, Ossi Ihalainen, Terttu Nevalainen, and Irma Taavitsainen (eds.), *History of Englishes: New Methods and Interpretations in Historical Linguistics* (pp. 144–55). Berlin: Mouton de Gruyter.

Lass, Roger (1999). Phonology and morphology. In Roger Lass (ed.), *The Cambridge History of the English Language*, vol. 3: *1476–1776* (pp. 56–186). Cambridge: Cambridge University Press.

McMahon, April (2000a). *Change, Chance, and Optimality*. Oxford: Oxford University Press.

McMahon, April (2000b). The emergence of the optimal? Optimality Theory and sound change. *The Linguistic Review* 17: 231–40.

McMahon, April (2002). On not explaining language change: Optimality Theory and the Great Vowel Shift. In Raymond Hickey (ed.), *Motives for Language Change* (pp. 82–96). Cambridge: Cambridge University Press.

Miglio, Viola (1998). The Great Vowel Shift: an OT model for unconditioned language change. Paper presented at the 10th International Conference on English Historical Linguistics, University of Manchester.

Miglio, Viola and Bruce Morén (2003). Merger avoidance and lexical reconstruction: an Optimality-Theoretic model of the Great Vowel Shift. In D. Eric Holt (ed.), *Optimality Theory and Language Change* (pp. 191–228). Amsterdam: Kluwer.

Minkova, Donka (1999). Review of Roger Lass (ed.) (1999) *The Cambridge History of the English Language*, vol. 3: *1476–1776*. *Journal of English Linguistics* 29: 83–92.

Minkova, Donka and Robert Stockwell (2003). English vowel shifts and "optimal" diphthongs: is there a logical link? In D. Eric Holt (ed.), *Optimality Theory and Language Change* (pp. 169–90). Amsterdam: Kluwer.

Stockwell, Robert P. (1975). Problems in the interpretation of the Great English Vowel Shift. In Didier L. Goyvaerts and Geoffrey K. Pullum (eds.), *Essays on the Sound Pattern of English* (pp. 331–53). Ghent: E. Story-Scientia.

Stockwell, Robert P. and Donka Minkova (1988a). The English Vowel Shift: problems of coherence and explanation. In Dieter Kastovsky and Gero Bauer (eds.), *Luick Revisited* (pp. 355–94). Tübingen: Gunter Narr Verlag.

Stockwell, Robert P. and Donka Minkova (1988b). A rejoinder to Lass. In Dieter Kastovsky and Gero Bauer (eds.), *Luick Revisited* (pp. 411–17). Tübingen: Gunter Narr Verlag.

Stockwell, Robert P. and Donka Minkova (1990). The Early Modern English vowels, more O'Lass. *Diachronica* 7: 199–214.

Stockwell, Robert P. and Donka Minkova (1997). On drifts and shifts. *Studia Anglica Posnaniensia* 31: 283–303.

Stockwell, Robert P. and Donka Minkova (1999). Explanations of sound change: contradictions between dialect data and theories of chain shifting. *Leeds Studies in English (New Series)* 30: 83–101.

FURTHER READING

Bermúdez-Otero, Ricardo and Kersti Börjars (forthcoming). Markedness in phonology and syntax: the problem of grounding. To appear in *Lingua*.

Flemming, Edward (1995). Auditory Representations in Phonology. PhD dissertation, University of California at Los Angeles.

Hammond, Michael (1999). *The Phonology of English: A Prosodic Optimality-Theoretic Approach* (The Phonology of the World's Languages). Oxford: Oxford University Press.

Lombardi, Linda (ed.) (2001). *Segmental Phonology in Optimality Theory: Constraints and Representations.* Cambridge: Cambridge University Press.

McCarthy, John (2002). *A Thematic Guide to Optimality Theory.* Cambridge: Cambridge University Press.

Prince, Alan and Paul Smolensky (1993). *Optimality Theory: Constraint Interaction in Generative Grammar.* Ms, Rutgers University / University of Colorado at Boulder.

2 Cuing a New Grammar

DAVID W. LIGHTFOOT

2.1 E-language Approaches

Our nineteenth-century predecessors developed linguistics as a distinct discipline and they were concerned exclusively with language change. They thought of texts as the essential reality and took languages to be entities "out there," existing in their own right, waiting to be acquired by groups of speakers. For them, languages were external objects and changed in systematic ways according to "laws" and general notions of directionality. Languages were related to each other to different degrees, modeled in tree diagrams (*Stammbäume*), and they changed at certain rates that could be discovered. Linguists of the time focused on the products of human behavior rather than on the internal processes that underlie the behavior, although other approaches were put forward towards the end of the century, particularly in the work of Hermann Paul and phoneticians like Eduard Sievers. By the end of the nineteenth century, the data of linguistics consisted of an inventory of sound changes, but there were no general principles: the changes occurred for no good reason and tended in no particular direction. The historical approach had not brought a scientific, Newtonian-style analysis of language, of the kind that had been hoped for, and there was no predictability to the changes. The historicist paradigm – the notion that there are principles of history to be discovered – was largely abandoned in the 1920s (Lightfoot 1999: ch. 2).

Languages were often seen as objects floating smoothly through time and space, and that persistent image survived the twentieth century. Despite the move away from historicism in the 1920s, linguists resumed the search for historical principles in the latter decades of the century. In the 1970s much work recast the notion of "drift," originated by Sapir (1921: ch. 7). The "typologists," working from Greenberg's (1963) word order harmonies, claimed that languages changed along universal diachronic continua, moving from one pure type to another via universally defined transitional stages. Languages change from one pure type to another by losing/acquiring the relevant orders in the sequence specified by the hierarchies. A pure subject–verb–object language, for example, has verb–object order, auxiliary–verb, noun–adjective, and preposition–DP, and these orders are ranked in a hierarchy. A subject–object–verb language is essentially the mirror image and has the opposite orders: object–verb, verb –auxiliary, adjective–noun, and DP–preposition, etc. If a language changes from the object–verb type to the verb–object type, it acquires all of the new orders harmonically, in the sequence prescribed by the hierarchy: first verb–object, then auxiliary–verb, and so on. The hierarchy is the substance of a historical law which stipulates how a language of one type changes to a language of a different type. The typologists argued that notions like the subject–object–verb-to-subject–verb–object continua constituted diachronic explanations (Vennemann 1975); for them, the drift was the explanatory force, rather than being something which required explanation, and no local causes were needed. The typologists remained faithful to the methods of the nineteenth century. They dealt with the products of the language capacity rather than with the capacity itself, and they retained the same kind of historical determinism, believing that languages of one type change inexorably to a language of another type, like their nineteenth-century predecessors. The goal remained one of finding "straightline explanations for language change" (Lass 1980), generalizations which would hold of history. And they were no more successful.

A more recent line of work has emphasized the alleged unidirectionality of change, also treating languages as external objects "out there," subject to change in certain inevitable ways. Grammaticalization, a notion first introduced by Antoine Meillet in the 1930s, is taken to be a semantic tendency for an item with a full lexical meaning to be bleached over time and to come to be used as a grammatical function. Such changes are said to be quite general and unidirectional; one does not find changes proceeding in the reverse direction, so it is said. I shall discuss an instance of grammaticalization in section 2.3 and there are many examples (Hopper and Traugott 1993). Grammaticalization is a real phenomenon but it is quite a different matter to claim that it is general, unidirectional, or an explanatory force. If there were a universal tendency to grammaticalize, there would be no counterdevelopments, when bound forms become independent lexical items (affixes becoming clitics or independent words – an example of this to be discussed later in this chapter is genitive endings in *-es* in Middle English being reanalyzed as *his*, yielding genitives like *Christ his sake, Mrs Sands his maid*). For further examples and discussion, see Gelderen (1997), Janda (2001), Joseph (2001), and Newmeyer (1998: ch. 5). When grammaticalization takes place, it is explained when one points to local factors which promoted the new grammar, new triggering experiences, changes in cues, or what Kiparsky (1996) calls the "enabling causes." Grammaticalization, interesting as a *phenomenon*, is not an explanatory force.

2.2 Focusing on I-language

In the 1970s, as the typologists were developing their determinist approach to change, others began to study language change in the context of the acquisition of grammars. If we switch our perspective from language change to new grammars, from the products of the language system to the system itself, from E-language to I-language (Chomsky 1986), we explain new grammars through the nature of the acquisition process. New grammars are just one part of language change, but a central part; language change goes beyond new grammars and may involve the changing *use* of grammars or social variation (see the introduction to Lightfoot 2002).

Grammars are formal characterizations of an individual's linguistic capacity, conforming to and exploiting the tools provided by a universal initial state ("Universal Grammar") and developing as a person is exposed to her childhood linguistic experience. A grammar, in this terminology, is a mental organ, in fact a person's language organ, and is physically represented somehow in the brain, "secreted" by the brain, in Darwin's terminology (Anderson and Lightfoot 2002). A grammar grows in a child from some initial state (UG), when she is exposed to primary linguistic data (PLD) (1).

(1) PLD (UG → grammar)

Furthermore, new grammars may emerge over time: people developed certain grammars in London in the thirteenth century and different ones in the fifteenth century. The only way a different grammar may grow in a different child is when that child is exposed to significantly different primary data. In that case, the linguist wants to find how grammars changed and how the relevant childhood experience might have changed just prior to the change in grammars, in such a way that the new grammar was the only possible outcome. In this perspective, the study of new grammars, of grammar change, is fused with work on variation and the acquisition of grammars. We explain the emergence of the new grammar and the explanation illuminates the nature of the child's triggering experience and the way in which children acquire their linguistic capacities; the study of new grammars has implications for grammatical theory and for theories of language acquisition.

Grammars differ sharply: a person either has a grammar with a certain property, or not. People's speech, on the other hand, is in constant flux and languages, conglomerations of the output of people's grammars, are inherently fluid, unstable, always changing. Speech is always in flux and no two people have the same initial experiences. While the primary linguistic data (PLD) are infinitely variable, grammars are not; under parameter theory, there is a finite number of grammars, resulting from different settings of a finite number of parameters. If we recast parameters in terms of cues (see below), there is a finite number of cues for which a child scans her linguistic environment. Grammars are generally supposed to be algebraic (finite and ranging over infinity) and modular (consisting of different types of mechanisms), and to involve computational operations of a special kind. For discussion of the three entities in (1), sometimes called "the analytical triplet," see Anderson and Lightfoot (2002).

Language change is a group phenomenon. Languages, whatever they may be precisely, reflect the output of grammars, the varying use of those grammars in discourse, and social variation in the set of grammars that are relevant for any particular language. Language change can sometimes be tracked geographically, seeing some new variant attested in different places at different times. And change at the level of languages often seems to take place gradually, spreading through the population socially and geographically.

The linguistic experience of young children (their PLD) varies constantly, but sometimes small variations have bigger, structural consequences, changes in grammars. Grammar change, involving new structures, is different; if grammars are abstract, then they change only occasionally and sometimes with dramatic consequences for a wide range of constructions and expressions; grammar change tends to be "bumpy," manifested by clusters of phenomena changing at the same time, as we shall see. Grammatical change is contingent, dependent on the details of the use of language (for example, changing morphology, changing distribution of words and construction types), language contact, perhaps even social attitudes and second language acquisition. Grammar change is linked to changes in people's speech, and we can only know about it by studying what people say, often through written texts, and it must be studied in conjunction with other kinds of change. But new grammars constitute a distinct type of change, a reaction to contingent factors of language use, and new grammars emerge subject to the usual principles of UG. The study of the contingent events is complementary to the search for the general organizing principles of UG, but there is a different focus. To focus on new grammars, on I-language, is to attend to one aspect of language change, one which illuminates the variation and acquisition of grammars by children, but one which is dependent on other kinds of language change.

The explanatory model is essentially synchronic and there will be a local cause for the emergence of any new grammar, namely a different set of primary linguistic data. I will offer two case studies.

2.3 English Auxiliary Verbs

English modal auxiliaries like *can, could, may, might, will, would, shall, should,* and *must* differ from ordinary verbs in their distribution. A modal auxiliary does not occur with a perfective (2) or present participle (3), unlike a verb; a modal does not occur in the infinitival complement to another verb (4), nor as the complement of another modal (5), unlike a verb such as *try*; and no modal may occur with a direct object, whereas some verbs may (6).

(2) a. *He has could understand chapter 4.
    b. He has understood chapter 4.

(3) a. *Canning understand chapter 4, . . .
    b. Understanding chapter 4, . . .

(4) a. *He wanted to can understand.
b. He wanted to understand.

(5) a. *He will can understand.
b. He will understand.

(6) a. *He can music.
b. He understands music.

The distribution of these modal auxiliaries is peculiar to modern English. For example, the French verb *pouvoir* 'can' behaves in the same way as a verb like *comprendre* 'understand': unlike *can, pouvoir* may occur as a complement to another verb (7), even to another modal verb (8), and may take a clitic direct object (9), and to that extent it behaves like ordinary, common-or-garden verbs in French. In French grammars, the words which translate the English modals, *pouvoir, devoir,* etc., are verbs, just like *comprendre.*

(7) Il a voulu pouvoir comprendre le chapitre.
'He wanted to be able to understand the chapter'

(8) Il doit pouvoir comprendre le chapitre.
'He must be able to understand the chapter'

(9) Il le peut.
'He can it,' i.e. understand the chapter

Furthermore, not only may languages differ in this regard, but also different stages of one language. Sentences along the lines of the nonexistent utterances of (2–6a) were well-formed in earlier English. If the differences between Old and Modern English were a function of separate features with no unifying factor (Ross 1969), we would expect these features to come into the language at different times and in different ways. On the other hand, if the differences between Old and Modern English reflect a single property in an abstract system, a categorical distinction, then we would expect the trajectory of the change to be very different. And that's what we find. If the differences between *can* and *understand* were a function of the single fact that *understand* is a verb while *can* is a member of a different category, Inflection (I), then we would not be surprised to find that (2–6a) dropped out of people's language in parallel, at the same time.

In Middle English *Kim can understand the chapter* had the structure (10) and in present-day English the structure (11). If in present-day English *can* is an I element, then one predicts that it cannot occur to the left of a perfective or present participle, as in (2a), (3a) (those participial markers are generated within the VP), that it is mutually exclusive with the infinitival marker *to* (which also occurs in I) (4b), that there may only be one modal per VP (5), and that a modal may not be followed by a direct object (6a). Simply postulating the structure of (11) accounts for the data of (2–6) in present-day English. Earlier English had structures like (10), where *can* is a verb and behaves like *understand,* moving to a higher functional position. If one thinks in terms of a certain kind of abstract system, then there is a single change which accounts for the phenomena of (2–6).

(10) Middle English

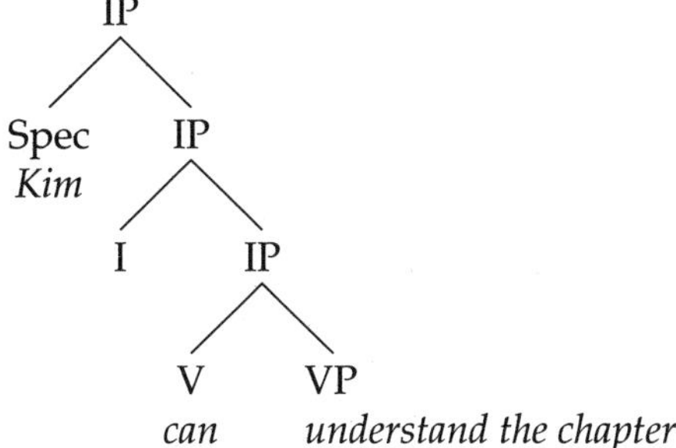

(11) Present-day English

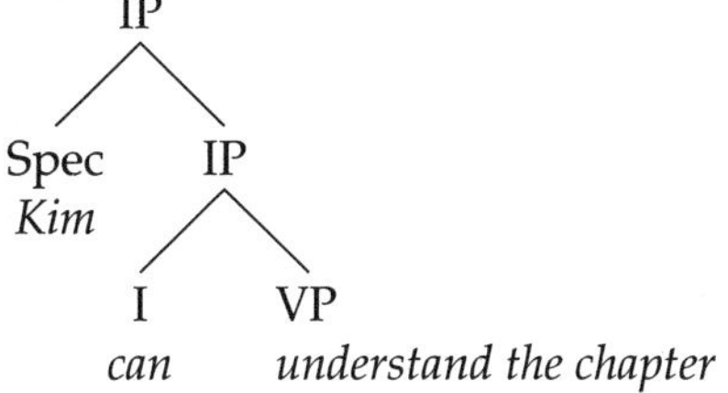

If we attend just to changing phenomena, the historical change consists in the *loss* of various forms, not in the development of new forms; people ceased to say some things which had been said in earlier times. Before the change, all of the utterances in (2–6) might have occurred in a person's speech, but later only those forms not marked with an asterisk. That fact alone suggests that there was a change in some abstract system. People might start to use some new expression because of the social demands of fashion or because of the influence of speakers from a different community, but people do not *cease* to say things for that sort of reason. There might be an indirect relationship, of course: people might introduce new expressions into their speech for external, social reasons, and those new expressions might entail the loss of old forms. Changes involving only the loss and obsolescence of forms need to be explained as a consequence of some change in an abstract, cognitive system. This methodological point is fundamental.

If one focuses on the final disappearance of the relevant forms, one sees that they were lost as a set and not individually. The most conservative writer in this regard was Sir Thomas More, writing in the early sixteenth century. He used all of the starred forms in (2–6a) and had the last attested uses of several constructions. His grammar treated *can*, etc., as verbs in the old fashion (10), and the fact that he used *all* the relevant forms and his heirs none, suggests that his grammar differed from theirs in one way and not that the new grammars accumulated unrelated features. Similarly for other writers: either they used all the forms of (2–6a) or none. The uniformity of the change suggests uniformity in the analysis. There was a single change, a change in category membership: *can*, formerly a verb that moved to I in the course of a derivation, came to be analyzed as an I element (11). The fact that there was a single change in grammars accounts for the bumpiness: already we see the advantages of thinking in terms of an abstract system, a grammar. Different verbs may have undergone the shift at different times and different people had the new properties at different times, but several phenomena clustered.

The change in category membership of the English modals explains the catastrophic nature of the change, not in the sense that the change spread through the population rapidly, but that phenomena changed together. The notion of change in grammars is a way of unifying disparate phenomena, taking them to be various surface manifestations of a single change at the abstract level. Tony Kroch and his associates (see Kroch 1989, for example) have done interesting statistical work on the spread of such changes through populations of speakers, showing that it is grammars which spread: competing grammars may coexist in individual speakers for periods of time. They have shown that the variation observed represents oscillation between two fixed points, two grammars, and not oscillation in which the *phenomena* vary independently of each other.

We do not appeal to historical forces as explanations under the cognitive view of grammars. The cause of the grammatical change can only be earlier changes in PLD. There were two. First, the modal auxiliaries became distinct morphologically, the sole surviving members of the preterite-present class of verbs. There were many verb classes in early English and the antecedents of the modern modals were preterite-presents. The preterite-presents (so called because their present tense forms had past tense or "preterite" morphology) were distinct in that they never had any inflection for the third person singular, although they were inflected elsewhere: *þu cannst, we cunnan, we cuðon*. Nonetheless, they were just another class of verbs, one of many, and the forms that were to become modal auxiliaries, sometimes called "premodals," belonged to this class, along with a number of other verbs which either dropped out of the language altogether or were assimilated to another more regular class of verbs. For example, *unnan* 'grant' was lost from the language and *witan* 'know' simply dropped out of the preterite-present class, coming to be treated like non-preterite-presents. They were not entirely normal verbs and there is evidence that the future modal auxiliaries were already developing some distinct properties in late Old English. Warner (1993) shows that some of these items were not attested with non-finite forms in Old English texts.

After the simplification of verb morphology, verb classes collapsed and the *only* inflectional property of present-tense verbs to survive was the *-s* ending for the third person singular, and the preterite-present verbs had always lacked that property. The preterite-presents did not change in this regard, but a great mass of inflectional distinctions had disappeared and now the preterite-presents were isolated; they looked different from all other verbs in lacking their one morphological feature, that *-s* ending. And the surviving preterite-presents were the elements that would be recategorized as Inflectional items.

The morphological distinctiveness of the surviving preterite-presents, the new modals, was complemented by a new opacity in their past tense forms. The past tense forms of the preterite-present verbs were phonetically identical in many instances to the subjunctive forms and, when the subjunctive forms were lost, past tense forms survived with subjunctive-type meanings rather than indicating past-time reference. While *loved* is related to *love* pretty much exclusively in terms of time reference in present-day English, the relationship between *can* and *could* is sometimes one of time (12a) and sometimes has nothing to do with time (12b). And *might* is never related to *may* in terms of time in present-day English (13a, b); in earlier times, *might* did indicate past time (13c) – but the thought of (13c) would need to be expressed as *might not have intended* in present-day English. So *might, could, should,* etc., came to take on new meanings which had nothing to do with past time, residues of the old subjunctive uses; the past tense forms became semantically opaque.

(12) a. Kim could understand the book, until she reached page 56.
b. Kim could be here tomorrow.

(13) a. *Kim might read the book yesterday.
b. Kim may/might read the book tomorrow.
c. These two respectable writers might not intend the mischief they were doing.
(Richard Hurd (1762), *Letters on Chivalry and Romance* 85)

As a result of these two changes, the preterite-present verbs came to look different from all other verbs in the language: they were morphologically distinct and had become semantically opaque. UG provides a small inventory of grammatical categories and elements are assigned to a category on the basis of their morphological and distributional properties. Consequently, morphological changes entail new primary linguistic data and they may trigger new category distinctions. In this case, we know that, following the morphological changes, the surviving verbs of the preterite-present class were assigned to a new grammatical category, and that change was complete by the early sixteenth century. The evidence for the new category membership is the simultaneous loss for each verb of the phenomena we discussed in (2–6a).

There were two stages to the history of English modal auxiliaries (Lightfoot 1999: ch. 6). First, a change in category membership, whereby *can,* etc., ceased to be treated as verbs and came to be taken as manifestations of the Inflection category; this change affected some verbs before others, but it was complete by the sixteenth century. For a sentence like *Kim can sing,* early grammars had structures like (10), where *can* is an ordinary verb which sometimes moves to I, but later grammars had structures like (11), where *can* is a modal, drawn from the lexicon and merged into a structure as an instance of I. As a result, sentences like (2–6a) dropped out of the language and no longer occurred in texts.

Second, English lost the operation moving verbs to a higher Inflection position (e.g. in (10)). This change was completed only in the eighteenth century, later than is generally supposed (Warner 1997). At this point, sentences with a finite verb moved to some initial position (14b), or to the left of a negative (15b), became obsolete and were replaced by equivalent forms with the periphrastic *do*: *Does Kim understand this chapter? Kim does not understand this chapter.*

(14) a. Can he understand chapter 4?
     b. *Understands he chapter 4?

(15) a. He cannot understand chapter 4.
     b. *He understands not chapter 4.

Again French differs: finite forms of both *pouvoir* and *comprendre* occur sentence-initially (16) and to the left of a negative (17).

(16) a. Peut-il comprendre le chapitre?
        'Can he understand the chapter?'
     b. Comprend-il le chapitre?
        'Does he understand the chapter?'

(17) a. Il ne peut pas comprendre le chapitre.
        'He cannot understand the chapter.'
     b. Il ne comprend pas le chapitre.
        'He doesn't understand the chapter.'

Also sentences with an adverb between the finite verb and its complement became obsolete: **Kim reads always the newspapers* (cf. French *Kim lit toujours les journaux*).

This change has been discussed extensively and Lightfoot (1999: sect. 6.3) argues that it was caused by prior changes in PLD, most notably the recategorization of the modal verbs just discussed and the rise of periphrastic *do* forms. These changes had the effect of greatly reducing the availability of the relevant cue, $_{\text{I}}$V, a verb occurring in an Inflection position.

The idea here is that children scan their linguistic environment for structural cues, such as $_{\text{I}}$V or $_{\text{VP}}$[V DP] (verb–object order), etc. Cues may be *expressed* in the utterances they hear. An utterance expresses a cue if, given everything that the child knows so far, it can only be analyzed with that cue present. So if a finite verb is separated from its DP direct object (by a negative particle, adverb, or other material), then it must have moved out of its VP and the only position that a finite verb may move to is the next highest head, necessarily a functional head like I under current assumptions. So (17a) can only be analyzed with the finite verb *peut* moved to some higher functional position. It therefore expresses the $_{\text{I}}$V cue for a child in a French-speaking milieu. Cues are elements of structure derived from what children hear. Cues are found in the mental representations which result from hearing, understanding, and "parsing" utterances. As a child understands an utterance, even partially, she has some kind of mental representation of the utterance. These are partial parses, which may differ from the full parses that an adult has. The learner scans those representations, derived from the input, and finds certain cues, elements of grammars, I-language.

If children acquire their grammars in this cue-based fashion, then they find the relevant structures and pay no attention to the set of sentences that grammars generate, comparing them to the set of sentences that they have heard. Lightfoot (1999: ch. 6) discusses the differences between that kind of input-matching and cue-based acquisition.

The two changes discussed so far are related in ways that we now understand: first, the Inflection position was appropriated by a subclass of verbs, the modal auxiliaries and *do*, and the V-to-I operation (10) no longer applied generally to all tensed clauses. Somewhat later, the V-to-I movement operation was lost for all verbs (other than the exceptional *be* and *have*) and I was no longer a position to which verbs might move. The relationship is that the first change dramatically changed the expression of the $_{\mathrm{I}}$V cue, leading to the loss of that structure.

A cue is expressed robustly if there are many simple utterances that can be analyzed only as $_{\mathrm{I}}$V. So, for example, the sentences corresponding to (16) and (17) can only be analyzed by the French child (given what she has already established about the emerging grammar) if the finite verb raises to I, and therefore they express the cue. A simple sentence like *Jeanne lit les journaux* 'Jeanne reads the newspapers,' on the other hand, could be analyzed with *lit* raised to I or with the I lowered into the VP in the English style; therefore it does not express the $_{\mathrm{I}}$V cue.

Early English grammars raised verbs to I, as in the grammars of modern French speakers, but later grammars did not; the operation was lost at some point. From our perspective, the operation ceased to be cued. The $_{\mathrm{I}}$V cue came to be expressed less in the PLD in the light of at least two developments in Early Modern English.

We have seen that modal auxiliaries, while once instances of verbs that raised to I (10), were recategorized such that they came to be merged into structures as I elements (11); they were no longer verbs, so sentences with a modal auxiliary ceased to include $_{\mathrm{I}}$V and ceased to express the cue. Sentences with a modal auxiliary, *Kim could not leave*, are very common in ordinary speech addressed to young children, and the recategorization meant that they no longer expressed the cue. Sentences of this type existed at all stages of English but they came to be analyzed differently after the change in category membership.

Second, as periphrastic *do* came to be used in interrogatives like *Does he understand chapter 4?* (cf. (14b)) and negatives like *He does not understand chapter 4* (cf. (15b)), so there were still fewer instances of $_{\mathrm{I}}$V. Before periphrastic *do* became available, sentences like (14b) and (15b) expressed the $_{\mathrm{I}}$V cue. Periphrastic *do* began to occur with significant frequency at the beginning of the fifteenth century and steadily increased in frequency until it stabilized into its modern usage by the mid-seventeenth century. For every instance of *do*, there is no verb in I.

By quantifying the degree to which a cue is expressed, we can understand why English grammars lost the V-to-I operation, and why they lost it after the modal auxiliaries were analyzed as nonverbs and as the periphrastic *do* became increasingly common. Grammars changed as the available triggering experiences, specifically those expressing the cue, shifted in critical ways. With the reanalysis of the modal auxiliaries and the increasing frequency of the periphrastic *do*, the expression of the $_I$V cue in English became less and less robust in the PLD. There was no longer much in children's experience which had to be analyzed as $_I$V, i.e. which *required* V-to-I movement, given that the morphological I-lowering operation was always available as the default. In particular, common, simple sentences like *Jill left* could be analyzed with I-lowering; meanwhile sentences like *Kim reads always the newspapers* with post-verbal adverbs and quantifiers had to be analyzed with a verb in I, but these instances of the cue were not robust enough to trigger the relevant grammatical property, and they disappeared quickly, a by-product of the loss of the V-to-I operation, a domino effect.

So the expression of the cue dropped below its threshold, leading to the elimination of V-to-I movement. The gradual reduction in the expression of $_I$V is not crucial. What is crucial is the point at which the phase transition took place, when the last straw was piled on to the camel's back. Children scan the environment for instances of $_I$V. This presupposes prior analysis, of course. Children may scan for this cue only after they have identified a class of verbs and when their grammars have a distinct inflection position, I.

This grammatical approach to diachrony explains changes at two levels. First, the cues postulated as part of UG explain the unity of the changes, why superficially unrelated properties cluster in the way they do. Second, the cues permit an appropriately contingent account of why the change took place, why children at a certain point converged on a different grammar: the expression of the cues changed in such a way that a threshold was crossed and a new grammar was acquired.

An intriguing paper by Anthony Warner (1995) shows that there is a third stage to the history of English auxiliaries, involving changes taking place quite recently affecting the copula *be*, and this turns out to be of current theoretical interest, discussed in Lightfoot (1999: ch. 7). The changes only involve the verb *be* but they have the hallmarks of grammatical change. There are several surface changes, all involving *be*, which can be attributed to one analytical notion concerning the way that elements are stored in the lexicon. The changes reflect quite general properties of the grammar. One can identify the structural property that is relevant and we can tell a plausible and rather elegant story about why and how the grammatical change might have come about.

That change, which I will not discuss here, is another illustration of the fact that morphology has syntactic effects. It is particularly important in defining category membership; children assign items to categories on the basis of their morphology. While morphology clearly influences category membership, one finds a stronger claim in the literature. It is sometimes argued that richly inflected languages differ in a fundamental, global way from poorly inflected languages like English, Swedish, and Chinese. Not many of the world's languages have a richly recorded history, but many that do have undergone morphological simplification, sometimes with category changes. If our historical records included languages with *increasing* morphological complexity, we would be in a stronger position to relate morphological and categorial changes. For discussion of this intriguing matter, see Lightfoot (2002).

In this section I have tracked some changes affecting the English modal auxiliaries, changes which might be labeled "grammaticalization." We have shown local causes for each of the two changes in grammars (the new category membership of the modal auxiliaries and the loss of V-to-I movement), taking grammars to be individual, internal systems existing in individual brains. There was nothing inevitable about these changes: the equivalent words in French and Swedish did not undergo parallel changes, because there were no parallel local causes.

This case study suggests that category changes may result from morphological changes. Let us now consider another structural change, which is cued by morphological changes in the case system.

2.4 Syntactic Effects of the Loss of Case

There is a theory of abstract Case, which determines the positions in which DPs may be pronounced (Anderson and Lightfoot 2002: ch. 3). DPs occur in positions in which they receive Case: as the subject of a finite clause (*They left*), as a specifier of a larger DP (*Their book*), or as a complement to a verb or a preposition (*Read them*, *Look at them*). These are positions that typically receive nominative, genitive, and accusative cases in languages with morphological case. If a DP is merged into a position where it does not receive Case (for example, as the complement to a noun or adjective or as the subject of an infinitival verb), it must move to a position where it does. Our abstract Case seems to be related to the overt, morphological case studied by earlier grammarians and one can probe that relationship by examining what happens syntactically when a morphological case system is eroded and eventually lost.

In this section I shall examine some curious syntactic effects resulting from the disappearance of the morphological case system in English. The loss of morphological case will enable us to understand to a significant degree the hitherto mysterious emergence of new "split genitives" in Middle English. What is striking is the tightness of the explanation, the way in which one element of Case theory explains the details of the development. We shall see that if one part of a child's linguistic experience changes, namely the case morphology, then other things must also change in the grammars that emerge (Lightfoot 1999: ch. 5).

The Case theory I adopt links Case to thematic roles: there is a one-to-one relationship in the sense that a DP has one Case and one thematic role (and not in the sense that there is a one-to-one relation between particular cases and particular thematic roles), and it is a single fact that a verb like *go* does not assign Case or a thematic role. Thematic roles define the semantic relationship of DPs to a head. In (18a) the subject DP is an Agent, a Theme in (18b), a Location in (18c), and an Instrument in (18d). These thematic roles are a function of the meaning of the verb and are "assigned" by the verb, so the DPs are thematically linked to the verbs. In a sentence like *Kay drove to NY, NY* is thematically linked to the preposition *to* and not to the verb *drove*; in a phrase *John's mother's house*, the DP *John's mother* is thematically related to *house* but the smaller DP *John* is thematically related only to *mother*.

(18) a. $_{DP}$[The striker] kicked the defender.
b. $_{DP}$[The striker] received the award.
c. $_{DP}$[The Indian Ocean] surrounds Madagascar.
d. $_{DP}$[The wind] blew the door open.

If UG stipulates that heads may assign Case to the left or to the right in accordance with the order of heads, one is not surprised to find Old English (OE) nouns assigning Case to the left *and* to the right. There is good reason to believe that the order of heads was shifting in late OE: one finds verbs preceding and following their complement, object–verb order alternating with verb–object. There is independent evidence that OE nouns assigned genitive Case not only to the left (19a) but also to the right (19b). One finds genitive–head order alternating with head–genitive. OE has a very simple analysis. It is more or less a direct manifestation of this UG theory of Case: nouns assigned Case to the left and to the right, and only to DPs with which they were thematically related, as we shall see. Case was assigned in that fashion and then was *realized* on both sides of the N with the morphological, genitive suffix.

(19) a. Godes lof
'praise of God'
(Ælfric)
Cristes læwa
'betrayer of Christ'
b. Lufu godes and manna
'love of God and of men'
(Ælfric, *Catholic Homilies* ii. 602.12)
Ormæte stream wæteres
'huge stream of water'
(Ælfric, *Catholic Homilies* ii. 196.5)

If OE nouns assigned Case to the left and to the right, and if in both positions it was realized as a morphological genitive, then one is not surprised to find that OE also manifested "split genitives." They were split in that a single genitive phrase occurred on both sides of the head noun. In (20) we see an example where the split element occurring to the right of the noun was a conjunct. Jespersen (1909: 300) notes that with conjuncts, splitting represents the usual word order in OE.

(20) a. Inwæres broþur ond Healfdenes.
Inwær's brother and Healfden's
'Inwær's and Healfden's brother.'
(*AS Chron.* 878)
b. Sodoma lande 7 gomorra.
'The Sodomites' and the Gomorreans' land.'
(*West Saxon Gospels* (Ms A), Matt 10.15)

In addition, appositional elements, where two DPs are in parallel, were usually split: the two elements occurred on either side of the head noun (21a–c), although (21d) was also possible, where *Ælfredes cyninges* is not split.

(21) a. Ælfredes godsune cyninges.
'King Alfred's godson'
(*AS Chron.* 890 (Laud (Peterborough) [E] 1122)
b. Þæs cyninges dagum herodes.
'In the days of Herod the king'
(*West Saxon Gospels* (Ms A), Matt 2.1)
c. Iohannes dagum fulwihteres.
'From the days of John the Baptist'
(*West Saxon Gospels* (Ms A), Matt 11.12)
d. Ælfredes cyninges godsunu.
(*AS Chron.* 890 (Parker c900))
e. *The book's cover about Rio (= 'The book about Rio's cover')
f. *Þæs cyninges godsune Frances
The king's godson of-France (= 'The king of France's godson')

Splitting within DPs was restricted to conjuncts (20) and to appositional elements (21a–c). In particular, OE did not show split constructions with a preposition phrase, along the lines of (21e). So there was no general rule "extraposing" a PP. Nor does one find anything like (21f), where *Frances* has no thematic relation to *godsune*.

Split genitives in OE had a structure along the lines of (22). *Ælfredes* was in the specifier of DP. *Godsune* assigned a thematic role and Case to the left and to the right (Allen 2002 argues that *cyninges* is an adjunct to *godsune*, not a complement).

(22) $_{DP}$[$_{Spec}$[Ælfredes] D $_{NP}$[$_{N}$godsune [cyninges]]]

These grammars had an overt genitive case on the right or on the left of the head noun; and they had split genitives, where the head noun assigned the same thematic role and Case in both directions. So much for splitting in OE grammars. Allen (chapter 9, this volume) argues that postnominal genitives began to decline in Old English and became restricted to positives, but I focus here on different changes.

Now for the mysterious changes. Middle and Early Modern English also manifested split genitives but they included forms which are very different from the split genitives of OE, as the examples of (23) show.

(23) a. The clerkes tale *of Oxenford*. (Chaucer, *Clerk's Tale*, Prologue)
b. The Wive's Tale *of Bath*. (Chaucer, *Wife of Bath's Tale*, Prologue)
c. Kyng Priamus sone *of Troy*. (Chaucer, *Troilus and Cressida*: I,2)
d. This kynges sone *of Troie*. (Chaucer, *Troilus and Cressida*: III.1715)
e. The Archbishop's Grace *of York*. (Shakespeare, *1 Henry IV* III.ii.119)

The meaning is 'The clerk of Oxford's tale,' 'King Priam of Troy's son,' etc., and the genitive is split: the rightmost part of the genitive phrase (italicized) occurs to the right of the head noun which the genitive phrase modifies. Mustanoja (1960: 78) notes that "the split genitive is common all through ME" and is more common than the modern "group genitive," *The clerk of Oxford's tale*. Jespersen (1909: 293), exaggerating a little, calls this splitting "the universal practice up to the end of the fifteenth century." However, these ME split forms are different from those of OE grammars, because the rightmost element is neither a conjunct nor appositional, and it has no thematic relation with the head noun, *tale, son, Grace*.

We can understand the development of the new ME split genitives in light of the loss of the overt morphological case system and the theory of Case related to thematic role (Culicover 1997: 37f. discusses the "thematic case thesis," under which abstract Case realizes thematic-role assignment quite generally). This is where we can connect work on abstract Case with the morphological properties discussed by earlier grammarians.

OE had four cases (nominative, accusative, genitive, and dative) and a vestigial instrumental, but they disappeared in the period of the tenth-to-thirteenth centuries, the loss spreading through the population from the north to the south – probably under the influence of the Scandinavian settlements (O'Neil 1978). In early ME, grammars emerged which lacked the morphological case properties of the earlier systems, in particular lacking a morphological genitive.

Put yourself now in the position of a child with this new, caseless grammar; your grammar has developed without morphological case. You are living in the thirteenth century; you would hear forms such as (21a) *Ælfredes godsune cyninges*, but the case endings do not register – that's what it means not to have morphological case in one's grammar. You are not an infant and you are old enough to have a partial analysis, which identifies three words. *Ælfredes* was construed as a "possessive" noun in the specifier of DP.

The modern "possessive" is not simply a reflex of the old genitive case. Morphological case generally is a property of nouns. On the other hand, "possessive" in Modern English is a property of the DP and not of nouns:

in (24a) *My uncle from Cornwall's cat* the possessor is the whole DP *My uncle from Cornwall*. Allen (1997) shows that the *'s* is a clitic attached to the preceding element and that the group genitive, where the clitic is attached to a full DP, is a late ME innovation.

(24) a. $_{DP}$[my uncle from Cornwall]'s cat
  b. Poines his brother (Shakespeare, *2 Henry IV* 2.4.308)
   For Jesus Christ his sake (1662 *Book of Common Prayer*),
  c. Mrs Sands his maid (OED, 1607)
  d. Job's patience, Moses his meekness, and Abraham's faith (*OED*, 1568)

As the case system was lost, the genitive ending *-es* was reanalyzed as something else, a Case-marking clitic. If *'s* comes to be a clitic in ME, which Case-marks DPs, this would explain why "group genitives" begin to appear only at that time, as Allen argued.

It is likely that there was another parallel reanalysis of the genitive *-es* ending, yielding the *his*-genitives that were current in the sixteenth and seventeenth centuries (24b) for 'Poines' brother', 'Jesus Christ's sake', etc. The genitive ending in *-s* was sometimes spelled *his*, and this form occurs even with females (24c) and occurs alongside possessive clitics (24d).

UG dictates that every phonetic DP has Case. The new caseless children reanalyzed the old morphological genitive suffix *-es* as a clitic, which was recruited as a Case-marker. The clitic *'s* Case-marks the element in the specifier of the containing DP. So *Ælfred* has Case and the Case is realized through the *'s* marker (usually analyzed as the head D, as in (25a')). In short, the *Ælfredes* of the parents is reanalyzed as *Ælfred's* (25a), although orthographic forms like *Ælfredes* occur in texts when mental grammars surely yielded *Ælfred's*. Orthographic *'s* is a recent innovation.

So now what about *cyninges* in (21a)? The evidence suggests that the phrase became (25a) *Ælfred's godsune king*. One finds phrases of just this form in (25b, c), where the postnominal noun is not overtly Case-marked, and Jespersen (1909: 283–4) notes that these forms are common in ME.

(25) a. Ælfred's godsune king
  a'. $_{DP}$[$_{DP}$[Ælfred] $_{D}$'s $_{NP}$[$_{N}$godsune [king]]]
  b. The kynges metynge Pharao.
   'Pharaoh the king's dream'
   (Chaucer, *Book of the Duchess* 282)
  c. The Grekes hors Synoun.
   'Sinon the Greek's horse'
   (Chaucer, *Squire's Tale*, 209)

The forms of (25), where the rightmost element is appositional, are direct reflexes of OE split genitives like (21), corresponding exactly, except that the split element, *Pharao*, *Synoun*, has no overt case. Despite the absence (for us new, caseless children – remember our thought experiment) of an overt, morphological genitive case, UG prescribes that the postnominal DP must carry some abstract Case. After the loss of the morphological case system, it can no longer be realized as a genitive case ending. That means that there must be another way of marking/realizing the abstract Case in (25). Perhaps *Pharao* receives its Case by coindexing with the Case-marked *kynges;* the two forms are in apposition and therefore are coindexed and share the same thematic role. This is what one would expect if there is a one-to-one relationship between Case and thematic role, the key element of the theory of Case adopted here. In that event, no independent Case-marker is needed for *Pharao.*

There is another option for realizing Case on the rightmost element. The dummy preposition *of* could be used as a Case-marker, as it is in (23). This is not possible in *Ælfred's godsune king* or the phrases of (25), because if *of* were to Case-mark the DP, one would expect it also to assign a thematic role (given a one-to-one relation between Case and thematic role) and in that event the DP could not be interpreted as an appositional element. The sentences of (23), on the other hand, are not like those of (25) and have different meanings. In (23b), for example, *Wive* and *Bath* are not appositional, not coindexed, and therefore an independent Case-marker and thematic-role assigner is needed; this is the function of *of*. Under this view, the emergence in ME of the new *N of DP* forms (23) is an automatic consequence of the loss of the morphological case system: *of* was introduced in order to Case-mark a DP which would not otherwise be Case-marked. In particular, the DP could not be Case-marked like the rightmost item in (25), which carries the same Case as *Ælfred's* because it has the same thematic role. *Of* assigns Case to a DP only if it has an independent thematic role.

With the introduction of the *of* Case-marker in these contexts, there is a further change and the split genitive construction is extended, as noted (23). In OE, the postnominal genitive always had a thematic relation with the head noun; one does not find expressions such as (21f) *Þæs cyninges son Frances* 'The king of France's son,' where *Frances* is neither a conjunct nor appositional and is thematically related to 'king' (Nunnally 1985: 148; Cynthia Allen, Willem Koopman, personal communication). In such a phrase, *Frances* could not be Case-marked by any adjacent element; in particular, it could not receive Case from *son* because it has no thematic relation with *son*. In ME, one does find postnominal, split DPs even where there is no thematic relation with the head noun, and the postnominal items are Case-marked by *of*. So, in (23a) *Oxenford* is construed with *clerkes* and not with *tale,* and it is Case-marked by *of*. It is crucial to note that the ME split expressions only involve *of* phrases: one does not find *The book's cover about Rio* for 'The book about Rio's cover,' mirroring the situation in OE and showing that there is no general operation "extraposing" PPs in ME, any more than there was in OE. Additionally – and this is crucial – the postnominal noun in (23) always has a thematic role of Locative/Source. I know of no claim to this effect in the literature but it has been pointed out by Cynthia Allen, Olga Fischer, and Willem Koopman in independent personal communications and it seems to be right. So, for example, one does not find forms like (26), where the postnominal noun is a Theme (26a) or a Possessor (26b).

(26) a. The portrait's painter of Saskia (= the portrait of Saskia's painter)
b. The wife's tale of Jim (= the wife of Jim's tale)

The fact that the *of* phrase is associated with a unique thematic role makes sense if UG prescribes a link between Case and thematic-role assignment. As we have noted, in OE (21a) *Ælfredes godsune cyninges, godsune* assigns the same Case to the right and to the left, realized in both instances as an overt, morphological genitive case; it also assigns the same thematic role to the two DPs to which it assigns Case. That is what it means for the two DPs to be appositional (same Case, same thematic role), and all of this is easy to understand if Case and thematic-role assignment are linked at the level of UG. Likewise for conjuncts (20). Consequently, the extension of these split genitives in ME (to the new forms with *of* – (23)) is not surprising under a theory which allows nouns to assign Case and which links Case to thematic-role assignment.

This much we can understand under the theory of Case. The properties of the new grammar must have emerged in the way that they did, if children (a) heard expressions like *Ælfredes godsune cyninges* (21a), (b) did not have the morphological case system of their parents, and (c) were subject to a Case theory requiring all DPs to have Case (assigned and realized) and linking Case with the assignment of thematic roles. We have a tight explanation for the new properties of ME grammars. In particular, we explain the distinction between (23) and (25), *of* occurring where there is no thematic relation with the head noun (23), but not where there is such a relation (25). We see that change is bumpy; if one element of a grammar changes, there may be many new phenomena (23). Children do not just match what they hear and they may produce innovative forms, as required by UG. UG defines the terrain, the hypothesis space, and a change in initial conditions (loss of morphological case) may have syntactic effects.

This is an explanation for the form of the split genitives of (23) in ME. They were around for four centuries and then dropped out of the language. This was probably a function of the newly available clitic *'s* that made possible group genitives like *The clerk of Oxford's tale*; these became possible only when *'s* was construed as a clitic, which Case-marked DPs, and that in turn was a function of the loss of morphological cases, including the genitive in *-es*.

Here I have taken a notion from traditional grammar and construed Case as an I-language element. Phonetic DPs, DPs that are pronounced, have an abstract Case that must be realized somehow. This is a function of UG, and abstract Cases are often realized as morphological cases. Children scan their linguistic environment for morphological cases and, if they find them, they serve to realize abstract Cases. If children do not find morphological cases, then different grammars emerge. In that event, a P or V (or other categories) may Case-mark a complement DP. We have examined here what happens when everything else remains constant. There came a point in the history of English when children ceased to find morphological cases. Those children were exposed to much the same linguistic experience as their parents but the transparency of overt case endings had dropped below a threshold such that they were no longer attained. Given a restrictive theory of UG, one linking Case-assignment by nouns to thematic-role assignment and requiring Cases to be realized on phonetic DPs, other things then had to change.

In this way our abstract theory of Case and our theory of cue-based acquisition enables us to understand how some of the details of ME grammars were shaped, why things changed as they did and why ME grammars had their odd split genitives.

2.5 Results

The emergence of a grammar in a child is sensitive to the initial conditions of the primary linguistic data. Those data might shift a little, because people came to use their grammars differently in discourse, using certain constructions more frequently, or because the distribution of grammars had shifted within the speech community. In that case, there may be significant consequences for the abstract system. A new system may be triggered, which generates a very different set of sentences and structures. Contingent changes in the distribution of the data (more accurately, changes in the expression of the cues) may trigger a grammar that generates significantly different sentences and structures, and that may have some domino effects.

Changes often take place in clusters: apparently unrelated superficial changes occur simultaneously or in rapid sequence. Such clusters manifest a single theoretical choice which has been taken differently. If so, the singularity of the change can be explained by the appropriately defined theoretical choice. So the principles of UG and the definition of the cues constitute the laws which guide change in grammars, defining the available terrain. Any change is explained if we show, first, that the linguistic environment has changed and, second, that the new phenomenon (*may*, *must*, etc., being categorized as I elements, for example) must be the way that it is because of some principle of the theory and the new PLD.

Sometimes we can explain domino effects. Loss of inflectional markings had consequences for category membership and changes in category membership had consequences for computational operations moving verbs to a I position. In that event, one establishes a link between a change in morphological patterns and changes in the positions of finite verbs.

Historical change is a kind of finite state Markov process, where each state is influenced only by the immediately preceding state: new grammars have only local causes and, if there is no local cause, there is no new grammar, regardless of the state of the grammar or the language some time previously. In that way, the emergence of a grammar in an individual child is sensitive to the initial conditions, to the details of the child's experience. The historian's explanations are based on available acquisition theories, and in some cases our explanations are quite tight and satisfying. Structural changes are interesting precisely because they have local causes. Identifying structural changes and the conditions under which they took place informs us about the conditions of language acquisition; we have indeed learned things about properties of UG and about the nature of acquisition by the careful examination of diachronic changes. So it is if we focus on changes in grammars, viewed as biological entities, and we gain a very different approach to language change than the ones which focus on E-language phenomena, on the group products of cognitive systems rather than on the systems themselves.

Linking language change to the acquisition of grammars in this fashion has enabled us to understand certain grammars better and has refined UG definitions. It has also been the source of two fairly fundamental notions: the idea of coexisting grammars and internal diglossia, whereby apparent optionality can be viewed as the effects of speakers using more than one grammar (Kroch 1989); and the idea that the PLD consist of structures instead of sets of sentences (Lightfoot 1999).

REFERENCES

Allen, C. (1997). Investigating the origins of the "group genitive" in English. *Transactions of the Philological Society* 95.1: 111–31.

Allen, C. (2002). Case and Middle English genitive noun phrases. In Lightfoot (2002).

Anderson, S. R. and D. W. Lightfoot (2002). *The Language Organ: Linguistics as Cognitive Physiology*. Cambridge: Cambridge University Press.

Chomsky, N. (1986). *Knowledge of Language: Its Nature, Origin and Use*. New York: Praeger.

Culicover, P. (1997). *Principles and Parameters: An Introduction to Syntactic Theory*. Oxford: Oxford University Press.

Gelderen, E. van (1997). *Verbal Agreement and the Grammar behind its "Breakdown": Minimalist Feature Checking*. Tübingen: Niemeyer.

Greenberg, J. H. (1963). Some universals of grammar with particular reference to the order of meaningful elements. In J. H. Greenberg (ed.), *Universals of Language*. Cambridge, MA: MIT Press.

Hopper, P. and E. Traugott (1993). *Grammaticalization*. Cambridge: Cambridge University Press.

Janda, R. (2001). Beyond "pathways" and "unidirectionality": on the discontinuity of language transmission and the counterability of grammaticalization. *Language Sciences* 23: 265–340.

Jespersen, O. (1909). *Progress in Language* (2nd edn.). London: Swan.

Joseph, B. (2001). Is there such a thing as grammaticalization? *Language Sciences* 23: 163–86.

Kiparsky, P. (1996). The shift to head-initial VO in Germanic. In H. Thráinsson, S. Epstein, and S. Peters (eds.), *Studies in Comparative Germanic Syntax* (vol. 2). Dordrecht: Kluwer.

Kroch, A. (1989). Reflexes of grammar in patterns of language change. *Language Variation and Change* 1: 199–244.

Lass, R. (1980). *On Explaining Language Change*. Cambridge: Cambridge University Press.
Lightfoot, D. W. (1999). *The Development of Language: Acquisition, Change and Evolution*. Oxford: Blackwell.
Lightfoot, D. W. (ed.) (2002). *The Syntactic Effects of Morphological Change*. Oxford: Oxford University Press.
Mustanoja, T. (1960). *A Middle English Syntax*. Helsinki: Société Néophilologique.
Newmeyer, F. (1998). *Language Form and Language Function*. Cambridge, MA: MIT Press.
Nunnally, T. (1985). The Syntax of the genitive in Old, Middle, and early Modern English. PhD dissertation, University of Georgia.
O'Neil, W. (1978). The evolution of the Germanic inflectional systems: a study in the causes of language change. *Orbis* 27.2: 248–85.
Ross, J. R. (1969). Auxiliaries main verbs. In W. Todd (ed.), *Studies in Philosophical Linguistics*. Evanston: Great Expectations.
Sapir, E. (1921). *Language*. New York: Harcourt.
Vennemann, T. (1975). An explanation of drift. In C. N. Li (ed.), *Word Order and Word Order Change*. Austin: University of Texas Press.
Warner, A. (1993). *English Auxiliaries: Structure and History*. Cambridge: Cambridge University Press.
Warner, A. (1995). Predicting the progressive passive: parametric change within a lexicalist framework. *Language* 71.3: 533–57.
Warner, A. (1997). The structure of parametric change, and V movement in the history of English. In A. van Kemenade and N. Vincent (eds.), *Parameters of Morphosyntactic Change*. Cambridge: Cambridge University Press.

FURTHER READING

Allen, C. (1995). *Case Marking and Reanalysis*. Oxford: Clarendon Press.
Clark, R. and I. G. Roberts (1993). A computational model of language learnability and language change. *Linguistic Inquiry* 24: 299–354.
Dresher, B. E. (1999). Charting the learning path: cues to parameter setting. *Linguistic Inquiry* 30: 27–67.
Fodor, J. D. (1998). Unambiguous triggers. *Linguistic Inquiry* 29.1: 1–36.
Haeberli, E. (2002). Inflectional morphology and the loss of verb-second in English. In Lightfoot (2002).
Kroch, A. (1994). Morphosyntactic variation. In K. Beals et al. (eds.), *Papers from the 30th Regional Meeting of the Chicago Linguistics Society: Parasession on Variation and Linguistic Theory*. Chicago: Chicago Linguistics Society.
Lightfoot, D. W. (1979). *Principles of Diachronic Syntax*. Cambridge: Cambridge University Press.
Pintzuk, S. (1999). *Phrase Structures in Competition: Variation and Change in Old English Word Order*. New York: Garland.
Pires. A. (2002). Cue-based change: inflection and subjects in the history of Portuguese infinitives. In Lightfoot (2002).
Roberts, I. G. (1993). *Verbs and Diachronic Syntax*. Dordrecht: Kluwer.
Rodrigues, C. (2002). Morphology and null subjects in Brazilian Portuguese. In Lightfoot (2002).
Thráinsson, H. (2003). Syntactic variation, historical development and Minimalism. In R. Hendrick (ed.), *Minimalist Syntax*. Oxford: Blackwell.

3 Variation and the Interpretation of Change in Periphrastic *Do*

ANTHONY WARNER

In this chapter I want to show how an understanding of variation can contribute to our understanding of earlier grammars and of linguistic change, including grammatical change. A crucial assumption here is that particular aspects of the way language is used will reflect aspects of its underlying grammar. So I will show how it is possible to argue for an underlying identity in grammar from an identity in rates of change shared by superficially distinct constructions. This uses the observed structuring of variation over time to form the basis of an argument about a grammatical abstraction. A second major topic will be to highlight one method of interpreting the sociolinguistics of an earlier linguistic situation. This leads to an understanding of a particular sociolinguistic change, which in turn clarifies the place of grammatical change in the more complex situation. A central theme of the chapter is necessarily methodological: how can we make best sense of historical variation? Historical data are impoverished as compared to modern data. We lack grammaticality judgments (hence straightforward, reliable statements about what was absent), and we have a sampling of only a proportion of the literate population, writing in circumstances about which typically little is known. So, a recurrent concern of this chapter will naturally be with appropriate methodology, with historical linguistics as "the art of making the best use of bad data," to use Labov's phrase (1994: 11).

The history of English auxiliaries contains several major instances of variation across time which seem to need different types of treatment. Modals as a group show an increase in grammatical status and subjective epistemic senses across the whole of the recorded history of English, with considerable variability among modals in syntactic properties at earlier periods. There follows an apparent point of change or abrupt restructuring at the beginning of the modern period, when properties such as the lack of nonfinite forms and failure to allow a direct object become systematic across the class. For different types of account see Warner (1993), Roberts and Rousseau (2003), and Lightfoot (chapter 2, this volume). The auxiliaries of the perfect, *have* and *be*, also show a long-term variation, as *have* increasingly takes over the domain of verbs of motion and change of state (*come, go, become, grow,* etc.) which earlier formed their perfect with *be*. The later phases of this variation have been chronicled by Rydén and Brorström (1987) and Kytö (1997). Variability clearly depended on a complex of factors, prominent among which were those relating to the semantics of the verb and the context. A third major locus of variation in the history of English auxiliaries is the rise of periphrastic (or supportive) *do*, as in *Do you see? – No, I don't see.* The establishment of *do* involves several centuries of variation, and it has been the subject of intensive investigation; see especially Rissanen (1999: 239ff.) for an authoritative descriptive overview of the situation in Early Modern English. Periphrastic *do* is especially interesting at this period because the choice between *do* and full verb is clearly open to treatment as a variable in the sense familiar within Labovian sociolinguistics, since *do* is apparently meaningless. It is, then, the most straightforward area in which to examine change and the possible involvement of both internal and external factors in change, using the type of quantitative methodology pioneered here by Kroch, that is, one based in the methods of quantitative sociolinguistics. Since these important issues of more general interest can be usefully discussed with respect to periphrastic *do*, this chapter will be devoted to discussing some aspects of its rise, and will focus on the interpretation of the data collected in Ellegård (1953).

3.1 Periphrastic *Do*: Background

There has been much discussion about the origin of periphrastic *do*. Recent proposals include the possibility that uses of *do* as a causative with an unspecified subject of the infinitive were reinterpreted as aspectual and then bleached further; and that periphrastic *do* arose as a reanalysis of *do* + noun sequences, which were interpreted as habitual, then identified with the *do* found in ellipsis. Contact with Celtic may also be involved, and an alternative suggestion has been that the form may be one that arises naturally at acquisition or through contact, so that it develops in English as a consequence of changing sociolinguistic conditions. See Denison (1993) and Garrett (1998) for major proposals, and for evaluative reviews of other possibilities.

At all events, the adoption of *do* involved a long period of variation between finite verbal forms and an apparently empty *do* plus infinitive. The two forms occur together in texts, as is illustrated in (1), and both are clearly available to individual users. The *do* form prevails and is the present-day form, with the exception that the earlier unstressed use of *do* in affirmative declaratives (as in (1.v.a)) has declined, leaving the present-day English use which emphasizes the polarity of the clause.

(1) Examples from Thomas Otway, *Cheats of Scapin; Friendship in Fashion*, 1677 (*Works* 1812; references by page and line)

(i) negative declarative sentences (with not)
  (a) she does not deserve it, (317–4)
  (b) I question not your friendship in the matter, (291–23)
(ii) negative imperatives (with not)
  (a) don't run yourself into danger thus rashly. (320–7)
  (b) get into the sack, and stir not, whatever happens; (237–31)
(iii) affirmative direct yes–no questions
  (a) Lord, madam, do you know what you do? (324–8)
  (b) Alas, sir, think you the captain has so little wit as to accept of such a poor rascally fellow as I am instead of your son? (229–37)
(iv) affirmative direct *wh*-adverbial questions
  (a) why do I spend my time in tittle-tattle with this idle fellow? (215–8)
  (b) Well, madam, how like you it, madam, ha? (301–13)
(v) affirmative declaratives
  (a) Why you must know, Frank, having a particular esteem for my family, (the nearest relation of which I would go fifty miles to see hanged) I do think her a very a – But no more, – mum, dear heart, mum, I say. (331–35)
  (b) Faith, bully, I think my dear kinswoman has mauled you to some purpose; . . . (331–27)

There is no reason to assume that *do* has any meaning in Early Modern English. Nevalainen (1991) lists some of the relevant possibilities, and points out that its frequency implies that it lacks a lexical meaning; see Klemola (1998) for a brief summary of views on the semantics of *do*. There are also claims in the literature that it has some pragmatic role in the sixteenth century, but as yet none is more than anecdotally supported, though it may have had particular discourse appropriacies (Rissanen 1999). So it is essentially semantically empty by 1500 at the latest, syntactically perhaps initially a bleached aspectual or causative.

Two major studies of this period have been based on substantial corpora. Ellegård's (1953) database was prose between 1390 and 1710. For the later period at least his data consist mostly of "literature" in the sense that it was written for publication in some form. His familiar graph is given as figure 3.1: the data are divided up into the major types shown in the key (and direct questions with *wh*-object which he did not include in the graph).

More recently Nurmi (1999) has published the results of investigations into the Corpus of Early English Correspondence (1410–1681), which has a sociolinguistically well-founded base. It contains the output of a large number of individuals, and for many of these writers (as often also for the recipients) we have information about social status, age, gender, level of education, and other factors. Nurmi's results are focused on sociolinguistic patterns and motivations, and are interestingly different in some respects from results based on Ellegård's less systematic material. Accounts for the seventeenth century can also be oriented with respect to the eighteenth, for which Tieken-Boon van Ostade

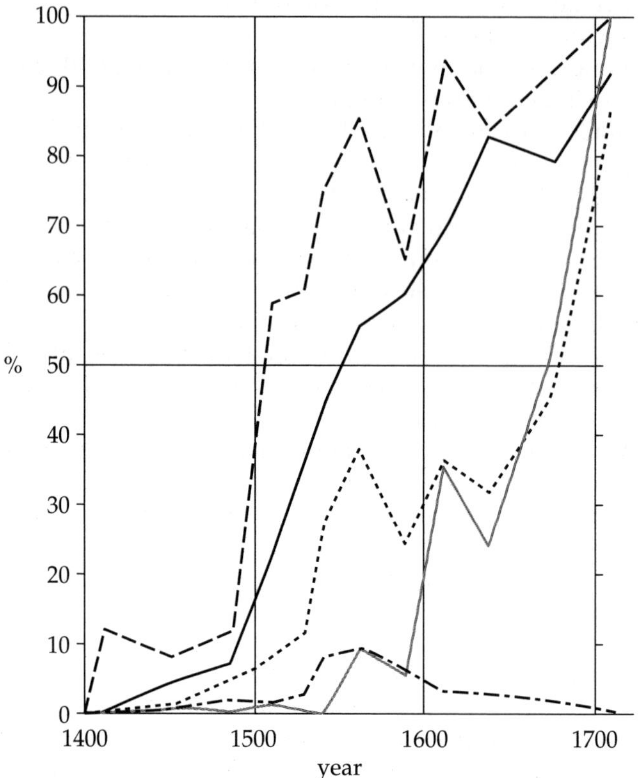

Key
negative yes–no and *wh*-adverbial questions (– – –)
affirmative yes–no and *wh*-adverbial questions (———)
negative declaratives (·········)
negative imperatives (———)
affirmative declaratives (–·–·–)

Figure 3.1 Percentage of *do* forms in different types of sentence (from Ellegård 1953: 162)

(1987) collected and analyzed a substantial and systematic corpus of material. She paid particular attention to the potential impact of social networks and to the oral-literate dimension, distinguishing "writing" from "speech in writing" with further subdivisions by genre.

3.2 Major Questions

When we examine Ellegård's results (and particularly those shown in his graph) and take account of the results of the other databases just mentioned, a series of questions becomes prominent.

(a) In Ellegård's graph you can readily see that the proportion of *do* varies between different construction types. What motivates such differences? Why should the incidence of *do* be higher in affirmative yes–no questions (as in (1.iii)) than it is in negative declaratives (as in (1.i))? One possible answer (given in Kroch 1989a) is that this type of difference is a consequence of functional or stylistic factors. Suppose, for example, that *do* was especially valuable in transitive questions because it permitted the retention of VO ordering with the object immediately after the lexical verb (*do*–S–V–O rather than V–S–O, as in (1.iv)) and that this made for simpler processing. This kind of advantage might lead to a higher incidence of *do* in questions than in negative declaratives. Another possibility is that *do* was spreading from the vernacular into prose. Then we might expect a higher incidence of *do* in texts which contained more interactive vernacular features such as questions, and this might also lead to a difference of incidence of *do* in the database between questions and negative declaratives. A further line of thinking is that properties of the underlying grammar may be responsible for such differences. One particular suggestion has been that *do* was proportionately less common in negative declaratives than in affirmative questions in the sixteenth century because *do*-support could occur without restriction in affirmative questions, but could only occur in a subset of negative declaratives. This follows from the claim that there were two underlying positions in which *not* could occur, and that conditions for *do*-support were only met when *not* was in the higher position. So in the sixteenth century those negative declaratives which had *not* in the lower position were not potential structures for *do*-support, hence the lower proportion of *do* in negative declaratives; see Han and Kroch (2000), Han (2001).

(b) Ellegård's graph apparently shows a rather orderly increase across all categories of *do* (except perhaps in imperatives) until the second half of the sixteenth century. It looks very much as if *do* is increasing in parallel across the different categories, which march in step. Kroch (1989a) argued convincingly that *do* was indeed increasing at the same rate of change in negative declaratives and different types of question up to 1575, so that the s-curves of change in each of these categories are parallel. This is the "Constant Rate Effect," which will be further discussed below. There is, however, the difficulty that the relationship between affirmative declarative *do* and the other contexts is not clear: Kroch's detailed results show that affirmative declarative *do* is changing more slowly than other contexts, and it is not obvious why this should be the case.

(c) After 1575 the graph shows apparently distinct developments in different categories. *Do* in questions continues to increase, in negative declaratives it declines and then behaves somewhat erratically before continuing to increase towards the end of the seventeenth century, and in affirmatives there is a clear decline. Kroch argued for a grammatical change in the second half of the sixteenth century, interpreting it as the loss of V-to-I raising. But then it is not so clear just what goes on after 1575, and not everyone has accepted that loss of V-to-I occurs at this point: both Lightfoot and I have argued that this loss is later (Warner 1997; Lightfoot 1999). Further questions here are: why does decline apparently start later in correspondence and in the Helsinki Corpus, and how is it that affirmative declarative *do* is not lost in all dialects, but survives into the twentieth century in southwestern dialects?

(d) Why does *do* in negative declaratives behave as it does? Why is there a big dip in the second half of the sixteenth century, followed by a partial recovery, then a further dip in 1625–50? Does initial dip also support the idea of a late sixteenth-century change, as suggested in (c) above? And why are negative declaratives so far behind affirmative questions in the seventeenth century: the gap is roughly 25 years before 1575, but is over 100 years in the seventeenth century? A further question arises from Nurmi's recent work. The Corpus of Early English Correspondence shows a single dip in negative declaratives which occupies the first four decades of the seventeenth century, instead of Ellegård's double dip (Nurmi 1999: 165ff.). Why should there be this difference between databases?

(e) Questions change their behavior between 1550 and 1600: throughout the seventeenth century there is a ranking of frequencies of *do*. Yes–no questions, as in (1.iii), have the highest incidence of *do*, adverbial *wh*-questions, as in (1.iv), are ranked next, and questions with a *wh*-object have the lowest incidence of *do*. But earlier, the rate of *do* in adverbial *wh*-questions is close to that in yes–no questions; later, it has dropped rather dramatically, so that it is close to that of *wh*-object questions. See the graph in Ellegård (1953: 205). Why should this be?

(f) A central and fundamental question is: Why does *do* make progress? This question has attracted a range of answers. One recent suggestion is Stein's (1986, 1990) claim that the use of *do* provides a strategy to avoid complex consonant groups, especially with *thou*: so, *thou did'st not flinch* was preferred to *thou flinch'd'st not*. A more broadly based claim is that processing difficulties associated with questions may have been involved (Kroch 1989b); recall the discussion above of the possibility that *do* was especially valuable in transitive questions for processing reasons. The line of argument here would be clear if structures where *do* was thought to be especially valuable (such as transitive questions) showed a higher rate of change than other categories (such as intransitive questions). But this is not what Kroch (1989a) found: instead, transitive and intransitive questions showed the same rate of change. In Warner (2004), however, I point out that when we take account of the ages of different authors, we see that at any point in time, older authors used *do* just as frequently in questions as younger authors did. Since the incidence of *do* was increasing with time, if the older authors had maintained the rate they adopted at acquisition, they would have a lower rate than younger individuals. The fact that they do not implies that the older authors increased their use of *do* as they grew older. This is consistent with what Labov (1994) calls "communal change," in which the usage of the entire community moves forwards together. It seems clear that communal change must involve accommodation, that is, that individuals must be adapting their behavior to conform to their interlocutors. In this context, a possible, indeed plausible, suggestion would be that the change is driven by some aspect of interaction between adults, and I concluded that some aspect of processing may have provided the motivation for the continuing increase in the use of *do*. This is, to be sure, an indirect line of justification, not a demonstration, but the nature of our historical data often requires such an oblique approach.

The questions listed in (a–f) are those that seem most prominent from the perspective of Ellegård's data: all involve some potential interconnections between variation, change, and grammar. There are, of course, many other questions that might be raised. I make no apology for adopting a particular focus, but will start with the problem that affirmative *do* seems not to be changing at the same rate as other constructions before 1575, and will examine the implications of this for our interpretation of the grammar of *do* at the period (the second and third questions in the list above). This interprets variation as evidence for underlying grammatical systems. Then I will tackle parts of the fourth question, the erratic behavior of *do* in negative declaratives after 1575.

3.3 The Constant Rate Effect as Evidence for the Grammar of *Do*

Ellegård's data for 1400–1575 was Kroch's central case for the Constant Rate Effect (also sometimes called the "Rate Identity Effect"). This claim involves cases where two linguistic options are in competition, and distinct surface syntactic contexts have different frequencies of use of the incoming form. The present case involves competition between *do* and the simple finite verb form (as reflex of V-to-I). We need to distinguish more than one surface context for the single underlying change (loss of V-to-I, or replacement of the simple finite by *do*), since negative declaratives and different types of question each show a distinct incidence of *do* at any particular point of time in the course of the change. Kroch's claim in the Constant Rate Effect is that the S-curves which characterize the change for each context are parallel to each other. This means that the change is proceeding at the same rate in each context: if *do* in one context has an incidence of 20 percent at one period, and 40 percent forty years later, other contexts will also take forty years to move from 20 to 40 percent. Note one particular consequence: affirmative transitive questions and affirmative intransitive questions are changing at the same rate, as noted above. This means that a context which shows some apparent functional motivation does not change faster than a context which lacks such motivation: their s-curves are parallel. So transitive questions are acquiring *do* at the same rate as intransitive questions, although we might suggest that *do* is potentially more valuable in processing terms in transitive questions. Given this, the identity of rate between contexts is initially puzzling. The point is that the grammar is unitary, and the user's choice in each context is subject to a weighting which belongs to that context and remains stable. This is the idea behind the former "variable rules" of sociolinguistics, in which the constraints remain stable within a community. So the grammatical change does not affect these constraints, but takes place at quite a high level of abstraction. The constructions are not moving forwards independently. Rather, the grammar is moving forwards as a whole.

In the case of *do*, Kroch gives coefficients for rate of change for a series of contexts (see table 3.1). A particular mathematical function, the logistic, characterizes an appropriate s-curve, and the coefficients were estimated by fitting this function to the data, using a logistic regression program. The curves are all virtually the same shape, and the coefficients in the table characterize their degree of "slope"; another set of coefficients, not given here, tells us their distance from one another along the date scale. For all contexts except the affirmative declarative type of (1.v), Kroch shows that the differences between their slopes are very likely to reflect random fluctuations in the data, and he argues that the curves should be interpreted as parallel. Since the slope corresponds to the rate of change, this shows the Constant Rate Effect. The underlying competition is between V-to-I and *do*: the verb could raise to Inflection (or some more specialized functional projection), as evidenced by the fact that it could precede *not*. As this movement was lost, *do* appeared instead. Thus the general rise of *do* reflected loss of V-to-I. This identical competition appears in each of the contexts of table 3.1 except the affirmative declaratives.

Affirmative declarative *do* made slower progress than *do* in other contexts before the last quarter of the sixteenth century. This is puzzling, and Kroch interpreted the difference in terms of a different competition for affirmative declarative *do* and the other contexts: he suggested that failure of V-to-I in affirmative declaratives led to either *do* or affix hopping (which lowered the morphology on to the verb), where these were in a stable relationship. So there was a different competition for this context, consequently a different rate of change. But there is a difficulty with this view which Kroch was forced to leave unresolved. On his account the later decline of affirmative declarative *do* depended precisely on competition between *do* and affix hopping, and it is not clear why

Table 3.1 Kroch's rates of change 1400–1575

Clause type	*Rate*
Affirmative transitive *wh*-adverbial and yes–no questions	3.62
Affirmative intransitive *wh*-adverbial and yes–no questions	3.77
Affirmative *wh*-object questions	4.01
Negative questions	3.45
Negative declaratives	3.74
Overall (without affirmative declaratives)	3.70
Affirmative declaratives	2.82

Coefficients of rate are given in logit units per century.
Range of variation of rates across question and negative categories: 0.56.
Source: Kroch (1989a: 225, 321).

this competition should have started when it did. Kroch noted that this "represents an important unresolved issue in our interpretation of the affirmative declarative context" (Kroch 1989a: 232–3).

I want to develop two lines of thinking in what follows. Both argue from rates of change to properties of underlying grammar, so both are equally concerned with demonstrating a methodology. The first accepts the figures of table 3.1 and interprets them grammatically. The second involves the claim that with some reinterpretation of Ellegård's data, the Constant Rate Effect can be seen to hold for all the categories of table 3.1, and considers the implications of this position.

First, then, let us accept the figures of table 3.1, and go on to make explicit the possibility that there was a grammatical difference between *do* in affirmative declaratives and *do* in other contexts. A grammatical difference could also underlie a difference of rate of change: if a single underlying grammar results in the same rate of change across contexts, the lack of a single underlying grammar may result in different rates of change. Let us try to characterize a relevant difference by distinguishing between "full auxiliary" *do* and "last resort" *do*. Full auxiliary *do* has an overall distribution like that of a modal, in that it may occur unstressed in affirmatives. It is presumably not yet fully grammaticalized, but is a lexical item selected from the lexicon; for a minimalist, it is present in the numeration. Last resort *do*, on the other hand, has the modern distribution. It is inserted automatically in some FP when it is needed to save a derivation. Clearly, English has last resort *do* today; and in the early sixteenth century it arguably had what I am calling full auxiliary *do*. So English has moved from full auxiliary *do* to last resort *do*. The questions relevant here are: when and how? Was there an abrupt transition, or did these options overlap with each other? Was there a change at the end of the sixteenth century? Could the possibility of overlap between analyses account for the different rates of change in the sixteenth century?

If these two characterizations of *do* were simultaneously present in the language before the last quarter of the sixteenth century, we might have a situation like the following: finite *do* was simultaneously a last resort item in questions and negatives, and a freely available lexeme in all constructions. If both of these types of *do* were increasing, we would reasonably expect a difference of rate of change: questions and negatives would be increasing on two fronts, affirmative declaratives only on one. And the general shape of developments shown by Ellegård is consistent with the possibility that full auxiliary *do* began to decline from the second half of the sixteenth century. From this point, affirmative declarative *do* declines, and questions and negatives show a slower and more erratic increase, perhaps also a consequence of combined developments: an increase in last resort *do*, coupled with a decline in full auxiliary *do*. Grammar competition would allow this, provided individuals could tolerate a situation in which *do* simultaneously had an entry as a lexical item and an entry as a grammatical formative. It seems likely that such a characterization will be required for the seventeenth century, when the last resort characteristics of *do* are prominent, and affirmative declarative *do* is infrequent and in decline. Then the difference of rate of change would be a consequence of the coexistence of these alternatives, and we might interpret the apparent exception to the Constant Rate Effect as showing instead this different type of grammatical distinction. We would have a plausible grammatical interpretation of the variation across time found in the basic data: not a knock down argument, but (as noted above) this may be the best we can do with historical data.

This analysis is coherent and plausible, given Ellegård's data, as he stated it. I want, however, to turn now to the second position mentioned above, in which the figures of table 3.1 are rejected. This will lead to an alternative interpretation in which *do* is unitary before 1575, and only involves the double analysis after that date. The general methodological point remains the same: that relationships between rates of change can contribute to an argument for and against particular grammatical analyses. In the present case, different treatments of *do* make different predictions about change, and these are open to test. My reasons for suggesting that *do* may have been unitary before 1575 follow from a detailed re-examination of Ellegård's database, which shows the need for some redating of Ellegård's fifteenth-century texts in line with recent philological assessments, and some correction of his figures. Furthermore, it is arguably appropriate to omit texts before 1425, which are predominantly western, whereas the sixteenth-century data are generally central and eastern. There is no space here for detailed discussion of the philological and statistical points which underlie these proposals and I shall simply give summary results for the period 1425–1575 in table 3.2, based on a conservative modification and reinterpretation of Ellegård's database.

If this is accepted, the result is a different estimate for the rate of change of affirmative declarative *do*. At 3.76 logit units per century this is indistinguishable from rates established for *wh*-adverbial and yes–no questions, and from the general rate for other categories taken together. Moreover, in each case, the

Table 3.2 Rates of change 1425–1575

Clause type	*Rate*
Affirmative transitive *wh*-adverbial and yes–no questions	3.78
Affirmative intransitive *wh*-adverbial and yes–no questions	3.71
Affirmative *wh*-object questions	4.33
Negative questions	3.81
Negative declaratives	4.14
Overall (without affirmative declaratives)	3.79
Affirmative declaratives	3.76

Coefficients of rate are given in logit units per century.
Range of variation of rates across question and negative categories: 0.62.

rate of change of each individual category was tested against the overall rate for all other categories: in no case was the difference significant. Thus, under this interpretation Kroch's Constant Rate Effect clearly holds for affirmative declarative *do* as well as for the other categories. Clearly, then, there is potentially a strong argument that *do* is changing at the same rate in all categories. *Do* is therefore open to interpretation as grammatically unitary.

Given this, *do* can be assigned a unitary interpretation in the period 1425–1575: it is simply an auxiliary that gives expression to tense, whether this follows from its grammar or as a matter of pragmatic equivalence. There is no need to suppose that there are two types of *do* interacting. Indeed, Occam's razor is against this, since we would need to make further assumptions: say, that the rate of change of each of these categories was virtually the same, and that the rate of occurrence of full auxiliary *do* in negatives and questions was very low (perhaps identical to that in affirmative declaratives). While such a position is not impossible, there is no obvious reason why this should be so.

If *do* is a unitary item before 1575 we are probably dealing with two changes. In the period 1425–1575 *do* is a functional equivalent to tense. It is optionally selected from the lexicon in the same way as other items. Early in the period it may have been a bleached aspectual; by the beginning of Early Modern English at the latest, *do* has undergone a minor reanalysis, after which it is a functional lexeme which represents tense. Throughout the period it is associated with the decline of V-to-I with non-auxiliaries in questions and negatives. *Do* makes steady progress until 1550/75, when we get the beginning of a decline in affirmative declarative *do*. This is the point at which the data give evidence of a reanalysis under which *do* acquires its last resort characteristics. This is a relatively sudden restructuring, a cataclysmic change in Lightfoot's sense, presumably taking place at acquisition. After this, *do* is a last resort item which is no longer freely selected from the lexicon, and this *do* is in competition with full auxiliary *do* which survives for a while, but declines in unstressed affirmative declarative contexts. Meanwhile the loss of V-to-I continues, to be completed in the nineteenth century.

This gives us a traditional view of grammaticalization: *do* is a bleached item used with what looks like a partial last resort distribution in questions and negatives before it is fully grammaticalized as a last resort item, integrated into the grammar in a distinctive way. See Roberts (1993: 296ff.), and Warner (1993) for accounts along these lines. There is also a suggestive parallel with the accounts of parametric change given by Roberts (1993) and Willis (1998), whereby preliminary shifts in performance and minor reanalyses alter the data available to learners, thereby aiding a subsequent major change (though I do not wish to suggest that the introduction of last resort *do* was necessarily a parametric change).

Methodologically, what we have here is the possibility of a line of argument for the structure of grammar from the nature of change. Two positions were contrasted in terms of their predictions for the fourteenth and fifteenth centuries to 1575. In the first, *do* was characterizable in two ways: either as a full auxiliary, or as a last resort item. The prediction was that affirmative declarative *do* should change more slowly than other categories, as is the case if we accept Ellegård's data as they stand. In the second, *do* was only a full auxiliary, and its rate of change was predicted to be the same as that of other categories. Under a reinterpretation of Ellegård's data, I claim that this latter prediction holds. In both cases we can therefore use aspects of change as part of an argument for aspects of the underlying grammar, making "best use of bad data." Logically, though, neither argument is fully watertight. The Constant Rate Effect says that if the same underlying change is manifested in different contexts, then those contexts will be seen to change at the same rate. We cannot simply deduce that where contexts show a distinct rate of change they are grammatically distinct, since some other factors might intervene. But if we set the possibility of interfering sociolinguistic (or other) factors to one side (and we will see immediately that this has dangers), we have a reasonably convincing line of argument in the first case. In the second case, too, we cannot strictly deduce the reverse implication: that an identical rate of change implies an identical mechanism. But the position becomes both possible and plausible, and in the present case, preferable.

3.4 Stylistic Variation and *Do*

I want now to turn to the second major topic of this chapter, and examine the curious behavior of *do* in negative declaratives from the late sixteenth century, pursuing the idea that this may be the consequence not of a grammatical change, but of a sociolinguistic re-evaluation of grammatical options.

Language is (of course) embedded in a social and stylistic context, and is liable to vary systematically according as that context changes, so the historian's data may reflect this kind of structured heterogeneity. Such variation is clearly a very interesting and important topic in its own right, and understanding it may also be crucial for the interpretation of change. Nurmi (1999) has shown clearly the relevance of gender and social status for the increasing occurrence of *do* in Early Modern English, and both she and others have shown the importance of a contrast between writing which is more oral (or "speech in writing") and writing which is more literate in type for the history of *do*.

Ellegård's database does not straightforwardly lend itself to investigation of social factors. But in his seventeenth-century data, there is a difference in the incidence of *do* in negative declaratives between plays and other kinds of texts. For example, Congreve's play *The Old Bachelor* has 89 percent *do*, but his novel *Incognita* has 77 percent *do*. This suggests that the distribution of *do* may differ systematically between those texts which are more oral and those which are more literate. So it is necessary to have some method of capturing this property of texts. One approach to this problem is based in the external identification of genres: this has been done (for example) by Tieken-Boon van Ostade for her eighteenth-century data. She set up an elaborate scale of lexical complexity, distinguishing representations of direct speech, and making further subdivisions (1987: 17–18). But her database was selected precisely in order to provide appropriate (and classifiable) types of language. Ellegård's database was not constructed in this way, and though the distinction "play or not play" is straightforward, more sophisticated genre-based distinctions can be difficult.

An alternative approach has been to characterize dimensions of variation not by assigning texts to genres, but in terms of the internal, linguistic properties of texts; see, for example, the recent work of Biber and his associates. I have used two properties which provide a measure of the lexical complexity of texts: average word length and type–token ratio. Type–token ratio is the ratio between the number of distinct abstract types or lexemes in a sample, and the number of tokens or typographical words. As a lexeme, *the* is counted once for each sample; as a typographical word it is counted as many times as it occurs in the sample, say 34 times. Texts with a more complex lexicon will show a higher average word length, and a higher type–token ratio; texts with a less complex lexicon will show a lower average word length, and a lower type–token ratio. I combined these two measures following Biber's (1988) method to obtain a single scale of lexical complexity. On this scale each text in Ellegård's database is associated with a coefficient of lexical complexity so that the texts are ranked in order.

Using average word length, and type–token ratio in this way seems a reasonable method of tackling the problem of characterizing stylistic level. These two properties are included among those contributing to what Biber establishes as his most important dimension of linguistic variation among texts, his "Factor 1." He says that it marks the contrast between "high informational density and exact informational content" on the one hand and "affective, interactional and generalized content" on the other (1988: 107). This factor is clearly closely related to the oral-literate parameter, and high values of the two lexical properties I have selected clearly characterize texts of "high informational density and exact informational content."

3.5 *Do* in Negative Declaratives, 1600–1710

Now let us see what relevance this measure of lexical complexity has to the distribution of *do* in negative declaratives. This can be tested by looking at Ellegård's database of sentences for 1600–1710 to see whether the scale of lexical complexity is a statistically significant factor for the choice between *do* and the full verb. It is necessary to take other major factors (date of text, transitivity of verb) into account. The answer is very clear: it is very highly significant ($p < 0.0001$), and *do* is substantially less frequent in negative declaratives in texts of higher lexical complexity.

What this means can be better appreciated if we look at figures for individual texts, and set date aside as a variable impacting on the analysis. This can be neatly done by using the estimated rate of change for the period to calculate what the figure for the incidence of *do* in negative declaratives would have

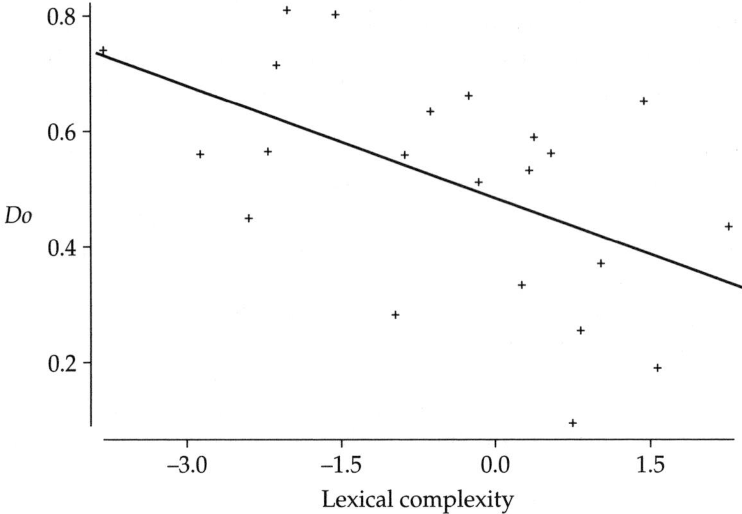

Figure 3.2 Proportion of *do* in negative declaratives versus the scale of lexical complexity, 1600–1700: proportion of *do* estimated for 1655

been for each text in some base year. So, for Beaumont and Fletcher's play *The Knight of the Burning Pestle*, there is 64.7 percent *do* in 1607. But given the overall rate of change across the period for negative declaratives, it is possible to work out that the corresponding percentage for 1655 is 81.0. Essentially this says that if the text had been written under the same conditions at the later date, it would have had 81.0 percent *do*. Similarly, Congreve's play *The Old Bachelor* has 88.9 percent *do* in 1693; the corresponding figure for 1655 is 80.4 percent. When corresponding figures are calculated for all the texts in the period, we can compare the results in respect of stylistic differentiation without interference from date.

A scatter plot for the 22 texts occurring in the period 1600–1710 is given in figure 3.2, with percentages of *do* estimated for the year 1655. The line on the graph, which shows the linear regression of *do* against the scale of lexical complexity, has a clear trend. If we divide the graph into four quadrants at the median of each parameter (percentage of *do* and the scale of lexical complexity), so that half the texts on each parameter fall into the one group and half into the other group, we find that most of the data occur in two quadrants: low lexical complexity and high percentage of *do*; high lexical complexity and low percentage of *do* (see table 3.3).

Comparing the averages can give us some real idea of the scale of this difference. Again, dividing at the median of the scale of lexical complexity, giving us 11 texts of low lexical complexity and 11 texts of high lexical complexity, we find that the average value of *do* for texts of low lexical complexity is 61.6 percent, while for the texts of high complexity it is 41.1 percent.

Table 3.3 Occurrence of *do* in texts of low/high lexical complexity 1600–1710

	Texts of low lexical complexity	*Texts of high lexical complexity*	*Total*
High *do* (%)	**8**	3	11
Low *do* (%)	3	**8**	11
Total	11	11	22
Do (%) average	61.6	41.1	

The scatter plot of figure 3.2 shows quite a wide range of variation, and there is some overlap between the categories high versus low lexical complexity in the values for *do* shown in individual texts, but the overall contrast is striking: on average texts of high lexical complexity show two-thirds of the incidence of *do* found in texts of low lexical complexity.

So there is a clear, consistent and substantial difference here in usage of *do* between texts of different levels: texts of low lexical complexity have more *do*, and texts of high lexical complexity have less *do*.

3.6 *Do* in Negative Declaratives, 1500–75

The situation is, however, interestingly different in the period 1500–75. Here when we examine Ellegård's database to see whether the scale of lexical complexity is a significant predictor of *do* in negative declaratives (taking other major factors – date of text, transitivity of verb – into account as before), we find that this factor is again very highly significant ($p < 0.0001$). But here there is more *do* in texts of higher lexical complexity, less *do* in texts with less complex lexis. This is apparently the reverse of the situation found in the following century.

This is also borne out when we look at figures for individuals, setting aside date in the manner described above, but this time taking 1535 as a base year. Estimates of proportions of *do* in negative declaratives for that year, plotted against lexical complexity, are given in the scatter plot of figure 3.3. The line in the graph shows the linear regression of the two properties. There is a clear trend which reverses the direction of the trend found in figure 3.2.

You can again see from the graph that there is quite a wide range of variation: some texts of low lexical complexity have fairly high rates of *do*, and some texts of high lexical complexity have fairly low rates of *do*. If we divide the graph into four quadrants, at the mid point, or median, of each scale, as before, we find that most of the data occur in two quadrants: high lexical complexity and high percentage of *do*; low lexical complexity and low percentage of *do*;

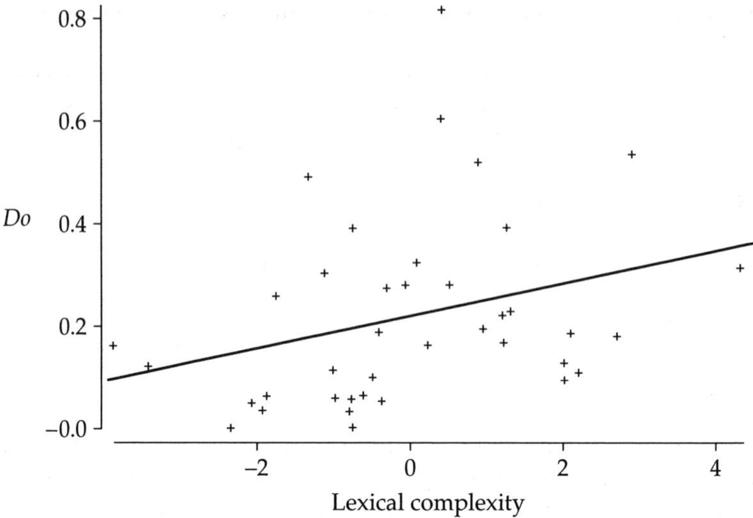

Figure 3.3 Proportion of *do* in negative declaratives versus the scale of lexical complexity, 1500–75: proportion of *do* estimated for 1535

Table 3.4 Occurrence of *do* in texts of low/high lexical complexity 1500–75

	Texts of low lexical complexity	*Texts of high lexical complexity*	*Total*
Higher *do* (%)	6	**14**	20
Lower *do* (%)	**14**	5	19
Total	20	19	39
Do (%) average	14.0	29.9	

Comparing the averages is again an interesting exercise. Dividing at the median of the scale of lexical complexity, giving us 20 texts of low lexical complexity and 19 texts of high lexical complexity, we find that the average percentage of *do* for the texts of low lexical complexity is 14.0, while for the texts of high lexical complexity it is 29.9. So there is a considerable difference here, and it is again clear that in Ellegård's data the incidence of *do* varies according to the lexical complexity of the text being composed.

What is very striking here is the reversal between the sixteenth and seventeenth centuries (contrast table 3.3 with table 3.4, the slope in figure 3.2 with that in figure 3.3). In the sixteenth-century data it is more lexically complex styles which show a higher incidence of *do*. In the seventeenth century such styles show a lower incidence. This apparent reversal is very interesting, because it implies that the situation in the seventeenth century is a new development.

How could we account for this? It looks very much as if there is some new evaluation impacting on negation, a conclusion which is also supported by the evidence of age-grading, not reviewed here but discussed in Warner (2000). This could be either a positive evaluation of the simple finite construction, or a hostile evaluation of the construction with *do not*: either would have been sufficient to result in the switch-over between the two centuries that we have seen.

3.7 *Do* in Negative Declaratives, 1500–1710

We can gain an understanding of what happened towards the end of the sixteenth century from graphs of change for the whole period 1500–1710, presented in figures 3.4 and 3.5. Here I have divided texts up into two groups of equal size by dividing the scale of lexical complexity at the median. In one are the texts of high lexical complexity, in the other the texts of low lexical complexity. In each case the value for the text is the percentage of *do* in negative declarative sentences, and a running average has been added to help the viewer discriminate the major trends. The difference between these graphs is striking. In texts of low lexical complexity there is no sign of the dip seen in Ellegård's original graph, though there is a gap in the data from 1565 to 1585. But the downward movement in texts of high lexical complexity is dramatic, and a lower level of *do* is maintained across the following century. Figure 3.6 simply imposes the two running averages on each other: it shows there is a difference

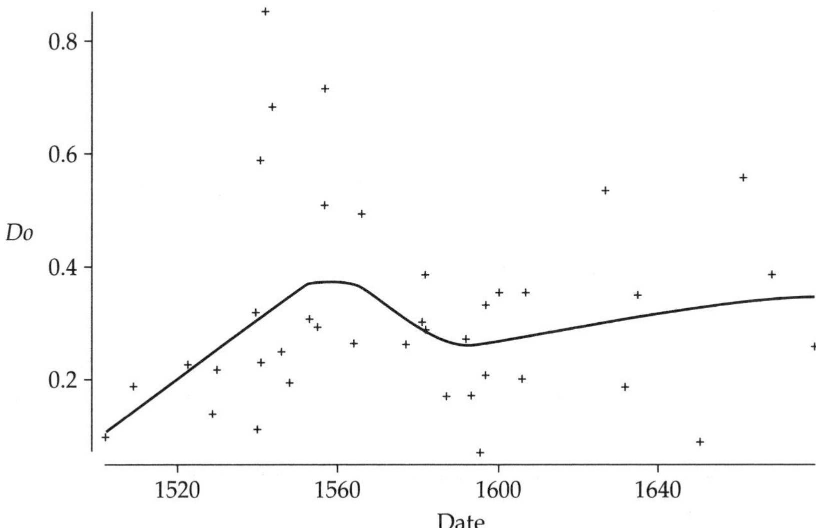

Figure 3.4 Proportion of *do* in negative declaratives in texts of high lexical complexity, 1500–1710

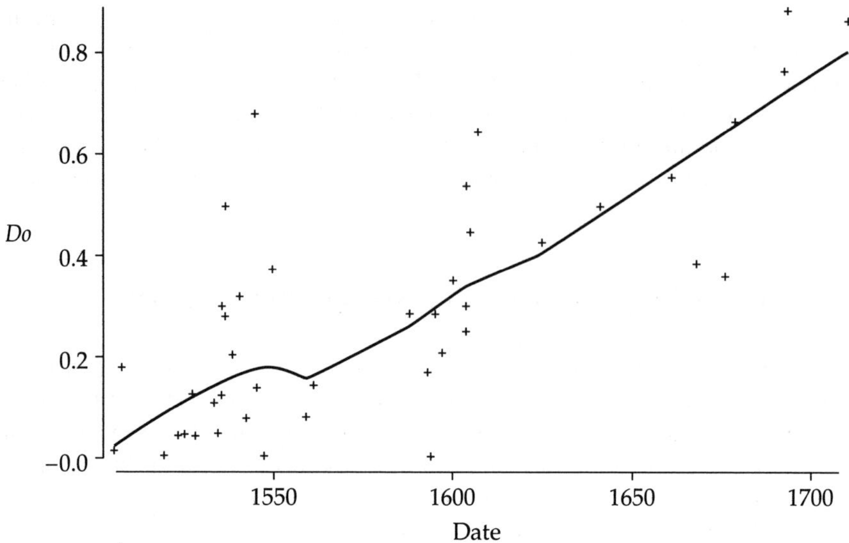

Figure 3.5 Proportion of *do* in negative declaratives in texts of low complexity, 1500–1710

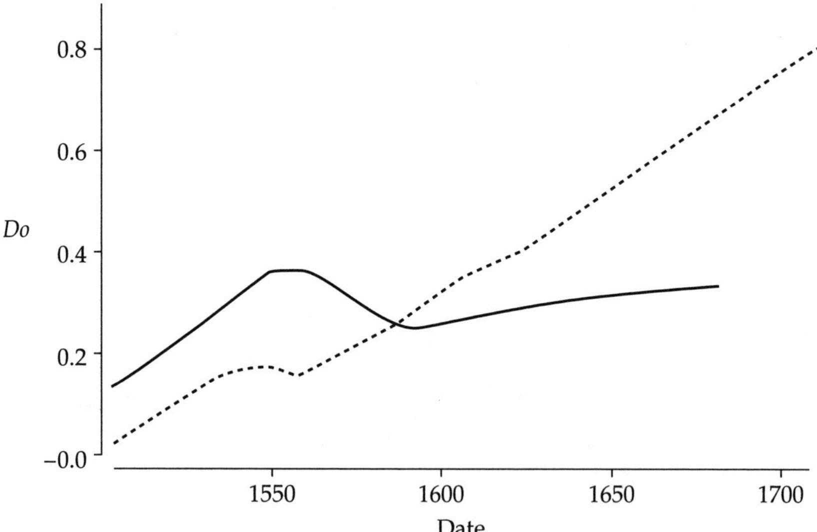

Figure 3.6 Proportion of *do* in negative declaratives in texts of high and low lexical complexity, 1500–1710

in the sixteenth century, and that the situation alters radically as we enter the seventeenth.

These different considerations point strongly to two conclusions:

1 A higher rate of *do not* is associated with texts of greater lexical complexity in Ellegård's data in the period 1500–75.
2 There is a sharp reversal of this association in the seventeenth century. In this period a lower rate of *do not* is associated with texts of greater lexical complexity.

This is consistent with a change in the stylistic value of *do* with *not* versus simple finite with *not*. For 1500–75, the evaluation of *do not* in texts of greater lexical complexity is more positive than that of the simple finite. But this reverses in the late sixteenth century, resulting in a situation where it is the simple finite whose evaluation in texts of greater lexical complexity is more positive than that of *do not*.

In texts of lower lexical complexity there seems to be a pretty steady increase across the period. This implies that there is likely to have been a relatively steady underlying development of *do not* in the vernacular, if we may extrapolate from the texts of lower lexical complexity in Ellegård's database. The drop during the period 1625–50 which can be seen in figure 3.1 does not appear in either graph: it is due to sampling differences (as Ellegård himself suggested), since Ellegård's period 1625–50 has a much higher proportion of texts of greater lexical complexity than the periods which precede and follow.

The Helsinki Corpus shows a similar stylistic switch in the use of *do not* between the period 1500–70 and the second half of the seventeenth century. The definition of oral used here differs, being genre-based. But the situation is clearly shown to be parallel (see table 3.5).

The situation in the Corpus of Early English Correspondence looks at first sight rather different: there is indeed a drop in the incidence of *do not*, but it is located in the first four decades of the seventeenth century (Nurmi 1999: 148–9, 165ff.). It is reasonable to suppose that the drop is stylistically motivated, and this gives us two possibilities for understanding the difference of timing. One is simply that the onset of the change in evaluation takes effect later in personal letters than in the more public types of writing in Ellegård's corpus. The other is that there is some variation in the types of letters written (or in the ages of writers) which affects the results. As Nurmi notes, "In the Correspondence Corpus the letters are personal, but not necessarily private,

Table 3.5 Incidence of *do* in negative declaratives in the Helsinki Corpus

Helsinki 1500–70	Non-oral texts > Oral texts
Helsinki 1570–1640	Non-oral texts = Oral texts
Helsinki 1640–1710	Non-oral texts < Oral texts

Source: Nurmi (1999: 147).

business letters and other less private types being included" (1999: 61). Further investigation will shed more light on this, and on possible relationships between stylistic evaluation and the age and gender differences noted by Nurmi (which also show apparent change in the early seventeenth century).

If this interpretation of the underlying, more vernacular trend is correct, then it has some impact on the interpretations of the history of the grammar of *do*. I have already agreed that there was a reanalysis of *do* in the second half of the sixteenth century. But it is clear that the substantial overall dip in negative declaratives in Ellegård's data as we cross 1575 does not supply any further support for such a reanalysis, since it is a fundamentally stylistic phenomenon. Similarly, if the seventeenth century is a period where evaluation prefers the simple finite over *do not*, then the fact that the development of *do not* seems to diverge from that of questions is not good direct evidence for a grammatical divergence. This line of argument was advanced by Kroch (1989a: 234), who claimed that *do* underwent three independently evolving processes after 1575, in affirmative declaratives, in negative declaratives and in question contexts, on the ground that each context shows a distinct rate of change. His general conclusion is absolutely correct: indeed, I have referred above to the distinct behavior of affirmative declaratives as evidence for grammatical change. But the status of negative declaratives is unclear, since we can now see that we need to take account of the contribution of stylistic evaluation in estimating the apparent rate of change in negative declaratives. In a similar vein, we need to re-examine the evidence for Roberts's account (1993: 303–6). He suggests that *not* occurs in SpecNeg until 1600, so that when obligatory *do* support entered the language in the late sixteenth century, the incidence of *do* with *not* represented the older optional *do*, and declined in tandem with affirmative *do*. Subsequently *not* was reanalysed as Neg^0, with which *do* support is obligatory, and the incidence of *do* recovered. But, again, if the decline of *do not* in the last part of the sixteenth century is a stylistic matter, then it no longer counts as rather compelling evidence for a particular interpretation for the interface of two grammatical developments (obligatory *do* support, and the reanalysis of *not* as Neg^0).

3.8 Conclusions

I have provided answers for some of the questions raised at the beginning of this chapter, but others have been left untouched. And (of course) further questions are raised by what has been said here: for example, what is the relevance of style to the history of *do* in other contexts (questions, affirmative declaratives, imperatives)? How can we better understand the relationships between the timing of events shown in Ellegård's corpus and those shown in the Corpus of Early English Correspondence? Among the conclusions, perhaps the most interesting general point is the demonstration of the value of quantitative, corpus-based methodology. In the first part of the chapter, two different interpretations of the historical data led to distinct arguments from rate(s) of change for specific characterizations of the grammar of *do*. In the second part, I was able to undertake a particular analysis of style, and establish its appropriacy and its limitations, using quantitative methods. These included using the rate of change for each period to calculate a simulation of the general situation for a particular time. Subsequently, I was able to show that major aspects of the apparently erratic behavior of *do* in negative declaratives are due to a dramatic change in the relevance of stylistic considerations. This has clear potential implications (not pursued here) for the interpretation of the grammar of *do*, as well as for the interface between the data of Ellegård's corpus and that in other corpora. Finally, it is worth noting that the series of tagged and parsed corpora for the history of English, initiated by Kroch and undertaken at the University of Pennsylvania and the University of York, will shortly be completed, and that a tagged and parsed version of the Corpus of Early English Correspondence is being compiled as a joint research project between the Universities of Helsinki and York. These are major developments, which will give us the opportunity to develop a much richer understanding of the history of English syntax.

ACKNOWLEDGMENTS

I am very grateful to the British Academy for the Research Readership which gave me time to pursue the matters discussed in this chapter. Thanks are also due to audiences at the Free University of Amsterdam, the 11th International Conference on English Historical Linguistics, the First York-Holland Symposium on the History of English Syntax, the Departmental Research Seminar at York and NWAVE32 for comments on the following material. Results here are derived from a version of Ellegård's database generously given to me by Tony Kroch. I am very grateful to him, to my colleague Ann Taylor who had compiled it, and to Celeste Tereczszuk, who completed it by entering text for the seventeenth century. I have made particular use of the logistic regression programs in Datadesk (Vellman et al. 1995) and SPSS since they allow continuous variables.

REFERENCES

Biber, D. (1988). *Variation across Speech and Writing*. Cambridge: Cambridge University Press.

Denison, David (1993). *English Historical Syntax: Verbal Constructions*. London and New York: Longman.

Ellegård, A. (1953). *The Auxiliary "Do": The Establishment and Regulation of its Use in English*. Stockholm: Almqvist and Wiksell.

Garrett, Andrew (1998). On the origin of auxiliary *do*. *English Language and Linguistics* 2: 283–330.

Han, Chung-hye (2001). The evolution of *do*-support in English imperatives. In Susan Pintzuk, George Tsoulas, and Anthony Warner (eds.), *Diachronic Syntax: Models and Mechanisms* (pp. 275–95). Oxford, New York: Oxford University Press.

Han, Chung-hye and A. Kroch (2000). The rise of *do*-support in English: implications for clause structure. *Proceedings of the 30th North East Linguistics Society*, GLSA: 311–25.

Klemola, J. (1998). Semantics of DO in southwestern dialects of English. In Ingrid Tieken-Boon van Ostade, Marijke van der Wal, and Arjan van Leuvenstijn (eds.), *DO in English, Dutch and German: History and Present-day Variation* (pp. 25–51). Munster: Nodus.

Kroch, A. (1989a). Reflexes of grammar in patterns of language change. *Language Variation and Change* 1: 199–244.

Kroch, A. (1989b). Function and grammar in the history of English: Periphrastic *do*. In R. W. Fasold and D. Schriffin (eds.), *Language Change and Variation* (pp. 132–72). Amsterdam and Philadelphia: John Benjamins.

Kytö, M. (1997). *Be/have* + past participle: the choice of the auxiliary with intransitives from Late Middle to Modern English. In M. Rissanen, M. Kytö, and K. Heikkonen (eds.), *English in Transition: Corpus-based Studies in Linguistic Variation and Genre Styles* (pp. 17–85). Berlin and New York: Mouton de Gruyter.

Labov, W. (1994). *Principles of Linguistic Change: Internal Factors*. Oxford: Blackwell.

Lightfoot, D. (1999). *The Development of Language: Acquisition, Change and Evolution*. Oxford: Blackwell.

Nevalainen, Terttu (1991). Motivated archaism: affirmative periphrastic *do* in Early Modern English liturgical prose. In D. Kastovsky (ed.), *Historical English Syntax* (pp. 303–20). Berlin and New York: Mouton de Gruyter.

Nurmi, Arja (1999). *A Social History of Periphrastic* Do. Mémoires de la Société Néophilologique de Helsinki 56.

Rissanen, Matti (1999). Syntax. In Roger Lass (ed.), *The Cambridge History of the English Language*, vol. 3: *1476–1776* (pp. 187–331). Cambridge: Cambridge University Press.

Roberts, Ian (1993). *Verbs and Diachronic Syntax*. Dordrecht: Kluwer.

Roberts, Ian and Anna Rousseau (2003). *Syntactic Change: A Minimalist Approach to Grammaticalization*. Cambridge: Cambridge University Press.

Rydén, M. and S. Brorström (1987). *The "Be/Have" Variation with Intransitives in English: With Special Reference to the Late Modern Period*. Stockholm: Almqvist and Wiksell.

Stein, Dieter (1986). Syntactic variation and change: the case of *do* in questions in Early Modern English. *Folia Linguistica Historica* 7: 121–49.

Stein, Dieter (1990). *The Semantics of Syntactic Change: Aspects of the Evolution of "Do" in English*. Trends in Linguistics 47. Berlin and New York: Mouton de Gruyter.

Tieken-Boon van Ostade, Ingrid (1987). *The Auxiliary* Do *in Eighteenth-century English: A Sociohistorical-Linguistic Approach*. Dordrecht: Foris.

Velleman, Paul et al. (1995). *DataDesk* (Software for Macintosh). Ithaca: Data Description.

Warner, Anthony (1997). The structure of parametric change, and V-movement in the history of English. In A. van Kemenade and N. Vincent (eds.), *Parameters of Morphosyntactic Change* (pp. 380–93). Cambridge: Cambridge University Press.

Warner, Anthony (2000). *Change and Rate of Change in* Do. ICEHL 11, University of Santiago.

Warner, A. R. (1993). *English Auxiliaries: Structure and History*. Cambridge: Cambridge University Press.

Warner, Anthony (2004). What drove DO? In Christian Kay, Simon Horobin, and Jeremy Smith (eds.), *New Perspectives on English Historical Linguistics* (pp. 229–42). Amsterdam and Philadelphia: John Benjamins.

Willis, David E. (1998). *Syntactic Change in Welsh*. Oxford: Oxford University Press.

FURTHER READING

Biber, D. and E. Finegan (1989). Drift and the evolution of English style: a history of three genres. *Language* 65: 487–517.

Biber, D. and E. Finegan (1992). The linguistic evolution of five written and speech-based English genres from the 17th to the 20th centuries. In Matti Rissanen, Ossi Ihalainen, Terttu Nevalainen, and Irma Taavitsainen (eds.), *History of Englishes: New Methods and Interpretations in Historical Linguistics* (pp. 688–704). Berlin and New York: Mouton de Gruyter.

Biber, D. and E. Finegan (1997). Diachronic relations among speech-based and written registers in English. In Terttu Nevalainen and Leena Kahlas-Tarkka (eds.), *To Explain the Present: Studies in the Changing English Language in Honour of Matti Rissanen* (pp. 253–76). Helsinki: Société Néophilologique.

Denison, David (1985). The origins of periphrastic *do*: Ellegård and Visser reconsidered. In R. Eaton et al. (eds.), *Papers from the 4th International Conference on English Historical Linguistics* (pp. 45–60). Amsterdam and Philadelphia: John Benjamins.

Kroch, A., J. Myhill, and S. Pintzuk (1982). Understanding DO. In K. Tuite et al. (eds.), *Papers from the 18th Regional Meeting of the Chicago Linguistics Society* (pp. 282–94). Chicago: Chicago Linguistics Society.

Miller, Gary D. and Katherine Leffel (1994). The Middle English reanalysis of *do*. *Diachronica* 11: 171–98.

Poussa, P. (1990). A contact universals origin for periphrastic *do*, with special consideration of Old English–Celtic contact. In S. Adamson, V. Law, N. Vincent, and S. Wright (eds.), *Papers from the Fifth International Conference on English Historical Linguistics, Cambridge 6–9 April 1987* (pp. 407–34). Amsterdam and Philadelphia: John Benjamins.

Rissanen, Matti (1985). Periphrastic *do* in affirmative statements in early American English. *Journal of English Linguistics* 18: 163–83.

Rissanen, Matti (1991). Spoken language and the history of *do*-periphrasis. In D. Kastovsky (ed.), *Historical English Syntax* (pp. 321–42). Berlin and New York: Mouton de Gruyter.

Stein, Dieter (1991). Semantic aspects of syntactic change. In D. Kastovsky (ed.), *Historical English Syntax* (pp. 355–66). Berlin and New York: Mouton de Gruyter.

Tieken-Boon van Ostade, Ingrid (1990). The origin and development of periphrastic auxiliary *do*: a case of destigmatization. *North-Western European Language Evolution* 16: 3–52.

Van der Auwera, Johan and Genee Inge (2002). English *do*: on the convergence of languages and linguists. *English Language and Linguistics* 6: 283–307.

Wright, S. (1990). Discourse, style and the rise of periphrastic *do* in English. *Folia Linguistica Historica* 10: 71–91.

Wright, S. (1991). On the stylistic basis of syntactic change. In D. Kastovsky (ed.), *Historical English Syntax* (pp. 469–91). Berlin and New York: Mouton de Gruyter.

4 Evolutionary Models and Functional-Typological Theories of Language Change

WILLIAM CROFT

4.1 Introduction

This chapter describes an evolutionary framework for analyzing language change (Croft 2000, in press) that integrates functional-typological and variationist sociolinguistic approaches to historical linguistics. The model is evolutionary in that it is a theory of how the generalized analysis of selection (Hull 1988, 2001) is to be applied to the processes of language change in contemporary human languages, such as the history of English. As such, the evolutionary framework is not a theory of how the (ultimately biological) ability for human language evolved, though it has important implications for such a theory. Nor is it a theory of the relationship between human linguistic prehistory and human biological prehistory, though it implies certain ways to apply biological methods to linguistic problems. Instead, it is a theory of language change that takes as its starting point variation across individual speech events, across speech communities in a society, and across languages. In this chapter, I will focus on functional-typological approaches to language and language change and how they are integrated in an evolutionary framework.

4.2 Functionalism: What it is, What it is Not

Functionalism can be described broadly as an approach to explaining linguistic structural phenomena in terms of their relationship to linguistic function. Functionalism suggests that there is a more intimate relationship between linguistic form and language function than is implied by formalism, in which explanations are sought internal to the structural system of a language.

There are basically two ways in which language function may, or may not, have an intimate relationship with linguistic form. The first is in the relationship between signifier (form) and the signified (function, in the sense of meaning) in the linguistic sign system. The meaning of a linguistic form is interpreted as functional because the purpose of a linguistic system involves communication, and what is communicated is the meaning denoted by the linguistic form. We will refer to meaning as semiotic function.

What does this mean in functionalist practice? An extreme form of functionalism would deny even the independence of linguistic form: formal syntactic behavior in particular would be wholly accounted for in terms of the meanings of the formal elements. This extreme position is easily falsified and is not held by any leading functionalist linguist. Functionalists frequently argue that a grammatical generalization which has been explained by a syntactic principle is in fact explainable by a semantic or pragmatic principle (see, for example, the work of Prince, Ward, and Birner, and the many semantic and pragmatic accounts of such phenomena as binding relations and so-called extraction constraints). But such an analysis would not refute the independence of form from function. That is, contemporary functionalism of all types accepts that form is an independent level of grammatical organization – in other words, that form is arbitrary.

Although linguistic form is independent of linguistic meaning, it is not a self-contained system in the functionalist approach. That is, the linguistic system is a system of signs or symbolic units, where form and meaning are related directly to each other. Functionalist models of grammatical organization make links between form and function central, in particular arguing for constructions as complex units pairing form and meaning (Fillmore et al. 1988; Goldberg 1995; Croft and Cruse 2004: chs. 9–11). In the constructionist model, all grammatical knowledge is represented as a pairing of form and meaning. Even the most general rule of syntactic combination is a highly abstract construction, and the rule of semantic interpretation associated with the rule of syntactic combination corresponds to the meaning of that construction in a construction grammar.

Functionalist approaches are more likely to explain grammatical generalizations in semantic-pragmatic terms where possible, leading to fewer generalizations formed in purely syntactic terms. Also, typological analyses frequently reveal cross-linguistic syntactic variation, which further reduces the number of remaining grammatical generalizations that can be hypothesized as language universals. The result of these two ways of attacking the problem of explaining grammatical generalizations (semantic-pragmatic and typological) is a radical simplification of syntactic structure (Croft 2001).

The second way in which language function may, or may not, have an intimate relationship with linguistic form is the relationship between grammatical knowledge and language use, or as some put it, between language and verbal behavior. The role of language use (verbal behavior) is seen as functional because communication – language use – is the purpose to which language is put. We will call this external function.

Again, what does this mean in functionalist practice? An extreme form of functionalism would deny the existence of any grammatical structures in the course of language use; that is, language as a system or even just a somewhat stable knowledge of grammatical rules or structures does not exist. No practicing functionalist believes this in the extreme form presented above. Instead, the specific hypothesis advocated by functionalists is that phenomena in language use influence the representation of grammatical knowledge. But evidence demonstrating the influence of language use on the representation of grammatical knowledge does not imply the absence of grammatical knowledge.

The most widely cited usage phenomenon that is argued to play this role is frequency, both token frequency of individual forms and the type frequency of grammatical patterns. This model of grammatical knowledge is called the usage-based model (see, for example, Langacker 2000; Bybee 2001). Activation network models are taken as offering a means to represent the usage-based model in a psychologically plausible form. Such models organize grammatical knowledge in a network (such as the taxonomic network of a construction grammar) and associate degrees of entrenchment with grammatical knowledge in the network. The degree of entrenchment, and the formation of more abstract or schematic grammatical patterns in the first place, is sensitive to frequency of use as well as structural similarity. In the usage-based model, grammar is dynamic and varies even in the lifetime of an adult speaker.

All of these features of the functionalist approach – arbitrariness, form–function linkage in a construction grammar model, typological variation, the usage-based model, and a dynamic, variable view of grammatical representation as well as language behavior – play a role in a functional-typological model of language change.

4.3 Language and Language Change

One cannot define a theory of language change without some hypothesis of what a language is. In order to understand the functionalist approach, it is useful to begin with two popular layperson's views of what a language is.

In the first view, a language is basically like a reference grammar plus dictionary: it is a stock of items and a system of rules for combining those items into sentences of the language. This lay view of a language has been formalized in linguistics as a grammar plus lexicon: a system of rules and oppositions that organizes basic elements – morphemes as well as words – syntagmatically (into sentences) and paradigmatically (into contrasting sets of elements). More precisely, of course, linguistic theory distinguishes between a grammar (the system) and a language (the set of sentences admissible by the grammar).

This view of language idealizes away from much variation both in language use and in grammars (knowledge of language by speakers). One principle of the functionalist approach is that the variation idealized away from in the first view is in fact essential for understanding language. For this reason, the second view of a language is more suited to the functionalist approach.

In the second view, a language is a historical entity. A language such as Hungarian arose at a certain time in a certain place, spread out over a certain area and persisted over a certain time, and will come to an end at a certain place and time, either through extinction or by splitting into two or more daughter languages. In this definition of a language, a language is a token, an empirically real entity; language as a type would be defined over the structures and processes common to languages so defined. In this definition of a language, a grammar is the knowledge that a specific speaker has about their language. Thus, neither a language nor a grammar is idealized in the way that these two entities are under the first definition described above.

An important task of the functionalist enterprise is to take the second lay view of what a language is, and turn it into a technical concept on which a functionalist theory of language change can be built. This chapter describes one proposal for doing so.

4.4 Variation in Language

The definition of a language as a historical entity is intended to confront a basic fact about language: variation. Variation is manifested at three levels in language, and in linguistic form, linguistic meaning and the pairing of form and meaning in grammar.

First-order variation is the variation that occurs in individual occasions of language use. The most obvious variation is in sound structure: as phoneticians and sociolinguists have discovered, the level of variation across productions, even of the same individuals, is quite large. For example, certain languages are standardly described as utilizing just the dental or alveolar place of articulation, such as French and English, respectively. However, in one study, 20–30 percent of French speakers produced an alveolar [t] while a similar proportion of English speakers produced a dental [t̪] (Ladefoged and Maddieson 1996: 23).

First-order variation is also pervasive in meaning. The information communicated by particular words and constructions is extremely variable across individual occasions of use. Grice described the unique meaning conveyed on a particular occasion of use as "utterer's occasion meaning" (Grice 1967/89: 90); Clark calls it "speaker's meaning" (Clark 1996: 126). Attempts have been made to construct a rigid semantic–pragmatics division which would exclude the variable portions of a speaker's conveyed meaning and leave an invariant semantic representation. However, these attempts have run against many problems, and functionalists (as well as many psychologists and philosophers) have instead argued that the relationship between conventional meaning and speaker's meaning is very flexible (the arguments are summarized in Croft 2000: ch. 4; see also Croft and Cruse 2004: chs. 2–4).

Finally, there is also grammatical variation: that is, there are many ways to say "the same thing" in a single language, but they vary in their conventionality (see below). For example, in a set of narratives of a silent film, speakers described the same event with different grammatical structures, some of which are illustrated in (1):

(1) a. Verb + finite complement: *and he notices the basket's missing*
 b. Verb + complementizer: *and he discovers that one of his baskets is gone*
 c. Verb + direct speech: *and notices "Whoa. My basket is gone."*
 d. Verb + coordinate clause: *he looks at the baskets, and there's one missing*

Examples (1a–b) are conventional variants: a finite complement with and without complementizer. But examples (1c–d) represent first-order variation, that is, nonconventionalized structures to communicate the meaning intended. (In fact, (1c–d) represent two common sources of complement constructions in grammaticalization.)

Second-order variation is built on first-order variation: certain first-order variant productions take on sociolinguistic value in the speech community. A simple example is the [n] and [ŋ] variants of the English present participle: *hunting* vs. *huntin'*. These variants no longer emerge from the production and comprehension processes of individual utterances. Instead, they are available to the speech community and are chosen for their social value – what they convey about the social context – as well as their communicative value – the content being communicated. As much sociolinguistic research has demonstrated, this variation is characteristic of the language of a speech community (in the second sense of 'language').

Finally, there is third-order variation, variation across languages and across varieties of language. Third-order variation is second-order variation that has become fixed conventions in different speech communities as these have diverged and/or entered into contact over the history of humankind. Third-order variation is manifested in the cross-linguistic and cross-dialectal variation that is the primary object of study of typology. Examples include the phonological variation of different "accents" of English, or the syntactic differences found in different varieties of English such as the well-advanced loss of verb-phrase ellipsis in British English vs. American English (*Who will take Jeff home? – I will* [Am. Eng.]/*I will do* [Br. Eng.]).

Taking variation as a central fact of language leads to a dynamic model of synchronic language and allows for a simple integration of synchrony and diachrony in language. Language change is simply linguistic variation at a broader scope, and more specifically, linguistic variation that proceeds from first-order innovations to second-order variants to third-order divergence. Although various linguists, both sociolinguists and functionalists, have argued for the centrality of variation in language (Weinreich et al. 1968; Heine et al. 1991; Bybee et al. 1994), it has proven more difficult to develop a model of language and language change that incorporates this idea. In the past decade, there has been an increase of interest in evolutionary models to fill this gap (e.g. Lass 1997; Nettle 1999; Haspelmath 1999; Croft 2000; Mufwene 2001).

4.5 The Generalized Analysis of Selection and Language Change

What is an evolutionary model of language and language change? Many attempts to apply evolutionary concepts to language change founder because of improper analogies. The evolutionary model was developed to describe diversification and change in the biological properties of organisms. It is obvious that many aspects of biological evolution are relevant to biology only. Nevertheless, there is something to the belief that there are aspects of biological evolution that transcend the specifics of biology. Without an understanding of what such a generalized evolutionary model should be, any attempt to apply biological theories to language change will merely be metaphors or analogies, not a systematic evolutionary theory of language change.

The evolutionary model is basically a framework for the analysis of change by replication (Hull 1988). Change occurs in (at least) two varieties: as inherent change or change by replication. Inherent change is the transformation of the properties of an object over time. Replication is a process producing copies of an object that largely preserves the structure of the original object in the replicate. Replication can lead to change if the copying process introduces changes, that is, the replication process is not perfect.

Copying with possible changes is only the kernel of a much more complex process. It is this more complex process which is found in biological evolution, and in language change. First, the replication process that is interesting from an evolutionary point of view allows iteration: copies are produced from copies indefinitely. The changes in the copying process are cumulative in the lineage of replications (that is, later replications do not automatically "revert" to the original's structure). The result of this iterated copying process is a set of replicators, with variation occurring in that set. In biological evolution, the paradigm replicator is the gene. It is a structured entity that is copied in biological reproduction. Changes can occur in the replication process, by random mutation or (in sexual reproduction) by recombination.

In language, replication occurs in language use. Every time we open our mouths to speak, we replicate grammatical structures – sounds, words, and constructions – that have occurred in prior utterances to which we have been exposed. Hence the paradigm replicator is a linguistic structure in an utterance. This entity has not played a major role in grammatical theories, which have dealt with idealizations – the phoneme /p/, or the periphrastic future construction, not specific realizations of /p/ or the future construction in particular utterances. A significant exception is variationist sociolinguistics, in which the basic data are tokens of linguistic structures, the variants of a linguistic variable, which are sampled, quantified, and correlated with various social and linguistic factors. The term *lingueme* is used to describe this entity (Croft 2000).

By taking the replicator as a lingueme, this evolutionary model is fundamentally usage-based, in keeping with the functionalist approach described above:

replication is language use. And as noted above, replication, that is, language use, produces variation, the first-order variation in form and meaning described above. This variation is the first step in a model of change by replication.

Replication leads to change, but change occurs at two levels in replication processes. There is change that occurs in a lineage of specific replications, such as replication of /p/ as [f] instead of the original [p]. This process is altered replication. But there is also change in the overall set of replicators: in this linguistic example, proliferation of [f]s at the expense of [p]s, that is, the increase in frequency of one variant of a linguistic variable at the expense of another variant in the speech community. This process is differential replication: some replicators are copied differentially compared to other replicators.

In biological evolution, the most important process of differential replication is selection. In selection, a distinct process from that which causes change in lineages causes differential replication in a set of replicators. In biological evolution, selection of genes is a consequence of the interaction of organisms with their environment. In biological evolution, organisms interact with their environment (including other members of their species), and their success or failure leads to the propagation or extinction of their genes. Hull generalizes the analysis of the selectional process as environmental interaction: environmental interaction causes differential replication of the relevant replicators. One mechanism for selection in biology is natural selection, in which organisms more adapted to the environment survive and reproduce at a greater rate, leading to the differential replication of their genes in the species.

In language change, the paradigm interactor is the speaker, or perhaps more precisely, the speaker's grammar (knowledge about their language). We cause the differential replication of lingueme variants every time we open our mouth to speak: we produce certain variants in our utterances instead of certain others. The choice of variants depends on what is being talked about and above all who is being spoken to. For example, out of the plethora of terms that were used to describe the then-new wireless phone that one carried around, American speakers increasingly selected *cellphone* – while British speakers increasingly selected *mobile phone*. The effect of differential production of variants – differential replication – is an increase in the frequency of certain variants and the decrease of others.

Evolution, and in this view language change, is therefore a two-step process: replication which produces variation among replicators, and environmental interaction by interactors which causes differential replication (selection) of replicators. This is the essential model of change by replication developed by Hull; he calls it the generalized analysis of selection, or GAS. Croft (2000) applies GAS to language change, identifying the lingueme as the paradigm replicator and the speaker as paradigm interactor.

There is a further level of organization in the biological evolution of sexual organisms which also forms a part of GAS, and is particularly relevant to language change. Organisms form species, and it is usually said that species are what evolves. A species is defined as a population in evolutionary biology. The population model replaces the previously assumed essentialist definition of a species. In the essentialist definition, membership in a species is defined by a set of essential properties (structural and/or behavioral). However, distinct species share the same supposedly essential properties in many cases, and in other cases, members of the same species are extremely diverse and no essential properties can be identified. Above all, species evolve and in so doing lose supposedly essential traits.

The problems with the essentialist definition of a species are paralleled exactly by problems in defining a language. Many languages are distinct although they share the same linguistic properties and are therefore mutually intelligible; examples include Bulgarian and Macedonian, or Danish and Norwegian. Some languages are considered to be a single language even though members of the speech community cannot understand each other; examples include the Chinese language, and, increasingly, English – an American speaker should not compliment her Southern British host on his *pants*, and a British speaker asking for a *guillotine* or a *torch* in a shop in the US will not get what he expects, if he gets anything at all. Finally, languages evolve and change their linguistic features (for example, an Old English speaker will fail to communicate with a Modern English speaker by saying, for example, *Ic gefremman sceal eorlic ellen* (Denison 1993: 38)). These phenomena all pose problems for a language defined in terms of structural properties or even in terms of mutual intelligibility.

The solution to the problem of essentialist definitions in biology is to redefine species as a population. The term *population* has a specific meaning in biology. A population is defined by some relational property between members, not inherent properties of members. In the case of species, it is interbreeding among the members, and (more critically) reproductive isolation from members of other species. A population is therefore unified by interbreeding.

The population definition of a species is tightly interwoven with the central processes of the evolutionary model: replication, variation (altered replication), and selection (differential replication). Interbreeding, of course, produces new members of the population. Interbreeding leads to replication of the relevant replicators as well. It also provides another mechanism for altered replication, that is, the production of variation: recombination of genes from the two parent organisms. Finally, success or failure in interbreeding leads to differential replication of the replicators.

The linguistic equivalent of the population definition of a species is a population definition of a language, or more precisely, the speech community. (Recall that speakers are interactors, like organisms.) A speech community is a group of speakers who engage in intercourse, that is, talk to each other and, more critically, are communicatively isolated from speakers in other speech communities. This definition of a language spoken by a speech community is therefore more "social" than "linguistic" (Chambers and Trudgill 1998: ch. 1). However, most "social" definitions of a language refer to speaker attitudes. The population definition presented here is defined in terms of what speakers actually do (or don't do, i.e. who they don't talk to). For example, despite mass media, an ocean still separates British and American English speakers: most speakers in one community don't talk to most of the speakers of the other, and hence linguistic divergence continues even with terms for new objects such as *cellphone / mobile phone.*

Of course, communicative isolation is never complete. People do talk to speakers of other dialects and other languages. However, this is not a problem for a generalized model of evolution. Reproductive isolation between biological species, especially plants, is incomplete as well. It is true that intercourse (in the linguistic sense) between speaker populations is undoubtedly of a higher degree than interbreeding across species, even plants: speakers of distant languages can communicate and borrow words, and even morphology and syntax. Nevertheless, this is a difference of degree, not kind.

The population definition of a speech community, like the population definition of a species, is also tightly integrated with the central processes of the evolutionary model: replication, innovation (altered replication), and propagation (differential replication). Conversation is the production of utterances. Hence, conversation leads to replication of linguemes. In particular, the production of utterances involves the recombination of linguemes from prior utterances heard and internalized by the speaker: most utterances are novel combinations of words and constructions. For example, it is unlikely that the speaker of example (1b), *And he discovers that one of his baskets is gone*, has ever produced that exact phrase before. But the speaker has certainly used the words before, and constructions such as [*And* S], [Sbj *discover that* S′], [*one of* X's Noun] [Sbj *be gone*]. Utterance (1b) is thus a recombination of the words and these constructions from probably different prior utterances. This recombination process is what is usually referred to as the creativity of language. Some of these novel combinations become the innovations for new constructions in grammaticalization, or for new word senses, or for new words themselves (e.g. derivational innovations). Hence the recombination process is a major source of innovations in language change. Finally, the production of utterances in conversation causes differential replication of the relevant linguemes.

A population of interactors is therefore defined by intercourse between members, and isolation from intercourse with other populations. (The term *intercourse* is introduced here to describe the specific sort of interaction that binds together populations.) Moreover, this intercourse brings about replication in the case of the interactors we have described in biological evolution and language change. The population of speakers is a historical entity. A population comes to exist when its ancestral population splits, and it continues to exist until it itself splits into new populations, or it becomes extinct.

Once we have identified a speech community – a population of speakers – then we may identify other associated populations or population-like entities. A language can now be defined as a population of utterances, that is, the population of utterances produced by members of a speech community. A population of utterances is a historical entity, consisting of the corpus of actual utterances produced. A population of utterances is thus the formalization of the second lay view of what a language is. It is born at a particular place and time, and extends over space and time until it splits into new populations or becomes extinct. A population of utterances is interconnected in that the linguemes in a particular utterance are replicated from prior utterances.

The other important population is the "lingueme pool," that is, all the linguemes occurring in a language. This is the data set that is sampled in variationist sociolinguistic research, yielding frequencies of variants in particular speech communities. The linguemes in a lingueme pool form lineages which trace the history of the sounds, words, and constructions of the language. These histories are sound changes, word etymologies, and grammaticalization chains of constructions – the basic facts of language change.

4.6 GAS: What it is, What it is Not

The generalized analysis of selection is an abstract model of change by replication. GAS is not a metaphor or analogy from biological evolution to language change. GAS in itself does not specify how it is instantiated in a particular phenomenal domain (it may even be the case that there are two distinct selection processes operating at once). The only constraint imposed by the generalized theory of selection is that all roles must be instantiated: replicator, interactor, environment; and that there are causal mechanisms linking those roles in the way specified by the generalized analysis.

The usage-based instantiation described above (called the Theory of Utterance Selection in Croft 2000) is an instantiation of GAS in language change. This theory is functionalist in that it is usage-based. The basic units of analysis, linguemes, are tokens of linguistic structure in language use. The process of change occurs in language use, that is, when speakers talk to each other. When speakers talk to each other, they replicate linguemes from prior occasions of language use. Language use can generate novel variants (altered replication), that is, innovation. Where alternative variants exist, language use involves selection or propagation of particular variants at the expense of other variants (differential replication).

GAS also does not specify what the causal mechanisms are that bring about selection in a particular domain. Causal mechanisms must be identified that produce novel variants, not to mention the even more fundamental mechanisms that lead to normal (identical) replication. Likewise, causal mechanisms must be identified that cause differential replication. These causal mechanisms are specific to the empirical phenomenon in which change by replication takes place. In this sense, GAS is not incompatible with many of the theories of mechanisms of language change. GAS tells us where we must look for such mechanisms; it does not tell us what we should find. The next section describes the causal mechanisms of the Theory of Utterance Selection and how they fit with the functional-typological approach to language change.

4.7 Convention and Functional-Typological Theories of Language Change

In the Theory of Utterance Selection, the most central fact about language is that it is a system of conventions. Language change represents the evolution of conventions. Normal replication, that is, more or less identical replication, is conformity to convention. Altered replication, that is, innovation, is breaking a convention. Differential replication, that is, propagation or selection, is the adoption (or abandonment) of a convention by a speech community.

A convention is defined in (2), following Lewis (1969) and Clark (1996; adapted from 1996: 71):

(2) a. a regularity in behavior
 b. that is partly arbitrary
 c. that is common ground in a community
 d. as a coordination device
 e. for a recurrent coordination problem

Lewis's theory of convention is based on a model of cooperative joint action. Language use is an example of cooperative joint action, namely to communicate in order to achieve various social-interactional goals of the interlocutors. In this respect, Lewis's theory of convention conforms to a functionalist approach to language, and in fact provides a firm theoretical foundation for it. Any cooperative action requires coordination, that is, speaker and hearer have to find a way to align their individual actions in order to achieve a joint goal. In fact, the fundamental function of language is to serve as a means to coordinate extralinguistic joint actions (Clark 1999). But language use itself is a joint action requiring coordination. The joint action is communicating a meaning. Clark uses a revised version of Grice's theory of meaning as a joint action, given in (3) (adapted from Clark 1996: 131):

(3) A speaker MEANS something for someone when:
 a. the communicative act includes (b) and (c)
 b. the speaker presents an utterance to the addressee intending that what is meant is part of the communicative act
 c. the addressee recognizes that what is meant is part of the communicative act

The definition of meaning in (3) makes clear that communication is a joint action, involving recognition by the hearer of the intentions of the speaker. For communication to succeed, speaker and hearer must (among other things) coordinate on the content of what is meant. This is the coordination problem that convention can be used to solve. Although a number of coordination devices are used in communication (see below), convention is one of the most important and distinctive of those devices.

We now return to the nature of convention by means of an example. One behavior that I exhibit as an English speaker is producing the string of sounds *butterfly* as a coordination device to solve the recurrent coordination problem of talking about butterflies. The employment of this behavior is common ground in the English speech community: we all know that we use *butterfly* for this purpose. And this behavior is partly arbitrary. For example, we could have used the string of sounds *Schmetterling* instead; that's what the German speech community did. The (partial) arbitrariness of convention is the means by which arbitrariness is integrated into a functionalist account of language: arbitrariness is a property of conventions, which serve the function of coordinating the act of communication. Conventions are also form–function relations, the central concern of functionalist theories of grammar: the regularity in behavior is form and the recurrent coordination problem is its (semiotic) function.

Convention is the foundation of the usage-based Theory of Utterance Selection. Conformity to convention is the absence of change. The absence of change is a phenomenon that requires explanation as much as change does. After all, language does not change rapidly in all of its dimensions, despite the ubiquity of variation in language use and in socially governed linguistic variables. The absence of change is a particularly important phenomenon in a usage-based theory such as the Theory of Utterance Selection. In such a theory, replication occurs every time we talk, and since we talk so much and so often, the "generations" are very short in absolute time (though still much longer than those of many biological organisms, such as bacteria and viruses). Hence, conformity to convention must be powerful in order to maintain language. In fact, the principle governing conformity to convention has been proposed a number of times in the history of linguistics; Keller describes it as "Humboldt's Law" (after the nineteenth-century linguist Wilhelm von Humboldt), and it corresponds to Roman Jakobson's referential function. Keller formulates the principle as one of his maxims of language use: "Talk in a way in which you believe the other would talk if he or she were in your place" (Keller 1990/4: 99).

The dynamic aspects of a theory of language change are the processes of altered replication (innovation) and differential replication or selection (propagation). The Theory of Utterance Selection hypothesizes that there is a strict separation of causal mechanisms for innovation and propagation. Innovation is functional, in the sense described for functionalism above: that is, it arises from the relationship between linguistic form and its meaning or "function" (or, in the case of phonological innovation, the relationship between phonological form and its phonetic realization). Propagation, on the other hand, is social, that is, it arises from the social structure of speech communities, and the social relations between speech communities. In other words, propagation is governed by the principles that variationist sociolinguistics has identified over several decades of research. This hypothesis in effect allows us to integrate two independent and seemingly incompatible research programs in historical linguistics, the sociolinguistic program and the "traditional" or philological program. These two programs are not incompatible but instead are studying different steps in the two-step process of language change in an evolutionary model. This "evolutionary synthesis" is one of the most important features of this approach to language change.

According to this separation of social and functional mechanisms of change, variationist sociolinguistics is compatible with functionalist approaches to language change, but an in-depth discussion is beyond the purview of this chapter. Nevertheless, certain aspects of propagation must be covered briefly before turning to functionalist mechanisms for innovation.

Some evolutionary functionalists have argued, contrary to the hypothesis presented above, that functional factors as well as social factors govern propagation (Nettle 1999; Haspelmath 1999). This position is motivated by the belief that the mechanism for propagation in language change should be analogous to the mechanism for selection in biological evolution, namely natural adaptation. But GAS does not specify mechanisms; it only identifies roles and causal relations between roles in selection (see above). Hence there is no a priori reason to try to relate mechanisms of language change to mechanisms of biological evolution.

Also, some functional models of language change are in fact one-step models: functional factors are innovations. Keller's (1990/4) invisible hand model is a one-step functional model of change. Each speaker independently innovates for a similar reason given the "ecological conditions" of their communicative situation. For example, speakers avoid the word *toilet* due to the taboo on bodily functions, and choose the euphemism *bathroom* instead. In this model, the "propagation" of language change is actually a cumulation of individual functional choices.

All of the empirical evidence in sociolinguistics points to a gradual and socially structured process of the propagation of an innovation through a speech community (see Labov 1994, 2001, for a survey of the literature). This evidence disconfirms the hypothesis of functionally motivated propagation. It also disconfirms one-step models: a one-step model would predict a relatively rapid process of innovation (recall that replication occurs every time a sentence is uttered), and of course the propagation would not be socially structured. The invisible hand model explains why speakers would choose a euphemism for *toilet*, but it does not explain why speakers converge on *bathroom* (or why British English speakers continue to use the older euphemism *toilet*).

Another motivation for the view that functional factors play a role in propagation is the belief that innovation must be random, because one of the chief mechanisms of innovation (variation) in biological evolution is random mutation. But GAS does not specify mechanisms, and in particular it does not specify that the mechanism must be random. Linguistic changes, phonological and morphosyntactic, tend to be broadly unidirectional (Croft 2003). Whatever their motivation, a two-step model must capture this fact. But as Kroch (1989) has demonstrated, one can separate the contribution of functional factors to directed (i.e. nonrandom) innovations from the contribution of social factors to propagation. Kroch's Constant Rate Hypothesis assumes that functional factors – the basic structure of communication and communicative interaction – remain the same over time, contributing to innovation (first-order variation) but not propagation. Social factors – the structure of the speech community – drive the change forward, and do vary over time (leading to propagation or even the halting of a change in progress).

Finally, it should be noted that we do not assume that every production of an innovation after the first one is socially motivated. The socially motivated propagation process begins only after a novel variant acquires a social value (that is, it is identified with a social group). This is the transition from first-order variation to second-order variation. A (functionally motivated) novel first-order variant may be produced independently many times before it acquires a social value, becoming a second-order variant, and is then propagated.

4.8 Functional Mechanisms for Innovation

Causal mechanisms for language change can be classified into three types. Teleological changes are changes for the sake of change, specifically changes intended to make the language system "better" in some respect. Selectional models do not support teleological changes. In fact, selection models in biology demonstrate how evolutionary changes can occur without organisms intending those changes to occur: once variation is generated, the relative fitness of organisms in an environment ensures that selection causes change to be directed towards increasing fitness. Likewise, in language, change does not take place because speakers intend to change their linguistic system (see, for example, Labov 1994: ch. 19; Lass 1997: 352ff.).

Some innovations are likely to have been intended by the speaker. However, these innovations were produced in the service of a communicative goal, not for the purpose of changing the linguistic system. These mechanisms are functional in that they serve a communicative purpose. For example, it has commonly been proposed that speakers innovate in order to be expressive for various reasons (e.g. to be noticed, to be amusing, to be charming, etc.; see Keller 1990/4: 101; compare Jakobson's poetic function). Expressiveness has been invoked in a variety of approaches to language change. Another widely invoked principle for innovation is economy, proposed for a wide variety of phonetic and grammatical processes. Economy is usually interpreted as a psychological phenomenon, the saving of energy on the part of the speaker. However, economy is more likely to have a communicative motivation: saving the speaker's and hearer's time, rather than saving the speaker's energy (compare Clark's (1996: 69) immediacy premise; see Croft 2000: 75). Finally, Keller observes that an important principle for innovation is to avoid misunderstanding (1990/4: 94); this principle may be at least as significant as expressiveness (Croft 2000: 75).

Finally, there are innovations that are not intended by the speaker. These are unintended side effects of a speaker's intention to conform to convention, i.e. not to innovate. The intention to conform to convention may lead to innovation because of the complexity of the encoding and decoding of language. For example, the phonetic realization of phonological articulations leads to complex coarticulation effects. When this is combined with the variability of speaker productions, the decoding of the auditory signal may lead to reanalysis of the mapping between phonological form and phonetic realization (see Ohala 1981, 1993). Likewise, the complexity of the morphosyntactic encoding of meaning, combined with the variability of the experiences communicated on particular occasions of use, may lead to the reanalysis of the mapping between morphosyntactic form in constructions and the semantic content that they denote (Croft 2000).

4.9 Form–Function Reanalysis and Intraference

This last process is described as form–function reanalysis (Croft 2000: chs. 5–6). Four types of syntagmatic form–function reanalysis and one type of paradigmatic form–function reanalysis are proposed. In the first syntagmatic type, hyperanalysis, a speaker analyzes out a semantic component from a syntactic element, typically a semantic component that overlaps with that of another element. Hyperanalysis accounts for semantic bleaching and eventually the loss of syntactic element.

There are a number of examples of hyperanalysis in the history of English; the examples here are from Allen (1995). In Old English, before the case system was lost, genitive phrases governed by the verb are occasionally found in the accusative: "although there are not a very large number of examples with accusative objects, they are nevertheless too frequent to be mistakes" (1995: 135; examples are from 1995: 133, 135):

(4) *Micel wund behofað micles læcedomes*
'A great wound requires great medicine'
([*COE*] Bede 4 26.350.19)

(5) *ac swa mare wund swa heo maran læcedomes behōfað*
'but the greater the wound, so it requires greater medicine'
([*COE*] ÆCHom I, 33 496.30)

In Middle English, the genitive object frequently is replaced by an accusative object (Allen 1995: 218). We can analyze this process as hyperanalysis: the meaning coded by the genitive case (presumably, some lesser degree of affectedness of the referent with "help") is redundant with the semantics of the verb and therefore is hyperanalyzed out, leading to the assignment of the more widely used and semantically less specific accusative case.

English also formed passives with verbs governing dative objects, in which the passive "subject" retained its dative case marking. These constructions were replaced by passives with nominative case. Interestingly, the passives with nominative case arose even when the dative/accusative distinction was still present, in at least some dialects (Allen 1995: 357–64). Allen treats this as problematic, because this change would complicate the grammars of those speakers (1995: 375). However, in a hyperanalysis account, it is a plausible remapping of the form–function relationship in these constructions: the semantic content of the dative case is hyperanalyzed out, and so the dative is replaced by the semantically less specific nominative.

In the second process, hypoanalysis, a semantic component is added to a syntactic element, typically one whose distribution has no discriminatory semantic value. Hypoanalysis is the same as exaptation (Lass 1990) or regrammaticalization (Greenberg 1991).

An example of multiple hypoanalysis is found in the history of English *do* and third person singular *-s*. The standard English third person singular present tense suffix *-s* is a minimal remnant of Old English subject agreement. Also, in earlier standard English (and lasting into the eighteenth century), "[periphrastic] *do* is simply used as an unstressed tense marker" (Ihalainen 1991: 148). Hypoanalysis (exaptation) of the combination of third singular *-s* and periphrastic *do* occurred in the traditional dialects of Somerset and Dorset (Ihalainen 1991; Trudgill 1990). In Somerset/Dorset traditional dialects, the simple present *-s* is used for specific or single events, while *do* is used for iterative or habitual events (Trudgill 1990: 95; Ihalainen 1991):

(6) a. *I sees the doctor tomorrow* [specific/single event, present]
b. *I do see him every day* [iterative/habitual, present]

It appears that the semantically minimal *-s* acquires the contextual semantic property of marking present tense; this hypoanalysis leads to its use beyond third person singular (as in (6a)). In addition, the semantically minimal *do* is attributed contextual properties of verbal aspect, and is reanalyzed as an iterative/habitual marker. As a consequence, present tense *-s* is attributed a semelfactive/nonhabitual semantic function. Again, we do not really know the usage contexts which might have led to this particular division of semantic labor between *-s* and *do*. But the use of periphrastic *do* plus the marginal grammatical status of *-s* probably gave rise to just the sort of complexity in the form–function mapping in language use that would invite hypoanalysis of these forms.

In the third process, metanalysis, a contextual semantic feature becomes inherent in a syntactic element while an inherent feature is analyzed out; in other words, it is simultaneous hyperanalysis/hypoanalysis. Metanalysis typically takes place when there is a unidirectional correlation of semantic features (one feature frequently occurs with another, but the second often does not occur with the first). Metanalysis underlies pragmatic inferencing (Traugott and König 1991), such as the shift of English *since* from a temporal to a causal meaning (Hopper and Traugott 2003: 82–3; they note that the causal meaning does not become widespread until the fifteenth century):

(7) *temporal meaning:*
þa, siþþan he irre wæs and gewundod, he ofslog micel þæs folces
'Then after/since he was angry and wounded, he slaughtered many troops'
(c.880, Orosius 4 1.156.11)

(8) *causal meaning:*
Ac ic þe wille nu giet getæcan ðone weg . . . siððan ðu ongitst þurh mine lare hwæt sio soðe gesælð bið and hwær hio bið
'But still I will now teach you the way . . . since you see through my teaching what true happiness is, . . . and where it is'
(c.880, Boethius 36 104.26)

Most contexts in which a temporal connective is used also denote a causal relation, and so the temporal and causal meanings were metanalyzed (i.e. the connective acquired an inherent causal meaning, and the temporal meaning became contextual). Metanalysis also motivates the negative cycle: negative contexts are frequently emphatic, and the emphatic marker replaces its emphatic meaning with a negative one.

In the fourth process, cryptanalysis, a covertly marked semantic feature is reanalyzed as not grammatically marked, and a grammatical marker is inserted. Cryptanalysis typically occurs when there is an obligatory transparent grammatical marker available for the covertly marked semantic feature. Cryptanalysis accounts for pleonasm (for example, pleonastic and paratactic negation) and reinforcement.

An example of contemporary language change in English that can be analyzed as cryptanalysis is pleonastic negation. The (a) and (b) sentences in (9–10), discussed on the LINGUIST list, mean the same thing, although the (b) sentence contains a negative that the (a) sentence lacks:

(9) a. *That'll teach you to come early.*
b. *That'll teach you not to come early.*
(a, b) = You came early, some unhappy consequence ensued, and you should not come early in the future
(Laurie Bauer, LINGUIST 4.873)

(10) a. *I really miss having a phonologist around the house.*
b. *I really miss not having a phonologist around the house.*
(a, b) = There used to be a phonologist around the house, there isn't any more, and I wish there were one around the house now.
(Dale Russell, LINGUIST 4.859)

Lawrence Horn made the following remarks on this class of examples:

> Now the negation that shows up pleonastically in *miss (not) VPing, surprised if it does(n't) . . . , prendre garde de (ne pas) tomber*, etc., is NOT, unlike the one in *so don't I*, ironic or sarcastic; . . . [it is] attributable to the difficulty of processing multiple negations especially when at least one is non-overt. (Horn on LINGUIST 4.898)

The (a) sentences in (9–10) have in common a covert negative, as Horn notes. However, polarity is something that is normally expressed overtly and grammatically in other sentences in English (and other languages). In (9a–10a), a listener recognizes the negative semantic component but there is no overt syntactic unit to which the negative semantic value can be linked; instead it is an entailment of some other syntactic unit. What has happened in (9b–10b) is that the hearer has reanalyzed the construction as "needing" an overt syntactic unit to convey the semantic value, and actualized the reanalysis by inserting a pleonastic negation. This is cryptanalysis.

Form–function reanalysis provides a link between the general functionalist model of language described above and widely occurring processes of morphosyntactic change. The general functionalist model places a central role on the mapping between form and function in language. This mapping is the basis of linguistic convention, the regularity in behavior (form) used to solve a recurrent coordination problem (function). The combination of variability and complexity in the form–function mapping leads to innovations as a consequence of the reanalysis of the form–function mapping in grammatical constructions.

The four types of form–function reanalysis illustrated above describe syntagmatic processes in innovation, namely form–function mappings in constructions. There are also paradigmatic contrasts in form–function mappings in the organization of linguistic elements – words and constructions – in a speaker's mind. In Croft (2000), the phenomenon of extension or spread – the use of a grammatical form or construction for new, semantically closely related functions – is also hypothesized to result from a non-intentional mechanism. In a functionalist model of grammar, the basic unit is a form-meaning pairing (a sign or construction, in the generalized sense of the latter term). The paradigmatic organization of grammatical forms and constructions is therefore determined by semantic as well as syntactic relations. (In typological theory, the semantic map model is used to represent the semantic relatedness of forms and constructions; Croft 2001, 2003; Haspelmath 2003.)

Grammatical forms and constructions are extended by the mechanism of intraference, the language-internal equivalent of interference. In external interference, bilingual speakers establish an interlingual identification of forms with overlapping functions in two different languages (Weinreich 1968: 7). The result is the introduction of a new form with a particular function into a language, or the addition of a new function to a linguistic form (a calque of the usage of the equivalent form in the other language). Intraference is the same process within a language: instead of interference from a form with a similar function from a second language, there is intraference from a form with a closely related function in the same language.

Besides various types of extension of forms and constructions, intraference also accounts for analogical leveling, where one stem in an irregular paradigm is extended to replace other stems in the paradigm. An example of analogical leveling is the evolution of the present tense paradigm of *do* from Old to Middle English (Bybee 1985: 64, from Moore and Marckwardt 1968):

(11)

		Old English	Middle English
Present Indicative:			
Singular	1st	*dō*	*do*
	2nd	*dēst*	*dost*
	3rd	*dēð*	*doth*
Plural		*dēð*	*do*

The meanings of the verb forms all overlap: they all denote the same type of event or state. Intraference is the consequence of identification of the meaning of one form with an overlapping meaning of another form: this leads to the introduction of the other form with the first meaning. The second and third person singular meanings are closely related to the first person singular meaning of the same verb in the same tense and mood. In the Middle English paradigm, the former Old English root for first person replaced the Old English root for second and third person, and so combines with the suffixes for second and third person. The resulting Middle English forms are fudged forms brought about by the paradigmatic form–function reanalysis of intraference, that is, intralingual identification of the first and second/third person singular present indicative forms.

4.10 Grammaticalization

Perhaps the most widely discussed phenomenon of language change in functional-typological theory is grammaticalization. Grammaticalization is the process by which grammatical forms and constructions evolve from ordinary lexical items in general syntactic constructions. A summary of the most common grammaticalization processes is given in (12) (Croft 2003: 254, drawn from several sources):

(12) a. full verb > auxiliary > tense-aspect-mood affix
b. verb > adposition
c. noun > adposition
d. adposition > case affix
e. adposition > subordinator
f. emphatic personal pronoun > clitic pronoun > indexation affix
g. cleft sentence marker > highlighter
h. noun > classifier
i. verb > classifier
j. demonstrative > article > gender/class marker
k. demonstrative or article > complementizer or relativizer
l. numeral "one" > indefinite article
m. numerals "two" or "three" > dual/paucal/plural affix
n. collective noun > plural affix
o. demonstrative > copula
p. positional verb > copula

Grammaticalization involves changes occurring more or less simultaneously at the phonological, morphosyntactic, and functional levels. Grammaticalization also involves both syntagmatic and paradigmatic processes. The processes generally accepted as belonging to grammaticalization are summarized in (13–15) (Croft 2003: 255):

(13) *Phonological processes:*
  a. Syntagmatic: coalescence (free morpheme > cliticization/compounding > affixation > loss); adaptation (including assimilation)
  b. Paradigmatic: attrition (reduction/erosion > phonological loss)

(14) *Morphosyntactic processes:*
  a. Syntagmatic: rigidification (word order); loss of syntactic independence > morphological fusion > loss
  b. Paradigmatic: obligatorification > fossilization > morphological loss; paradigmaticization (open class element > closed class element > invariant element)

(15) *Functional processes:*
  a. Syntagmatic: idiomaticization (compositional and analyzable > "noncompositional" [by general rules] but analyzable > unanalyzable
  b. Paradigmatic: subjectification > loss of function

Space prevents detailed discussion of these processes; but they have been extensively analyzed elsewhere (Lehmann 1982/95; Heine and Reh 1984; Heine et al. 1991; Hopper and Traugott 2003; Croft 2003).

Various explanatory models for grammaticalization have been proposed. The most general of these models is the periphrasis–fusion–erosion cycle (Lüdtke 1986; Keller 1990/4; Croft 2000). We will describe a recent English change, the rise of the periphrastic future *be going to*, in terms of this explanatory model. In the periphrasis stage, a periphrastic construction is employed for a particular function. In the case of the English future, a combination of a motion verb (*go*) and a purpose clause (*to* + infinitive) is employed for a future function. This stage is motivated most likely to avoid misunderstanding, although expressiveness is also sometimes invoked. The mechanism that leads to the choice of the construction is pragmatic inference, interpreted above as a type of metanalysis; a construction may also spread from a closely related function by intraference. The construction *be going to* probably spread from the closely related meaning of a motion event undertaken with an intended future outcome (the purpose clause). In the fusion stage, the periphrastic construction becomes a fixed, distinct, independent construction employed specifically for the function in question. That is, the construction becomes conventionalized or idiomatized in that function. This stage has clearly occurred with future *be going to*: it is fixed in the use of the specific verb *go* and the present progressive form. Finally, erosion occurs: as the construction becomes entrenched, it is phonologically and morphologically reduced in the ways described in (4–6). The future *be going to* has commonly been reduced to the contracted form of *be* plus the reduced unit *gonna* [gʌnə].

Certain theoretical issues have provoked debate in the grammaticalization literature; these are touched upon briefly here. First, empirical evidence indicates that phonological, morphosyntactic and functional grammaticalization processes are not exactly synchronized in language change: sometimes one advances while another does not change. Second, the central hypothesis of grammaticalization theory is that grammaticalization processes are unidirectional. This hypothesis has been challenged by a number of putative counterexamples. Many of these counterexamples violated a putative morphosyntactic grammaticalization process, reduction of syntactic scope; but this process has been rejected for more general reasons (Tabor and Traugott 1998). Third, grammaticalization has also been associated with syntactic reanalysis (not the same phenomenon as the form–function reanalysis discussed above), but this association may be an artifact of the syntactic theory assumed (Haspelmath 1998). Fourth, grammaticalized constructions also undergo semantic change. This change is sometimes described as "bleaching" or "loss," but in fact the appearance of "bleaching" is because of the spread of a construction across several functions, not loss of meaning. The direction of extension of a grammaticalizing construction is difficult to characterize semantically; the most satisfying analysis is that the process involves subjectification (Traugott 1989, 1990).

4.11 Conclusion

Towards the beginning of this chapter, it was noted that one's theory of language change depends on what one's theory of language is. A functional-typological approach to language argues that the relationship between form and (semiotic) function is central to grammatical representation, and the relationship between grammar and use is central to understanding language change. But functional-typological theory has only recently begun to integrate its various hypotheses and empirical results into a coherent synthesis.

Variation is the key concept linking synchronic and diachronic functional analyses of language and language change. Language use is undoubtedly highly variable (first-order variation), and that variation becomes part of the social fabric of language (second-order variation). A functionalist model also posits grammatical knowledge as variable. In this respect functionalism joins with variationist sociolinguistics. But variation and change has to be understood in a suitable framework.

Evolution provides a suitable framework for integrating grammatical variation and social variation, and synchrony and diachrony. An evolutionary model describes change by replication, and change by replication occurs via variation in the replication process. An evolutionary model, specifically Hull's generalized analysis of selection, can be instantiated in language by analyzing language use as the replication of grammatical structures in utterances. Language use generates variation, and selection then operates on the variation to yield change and ultimately diversity across dialects and languages as speech communities differentiate themselves over time. Evolution with selection is a two-step process: the first step, innovation, is driven by functional mechanisms while the second step, propagation, is driven by social mechanisms of the sort analyzed by sociohistorical linguists. Linguistic convention governs all processes of change: maintenance of language (conformity to convention), innovations (breaking conventions), and propagation (adoption of conventions).

Innovations in a functionalist model of language change are motivated by a series of principles or maxims for achieving successful communication. These principles are themselves founded on pragmatic theories of language use including theories of conventional coordination and joint action. Teleological mechanisms for language change are rejected, but change may be intentional (serving the goals of communication) or nonintentional (a side effect of conforming to convention). Besides the intentional mechanisms of avoiding misunderstanding, economy, and expressiveness, form–function reanalysis of various kinds may occur non-intentionally. Finally, one can account for such widely attested language changes as grammaticalization processes using this model.

REFERENCES

Allen, Cynthia L. (1995). *Case Marking and Reanalysis: Grammatical Relations from Old to Early Modern English.* Oxford: Clarendon Press.

Bybee, Joan L. (1985). *Morphology: An Inquiry into the Relation between Meaning and Form.* Amsterdam: John Benjamins.

Bybee, Joan L. (2001). *Phonology and Language Use.* Cambridge: Cambridge University Press.

Bybee, Joan L., Revere D. Perkins, and William Pagliuca (1994). *The Evolution of Grammar: Tense, Aspect and Modality in the Languages of the World.* Chicago: University of Chicago Press.

Chambers, J. K. and Peter Trudgill (1998). *Dialectology* (2nd edn.). Cambridge: Cambridge University Press.

Clark, Herbert H. (1996). *Using Language.* Cambridge: Cambridge University Press.

Clark, Herbert H. (1999). On the origins of conversation. *Verbum* 21: 147–61.

Croft, William (2000). *Explaining Language Change: An Evolutionary Approach.* Harlow: Longman.

Croft, William (2001). *Radical Construction Grammar: Syntactic Theory in Typological Perspective.* Oxford: Oxford University Press.

Croft, William (2003). *Typology and Universals* (2nd edn.). Cambridge: Cambridge University Press.

Croft, William (in press). The relevance of an evolutionary model to historical linguistics. In Ole Nedergård Thomsen (ed.), *Different Models of Linguistic Change.* Amsterdam: John Benjamins.

Croft, William and D. Alan Cruse (2004). *Cognitive Linguistics.* Cambridge: Cambridge University Press.

Denison, David (1993). *English Historical Syntax.* London: Longman.

Fillmore, Charles J., Paul Kay, and Mary Kay O'Connor (1988). Regularity and idiomaticity in grammatical constructions: the case of *let alone*. *Language* 64: 501–38.

Goldberg, Adele E. (1995). *Constructions: A Construction Grammar Approach to Argument Structure*. Chicago: University of Chicago Press.

Greenberg, Joseph H. (1991). The last stages of grammatical elements: contractive and expansive desemanticization. In Elizabeth Traugott and Bernd Heine (eds.), *Approaches to Grammaticalization* (pp. 301–14). Amsterdam: John Benjamins.

Grice, H. Paul (1967/89). Logic and conversation. In *Studies in the Way of Words* (pp. 1–143). Cambridge, MA: Harvard University Press.

Haspelmath, Martin (1998). Does grammaticalization need reanalysis? *Studies in Language* 22: 49–85.

Haspelmath, Martin (1999). Optimality and diachronic adaptation. *Zeitschrift für Sprachwissenschaft* 18: 180–205.

Haspelmath, Martin (2003). The geometry of grammatical meaning: semantic maps and cross-linguistic comparison. In Michael Tomasello (ed.), *The New Psychology of Language* (vol. 2; pp. 211–42). Mahwah, NJ: Lawrence Erlbaum Associates.

Heine, Bernd, Ulrike Claudi, and Friederieke Hünnemeyer (1991). *Grammaticalization: A Conceptual Framework*. Chicago: University of Chicago Press.

Heine, Bernd and Mechthild Reh (1984). *Grammaticalization and Reanalysis in African Languages*. Hamburg: Helmut Buske Verlag.

Hopper, Paul and Elizabeth Traugott (2003). *Grammaticalization* (2nd edn.). Cambridge: Cambridge University Press.

Hull, David L. (1988). *Science as a Process: An Evolutionary Account of the Social and Conceptual Development of Science*. Chicago: University of Chicago Press.

Hull, David L. (2001). *Science and Selection: Essays on Biological Evolution and the Philosophy of Science*. Cambridge: Cambridge University Press.

Ihalainen, Ossi (1991). Periphrastic *do* in affirmative sentences in the dialect of East Somerset. In Peter Trudgill and J. K. Chambers (eds.), *Dialects of English: Studies in Grammatical Variation* (pp. 148–60). London: Longman.

Keller, Rudi (1990/4). *On Language Change: The Invisible Hand in Language*. London: Routledge. (Translation and expansion of *Sprachwandel*, 1990.)

Kroch, Anthony S. (1989). Reflexes of grammar in patterns of language change. *Language Variation and Change* 1: 199–244.

Labov, William (1994). *Principles of Linguistic Variation*, vol. 1: *Internal Factors*. Oxford: Basil Blackwell.

Labov, William (2001). *Principles of Linguistic Change*, vol. 2: *Social Factors*. Oxford: Blackwell.

Ladefoged, P. and Maddieson, I. (1996). *The Sounds of the World's Languages*. Oxford: Blackwell.

Langacker, Ronald W. (2000). A dynamic usage-based model. In Michael Barlow and Suzanne Kemmer (eds.), *Usage-based Models of Language* (pp. 1–63). Stanford, CA: Center for the Study of Language and Information.

Lass, Roger (1990). How to do things with junk: exaptation in language change. *Journal of Linguistics* 26: 79–102.

Lass, Roger (1997). *Historical Linguistics and Language Change*. Cambridge: Cambridge University Press.

Lehmann, Christian (1982/95). *Thoughts on Grammaticalization: A Programmatic Sketch* (vol. 1). (Arbeiten des Kölner Universalien-Projekts, 48.) Cologne: Institut für Sprachwissenschaft.

(Reprinted by LINCOM Europa, München, 1995.)
Lewis, David (1969). *Convention*. Cambridge, MA: MIT Press.
Lüdtke, Helmut (1986). Esquisse d'une théorie du changement langagier. *La linguistique* 22: 3–46.
Moore, Samuel and Albert H. Marckwardt (1968). *Historical Outline of English Sounds and Inflections*. Ann Arbor: George Wahr Publishing.
Mufwene, Salikoko (2001). *The Ecology of Language Evolution*. Cambridge: Cambridge University Press.
Nettle, Daniel (1999). Functionalism and its difficulties in biology and linguistics. In Michael Darnell, Edith Moravcsik, Frederick Newmeyer, Michael Noonan, and Kathleen Wheatley (eds.), *Functionalism and Formalism in Linguistics* (vol. 1; pp. 445–67). Amsterdam: John Benjamins.
Ohala, John J. (1981). The listener as a source of sound change. In Carrie S. Masek, Roberta A. Hendrick, and Mary Frances Miller (eds.), *Papers from the Parasession on Language and Behavior, Chicago Linguistic Society* (pp. 178–203). Chicago: Chicago Linguistic Society.
Ohala, John (1993). The phonetics of sound change. In Charles Jones (ed.), *Historical Linguistics: Problems and Perspectives* (pp. 237–78). London: Longman.
Tabor, Whitney and Elizabeth C. Traugott (1998). Structural scope expansion and grammaticalization. In Anna Giacolone Ramat and Paul J. Hopper (eds.), *The Limits of Grammaticalization* (pp. 229–72). Amsterdam: John Benjamins.
Traugott, Elizabeth Closs (1989). On the rise of epistemic meanings in English: an example of subjectification in semantic change. *Language* 65: 31–55.
Traugott, Elizabeth Closs (1990). From less to more situated in language: the unidirectionality of semantic change. In Sylvian Adamson, Vivien Law, Nigel Vincent, and Susan Wright (eds.), *Papers from the 5th International Conference on Historical Linguistics* (pp. 497–517). Amsterdam: John Benjamins.
Traugott, Elizabeth Closs and Ekkehart König (1991). The semantics-pragmatics of grammaticalization revisited. In Elizabeth C. Traugott and Bernd Heine (eds.), *Approaches to Grammaticalization* (pp. 189–218). Amsterdam: John Benjamins.
Trudgill, Peter (1990). *The Dialects of England*. Oxford: Basil Blackwell.
Weinreich, Uriel (1968). *Languages in Contact: Findings and Problems* (2nd edn.). The Hague: Mouton.
Weinreich, Uriel, William Labov, and Marvin I. Herzog (1968). Empirical foundations for a theory of language change. In Winfrid P. Lehmann and Yakov Malkiel (eds.), *Directions for Historical Linguistics* (pp. 95–195). Austin: University of Texas Press.

II Words: Derivation and Prosody

5 Old and Middle English Prosody

DONKA MINKOVA

Definition of Terms

This chapter addresses the early history of English *prosody*. *Prosody* is used here to mean the study of the suprasegmental phenomena of speech, such as syllabicity, stress, intonation, and juncture. Our focus will be primarily on word stress. The terms *meter* and *metrical* will be applied to the properties of the verse template, including ictus, foot type (trochee, iamb), and lineation. Much of our historical knowledge of the prosody of English depends on verse evidence; the reconstruction of the forms of verse, on the other hand, rests on assumptions about the prosodic system. To avoid circularity, we will seek support from independently attested historical linguistic facts and typological observations.

5.1 Main Stress Assignment in Old English

5.1.1 The fixed main stress of Old English

Departing from the analyses dominant in the specialized literature of the last decade (e.g. McCully and Hogg 1990; Moon 1996; Gąsiorowski 1997; Hutton 1998a, 1998b; Getty 2002), Old English (OE) stress will be treated here as morphologically determined, in the spirit of more traditional accounts, of which the sections on stress in the *Cambridge History of the English Language*, volume 1 (Hogg 1992: 98–9) and volume 2 (Lass 1992: 85–6) are representative. On our starting point there is no disagreement: main stress in Old English was placed on the first syllable of the root of major class words:

(1) *bére* 'barley' *gánian* 'to yawn'
betwéox 'between' *gúttas* 'entrails'
forwérod 'worn out' *ofstícian* 'stab to death'

The facts and arguments that support this assertion are as follows. Typologically, OE shares root-initial stress with the other Germanic languages. In English root-initial stress was powerful enough to reshape the prosody of Romance loanwords in early Middle English (ME), and it characterizes the native vocabulary of Present-day English (PDE). Positing root-initial stress is consistent with the phonological behavior of the segments in root-initial syllables: the vowels resist reduction and the onset consonants are comparatively stable. The reconstruction of root-initial stress is supported by the metrical organization of alliterative verse; in it the onsets of the root-initial syllables of nouns, adjectives, and many adverbs alliterate obligatorily in the first foot of the verse, as in (2).

(2) **m**onegum mǣgþum, / **m**eodosetla oftēah (*Beo.* 5)
fromum feohgiftum / on **f**æder bearme (*Beo.* 21)
Þurh **s**līðne nīð / **s**āwle bescūfan (*Beo.* 184)
on **b**earm nacan / **b**eorhte frætwe (*Beo.* 214)

The first syllable of the root is stressed regardless of weight: in *mónegum* 'from many', *méodosetla* 'mead-benches' in *Beowulf* 5, and in *fromum* 'fine' and *fæder* 'father' in *Beowulf* 21, the stressed and alliterating syllables are light, while *slīðne* 'searing', *sāwle* 'soul', *beorhte* 'bosom' start with a heavy syllable.

5.1.2 Compounding and main stress

Compounding in Old English preserves the prominence of the first syllables of the individual roots. Within the larger domain of the compound word, however, the second stress is subordinated to the first; again, main stress invariably falls on the first syllable of the leftmost root, as in the following examples – using the acute accent (´) for primary, and the grave accent (`) for secondary stress:

(3) *lúfu* 'love' + *táken* 'token' *lúfutàcen* 'love-token'
héafod 'head' + *gemáca* 'mate' *héafodgemàca* 'companion'

This process is similar to the default stress contour of PDE compounds, the difference being that the modern language allows end-stress in some adverbial compounds: *hereáfter, wheréver, upón,* and in some nominal compounds (*mankind, cotton dress, Lord Mayor*). The evidence for positing a subordinate level of stress on the second elements of OE compounds comes from the history of the so-called "obscured" compounds, e.g. *bridal* < *brȳd* 'bride' + *ealo* 'beer', *garlic* < *gār* 'spear' + *lēac* 'leek', *forehead* < *for(e)* '(be)fore' + *hēafod* 'head', where the right-hand part of the compound shows more drastic phonological reduction than the initial stressed syllable, and from verse. Metrically, the second elements of compounds retain sufficient prominence to be regularly matched to ictic positions in the line. Their alliterative behavior, however, suggests that the second prominence was weaker compared to that on the leftmost edge of the first root. Unlike the obligatory alliteration on the first root syllable, the second part of a compound alliterates only optionally in the on-verse and may not alliterate in the off-verse:

(4) ofer **h**ronrade / **h**yran scolde (*Beo.* 10)
folce to **f**rofre; / **f**yrenðearfe ongeat (*Beo.* 14)

On the other hand, the preservation of significant stress on the second root in compounding is confirmed both by the systematic ictic placement of those roots in the verse, and by the fact that in the on-verse they can co-alliterate with the first part of the compound:

(5) wið þeodþreaum. / Swylc wæs þeaw hyra (*Beo.* 178)
heard**h**icgende / **h**ider wilcuman (*Beo.* 394)

The unattested pattern is that of alliteration *only* on the second element of a compound. Double-alliterating compounds as in (5) might suggest "level" stress; this is of no consequence for the present account. What matters is that the absence of compounds alliterating exclusively on their second roots testifies to the stability of the correspondence between stress and the leftmost root-edge on the word level. For the rest of this chapter compounds will be treated, non-controversially, as sequences of independently stressable units, with the second one subject to stress reduction within a larger prosodic domain.

5.1.3 *Affixation and main stress*

The alignment of the main stress with the left edge of the root in Old English persists in derived words; the addition of affixes does not affect the placement of primary stress in the word. Unlike the familiar processes of suffix-driven stress-shifting in the loan vocabulary of Present-day English (e.g. *acid–acidic*), there are no OE suffixes that attract primary stress away from the root of the word. This is illustrated in (6):

(6) Preservation of main stress in OE suffixation:

ǽðel	ǽðeling	mánig	mánigfeald
ánda	ándian	mártyr	mártyrdom
déofol	déofolcund	mýcel	mýcelnesse
géogoð	géogoðhad	wóruld	wóruldlic
hláford	hláfordscipe	wúldor	wúldorfull

The persistence of main stress under suffixation is supported by the stability of the vowel quality in the root against incipient vowel reduction in the suffixes already in Old English, and by the fact that even when suffixes fill a metrical ictus, like the underlined suffixes in (7), they can never carry functional alliteration:

(7) þæt ða liðende / land gesawon (*Beo*. 221)
in ecnesse / agan mosten (*Chr*. 1203)
mid wynsume / wine drenctest (*Pps*. 59. 3.3)

By way of comparison, in Present-day English certain derivational affixes can "steal" the primary stress away from the root, as in (8).

(8) ábsent àbsentée vélvet vèlvetéen
míllion mìllionáire Róman Ròmanésque

Also, unlike anything of that kind in Old or Middle English, in the modern language the main stress can shift to the right as in (9a), or to the left as in (9b), deleting the original root stress altogether:

(9a) sýmbol symbólic (9b) repúte réputable
párent paréntal revére réverence

Such paradigmatic stress changes are entirely alien to Old English. The alignment of the main stress with the leftmost syllable of the (first) root was never violated. Predictably, expanding the morphological content of a word by affixation could trigger the addition of secondary prominences. We will return to this issue after a brief discussion of the parameters involved in the assignment of main stress.

5.2 Modeling Main Stress in Old English

A framework within which the facts laid out in section 5.1 are straightforwardly handled is Optimality Theory (OT). In that theory, the production of forms is governed by filters, or constraints, of universal validity; the speakers of a particular language at a particular time hierarchize those filters in different ways in response to structural or social pressures. All constraints are violable in principle, though the recoverable data from a particular period in a specific language may not include forms that violate some of the constraints. Such constraints are ranked at the top of the hierarchy. The inventory of constraints for a set of forms normally includes also weaker filters, which can privilege one form over another, but which do not rule out the production of either form completely. In OT-based Prosodic Morphology (McCarthy and Prince 1995) the features of the output form are computed with reference to the interaction of constraints on both the morphological and the phonological component of that form. The types of constraints that will be used in our account are constraints on the *alignment* of the morphology to the prosody (stress), and prosodic *markedness* constraints which inhibit the realization of ill-formed surface strings.

The morphological entity to which Old English main stress attaches is the *lexical* Root which converts into a major class word: noun, adjective, verb, or adverb. For the purposes of stress, monosyllabic function words are treated in the same way as non-root affixes (see below) and inflections, i.e. their morphological status is below that of the lexical root and their prosodic alignment to the Foot is not enforced. A root is the core building block in the morphological hierarchy; it can be formally identical with the word, or it can be embedded into a word through compounding and affixation. Words are part of the syntax; they combine in phrases and larger syntactic units. Parallel to these entities is a hierarchy of prosodic units: the syllable (σ), the foot (F), the prosodic word (PrWd), etc. This is shown in (10):

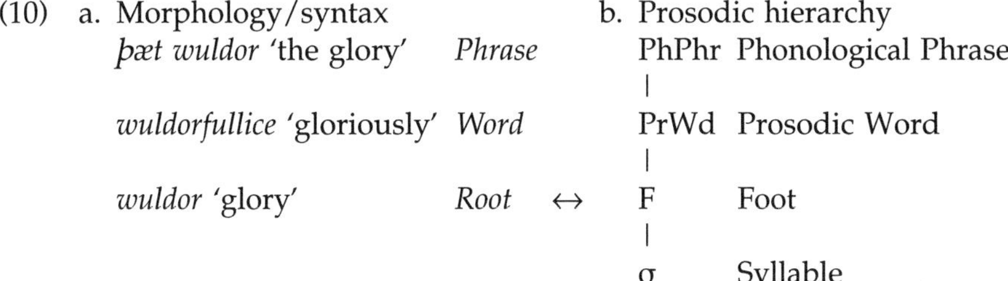

(10) a. Morphology/syntax

þæt wuldor 'the glory' *Phrase*

wuldorfullice 'gloriously' *Word*

wuldor 'glory' *Root* ↔

b. Prosodic hierarchy

PhPhr Phonological Phrase

PrWd Prosodic Word

F Foot

σ Syllable

Prosodic Morphology relates the two hierarchies by aligning morphological material and prosodic structure in a particular way. In the account of stress assignment pursued here, the OE morphological category Root is matched to the Foot, a fairly common cross-linguistic option of pairing grammatical and prosodic information. This alignment is congruent with the delimiting function of stress: stress here marks the beginning of the lexical core of the word. Any major class word in Old English must be aligned to a minimum of one Foot.

The constraint aligning the edges of the morphological domain of the Root and the prosodic domain of the Foot is defined in (11):

(11) ALIGNLEFT (ROOT, F):
The left edge of the root must be flush with the head of the Foot F

The head of the Foot is the strong syllable of a disyllabic (σ́ σ) string. Put differently, the constraint in (11) requires the assignment of a syllabic trochee starting with the first syllable of the root. Any other alignment will produce an unacceptable stress contour. In derived words and in compounds the alignment is preserved by virtue of "upward inheritance" (McCarthy and Prince 1995: 323–4). This means that all morphological strings above the Root will necessarily contain a Foot. It also implies that in any surface string the number of roots should correspond to the number of prosodic feet, and also stresses.

Stress is a relational property. Rhythmically, English is a language in which stressed and unstressed syllables tend to alternate in a regular fashion. This alternation is captured by the notion of the prosodic Foot, which groups stressed and unstressed syllables into recursive rhythmic units. One of the basic rhythmic requirements of prosodic phonology is that feet must be binary.

(12) FT-BIN: Feet are binary

Unlike the alignment constraint in (11) which is defined within the grammar of a single language, (12) is a phonological well-formedness constraint of universal applicability; each well-formed trochee is therefore not just left-headed, but also disyllabic or binary-branching. The trochaic nature of Old English speech rhythm is undisputed; all previous accounts assume that the trochee is the unmarked foot type for Old English. The departure from analyses proposed over the last two decades in this reconstruction is that the trochaic foot posited here is based on the binary prosodic relation of two *syllables*, rather than on smaller units of potential prosodic significance. This agrees with the intuition that the basic stress-bearing unit in the language is the syllable. Diagram (13) shows the prominence relations within the syllabic trochee; subscript s = Strong, and subscript w = Weak branch of the Foot. The strong branch (σ_S) is the *head* of the Foot which the constraint ALIGNLEFT (ROOT, F) refers to.

(13)

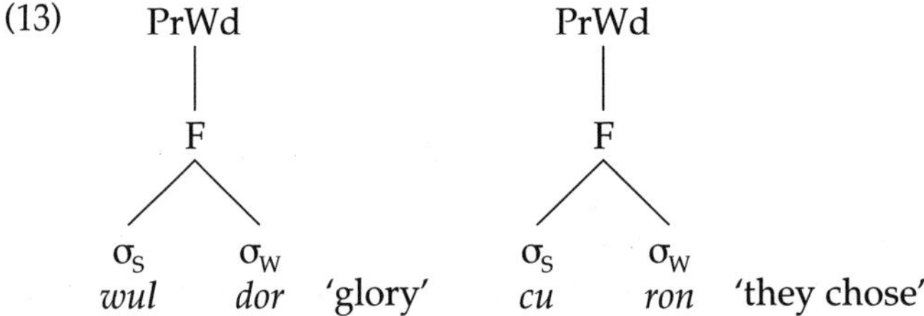

OE disyllabic unprefixed words automatically satisfy the requirement of foot binarity. However, not all morphological strings fit this "ideal"; it is not obligatory to incorporate every syllable into a binary metrical structure. Inflected single-root disyllabic words, for instance, have the metrical structure as in (14a), where the inflectional syllable is *extrametrical*, i.e. external to the process of stress assignment. Similarly, as in all other accounts of Old English stress, unstressable prefixes, such as *ge-* (e.g. *ge*síttan 'inhabit', *ge*þríng 'crowd', *ge*hwílc 'each'), also *a-*, *be-*, *for-*, remain outside the metrical structure, as in (14b), where parentheses enclose feet and angled brackets enclose unfooted syllables:

(14)

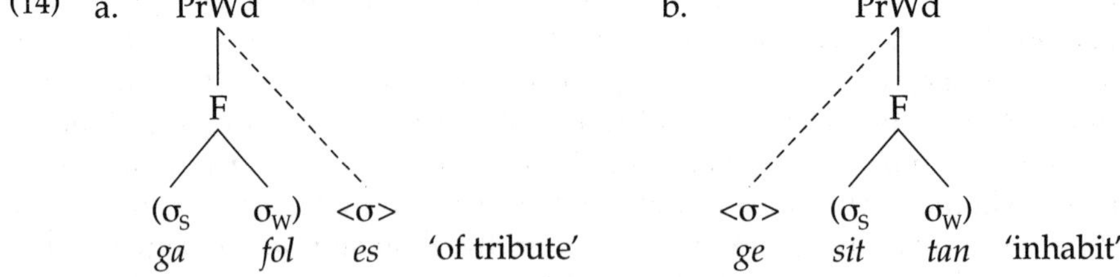

Only unstressed syllables at the edges of a morphological domain can be extrametrical. Since monosyllabic function words can behave like inflections, they may be incorporated into trochees headed by monosyllabic uninflected roots.

The incorporation of an adjacent function word into the domain of the Foot is shown in (15):

(15)
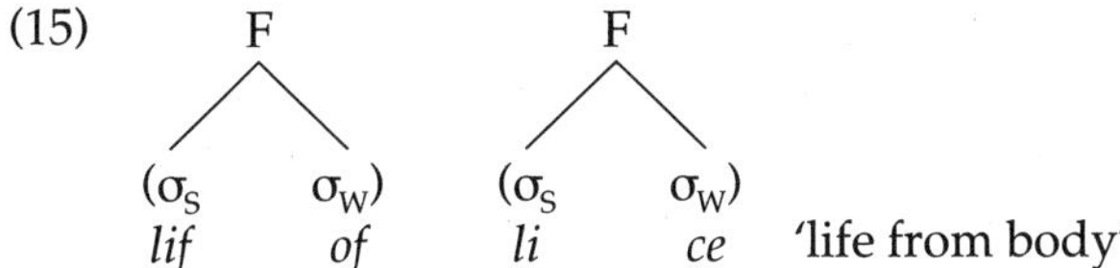

'life from body'

As in PDE, rhythmic alternation (which is consistent with the language's *stress timing* character) is imperfect and tolerates extended stretches of unstressed syllables. In OE such stress lapses are manifested as "extended" dips in the alliterative verse form.

If each lexical root is left-aligned with the head of a binary Foot, the occurrence of a monosyllabic lexical word not followed by a weak syllable produces a defective metrical configuration; technically, we cannot assign stress to monosyllables in isolation such as *bead* 'I offered', *gram* 'fierce', *hond* 'hand'. In connected speech, however, such lexical items commonly acquire prosodic prominence by virtue of the contrast to adjacent weak syllables, as in *lif of* 'life from' in (15). Another way of guaranteeing that a monosyllabic lexical item is prosodically well formed is by the insertion of a slight pause after the stressed syllable. Typologically, interpreting the stress domain for a lexical monosyllable as a binary-branching foot containing the syllable itself plus a pause is supported by phonetic studies showing manipulation of stressed syllable duration depending on the composition of the weak branch of the Foot (Gimson 1973 [1970]: 262; Fowler 1977: 33; Bolinger 1981: 17–18).

The representation of unfilled structure can refer to a zero syllable (Giegerich 1980, 1985; Suphi 1988; Lass 1992) for English, to the conceptually similar idea of empty structure (Burzio 1994), or to catalexis (Hammond 1999), which in metrics means a missing syllable in the last foot of a verse. All versions use an abstract representation for an unrealized surface syllable to produce an account which generalizes over sets of words whose prosodic behavior would otherwise be exceptional. The term that will be used for this theoretical device here is *catalexis*, defined as the insertion of an unrealized weak branch after monosyllabic lexical roots. The proposed structure for lexical monosyllables is shown in (16):

(16) Catalexis:
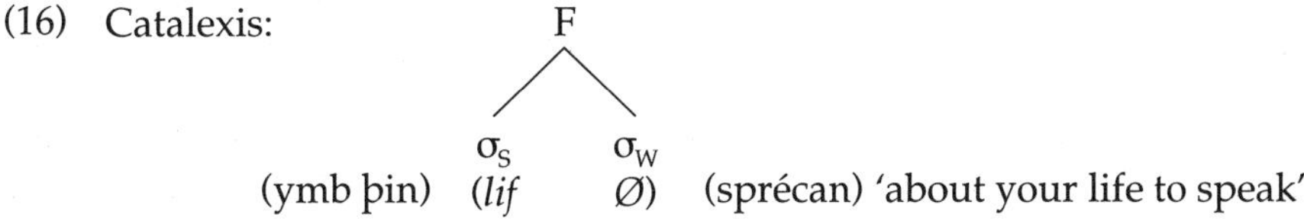

As noted, the assumption of an empty terminal node is typically manifested in the special properties of the syllable located in the head of the foot. For Old English this correlates with the absence of light lexical monosyllables; it parallels the extra length on lexical monosyllables observed in modern phonetic studies. In compounds with a monosyllabic first element the catalectic syllable was arguably realized as a pause. This is suggested by the behavior of compounds like OE *cofincel* 'little chamber', *cwicǣht* 'livestock', *friþāþ* 'peace-oath', *frumieldo* 'first age', *twi-ecge(de)* 'two-edge(d)', *wynele* 'pleasant oil': they resist obscuration, possibly because the pause after the first root allows glottal stop insertion before the second root and inhibits resyllabification, in spite of the fact that the first syllable has a short vowel. In verse such compounds regularly fill two ictic positions and behave in the same way as compounds whose first element is disyllabic. Consider the examples in (17):

(17) <u>healØærna</u> mæst; / scop him Heort naman (*Beo*. 78)
<u>sibØæðelingas</u>. / Swylc sceolde secg wesan (*Beo*. 2708)

Following the universal principle that consonants syllabify as onsets to the maximal possible extent, the syllabification of the underlined words in (17) would be *hea-lær-na* 'of hall rooms' and *si-bæ-ðe-lin-gas* 'kin-nobles', producing, in both cases, unacceptable scansions of these verses (the first two syllables have to be counted as a single position). The assumption of compound-internal catalexis allows the first roots metrical independence; syllabification cannot respect the maximal onset principle.

Although OE had no minimal-word requirement with respect to syllable count, due to the inflectional nature of the language, the lexicon was largely realized as non-monosyllabic in usage. Getty (2002: 213) found that only 23.9 percent of his 7,920-word prose sample, and 28.4 percent of his 5,866-word *Beowulf* sample are lexical monosyllables, including counting the elements of compounds as separate entities. Thus the statistical dominance of fully realized trochaic feet in the language is likely to trigger analogical insertion of a pause after monosyllabic roots.

In this analysis catalexis is *restricted to the right edge of monosyllabic roots*. Put differently, binarity is an obligatory *minimal* requirement for roots, but it is not obligatory for non-root material. Inflections are footed optionally and do not affect the prosodic contour of a word. The binarity of the trochaic foot ($\sigma_S\ \sigma_W$) is based on the prominence contrast between two adjacent syllables, irrespective of their weight, or on the contrast between a heavy syllable and a pause. Except for rare borrowed names, the size of OE underived words does not exceed three syllables, and the rightmost syllable is most commonly an inflection; a syllabic trochee is therefore sufficient to account for the placement of main stress in underived words.

Another constraint on the prosodic organization, namely that all available syllables should be parsed into feet, is also part of the well-formedness of the string. This is covered by the constraint PARSE SYLLABLE (PARSESYLL):

(18) PARSE SYLLABLE (PARSESYLL):
Incorporate all syllables into feet

This constraint is automatically satisfied by structures like the ones in (13). Exhaustive parsing, however, is not obligatory. PARSESYLL is a weak constraint, regularly violated by inflected disyllabic words, as in (14a, 14b), where the unparsed syllables are immediate daughters of the Prosodic Word, not the Foot. Its violability is well defined, however. Recall that only function words, inflexions, and inflexion-like affixes can be extrametrical. Unparsed syllables can occur only at the edges of a morphological domain. Finally, only one syllable on either side of the foot can be left unparsed. Further prominence adjustments, e.g. making sure that *gesiþþe* 'companion' is the strongest prominence in *hæfde him to gesiþþe* (*Deor* 3), 'had him for company' are handled above the Prosodic Word level where the phrase-final branch (*gesiþþe*) is stronger than *hæfde him to*, no matter how the latter is footed.

Though not necessary for the assignment of main stress, PARSESYLL is useful in assessing the prosodic complexity of various strings. In a framework which accounts for the non-occurrence of forms and evaluates their *relative* well-formedness, morphological strings which satisfy PARSESYLL can be predicted to be the more common word shapes in the language. This is indeed true: only 4.6 percent of the words in the prose sample in Getty (2002: 214) are words of three syllables. Thus, though not essential for the basic morphology–prosody alignment, PARSESYLL will be kept here as an indicator of prosodic complexity.[1]

The interaction of these three constraints is sufficient to model the prosodic structure of single-root words in Old English; parentheses enclose feet, the symbol *! (fatal violation) bans a candidate from surfacing, an asterisk * indicates a violation that is tolerated, and the pointing finger ☞ identifies the optimal candidate. Shaded cells mean that the satisfaction of a particular constraint is irrelevant for that candidate. The simplest cases are shown in (19):

(19) Stress assignment for *scip* 'ship' and *deofol* 'devil'

		ALIGNL (R, F)	FT-BIN	PARSESYLL
a.	(scíp)		*!	
b. ☞	(scíp. Ø)			
a.	(déo). fol		*!	*
b.	(deo. fól)	*!		
c. ☞	(déo. fol)			

The prosodification of inflected forms is shown in (20). In the interest of simplicity not all logically possible non-occurring forms have been included in the candidate set.

(20) Stress assignment for *scipu* 'ships' and *namena* 'of the names'

		AlignL (R, F)	Ft-Bin	ParseSyll
a.	(scíp). u		*!	*
b.	(scip. ú)	*!		
c. ☞	(scí. pu)			
a.	(ná). me. na		*!	**
b.	(na. mé). na	*!		*
c. ☞	(ná. me). na			*

Note the precarious position of the final syllable of *namena*. By late OE unparsed final vowels would have been reduced, and in that position they would be more subject to loss than word-final -*es* which are part of a normal foot. There is, indeed, evidence that -*e* was lost in trisyllabic words earlier than in disyllables (Minkova 1991: 136, 158). The same hierarchy of constraints as in (20) can model stress assignment in compounds. In (21) the violations are marked for *scip-* 'ship' in *sciphere* 'fleet', and for -*hus* 'house' in *ealo-hus* 'ale-house':

(21) Stress assignment for *sciphere* 'fleet' and *ealo-hus* 'ale-house'

		AlignL (R, F)	Ft-Bin	ParseSyll
a.	(scíp).(hé. re)		*!	
b.	scip. (hé. re)	*!	*	*
c. ☞	(scíp. Ø) (hé. re)			
a.	(éa. lo). (hús)		*!	
b.	(éa. lo). (hus. Ø)	*!		
c. ☞	(éa. lo). (hús. Ø)			

As noted in section 5.1.2, the metrical difference between primary and secondary stress will be handled by linear precedence privileging the prominence at the left edge of the word.

As in all other accounts, the primarily grammatical prefixes *a-*, *be-*, *ge-*, *for-* lie outside the prosodic stress template. This behavior is enforced by the high ranking of AlignL (R, F); prosodically such affixes are the mirror image of inflexions. The table in (22) shows how the minimal set of constraints used in (19–21) above handles forms with unstressable prefixes:

(22) Stress assignment for *gemæne* 'common' and *acenned* 'born'

		ALIGNL (R, F)	FT-BIN	PARSESYLL
a.	ge. (mǽ). ne		*!	**
b.	(gé. mæ). ne	*!		*
c. ☞	ge (mǽ. ne)			*
a.	a. (cén). ned		*!	**
b.	(á. cen). ned	*!		*
c. ☞	a. (cén. ned)			*

It is often noted that in Old English one and the same prefix can be stressed or unstressed depending on the morphological nature of the root to which it attaches, e.g. *ymb*sǽton 'they besieged', but *ýmb*sittend 'besieging', *ýmb*setnung 'siege'. The patterns are in fact much less clear than the example suggests. As Minkova (2003) argues, the reconstruction of variable stress on a small subset of initial adverbial elements is an artifact of the "rule of precedence" in Old English verse, which privileges nouns and adjectives over finite verbs for the purposes of alliteration and the fact that verbal prefixes in general are associated with grammatical functions. For all nouns and adjectives, and variably for inflected verbs, adverbial prefixes mimic roots: the filters producing *ýmb*setnung 'siege' will be identical to the ones selecting *sciphere* 'fleet'.

In summary: OE primary stress is controlled by two constraints, both of which refer to the interplay between morphology and prosody. Main stress must be aligned with the left edge of a root. Catalexis ensures that monosyllabic lexical items are prosodically equivalent to binary sequences elsewhere in the lexicon. The violability of PARSESYLL allows inflexions and a subset of monosyllabic prefixes, defined morphologically, to be ignored for the purposes of stress assignment. No aspect of the account requires reference to the weight of the stressed syllable.[2]

A morphologically determined stress system can, however, coexist with the universally robust preference for the co-occurrence of weight and stress. We have already seen how phonological strength correlates with the absence of monosyllabic lexical items in the language. Diachronic syncopations of unstressed vowels also show some sensitivity to the moraic composition of the preceding stressed syllable. Disyllables with a heavy or superheavy stressed syllable (HL, SL, SH, HH) in the OE prose sample reported in Getty (2002: 213) account for 82.2 percent of the total, while disyllables with a stressed light syllable (LL and LH) are the minority. The high incidence of stressed syllables that are also etymologically heavy increases the probability of analogical change in the minority pattern. This is the kind of evidence that proved crucial in the segmental history of the low and mid non-peripheral vowels in ME when loss of the vowel in the second syllable was often compensated for by strengthening of the orphaned left branch of the trochee (Minkova 1982). Such processes, however, are contingent upon morphologically fixed trochaic stress, and not its trigger, as will become clear also from the weight-insensitive adaptation of loan-words in Early ME.

5.3 Secondary Stress in Old English

5.3.1 *Campbell's half-stress*

Items whose prosodic contour requires more than a single stress comprise approximately 55 percent of the OE lexicon.[3] The assignment of secondary stress in the derived portion of the vocabulary is a subject of considerable scholarly interest. Campbell (1959: 34–5) is responsible for the most widely discussed statement on secondary stress ("half-stress" in his terminology) in the literature:

(23) The verse shows that the general rule is that they [second elements] retain a half-stress only when they are either themselves disyllabic (e.g. *-bǣre, -rǣden, -scipe, -wende*) or have an inflexional syllable added.... The principal monosyllabic suffixes which are ... reduced to low stress in the uninflected form, but which recover half-stress followed by an inflexion, are: *-dōm, -cund, -fæst, -feald, -full, -hād, -lāc, -lēas, -līc, -sum, -weard, -wist*.

Similarly, heavy derivative suffixes have a half-stress after a long syllable ... or its equivalent ... when followed by an unaccented syllable. This applies to *-els, -en, -end-, -ere, -erne, -estre, -ig, -ing, -ung, -isc, -ness, -oþ*; the endings *-ende* (participle), *-enne* (inflected inf.), *-est, -ost* (superlative); the medial *-i-* and *-od-* of weak verbs of the second class.

As well as these suffixes, any long final syllable or its equivalent acquires half-stress when it becomes internal by the addition of an inflexion: *Héngèstes, ǽghwèlcne*. Short final syllables which become long in inflexion are similarly treated: *óþèrne*.

For a whole generation of scholars, Campbell's description has been a source of frustration; it mixes syllable count, distance from the right edge, and syllable weight, and conflates affixes with morphologically inseparable syllables. It also builds on the assumption that every syllable capable of filling an ictic position in one particular account of verse was stressed in speech.[4] Nevertheless, the core of the observations in (23) has withstood the scrutiny of critics.

Campbell's patterns are illustrated in (24). The verses in (a) require the suffix to have reduced or no stress because it is in a dip, while in (b) the inflected forms of the same suffixes have to be stressed because they correspond to an ictic position in the verse.

(24) a. wig ond wísdom: / Ic þæs wine Deniga (*Beo*. 350)
b. wide geweorðod, / wísdòme heold (*Beo*. 1959)

a. heah ond halig, / héofoncund þrynes (*Chr*. 379)
b. héofoncùndne hyht, / hælu geræhte (*Glc*. 171)

a. Neb is min níþerweard; / neol ic fere (*Riddle* 21.1)
b. híndewèardre, / þæt biþ hlaford min (*Riddle* 15)

Occasionally, the pattern breaks down, however. As is clear from the metrical deployment of the uninflected monosyllabic suffixes in the verses underlined in (25) below, secondary stress must be assumed on them so that they can fill a lift:

(25) wísdòm onwreah. / Ic wæs weorcum fah (*Ele*. 1242)
þæt ge swa mónigfèald / on gemynd witon (*Ele*. 644)
þæt he gesette / on sácerdhàd (*Ele*. 1054)

5.3.2 *Russom's data on secondary stress*

The type of inconsistency illustrated in (25), coupled with the problematic features of the scansion system which Campbell used, prompted the thorough re-examination of the verse data on OE subordinate stress in Russom (2001). Russom's findings, based on his own scansion system, confirm the widespread assumption of instability of secondary stress, its dependence on metrical context, and support the author's hypothesis that such stress was "indeterminate." That cover label, however, conceals a high level of consistency in the morphology–prosody interface which presumably reflects the stochastic nature of secondary stress assignment in speech. The probability of secondary stress can be captured in the OT framework of constraint ranking. We will proceed to the formal modeling after a summary of the distributional facts concerning subsidiary stress based on Russom (2001).

Like other scholars before him (e.g. Suphi 1988; Colman 1994; Minkova 1996; Hutton 1998a, 1998b), Russom divides the OE suffixes into two major groups, Root Affixes and Derivational Affixes. The first group consists of synchronically recognizable roots, also used as affixes. The most important Root Affixes, as in Campbell's first group in (23) are: *-dōm, -cund, -fæst, -feald, -full, -hād, -lāc, -lēas, -līc, -sum, -weard, -wist*. The Derivational affixes are divided into two subgroups: Heavy Affixes, ending in two consonants (*-ende, -ing, -enne, -est, -ost*) and Light Affixes which have a synchronically short vowel followed by a single consonant (*-ig, -er*).

The statistics compiled and cited in Russom (2001: 56–61) are tabulated in (26). The first column lists the morpheme type. The second column shows the linear location of the morpheme, where Penultimate corresponds to Campbell's "followed by an inflexion." The third column records the metrical behavior of the morpheme in verse as determined by Russom's scansion. The fourth column compares Russom's data to Campbell's predictions on the stress of the relevant morpheme. The fifth column shows the numerical count. The total number of lines in which the stress behavior of the words in question can be tested reliably is shown in the sixth column.

(26) Metrical behavior of affixes (counts from Russom 2001: 56–61)

Morpheme type	*Location*	*Stress*	*Campbell's prediction*	*No. of instances*	*Metrical pool*
Root affix	Word-final	No	No	48	7,126
Heavy affix	Word-final	No	No	92	7,126
Light affix	Word-final	No	No	76	7,127
Root affix	Word-final	Yes	**No**	**43**	409
Heavy affix	Word-final	Yes	**No**	**8**	413
Light affix	Word-final	**Yes**	**No**	**1**	—
Root affix	Penultimate	No	**Yes**	**18**	106
Heavy affix	Penultimate	No	**Yes**	**3**	107
Light affix	Penultimate	No	**Yes**	**8**	107
Root affix	Penultimate	Yes	Yes	119	1,316
Heavy affix	Penultimate	Yes	Yes	192	1,316
Light Affix	Penultimate	Yes	Yes	80	1,316

Total: 688 instances. Campbell's predictions violated in 81 cases (11.7%).

These are extremely interesting results. The density of some patterns that run against Campbell's predictions (e.g. 43/409, or 10.5 percent of stressed word-final Root Affixes) makes a good case for "indeterminacy" in the realization of secondary stress. Nevertheless, the overall incidence of stress in agreement with Campbell is the dominant one, accounting for over 88 percent of the data. The morphological status of the affixes makes a difference: the data for Root Affixes confirms Campbell in about 74 percent of the cases, while for Derivational Affixes Campbell's predictions are realized at an impressive 96 percent. This is an empirical difference that any model of stress should reflect. Both types of Derivational Affixes behave in a comparable manner; however, the label "light" can be misleading since the attested cases of stressed light affixes are all cases where a consonant-initial inflexion preserves the segmental integrity of the "light" affix, as in *-ig* + *-ra*.

Russom's "indeterminate" stress has a corollary in the treatment of OE secondary stress as a gradient property of the syllable. As argued in Minkova (1996), the realization of secondary stress is a function of the interaction of morphological salience, syllabic composition, and syllable weight. The latter, as will be shown below, is the least important of these constraints. There is no doubt, however, that within the landscape of "gradience" or "indeterminacy" some realizations are more likely than others, making the probability stochastic rather than random. The OT model of ranked and violable constraints allows us to pursue an account that accommodates both the majority and the minority patterns.

5.3.3 *Secondary stress on* Root Affixes

The prosodic shape of affixed words is subject to the same constraints that control the stress realizations of underived words, plus constraints that refer specifically to the prosodic alignment of affixes. The first such constraint aligns Root Affixes with the head of the prosodic Foot:

(27) AlignLeft (RootAffix, F)
The left edge of a Root Affix must be flush with the head of the Foot F

The Root Affix-to-Foot left-alignment is an analogue of AlignLeft (Root, F). Unlike roots, however, Root Affixes do not require the rigorous prosodic delineation of their left edge; they can be obscured, delexicalized, in which case their morphological status will be closer to that of Derivational Affixes.

Disyllabic and inflected Root Affixes were preferentially stressed: *-rǽden, wénde, -cúndne, -wéardre* are typical, with a ratio of 119 stressed to 18 unstressed attestations in (26). The imbalance cannot be accounted for solely by reference to their morphological status. The very strong tendency for stress to be aligned with the affix when the affix is non-final in the word is covered by the familiar constraint of Nonfinality.

(28) Nonfinality: No prosodic head is final in PrWd

The effect of this constraint is to prevent the final syllable in a derived word from carrying stress. For monosyllabic lexical items Nonfinality is vacuously satisfied because of the higher ranking prosodic markedness constraint of foot binarity (Ft-Bin), which triggers catalexis. For Root Affixes catalexis is not an option because there is no phonetic evidence for strengthening of affixes parallel to that of monosyllabic roots; recall that in section 5.2 we restricted the application of catalexis to lexical roots. Moreover, in expanded strings, the second foot is in a subordinate relation to the primary foot to the left, another rationale for allowing the binarity of the second foot to be violable. The combined effect of AlignLeft (RootAffix, F) and Nonfinality is shown in (29); for simplicity the first root is enclosed in square brackets and is not included in the account:

(29) Stress assignment for *-weard* and *-weardre* 'wards' in *hindeweard* 'behind'

		AlignL (RA, F)	Nonfinality	Parse-Syll	Ft-Bin
a.	[hinde] weard	*		*	*
b.	[hinde] (wéard)		*		*
c.	[hinde] (wéar. dre)				

All three candidates are possible realizations of the prosody of ROOT AFFIXES. The argument for ranking ALIGNL (RA, F) at the top of the hierarchy is that the number of instances that violate it, i.e. the unstressed word-final ROOT AFFIXES, is proportionately small. Within the relevant metrical pool in Russom's database it is 48/7,126, or 0.7 percent. This corresponds to the form in (a), which, in addition, is ill-formed also in terms of two other filters; it has the least chance of surfacing. NONFINALITY is a weaker constraint. It is violated at a relatively higher rate, 43/409 in Russom's database, or in 10.5 percent of the cases; this is candidate (b) which takes an intermediate position in terms of probability of being realized. The optimal structure is shown in (c); this is the pattern that Campbell described as normative and for which Russom cites 119 attestations. The interaction of constraints thus models successfully the statistical distribution of secondary stresses observable in the verse.

Unlike other accounts, this account does not have to treat disyllabic affixes as a separate group. The consistency of secondary stress on such affixes is predicted by the interaction of the same set of filters as in (29). The table in (30) shows how the same hierarchy selects the right metrical shape for the disyllabic suffixes singled out by Campbell (1959: 34):

(30) Stress assignment for *-ræden* and *-rædenne* 'state, act' in *gafolræden* 'tribute, rent'

		ALIGNL (RA, F)	NONFINALITY	PARSE-SYLL	FT-BIN
a.	[gafol] ræ. den	*		*!*	*
b.	[gafol] (rǽ. den)				
c.	[gafol] (rǽ. den). ne			*	

In (30) the candidate in (a) is excluded by a restriction on multiple PARSESYLL violations; only one unparsed syllable can be tolerated on either side of the foot. The same effect will be achieved by *LAPSE, not introduced here for the sake of simplicity, but see section 5.4.2. The strength of ALIGNL (RA, F) guarantees that the first syllable of the affix will be stressed. This applies also to disyllabic prefixes: *ofer-* 'over', *under-* 'under', and *ymbe-* 'about' are provably stressed in all derivatives except for a handful of attestations in inflected verbs where the evidence is ambiguous. The uninflected variant of the suffix in (b) parses into a perfect disyllabic foot. In fact, *all* attested cases of unstressed usage in penultimate position, as observed by Russom (2001: 60), involve the high-frequency suffix *-lic(e)*, a significant observation in terms of the morphological history of ROOT AFFIXES. The inflected suffix in (c) satisfies the high-ranking constraints; a single unparsed final syllable is a minor violation, parallel to the one incurred by *(ná. me). na* 'of the names' in (20).[5]

5.3.4 *Secondary stress on* Derivational Affixes

As described by Campbell, see (23) above, "[half-stress] applies to *-els, -en, -end-, -ere, -erne, -estre, -ig, -ing, -ung, -isc, -ness, -oþ*; the endings *-ende* (participle), *-enne* (inflected inf.), *-est, -ost* (superlative); the medial *-i-* and *-od-* of weak verbs of the second class." The picture is complicated by the further assumption of penultimate stress in *any* morphological string where the penultimate syllable is heavy.

Russom's (2001) statistics on Derivational Affixes cover all of Campbell's types, including words in which the middle syllable has no synchronic morphological status, e.g. *oðerne* 'other', acc. sg. masc., which he counts as equivalent to Light Affixes. Let us first look at the behavior of these affixes in word-final position. The table in (31) extracts the data from (26) for Derivational Affixes in word-final position:[6]

(31) Derivational Affixes in word-final position

Morpheme type	*Location*	*Stress*	*Campbell's prediction*	*No. of instances*	*Metrical pool*
Heavy affix	Word-final	No	No	92	7,126
Light affix	Word-final	No	No	76	7,127
Heavy affix	Word-final	**Yes**	**No**	**8**	413
Light affix	Word-final	**Yes**	**No**	**1**	—[7]

Only 0.05 percent of the total number of attestations are in disagreement with Campbell's statement; stress on all of them can be seen as a metrically induced license. All of the data here are "metrically induced," but the difference between minority and majority patterns is significant: the probability that 166 instances have no prosodic grounding is smaller than the probability that 9 instances are "special." There is no evidence here that weight is prosodically significant. The consistent lack of stress correlates best with a strong Nonfinality constraint: for Derivational Affixes, Nonfinality is inviolable. A morpheme's ability to form a prosodic foot by itself decreases in tandem with the decrease of its morphological independence: from Root to Root Affix, to a Derivational Affix of vague semantic content.

In penultimate position the overwhelming pattern is that of stress on the Derivational Affix. The potential of derivational affixes to attract some stress in penultimate position is covered by the constraint AlignLeft (Derivational Affix, F):

(32) AlignLeft (Derivational Affix, F)
The left edge of a Derivational Affix must be flush with the head of the Foot F

The table in (34) shows the constraint rankings and violations for the affix *-est* in *æðelest* 'the noblest' (nom. sg.) vs. *æðelestan* 'the noblest' (pl.):

(33) Stress assignment for [*æðel*]*est* 'the noblest' vs. [*æðel*]*estan* 'the noblest'

		NONFINALITY (DA, F)	ALIGNL	PARSE-SYLL	FT-BIN
a.	[æðel]. (ést)	*!			*
b.	☞[æðel]. est		*	*	*
c.	[æðel]. (es. tán)	*!	*		
d.	[æðel]. es. tan		*	*!*	*
e.	☞[æðel]. (és. tan)				

For DERIVATIONAL AFFIXES the two filters crucial in blocking realizations like the ones in (a), (c), and (d) are NONFINALITY and multiple unparsed syllables.

This concludes the survey of the principles of stress placement in Old English. Some verse-specific problems remain, but they do not affect the basic tenets of morphology–prosody alignment outlined here. The probability of stable foot structure marking the left edge of a morpheme matches a morphological hierarchy of stressability: roots > root affixes > derivational affixes > inflexional affixes. As in all other accounts, the boundaries between the morphological classes are sometimes fuzzy, especially in the dynamic circumstances of unstressed vowel reduction and deletion triggering reanalysis of the prosodic alignment. At no point in the stress assignment is weight instrumental; the association between main stress and weight is a *consequence* of the way Old English words were stressed, not a trigger of stress.

5.4 Stress Placement in Middle English

The morphological model of stress placement presented in sections 5.1–5.3 covers a lexicon which was etymologically largely homogeneous. The Norman Conquest of 1066 affected not just the social and demographic scene, but it changed the course of the prosodic history of English. Speakers of English who had the education and leisure to engage in literary or scribal activities were often proficient in Anglo-Norman and Latin. The socially privileged status of these speakers and the prestige of the continental literary tradition created favorable conditions for lexical borrowing, either through translation or through direct contact with the Romance vernacular. While estimates of the composition of the Old English vocabulary place the non-Germanic component at about 3 percent, by the end of Middle English the share of Romance words in the language of the documents that have survived rose to about 25 percent. The absorption of the new vocabulary proceeded simultaneously with important phonological changes within the native lexicon, most significantly the attrition and loss of final unstressed vowels. Together, borrowing and internal change created conditions for the introduction of a new prosodic template in the language. The new template, known as the Romance Stress Rule (RSR), is controlled by a different set of constraints on the prosody–morphology alignment. The prosodic stratification of the English vocabulary which characterizes PDE was only beginning in Middle English, however. Throughout Middle English the OE morphological patterns of stress assignment continued to dominate; the competing foreign model did not become robust until the Renaissance. Section 5.4 addresses the stability of the OE pattern in ME, the conditions leading to the strengthening of the prosodic constraint associating weight-to-stress (WtS), and the rise of the RSR at the end of ME/beginning of early Modern English.

5.4.1 *The stability of morphological left-edge marking in Middle English*

The placement of main stress for the native vocabulary of Middle English continued the patterns described in sections 5.1–5.2. The organization of the morphology of Middle English differed from Old English in one important typological aspect: the variability that had characterized the root-based morphology, especially of earlier OE, was obscured due to loss of phonological conditioning, resulting in stem invariancy and a collapse of the two categories of stem and root (Kastovsky 1992: 298, 397ff.). The prosodic effect of this restructuring was that in ME the prosodic Foot F became co-extensive with the Stem (S), which was the same as the domain of the Word (W) for the classes that were rapidly abandoning their inflexions. For ME, then, the constraint that controls the morphology–prosody alignment is ALIGNLEFT (STEM, F):

(34) ALIGNLEFT (STEM, F):
The left edge of the Stem must be flush with the head of the Foot F

The other constraints on main stress, FOOT BINARITY and PARSE SYLLABLE, were rank-ordered in the same way as in Old English. Following (34), FOOT BINARITY, was defined over the domain of the Stem.

The influx of French vocabulary in Middle English is treated in the literature as an event of devastating consequences for the core principles of English prosody. The roots of the two-layer stress system of PDE must, indeed, be sought in Middle English. What is often overlooked, however, is the enormous vitality of the morphological alignment inherited from OE. Since part of the scholarly territory is still unexplored, and the findings that we do have are relatively new, I will summarize briefly the data and the arguments in Minkova (1997, 2000).

A widespread philological position on the accentuation of French loanwords in Middle English is that "such words commonly vary between French and native stressing – thus, *natúre* beside *náture*" (Burrow and Turville-Petre 1996: 13). The line "In *dívers* art and in *divérse* figúres" from Chaucer's *Friar's*

Tale (III 1486), mentioned in Jespersen (1909: 161) has been repeatedly cited as representative of the accentual instability of Romance loanwords in Middle English. A more careful scrutiny of the verse data demonstrates the unreliability of these isolated examples as the "paradigm case" for ME. More specifically, the combined evidence of the use of underived nouns and adjectives in alliterative and syllable-counting verse indicates an overwhelming pattern of initial stress: for a large subset of the new arrivals the assignment of main stress is undistinguishable from the native model. The table in (35) extracts some data on the stress patterns of Romance loanwords in ME verse compositions from Minkova (2000):

(35) Romance loans in Middle English verse

Text	*Tokens*	*Initial stress*	*Non-initial stress*
Sir Gawain and the Green Knight	283	276/97.5%	7/2.5%
The Siege of Jerusalem	87	84/96.5%	3/3.4%
Troilus and Criseyde	266	223/84%	43/16%
Henryson's poetry	151	137/90.7%	14/9.3%

Stress on the initial syllable occurs irrespective of the weight of either syllable, as illustrated by the prosodic history of *baron, courage, finish, manner, pity, ponder, reason, rigor, sermon, travel, virtue,* etc. The conclusion suggested by the distribution in (35) is that throughout Middle English the main stress of underived borrowed words was assimilated to the native model of left alignment of stem-to-stress. Moreover, stem-initial stress was not restricted to disyllabic words, where initial stress would be a default case in words with a light second syllable by any account. Leftward stress in early trisyllabic borrowings with a heavy middle syllable, e.g. *harbinger* (1175), *character* (1315), *interval* (1300), *manacle* (1350), *galaxy* (1384).[8] Predictably, borrowed prefixes: *a(d)-, con-, de-, dis-, ex-, en-, in-, per-, pre-, pro-, re-, sub-, trans-,* etc., as long as they were recognizable as such, were treated as extrametrical, falling in line with the unstressed native prefixes *a-, be-, ge-, for-, of-, oð-, to-*.

5.4.2 *Innovations:* Stress-to-Weight (StW), *Lapse

Recall from section 5.2.1 that all OE lexical monosyllables were heavy, either by virtue of having a –VC # rhyme, or by having a long vowel. Moreover, in a high proportion of the polysyllabic lexical items in the language (82.2 percent of the disyllabic lexical items in Getty's (2002: 213) prose sample) the stressed syllable was also heavy. During Middle English the stressed vowels in a significant number of etymologically light-light (LL) items, e.g. *talu* 'tale', *nosu* 'nose', *etan* 'eat', were lengthened by way of compensation for the loss of the final unstressed syllable. The process, known as Middle English Open Syllable Lengthening (MEOSL), started in the Northern dialects in the thirteenth century and had spread southwards by the end of the ME period. Stress-bearing light syllables remained, of course, both in native and borrowed words: *barrow, body, happy, gammon, talent,* but they are the rarer pattern. The frequent association of stress and weight in the lexicon prepared the ground for the more active role of weight in the characterization of a stressed syllable in the language. The link is expressed by "Prokosch's Law" (1939), Vennemann's Weight Law (1988), and, within OT, the prosodic markedness constraint STRESS-TO-WEIGHT:

(36) STRESS-TO-WEIGHT (STW)
The head of the prosodic FOOT should be a heavy syllable

The co-occurrence of weight and stress is a broadly attested linguistic phenomenon. The already robust presence of STW in the OE lexicon was further strengthened by MEOSL. While for the native vocabulary STRESS-TO-WEIGHT has never displaced ALIGNLEFT (STEM, F), as we shall see in section 5.5 below, in the later prosody of English it took center stage as a component of a radically different stress system where it was crucial for the acquisition of (X)H(X) structures.

Another constraint, probably latent in the prosody of OE, but acquiring more importance in ME, is the rhythmic well-formedness constraint restricting the occurrence of long strings of unstressed syllables, the *LAPSE constraint:

(37) *LAPSE
Avoid adjacent unstressed syllables

The effect of *LAPSE is equivalent to banning two unparsed syllables in a row, as in (30a) or (33d). Rhythmically it means that foot-heads should alternate with non-heads. In the underived native vocabulary of ME *LAPSE was observed by default since stems were maximally disyllabic. In compounding, the addition of a stem would trigger the formation of a new foot: *éuen-sòng* 'even-song', *fínger-nèile* 'fingernail', stressed like *scíphère* and *éalo-hùs* in (21). Suffixed forms are more complex: some non-root affixes became part of the stem and the independent word status of the earlier ROOT AFFIXES was obscured (Kastovsky 1992: 382–400), pushing NONFINALITY above ALIGNL (RA, F) in the constraint hierarchy, as in (33). Nevertheless, derivatives such as *mártyrdòm, máidenhòd, tónnefùl, stédefàst(e)* were still predominantly stressed like *híndewèard* in (29), a pattern which respects *LAPSE. The order of the prominences, as in OE, was main stress at the left edge, followed by a secondary stress.

For a similar phenomenon in the borrowed vocabulary of Middle English, Danielsson (1948: 26–9, 39–54) coined the term "countertonic accentuation," e.g. *mélanchòly* < Latin *melancholia* (1375). The countertonic principle not only ensures that polysyllabic Latin borrowings respect *LAPSE, but it also switches the position of the primary and the secondary stress in the input word. According to Danielsson, it "originated in the school pronunciation of Latin in Middle English" (1948: 27). The rhythmic alternation applies also to derived loanwords. Middle English borrowed a large number of Romance suffixes such as *-able, -ance/-ence, -esse, -(i)er, -io(u)n, -ité(e), -ment, -ory, -ous, -ude*, which carried the main stress of the word; in ME the order of the prominences was presumably reversed: *éloquènce, partículèr, humánitèe, párlemènt*, aligning the prosody of these borrowed words with the native model of *máidenhòd*.

5.5 The Hybrid Stress Patterns of Polysyllabic Romance Words

Following an earlier suggestion of Luick's, Halle and Keyser (1971: 100–9) posited the introduction of a new stress rule, the Romance Stress Rule (RSR), for the Romance loanwords in Middle English. As the data in (35) show, dating the RSR to Middle English is premature. In ME the principles of morphological stress placement continued to be very powerful, so that the relatively small Romance portion of the vocabulary, 12.5 percent of the tokens and 21.2 percent of the types in late ME (Dekeyser 1986: 262), could still undergo prosodic assimilation as part of the overall nativization process. Monosyllabic loanwords, e.g. *psalm* (1200), *desk* (1363), *lamp* (1386), etc. fell naturally into the prosodic pattern of native monosyllables, the pattern of *scip* 'ship' in (19); the number of such words in the language was rapidly increasing due to the loss of final unstressed vowels. Disyllables, too, would easily fit the native prosodification in (19) and (20); that's how words of the type *manner, palace, vigil, volume*, etc. get their initial stress irrespective of the weight of the second syllable. Nevertheless, the increased density of Romance trisyllabic or longer words must be recognized as the basis of a new system which assigns metrical structure from the right edge of the word. The relevant stress patterns covered by the RSR are as in (38):

(38) Romance Stress Rule:[9]
  (a) Stress the penult if it is heavy and in disyllables (*vigil* (1225), *meménto* (1400))
  (b) Stress the antepenult if the penult is light, e.g. *málady* (1275)

For Latin the pattern is shown in (39), where again S = stressed, and W = unstressed syllable.

(39)	σ_S	σ_W	σ	σ_S	<σ_W>	σ_S	σ_W	<σ>
	vi	*gil*	*me*	*men*	<*to*>	*ma*	*la*	<*dy*>
	L	H	L	H	<H>	L	L	<H>

The angled brackets enclose the final syllables which, according to (38), are irrelevant for the assignment of stress. Under the pressure of FOOT BINARITY, however, the rightmost syllable of the word will have to be included in the prosodic structure when there is no other syllable to fill out the foot, as in *vigil*.[10]

The simplified table in (40) – all winning candidates satisfy FT-BIN, and therefore it is left out – models the effect of the RSR with the help of the familiar constraint on NONFINALITY, plus the STW constraint:

(40) The RSR system: stress assignment for *vigil, memento, malady*

		NONFINALITY	STW
1a.	(vi. gíl)	*!	
1b. ☞	(ví. gil)		*
2a.	me. (men. tó)	*!	
2b.	(mé. men). to		*
2c. ☞	me. (mén. to)		
3a.	ma. (la. dý)	*!	
3b.	ma. (lá. dy)		*
3c. ☞	(má. la). dy		*

The STW violations for (1b) *(ví. gil)*, (2b) *(mé. men). to*, (3b) *ma. (lá. dy)*, and 3c *(má. la). dy* are non-fatal. This licenses stress patterns which are indeed attested: like (2b) are e.g. *character* (1315), *manacle* (1350), *galaxy* (1384), and like (3b) are e.g. *cadaver* (1398), *enamel* (1463), though it is clear that additional factors must account for the rarity of the latter pattern. The weight of the initial syllable in all three types is irrelevant, in the same way that the weight of the initial syllable of the stem was irrelevant for the native lexicon. Of the three successful outputs, only the (X)H(X) type, as in *memento*, will *not* fit the native model in (20).

Though this is an unorthodox way of addressing the prosodic status of Romance borrowings in ME, it is adopted here because it highlights a very important question, that of the compatibility of the native and the foreign prosodic patterns; on this see also Lass (1992: 85–90). The host language already used constraints which made a large portion of the monomorphemic borrowed lexicon unrecognizable as "foreign." Disyllabic words and trisyllabic words with a light middle syllable, e.g. *emperor* (1225), *medicine* (1230), *policy* (1386), *animal* (1398), etc. behaved like native words. The group of "stress-conforming" loanwords was enlarged by the loss of the final syllables in originally trisyllabic words, e.g. *órgan* (1000), *fígure* (1300), *trumpet* (1390), which acquired stem-initial stress irrespective of the weight of the second syllable. Again, except for the (X)H(X) subset of Romance words, all monomorphemic words in ME of three syllables or less automatically obeyed the alignment constraint ALIGNLEFT (ST, F); stress was on the first syllable of the stem.[11] It is not surprising, then, that for the largish subset of words that violate the stress patterns of the donor language: *character, orator, principle, plethora, minister, sinister, calendar, cylinder,* etc., the account should make reference to the left-alignment with the stem, rendering any quantitative considerations redundant. This group is quite robust and is regularly commented on in studies of English stress, starting with Walker (1791: 67), who attributes the pattern correctly to "the invasion of the Gothic accent."

In the table in (41) the StW constraint of (40) is replaced by AlignLeft (St, F), showing how a constraint set mixing the RSR ranking and the natively present filters accounts for regular Germanic stressing of disyllables (as in *gammon*) and for the initial stress on all types of Latinate words, irrespective of the weight of the middle syllable:

(41) Hybrid system (I): stress assignment for *gammon, calendar, malady*

		Nonfinality	AlignLeft (St, F)
1a.	(ga. món)	*!	*
1b. ☞	(gá. mon)		
2a.	(ca. lén). dar	*!	*
2b.	ca. (lén. dar)		*!
2c. ☞	(cá. len). dar		
3a.	ma. (la. dý)	*!	*!
3b.	ma. (lá. dy)		*!
3c. ☞	(má. la). dy		

The property that allows new loans to become weight-*in*sensitive despite a low initial rate of weight-insensitivity in the language is primarily the robustness of stress as a marker of morphological constituency – the well-known demarcative property of stress (Kager 1999: 167). The two systems shown in (40) and (41) must have coexisted during Early Modern English. The infiltration of Romance vocabulary continued at a faster pace after 1500. According to an estimate based on Barber's (1997: 220) count of 2 percent of the OED entries, as many as 4,500 new words were recorded in English during each decade between 1500 and 1700. Eliminating new words of unknown origin, and words not recorded after 1700, English adopted for permanent use over 20,000 borrowings in two centuries, of which over 85 percent were Latin or French, with Latin outnumbering French at a ratio of 3.5 : 1. By 1700, the balance of power in the polysyllabic vocabulary of English had shifted in favor of the "foreign" words. The "critical mass" of foreign prosodic evidence created conditions for the spread of the stress principles based on the Latin system of accentuation shown in (40). This is the system described in detail in Walker's famous *Principles of English Pronunciation* (1791). It is also at the core of the numerous accounts of PDE stress in various frameworks over the last century.

A third subsystem, one in which simple roots can take final stress, switching the ranking of StW and Nonfinality, became possible through the loss of the original Latin endings, e.g. *cement* < Lat. caementum (1300), *molest* (1425) < Lat. *molestus*, etc. This pattern is represented sparsely – less than two pages of words other than proper nouns in Fudge (1984: 34–6), with most of the words exhibiting alternative pronunciations. It does, however, match the prosodic contour of a large number of prefixed native (e.g. *beget, mistake, forswear*) and Latinate (e.g. *delude, perceive, resume*) verbs. These types get a unified treatment under the assumption that the Stress-to-Weight principle is the only inviolable constraint; Nonfinality is violable, and the alignment refers to the roots of the words, as in the accounts of OE main stress. This second hybrid system is shown in (42):

(42) Hybrid system (II): stress assignment for *cement, delude*

		StW	Nonfinality	AlignL(R, F)
1a. ☞	(ce. mént)		*	*
1b.	(cé. ment)	*!		
2a. ☞	de. (lúde)		*	
2b.	(dé. lude)	*!		
2c.	(de. lúde)		*	*

The ranking between Nonfinality and AlignL (R, F) is indeterminate. As in the previous tables, this table simplifies matters by avoiding reference to foot well-formedness constraints. I have focused on the main distinction: non-quantitative vs. quantitative stress. One advantage of the hybrid model in (42) is that it sheds light on the familiar difference between monomorphemic words like *cement*, which are unusual (they violate *both* Nonfinality and AlignL (R, F), and prefixed verbs which are regularly stress-final – they violate only Nonfinality, and that only in non-inflected forms, see also Minkova (1997).

Hybrid systems (I) and (II) account for the stress of all disyllabic words and for initial or penultimate stress on (X)H(X) words (*calendar, memento*). The last option for trisyllabic words, which is also a common ME and later pattern for four-syllable words, relies on more powerful Foot Binarity, as well as the rhythmic constraint *Lapse for the avoidance of strings of unstressed syllables. The resulting prosodification respects and reinforces the left-alignment with the stem. These are the patterns represented by *advertise* (v. 1430) and *memorandum* (1394); the relative prominence of the foot-heads is ignored here:

(43) Hybrid system (III): stress assignment for *advertise, memorandum*

		ALIGNLEFT (ST, F)	FT-BIN	*LAPSE
1a.	ad. (vér. tise)	*!	*	
1b.	(ád). (vér. tise)		*!	
1c. ☞	(ád. ver). (tíse)		*	
2a.	me.(mó.ran). dum	*!		
2b.	(mé). (mó.ran). dum		*!	
2c	(mé. mo). ran. dum			*!
2d. ☞	(mé. mo). (rán. dum)			

The history of another major rhythmic adjustment constraint, *CLASH, cannot be developed here, but see Minkova and Stockwell (forthcoming). Indeed, (1b) and (2b) in (43) could be eliminated equally well by *CLASH. I have chosen to refer to FOOT BINARITY and *LAPSE because the former provides a useful link to the OE system as presented in section 5.2, and the latter is characteristic of ME, as argued in section 5.4.2.

The hybrid systems in (41–43) presented a serious challenge for the acquisition of stress in the rapidly expanding Latinate vocabulary of Early Modern English. As is evident from contemporary records from the sixteenth to the late eighteenth centuries, and even to this day (Lass 1999: 128–33; MacMahon 1998: 493–517), all three systems were in competition and the end result is not always predictable on linguistic grounds. Stress in post-ME loans or new formations, e.g. *harass* (1618), *cascade* (1641), *synergy* (1660), *badminton* (1845), *allergy* (1911), *boondoggle* (1935) will fit one of the three models above, but not predictably so. Why *hostel* but *hotel,* when John Walker (1791) has only one entry: [ho-stel'] 'a genteel inn'? Walker also has *cáprice, cónfessor, decórous, excávate, vertígo. . . .* This point is highlighted by the often discussed differences between British and American accentuation (Berg 1999). As Lass (1999: 128) wrote: "The Present-Day English stress system, as ongoing controversy about how to treat it synchronically shows, is in fact the relic of an 'unresolved' history, each problematic area a scar left by its evolution." Whether the historical "scars" become healthy transplant tissue or whether the system accommodates old scars and constantly creates new ones is still a hot research topic, of which Halle (1998), Hammond (1999), Pater (2000), and McCully (2002), are some of the most recent examples.

The complexities of stress under affixation in the modern system are beyond the scope of this chapter. I have deliberately avoided references to lexical strata, or cyclicity, though the OE sections refer implicitly to different levels of representation. Another shortcut was taken in addressing the details of the STRESS-TO-WEIGHT, i.e. how vowel quality, quantity, and the syllabic association of an intervocalic consonant are adjusted depending on the presence or absence of stress. Crucially, such segmental and analytical processes are seen as consequences of a historical stress system which is predominantly morphological.

In conclusion, there are two ways in which the location of the stress in English can be determined. Morphologically assigned stress, which aligns the prosodic prominence with the left edge of a root or a stem, was the leading force in determining stress in Old and Middle English. Massive borrowing of Latin vocabulary during the Renaissance led to a hybridization of the stress system allowing for some weight-driven distinctions in Present-day English.

ACKNOWLEDGMENTS

I am grateful to Michael Getty, Heinz Giegerich, Robert Stockwell, and the editors of this volume for a close critical reading of an earlier version of this chapter. Any errors of fact and judgment are mine.

NOTES

1 Following the principle of FIT, namely that "Languages select meters in which their entire vocabularies are usable in the greatest variety of ways" (Hanson and Kiparsky 1996: 294), we can expect forms that satisfy PARSESYLL to be more frequently utilized in verse. The validity of the observation that trochaic words are the optimal verse feet has been defended independently in Russom (1987).

2 Metrical resolution, the main motivation for weight-sensitive accounts of OE stress, is treated here as a parametrical rule, similar to alliteration. Russom (1995) shows that the probability of resolution is directly related to verse structure. The circularity of the evidence for prosodic resolution in simplex words is discussed in Minkova and Stockwell (1994), Stockwell and Minkova (1997). Treating OE resolution as a metrical device has the advantage of aligning it with metrical equivalences found in the later forms of English verse; see for Middle English Fulk (2002), for Chaucer Youmans (1996), and Kiparsky (1977) for the later pentameter.

3 See Morohovskiy (1980: 116). The estimate is based on a sample of 2,600 words in continuous texts. The "main stress only" portion of the data includes about 30 percent of simple forms and 15 percent compounds.

4 Recent critiques from different theoretical points of view appear in Suphi (1988), McCully (1992), Fulk (1992) Minkova (1996), Russom (2001), and Getty (2002).

5 Stress assignment on the second elements of personal names will not be addressed here. At the risk of oversimplifying, we can say that these are treated either as ROOT AFFIXES (Ecg*ðeow*, Hro*þgar*, Beo*wulf*, Healf*dene*), or as DERIVATIONAL AFFIXES (Hrunt*ing*, Wylf*ing*). On this see also Russom (2001).

6 Affixes are defined as "heavy" if they end in two consonants. Light affixes have a short vowel followed by a single consonant (Russom 2001: 56–7).

7 *Jul* 242a: *singal gesið* 'a constant companion'. Russom (2001: fn.31) bundles this case together with the heavy affixes.

8 Dates in parentheses here and below refer to the earliest attestations recorded by the OED.

9 The traditional RSR as defined in Halle and Keyser (1971: 101) and Lass (1992: 87, 1999: 126) provides for stress also on any final syllable if it is heavy. I do not believe that this subpart of the rule was ever functional for underived words in Middle English. Old French words ending in short open *-e*: *mirácle, prudénce, solémpne*, or words ending in a long vowel: *honóur, mercí, sesún, vertú*, etc. did not retain their "Romance" stress, unless they were verbs, for which the inflected forms satisfied NONFINALITY. On this see Minkova (1997: 158–61).

10 This device is similar to the "extrametricality revocation" in Prince and Smolensky (1993: 4.3). Unlike the analysis there and its modified version in Jacobs (2003), the trochaic foot here is not a quantitative, but a syllabic foot.

11 The quantity-insensitivity of Latin secondary stress is discussed in Jacobs (2000: 344), who also points out that "in Latin the penultimate syllable was the only syllable where weight mattered for stress distribution."

FURTHER READING

Barber, Charles (1997). *Early Modern English*. Edinburgh: Edinburgh University Press.

Berg, Thomas (1999). Stress variation in British and American English. *World Englishes* 18.2: 123–43.

Bolinger, Dwight L. (1981). *Two Kinds of Vowels, Two Kinds of Rhythm*. Bloomington, IN: Indiana University Linguistics Club.

Burrow, J. and T. Turville-Petre (1996). *A Book of Middle English* (2nd edn.). Oxford: Blackwell.

Burzio, Luigi (1994). *Principles of English Stress*. Cambridge: Cambridge University Press.

Campbell, Alistair (1959). *Old English Grammar*. Oxford: Clarendon Press.

Colman, Fran (1994). On the morphology of Old English word stress. *Lingua* 93: 141–81.

Danielsson, Bror (1948). *Studies on the Accentuation of Polysyllabic Latin, Greek, and Romance Loan-Words in English*. With special reference to those ending in *-able, -ate, -ator, -ible, -ic, -ical*, and *-ize*. Stockholm: Almqvist and Wiksell.

Dekeyser, Xavier (1986). Romance loans in Middle English: a reassessment. In D. Kastovsky, and A. Szwedek (eds.), *Linguistics across Historical and Geographical Boundaries* (pp. 253–65). Berlin: Mouton de Gruyter.

Fowler, Carol Ann (1977). *Timing Control in Speech Production*. Bloomington, IN: Indiana University Linguistics Club.

Fudge, Eric (1984). *English Word-Stress*. London: George Allen and Unwin.

Fulk, Robert D. (1992). *A History of Old English Meter*. Philadelphia: University of Pennsylvania Press.

Fulk, Robert (2002). Early Middle English evidence for Old English meter: resolution in *Poema Morale*. *Journal of Germanic Linguistics* 14.4: 331–57.

Gąsiorowski, Piotr (1997). *The Phonology of Old English Stress and Metrical Structure*. Frankfurt am Main: Peter Lang.

Getty, Michael (2002). *A Constraint-based Approach to the Metre of* Beowulf. Berlin: Mouton de Gruyter.

Giegerich, Heinz (1980). On stress-timing in English phonology. *Lingua* 51: 187–221.

Giegerich, Heinz (1985). *Metrical Phonology and Phonological Structure: German and English*. Cambridge: Cambridge University Press.

Gimson, A. C. (1973 [1970]). *An Introduction to the Pronunciation of English* (2nd edn.). London: Edward Arnold.

Halle, Morris (1998). The stress of English words 1968–1998. *Linguistic Inquiry* 29.4: 539–68.

Halle, Morris and S. J. Keyser (1971). *English Stress: Its Form, Its Growth, and Its Role in Verse*. New York: Harper and Row.

Hammond, Michael (1999). *The Phonology of English*. Oxford: Oxford University Press.

Hanson, K. and P. Kiparsky (1996). A parametric theory of poetic meter. *Language* 72.2: 287–336.

Hogg, Richard (1992). Phonology and morphology. In Richard Hogg (ed.), *The Cambridge History of the English Language*. Vol. 1: *The Beginnings to 1066* (pp. 67–164). Cambridge: Cambridge University Press.

Hutton, John (1998a). The development of secondary stress in Old English. In Richard M. Hogg and Linda van Bergen (eds.), *Historical Linguistics 1995*, vol. 2: *Germanic Linguistics* (pp. 115–30). Amsterdam: John Benjamins.

Hutton, John (1998b). Stress assignment in Old English, giet ongean. *Linguistics* 35–6: 847–85.

Jacobs, Haike (2000). The revenge of the uneven trochee: Latin main stress, metrical constituency, stress-related phenomena and OT. In A. Lahiri (ed.), *Analogy, Levelling, Markedness* (pp. 333–53). Berlin: Mouton de Gruyter.

Jacobs, Haike (2003). Why preantepenultimote stress in Latin requires an OT account. In Paula Fikkert and Haike Jakobs (eds.), *Development in Prosodic Systems* (pp. 395–419). Berlin: Mouton de Gruyter.

Jespersen, Otto (1909). *A Modern English Grammar on Historical Principles*. Part I: *Sounds and Spellings*. Heidelberg: Carl Winter's Universitätsbuchhandlung.

Kager, René (1999). *Optimality Theory*. Cambridge: Cambridge University Press.

Kastovsky, Dieter (1992). Semantics and vocabulary. In Richard Hogg (ed.), *The Cambridge History of the English Language*. Vol. 1: *The Beginnings to 1066* (pp. 290–409). Cambridge: Cambridge University Press.

Kiparsky, Paul (1977). The rhythmic structure of English verse. *Linguistic Inquiry* 8: 189–247.

Lass, Roger (1992). Phonology and morphology. In Norman Blake (ed.), *The Cambridge History of the English Language*. Vol. 2: *1066–1476* (pp. 23–156). Cambridge: Cambridge University Press.

Lass, Roger (1999). Phonology and morphology. In Roger Lass (ed.), *The Cambridge History of the English Language*. Vol. 3: *1476–1776* (pp. 56–187). Cambridge: Cambridge University Press.

McCarthy, John and Alan Prince (1995 [1966]). Prosodic morphology. In J. Goldsmith (ed.), *A Handbook of Phonological Theory* (paperback reprint 1996). Cambridge, MA: Blackwell.

McCully, Christopher (1992). The phonology of resolution in OE word-stress and metre. In Fran Colman (ed.), *Evidence for Old English: Material and Theoretical Bases for Reconstruction* (pp. 117–41). Edinburgh: John Donald.

McCully, Christopher (2002). Exaptation and English stress. *Language Sciences* 24: 3–4, 323–44.

McCully, Christopher and Richard Hogg (1990). An account of Old English stress. *Journal of Linguistics* 26: 315–39.

MacMahon, Michael K. C. (1998). Phonology. In Suzanne Romaine (ed.), *The Cambridge History of the English Language*. Vol. 4: *1776–1997*

(pp. 373–535). Cambridge: Cambridge University Press.
Minkova, D. (1982). The environment for Middle English open syllable lengthening. *Folia Linguistica Historica* 3.1: 29–58.
Minkova, D. (1991). *The History of Final Vowels in English*. Berlin: Mouton de Gruyter.
Minkova, D. (1996). Verse structure as evidence for prosodic reconstruction in Old English. In Derek Britton (ed.), *Amsterdam Studies in the Theory and History of Linguistics Science* (pp. 13–38) (series 4, issue 135). Amsterdam: John Benjamins.
Minkova, D. (1997). Constraint ranking in Middle English stress-shifting. *English Language and Linguistics*, I. 1: 135–75.
Minkova, D. (2000). Middle English prosodic innovations and their testability in verse. In I. Taavitsainen et al. (eds.), *Placing Middle English in Context* (pp. 431–61). Berlin: Mouton de Gruyter.
Minkova, D. (2003). Prefixation and stress in Old English. Paper presented at the 16th International Conference on Historical Linguistics, Copenhagen, August 2003.
Minkova, D. and R. Stockwell (1994). Syllable weight, prosody, and meter in Old English. *Diachronica* 11.1: 35–65.
Minkova, D. and R. Stockwell (forthcoming). Clash avoidance in morphologically derived words in Middle English. Why [-hʊd] but [-dm]? In Nikolaus Ritt et al. (eds.).
Moon, An-nah (1996). Aspects of Old English prosody: an optimality-theoretic analysis. PhD thesis, New York University.
Morohovskiy, A. N. (1980). *Slovo i predlojenie v istorii angliiskogo yazika* [Word and clause in the history of the English Language]. Kiev: Vyssha Shkola.
Pater, Joe (2000). Non-uniformity in English secondary stress: the role of ranked and lexically specific constraints. *Phonology* 17.2: 237–74.
Prince, A. and P. Smolensky (1993). *Optimality Theory: Constraint Interaction in Generative Grammar* (Technical Report 2). Center for Cognitive Sciences, Rutgers University, New Brunswick, NJ and Computer Science Department, University of Colorado, Boulder.
Prokosch, Eduard (1939). *A Comparative Germanic Grammar*. Baltimore: Linguistic Society of America.
Russom, Geoffrey (1987). *Old English Meter and Linguistic Theory*. Cambridge: Cambridge University Press.
Russom, Geoffrey (1995). Constraints on resolution in Beowulf. In Jane Toswell (ed.), *Prosody and Poetics in the Early Middle Ages*, (pp. 147–63). Toronto: University of Toronto Press.
Russom, Geoffrey (2001). Metrical evidence for subordinate stress in Old English. *Journal of Germanic Linguistics* 13.1: 39–64.
Stockwell, Robert and D. Minkova (1997). Old English metrics and the phonology of resolution. In *Germanic Studies in Honor of Anatoly Liberman* (pp. 389–406). NOWELE 31/32.
Suphi, M. (1988). Old English stress assignment. *Lingua* 75: 171–202.
Vennemann, Theo (1988). *Preference Laws for Syllable Structure and the Explanation of Sound Change*. Berlin: Mouton de Gruyter.
Walker John (1791/1831). *A Critical Pronouncing Dictionary and Expositor of the English Language*. Edinburgh: Thomas Nelson and Peter Brown.
Youmans, G. (1996). Reconsidering Chaucer's prosody. In C. B. McCully and J. J. Anderson (eds.), *English Historical Metrics* (pp. 185–210). Cambridge: Cambridge University Press.

6 Prosodic Preferences: From Old English to Early Modern English

PAULA FIKKERT, B. ELAN DRESHER, AND ADITI LAHIRI

6.1 Introduction

This chapter discusses the prosodic organization of the phonological and morphological system of Old English, and investigates how this system changed up to early Modern English. By *prosody* we mean primarily aspects of the grammar related to the weight of root syllables, syllable structure, and stress.[1] Although the changes we will discuss are primarily phonological, a proper understanding of prosodic change in the history of English requires that we take into account morphological class membership, particularly as stem extensions and endings played a significant role in many of the phonological rules that ultimately affected the prosodic organization of the language. In addition, the quantity of root syllables played a crucial role in constraining prosodic changes throughout the history of English.

We assume that the major developments under review here came about in the process of transmission of the language from one generation to the next, that is, in the course of language acquisition. Prominent in our account will be a characteristic of grammars called *pertinacity* (Lahiri 2002). A rule or pattern in the native speaker's grammar may persist over time, though its outward realization may change. An example is the persistence of a particular metrical pattern in English, the Germanic foot. We will show that this foot pattern came to apply to new forms, such as Romance loans in Middle English, and applied in a new way to certain older forms. This type of prosodic change occurs when learners extend a grammatical pattern to new forms. The grammatical pattern is transmitted to the next generation, but sometimes with different outward manifestations due to other changes in the grammar.

Another type of pertinacity concerns the persistence of the native output forms despite changes in the grammar. We will show that despite major changes in the metrical system in early Modern English, native English words retained the original position of main stress, while the grammar restructured all around them. Since learners acquire their grammar guided by the output forms they are exposed to, we do not expect the forms that make up the 'core' or 'primary' data to change in the course of acquisition. However, when such core forms fail to provide unambiguous evidence as to the nature of the underlying grammar, the way is opened for new forms to cause a change in the grammar.

Both types of pertinacity imply conservatism, either in the grammar or in the surface forms. But the acquisition process can also result in radical changes where neither grammar nor outputs remain the same. Such upheavals occur when, due to the interaction of various phonological and morphological processes, the underlying forms become *unrecoverable* (Kaye 1974), or the grammatical principles that give rise to the surface forms become *opaque* (Kiparsky 1982, 2000). When the opacity is such that language learners cannot reconstruct the old system, they may instead adopt strategies, such as paradigmatic leveling, that lead to dramatic changes in both grammar and output.

In this chapter we first discuss the prosodic system of West Germanic, which remained largely unchanged in Old English. Subsequently, we will show how a number of phonological rules directly or indirectly influenced the West Germanic nominal paradigms which led to the Old English situation. Many of these rules affected light and heavy root syllables differently and consequently affected morphological paradigms as well. In this chapter we will restrict ourselves to the nominal system, but it is important to note that the effects also hold for the verbal system. From Old English to Middle English the prosodic system underwent processes such as High Vowel Deletion (HVD), Trisyllabic Shortening (TSS) and Open Syllable Lengthening (OSL). While the last two processes served to optimize metrical structures in ways we will discuss, they also gave rise to new types of vowel length alternations in morphological paradigms. Furthermore, subsequent processes such as final vowel deletion often obscured the contexts of these vowels' length alternations, making the phonology opaque. This opacity lead to paradigm leveling, simplifying the morphological system, but altering the prosodic system.

Despite the fact that many words changed their prosodic word structure, we present evidence from Romance loan words into Middle English showing that the prosodic system in Middle English was still essentially the same as that of Old English. In other words, no new stress rules were taken over from the donor language. However, loans may ultimately have an effect on the stress system, which we argue is the case when long Latin words were borrowed into early Modern English. When the native stress rules are indecisive, loan words can trigger a change. This, we argue, led to the modern English Latinate stress system.

6.2 The Word Prosodic System of West Germanic

Stress in West Germanic and in Old English invariably falls on the first syllable of the word, unless the word is prefixed, in which case the prefix is stressed in nouns, but not in verbs. The stress system of Old English is much debated (cf. Dresher and Lahiri 1991, 2005; Kiparsky 1998; see also Minkova, chapter 5, this volume). Here, we will follow Dresher and Lahiri (1991), who argue that the metrical foot is a resolved and expanded moraic trochee ([μ μ̣μ̣] μ), where the head, indicated by square brackets, must dominate at least two moras. When the stressed syllable is light, that is, when the two moras of the head could not have come from one syllable, it is "resolved." In that case the head is formed by the first two syllables regardless of the weight of the second syllable. In parametric terms, the Germanic metrical structure is as in (1) with sample parsings from Old English.

(1) The Germanic Foot (Dresher and Lahiri 1991)
Foot type: resolved (expanded) moraic trochee ([μ μ(μ)] μ)
Direction of parsing: left to right
Main stress: Left

Sample parsings

(x .)	(x .)	(x .)
([μμ] μ)	([μ μ] μ)	([μ μμ] μ)
H L	L L L	L H L
wor da	we ru da	cy nin ga

Given this formulation of Old English metrical structure, we would expect all heavy syllables, except those following an initial light syllable, to be stressed. This might have been the case in earlier times, but in Old English no final syllable, whether heavy or light, bears secondary stress (Campbell 1959: §§87–92). A non-initial foot can bear secondary stress only if it is branching. Thus, we find alternations such as *ṓðer* ~ *ṓðèrne* 'other, NOM. SING. ~ ACC. SING.' and *ǣ́ðeling* ~ *ǣ́ðelìnges* 'prince, NOM. SING. ~ GEN. SING.' Their metrical structures are shown in (2), where an underlined x indicates a syllable that lacks secondary stress, despite being the head of a foot:

(2) Lack of secondary stress in final syllables (Dresher and Lahiri 1991)

(x) (x̲)	(x) (x .)	(x) (x̲)	(x) (x) (x̲)
([μμ]) ([μμ])	([μμ])([μμ] μ)	([μ μ])([μμ])	([μ μ])([μμ])([μμ])
H H	H H L	L L H	L L H H
ō ðer	ō ðer ne	æ ðe ling	æ ðe lin ges

This systematic failure of final syllables to be stressed suggests a rule such as Final Destressing (FD):

(3) Final Destressing (FD)
Defoot a final weak non-branching foot.

In Old English all unstressed long vowels, including those in final syllables, were shortened, which made a subtle reanalysis of the prosodic system possible.

In the absence of unstressed long vowels, the only word-final syllables that appeared to be heavy were those ending in a consonant. The fact that such syllables did not receive secondary stress could then be accounted for in terms of Final Consonant Extrametricality (CEM):

(4) Final Consonant Extrametricality (CEM)
Word-final consonants are extrametrical.

Dresher and Lahiri provide several types of evidence supporting the Germanic foot, including main and secondary stress, High Vowel Deletion in Old English, and Sievers' Law in Gothic. Additional evidence for the Germanic foot and the reanalysis of Final Destressing (3) as Consonant Extrametricality (4) comes from OSL (Lahiri and Dresher 1999), TSS (Lahiri and Fikkert 1999) and the dental preterit (Lahiri 1999, 2004). We will discuss some of the evidence below.

A key concept in the discussion of the prosodic systems of Germanic and their change is weight or quantity. It played a crucial role in the changes in the old inherited morphological paradigms from West Germanic to Old English. Syllables in Old English can be characterized as either light, heavy, or superheavy. Light syllables contain a non-branching rhyme (V). Heavy syllables have rhymes with either a branching nucleus (VV) or a branching rhyme (VC). Superheavy syllables contain VVC or VCC rhymes. All these syllable types occur in Old English, but an important further restriction is that *root*[2] syllables cannot consist of a single light syllable. The minimal requirement for a monosyllabic root is a heavy syllable: VV or VC_1.[3] Roots consisting of a heavy CVC syllable are called *light* roots: a CVC root plus a vowel-initial ending would syllabify as CV.CV, making the initial (root) syllable light. All other root syllables are heavy. Most roots in Old English are monosyllabic – which explains the term root syllable – although there are longer roots, too.

The table in (5) presents the nominative singular and plural forms as they are attested in Old English. The first column gives the traditional name of the nominal class (after their stem extensions), and the genders it came in: masculine (m.), feminine (f.), or neuter (n.). The main Proto-Germanic stem extensions were *a-*, *ja-* for masculine and neuter nouns, *ō-*, *jō-* for feminines, and *i-* and *u-* in all genders, although *u*-neuters went over to the *a*-nouns at an early stage.

(5) Survey of strong nominal classes – light and heavy roots[4]

Class	*Sing.*	*Plur.*	*Gloss*
a- (m.)	dæg	dagas	'day'
	stān	stānas	'stone'
ja- (m.)	hyll	hyllas	'hill'
	ende	endas	'end'
a- (n.)	hol	holu	'hole'
	word	word	'word'
ja- (n.)	bedd	bedd	'bed'
	gewǣde[5]	gewǣdu	'clothing'
ō- (f.)	talu	tale, -a	'tale'
	ār	āre, -a	'honor'
jō- (f.)	synn	synne, -a	'offense'
	sprēc	sprēce, -a	'speech'
i- (m.)	byre	byras	'son'
	gylt	gyltas	'guilt'
i- (n.)	spere	speru	'spear'
	gecynd	gecyndu	'nature'
i- (f.)	wyrd	wyrde, -a	'fate'
u- (m., f.)	sunu	suna	'son'
	feld	felda	'field'

Old English inherited from its Germanic and ultimately Indo-European ancestors a system of noun classes that took the form Root + Extension + Suffix, which is reflected in (6). The table in (6) gives a sample of some of the nominal classes of pre-Old English with examples of their nominative singular–plural suffixes. Reconstructed underlying stems are given.[6]

(6) Survey of strong nominal classes – light and heavy roots

Class	*Sing. suffix*	*Plur. suffix*	*Weight*	*Root + Extension*	*Gloss*
a- (m.)	/+Ø/	/+as/	*light*	/dæg/	'day'
			heavy	/stān/	'stone'
ja- (m.)			*light*	/hul+j/	'hill'
			heavy	/and+j/	'end'
a- (n.)	/+Ø/	/+u/	*light*	/hol/	'hole'
			heavy	/word/	'word'
ja- (n.)			*light*	/bad+j/	'bed'
			heavy	/gewād+j/	'clothing'
ō- (f.)	/+Ø/	/+e~a/	*light*	/tal+u/	'tale'
			heavy	/ār+u/	'honor'
jō- (f.)			*light*	/sun+ju/	'offense'
			heavy	/sprāc+ju/	'speech'
i- (m.)	/+Ø/	/+e~as/	*light*	/bur+i/	'son'
			heavy	/gult+i/	'guilt'
i- (n.)	/+Ø/	/+u/	*light*	/sper+i/	'spear'
			heavy	/gecund+i/	'nature'
i- (f.)	/+Ø/	/+e~a/	*light*	—[7]	
			heavy	/wurd+i/	'fate'
u- (m., f.)	/+Ø/	/+a/	*light*	/sun+u/	'son'
			heavy	/feld+u/	'field'

The largest classes in Old English came to be the *a-* and the *ō*-nouns. In early times the *a*-extensions were reanalyzed as being part of the suffixal inflection; thus, stems in these classes appear in the chart without any extension. All other classes show a stem extension in (6). A significant subclass of these nouns, called *ja-* and *jō*-nouns, had a formative we represent as an extension *-j*. Although the stem extension and nominative suffixes of *ō-* and *jō*-nouns are alike, the words in each class are distinguished by genitive and dative case suffixes. The table in (6) further gives the singular and plural endings of the nominative and the weight of the root.

The symmetrical West Germanic system represented in (6), with light and heavy roots for each class, would later be disturbed by the effects of several phonological rules, as can be seen in (5). We discuss these rules in the next section. We shall see that the distinction between light and heavy roots plays a central role in many of the main phonological-prosodic processes of Old English. Also of prosodic interest is the distinction between the formatives designated as *j-* and *i-*; we will see evidence that these must have different representations, but for now we assume that the *j-* is a floating *i* (following Kiparsky 1998, 2000, 2002). We will come back to this issue.

6.3 From West Germanic to Old English

6.3.1 *Sievers' Law*

The distinction between light and heavy roots had been reinforced by Sievers' Law (Sievers 1885) in the ancestor of the Germanic languages. In the formulation of Edgerton (1934, 1943), the *-j* extension takes the form *j* after a light stem and *ij (ii)* after a heavy stem. Therefore, the *ja-* and *jō-*nouns, at an early stage, would have appeared as in (7). This alternation did not affect the *-i* extension, showing it was a distinct element from *-j*.

(7) Sievers' Law – light and heavy roots

Class	*Weight*	*Sievers' Law*	*Gloss*
ja- (m.)	*light*	hul+^{i}	'hill'
	heavy	and+i^{i}	'end'
ja- (n.)	*light*	bad+^{i}	'bed'
	heavy	gewād+i^{i}	'clothing'
jō- (f.)	*light*	sun+^{i}u	'sin'
	heavy	sprāc+^{i}u	'rest'

We will assume that Sievers' Law optimized the prosodic structure by avoiding Cj-clusters (Dresher and Lahiri 1991; Riad 1992; Kiparsky 1999). In *sprāc+*^{i}*u* Sievers' Law could not improve the prosodic structure, but rather would have created a sequence of too many high vowels in a row; hence, no extra vowel was added here.

6.3.2 *i-Umlaut (i-Mutation)*

A high front vowel or glide (*i* or *j* in the table in (6)) causes fronting (and in some cases raising) of a preceding stressed vowel. This rule of Umlaut is evidently an early rule, as it affects all the West Germanic dialects. In Old English it applies before High Vowel Deletion or apocope, as it affects the singular of heavy *i*-stems, as in *gesti* 'guest', unlike in Old High German, where *gast* is not umlauted. In terms of morphological classes, umlaut systematically affected *ja-*, *jō-*, and *i*-nouns, as shown in (8):

(8) Effects of *i*-Umlaut on stressed vowels

Class	*Root + Extension*	*i-Umlaut*	*Gloss*
ja- (m.)	/hul+^{i}/	hyl+^{i}	'hill'
	/har+^{i}/	her+^{i}	'army'
	/and+i^i/	end+i^i	'end'
ja- (n.)	/bad+^{i}/	bed+^{i}	'bed'
	/stucc+i^i/	stycc+i^i	'stick'
	/ gewād+i^i/	gewǣd+i^i	'clothing'
jō- (f.)	/sun+^{i}u/	syn+^{i}u	'offense'
	sprāc+^{i}u	sprēc+^{i}u	'rest'
i- (m.)	/bur+i/	byr+i	'friend'
	/gult+i/	gylt+i	'guilt'
i- (n.)	/sper+i/	sper+i	'spear'
	/gecund+i/	gecynd+i	'nature'
i- (f.)	/wurd+i/	wyrd+i	'fate'

Because the umlauting element was present throughout the nominal paradigm no alternations are created within these classes. However, alternations were created in other classes, such as in the consonantal stems, where high front vowels or glides appeared in certain suffixes but not others, giving rise to alternations in singular–plural pairs like *fōt* – *fēt*, and in derivationally related words belonging to different lexical classes, such as *lang* – *lengð(u)* ('long' – 'length').

Therefore, *i*-Umlaut remained as a synchronic rule in Old English for some time, at least in paradigms where it created alternations. Where there were no alternations the matter is less clear-cut. As long as vowels newly created by umlaut, such as *y* and *æ*, were recognized as positional allophones of *u* and *o*, forms such as *gylt-* would be interpreted as deriving from /gult-/. As long as the umlauting element remained detectable, it should not have been difficult for the learner to discern that umlauted vowels were in complementary distribution with corresponding non-umlauted vowels. However, the intervention of further changes would considerably complicate the situation.

6.3.3 West Germanic Gemination

Another early process that applied throughout West Germanic is West Germanic Gemination (WGG). Gemination applied to all root-final consonants other than *r* when *j* followed. Since gemination adds a mora to the first syllable, forms could undergo gemination only if the prosodic structure of the root syllable was able to include another mora. If the root syllable already contained two moras (i.e., was heavy, as in *end, stucc,* or *sprēc*), gemination could not take place. We refer to this as the bimoraicity constraint on root syllables (*μμμ). If the root syllable contained a single mora, as in the case of *hyl, bed,* or *syn,* the root underwent gemination.

(9) Effects of gemination on light roots

Class	*Weight*	*Umlaut*	*Gemination*	*Gloss*
ja- (m.)	*light*	hyl+^{i}	hyll	'hill'
		her+^{i}	her+^{i}	'army'
ja- (n.)	*light*	bed+^{i}	bedd	'bed'
jō- (f.)	*light*	syn+^{i}u	synnu	'offense'

The effect of WGG is to turn light roots into heavy ones. This change significantly alters the original symmetry of the morphological classes.

Note that the geminating element *j* in the representations in (9) seems to disappear after gemination, as the surface forms in Old English are respectively, *hyll, here, bedd,* and *synn*. There is evidence that in West Germanic, *j* did not delete in the process of WGG; hence Old High German *kunni* from /cun+j/. In Old English, too, there are traces left of the *j*, particularly in the heavy *ja-* and *jō*-stems, but not after gemination, as we shall discuss in the next section.

Significantly, the *i*-nouns do not undergo West Germanic gemination. This is a principled motivation for the claim that the element we have been designating as *j* differs from the extension we have been writing as *i*: otherwise, it would be hard to explain why /hyl+j/ geminates, whereas /byr+i/ does not. Under the assumption that the distinction is, as the notation suggests, one between an underlying glide and an underlying vowel, there would be an underlying moraic contrast between *j* and *i*. Such a contrast is unusual, because it is usually assumed that moraicity falls out from syllabification. Whether a segment surfaces as a vowel or glide in Old English is to a large extent predictable. For example, the *j* extension surfaces as a glide in *herjas* 'armies NOM., ACC. PL.' but as a vowel *e* (lowered from *i*) in the singular *here* 'army'.

(10) Syllabification of *j*

Underlying	Umlaut	Syllabification	i>e	
har-^{i}	her-^{i}	he.ri	here	'army' SG.
har-^{i}-as	her-^{i}-as	her.jas	—	'army' PL.

Nevertheless, some distinction must be made to account for the different behavior of the *-j* and *-i* extensions, as Germanic *harj* 'army' (light *ja*-noun) and *mari* 'see' (light *i*-noun) pattern differently. One possibility is to specify that the *i* is underlyingly moraic, as in (11a), or equivalently, that it is associated to a nuclear position, whereas *j* is not. Another possibility, suggested by Kiparsky (2000, 2002), is that this contrast rests on the difference between an ordinary segment (*i*) and a floating one (*j*), as shown in (11b).

(11) j-i stem extensions

a.

μ	
i	i(= j)
/hyp + i/	/stycc + j/

b.

x	*floating*
i	^{i}(= j)
/hyp + i/	/stycc +^{i}/

We will assume the latter possibility. The floating *j* of the stem extension is syllabified as a glide when other (vowel-initial) suffixes follow, that is, when it is no longer word edge, but only if syllabification is possible. If it cannot be syllabified it disappears. If the *j* of the stem extension is word-final, it surfaces as a vowel *i*, which is lowered to *e*.

6.3.4 *High Vowel Deletion and hiatus*

High Vowel Deletion (HVD) is a rule that deletes an unstressed high vowel or glide following a heavy syllable. This is only one of its contexts, however; HVD also deletes an unstressed high vowel or glide following two light syllables, or a light followed by a heavy syllable. The generalization is that HVD applies in the weak branch of a foot, leaving unfooted high vowels intact. In (12), the underlined vowels are in the weak branch of a foot and undergo HVD.

(12) High Vowel Deletion in Old English

(x .) .	(x .)	(x .)
([μμ] μ) μ	([μμ] μ)	([μ μμ] μ)
H L L	H L	L H L
hēa fu̲ de	wor du̲	fæ rel du̲
'head-DAT.SG'	'word-NOM.PL'	'journey-NOM.PL.'
(x .)	(x)	(x .)
([μ μ] μ)	([μ μ])	([μμ] μ) μ
L L L	L L	H L L
we ru du̲	ho lu	cī ce nu > cicenu (TSS)[8]
'army-NOM.PL'	'hole-NOM.PL'	'chicken-NOM.PL.'

Lahiri (1982) notes that there are two conditions under which HVD did not take place. First, HVD did not take place if the high vowel was part of a syllable without an onset. For instance, in the light neuter *i*-noun *sper-i+u*, the *u* is not deleted. Second, if the high vowel was preceded by a glide HVD was also blocked; in that case the glide was deleted, as we will see when discussing the *ja*-nouns. These conditions were probably more general strategies to avoid hiatus of unstressed vowels. High vowels were more prone to deletion than other vowels. In the case of two high vowels, usually the first deletes.

(13) Effects of HVD and avoidance of hiatus on *a*-, *ō*-, *i*-, and *u*- nominal classes

Weight	*Root + stem extension*	SING.	PLUR.	*Gloss*
a- (n.)		+Ø	+u	
L	/hol-/	hol	hol**u**	'hole'
H	/word-/	word	word Ø	'word'
ō- (f.)		+Ø	+e/a	
L	/tal-u/	tal**u**	tal _ e, -a	'tale'
H	/ār-u/	ār Ø	ār Ø e	'honor'
i- (m.)		+Ø	+as(/e)	
L	/byr-i/	byr**e**	byr _ as, -e	'son'
H	/gylt-i/	gylt Ø	gylt Ø as	'guilt'
i- (n.)		+Ø	+u	
L	/sper+i/	sper**e**	sper _ u[9]	'spear'
H	/gecynd+i/	gecynd Ø	gecynd Ø **u**	'nature'
i- (f.)		+Ø	+a/e	
H	/wyrd-i/	wyrd Ø	wyrd Ø e, -a	'fate'
u- (m., f.)		+Ø	+a	
L	/sun+u/	sun**u**	sun _ a	'son'
H	/feld+u/	feld Ø	feld Ø a	'field'

HVD creates a further difference between heavy and light roots in classes in which a high vowel or glide occurs as either an extension or as part of the suffix. Let us consider first the effects on members of the *a*-, *ō*-, *i*-, and *u*- classes, where Ø indicates HVD and _ a vowel deleted to avoid hiatus. The bolded high vowels do not undergo HVD.

HVD creates an alternation in the neuter *a*- class whereby a final -*u* appears in the nominative plural after a light root but not after a heavy. The rest of the inflections would have been identical in the light and heavy roots. Moreover, because the *a*- class was the major nominal class, such words were not inclined to be reanalyzed as belonging to any other class. Thus, we expect that learners would recognize that nouns with and without a -*u* suffix in the relevant cases belong to the same declension. From this, it would be fairly easy to recover underlying -*u* following heavy stems, and with it, the rule of HVD. A similar situation arose in the *ō*-class nouns, but here the *u* of the stem extension surfaces in the nominative singular after light roots, but not after heavy ones. As this was also a major class, no reanalysis took place.

Matters were somewhat different in the smaller *i*- and *u*-classes. To start with the latter, the appearance of -*u* in the nominative of masculine *u*-nouns served to distinguish these nouns from the major *a*-class. Once this suffix was deleted after heavy stems, however, the latter were liable to look, in the nominative singular, like *a*-nouns; thus, *feld* looks like *stān*. Despite the distinctiveness of the oblique and plural case endings, heavy *u*-nouns were prone to be reanalyzed as *a*-nouns if they were masculine. Even without HVD, the feminine *i*-stems looked, in the nominative singular (and in some dialects also the nominative plural), like *ō*-stems, and were prone to be reanalyzed as such.

Similar challenges faced the other heavy *i*-nouns. Once the distinctive -*i* suffix had deleted, only the presence of umlauted vowels could, in some cases, signal that a heavy noun was not simply a member of the *a*- or *ō*-stems. If umlauted vowels at some point became phonemic (as argued by Dresher 1985, for the Mercian dialect), then there would be no reason to keep these nouns distinct from the major classes.

(14) Singular–plural alternations in neuter *ja*-class nouns

Gothic	*Stem*	NOM SG Ø	NOM PL *u*
*stucc-i	stycc+^{i}	stycc-e	stycc-u
*gawad-i	gewǣd+^{i}	gewǣd-e	gewǣd-u
*aθal-i	æθel+^{i}	æθel-e	æθel-u
bad-i	bed+^{i}	bedd	bedd-Ø
kun-i	cyn+^{i}	cynn	cynn-Ø

The *ja-* and *jō*-stems exhibit more complex interactions with HVD. We repeat the singular–plural forms of the neuter *ja*-nouns along with the Gothic forms for comparison. Note that Gothic shows no gemination and umlaut.

Formerly light roots that had undergone WGG, such as *bedd* 'bed' and *cynn* 'race', became indistinguishable from neuter *a*-nouns. The difference between words like *bedd* and *stycce* is that the latter was a real heavy root, whereas the former became heavy after gemination. Neuter *ja*-nouns, such as *stycce-styccu* 'stick', which were originally heavy, create apparent exceptions to the rule of HVD. There are, in fact, two types of apparent exceptions. In the plural, we find *-u* immediately following a heavy syllable. In the nominative singular, these nouns surface with a final *-e*, which originates from *-i*.

It has been proposed that these *ja*-nouns joined with the light *i*-nouns to create a new class of nouns with a nominative singular suffix *-e* (Keyser and O'Neil 1985). A major problem with this analysis is that it does not account for the plurals with *-u* after a heavy syllable. Though HVD did have various exceptions here and there, particularly after bisyllabic roots (see Dresher 1985), the application of HVD after heavy roots was virtually without exceptions. Moreover, nouns such as *styccu* and *gewǣdu* showed the suffix *-u* with great

(15) Gemination, HVD, and restructuring of feet in OE neuter nouns

			Gemination	*HVD*		
a.	*a*-stems *H*					
	SG.	word – Ø	—	—	→	word
		([μμ])				([μμ])
	PL.	word – u	—	word – Ø	→	word
		([μμ] μ)		([μμ])		([μμ])
b.	*ja*-stems *H*					
	SG.	stycc – i^{i} – Ø	—	stycc–Ø^{i} – Ø	→	stycc – i(>e)
		([μμ] μ)				([μμ] μ)
	PL.	stycc – i^{i} – u	—	stycc – Ø^{i} – u	→	stycc – u
		([μμ] μ) μ		([μμ]) μ		([μμ] μ)
	SG.	æθel – i^{i} – Ø	—	æθel – Ø^{i} – Ø	→	æθel – i(>e)
		([μ μμ])				([μμ] μ)
	PL.	æθel – i^{i} – u	—	æθel – Ø^{i} – u	→	æθel – u
		([μ μ] μ) μ		([μ μ]) μ		([μμ] μ)
c.	*ja*-stems *L*					
	SG.	bed – ^{i} – Ø	bed – d	bedd	→	bedd
		([μμ])	([μ μ])			([μ μ])
	PL.	bed – ^{i} – u	bed – d – u	bedd – Ø	→	bedd
		([μ μ])	([μμ] μ)	([μ μ])		([μ μ])

regularity, and no tendency to "regularize" it. Therefore, the persistence of surface *-u* in these cases points to regular, not exceptional, behavior. Rather, the survival of the *-u* in these cases can be explained if we assume that these stems maintained their *j* extension. Therefore, in the plural, it was this element and not the *-u* which was deleted by HVD. This is the condition in which HVD is blocked before a glide, and is shown in (15).

The second apparent exception to HVD occurs in the singular, where the *j* extension surfaces as *-e*. Unstressed *i* in Old English systematically lowers to *e*; thus, the occurrence of *-e* is compatible with deriving it from *j*. But why does this element not delete after a heavy syllable, as it does in the plural, deriving **stycc*, **gewǣd*, and **æθel*? The diachronic explanation for this involves an intricate though straightforward interaction between Sievers' Law, which provided these forms with an extra high vowel, and High Vowel Deletion. Assuming that the *j* extension could be recovered in these nouns (an assumption based on the widespread evidence for HVD and *i*-lowering, as well as the persistence of *-u* following heavy stems in these nouns), what a learner could glean is that it deletes like a regular high vowel when medial, but escapes HVD when final. Thus, because of Sievers' Law, HVD had different results on originally light *ja*-stems which became heavy by WGG and *ja*-stems that were originally heavy. Therefore, at a certain period it must have looked to learners of Old English that WGG invariably involved the loss of the triggering *j*. Thus, the loss of the *j* was folded into the rule of WGG in Old English (Lahiri 1982).

6.4 From Old English to Middle English

6.4.1 Nominal paradigms in Old English

After all these changes the resulting paradigms in (16) differ in a number of aspects from the original West Germanic paradigms given in (6). In (16) the forms are arranged by gender.

Compared to the original symmetrical system of long and short stems there are a number of important changes. First, masculine endings are Ø or *-e* (from *i*) in the singular, and *-as* in the plural. Neuter singulars either end in Ø or *-e* (from *i*); plurals in Ø or *-u*. Feminine singular forms end in either *-u* or Ø; plural endings always *-e*, *-a*. Thus, any variation in the singular invariably involves the presence or absence of a high vowel, which originates from the stem extension, as all classes have a Ø ending in the nominative singular. In the plural each gender has its own ending: *-as*, *-e/a*, and *-u* for masculine, feminine, and neuter, respectively.

In the forms with an underlying *j*, the *-e* or *-u* ending is maintained after originally heavy stems, but not after originally light stems made heavy by WGG. In both cases, the stem invariably has a front vowel due to Umlaut. In other words, the original heavy–light distinction is preserved, as well as the Umlaut

(16) Survey of strong nominal classes – light and heavy roots

Class	*Weight*	SING.	PLUR.	*Gloss*
a- (m.)	*light*	dæg	dag-as	'day'
	heavy	stān	stān-as	'stone'
ja- (m.)	*light*	hyll	hyll-as	'hill'
	heavy	end-**e**	end-as	'end'
i- (m.)	*light*	byr-**e**	byr-as	'son'
	heavy	gylt	gylt-as	'guilt'
a- (n.)	*light*	hol	hol-**u**	'hole'
	heavy	word	word	'word'
ja- (n.)	*light*	bedd	bedd	'bed'
	heavy	gewǣd-**e**	gewǣd-**u**	'clothing'
i- (n.)	*light*	sper-**e**	sper-**u**	'spear'
	heavy	gecynd	gecynd-**u**	'nature'
ō- (f.)	*light*	tal-**u**	tal-e, -a	'tale'
	heavy	ār	ār-e, -a	'honor'
jō- (f.)	*light*	synn	synn-e, -a	'offense'
	heavy	sprēc	sprēc-e, -a	'speech'
i- (f.)	*light*	—	—	
	heavy	wyrd	wyrd-e, -a	'fate'
u- (m., f.)	*light*	sun-**u**	sun-a	'son'
	heavy	feld	feld-a	'field'

factor. In the other cases with variable endings, the ending *-e* or *-u* shows up after light stems, but not usually after heavy stems. If the *-u* is preserved after heavy stems the stem vowel is umlauted. Again, the original heavy–light distinction is maintained, as well as the source for Umlaut. Thus, there definitely is a relationship between the quality of the root vowel and the overt suffixes, which must have been obvious to the language learner. The morphological classes were clearly still – to a large extent – transparent to the learners of Old English. The singular has no overt suffix, while the plural suffix depends on gender and class: *-as* for the masculines, *-u* for the neuters, and *-e*, *-a* for the feminines. In addition, we assume the stem extensions *-j* and *-i*, which contrast, underlyingly as shown in (11b).

Of interest is that despite all the changes the underlying contrasts are still recoverable to the Old English learner. Indeed, the learner appears to be quite conservative. However, a number of other prosodic rules took place, which affected the recoverability to a great extent, which we will discuss next.

6.4.2 *Prosodic preferences and the pertinacity of the Germanic foot*

The Old English metrical structure, inherited from its Germanic ancestor, served as a template that influenced a number of further prosodic developments. In these developments we will observe the pertinacity of a basic metrical structure, even if its application to particular forms results in new output forms, due to novel interactions with new phonological processes.

The Old English metrical structure, discussed in section 6.2, is relevant for the phenomenon of Trisyllabic Shortening (TSS): in a three-syllable word, the vowel of the first stressed syllable is shortened. TSS was already present in Old English (Hogg 1992: §5.199–5.201). In the early stages, TSS applied when the long vowel was followed by two consonants or a geminate, that is, in closed syllables; later the process also affected long vowels before single consonants, that is, in open syllables (Luick 1914: §204, §353). This shortening occurred primarily in inflected forms, although there are also some early examples with derivational suffixes, as in *blīθe* – *blĭθeliche* 'happy', and in compounds: *hālig* 'holy' – *hăligdæg* 'holiday'. In disyllabic nouns TSS created a short vowel in trisyllabic plural forms where the nominative singular had a long vowel. The following examples illustrate the alternations:

(17) TSS in late Old English

Singular	*Plural*	
cīcen	cĭcenu	'chicken'
hēafod	hĕafodu	'head'
ǣnig	æ̆nige	'any'
clōver	clăvere	'clover'
hǣring	hæ̆ringas	'herring'

TSS changed the prosodic shape of a word of the form ([H] L) L to ([L L] L). Whereas the older form contained a foot plus a syllable, the newer form makes up a maximal foot.

Another rule that redistributed the syllables of a word within a foot was Open Syllable Lengthening (OSL), which became established in Early Middle English. OSL caused a stressed vowel to lengthen in an open syllable, and affected native words like *beofor* > *bēofor* 'beaver' as well as Latin loans such as *vāne* ([vɑ:nə], not **vǎne*). This rule primarily affected bisyllabic words; in trisyllabic words, TSS ensured that the stressed vowel would remain short. The effect of OSL was to convert a word of the form [L L] to [H L]; like TSS, this rule also resulted in a maximal foot.

We hypothesize that these changes are in keeping with a set of *prosodic preferences*, defaults that learners adhere to, or tendencies that exert a pressure in a certain direction. Lahiri and Dresher (1999) posit the following preferences:

(18) Prosodic preference scales and principles of interpretation
- a. Maximization of foot: (Hd Dep) >> (Hd)
- b. Incorporate unfooted syllables into feet
- c. Maximization of head:
([H]) >> ([L H]) >> ([L])
- d. Main stressed foot not less complex than secondary stressed feet

The notable preferences are to maximize the foot size (18a) and minimize the number of unfooted syllables (18b). However, as a result quantity alternations appeared in the nominal paradigms. Romance loans in Middle English were subject to the same preferences and hence show quantity alternations in morphologically related words, as shown in (19) (see Lahiri and Fikkert 1999).

(19) Prosodic preferences giving rise to quantity alternations

a.	([H] L) >> ([L L])	(OSL)	*vāne* rather than *vǎne*	(18a)
b.	([L L] L) >> ([H] L) L	(TSS)	*vǎnity* rather than *vānity*	(18b)

6.4.3 *Leveling in Middle English: the collapse of the quantity distinctions in nouns*

In the preceding sections we observed a series of prosodic changes that, while resulting in changes in surface forms, exhibited a certain conservatism, or pertinacity, in the grammar. But radical upheavals in the grammar also occur. In this section we will observe how the interaction of OSL and TSS caused the long-enduring underlying quantity distinction between light and heavy roots in nouns to finally become obscure to the point where it could no longer be maintained by language learners.

In early Old English there were no rules that created alternations of the quantity of root syllables in nominal paradigms. WGG had changed light syllables into heavy ones, but this rule tended to affect entire nominal paradigms.

Once OSL and TSS became established, however, quantity alternations within nominal paradigms were created. The nature of the alternation depended on the number of syllables in the root and inflectional suffixes. The expected quantity alternations of some representative noun classes are given in the table in (19); "expected" because, as the reader will immediately notice, the Present-day English (PDE) reflexes of these nouns do not display any quantity alternations. The reason for this is the subject of this section. "L" stands for long vowels, "S" for short ones.

(20) Predicted effects of OSL and TSS on Old English noun classes in Middle English

		Old English		*Expected ME vowel length*		*PDE vowel*
	Endings	*Singular*	*Plural*	*after OSL/TSS*	*Gloss*	*length*
a.	V – V	talu	tala	L – L	'tale'	L
b.	Ø – V	hwæl	hwalas	S – L	'whale'	L
c.	Ø – V	beofor	beoferas	L – S	'beaver'	L
d.	Ø – V	dēofol	dēofelas	L – S	'devil'	S
e.	Ø – V	hyll	hyllas	S – S	'hill'	S

The most straightforward classes are (20a), which are the OE *n*-class nouns and light *i*-, *u*-, *ō*-nouns, and (20e), which typically are the OE light *ja*- and *jō*-class nouns, in which the coda consonant was geminated after a short vowel (WGG). We expect OSL in both the singular and the plural for (20a), and no OSL in (20e). Thus, no alternations are expected in ME. Because the root vowels in (20a) were long throughout the paradigm, with no indication that they remained underlyingly short, learners would have learned them as long vowels. If we look at some of the Old English words with short root vowels in disyllables throughout the paradigm, they are almost all long vowels in Present-day English: OE *apa* 'ape', *blæse* 'blaze', *bracu* 'brake', *cwene* 'queen', *fola* 'foal', *nama* 'name', *nosu* 'nose', *slege* 'slay', *smoca* 'smoke', *snaca* 'snake', *stole* 'stole', etc. In contrast, words with geminates following short vowels are nowadays all short, as in Old English *bridd* 'bird', *cnyll* 'knoll', *dynn* 'din', *hrycg* 'ridge', etc.

The monosyllabic stems in (20b) descend from the *a*-nouns, which have a closed syllable in the singular and an open syllable in the plural. We expect OSL to apply only in the plural. Thus, the singulars should have emerged with short vowels and the plurals with long vowels. But such alternations do not exist in Modern English.

If we look systematically at this noun class, we find that these nouns have leveled in both directions. Lahiri and Dresher (1999) and Dresher (2000) report that in their collection of *a*-nouns 19 nouns have a short vowel in Modern English and 17 have a long vowel (cf. (21)), a proportion of 53 percent short to 47 percent long.

(21) Examples of OE monosyllabic *a*-stems with short vowels

a. *Short in PDE*: back, bath, black, brass, broth, chaff, glass, god, grass, lock, lot, path, sap, shot, staff, swath, thatch, vat, wer[wolf]

b. *Long in PDE*: bead, blade, coal, crate, dale, day, door, fare, gate, grave, hole, hope 'recess', meet, sole 'mud', way, whale, yoke

The data in (20c) represent Old English disyllabic stems with short stressed vowels in open syllables. Such nouns are disyllabic in uninflected forms, and trisyllabic when an inflectional suffix is added. According to Lahiri and Dresher, the first vowel in the disyllabic forms would have been lengthened by OSL, but the trisyllabic forms would have been subject to the overriding effects of TSS: expected ME *bēofər/beofərəs*. The pattern in (20d) represents Old English disyllabic nouns with an original long vowel. Such nouns would have been subject to TSS in the plural (expected ME *dēofəl/deofələs*) and should thus have become identical in vowel quantity to the disyllables with original short vowels in (20c).

Assuming that the hypothesized length alternations were subsequently leveled, the leveling should again go in both directions. The descendants of these nouns are indeed found as both long and short in Modern English, as shown in (22).

(22) OE disyllabic nouns (20c, 20d)

With short vowels in open syllables

a. *Long in PDE*: *bydel* 'beadle', *beofor* 'beaver', *cradol* 'cradle', *efen* 'even', *nacod* 'naked'

b. *Short in PDE*: *camel* 'camel', *canon* 'canon', *copor* 'copper', *fæder* 'father'

With long vowels in open syllables

a. *Long in PDE*: *bēacen* 'beacon', *bītel* 'beetle', *stȳpel* 'steeple', *tācn* 'token', *fēfor* 'fever'

b. *Short in PDE*: *brōθor* 'brother', *fōdor* 'fodder', *hǣring* 'herring', *wǣpen* 'weapon'

In sum, in the forms in (20a, 20e) quantity variation is neither expected nor attested in PDE. The cases in (20b–d) where we expected variation indeed show variation in PDE. These results are entirely consistent with our hypothesis of OSL and TSS followed by leveling. Reflexes of original short vowels are short in 58 percent of the words and long in 42 percent. Original long vowels come out 53 percent short and 47 per cent long. We therefore conclude that paradigmatic leveling of quantity plays an important role in the outcome of vowel length in English.

What can we say about the bidirectionality of the leveling? We know that at some point after OSL and TSS, the inflectional vowel was deleted. Then we would expect alternations such as: *nām* ~ *nāms*, *god* ~ *gōds*, and *bēver* ~ *bevers*. For *nām* ~ *nāms*, the vowel length is entirely consistent; but with the loss of the inflectional vowel in *god* ~ *gōds* and *bēver* ~ *bevers*, the motivation for the length alternation disappears.

Assuming no further adjustment of vowel length, the loss of the inflected vowel leaves the vowel length situation in a confused state. In some words, there is lengthening in the plural, but no change in syllable structure, while in other words the plural is associated with shortening. Some nouns have long vowels in both singular and plural, like *name*, and others are always short, like *bed(d)*. But in the majority of cases, the alternation has become phonologically incoherent. Even a morphological rule appears to be unavailable: we cannot, for example, associate length with any particular morphological category. In such circumstances, paradigm uniformity may step in. On this account, language learners choose a consistent vowel quantity. This may proceed on a word-by-word basis, in which case we might expect a fairly even split in outcomes.

In other words, once underlying contrasts are no longer recoverable, the situation is open to reanalysis by the learner. This happened in Middle English. Interestingly, although quantity alternations also appeared in derivationally related words, such as in *vain* – *vanity*, these have not been leveled out. However, these loans were not borrowed as derivationally related (Lahiri and Fikkert 1999). The "suffixed" trisyllabic words like *vanity* (1230) and *sanity* (1432) were borrowed as independent words and, in fact, often borrowed earlier than the adjectives *vain* (1300) and *sane* (1628). The fact that these words were borrowed according to the prosodic system of Middle English provides evidence that direction of parsing and placement of main stress had not changed in Middle English.

6.5 Changes in Stress: Middle English to Early Modern English

Although the changes sketched above had a dramatic effect on nominal paradigms, they had no effect on the position of main stress, and the stress system in Middle English remained essentially as in Old English. However, the various changes did have the effect of metrically "shortening" many words. Thus, words which in Old English had more than one foot were often reduced to a single foot in Middle English, as shown in (23).

(23) Metrical shortening from Old to Middle English

	a. *hḗringes	b. *lā́verke	c. *cī́cenes	d. *clā́vere
OE	(H)(H)(H)	(H)(HL)	(H L)(H)	(H L)L
CEM	(H) (HL)	—	(H L) L	—
TSS	([L H] L)	([L H]L)	([L L] L)	([LL]L)
ME	hĕringes	lăverke	cĭcenes	clăvere

Old English words already tended to be short. Moreover, many Old English suffixes were, as they still are today, "stress-neutral," meaning they do not participate in the stress domain. Adding the further metrical shortenings described above, native English words tended to be no longer than a single foot. Therefore, evidence for setting the parameters of directionality and main stress was in relatively short supply. Both Old English and Middle English had stress on the root-initial syllable, regardless of quantity. Feet were built iteratively from left to right, resulting in secondary-stressed feet in longer words, which, however, were becoming increasingly rare. Recall that final syllables did not have secondary stress, a fact we accounted for in the earlier period by defooting (3), and in the later period by consonant extrametricality (CEM) (4).

In Modern English stress is Latinate (Hayes 1995): stress falls on the penultimate syllable if heavy, otherwise on the antepenultimate syllable. Final syllables are extrametrical and stress is assigned from right to left. The old and new systems are sketched in (24).

(24) OE/ME to PDE stress shift
a. Stress in Old and Middle English: Left to right, main stress left
(i) (L L) (H L) (ii) (L H L) (iii) (L L L)
b. Stress in Modern English: Right to left, main stress right (and final syllable extrametricality)
(i) (L L) (H) <L> (ii) L (H) <L> (iii) (L L) <L>

Despite the changes in the stress system, all native Old English words have retained their output stress contours in Modern English, such as *wáter*, *hópefulness*, *begín*, even though the metrical structures that underlie them have changed. Contrary to Halle and Keyser (1971), who place the origins of the change in the time of Chaucer, Lahiri and Fikkert (1999), Fikkert (2003), and Dresher and Lahiri (2005) date the important innovations to a later time, due to the influence of Latin borrowings.

Among the Latin words that began entering the language in great numbers in the sixteenth century were many that were relatively long, that is, contained more than one foot. These Latin loan words were thus able to fill the gap left by the native words. Without contradicting the majority of the native words, the loan words eventually caused the resetting of the directionality and main stress parameters. Thus, borrowings can be decisive when the core native vocabulary cannot decide between grammars. We argued that Romance loans into Middle English were borrowed with the native prosodic preferences at the time of borrowing and did not come in with their foreign stress pattern. However, where the evidence for directionality and main stress is no longer clear from the native vocabulary, the learner may use the stress pattern of loan words to determine directionality and stress.

However, there is no evidence that either the Old French or the Latin stress *rule* gained a foothold in English at the time of Chaucer (see also Minkova 1997; Redford 2003). In other words, language users do not adopt a prosodic system of another language. But, large-scale borrowing did affect the language system as a whole, because the make-up of the vocabulary changed considerably.

The native vocabulary, which mainly consisted of words of the prosodic shape of one foot (see also Minkova, chapter 5, this volume), was extended with longer Latin words. These longer Latin words did not all enter the language at the same time nor with the same prosodic structure, as can be seen in (25). Early borrowings had the Old and Middle English leftward directionality, as shown in (25a, 25b), whereas in later borrowings directionality seems to have shifted rightwards (25c, 25d). The dates refer to the first occurrence according to the OED.

(25) Change in directionality
Early borrowings: Foot direction Leftward, Main stress Left

```
a. (x      .) (x  .)           b. (x     .)
   μμ   μ   μ   μ                 μ  μ  μ
   com pa ra ble (1413)           re si dence (1386)
```

Later borrowings: Foot direction Rightward, Main stress Left

```
c.  . (x     .)                d. (x     .)
   μ  μ   μ μ                     μ  μ  μ
   se ve ri ty (1530)             ra ri ty (1560)
```

Borrowing Latin words alone could not provoke the native speakers to change directionality. This change in direction came with the introduction of words with Latin suffixes such as *-ation, -ic(al), -ity, -ator, -able/-ible,* etc. In such forms, stress is computed from the right side. Compare the analyses of *cómparable* and *résidence,* borrowed when direction of parsing was still from the left, with those of *sevérity* and *rárity,* borrowed after the change in parsing direction. Notice that the change in direction is evident only in (25c) and not in the others (underlined consonants are extrametrical).

These long Latin loan data in early Modern English suggest that (i) the directionality of parsing changed from leftwards to rightwards, and (ii) that the main stress parameter did not immediately change together with the directionality parameter. Approximate dates of changes in metrical structure are given in (26), where the foot still is the Germanic resolved moraic trochee throughout:

(26) Sequence of changes in stress parameters
1400: Foot direction Leftward, Main stress Left (as in OE)
1530: Foot direction Rightward, Main stress Left.
1660: Foot direction Rightward, Main stress Right

Classical words were pronounced by native speakers in the English pronunciation, with alternating secondary stresses two syllables before the tonic (e.g. Latin *àcadémia;* see Danielsson 1948; Walker 1791/1831). When "Englished," the tonic and countertonic change places to conform to English "speech habits" (e.g. *ácadèmy*). Thus, a word like *ácadèmy* clearly shows two feet, of which the left has the main stress. Therefore, it is not correct to say that English gradually moved from a "Germanic" to a "Romance" stress system. In this case, the same words that provoked a change of directionality to the right reinforced the evidence for main stress left.

What exactly caused the main stress parameter to finally switch to the right is not entirely clear to us. However, a likely place to look is around or before 1660. According to Danielsson (1948: 29), that year was the "turning point" when French words kept final accent in English, as with suffixes like those in (27) below.

(27) Suffixes retaining main stress: *-eer, -ee, -ade, -esque, -ette, -oon* cannoneer (1562), grenadier (1676), payee (1758), parade (1656), arabesque (1611)

Though some words may have entered the language before 1660, they may not have systematically retained final stress until around that date. It is plausible to suppose that final stress in words with these suffixes became more systematic after the change of main stress to the right.

6.6 Conclusion

We have discussed the phonological and morphological system from Old English to early Modern English with reference to constraints on prosodic structure, the quantity of root syllables, foot structure, and prosodic preferences. In Old English, both the weight of root syllables and morphological class membership were still important factors in prosodic change. To the language learner these classifications clearly still were transparent to a large extent. In Middle English, morphological class membership became opaque due to the reduction of morphological endings. Moreover, the weight of root syllables became less transparent, due to the interaction of various phonological processes, such as TSS and OSL. In the face of such opacity the language learner could not reconstruct the old system and instead opted for paradigmatic leveling of quantity in the nominal paradigms. However, these reanalyses did not affect prosodic preferences, nor did the foot structure change.

Crucial evidence comes from loans, which are adapted by the adult native speaker, conforming to the prosodic system of the native language. The language learner is indeed quite conservative and will only change the system if (s)he is faced with more than one conflicting prosodic option. After metrical weakening reduced most native words to one foot, the prosodic system had no way of deciding on directionality for words that were longer. In this case, the non-native vocabulary played a decisive role for the language learner. Importantly, the loans were not adopted with the prosodic system of the donor language. Language learners are conservative and do not change the prosodic preferences, nor do they change underlying representations as long as they are still recoverable. Only if underlying representations are no longer recoverable – because of the interaction of phonological rules – will the learner resort to innovative strategies such as paradigm leveling, which can have dramatic consequences for both underlying representations and the grammar.

ACKNOWLEDGMENTS

Paula Fikkert would like to thank both KNAW and NWO for respectively funding the research projects "The development of prosodic systems of West Germanic: learnability and change" and "Changing lexical representations in the mental lexicon." Elan Dresher wants to acknowledge support from the Social Sciences and Humanities Research Council of Canada (SSHRCC). The research of Aditi Lahiri was partly supported by funds from the Deutsche Forschungsgemeinschaft (Sonderforschungsbereich 471 and the Leibniz Prize).

NOTES

1 We will not be concerned here with intonation and other aspects of speech rhythm, which are also commonly considered to be part of prosody.
2 The philological literature refers to noun stems and verb roots. A "stem-extension" was added to all Proto-Germanic nominal roots. Here, by stems we mean nominal roots plus their extensions. That is, the stem is the element to which gender/number/case suffixes are added.
3 Modern English still does not allow monosyllabic words with a non-branching rhyme (V), even though light syllables can occur in the language.
4 There are other morphological classes in Old English which we have not discussed for reasons of space. There is a *wa*-class as well as the weak declension, *n*-class, and the consonantal stems. These classes also follow the weight-sensitive processes.
5 The prefix *ge-* in *gewæd* and *gecynd* is unstressed. Stress falls on the root in nouns.
6 All forms mentioned in this chapter actually occur according to Bosworth and Toller (1898 [1921]).
7 There are no OE feminine *i*-nouns with light roots; the ancestors of such forms had all been reanalyzed into other classes.
8 The nominative singular has the long vowel: *cīcen*. In the plural there are three syllables because the *u* is retained; the word is then subject to trisyllabic shortening (TSS – see section 6.4).
9 Wright and Wright (1925: §392) suggest that *speriu* became *speru* by analogy to the light neuter *a*-nouns and the heavy neuter *i*-nouns. However, one condition for HVD was that the vowel to be deleted had an onset. In the case of *speriu* the *u* did not have an onset.

REFERENCES

Bosworth, Joseph and T. Northcote Toller (1898 [1921]). *An Anglo-Saxon Dictionary*. Oxford: Oxford University Press.

Campbell, Alistair (1959). *Old English Grammar*. Oxford: Clarendon Press.

Danielsson, Bror (1948). *Studies on the Accentuation of Polysyllabic Latin, Greek, and Romance Loan-Words in English. With special reference to those endings in -able, -ate, ator, -ible, -ic, -ical, and -ize.* Stockholm: Almquist and Wiksell.

Dresher, B. Elan (1985). *Old English and the Theory of Phonology.* PhD dissertation, University of Massachussetts. Appeared in Outstanding Dissertations in Linguistics. New York: Garland Publishing.

Dresher, B. Elan (2000). Analogical levelling of vowel length in West Germanic. In Aditi Lahiri (ed.), *Analogy, Levelling, Markedness: Principles of Change in Phonology and Morphology* (pp. 47–70). Berlin: Mouton.

Dresher, Elan and Aditi Lahiri (1991). The Germanic foot: metrical coherence in Old English. *Linguistic Inquiry* 22: 251–86.

Dresher, Elan and Aditi Lahiri (2005). Main stress left in Early Middle English. In Michael Fortescue, Eva Skafte Jensen, Jens Erik Mogensen, and Lene Schøsler (eds.), *Historical Linguistics 2003: Selected Papers from the 16th International Conference on Historical Linguistics, Copenhagen, 10–15 August 2003* (pp. 75–85). Amsterdam: John Benjamins.

Edgerton, Franklin (1934). Sievers' Law and IE weak-grade vocalism. *Language* 10: 235–65.

Edgerton, Franklin (1943). Indo-European semi-vowels. *Language* 19: 83–124.

Fikkert, Paula (2003). The prosodic structure of prefixed words in the history of West Germanic. In Paula Fikkert and Haike Jacobs (eds.), *Development in Prosodic systems.* Berlin: Mouton.

Halle, Moris and Samuel J. Keyser (1971). *English Stress: Its Form, Its Growth, and Its Role in Verse.* New York: Harper and Row.

Hayes, Bruce (1995). *Metrical Stress Theory: Principles and Case Studies.* Chicago: University of Chicago Press.

Hogg, Richard (1992). Phonology and morphology. In Richard Hogg (ed.), *The Cambridge History of the English Language.* Vol. 1: *The Beginnings to 1066* (pp. 67–164). Cambridge: Cambridge University Press.

Kaye, Jonathan (1974). Opacity and recoverability in phonology. *Canadian Journal of Linguistics* 19: 134–49.

Keyser, Samuel J. and Wayne O'Neil (1985). *Rule Generalization and Optionality in Language Change.* Dordrecht: Foris.

Kiparsky, Paul (1982). *Explanation in Phonology.* Dordrecht: Foris.

Kiparsky, Paul (1998). Sievers' Law as prosodic optimization. In Jay Jasanoff, H. Craig Melchert, and Lisi Oliver (eds.), *Mír Curad: Studies in Honor of Calvert Watkins.* Innsbruck: Innsbrucker Beiträge zur Sprachwissenschaft.

Kiparsky, Paul (1999). Analogy as optimization. In Aditi Lahiri (ed.), *Analogy, Levelling, Markedness: Principles of Change in Phonology and Morphology* (pp. 15–46). Berlin: Mouton.

Kiparsky, Paul (2000). Opacity and cyclicity. *The Linguistic Review* 17: 351–67.

Kiparsky, Paul (2002). *Paradigms and Opacity* (CSLI Lecture Notes). Chicago: Chicago University Press.

Lahiri, Aditi (1982). Theoretical Implications of Analogical Change: Evidence from Germanic Languages. PhD dissertation, Brown University.

Lahiri, Aditi (1999). Hierarchical restructuring in the creation of verbal morphology in Bengali and Germanic: evidence from phonology. In Aditi Lahiri (ed.), *Analogy, Levelling, Markedness: Principles of Change in Phonology and Morphology* (pp. 71–124). Berlin: Mouton.

Lahiri, Aditi (2002). Pertinacity in representation and change. Paper presented at the Workshop on Pertinacity, Schloss Freudental, July 10–14.

Lahiri, Aditi (2004). Phonological and morphological grammaticalisation and the prosodic word: phonological evidence for morphological decomposition in grammaticalisation. Ms., University of Konstanz.

Lahiri, Aditi and B. Elan Dresher (1999). Open syllable lengthening in West Germanic. *Language* 75: 678–719.

Lahiri, Aditi and Paula Fikkert (1999). Trisyllabic shortening: past and present. *English Language and Linguistics* 3.2: 229–67.

Luick, K. (1914 [1964]). *Historische Grammatik der Englischen Sprache. Erster Band, I Abteilung* (Fotomechanischer Nachdruck der ersten Auflage 1914). Oxford and Stuttgart: Bernhard Tauchnitz.

Minkova, D. (1997). Constraint ranking in Middle English stress-shifting. *English Language and Linguistics* 1: 135–75.

Redford, Michael (2003). Middle English stress doubles: new evidence from Chaucer's meter. In Paula Fikkert and Haike Jacobs (eds.), *Development in Prosodic Systems* (pp. 159–96). Berlin: Mouton.

Riad, Tomas (1992). *Structures in Germanic phonology: A Diachronic Study with Special Reference to the Nordic Languages*. PhD dissertation, Stockholm University.

Sievers, Eduard (1885). *An Old English Grammar* (tr. and ed. A. S. Cook, 1903). Boston, New York, Chicago, London: Ginn.

Walker, John (1791 [1831]). *A Critical Pronouncing Dictionary and Expositor of the English Language*. Edinburgh: Thomas Nelson and Peter Brown.

Wright, Joseph and Elizabeth M. Wright (1925). *Old English Grammar* (3rd ed.) Oxford: Oxford University Press.

7 Typological Changes in Derivational Morphology

DIETER KASTOVSKY

7.1 Introduction

In this chapter I will discuss some basic typological changes in English derivational morphology. The chapter will not be organized strictly chronologically, but according to levels at which important changes happened, e.g. the demarcation of inflectional and derivational morphology, the question of stem-based vs. word-based morphology, native and non-native word-formation, or the role of morphophonemic alternations.

7.1.1 Derivational and inflectional morphology

Morphology is conventionally subdivided into the two subdomains of inflectional and derivational morphology, which, however, in the older stages of the Indo-European (IE) languages cannot always be neatly separated from each other, whereas in the modern daughter languages the distinction is more clear-cut. The two domains interact with each other: the typological structure and status of inflectional morphology determines the typological properties of derivational morphology. Therefore, both domains will be taken into account here, even though the emphasis will be on the latter. In this connection it is useful to distinguish between the levels of "lexeme," "word-form," and "word" as proposed in Matthews (1974: 20ff.) and Lyons (1977: 18ff.). This distinction on the one hand provides a clear functional demarcation: derivational morphology (often also called word-formation; I will use the two terms interchangeably) deals with the creation of new lexemes (it should therefore actually be called "lexeme-formation"), and inflectional morphology deals with the derivation of word-forms from uninflected simple or complex bases. On the other hand, it is the basis for distinguishing between two types of morphology, that is, word-based and stem-based.

The output of word-formation processes are complex lexemes, which are analyzable on the basis of the meaning of their constituents and some underlying formal-semantic pattern shared by other parallel formations, i.e. they follow the general compositionality principle of language. This principle is counteracted by the diachronic phenomenon of lexicalization/idiomatization, through which complex lexemes may develop noncompositional meanings (e.g. *blackboards* are now usually green or white and not black), or their constituents have become semantically and formally obscured, e.g. OE *hūs-wīf* 'house-wife' > ME / Modern English *hussy*, or the word *cupboard*, pronounced /'kʌbəd/, which was originally a regular compound *cup-board* 'board for cups' pronounced /kʌp'bɔ:d/, but is now semantically opaque (*cupboards* don't often contain cups); the second constituent has lost its full pronunciation, being reduced to /bəd/ with concomitant simplification/assimilation of /pb/ to /b/.

In Modern English, derivational morphology and inflectional morphology seem to be neatly separated, but there is no consensus on the status of adverbs in *-ly*. Since the addition of *-ly* involves a change of word-class from adjective to adverb, and since word-class change is a typical feature of derivational morphology, adverb-formation tends to be regarded as derivational (cf. e.g. Francis 1958: 282; Huddleston and Pullum 2002: 1667–8); but Marchand (1969) did not include adverb-formation in his handbook, perhaps because he regarded it as grammatical rather than lexical, unlike Nevalainen (1999: 405–6). And in view of pairs such as *smoke heavily* ~ *heavy smoker*, *rise early* ~ *early riser*, where the alternation between adverb and adjective is context-dependent, adverb-formation might also be taken as an instance of inflectional morphology (cf. Hockett 1958: 211).

This ambivalence can be explained historically, because adverb-formation is the result of the grammaticalization of a derivational process. The suffix *-ly* goes back to OE *-lic*, which was an independent noun meaning 'body, form'. Thus, *-lic*-formations started out as nominal compounds, but then developed an adjectival function (probably via the status of *bahuvrihi*-formations of the type OE *ān-hyrne* 'having one horn' (cf. Kastovsky 2002a)). An OE formation *cildlic* was therefore structurally parallel to its Modern English equivalent *childlike*. From such adjectives adverbs could be formed by adding the suffix *-e*, e.g. *cildlice*. In Early Middle English this *-e* was lost, and the suffix *-ly* also adopted an adverbial function as in *slowly*, *royally*, besides continuing to act as an adjective-forming suffix, cf. *manly*, *princely*, etc. German and the Romance languages have undergone similar developments. Such grammaticalization processes obviously fudge the boundary between derivational and inflectional morphology.

7.1.2 Word-formation structures

The result of word-formation processes is usually a binary structure based on a determinant (dt) / determinatum (dm) (= head / modifier) relationship, i.e. it constitutes a syntagma (cf. Marchand 1969: 2ff.; Kastovsky 1999: 34f.).

7.1.2.1 Morphological structure

On the basis of the morphological status of the constituents dt and dm, word-formation is usually subdivided into two subcategories: (1) compounding (both constituents are actual or potential lexemes, as in *bird/cage, letter/writer, astro/naut, biblio/phile, color/blind, heart/breaking, home/sick*), and (2) affixation or derivation (a bound morpheme is added to a lexeme/stem), with the additional division into prefixation and suffixation.

A further possibility is so-called conversion or zero-derivation, by which a lexeme belonging to one word-class is "converted" to a member of a different word class, e.g. *bridge* sb. > *bridge* vb., *cheat* vb. > *cheat* sb., or *clean* adj. > *clean* vb., with a concomitant shift of meaning. The meaning difference matches the type of semantic contrast found with suffixation, cf. *cheat* vb. : *cheat* sb. = *write* vb. : *write/r* sb., *clean* adj. : *clean* vb. = *legal* adj. : *legal/ize* vb.; this parallelism is the basis for postulating a zero morpheme.

It is sometimes claimed that this type of word-formation is restricted to Modern English or is particularly characteristic of Modern English. This is incorrect, since it exists also in languages with a full-fledged inflectional system such as OE (cf. Kastovsky 1968, 1996), cf.

(1) a. *cum-an* 'to come' : *cum-Ø-a* 'one who comes, a guest'; *ġief-an* 'to give' : *ġief-Ø-u* 'what is given, gift'; *hunt-an* 'to hunt' : *hunt-Ø* 'hunting' : *hunt-Ø-a* 'hunter'
  b. *beorht* 'bright' : *beorht-Ø-ian* 'to make bright'; *ār* 'honor' : *ār-Ø-ian* 'to honor'; *munuc* 'monk' : *munuc-Ø-ian* 'to make into a monk'

Here, the endings are part of the inflectional system and thus do not have any derivational function. Formations such as *cuma, ġiefu, beorhtian* thus lack an overt derivational affix just as their Modern English counterparts do.

A further word-formation type is back-derivation, which has partly diachronic, partly synchronic relevance. In the diachronically relevant instances a phoneme sequence which resembles a suffix but isn't one is cut off from a monomorphemic lexeme, resulting in a new, phonetically shorter lexeme. The phenomenon is based on a reverse analogy in which derivationally related word-pairs have a similar phonological structure. Thus, just as children might derive a verb *to butch* from *butcher*, a verb *to peddle* 'act like a pedlar' is derived from monomorphemic *pedlar* by reverse analogy with pairs such as *rob* : *robber*. But since this direction of derivation (agent noun → verb) goes against the normal direction (verb → agent noun), the original direction of the derivation was eventually reversed analogous to the majority pattern. Further examples are *scavenge* (1644) : *scavenger* (1503); *edit* (1791) : *editor* (1712); *sculpt* (1864) : *sculptor* (1634) (the dates in parentheses give the first OED quotation).

These instances are back-derivations only from a diachronic point of view but have been reinterpreted as being based on the normal agent noun pattern V → N. A very productive synchronic Modern English pattern has a similar origin, namely *stage-manag/er* → *to stagemanage* 'act as stage manager'; *proof-read/ing* → *to proofread* 'do proofreading'; *new-creat/ed* → *to new-create* 'cause to become new-created'. Marchand (1969: 101ff.) calls these "pseudo-compound verbs," since they look like compounds. For historical reasons, these verbs are not naturally analyzable as 'manage the stage', 'read proofs', 'create newly'. English, like the other Germanic languages, had not developed verbal compounds as a derivational pattern. As indicated by standard dictionary definitions, the bases of these verbs are nominal or adjectival compounds, from which the verbs are back-derived by cutting off the suffix. But since these compounds contain a deverbal noun or adjective as their morphological determinatum, this truncation process leaves behind a verbal base, which can now act as a formal determinatum. This would also account for the morphological behavior of such formations, which adopt any irregularity features of the underlying verb, cf. the preterit *He proofread/typewrote the article*. This has developed into a productive pattern. Moreover, since the base is itself morphologically complex, truncation of the suffix is facilitated, because after truncation we are still left with an existing verb which may act as a formal determinatum. Perhaps the current productivity of this pattern in technical jargon is due to a reinterpretation of such verbs, especially since in the last decades they have multiplied. There seems to be an incipient tendency to analyze them no longer as back-derivations, but as genuine compound verbs, i.e. to interpret *to proofread* as 'to read proofs' rather than as 'to do proofreading'. Additional corroboration for this idea comes from the fact that an increasing number of such verbs come into being without an appropriate nominal basis. Thus, while *to chainsmoke* can be derived from *chainsmoker* or *chainsmoking*, no such basis exists for *to chaindrink*. Likewise, *to half-close, half-rise, consumer-test, handwásh, coldrínse, shortspín, warmíron*, etc., although the stress pattern in *coldrínse, warmíron* still suggests a nominal group origin. If this tendency continues, English may be in the process of developing a genuine compound-verb type, which would mean that it is undergoing a major typological change, developing a pattern where the first member of the compound is incorporated into the verbal construction. For the time being, however, the majority of speakers still seem to treat these formations as back-derivations rather than as compounds.

7.1.2.2 Functional structure

Cutting across this formal-morphological division of compounding and derivation is a functional one, which depends on the lexeme status of the determinatum.

In the Germanic languages, where we always have a dt/dm sequence, suffixes but not prefixes can change the word-class affiliation of the basis. This means that suffixes as determinata can iteratively transpose a free lexeme, a complex lexeme, or a syntactic word-group, which then act as a determinant, into another word-class, or at least into another semantic class, cf. *write* vb. > *writ/er* sb. (agent noun); *white* adj. > *whit/en* vb. (causative = 'cause to become white'); *pot* sb. (non-animate) > *pott/er* sb. (human, agent noun); *vicar* sb. (human) > *vicar/age* sb. (non-animate, place).

Prefixes cannot normally do this in the Germanic languages. They only modify a dm., which is always a lexeme, without changing word-class affiliation or appurtenance to a semantic class, cf. *write* vb. > *re/write* vb.; *fair* adj. > *un/fair* adj. There are some instances such as *befriend, delouse, disbar,* which have been taken to be exceptions to this rule (cf. Lieber 1981, 1983). But these can be interpreted as containing a zero-derived verb as determinatum, modified by the prefix (cf. Kastovsky 1986b).

On the other hand, prefixations share an important functional property with compounds: their rightmost member may substitute for the whole combination. Prefixed words thus satisfy the formula AB = B, which also holds for compounds, but not for suffixations, cf.:

(2) a. *A co-author is an author.*
    b. *A bird cage is a cage.*
    c. **A writer is an -er.*

This results in a subdivision of word-formation into "expansion" (compounding and prefixation), and "derivation" (= suffixation), cf. Marchand (1967: 323), although from a diachronic (or even synchronic) point of view, this division is far from neat, cf. the development of *-hood* (OE *hād*), *-dom* (OE *dōm*).

7.2 Morphological Typology

7.2.1 *Traditional parameters*

Let us now turn to the question of morphological typology, i.e. the factors that determine the typological shape or *gestalt* of a morphological system. Here we have to include inflectional morphology, since the typological status of derivational morphology depends on the structure of inflectional morphology. Furthermore, it is important to know whether inflectional and derivational morphology follow the same typological principles or not.

In the nineteenth century, typological studies in morphology, inspired by the work of Humboldt and Schlegel, and involving language types, classified languages as analytic, synthetic, agglutinating, inflecting, or incorporating. Such classifications are, however, very general, and partly overlap, since the criteria used intersect with each other. Thus the distinction between analytic and synthetic languages is based on the question as to where grammatical, i.e. mainly syntactic, functions are expressed, namely word-externally by particles or word-internally by morphological means. The former type would not have any, or hardly any, morphology (cf. e.g. Chinese, or, to a certain extent, Modern English), the latter would (cf. Latin or Old English).

The contrast involving the distinction between isolating, agglutinating, inflectional, and incorporating languages is based on how morphological and syntactic categories are expressed formally, and intersects with the previously discussed dimension. Thus, the isolating language type coincides with the analytical type, since neither has any morphology. The other three types are a subclassification of the synthetic type.

In agglutinative languages there is a one-to-one correspondence between morphological exponent and category and vice versa, that is, each morphological exponent expresses one and only one morphosemantic category, and each morphosemantic category has its own exponent. Typical examples are Hungarian or Turkish, but both English and German noun inflection also have developed agglutinative structures. Thus the categories of case and number are always expressed separately, if they are both marked overtly (which in many instances they are not, however, cf. Ø in the following examples):

(3)	E	*ox*	*en*	*s*	*child*	*ren*	*s*	*mice*	*s*	*boy*	*s*	*Ø*
			Pl	Gen		Pl	Gen	Pl	Gen		Pl	Gen

Here, the singular is always morphologically unmarked, whereas the plural is usually marked overtly (except if it is zero as in *fish-Ø*). Case is reduced to the genitive, which is normally expressed overtly in the singular. However, when the plural is expressed by its regular, phonologically determined sibilant allomorphs /z, ɪz, s/, the genitive is not marked overtly, i.e. it is zero, cf. *boys'*; but when it is represented by one of its irregular allomorphs such as *-en* or vowel alternation, the genitive is expressed overtly by one of its sibilant allomorphs, i.e. we get an agglutinative sequence: number + case.

In inflectional languages, one formal exponent usually represents more than one grammatical category. Examples are Old English forms like *cyning-as* (Nom. Pl.), *cyning-um* (Dat. Pl.), in which number and case are expressed jointly by one unanalyzable exponent.

Incorporating languages, finally, are characterized by very complex verbal structures, into which objects, adverbials, etc. are incorporated morphologically. Verbs like *chainsmoke, proofread, babysit, dryclean, joyride,* etc., discussed above, seem to suggest that English is in the process of developing one such morphological pattern.

7.2.2 *Additional parameters*

The distinction between isolating, agglutinative, inflectional, and incorporating languages is useful, but it only deals with aspects of inflectional morphology and thus characterizes only one part of what determines the overall *gestalt* of the morphology of a language. It does not tell us anything about the typological properties of derivational morphology and its interdependence with inflectional morphology. In order to characterize these two aspects, it is necessary to add further parameters which apply to both domains, which also play an important role in the historical development. These additional parameters are:

1 the morphological status of the input to the morphological processes (word, stem, or root);
2 the existence and status of morphological levels/strata (native vs. non-native);
3 the status and function of morphophonemic alternations;
4 the position of affixes.

7.2.2.1 Status of the base form

Of these parameters, the most important is the first, i.e. the status of the base form, on which inflectional and derivational processes operate. The base form of an inflectional paradigm can be defined as that formal representation of a lexeme, from which all other word-forms can be derived by appropriate processes, cf. *cat* → *cat-s, cat's*; *cheat* → *cheat-s, cheat-ed, cheat-ing,* where *cat* and *cheat* act as base forms. The base form can be a word, a stem, or a root, and accordingly one can distinguish between word-based, stem-based, or root-based morphology.

A word in this sense is basically a free form, and can occur in an utterance without additional material such as inflectional or derivational morphemes.

A stem is a bound, word-class-specific lexeme representation stripped of any inflectional endings, but potentially containing derivational affixes or stem-formatives, which determine the inflectional category of the lexeme in question, e.g. Lat. *coron-a-(-re)*, G *bind-(-en, -est,* etc.), E *scient-(-ist)* vs. *science, dramat-(-ic, -ist)* vs. *drama*. Stems always need additional morphological material in order to function as words.

A root is the element that is left over when all derivational, stem-forming, and inflectional elements are stripped away. Such roots can either be affiliated to a particular word-class, or they can be word-class-neutral. In the latter case the word-class affiliation is added by a word-formative process, cf. IE roots like **gVn* (as in Lat. *genus, gignere, cognatus*), **mVd-* 'measure' (cf. OE *metan*), **Vd-* 'eat' (cf. OE *etan*), **wVr-* 'turn' (cf. Lat. *uer-t-ere, uer-m(-is)*, OE *weor-þ-an, wyr-m,* etc.), with *V* standing for the ablaut vowel, cf., e.g., Kuryłowicz (1968: 200ff.), Szemerényi (1990: 102ff.). The distinction between root and stem is not always necessary; in Modern English the two categories coincide, but it is relevant in other languages such as Indo-European or the Semitic languages, whose morphology is based on abstract lexical entities that should be kept apart from the stems derived from them.

In word-based morphology, the categories of word and lexeme coincide, i.e. the lexeme can be represented by at least one word-form without any inflectional ending, which will usually act as base form, and can also function as a word. In stem-based morphology, no word-form of the paradigm occurs without an inflectional ending, i.e. the base form itself also contains an inflectional ending and must therefore be extracted from the paradigm. Thus it is not directly accessible, as in word-based morphology, but is an abstraction. Besides this aspect involving inflection, we also have to recognize stem-based morphology in those instances where the base does not occur without a derivational morpheme, as in *scient-ist, sol-ar, auto-crat.* In root-based morphology, roots usually have to be converted into stems before inflectional endings can be added. Very often, there is no clear-cut demarcation between derivation and inflection in this case, cf. Kastovsky (1996). Note that a language need not necessarily be homogeneous with regard to these types and that inflection and derivation might exhibit different properties.

7.2.2.2 *Lexical strata*

Thanks to language contact and massive borrowing, a language may develop lexical strata characterized by different properties. These are usually called "native" and "non-native" in view of their different etymological origins, but sometimes are just given descriptive labels such as Stratum or Level 1, Stratum or Level 2, as in lexical phonology (cf., e.g., Giegerich 1999), since it is their different morphological and phonological properties and not their historical origin which is important, cf. Marchand (1951: 92, 1969: 5f.).

7.2.2.3 *Morphophonemic alternations*

Morphophonemic alternations produce allomorphs. The triggering factors can be phonological or morphological, the alternation can be functional or non-functional, and the change itself can be described as a phonological process or as a purely allomorphic alternation (cf. Dressler 1985; Kastovsky 1989a, 1989b).

7.2.2.4 *Affix position*

Finally, languages differ with respect to the position of affixes. Beside prefixes or suffixes there may be infixes (e.g. *im-fucking-possible, abso-blooming-lutely;* L *fra-n-g-(ere) ~ frēgi ~ fractus*), or circumfixes, i.e. an affix consisting of a prefixal and a suffixal part as in G *ge-frag-t, Ge-schreib-sel* 'scribbling'.

7.3 Modern English

7.3.1 *Word-based versus stem-based*

I begin the descriptive part of this contribution with a sketch of the Modern English situation, starting with the distinction between word-based and stem-based morphology.

With regard to this parameter Modern English is heterogeneous in two respects. First, there is a difference between inflection and word-formation. Inflection is almost completely word-based. The only exceptions are some non-native plurals, which as loans from Latin or Greek have kept their stem-based status, cf.

(4) a. *cat*$_{\mathrm{N}}$ > *cat-s, cat-s'* (= *cat-s-Ø*); *cheat*$_{\mathrm{Vb}}$ > *cheat-s, cheat-ed, cheat-ing; long*$_{\mathrm{Adj}}$ > *long-er, long-est* (word-based)
b. *cact-us : cact-i* (vs. *cactus-es*); *hippopotam-us : hippopotam-i* (vs. *hippo-s*); *bacill-us : bacill-i; strat-um : strat-a; lacun-a : lacun-ae* (stem-based)

In word-formation, on the other hand, there is a dual system with fuzzy boundaries, namely word-formation on a native and word-formation on a non-native, usually Latin/Neo-Latin or French basis. Native word-formation patterns have the same properties as regular inflectional morphology, and are therefore always word-based; non-native word-formation is partly word-based, partly stem-based. Non-native derivational morphology exhibits properties not shared by the native patterns; this is a structural and not an etymological question, since originally non-native lexemes and patterns can be and have been nativized. Here are some examples of the various typical patterns:

(5) a. *help : help-er, help-ing; read : read-able; re-write; un-tie; in-come; house-door; atom bomb; sun ray* (native, word-based);
b. *Japán : Japanése; históric : historíc-ity; delímit : delìmit-átion* (non-native, word-based);[1]
c. *science : scient-ist; dráma : drámat-ist, dramát-ic; návig-ate : návig-able* (vs. *návigàtable*); *sol-ar; leg-ible; eléctr-ic : eléctr-ify, èlectr-íc-ity, elèctr-ific-átion* (non-native, stem-based);
d. *astro-nomy, astro-botany; cosmo-logy, cosmo-naut, cosmo-graphy, cosmo-biology; tele-gram, tele-pathy* (non-native stem-based compounds involving so-called "combining forms").

7.3.2 *Native versus non-native*

The existence of two lexical strata, a native and a non-native one, is also reflected by the kind, frequency, distribution, conditioning, and functioning of morphophonemic alternations.

Two extreme possibilities are conceivable, with a transitional area in between. Either the morphemes of a language are basically invariable, or at best subject to very superficial phonological alternations with phonological conditioning, or they are basically variable, i.e. there is widespread morphophonemic alternation with phonological and/or morphological conditioning. Modern English is basically invariable, with one exception, namely word-formation on a non-native basis. This involves morphophonemic or allomorphic alternations, that is, this feature, together with the stem-based status of many of the formations distinguishes word-formation on a non-native basis from word-formation on a native basis.

Morphophonemic/allomorphic alternations constitute a scale with purely automatic, allophonic alternations such as *kill* [kɪɫ] ~ *killing* [kɪlɪŋ] (dark vs. clear /l/ in some varieties such as Southern British English, but not in others, which have one realization of /l/ only) at the one end and suppletion like *sun ~ solar, mouth ~ oral*, at the other. In between, we might recognize as further prototypical instances phonemic alternations with phonological or morphological conditioning, and allomorphic alternations, which are typically morphologically conditioned (cf. Dressler 1985).

There is again a significant distinction between inflection and derivation in this respect. In inflection, there is a division that coincides with the distinction between regular and irregular nouns, verbs, and adjectives. Regular inflection is base-form-invariant except for some subphonemic processes, but it allows morphophonemic alternations of the inflectional morphemes, cf. /z ~ ɪz ~ s; d ~ ɪd ~ t/, which are fully predictable on the basis of phonologically conditioned vowel insertion and voice assimilation triggered by the base-final phoneme.

Irregular inflection is characterized by morphologically conditioned alternations of both bases and affixes, and may be either morphophonological or strictly allomorphic:

(6) a. irregular, morphologically conditioned affix allomorphy: *fish, trout, grouse, deer* (= Ø); *ox-en, childr-en* (= *-en*); *burnt, spoilt, built, sent* (/t/);
b. base alternation (non-functional): *child ~ child-r-en, brother ~ brethr-en; keep ~ kept, lean ~ leant, deal ~ dealt, lose ~ lost; shelf ~ shelves, house ~ houses* (/s/ ~ /z/);
c. base alternation (functional = morpheme representation (replacive)): *mouse ~ mice, foot ~ feet, sing ~ sang ~ sung, write ~ wrote ~ written, choose ~ chose ~ chosen.*

In word-formation, there is a distinction between native and non-native patterns. Native word-formation has the same properties as regular inflection, i.e. it is base-form-invariant, with phonologically conditioned alternations of suffixes, cf. *white-haired* vs. *bearded* (/d/ ~ /ɪd/). Whatever there is in the way of base-form alternations, are relics of older alternating types, e.g. the voicing involved in *north* /θ/ ~ *northern* /ð/ (as against *earth ~ earthen* without voice alternation), *shelf ~ to shelve, glass ~ glazier*, etc.

Non-native word-formation is typically characterized by both suprasegmental and segmental alternations. The two are usually interdependent, i.e. segmental alternations are often, though not always, the consequence of stress alternations with concomitant reduction of the originally stressed vowel to schwa, cf. *Japán* /dʒə'pæn/ ~ *Japanèse* /dʒæpə'ni:z/, *hístory* /'hɪstəri/ ~ *historic* /hɪs'tOrɪk/, etc. The suprasegmental alternations involve the position of the main stress, which is triggered by the suffix. There are two possibilities. Either the suffix is stressed itself, as in *refugée, profitéer, admirátion, Japanése*, or it is stress-determining, as in *hístory ~ históric ~ hìstorícity*. Stress placement is more variable than usually assumed (cf., e.g., *ádmirable ~ admírable, lámentable ~ laméntable, télevision ~ televísion*, etc.). It involves the continued rivalry between the old left-to-right Germanic principle and the new Romance right-to-left weight-based principle existing since Middle English, as shown by Dalton-Puffer (2002), cf. also Lass (forthcoming). There is considerable room for further work here. Such stress alternations automatically entail the segmental alternation of vowels, which is rather similar to the Indo-European ablaut alternation between full, reduced, and zero grade stems, which was also triggered by stress position.

Beside the stress-conditioned segmental alternations, there are also purely morphologically conditioned segmental alternations such as trisyllabic laxing (*sane : sanity* (/eɪ/ ~ /æ/)), which is probably unproductive (cf. Minkova and Stockwell 1998), or velar softening (*historic ~ historicity* (/k/ ~ /s/), *didactic ~ didactician* (/k/ ~ /ʃ/)).

Furthermore, non-native prefixes can be subject to morphophonemic alternation, cf. *a-* as in *atonal* vs. *anelectric, in-* in *intolerant*, as against *illegible, incongruous, impossible, irreplaceable.*

7.3.3 *Affix position*

Inflection is basically affixal, except for irregular cases, which might involve zero (e.g. *fish, cut*) or vowel alternations of the type *sing : sang : sung; mouse : mice* and which might be regarded as a subtype of an infix. The combination of vowel alternation with affixal representation results in a discontinuous morpheme representation as in *write ~ writt-en, choose ~ chos-en.*

In word-formation, we find both prefixation (*un-true, im-possible, dis-en-tangle, pre-cook*) and suffixation (*writ-er, hair-less, disestablish-ment-arian-ism*) as well as zero-derivation (*walk*$_{V}$ > *walk-Ø*$_{N}$, *cook*$_{V}$ > *cook-Ø*$_{N}$; *bottle*$_{N}$ > *bottle-Ø*$_{V}$, *father*$_{N}$ > *father-Ø*$_{V}$; *clean*$_{Adj}$ > *clean-Ø*$_{V}$), while infixation is restricted to expletives as in *abso-blooming-lutely, im-fucking-possible* (the treatment of these expletives as infixes is not unproblematic, since they constitute free lexical items). Some formations, such as *demilitarize, delouse,* might be interpreted as circumfixation, i.e. as a discontinuous representation of the derivational marker with the structure *de-militar-ize, de-louse-Ø,* where the prefix and the suffix operate together (cf. Marchand 1969: 136; Kastovsky 1986b).

Finally, English word-formations always have the sequence modifier/head, with the exception of the French loan pattern of *Secretary-General, letters patent* (due to borrowing from French in Middle English), which preserves the head/modifier sequence of the source language, but is unproductive.

7.4 The Historical Perspective

7.4.1 *Introduction*

In the following approach to the historical perspective on the changes responsible for the morphological shape of English today, I will take the various parameters proposed above one by one and investigate their diachronic development as well as their interaction in the typological changes under discussion. This approach, rather than the usual treatment discussing changes in historical order, has the advantage of highlighting the intricate mechanisms at work in the transformation of the morphological system under investigation. Moreover, it allows a close look at the interaction of the various factors and levels at work in the restructuring of morphology. To use a metaphor, it is like following the various intertwining threads in a tapestry until one finally ends up with a glimpse of what these intertwining threads produce: a representation of a major pattern, a tapestry from a synchronic point of view, which still lets us recognize its genesis. In this sense, synchrony and diachrony are not treated as totally separate, but as interacting, panchronic phenomena.

7.4.2 *Status of the base form*

I will begin with a look at the type of input into morphology, because this is where we observe the most important typological changes due to changes in the system of inflectional morphology. This parameter requires considerable historical depth, as the structure of Old English derivational morphology cannot be understood without some knowledge of its Indo-European and Germanic antecedents, with relics of root-based morphology especially in the domain of ablaut formations.

Indo-European morphology was root-based, the root usually being represented as a consonantal skeleton, and the vowel being supplied by ablaut alternations. This consonantal skeleton could be followed by so-called root-determinatives, which probably had some kind of derivational or word-class-specifying function. For our purposes, we can treat these root-determinatives as integral parts of the IE roots. The actual nominal, adjectival, or verbal paradigms are derived by first adding stem-formatives and then inflectional endings proper, that is, the basic structure of IE morphology is

(7) root (+ root determinative) + stem-formative + inflection proper (± secondary stem-formative elements)

Since word-class-specific properties were added to the roots by the various morphological processes which derived word-class-specific stems, there was an ambivalence of the stem-formatives between having a derivational and an inflectional function.

The addition of stem formatives and of the appropriate endings produces primary nouns and primary verbs. Therefore, at this stage there is no direct derivational connection between verb and derived noun or noun and derived verb; both are only related via their common root, i.e. there is no directional verb > noun or noun > verb derivation. This relationship is the origin of the Germanic (and Old English) strong verbs and ablaut nouns or adjectives related to them. From these primary derivatives further, secondary derivations could be formed by adding further derivational and stem-forming affixes, i.e. by directional derivation, resulting in the following complex morphological system:

(8)

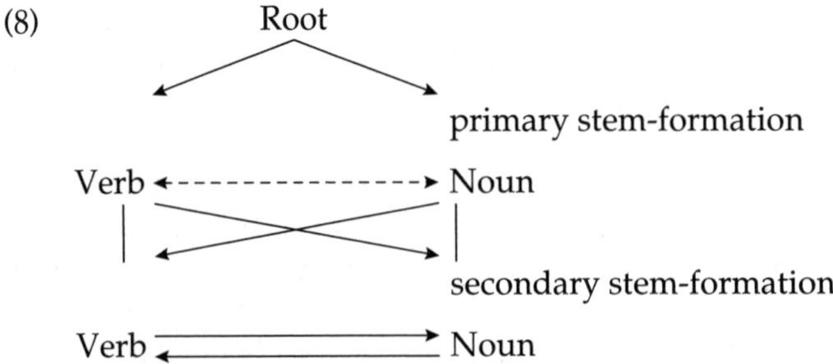

The Indo-European verb system was characterized by a mixture of aspectual and temporal categories such as Present, Imperfect, Perfect, Aorist, etc., and mode of action categories such as iterative, intensive, durative, inchoative, etc. In Modern English or German these categories are neatly separated as either belonging to inflection (Tense, Aspect) or derivation (mode of action/*aktionsart*). In Indo-European, however, apparently no such separation was possible, cf., e.g., Watkins (1969: 19). It is therefore a moot point to ask whether these present, perfect or aorist stems were separate words or word-forms, since they were ultimately related to one and the same root. Clearly, they served a dual function if looked at from our modern perspective, where aspects and modes of action are separate grammatical and lexical categories, respectively.

Primary root-based verbs normally accepted quite a variety of stem-formatives, which resulted in the whole gamut of aspectual/temporal categories. But secondary verbs usually occurred in one category only, namely in the present. These secondary verbs are the ancestors of our modern "weak" verbs (for details, cf. Kastovsky 1996: 111–12). According to Bammesberger (1986: 36ff.), these verbs had originally the meaning 'perform an action', 'act like an agent', etc., the action or agent being represented by a root-based action or agent noun, i.e. they are similar to Mod E *to curtsy, to sabotage, to author, to doctor*, which are derived from primary action or agent nouns. The verbal stem-formatives allowed the derivation of an imperfectivum, but not of a perfect or aorist. This explains the development of new preterite forms in the Germanic languages (the "dental preterite") in connection with the shift from an aspectual to a tense-oriented system, which was one of the innovations of Germanic. The stem-formative thus originally combined the function of a derivative morpheme with that of creating an inflectional stem. This legacy of Indo-European morphology was lost in connection with the erosion of final syllables and the concomitant restructuring of the morphology toward a stem-based system during the evolution of the Germanic language family.

The situation with nouns is similar, that is, they have the same morphological structure as the verbs. The stem-formatives thus also function both as derivational suffixes and as inflectional class markers characterizing the nouns as members of a particular inflectional class, e.g. *-o*-stems, *-ō*-stems, *-i*-stems, *-n*-stems, etc.

7.4.2.1 Historical background

The evolution of the Germanic language family is characterized by a profound transformation of its phonological and morphological systems. Indo-European had been characterized by movable stress, which influenced the quality and quantity of the root vowel and was responsible for the ablaut alternations. In Germanic, stress came to be fixed on the first syllable, which rendered ablaut alternations unpredictable. This, and the increase of secondary derived verbs and nouns (implying directional non-root-based derivation), led to a gradual shift from root-based to stem-based morphology with the establishment of a base form (stem) from which the other morphological forms could be derived.

The stress shift eventually led to a weakening and ultimate loss of medial and final unstressed syllables, which in turn resulted in a growing loss of morphological contrasts. This development ultimately establishes word-based morphology in Old and Middle English, cf. the following examples.

The weak verbs were originally derived from nouns, adjectives, or verbs, i.e. they were characterized by stem-formatives which had the dual function of a derivational element and an inflectional marker, assigning the resulting form to a specific inflectional class. For Germanic, four different stem-formatives have been postulated as the basis of four classes of weak verbs, which are still fairly transparent in Gothic, cf.

(9) class 1: *-j-/-i-* (Goth. *satjan*, OE *settan*), class 2: *-ōi-/-ō-* (Goth. *salbôn*, OE *sealfian*), class 3: *-ē(j)-* (Goth. *haban*, OE *habban*), class 4: *-nō-* (Goth. *fullnan*, OE *beorhtnian*).

Of these, only classes 1 and 2 are relevant here. The forms reconstructed for fifth-century pre-Old English in Hogg (1992: 157) and Kastovsky (1996: 104f.) still allow a segmentation of the underlying stem-formatives, cf. class 1 inf. **trum+j+(an+az)* 'to strengthen', 1st pers. pres. **trum+j+(u)*, 1st, 3rd pers. pret. **trum+i+(d+æ)*; class 2 inf. **luf+ōj+(an+az)*, 'to love', 1st pers. pres. **luf+ōj+(u)*, 1st, 3rd pers. pret. **luf+ō+(d+a)*.

In the paradigms of Early and Late West Saxon, the stem extensions are no longer genuinely segmentable, however, because they have either fused with the person/number endings, or they syncopated according to Sievers' Law, leaving a trace in class 1 in the form of *i*-umlaut of the stem where possible, cf. the following partially segmented paradigms:

(10)					
	trymman (< *trum*)		*lufian* (< *luf+u*)		inf.
	trymme	*trymede*	*lufie*	*lufode*	1st pers. sg. pres./pret.
	trymest	*trymedest*	*lufast*	*lufodest*	2nd pers. sg. pres./pret.
	trymeð	*trymede*	*lufað*	*lufode*	3rd pers. sg. pres./pret.
	trymmað	*trymedon*	*lufiað*	*lufodon*	plural pres./pret.
	Class 1		Class 2		

At this stage a morphological reanalysis must have taken place. In the present, any morphological analysis without historical bias would certainly result in a structure consisting of a stem + person/number, infinitive or participle marker along the following lines: *trymm+an, trymm+e, trym+að*; *luf+ian, luf+ie, luf+iað*. This means that the stem-formative had been lost, which of course had morphological consequences, because its derivational function could not simply have disappeared, since most of these verbs must still have been analyzed as synchronically derived from adjectives or nouns. Now that this derivational relationship no longer had a formal marker, it had been replaced by zero (cf. Kastovsky 1980, 1996). Note that this seemingly innocuous reanalysis had a much more far-reaching consequence of replacing the original functional duality of the stem extension (derivational morpheme and inflectional class marker) by a new systematic formal/functional separation of inflection and derivation. The inflectional class became an inherent feature of the stem and was no longer necessarily predictable on the basis of its form. The derivational function, on the other hand, must now be attributed to a zero element commutable with other derivational suffixes, although these were an absolute minority in Old English, as in many other Indo-European languages. This was a major morphological reorientation and consolidated stem-based morphology.

The same reanalysis also happened in the preterit and past participle forms. The original stem extensions preceding the preterit/past participle morpheme /d/ (in Old English /e/ and /o/), came to be reinterpreted as part of the preterit and past participle morphemes. This process was certainly gradual and there must have been a transition period of morphological indeterminacy. But by the end of the ninth century, if not even earlier, the change *trym+e+d+e* > *trym+ed+e*, *luf+o+d+e* > *luf+od+e* had been completed. When finally /e/ and /o/ merged into schwa, this reanalysis was also complete at the morphophonological level, since inflectional class was now determined by the presence vs. absence of a vowel in the preterite/past participle morphemes rather than the quality of the preceding vowel (cf. Kastovsky 1998: 142), resulting in a realignment of inflectional classes. Thus, this development led to a strict separation of inflection and derivation, which is still the characteristic feature of Modern English. The few Old English verbal suffixes (*-ett(an)*, *-lǣċ(an)*, *-n(ian)*, *-s(ian)*) died out, with the exception of *-n(ian)* as in *fasten*, *redden*, etc. The Modern English suffixes *-ate*, *-ify*, *-ize* are predominantly restricted to non-native bases, so that Modern English verbal derivation is primarily affixless. Nevertheless, in Old English, verbal inflection, and with it deverbal derivation, remained stem-based, because the verbs maintained a full-fledged inflectional paradigm. This only changed at the end of the Old English period, when in the North the infinitive gradually lost its ending, turning into an uninflected base form and thus introducing word-based inflection and derivation into the verbal domain.

With nouns, the development is similar, although somewhat more advanced than with verbs. In Germanic the original stem-formatives had begun to merge with the case/number exponents, losing their class-marking function. Taking masculine *a*-stems and comparing forms such as **dagaz* (Nom. Sg.), **dages* (Gen. Sg.), **dage:* (Dat. Sg.), **dago:s* (Nom. Pl.), consistent representation of the original stem-formative is a thing of the past, and the forms have to be analyzed simply as stem **dag-* + case/number endings *-az*, *-es*, *-e:*, *-o:s*. Similar analyses can be postulated for the other inflectional classes. Clearly, this implies a shift from root-based to stem-based inflection and the loss of the stem-formatives as morphologically relevant. But, all inflected forms are still overtly marked for case and number, i.e. we have stem-based morphology both in inflection and denominal derivation. The same also holds for adjectives.

The next stage is the loss of the nominative/accusative singular endings with the strong masculines and the neuters. This introduces inflectionless forms into some of the nominal (and adjectival) paradigms. Since the nominative is usually regarded as the semantically most neutral case, these uninflected forms can also be interpreted as unmarked base forms, in which case we can now speak of word-based inflection and derivation. But since in Old English, we find endingless nominatives like *cyning, dæġ, stān* beside nominatives like *luf-u, end-e, gum-a,* the inflectional and derivational system is partly word-based, e.g. *dag-ian* 'to dawn', partly stem-based, e.g., *luf-ian, end-ian.* But the word-based type was numerically dominant (with over 50 percent of the nouns) and therefore prompted a reinterpretation of other paradigms. This is certainly the case with *i*-stems of the type *ende, here,* which on the whole had the same inflectional endings as the *a*-stems. Here *-e* must have been reinterpreted as part of the stem too, losing its inflectional function. And when in late Old English and early Middle English, final vowels were reduced to schwa, this schwa must have been reinterpreted as part of the base (i.e. *luf-u* > *luf-e* > *lufe; gum-a* > *gum-e* > *gume*) by analogy. This rendered both nominal inflection and denominal derivation word-based throughout. In all likelihood, this typological shift affected the development of the verbs as well, since the loss of the infinitive ending *-an* > *-en* > *-e* cannot be attributed solely to phonetic erosion. It is therefore likely that some typological "pressure" was at work transforming the whole morphological system into word-based morphology. This state of affairs was reached in the Middle English period and still characterizes Modern English inflection and derivation on a native basis.

7.4.2.2 Borrowing

This development was basically governed by language-internal factors, primarily by the impact of phonology on morphology (weakening of unstressed syllables due to prosodic factors). But once a certain amount of morphological material had been lost, and unmarked base forms emerged, this development apparently gained momentum, until the emerging word-based typological pattern was generalized in Late Middle English. The process was further promoted by language contact and increased borrowing. The first stage was borrowing from French after the Norman invasion. This borrowing became a flood in Early Modern English and continued into Modern English, especially in scientific terminology. French and Latin both have stem-based morphology, and once their derivational patterns became established, stem-based morphology became part of English derivational morphology once more.

Thus, with French *-able,* borrowed in early Middle English, we find word-based *allow-able, understand-able, believ-able* beside stem-based *charit-able, navig-able* (besides *navigat-able*), *cultiv-able* (besides *cultivat-able*). The alternation *-ate* ~ *-acy* as in *pirate* ~ *pira-cy, obstinate* ~ *obstina-cy* is also of French origin and was adopted in Middle English, similarly *-ant* ~ *-ancy* in *sergeant* ~ *sergean-cy, innocent* ~ *innocen-cy.* For the latter, it is not quite clear whether such instances should be handled in terms of stem-based derivation, or just as a morphologically conditioned morphophonemic alternation involving /t ~ s/ with /t/ characterizing the derivational base, in which case the derivation would be word-based; this would then be parallel to *histor-ic* ~ *historic-ity*, etc. The same duality exists with suffixes adopted from Latin in Late Middle and Early Modern English. Thus *-al* operates both on a word-based (e.g. *accident-al, post-al, tid-al*) and a stem-based principle (e.g. *horizont-al, societ-al, matern-al, terrestr-ial*), also *-ic* (*chlor-ic, Iceland-ic* vs. *dramat-ic, geolog-ic, lunat-ic*), and many others. For a detailed survey the reader is referred to Marchand (1969: 209–355).

Both the development of these stem-based formations and the competition between stem-based and word-based derivation with one and the same suffix in the earlier stages as well as in Modern English are still in need of a more thorough investigation, aided by the electronic corpora now available.

7.5 Native versus Non-native Word-formation

With these remarks we have entered the domain of the existence and status of morphological strata, namely native vs. non-native.

Old English was characterized by a homogeneous lexicon from this point of view, and consequently also by a homogeneous morphology and phonology. Only about 3 percent of the lexical items recorded were non-native (usually loans from Latin), but they had all been completely integrated into the phonological and morphological system of the language. This continued until the late eleventh century and the most frequent means of expanding the lexicon was by derivation (often in the form of loan-translations) or semantic transfer (cf. Kastovsky 1992a: 355–400). It was only in the wake of the Benedictine Reform that loans from Latin increased considerably (often as technical ecclesiastic terms); these were no longer phonologically and morphologically integrated and were easily recognizable as loans. Most of them belonged to the written language and therefore did not yet materially change the structure of the vocabulary, nor did they introduce non-native derivational patterns. This started with the impact of French in Middle English, and increased even more with the large-scale borrowing from Latin in Late Middle English and especially in Early Modern English, which transformed the once homogeneous vocabulary into the dual-stratum system that we have today. It is estimated that about 80 percent of the Modern English vocabulary (derivatives included) is of non-native, predominantly Romance or Latin/Greek origin. One of the consequences of this development was the introduction of stem-based derivational morphology, the other, dealt with in section 7.6 below, was the rise of new morphophonemic and allomorphic alternations in the derivational system.

In this connection, it is of interest how these non-native derivational patterns came into being, and especially how and when they became productive in English and what impact they had on the derivational system in general. Obviously, borrowing began with individual lexical items, some of which had already been derivationally related in the donor language. Thus, once a certain number of such derivationally related pairs had been borrowed, a derivational, i.e.

formal-semantic relationship could also be established in English. On this basis, the pattern could be extended to new formations which had no parallel in the source language, probably first by individual analogical formations, until the pattern finally became productive (cf. Kastovsky 1986a). This emergence of productive patterns is of particular interest here.

Traditionally, it has been assumed that non-native, especially French patterns had become productive fairly early. However, in a pioneering, corpus-based study dealing with nominal derivation, Dalton-Puffer (1996) argues that the Romance suffixes had not really become productive in Middle English. Hybrid formations of a Germanic base and a Romance affix, such as *spekable, knowable, bondage, aldermanrie, outlawery, hunteresse,* might be indicative of productivity beginning, but may be due to direct analogy; only with *-able* "we must indeed be observing a budding derivational rule for deverbal adjectives" (Dalton-Puffer 1996: 221). Thus, the real productivity of Romance and Latin derivational patterns would seem to have started during the Early Modern English period, when a certain critical mass of borrowings and analogical formations had accumulated to get the derivational processes going (cf. also Nevalainen 1999: 378ff.). Dalton-Puffer may well be right in this respect, but further work on a larger and more representative corpus is needed. This seems especially true if we consider the following list of prefixes and suffixes, which according to Marchand (1969) have their roots in Middle English loans, but the stage at which they became productive has not been established: *dis-* (*displease, disfigure,* fourteenth century), *en-* (*embow, encrown,* fifteenth century), *in-* (*incomprehensible, infinite,* fourteenth and fifteenth centuries), *inter-* (*interchange, interspace,* fourteenth and fifteenth centuries), *non-* (*non-age, non-payment,* fourteenth century), *re-* (*re-enter, re-establish,* fifteenth centuries); *-able* (*understandable, unknowable,* fourteenth centuries), *-acy* ~ *-ate* (*prelacy, obstinacy,* fourteenth century), *-age* (*baronage, parsonage,* fourteenth century), *-al* (*arrival, supposal,* fourteenth century), *-al* (*poetical, textual,* fourteenth century), *-ance/-ence* (*acceptance, accordance,* fourteenth century), *-ancy/-ency* ~ *-ant/-ent* (*sergeancy, innocency,* fourteenth century), *-ant/-ent* (*defendant, inhabitant,* fifteenth century), *-ation* (*edification, justification,* fourteenth and fifteenth centuries), *-ee* (*assignee, grantee,* fifteenth century), *-ery* (*robbery, sophistry*; fourteenth century), *-ess* (*adulteress, huntress,* fourteenth and fifteenth centuries), *-ic* (*Arabic, choleric,* fourteenth century), *-ician* (*physician, musician,* thirteenth and fourteenth centuries), *-ify* (*amplify, verify,* fourteenth and fifteenth centuries), *-ity* (*ability, diversity,* fourteenth and fifteenth centuries), *-ive* (*affirmative, expressive,* fourteenth century), *-ise* (*canonise, moralise,* fourteenth century), *-ment* (*achievement, advancement, increasement,* fourteenth century), *-ous* (*poisonous, villainous,* fourteenth century). This area is still in need of more detailed empirical investigation using the growing set of text-type-specific corpora, which should provide a deeper insight into the way in which these patterns were gradually implemented in the various registers until they finally "exploded" in the Early Modern English period.

Many of the Old English compound patterns continued, but a few new ones emerged as well. Thus, as of about 1300, sex-denoting compounds of the type *he-lamb, she-ass* begin to appear, and in the fourteenth century we find the first instances of the type *Tom Fool, tomcat.* Also in the early fourteenth century the exocentric compound pattern *spillbread, cutpurse, pinchpenny, pickpocket*, etc. makes its appearance, possibly influenced by the French pattern *coupe-gorge, tire-bouchon.* But since German has a similar pattern with names, cf. *Fürchtegott, Habedank*, etc., the origin might be native spoken language, from where it was introduced into written language under French influence.

Most of the Old English verbal prefixes had disappeared in Middle English, having already been very weak and semantically non-transparent in Old English. This paved the way for the large-scale adoption of the Romance and Latin prefixes in Late Middle and Early Modern English (cf. the above list), which filled a number of semantic gaps such as ablative verbs of the type *dislodge* (1450), *displace* (1551), which had no Old English counterpart and which may have caused the extension of privative *un-* as in *unsaddle* 'remove the saddle' to ablative *un-* as in *unsaddle* 'remove the rider from the saddle' (cf. Kastovsky 2002b: 106ff.; Nevalainen 1999: 378ff.).

It was the Early Modern English period during which the non-native word-formation patterns finally gained a real foothold in English and began to seriously compete with the native patterns, cf. Nevalainen (1999: 378ff.). This is in line with the general explosion of the size of the vocabulary thanks to nearly unconstrained borrowing (cf. the Inkhorn controversy), which in turn provided many more analyzable examples on the basis of which new formations could be produced that had no counterpart in the source languages. As a result, the patterns mentioned in section 7.5.2. above were strengthened, and if they had not already been productive on a limited scale, they now finally became productive, with a few more affixes added to the existing stock. More interesting is the question of what that meant to the overall structure of the word-formation system. The answer is in fact very simple: it meant competition (cf. Kastovsky 1985). This competition not only concerned the rivalry between native affixes (*fore-, mid-, un-; -dom, -ed, -en, -er, -ful, -hood, -ing, -ish, -less, -let, -like, -ling, -ness, -ship*, zero) and non-native affixes (*ante-, circum-, dis-, extra-, in-, inter-, non-, post-, pre-, re-, sub-, super-, trans-; -able, -acy, -age, -al, -an, -ance, -ancy, -ant, -arian, -ate, -ation, -ee, -eer, -ery, -ese, -ic, -ical, -ician, -ify, -ize, -ism, -ist, -ment, -ory, -ous, -ure*), but also between the non-native affixes themselves. Thus, to give just one example, Old English had had only one productive negative prefix, namely *un-* as in *un-wīs*. In Middle and Early Modern English four competing non-native prefixes were added: *a-, dis-, in-, non-*, which now competed with *un-* and among themselves. This situation in fact has persisted until today and, despite the work of e.g. Aronoff (1980), Anshen and Aronoff (1988), Baayen (1989), Plag (1999), Riddle (1985), it is still in need of more thorough investigation, especially on the gradually emerging semantic and distributional restrictions. In Early Modern English we often find rivaling forms from one and the same basis, e.g. *frequency ~ frequentness, immaturity ~ immatureness, immediacy ~ immediateness; light/Ø ~*

lighten ~ *enlighten*; *length*/Ø ~ *lengthen* ~ *enlength*/Ø; *disthronize* ~ *disthrone* Ø ~ *dethrone*/Ø ~ *dethronize* ~ *unthrone*/Ø. Eventually, one of the forms survived, whereas the others were discarded, or else some semantic differentiation took place. Again, the rivalry of these competing patterns and their sorting out in the eighteenth and nineteenth centuries are in need of further investigation, especially with regard to their distribution among text types and the influence of prescriptive grammar.

This process continued in Modern English, especially furthered by scientific terminology, which relied heavily on Latin and Greek models. Examples are: *ante-* (*anteroom*, *ante-orbital*), *auto-* (*autobiography*, *auto-infectant*), *bi-* (*biangular*, *biforked*), *di-* (*dipetalous*, *dioxide*), *epi-* (*epibasal*, *epidermis*), *hyper-* (*hyperactive*, *hyper-emphasize*), *hypo-* (*hypodermic*, *hypo-acid*), *intra-* (*intra-abdominal*, *intra-state* (*traffic*)), *meta-* (*meta-arthritic*, *metatheory*), *micro-* (*microbacillus*, *microcosmos*), *multi-* (*multi-angular*, *multi-bladed*), *neo-* (*Neoplatonism*, *Neo-Cambrian*), *per-* (*perchloride*, *perchloric*), *poly-* (*polychromatic*, *polygrooved* (*rifle*)), *post-* (*post-biblical*, *post-war*), *pro-* (*pro-ethnic*, *pro-British*), *retro-* (*retro-act*, *retro-buccal*), *semi-* (*semi-fluid*, *semi-ape*); *-ate* (*acetate*, *citrate*), *-ine* (*bovine*, *chlorine*). Note that here the number of prefixes by far outnumbers the suffixes, and an investigation of this nomenclature in connection with the development of the sciences is still pending, especially since there had also been uncertainties with regard to the development of this kind of terminology.

Summing up this section, the net result is that the influx of non-native material has substantially changed the structure of the English lexicon. It has created a two-level system in both the simple and the complex dictionary with a native stratum inherited from Old English and a (partially integrated) non-native system adopted from Romance, Latin, and Greek. As a consequence, the derivational patterns available have increased tremendously, partly rivaling each other, partly restricting each other according to etymological domains. This also has consequences for the question of productivity of the rivaling patterns, both in Modern English and with regard to the historical development. Here, a lot of empirical spadework still needs to be done, but with the help of the emerging computer-readable corpora more specific analyses seem to be possible.

7.6 Morphophonemic Alternation

I now turn to the parameter of the status of morphophonemic alternations, which is tied up with the developments discussed in the previous section.

Old English was characterized by pervasive stem variability because of widespread morphophonemic and allomorphic alternations. Their origin was twofold. First of all, Old English, as all the other Germanic languages, had inherited Indo-European ablaut alternations. In the verbal system (i.e. the so-called "strong verbs") these alternations had become functionalized as indicators of the past tense and the past participle, cf. *wrītan ~ wrāt ~ writon ~ ġewriten, helpan ~ healp ~ hulpon ~ ġeholpen*. But they also characterized nouns and adjectives that were related to these strong verbs, echoing the original root-based derivational relationship, cf. the derivatives related to *brecan ~ bræc ~ bræċ ~ brecen/broken* or *drincan ~ dranc ~ druncon*:

(11) *brecan: æw–brecþ* 'sacrilege, lit. law-breach', *æw–breca* 'adulterer, lit. law-breaker', *brecness* 'breach', *brecþa* 'broken condition'; *(ġe-)bræc* 'noise, sound'; *bræċ* 'breaking, destruction', *æw–bræċe* adj. 'adulterous, despising the law', *æw-brucol* 'sacrilegious', *broc* 'breach, fragment', *bryċe* 'break, fragment', *hūs-bryċe* 'burglary', *hūs-bryċel* 'burglarious', *bryċe* 'fragile';
drincan: drinc 'drink, drinking', *ġedrinca* 'one who drinks with another', *drincere* 'drinker', *drenċ* 'drink, drinking', *drenċan* 'give to drink', *drenċ–hus* 'drinking-house'; *druncen* 'drunkenness', *druncennis* 'drunkenness', *druncnian* 'be, get drunk', *druncning* 'drinking', *drynċ* 'drink, potion, drinking'.

Although these patterns probably were no longer productive, since the strong verbs were basically a closed class (although there were the odd new additions like *śċrīfan* 'to shrive'), the related nouns and adjectives still formed a major part of the core vocabulary and must have been interpreted as derivationally related to these verbs, much as they are in Modern High German, where we still have the same situation.

But in addition to this Indo-European legacy, a number of sound changes had left their traces in the form of first morphophonemic, but ultimately allomorphic alternations, e.g. *i*-umlaut (*full ~ fyllan, dōm ~ dēman, curon ~ cyre, seċġan ~ sagu, trum ~ trymþ*), consonant gemination (*gram ~ gremman, wefan ~ webba*), palatalization and assibilation (*ċēosan ~ curon ~ cyre, lugon ~ lyġe, brecan ~ brucon ~ bryċe, gangan ~ genġe, genġa, fōn ~ fangen ~ fenġ*), Anglo-Frisian Brightening and Retraction (*grafan ~ græf, græft, bacan ~ ġebæc*). These had started out as purely phonologically conditioned allophonic alternations, then became phonemicized and by the end of the Old English period ended up as morphologically conditioned unpredictable alternations (cf. Kastovsky 1989a, 1989b). To these have to be added quantitative alternations that arose in Late Old English due to vowel shortening before consonant clusters (e.g. *cēpan ~ cēpte > cepte*) or vowel lengthening before other clusters (e.g. *ċild > ċīld ~ cildru*), which so far have hardly ever been investigated as to their morphological consequences (cf. Minkova and Stockwell 1998). In any case, towards the end of the Old English period, the language was characterized by large-scale allomorphic variation, with most of these alternations being unpredictable. This eventually led to considerable analogical leveling in the Middle English period with the result of eliminating most of these alternations, a development that might have been enhanced by the contact situation with

Scandinavian and French, again largely uninvestigated. A further factor which must have played a role was the generalization of word-based inflection and derivation. This morphological type would seem to favor a system without alternations, i.e. morphology with base-invariancy. There are two factors which corroborate this. First of all, in English many more originally strong verbs became weak than in German, which preserved stem-based inflection in the verbal system. And secondly, during Middle English almost all of the ablaut nouns of the type exemplified in (11) were lost and were replaced either by equivalent non-alternating instances or by loans. Thus, apart from instances such as *song*, *writ*, *road*, and a few others hardly any of these survive into Modern English. As a result, stem-alternation became a characteristic feature of the irregular part of inflection (e.g. *keep* ~ *kept*, *write* ~ *wrote* ~ *written*), whereas it disappeared from word-formation on a native basis except for some unproductive cases such as *long* ~ *length*, *north* /θ/ ~ *northern* /ð/. Thus Modern English word-formation on a native basis is stem-invariant as a consequence of this leveling process.

During the Middle English and Early Modern English periods, however, the situation changed drastically as a result of the borrowing process discussed above. The loans from French and Latin had a different prosodic structure, namely non-initial, partly movable stress as against fixed initial stress, which was characteristic of the Germanic languages. The latter assigns stress from left to right and stresses the first syllable of the lexical root (except for certain verbal prefixes), regardless of its phonological structure. For Romance and Latin loans, however, stress assignment operates from right to left, taking into account syllable weight. Stress could therefore be placed on the final (*licóur*), penultimate (*engéndred*) or antepenultimate (*párdoner*) syllable, depending on weight distribution. This automatically leads to movable stress in derivationally related patterns, especially since suffixes could bear stress themselves or determined the position of stress, cf. *Japán* ~ *Japanése*, *hístory* ~ *históric* ~ *historícity*, *admíre* ~ *ádmirable*/*admírable*, etc. This affected the English phonological system profoundly, especially since stress position led to phonological alternations between full vowels and schwa. It has been claimed that this led to a change from Germanic right-to-left ("left-handed") to left-to-right ("right-handed") Romance stress assignment (cf., e.g., Lass 1992: 85ff.). I would rather argue that we have two competing stress assignment rules in the non-native vocabulary, see also Lass (to appear).

A further trigger for alternations due to stress assignment were shortening processes sensitive to syllable number, such as trisyllabic laxing, e.g. *sān* ~ *sǽnity*, *divīn* ~ *divínity*, which after the Great Vowel Shift led to alternations such as /seɪn/ ~ /ˈsænɪti/, /dɪvaɪn/ ~ /dɪvɪnɪti/. Whether such alternations have really become productive in English is questionable (cf. Minkova and Stockwell 1998). But the alternation called Velar Softening, i.e. the alternation between a velar stop and a palatal or alveolar fricative or affricate, characterizing *historic* ~ *historicity*, *magic* ~ *magician*, *concept* ~ *conceptual*, etc., certainly is productive, although tied to the respective suffixes, which are non-native.

Thus, the borrowing process not only changed the overall phonological system of English, especially with regard to stress alternations and concomitant segmental alternations, but also the morphophonemic system of derivational morphology, establishing two levels here as well.

7.7 Affix Position

Little need be said as to the last parameter, the position of affixes, because there have been no major changes. The language has always had prefixes and suffixes, as well as circumfixes. As to the latter, it might be added, however, that the pattern *beorcan* ~ *ġe-beorc-Ø* 'barking' (repetitive action), *ġebrōþor-Ø* 'brethren' (collectivity), *ġefar-Ø-a* 'one who travels with another' (associativity) involving the combination of the prefix *ġe-* with zero was lost in Middle English, probably together with the loss of the prefixal part of the past participle, cf. Old English *ġe-writ-en, ġe-luf-od(-e)* vs. *writt-en, lov-ed*.

7.8 Concluding Remarks

I hope that this sketch has demonstrated that morphological typology both from a synchronic and a diachronic point of view is much more complex than traditional typological approaches have implied. Moreover, especially from a historical perspective, inflection and derivation have to be treated as interacting. And the same holds for the relationship between morphology and phonology, especially as regards the importance of morphophonemic alternation, which have so far been sorely neglected in the existing handbooks, including the *Cambridge History of the English Language*.

ACKNOWLEDGMENTS

I would like to thank Ans van Kemenade, Bettelou Los, and Roger Lass for their helpful comments.

NOTE

1 It is the stress-alternation which marks these as non-native, whereas native formations have non-alternating stress.

REFERENCES

Anshen, Frank and Mark Aronoff (1988). Producing morphologically complex words. *Linguistics* 26: 641–55.

Aronoff, Mark (1980). The relevance of productivity in a synchronic description of word formation. In Jacek Fisiak (ed.), *Historical Morphology* (pp. 71–82) (Trends in Linguistics. Studies and Monographs 17). The Hague: Mouton.

Baayen, Rolf H. (1989). *A Corpus-based Approach to Morphological Productivity: Statistical Analysis and Psycholinguistic Interpretation*. Amsterdam: Centrum voor Wiskunde en Informatica.

Bally, Charles (1944). *Linguistique générale et linguistique française* (2nd edn.) Berne: Francke.

Bammesberger, Alfred (1986). *Untersuchungen zur vergleichenden Grammatik der germanischen Sprachen*. Band 1: *Der Aufbau des germanischen Verbalsystems*. Heidelberg: Winter.

Bauer, Laurie (1983). *English Word-formation* (Cambridge Textbooks in Linguistics). Cambridge: Cambridge University Press.

Bauer, Laurie (1992). *Introducing Linguistic Morphology*. Edinburgh: Edinburgh University Press.

Chomsky, Noam and Morris Halle (1968). *The Sound Pattern of English*. New York: Harper and Row.

Cowie, Claire and Christiane Dalton-Puffer (2002). Diachronic word-formation and studying changes in productivity over time: theoretical and methodological considerations. In Javier E. Díaz Vera (ed.), *A Changing World of Words: Studies in English Historical Lexicography, Lexicology, and Semantics*. Amsterdam and New York: Rodopi, 410–37.

Dalton-Puffer, Christiane (1996). *The French Influence on Middle English Morphology: A Corpus-based Study of Derivation* (Topics in English Linguistics 20). Berlin and New York: Mouton de Gruyter.

Dalton-Puffer, Christiane (2002). Is there a social element in English word-stress? Explorations into a non-categorial treatment of English stress: a long-term view. In Dieter Kastovsky and Arthur Mettinger (eds.), *The History of English in a Social Context: A Contribution to Historical Sociolinguistics* (Trends in Linguistics 129) (pp. 91–113). Berlin/New York: Mouton de Gruyter.

Dressler, Wolfgang U. (1985). *Morphophonology: The Dynamics of Derivation*. Ann Arbor: Karoma.

Francis, W. Nelson (1958). *The Structure of American English*. New York: Ronald Press.

Giegerich, Heinz J. (1999). *Lexical Strata in English: Morphological Causes, Phonological Effects*. Cambridge: Cambridge University Press.

Hockett, Charles (1958). *A Course in Modern Linguistics*. New York: Macmillan.

Hogg, Richard M. (1992). Phonology and morphology. In Richard M. Hogg (ed.), *The Cambridge History of the English Language*. Vol. 1: *The Beginnings to 1066* (pp. 67–167). Cambridge: Cambridge University Press.

Huddleston, Rodney and Geoffrey K. Pullum (2002). *The Cambridge Grammar of the English Language*. Cambridge: Cambridge University Press.

Kastovsky, Dieter (1968). *Old English Deverbal Substantives Derived by Means of a Zero Morpheme* [Tübingen University PhD dissertation 1967]. Esslingen/N: Langer.

Kastovsky, Dieter (1980). Zero in morphology: a means of making up for phonological losses? In Jacek Fisiak (ed.), *Historical Morphology* (pp. 213–50) (Trends in Linguistics. Studies and Monographs 17). The Hague: Mouton.

Kastovsky, Dieter (1985). Deverbal nouns in Old and Modern English: from stem-formation to word-formation. In Jacek Fisiak (ed.), *Historical Semantics – Historical Word-Formation* (pp. 221–61) (Trends in Linguistics. Studies and Monographs 29). Berlin and New York: Mouton de Gruyter.

Kastovsky, Dieter (1986a). Diachronic word-formation in a functional perspective. In Dieter Kastovsky and Aleksander Szwedek (eds.), *Linguistics across Historical and Geographical Boundaries: In Honour of Jacek Fisiak on the Occasion of his Fiftieth Birthday* (pp. 409–21) (Trends in Linguistics. Studies and Monographs 32). Berlin: Mouton de Gruyter.

Kastovsky, Dieter (1986b). Problems in the morphological analysis of complex lexical items. *Acta Linguistica Academiae Scientiarum Hungaricae* 36: 93–107.

Kastovsky, Dieter (1989a). Morphophonemic alternations and the history of English: examples from Old English. In Manfred Markus (ed.), *Historical English: On the Occasion of Karl Brunner's 100th Birthday* (pp. 112–23) (Innsbrucker Beiträge zur Kulturwissenschaft. Anglistische Reihe 1). Innsbruck: University of Innsbruck.

Kastovsky, Dieter (1989b). Old English morphonological processes and morphology. In Wolfgang Grosser, Karl Hubmayer, Franz Wagner and Wilfried Wieden (eds.), *Phonophilia: Untersuchungen zur Phonetik und Phonologie. Festschrift für Franz Zaic* (pp. 83–94). Salzburg: Abakus.

Kastovsky, Dieter (1992a). Semantics and vocabulary. In Richard M. Hogg (ed.), *The Cambridge History of the English Language*. Vol. 1: *The Beginnings to 1066* (pp. 290–407). Cambridge: Cambridge University Press.

Kastovsky, Dieter (1992b). Typological reorientation as a result of level interaction: the case of English morphology. In Günter Kellermann and Michael D. Morrissey (eds.), *Diachrony within Synchrony: Language History and Cognition* (pp. 411–28) (Duisburger Arbeiten zur Sprach- und Kulturwissenschaft 14). Frankfurt: Lang.

Kastovsky, Dieter (1994). Historical English word-formation: from a monostratal to a polystratal system. In Rolando Bacchielli (ed.), *Historical English Word-formation: Papers Read at the Sixth National Conference of the History of English* (pp. 17–31). Urbino: QuattroVenti.

Kastovsky, Dieter (1996). Verbal derivation in English: a historical survey. Or: Much ado about nothing. In Derek Britton (ed.), *English Historical Linguistics 1994* (pp. 93–117) (Current Issues in Linguistic Theory 135). Amsterdam/Philadelphia: Benjamins.

Kastovsky, Dieter (1998). Morphological restructuring: the case of Old English and Middle English verbs. In Richard Hogg and Linda van Bergen (eds.), *Historical Linguistics 1995*. Vol. 2: *Germanic Linguistics* (pp. 131–47). Amsterdam/Philadelphia: Benjamins.

Kastovsky, Dieter (1999). Hans Marchand's theory of word-formation: genesis and development. In Uwe Carls and Peter Lucko (eds.), *Form, Function and Variation in English: Studies in Honour of Klaus Hansen* (pp. 19–39). Frankfurt: Peter Lang.

Kastovsky, Dieter (2000). Words and word-formation: morphology in the *OED*. In Lynda Mugglestone (ed.), *Lexicography and the* OED: *Pioneers in the Untrodden Forest* (pp. 110–25). Oxford: Oxford University Press.

Kastovsky, Dieter (2002a). The "haves" and the "have-nots" in Germanic and English: from *bahuvrihi* compounds to affixal derivation. In Katja Lenz and Ruth Möhlig (eds.), *Of Dyuersitie and Chaunge of Language: Essays Presented to Manfred Görlach on the Occasion of his 65th Birthday* (pp. 33–46). Heidelberg: C. Winter.

Kastovsky, Dieter (2002b). The derivation of ornative, locative, ablative, privative and reversative verbs in English. In Teresa Fanego, María José Lopez Couso, and Javier Pérez-Guerra (eds.), *English Historical Syntax and Morphology: Selected Papers from 11 ICEHL. Santiago de Compostela. 7–11 September 2000* (pp. 99–109). Amsterdam and Philadelphia: Benjamins.

Kuryłowicz, Jerzy (1968). *Indogermanische Grammatik.* Band 2: *Akzent, Ablaut.* Heidelberg: Winter.

Lass, Roger (1990). How to do things with junk: exaptation in language evolution. *Journal of Linguistics* 26: 79–102.

Lass, Roger (1992). Phonology and morphology. In Norman Blake (ed.), *The Cambridge History of the English Language.* Vol. 2: *1066–1476* (pp. 23–155). Cambridge: Cambridge University Press.

Lass, Roger (1994). On 'root-based' Indo-European: an embryological or phylogenetic note. *VIEWS* 3: 31–4.

Lass, Roger (forthcoming). Phonology and morphology. In *The Shorter Cambridge History of the English Language.* Cambridge University Press.

Lieber, Rochelle (1981). *On the Organisation of the Lexicon.* Bloomington: Indiana University Linguistics Club.

Lieber, Rochelle (1983). Argument linking and compounds in English. *Linguistic Inquiry* 14: 251–85.

Lyons, John (1977). *Semantics* (2 vols.). Cambridge: Cambridge University Press.

Marchand, Hans (1951). Phonology, morphophonology and word-formation. *Neuphilologische Mitteilungen* 52: 87–95.

Marchand, Hans (1967). Expansion, transposition and derivation. *La Linguistique* 1: 13–26. (Reprinted in Hans Marchand (1974) *Studies in Syntax and Word-formation: Selected Articles.* On the Occasion of his 65th Birthday on October 1st, 1972, ed. Dieter Kastovsky. (Internationale Bibliothek für allgemeine Linguistik 18.) München: Fink, pp. 322–37.)

Marchand, Hans (1969). *The Categories and Types of Present-day English Word-formation* (2nd rev. edn.). München: Beck.

Matthews, Peter H. (1974). *Morphology* (Cambridge Textbooks in Linguistics). London: Cambridge University Press.

Minkova, Donka and Robert P. Stockwell (1998). The origins of long–short allomorphy in English. In Jacek Fisiak and Marcin Krygier (eds.), *Advances in English Historical Linguistics* (pp. 211–39) (Trends in Linguistics. Studies and Monographs 112). Berlin and New York: Mouton de Gruyter.

Nevalainen, Terttu (1999). Early Modern English lexis and semantics. In Roger Lass (ed.), *The Cambridge History of the English Language.* Vol. 3: *1476–1776* (pp. 332–458). Cambridge: Cambridge University Press.

Plag, Ingo (1999). *Morphological Productivity: Structural Constraints in English Derivation* (Topics in English Linguistics 28). Berlin and New York: Mouton de Gruyter.

Riddle, Elizabeth M. (1985). A historical perspective on the productivity of the suffixes *-ness* and *-ity*. In Jacek Fisiak (ed.), *Historical Semantics – Historical Word-Formation* (pp. 435–61) (Trends in Linguistics. Studies and Monographs 29). Berlin and New York: Mouton de Gruyter.

Štekauer, Pavol (1996). *A Theory of Conversion in English.* Frankfurt am Main: Lang.

Szemerényi, Oswald (1990). *Einführung in die vergleichende Sprachwissenschaft.* 4., durchgesehene Auflage. Darmstadt: Wissenschaftliche Buchgesellschaft.

Watkins, Calvert (1969). *Indogermanische Grammatik.* Band 3.1: *Formenlehre. Geschichte der indogermanischen Verbalflexion.* Heidelberg: Winter.

8 Competition in English Word Formation

LAURIE BAUER

8.1 Introduction

If we look back at the history of English word-formation, we can see two types of change: individual words which instance various word-formation patterns come and go, and various processes (specific patterns of affixation, compounding or conversion) come and go. Although we have well-attested instances of processes disappearing entirely between Old English and Modern English (sometimes taking with them all the words coined by the process), in the Modern English period, there have been more gains in processes than losses. There has also been a great deal of variation in the number of words that are coined using particular processes at various times in history. In the modern period, it might be fair to say that no process has vanished entirely, since the individual processes have left traces behind in the form of words which are still known. Even though it may not be clear to most speakers that words such as *snigger* and *titter* were in origin morphologically complex, we must leave open the possibility that such processes could be resurrected.

There are a vast amount of data on the development of the vocabulary of English available through sources such as *The Oxford English Dictionary*. These make it easy to trace the development of an individual word but, partly for reasons which will be explored here, difficult to follow and evaluate the changes in a word-formation process. Yet while the fate of an individual word may depend upon factors unique to that word, we would predict that changes in word-formation patterns would be more systematic and of more interest to linguists. Accordingly, it is such changes which will be the focus of attention in this chapter.

The studies presented here are all based on an analysis of the data from the electronic (on-line) version of the second edition of *The Oxford English Dictionary*. Words with a particular suffix were found by searching for the suffix in the etymology section of the dictionary entries. Because the search software does not allow a hyphen to be specified in the search parameters, this often found too many words (for example where a word used in the etymology section happened to end in the same sequence of letters as the suffix that was being searched for), but the excess entries were relatively easy to remove. It also found too few words, but in ways which are not predictable. For example, sometimes an entry in the dictionary will simply list derivatives as sub-entries without a great deal of explanation. *Dispauperization*, for instance, can be found only by looking up *dispauperize* and working out the implications of the note "Hence . . . *-ization*." Such words were all missed by this method. Where etymologies simply say "from last" or "from next" these were also missed. However, relatively large samples were obtained from the dictionary by this method, and there does not seem to be any great danger to the gaps, provided that their existence is recognized. With the software for *The Oxford English Dictionary* now able to accept left-truncated searches, so that it is now possible, in a way which it used not to be, to search for headwords ending in *-ation*, for example, this might provide better data, though it would also provide more in the way of excess (in this instance, words like *nation* alongside words like *expectation*).

Because *The Oxford English Dictionary* is the source of the data used here, dates given for particular words are the dates of first or last occurrence in that dictionary. These dates have to be used with some care, since a first attestation may arise some time after a first use in the wider community, and a last attestation some time before a last use (or indeed some time after a word has passed out of general use). These dates are thus useful as a general guide to period of use, but small differences in dates may not be significant.

While this chapter is concerned with word-formation patterns, it is mainly concerned with slots in the derivational paradigms of English and the ways in which individual patterns compete with each other to fill those slots. This seems to imply some kind of variationist view of word formation which cannot strictly be maintained: word formation is almost by definition not necessary, so that there can never be a closed set of potential forms competing for some slot. Rather, we need to assume that word formation takes place, and then look at the alternative forms which arise. Some competition in this rather loose sense will be shown to be more apparent than real, while other cases of competition are genuine. This raises questions about the origins of competition and the outcomes of competition.

This chapter begins with a study of the suffix *-ster*, which behaves in a relatively predictable way in the course of its history, changing its meaning in the light of changing society and in the light of competition from other suffixes. Then the notion of competition between word-formation processes is considered in more detail, and illustrated with a set of English deverbal nominalizations. On the basis of this set of examples some tentative principles are discussed. These are then further illustrated on *behead*-class words and English diminutives. Finally, a conclusion about the origins and outcomes of competition is attempted.

8.2 A Case Study: The Rise and Rise of *-Ster*

This case study shows us something of the way an affix can be expected to change under the influence of societal change and linguistic competition. The affix in question is the *-ster* which appears in words like *webster* and *youngster*. The suffix *-ster* is of some interest, having apparently changed not only its meaning but also its connotations several times in the course of its history. The semantics of this suffix are discussed in detail by Lubbers (1965), and no attempt is made here to rework his analysis. Rather, the aim is to look at the way in which the changes have taken place and what has caused the changes.

The suffix *-ster* is cognate with Dutch *-ster* which is a marker of feminine gender, and the earliest coinages with *-ster* in *The Oxford English Dictionary* (*OED*) show that meaning, but with an extra semantic element: words in *-ster* denote professions, or if not, then habitual behavior. In this, they are like words in *-er*, a suffix which is frequently said to mark a profession. Whether the idea of profession is actually part of the meaning of the suffix, or whether it is part of the pragmatics attached to habitual performance of an action is an open question.

The earliest words cited by the *OED*, such as *seamster* (995), *baxter* 'female baker' (*c*.1000), *webster* 'female weaver' (*c*.1100) are all nouns denoting women, although they later lose their female meaning and simply become the names for professions. Words from the *OED* with first attestations after 1350 start to carry this more general meaning, although the female meaning appears to remain predominant until about 1430. After that, *-ster* words seem to be predominantly sex-neutral (or masculine, depending on the profession): *plumster* ('plumber', *c*.1440), *thackster* ('thatcher', *c*.1440), *woolster* (1577), *drumster* ('drummer', 1586). The addition of *-ess* to *seamster* to give *seamstress* from the seventeenth century is an indication that *-ster* was no longer felt as a female marker at that time. Occasional female nouns are found until the late nineteenth century (*spokester*, 1850; *nagster*, 1873) but these are exceptional at that period.

Starting in the mid-sixteenth century, we find *-ster* derivatives which show habitual actions which are not (or are not necessarily) professions. The first such word is *gamester* (1553), but we also find words such as *rimester* (1589), *lewdster* (1598), *youngster* (1589), *scoldster* (*c*.1600), *lamester* (1639), and so on. Note the unusual adjectival bases in this set. About the same time, words start appearing with pejorative connotations. It can be difficult to distinguish words which have pejorative connotations because they use the suffix *-ster* from words which have pejorative connotations because of their denotatum, but in the end these go hand-in-hand to a certain extent. Despite the negative connotations of many *-ster* words, there are others which have positive connotations: *dabster* ('one who is a dab hand at something', 1708) and the musical *-ster* words which arise in the twentieth century: *hepster*, *hipster*, *beatster*, etc.

From the late seventeenth century onwards, there is a trickle of *-ster* words which do not denote human beings. The earliest of these, *rubster* (1697), is of uncertain etymology, and may not have been formed with the *-ster* affix, but we find *roadster* (1744, originally a ship or a horse), *gigster* (a. 1812, a horse), *haulster* (1882, a horse), *speedster* (1918, person or vehicle), *dragster* (1954, vehicle), *sportster* (1963, vehicle or garment) and *hipster* (1962, garment). Of interest here are the facts that other word-formation processes which produce person nouns (such as *-er* affixation and conversion) are also used for instruments, and that *-er* is also used for garments (*drawers, slipper, stomacher, wader*). There is thus some generalization of pattern of semantic expansion in these affixes. It is assumed in the way these words are presented here that the affix exists independent of the meaning slots into which words with the affix fit. It might be argued that the slots have a prior existence (see section 8.4, below) and that at any given period of history, the most appropriate affix is sought to fill a particular slot. This alternative will not be explored here.

In the last hundred and fifty years, the value of the *-ster* affix appears to have become less fixed. As mentioned above, there are musical *-ster* words; there are criminal *-ster* words (*gangster*, 1896; *mobster*, 1917; *dopester*, 1938; *fraudster*, 1975); there are jocular *-ster* words (*lobster* 'person who bowls lobs in cricket', 1889; *gagster*, 1935; *prepster*, 1965); and there are perfectly serious *-ster* words (*beamster* 'job in a tannery', 1885; *skister*, 1898; *pollster*, 1939). This apparent loss of consistency or focus in new formations is unexpected, though we see new uses for the affix opening up, any of which might become a new norm.

The suffix *-ster* has competition in some of the areas it covers. Most clearly we find *-ess* in competition with *-ster* in its female meaning. The suffix *-ess* first appears in English in the early fourteenth century, sometimes to denote what might be thought of as a profession (*prioress*, *c*.1290; *abbess*, 1297; *herdess*, 1374), but more often to denote a female without any implication of profession (*charmeress*, *c*.1340; *cousiness*, *c*.1350; *adulteress*, 1382). Nevertheless, the two suffixes are apparently in competition, as can be seen in table 8.1. At the same time, *-ess* has its own domains, in denoting the spouses of titled men (*countess*, 1154; *princess*, a. 1380; *marquisess*, *c*.1386; *mayoress*, *c*.1430) and the female of non-human animals (*wolfess*, 1387; *dovess*, 1432; *leopardess*, 1567).

The suffix *-ess* is well established in English by 1400, and continues in widespread usage until the end of the nineteenth century. It is thus interesting to see that the period of the rise of *-ess* corresponds with the period of the fall of *-ster* in the meaning 'female'. It is also of interest that *-ette*, used only sporadically before the beginning of the nineteenth century, starts to be used

Table 8.1 Early competition between *-ster* and *-ess*

songster, *c*.1000; singster, 1388	singeress, 1382; chantress, 1430
hoppestere, *c*.1000	leaperess, 1382; danceress, 1388
chidester, *c*.1386	chideress, *c*.1400
slayster, 14??	murderess, 1390

Source: OED.

to derive female nouns in the early twentieth century (*suffragette*, 1906), just when *-ess* appears to be failing. While *-ette* has never been strong in this meaning, it continues to be more productive than the alternative *-ine* (or *-ene*) which is found only in a few words (*heroine*, a. 1659; *chorine*, 1922; *leaderene*, 1980).

The history that has just been outlined is precisely what we would expect to find: the meaning of a suffix (or other word-formation process) changes gradually, focusing sometimes on one part of its denotation, sometimes on another, and sometimes taking connotations to be more important than denotation. At the same time, it is in competition with other suffixes, and as new suffixes become popular for a particular meaning, so old suffixes with the same meaning become less commonly used to coin words and may lose the relevant meaning in established words. The only thing we would probably not expect is the apparent loss of focus of *-ster* commented on above, where it is no longer clear what the core meaning of the suffix should be taken to be. Either this is a sign that the suffix is moribund (which is possible, though it has apparently been moribund before and still survives!) or that there is currently a process of change on-going, and a new pattern will eventually emerge.

8.3 Competition

Having seen competition in action between various gender-marking suffixes in the last section, we now turn to view the notion more generally. Competition takes place on two levels. There is competition between individual words (such as the ones illustrated in table 8.1) and there is competition between word-formation patterns. It might seem that the former type of competition would resolve the second type: if sufficient doublets are formed and word-formation process *x* wins out in the majority of cases, then word-formation process *x* will become the dominant process. This is not necessarily true, however, because of blocking (Aronoff 1976: 43). Aronoff defines blocking as "the nonoccurrence of one form due to the simple existence of another" and in Aronoff's (1976) discussion it is restricted to words which share the same base. Blocking leads us to expect an earlier word to be preferred to a later word when there is competition between them. Word-formation pattern competition might lead us to expect the newer word to win out (as when *-ess* takes over from *-ster*, for instance). There is a tension here which has not been resolved: how should we expect individual words to react given the contrary demands of two types of pressure? Several points should be made about this.

First we need to comment on the validity of the data available when we start to consider competition between word-formation processes in earlier periods of the history of English. We need to be aware that data, even from as good a source as the *OED*, may not be reliable on the relative order of coining of two words, particularly if they are said to have been coined within a short time of each other. This is important because blocking can only work if the earlier word is well established by the time the later word enters general use. We also need to note that because a source such as the *OED* is so inclusive, it may not be clear how long a word was used for or how frequent it was: first citations can be earlier than the general use and last citations can postdate the vitality of the pattern by a long way; rare persisting words may have as many citations as common but short-lived words. Other things being equal, we would expect the more frequent of two words in competition to persist (Rainer 1988), although why one is more frequent than the other may be an interesting question. Some words listed in the *OED* are too rare to have influenced a competitor greatly.

If words with competing affixes were distinguished according to predictable patterns, we might expect both affixes to survive with new, more specific meanings. But while this happens in the competition between individual words, it seems to be less usual as the resolution of competition between word-formation patterns. Gender-marking *-ster* yielding to *-ess* but continuing as a profession marker seems atypical in this regard. Nevertheless, in principle it is always possible to solve the problem of competition between words by specializing one or both of them so that the two are no longer synonymous. In inflectional instances it has sometimes been pointed out (see e.g. Campbell 1998: 93, 95) that the regular form takes on the regular meaning, while the irregular (because archaic) form takes on a specialized meaning: thus the distinction between *brothers* and *brethren*, *older* and *elder*, etc. Even if the denotation of two words remains the same, they may be distinguished stylistically. This is a regular feature of clippings, for example, with the clipped form at first being less formal than the unclipped base, although the clipping may go on to become the usual term (as, for example, has happened with *photo*, *piano*, and possibly even *flu*).

Finally, it must be recalled that words can coexist for quite some time before the competition between them is resolved. *Mirror* and *looking-glass* have been in competition since the sixteenth century. Originally, they seem to have been distinguished in terms of the material from which they were made, but that ceased to be true when amalgam-coated glass became the norm. The *OED* shows both being used in the nineteenth century (though Alice went through the looking-glass, not the mirror), but in the mid-twentieth century we find Ross (1956) citing *looking-glass* as being U[pper-class] as opposed to Non-U *mirror*. In the late twentieth century *mirror* was the norm. Although these are not derived from the same base, as blocking requires in Aronoff's definition, neither do they suggest a quick solution to synonymy. The instances being dealt with in this chapter are, because of the method used, all competing processes on the same base (or bases deemed to be equivalent), so that instances like *looking-glass* and *mirror* are not entirely relevant. Nevertheless, they suggest that a label such as the "Avoid Synonymy Principle" used by Kiparsky (cited in Rainer 1988) might be more explanatory and more general than the label "blocking," which is the usual term in word-formation study.

We also need to consider the roles played by lexicalization and by borrowing in the way in which morphological structure is perceived and used. This is well illustrated by the next case study.

8.4 Another Example: Apparently Chaotic Nominalizations

In morphology (much more than in syntax) we have to consider the force of lexicalization. Established words tend to persist, even when their morphology is no longer productive. We can explain this by pointing out that we do not have to understand the morphological make-up of a word to use it felicitously, so that awareness of motivation does not have to be maintained. There is plenty of evidence to support this (Bauer 2001: 43–6), from the fact that people can be surprised that hedgehogs should have anything to do with hedges to the fact that phonological change can affect morphologically complex structures in ways distinct from those in which the same elements are affected in isolation, with the result that transparency is lost (consider such well-discussed examples as *lord* < *loaf ward*, *lammas* < *loaf mass*, *hussy* < *house wife*, and so on).

Where borrowing is concerned, a little care is needed in the way in which the processes are described. Although it is possible to borrow an affix as such from some other language, the more usual pattern is to borrow a lot of words from another language which are subsequently analyzed as containing an affix (which may or may not be a genuine affix in the donor language). Most English borrowing of French, Latin, and Greek affixes has happened in this way. We can talk about English affixation only once the affix starts appearing on native bases or on foreign bases where it has no counterpart in the donor language. Thus while *countess* and *abbess* are not good examples of the English use of *-ess*, existing as such in French, *disheress* (*c*.1300) and *cousiness* (*c*.1350) do show the early adoption of the suffix in English.

In any diachronic study of word formation, we might expect to find some kind of force towards what is sometimes called Humboldt's Universal (Vennemann 1972): a one-to-one relation between form and meaning. Thus where we have several forms, there is a tendency to try to distinguish them semantically, and where we have a single meaning, there is a tendency to try to express that consistently with a single form.

To a certain extent, there seem to be culturally determined paradigm slots which speakers feel a need to fill. In Dutch and German, these include diminutives, which are rare in English. As far as English is concerned, we seem to have at least the paradigm slots shown in table 8.2. These may not all be available in any given case, but they are frequently available.

As well as these categories there are others which seem more peripheral to the system: *-ism* marking a philosophy, *-ful* yielding a measure, *-fold* showing repetition. It should be stressed that the division drawn here is not based on any experimental data, and that it may well be that certain categories should be included or excluded. Nothing will depend on this in this chapter. The point about the above list is to illustrate how badly English seems to do when faced with Humboldt's Universal: the same meaning regularly has several possible exponents, and the same affix often occurs in more than one place in the list.

Table 8.2 The derivational paradigms of English, a tentative sketch

Noun base
- collective (*-ery, -age*)
- abstract noun from common noun (*-dom, -hood, -ship*)
- female (*-ess, -ette*)
- personal noun connected with base (*-er, -ist*)
- adjectivalizer (*-al, -(i)an, -en, -esque, -y*)
- verbalizer (*en-, -ify, -ise,* conversion)
- resembling (*-like, -y*)
- lacking (*-less*)

Verb base
- nominalization (*-ance, -ation, -ment, -ure,* conversion)
- agent (*-er*)
- instrument (*-er,* conversion)
- patient (*-ee*)
- modalizer (*-able*)

Adjective base
- nominalization (*-ness, -ity*)
- causative verb (*en-, -ify, -ise*)
- collective (*-ery*)
- attenuative (*-ish*)
- negator (*in-, un-*)
- intensifier (*super-, mega-*)
- adverbializer (*-ly*)

Note: It may be misleading to include "patient" in this list, since (a) the suffix *-ee* has gained in productivity relatively recently, (b) the suffix cannot be used freely to denote any patient (except in technical vocabularies, the suffix denotes human patients), and (c) more is implied in this suffix than just patient-ness (see Barker 1998).

Even if we assume that for certain purposes adjectives and nouns are treated together as a single class, we might expect to do better.

To some extent, this appearance is deceptive. Plag (1999), for instance, argues that *-ify* and *-ize* are in complementary distribution, depending on the phonology of the base, while *en-* and *-en* (or their combination) are simply unavailable. This means that, in most cases, there is no choice of verbalizer for modern speakers. (The hedge of "most cases" is necessary because this fails to take conversion into account; Plag's argument on conversion is perhaps less convincing.) Similarly, Bauer (2001) argues that nominalizations of verbs are determined by the morphology of the verb, with very little choice for the speaker producing a nominalization on the spot (though, of course, established nominalizations may make use of lexicalized patterns). Here, the "little" choice depends upon the status of *-ing*, which often appears to compete with other nominalization markers, and which is available for all verbs. So here we may be said to have well-behaved derivational morphology with the apparent multiplicity of choice in fact so restricted that we can talk about rule-governed behavior. But this type of pattern is not always found, and has not always been found.

An example where it is not found is in the adjectivalization of proper names (Bauer 1983: 268–70). While it may be perfectly clear that *-ian* is the default suffix in such cases, examples such as *Dickensian, Dickensesque, Dickensish, Dickensy, Dickeny; Ibsenian, Ibsenesque, Ibsenish, Ibsenist, Ibsenite* show that things are not necessarily that simple. The problem here is that there is no point in setting up a series of Optimality Theoretic constraints and finding an optimal output: all outputs appear to be permitted. And while it must be admitted that not all of these forms are likely to persist as established forms, and that some of the forms may be intended to contrast with established forms in order to make some stylistic or semantic point, it is difficult to evaluate what is going on without some temporal perspective.

An example where good behavior on the part of derivational morphology has not always been found is in the nominalization affixes mentioned above. A search through the *OED* turns up 715 nominalizations of verbs created during the seventeenth century with the suffixes as set out in table 8.3. Note that instances of conversion are not included in this list, since they cannot be found in an electronic search of the *OED*.

The fact that so many suffixes are in competition for the same meaning is not necessarily significant; it could be the case, for instance, that each of the suffixes has its own domain, and that between them they divide up possible verbs neatly – that they are, in fact, in complementary distribution. This is not the case, however, as the list of doublets and triplets in table 8.4 shows.

Table 8.3 Seventeenth-century nominalizations with various suffixes

Suffix	*Number*
-y	2
-ery	8
-ancy	10
-ency	10
-ence	18
-ion	20
-ance	49
-al	56
-ure	96
-ation	190
-ment	258

Source: OED.

Table 8.4 Pairs of deverbal nominalizations of contrasting form coined during the seventeenth century

abutment	abuttal	
bequeathal	bequeathment	
bewitchery	bewitchment	
commitment	committal	committance
composal	compositure	
comprisal	comprisement	comprisure
concumbence	concumbency	
condolement	condolence	condolency
conducence	conducency	
contrival	contrivance	
depositation	depositure	
deprival	deprivement	
desistance	desistency	
discoverance	discoverment	
disfiguration	disfigurement	
disproval	disprovement	
disquietal	disquietment	
dissentation	dissentment	
disseveration	disseverment	
encompassment	encompassure	
engraftment	engrafture	
exhaustment	exhausture	
exposal	exposement	exposure
expugnance	expugnancy	
expulsation	expulsure	
extendment	extendure	
impartment	imparture	
imposal	imposement	imposure
insistence	insisture	
interposal	interposure	
pretendence	pretendment	
promotement	promoval	
proposal	proposure	
redamancy	redamation	
renewal	renewance	
reposance	reposure	
reserval	reservancy	
resistal	resistment	
retrieval	retrievement	
returnal	returnment	
securance	securement	
subdual	subduement	
supportment	supporture	
surchargement	surchargure	

Source: OED.

Some of the forms in table 8.4 are still standard forms; others have vanished. Some had only a very short life; others appear to have been widely used. Some of them compete with nominalizations coined in other centuries; others do not. Nevertheless, the fact that all of them could be formed in the same hundred-year period (and sometimes within a very few years of each other, according to the *OED*) suggests that the various affixes were not in complementary distribution at the time. If loan words were added to the table (many of which use the same affixes), the problem would be magnified. The same message is given by the rather longer list (not reproduced here) of seventeenth-century nominalizations which have not persisted to the present day.

There are, of course, other possible interpretations of the data in table 8.4. It could be that the norms were changing at precisely that period; it could be that individuals had aberrant norms of productivity; it could be that the alternate forms were always intended to reflect distinct meanings; some mixture of these could account for the resultant confusion. All of these are true to a limited extent. But the extent of the problem illustrated in table 8.4 suggests that noun formation in the seventeenth century was a rather freer process than it is in the twenty-first. We can see this if we consider the words in table 8.4 more closely.

There are pairs of words in the table of which neither survives more than briefly. This is true whether or not they are subject to blocking. Cases which appear to be prevented by blocking are the following: *composal* and *compositure* are both blocked by an older *composition*; *comprisal*, *comprisement*, and *comprisure* are all blocked by earlier synonymous forms *comprehension* or *compass*; *discoverance* and *discoverment* are both blocked by the slightly earlier *discovery* (1586); *expulsation* and *expulsure* are both blocked by an earlier *expulsion*; *extendment* and *extendure* (as well as *extensure*, which the *OED* lists from the late sixteenth until the mid-seventeenth century) yield before *extent* and *extension*, both of which are older; *promotement* and *promoval* are both blocked by an earlier *promotion*; *reposance* and *reposure* are both blocked by an earlier *repose*; *resistal*, *resistment*, and also *resistancy* (another seventeenth-century formation) are blocked by an earlier *resistance*; *returnal* and *returnment* are both blocked by the earlier *return*.

All of this sounds like the kind of pattern that would be predicted. However, we might ask whether the very formation of these nominalizations ought to have been prevented if blocking were working as expected. As noted by Bauer (1983: 88) it is the institutionalization of new words which is prevented by blocking, not their coinage. So the counter-argument would have to be that because of the inclusiveness of the *OED*, we are seeing traces of individual productivity (see Bauer 2003) as opposed to societal productivity here. This is not entirely satisfactory as a response. *Composal* and *compositure*, for example, have more than one citation each; they may never have been very common, and the *OED* claims that they had died out by 1700 and 1720 respectively, but they were used by more than one individual. If this is an instance of blocking, we need to consider the mechanism of blocking rather more carefully than has been done in the past. What we see is not blocking as defined by Aronoff (1976) (though Aronoff, 1994, is in line with the present suggestion), but blocking as the disfavoring of rare (probably meaning 'token-infrequent') words in the face of a more common (more token-frequent), previously established synonymous word.

If we return to the words in table 8.4, we also find cases where both competing nominalizations disappear despite the fact that there is no blocking involved. *Concumbence* and *concumbency* (on a Latin base) both vanish, as do *conducence* and *conducency*, *expugnance* and *expugnancy*, *redamancy* and *redamation* (again on a Latin base). Such cases are perhaps easily explained: neologisms were coined but failed to meet a societal need and so were not reused. Because affixes were not in strict complementary distribution at the time, there was room for some variation in the coining process, and again the completeness of the *OED* records these superfluous words.

We also find instances where the two nominalizations persist, but with distinct meanings. This again is expected: blocking should not occur where the two words are not synonyms. Examples are *abutment* versus *abuttal*, *commitment* versus *committal*, although neither case is as clear-cut as I have made it sound: both pairs have a certain amount of overlap in meaning, but take on specialized meanings, sometimes quite late – the 'burial' meaning of *committal* (which is not shared with *commitment*), for instance, does not arise until the nineteenth century. Note also that the older loan *commission* complicates the picture for this latter pair.

Next we find pairs where one of the pair survives and the other does not. Again, this is expected, at least if we do not interpret the dates provided by the *OED* as first citations too seriously, or necessarily expect the older always to survive the newer: it must be the more frequent which survives the less frequent, though the *OED* does not allow us any serious measure of frequency. Thus *committance* dies out at the expense of other nominalizations on the same base; *contrival* yields to *contrivance*, *desistency* gives way before *desistance*, *engrafture* gives way to *engraftment*, *exposal* and *exposement* yield to *exposure*, *insisture* vanishes in the face of *insistence*, *renewance* vanishes in the face of *renewal*. Sometimes the non-persisting member of the set may take some time to disappear, but not, in the cases cited, surprisingly long.

We also find instances where none of the words from table 8.4 survive, though a later word with the same meaning does survive. The clearest case of this is the disappearance of *exhaustment* (by 1650 according to the *OED*) and *exhausture* (by 1800) in the face of *exhaustion* (1661) and *exhaust* (nineteenth century). This seems to run counter to the predictions made under a theory of blocking, but if blocking is the victory of the most frequent, we can see that no real problem is raised by such cases: it all becomes a matter of the period at which the need for this particular nominalization becomes greatest, and the form which appears most suitable at that period.

More surprising are the instances where both (or, in some cases, all) of the relevant words continue to be used, at least for the period over which the *OED* provides solid data. In this context, this is taken to mean that we cannot necessarily trace developments which took place in the twentieth century, because we would not necessarily have twentieth-century citations in the *OED* anyway. But both *bequeathal* and *bequeathment* appear to be synonymous and to persist until the end of the nineteenth century, as do *bewitchery* and *bewitchment, condolement* and *condolence, depositation* and *depositure, disproval* and *disprovement* (both are rare, but continue despite an earlier *disproof*), *imposement* and *imposure* (again both rarer than the earlier *imposition*), *subdual* and *subduement*. Some of these may seem rare or unlikely from a twenty-first-century viewpoint, but many of them have never been particularly common, so that while it may be that they have become obsolete in the last century, their non-occurrence in a particular corpus or the lexicon of a single speaker is not necessarily sufficient to guarantee the point.

All of this might make it look as if there are no principles operating in the formation of seventeenth-century nominalizations. But that is certainly not true. All verbs in *-ize* took the nominalization ending *-ation* in the seventeenth century as they do today (*aggrandizement* is a loan). All verbs in *-ify* have corresponding nominalizations in *-ification*, as today. And the suffix *-al* is added only to verbs with final stress (the *OED* even lists *supervise*, the base of *supervisal* – now usually *supervision* – as having final stress).

What we need to know is how we get from the apparent chaos of the seventeenth century to the apparent orderliness of the system which applies now.

8.5 Explaining Solutions to Competition

When it comes to providing explanations of the changes that have affected English morphology over the last 300 years, we can do little more than speculate. Speculation provides us with hypotheses, but does not allow us to test those hypotheses. We will see that some of the possible hypotheses are so distinct that a really good test would be desirable.

8.5.1 History as simplification

Given the scenario that has been sketched in the previous section about the way in which deverbal nominalizations were extremely unpredictable in the seventeenth century but are extremely predictable now, an obvious conclusion is that the system has changed by imposing pattern. This is a very satisfying conclusion: gradually, English speakers have collectively solved the problem posed by the plethora of nominalization markers and have created a predictable system. This looks like progress.

We can even set up an argument as to why this should be the case. The seventeenth century was a period of great change in English, with many words being borrowed from French and Latin in order to "improve" English. These loans were inevitably reanalyzed, and made available a new range of potential nominalization endings. However, the various endings or processes were not clearly in complementary distribution. Once the flood of loans had diminished, it became impossible for the situation to continue: for one thing, such a situation is inimical to the notion of rule-governed morphology. Gradually, complementary distribution was re-established as the expected norm, but because so many processes were in competition in the seventeenth century, it took a long time for the situation to resolve itself, the final resolution not coming until the twentieth century. Thus the history of the past 300 years of English morphology is a reaction against the plethora of potential processes arising from the introduction of overwhelming loan morphology.

8.5.2 *History as complication*

But of course, other interpretations are possible. An alternative view would be to see the seventeenth century as less different from the twenty-first than is implied in the hypothesis outlined above. A priori, it must be an advantage to view any period as subject to the same set of pressures and constraints, despite the fact that this prevents us from seeing any change as progress.

Let us assume a rule-governed approach to morphology, which specifies a default form for any of the categories listed earlier. The rules may change over time as the result of loans, societal needs, the exhaustion of potential bases, or other factors, but at any given period there is a set of expected ways of forming particular categories which are more or less in complementary distribution. In other words, the situation we see with twenty-first-century nominalizations is typical. This situation may, of course, be upset by loanwords. Loanwords arise as unanalyzed entities, but eventually may become numerous enough to establish new patterns of regular behavior, thus giving rise to changes in the default patterns. Any speaker, at any period, who needs to coin a new lexeme is faced with at least two solutions: rule-governed formation and borrowing. The rule-governed formation is fairly automatic; borrowing demands knowledge that goes beyond competence in one's own native system. Speakers are faced with difficulties in this system under three sets of circumstances:

1 there is conflict between the rule-governed formation and the borrowing solution;
2 new bases do not fit into the categories for which there is an automatic rule-governed solution;
3 the rule-governed solution has already been pre-empted with a different meaning.

In situation (1) we might find variation between two outputs over an apparently coherent set of inputs. In situation (2) we find that speakers are forced to select from the processes they perceive as being available to them in such a way as to maximize euphony (something which ought to be more closely definable, though no such attempt will be made here). In situation (3) speakers have the choice of either using the rule-governed solution, despite the meaning (in which case they may add some kind of gloss) or creating a new word by the processes just described for (2).

In this view, there is a constant application of unproductive morphology in order to solve problems provided by productive morphology, so that the language is continually having new words added to it which are not the forms which would be the predicted ones, as well as a number of predicted forms. That is, the processes of history add irregularities (which are available to turn into regularities if enough of them are coined). History, rather than simplifying matters (or rather than merely simplifying matters), reflects a process of building in extra complications.

8.5.3 Complications on complications

Whichever of these views is correct (if either), there are a number of factors which are likely to muddy the waters for the analyst. Specifically, words are likely to be coined which cannot be taken to show societal solutions to morphological problems when they arise in poetry and highly literary contexts, in advertising, in headlines, in the creation of technical terms, or in other places where the patterns found in the speech/writing of a single individual are considered (see Bauer 2001: 57–8). In order to eliminate such potentially misleading data, a very large database is required in attempting to discover how word formation is really used.

Alternatively, words may be coined according to different norms in different varieties. Since different varieties may be distinct in terms of their regional origin, or in terms of the usual sociolinguistic variables of gender, socioeconomic status, ethnicity, and age, the variation in a source like the *OED* may reflect a lack of homogeneity in the community of speakers of "English." However, any such variation is masked by the presentation in the *OED*, where attestation (as opposed to, say, attestation in a particular genre) is the decisive factor in a listing. Again, it may be impossible to sort out the real patterns without large and specialized corpora illustrating particular genres or varieties.

8.6 Some Hints as to the Solution

8.6.1 Behead*-class words*

This section considers verbs like *behead* which are created by prefixation to a noun base, usually with a meaning of removal (but also with meanings such as 'leave, descend from a vehicle'). *Behead* is the only relevant word using the prefix *be-*; *de-*, *dis-*, and *un-* are the usual prefixes for this function in English. Of these, *un-* is the most frequent in terms of number of types listed in the *OED*. Interestingly, there are a number of doublets with the same base but different prefixes (see table 8.5). These appear to be synonymous.

We can view the data in a number of ways. Table 8.6 presents the numbers of each type found introduced in each century (according to the first citation dates

Table 8.5 Examples of synonymous doublets in *behead*-class

debark 1742	disbark 1578	unbark 1557
debowel 1375	disbowel 1440	unbowel 1552
decrown 1609	discrown 1586	uncrown 1300
dehair 1902	unhair 1382	
deleave 1591	unleaf 1598	unleave 1589
disfrock 1837	unfrock 1644	
dethrone 1609	disthrone 1591	unthrone 1611
dismast 1747	unmast 1611	
dispeople 1490	unpeople 1533	

Table 8.6 Numbers of *behead*-class words coined in each century

	14th cent.	*15th cent.*	*16th cent.*	*17th cent.*	*18th cent.*	*19th cent.*	*20th cent.*
de-	1	0	5	9	2	12	40
dis-	0	5	29	48	4	16	0
un-	10	19	42	48	8	10	1

Source: OED.

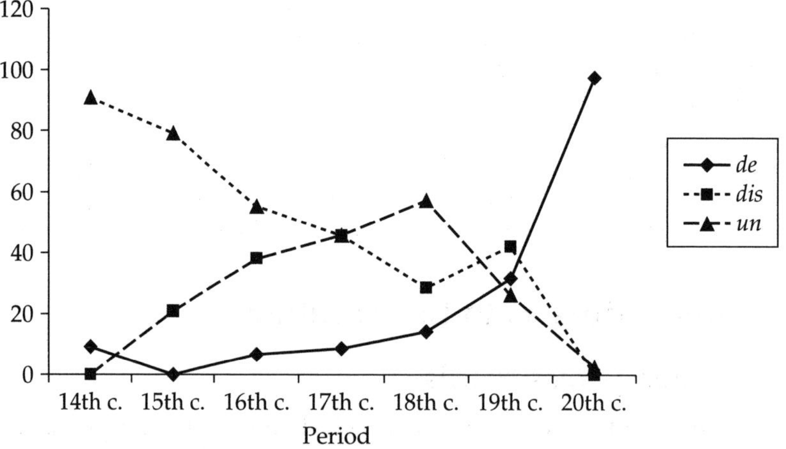

Figure 8.1 Percentage of *behead*-class words from each century using each prefix

given in the *OED*). An alternative view, an attempt to cope with the different absolute numbers in each century, is to see what proportion of the words in each century are created using which suffix, which is shown in figure 8.1.

With a set like *debark*, *disbark*, and *unbark* from table 8.5, the usage of the three words seems to be explicable in terms of figure 8.1. *Unbark* is the earliest coinage (1557) and its last citation in the *OED* is for 1719. *Disbark* is the next coinage

(1578), so the two were in competition for a long time, but *disbark* (following the trends in figure 8.1 which show the gradual demise of *un-* in the nineteenth century) seems to have lasted into the nineteenth century, outliving *unbark. Debark* started later than the others (1742), but is the only one of the three for which the *OED* gives a twentieth-century citation (1970), in line with the preference for *de-* in this meaning in the twentieth century. *Disembark,* now probably the usual term, arises at about the same time as *disbark,* but has persisted longer.

Other sets from table 8.5 give a more confused picture, though. *Debowel* is an earlier coinage than its competitors, and appears to have died out first, although all three of the cited forms yielded ground to *disembowel* (1613), the only one of the words for which the *OED* has citations after the eighteenth century. *Dethrone, disthrone,* and *unthrone* were all coined at about the same period, and all have nineteenth-century citations in the *OED,* outliving their competitor *disthronize* (1583–1689). While *disfrock* was coined in the nineteenth century, when *dis-* was the most frequent prefix used to coin *behead*-class words, it remains in competition with *unfrock* and with the earlier *defrock,* which is not listed in table 8.5 because it is a loan rather than an English coining.

Although the graph in figure 8.1 seems to show the simplification theory holding sway, it is interesting that three competing processes have managed to survive side-by-side for 700 years without their bases being in complementary distribution and without the blocking principle apparently having had a great deal of effect. Perhaps these words are too rare for blocking to be a real force.

8.6.2 Diminutives

In this section diminutives in *-ette, -kin, -let,* and *-ling* are considered. There are other diminutive markers in English, as illustrated in such words as *adagietto, babe, chicken, cockerel, concertino, drinky-poo, ducks, dunnock, kiddie-wink, lochan, nodule, piggie, poetaster, tootsies,* etc. Most of these, however, are rare and/or unproductive, while *-ie* is so productive (at least in some varieties of English) that dictionaries are unlikely to list relevant words. The productivity of *-s* (or *-sies* if this is an independent synaffix) appears to be largely in spoken genres (see Bauer and Bauer 1996), so that relevant words are again frequently not listed in dictionaries. The forms considered here are of sufficient productivity to give reasonable numbers of forms to consider, while being of limited enough productivity to make lexical listing a possibility.

In by far the majority of cases in which these endings occur, the affixes are in complementary distribution on their bases. To some extent the complementarity is semantically determined, with *-ling,* for example, being the affix of choice for denoting people when contemptuous connotations are required, but a great deal of the complementarity is not so easily described, and some of it may be due to blocking. It is not necessary here to determine how the various affixes are selected, though that might make an interesting study. Rather, we need to consider what happens when the complementarity breaks down.

Words where the four affixes are (superficially, at any rate) not in complementary distribution are listed in table 8.7. Each form is listed with the year

Table 8.7 Competing diminutives in English

-(i)kin		-ling		-let		-et(te)		*Mng*	*Comp*
		bardling	1813	bardlet	1867				A
birdikin	1864	birdling	1856	birdlet	1867				R
bodikin	1589			bodylet	1870			NS	
		bookling	1803	booklet	1859			C	
		budling	1577	budlet	1864			NS	R
		bushling	1562	bushlet	1822				R
		cockling	1580	cocklet	1834				R
		crabling	1822	crablet	1841				A
		crownling	1884	crownlet	1805	coronet	1494	NS	R
devilkin	1510	deviling	1616					NS	
		dishling	1811	dishlet	1884				R
		dropling	1605	droplet	1607			NS	
		dukeling	1612	dukelet	1870				R
essaykin	1860			essaylet	1872	essayette	1877	NS	
		frogling	1742	froglet	1907			NS	
		fruitling	1876	fruitlet	1882			NS	
godkin	1802	godling	1500	godlet	1877				
		gosling	1425	goslet	1884			NS	
heartikin	1540	heartling	1598	heartlet	1826			NS	R
		houseling	1598	houslet	1802			NS	R
		kidling	1586	kidlet	1899			NS	
		kingling	1598	kinglet	1603			C	
ladykin	1853	ladyling	1855					NS	
lambkin	1579	lambling	1591						R
lordkin	1855	lordling	1275	lordlet	1884			C	R
lovekin	1922	loveling	1606						A
maidkin	1440	maidling	1831						R
mankin	1820	manling	1637					C	
		moonling	1616	moonlet	1832			NS	R

mousekin	1859	mouseling	1832	mouselet	1832				R
				novelet	1592	novelette	1814	C/Sp	
		oakling	1664	oaklet	1871				A
		odeling	1845	odelet	1871			C	R
		pigling	1713	piglet	1883				A
		plantling	1766	plantlet	1816				A
		poetling	1772			poetette	1913	NS	R
		pointling	1840	pointlet	1847			NS	R
popekin	1890	popeling	1561						R
		priestling	1629	priestlet	1880				A
princekin	1855	princeling	1618	princelet	1682				
		riverling	1591	riverlet	1674				R
		rockling	1602	rocklet	1845			NS	
				roomlet	1880	roomette	1938	NS	R
		scrapeling	1629	scrapelet	1615			NS	R
		scrapling	1843	scraplet	1519				R
		seedling	1660	seedlet	1863			NS	
		sharkling	1900	sharklet	1898				R
		shredling	1674	shredlet	1840				R
		shrubling	1851	shrublet	1886				R
		snakeling	1868	snakelet	1887				R
		speechling	1880	speechlet	1881				R
		squibling	1884	squiblet	1820				R
		starling	1839	starlet	1830			NS	R
		stripling	1398	striplet	1839			NS	
thumbikins	1684	thumbling	1867					NS	
		toadling	1440	toadlet	1817				
		townling	1887	townlet	1552				
worldkin	1831	worldling	1549	worldlet	1926			NS	
		wormling	1598	wormlet	1611			NS	R
		youngling	900	younglet	1855				

Mng = Meaning; Comp = competition (see text); NS = not synonymous; C = different connotations; A = adjacent (non-overlapping) periods of history; R = at least one is rare; Sp = spelling difference only.
Source: OED.

of its first citation in the *OED*. Although the list looks substantial, it represents a small proportion of the relevant set of words.

By far the majority of the cases in table 8.7 are not synonymous (marked by NS in the penultimate column of the table) or have different connotations (marked by C). For instance, while a *bodikin* is a small body, a *bodylet* is a piece of jewellery (cf. *anklet*, *bracelet*, etc.); while a *mankin* is a term of contempt, a *manling* may be a term of approbation. These are thus examples where the default or expected choice of affix could be overruled by the demands of semantic distinctness. There are also a number of sets (marked R in the final column of the table) where at least one of the words is rare, either marked as such by the *OED*, or having only a single citation there. In these cases, we could be seeing the effect of individual rather than societal productivity. And the words marked with an A in the final column of the table have the two derivatives more or less in distinct adjacent time periods, so that the two do not really compete. It will be seen that very few pairs of diminutives are actually in competition.

In terms of the categories given above, this seems to be a case where the listings in the *OED* provide a database which is more complicated than the actual processes of formation would justify: history has masked the fundamental simplicity of the processes.

8.7 Conclusion

While speakers and lexicographers are probably aware of competition between affixes at the level of the individual pairs of lexemes, morphologists need to take a broader view of the issue. Though it may not be clear that micro-level competition between lexeme pairs has any effect at the macro-level of derivational patterns, all the examples that have been considered here show that such an effect is likely.

The main disrupting influence to English morphological patterns, in all the examples that have been considered here, is the impact of borrowing. Borrowing introduces the potential for widespread affix-synonymy. (Limited affix-synonymy is possible without borrowing, cf. *Dickensish* and *Dickensy* if these two are strictly synonymous, but it does not appear to be the rule.) There are cases where the borrowed affix becomes the new dominant one (e.g. *-ess*) and there are cases where the borrowed affix eventually fades out (e.g. *-ture* and *-ment* in the face of conversion). The survival of the borrowed affix depends upon its creating for itself a domain which, by whatever means, is distinguished from the domain of the competing affix. Gender-marking *-ess* succeeded because *-ster* lost its gender-marking role; nominalizing *-ation* succeeded because it became specialized in the domain where verbs are productively formed. The nominalizing *-ture* has no domain, and has vanished.

The disruption caused by the introduction of competing morphology is long-lasting. Even the domain of *-ster* words was not entirely clear until after the nineteenth century, and the patterns of nominalization may not yet be clear, but to the extent that they are, they have become settled within living memory. The reason that the system for creating adjectives from proper names has not yet become fixed is that the fashion for such adjectives appears not to predate the eighteenth century and is mainly a phenomenon of the nineteenth and later centuries (see the *OED* at *Homeric, Shakespearian, -ish, -ian,* etc.). We can expect another 300 years or so of confusion before the system settles down.

The process of sorting out the systems after the borrowing of synonymous affixes is one of both complication and simplification. Individual ad hoc decisions on relevant forms may or may not be picked up widely in the community. Where the relevant word is of very low frequency, the likelihood is that it will not become fixed as part of the community standard. It may be that the advent of broadcasting will affect this phase in the longer term, by making some neologisms available to a larger part of the community despite their low frequency, and also by making them available within a shorter period of time. However, it is clear from the history which the *OED* presents that the need of the individual for a particular word is not always matched by the need of the community for the same word, with the result that multiple coinages are possible.

At another level, the possibility of multiple heterophonous coinages is made possible by the fact of borrowing. While we can find native affixes which contravene Humboldt's Universal by having several functions, contraventions where a single meaning has several distinct morphemes to represent it seem to arise mainly if not exclusively from borrowing.

We must presume that there is some rule at work in a community which constrains new forms: new forms receive the communal blessing only when they are sufficiently parallel to established forms to be seen as well-motivated. In a period of catastrophic change like the seventeenth century, virtually any Romance form could be motivated by foreign parallels. In the twenty-first century, we have a community of speakers of "English" which is heterogeneous enough for different parallels to be accepted in different parts of that community. The result is that a form such as *tread* can be accepted as the past tense of TREAD in some parts of the community but not in others. Equally, *Pinteresque, Pinterian,* and *Pinterish* can all be accepted as "English" (see the *OED* at *Pinteresque*), and there may be more than one solution for the nominalization of the verb *to English.*

Accordingly, we can hypothesize that the smaller and more homogeneous the community, and the less susceptible to immoderate loans, the more likely it is to show word-formation patterns which conform to at least half of Humboldt's Universal. A comparison of English and Icelandic derivational morphology seems called for.

ACKNOWLEDGMENTS

I should like to thank Claire Cowie and Winifred Bauer, as well as the editors, for comments on an earlier draft, and Adam Albright for the reference to Vennemann. They are not to be held responsible.

REFERENCES

Aronoff, M. (1976). *Word Formation in Generative Grammar*. Cambridge, MA: MIT Press.

Aronoff, M. (1994). Blocking. In R. E. Asher (ed.), *The Encyclopedia of Language and Linguistics*. Oxford: Pergamon.

Barker, C. (1998). Episodic *-ee* in English: a thematic role constraint on new word formation. *Language*, 74: 695–727.

Bauer, L. (1983). *English Word-formation*. Cambridge: Cambridge University Press.

Bauer, L. (2001). *Morphological Productivity*. Cambridge: Cambridge University Press.

Bauer, L. (2003). *Introducing Linguistic Morphology* (2nd edn.). Edinburgh: Edinburgh University Press.

Bauer, L. and I. Bauer (1996). Word-formation in the playground. *American Speech*, 71: 111–12.

Campbell, L. (1998). *Historical Linguistics*. Edinburgh: Edinburgh University Press.

Lubbers, K. (1965). The development of *-ster* in modern British and American English. *English Studies* 46: 449–70.

Plag, I. (1999). *Morphological Productivity*. Berlin and New York: Mouton de Gruyter.

Rainer, F. (1988). Towards a theory of blocking: the case of Italian and German quality nouns. *Yearbook of Morphology 1988*: 155–85.

Ross, A. S. C. (1956 [1954]). U and Non-U: an essay in sociological linguistics. In N. Mitford (ed.), *Noblesse Oblige* (pp. 9–32). Harmondsworth: Penguin.

Vennemann, T. (1972). Phonetic analogy and conceptual analogy. In T. Vennemann and T. H. Wilbur (eds.), *Schuchardt, the Neogrammarians, and the Transformational Theory of Phonological Change: Four Essays*. Frankfurt: Athenaeum.

III Inflectional Morphology and Syntax

9 Case Syncretism and Word Order Change

CYNTHIA L. ALLEN

9.1 Introduction

One of the most striking grammatical differences between Old English (OE) and Present-day English (PDE) is that in OE, word order was reasonably free in that the syntactic and semantic roles of NP/DPs were not conveyed by the order of those NP/DPs, but rather by their case morphology. There is a long tradition of attributing the fixing of word order (and the increase in the use of prepositions) in English to loss of case-marking distinctions or syncretism which led to a (nearly) complete absence of case morphology (see e.g. Kellner (1892: §483 and *passim*; Meillet 1949: 187–92; Mossé 1952: §106, etc.). However, these traditional treatments do not offer explanations of the specific mechanisms involved, and as Jespersen (1894: §75) pointed out, the idea that fixed word order "stepped in" to make up for lost inflections suffers from the problem that "we should have to imagine an intervening period in which the mutual relations of words were indicated in neither way; a period, in fact, in which speech would be unintelligible." Jespersen concludes that "a fixed word order was the *prius*, or cause, and grammatical simplification, the *posterus*, or effect".

More recently, much attention has been devoted within generative frameworks to formal treatments of the interaction of case and constituent order in universal grammar (UG) and some very precise mechanisms have been proposed to link reduced case morphology with more fixed word order; see the introduction to Lightfoot (2002) for a useful overview. These proposals are an advance over the traditional discussions in making some explicit predictions which can be tested.

Much recent attention has focused on the shift from OV to VO order, a topic which is dealt with elsewhere in this volume. In this chapter, we will not concern ourselves with the possible role of the loss of case marking in this shift, but will rather focus on the disappearance of two orders which are found in OE but not in the Middle English (ME) period. The first is the fixing of the order of two bare nominal NP/DP objects of ditransitive verbs. While this order was variable in OE and ME, only one order is now possible. The second is the postnominal positioning of a phrase in the genitive case. While both prenominal and postnominal genitive phrases were possible in OE, postnominal genitives which are NP/DPs rather than PPs disappear from the texts early in the ME period.

These changes have both been attributed to case syncretism (contrary to Jespersen's argument) and have both been the subject of specific proposals to link the syntactic changes to morphological change. The mechanisms which have been proposed avoid the problem which Jespersen noted of having to assume a period of chaos, as should be clear from the discussion below. In this chapter, we will examine the evidence for the relative timing of the fixing of these orders and the loss of the relevant morphology, testing where possible some predictions made by some of these recent proposals. We will see that while there is a broad correlation between more fixed order and reduced morphology, the connection between case syncretism and increased restrictiveness of constituent order is not as direct as is often assumed. While the reduction of case marking surely had an important role in the final loss of some word orders, nevertheless the movement toward less variation in word order seems difficult to explain as a result of the loss of case marking on its own.

We begin with a very brief review of the case-marking system of OE and a more detailed look at the case syncretism in ME. We then examine the fixing of the order of two nominal NP/DP objects and finally turn to the genitives.

9.2 Case in OE and ME

It is important to make a distinction between abstract categories and the forms which represent these categories. It is common to make this distinction typographically, with *Case* referring to the abstract features relevant to syntax and *case* referring to overt morphology, and we will adopt this convention here. Old English (OE) was a language in which four cases, namely nominative, accusative, genitive, and dative, were distinguished by morphology on nouns and their modifiers, although there was already a good deal of syncretism; for example, the nominative/accusative distinction was already greatly obscured for nouns in OE and while the dative/accusative distinction was clearly marked in the third person pronouns, it was not in the other persons. The amount of syncretism varied with the noun class, and there was generally less syncretism in the determiner system than with nouns. Fairly early in ME, this syncretism had become so widespread that there was a general collapse of the case marking system, with the difference between the nominative, accusative, and dative cases disappearing entirely from the nominal, determiner, and adjectival systems. The dative/accusative distinction disappeared in the pronominal system, resulting in the complete disappearance of a morphological dative/accusative distinction, although a general object case remains to this day in the pronominal system.

It is a matter of current debate whether the genitive "case" of Early Middle English (EME) is to be treated as a case (i.e. inflection) or as some sort of clitic where nouns are concerned; depending on our stand on this issue, we can say either that in EME most dialects of English had either no morphological marking of Case in the nominal system or had only an opposition between genitive and "general" case (although the optional marking of the objects of prepositions complicates this picture; see below). This general reduction of morphology is commonly referred to as "deflexion."

For an overview of deflexion in ME, see Lass (1992). Here, we will focus on the disappearance of the dative/accusative distinction, because this morphological change has been implicated in both of the changes in word order discussed here. We will see that one of the problems with some proposals which have been made concerning the fixing of word order is the broad-brush approach which has been taken to deflexion, and that a more detailed empirical base is needed in order to evaluate the hypotheses which have been put forward.

The loss of the dative/accusative distinction took place at different times in different dialects; all traces of any overtly marked distinction are already gone in the Second Continuation of the *Peterborough Chronicle* (*PC II*), which was written around the middle of the twelfth century in a dialect of the northern edge of the Southeast Midlands, while the category distinction is still frequently marked in the *Aȝenbite of Inwit*, written in 1340 in the Kentish dialect. We can say that, by 1250, an overt distinction had entirely disappeared except in the most southern dialects, and the marking of the distinction was optional even in the dialects which retained the category distinction. Nouns and adjectives generally lost the overt marking of this category distinction before determiners did, and the distinction was maintained in the pronominal system (but only in the third person) longest of all. Within the pronominal system, the masculine singular pronoun was usually more resistant to the loss of the overt distinction than the other forms; we still find some remnants of the distinction between *hine* (the old accusative form) and *him* (the old dative) in the First Continuation of the *Peterborough Chronicle* (*PC I*), written around 1131, although *hine* has disappeared in *PC II*, presumably written less than 25 years later.

In looking at deflexion in ME, it is useful to classify texts into "case-rich" texts and "case-impoverished" ones. The case-rich texts maintain at least some formal dative/accusative distinctions, although syncretism may greatly obscure this distinction. For these texts, the assumption of a more abstract dative/accusative category distinction is unproblematic. The case-impoverished texts give no morphological evidence for a dative/accusative distinction at all, and whether we want to assume an abstract Case distinction here will depend largely on theoretical considerations such as the nature of the evidence necessary to support Case as features in the syntax.

This classification into case-rich and case-impoverished texts is not entirely unproblematic. It is often not a simple matter to determine the morphological case distinctions of a given text, and it is even more difficult to be certain what abstract Cases the forms represent. One problem is that forms which are historically reflexes of a given case marker do not always represent that case any more at a later stage. For example, the ending *-e* frequently shows up on nouns in ME texts, even as late as Chaucer, giving the impression of the continued possibility of marking dative case on nouns. But in some of these texts, this ending appears to be a purely metrical device. In others, it is found only on the objects of prepositions, and we appear to be dealing with a case system which is different from the OE system in that there is a single "direct" case (lacking any overt marking) which is used for bare NP/DPs and another case (optionally marked with *-e*) which is carried by the objects of prepositions; the old dative/accusative distinction is no longer a part of the nominal system. Similarly, in some texts, such as the *Ormulum*, the decline of nominal morphology is well advanced, but we still find reasonably frequent examples of agreement of a quantifier and a noun:

(1) Att ænne time . . .
at one time . . .
'On one occasion . . .'
(*Ormulum* 133)

The form *ænne* is inflected (optionally) in agreement with the noun *time*, and the *-ne* suffix looks accusative. However, a closer analysis of the *Ormulum* indicates that there is no longer any dative/accusative distinction, and that this form represents a general *object* case. This conclusion requires careful examination of the text, since we cannot rely on the glossary to the edition of this text, as it uses terms like "dative" in a way which reflects etymology and function (e.g. "indirect object") rather than formal categories. Similarly, in Robert of Gloucester's *Chronicle* of the early fourteenth century, we find some examples of inflected determiners, but it appears that they represent a general object case.

Another difficulty in determining the morphological system of a text arises from the fact that many of the remaining ME texts are extant only as copies of earlier works. Of particular relevance to the discussion below is the fact that the remaining copy of the *Ancrene Wisse* is a copy of a text which was presumably written at a time when the dative/accusative distinction was still a real morphological distinction and copied by a scribe who lacked this distinction. Some EME texts are even further removed from their originals; for example the *Lambeth Homilies* are found in a manuscript of the late twelfth or early thirteenth century, but their composition is at least partly OE, so they can only be used with caution.

Finally, we have texts like *PC I*, which show very little overt marking of the dative/accusative distinction but still have some *hine* forms, which suggest the retention of the accusative as a morphological category. It is a bit odd to categorize this text as case-rich, but that is how we must group it by this scheme.

Nevertheless, this simple bipartite classification is a useful one for our purposes, and we will adopt it in the following discussion of the loss of the word orders in question. Where not otherwise specified, the statements below

Table 9.1 Middle English texts investigated for this study

Case-rich texts	*Date*	*Case-impoverished texts*	*Date*
PC I (not very rich)	*c*.1131	*PC II*	*c*.1155
Kentish Homilies	*a*.1150, *c*.1125	*Ormulum* (Vol. II)	*c*.1180
Lambeth Homilies	*c*.1200, mostly OE	*Ancrene Wisse* (Parts 1–5)	*c*.1230, somewhat earlier
Poema Morale (Lambeth version)	*c*.1200, *c*.1170–90	Katherine Group	*c*.1225, 1200–20
Trinity Homilies	*a*.1225, ?OE	Wohunge	*c*.1220, post 1200
Brut (C MS) (1st 3,000 lines)	s.xiii^2, post 1189	*Cursor Mundi* (Vesp. MS, Vol. I)	*c*.1350
Vices and Virtues	*c*.1200, *a*.1225	*Havelok the Dane*	*c*.1300, *c*.1295–1310
Owl and Nightingale (C MS)	s.xiii^2, 1189–1216	Robert of Gloucester's *Chronicle* (A MS, Vol. I)	*c*.1325, c.1300
Kentish Sermons	*c*.1275, pre-1250	Genesis and Exodus	*a*.1325, c.1250
Aȝenbite of Inwit	1340	*Sir Orfeo* and *Amis and Amiloun* (Auchinleck MS)	*c*.1330
		Early Prose Psalter	*c*.1350

concerning the situation in the two types of texts are made specifically on the basis of the author's examination of the texts listed in table 9.1 (where the later fourteenth-century texts are not listed because there is general agreement on the situation there). The entire text has been read except where noted. Examples will sometimes be used from other texts. Searches for double objects and post-head genitives have been carried out where possible on the *Penn-Helsinki Parsed Corpus of Middle English, second edition* (*PPCME2*, Kroch and Taylor 1999) using CorpusSearch (Randall 2000). In table 9.1, when more than one date is given for a single text, the later date refers to the presumed date of the manuscript, while the earlier date refers to the date of composition.

9.3 The Objects of Ditransitive Verbs

In OE, a typical ditransitive verb such as *gifan* 'give' was subcategorized for two objects, with one usually having the thematic role Recipient (although other roles were possible) and taking dative Case and the other, with the thematic role of Theme, receiving accusative Case. Other combinations of Case for the two objects were possible, depending on the meaning of the verb, but we limit our discussion to the dative-accusative type. We will use the traditional label IO (indirect object) for the dative-marked object and DO (direct object) for the accusative-marked object.

These objects could appear in either order, as in these two clauses from the same sentence:

(2) a. Se mennisca crist dælde his god his ðeowum
The human Christ distributed his goods(N/A) his servants(D)
'The human Christ distributed his goods to his servants'
(*ÆCH II* XXXVIII.44)
b. for ðon he forgeaf his geleaffullum þa gastlican gife
for that he gave his faithful(D) the(A) spiritual grace
'because he gave his faithful the spiritual grace'
(*ÆCH II* XXXVIII.45)

It was also possible for either one or both of these objects to be preverbal, depending on such factors as whether the clause was a main clause or a subordinate one, discourse factors, etc. We will not give examples of all attested orders here. The point is that either order, DO IO or IO DO, was possible, whatever the position of the objects with respect to the verb. Neither order was clearly dominant in OE; as reported in Allen (1995: 48), approximately 54 percent of the clauses with two nominal (as opposed to pronominal) NP/DP objects in the late OE (c.995) Second series of Ælfric's *Catholic Homilies* (*ÆCH II*) had (surface) DO IO order.

One other fact which should be noted is that already in OE, some verbs, such as verbs of saying, allowed the IO to be either a bare NP/DP (with dative Case) or the object of a preposition (again with dative Case). Thus, the precursor of the modern *to*-dative was already in competition to some extent with the bare IO in OE, although this variation was lexically limited at that time; it was not found, for example, with *ʒifan* 'give'. In EME, the *to*-dative (with or without case marking on the NP/DP) becomes more common and lexically less restricted, although it is still relatively frequent at that time.

By the late fourteenth century, the order DO IO had entirely disappeared for two bare nominal objects (although it was still the norm when both objects were pronouns, and pronominal objects still normally preceded nominal objects, whatever the semantic role). The only possibilities for two nominal NP/DPs were (1) IO DO and (2) the *to*-dative, i.e. DO *to* IO.

Can this fixing of the order of two non-prepositional nominal objects be attributed to the decline of case marking, specifically to the loss of the dative/accusative distinction? Traditionally, it is assumed that languages generally use either case marking or word order to keep track of semantic roles, and it is normally assumed that when the dative/accusative distinction was lost in English, the inevitable result was that the old function of this case morphology was taken over by other means. There has been a considerable focus recently in syntactic theory on attempts to formalize the often-made observation that languages with reasonably robust case morphology tend to have rather free word order, while languages which lack this morphology usually have fairly fixed word order. In order to explain this correlation, it is widely assumed that NP/DPs must be somehow "licensed" to appear where they do, and that having some sort of specification for Case is an important part of this licensing. It is further assumed that this licensing may be accomplished in more than one way, or to put it another way, there is more than one type of Case. The licensing may be achieved through overt morphology or adpositions (inherent Case) or through structural relations with heads of the right sort (structural Case). While this licensing can be seen as having a functional basis to it – that language users need to be able to identify the semantic and grammatical roles of participants somehow – it goes beyond simple functionalism because NP/DPs must be licensed even if a listener should arguably be able to reconstruct the semantic roles from the context in a given sentence. Thus, if one way of licensing the NP/DPs (such as case marking) disappears, another device must take its place. There are, of course, different views on Case; see Lightfoot, chapter 2, this volume. For our purposes, it does not matter whether we treat Case as being assigned, as assumed by earlier generative frameworks, or checked, as suggested by Chomsky (1995) and adopted in much recent work.

In the case of ditransitive verbs, various analyses have been proposed for PDE. These analyses vary a great deal in important ways, but abstracting away from details, the most widely held analyses assume that the DO is generated with a structural relationship to a verbal element which is able to license it whether its surface position is directly next to the verb or after the IO (i.e. in the IO DO construction); it always has structural Case; in contrast, the IO is licensed by the verb only when its surface position is directly adjacent to it, i.e. when some sort of movement has taken place so that it is licensed for structural case; otherwise, the IO needs to have an overt expression of (inherent) Case, i.e. a preposition.

Given such a point of view, it is natural to assume that dative morphology performed the function in OE that the preposition performs in PDE, namely, that it licensed the IO, and that once this case marking was lost, DO IO order (without *to*) became impossible because an IO in this position was not in the right relationship to be licensed structurally, and did not have the morphology necessary to license it inherently. This is an assumption which can be tested empirically, and we can discern at least three hypotheses which can be treated as variants of the assumption that the connection between the deterioration of the morphological distinctions and the loss of DO IO order is straightforwardly accounted for by current licensing theory. Making the usual assumption within generative grammar that such changes occur as children learning the language construct new grammars, we can say that these hypotheses reflect different assumptions about how much morphological evidence a language learner needs to construct a grammar in which the relevant Case features are available in the syntax.

Hypothesis (1) is that there is a very direct relationship between these two changes; as soon as the surface dative/accusative distinction was no longer marked on an NP/DP, variable order of two bare nominal NP/DPs became impossible. By this hypothesis, we assume that if Case is not overtly marked by morphology or an adposition, it must be licensed by structural relationships, i.e. IO DO order. This hypothesis reflects a view, held by many generativists but by no means all, that the relationship between abstract, syntactic Case and concrete, morphological case should be highly transparent. In its strongest form, this hypothesis predicts that we should never find DO IO order when the IO is not overtly case-marked; that is, even in the case-rich texts of ME, we should only find DO IO order when the accusative NP/DP is distinguished by overt morphology from the dative NP/DP.

Hypothesis (2) is that there was direct causal relationship in that the loss of *category* distinctions triggered the loss of variable order, but variable order remained possible even after the syncretism of certain distinctions of *form* was complete; the retention of abstract Case categories was possible as long as some formal distinctions remained between dative and accusative, e.g. in determiners or the pronominal system, and variable order remained possible as long as the abstract distinctions remained. With this hypothesis, we are still assuming that the acquisition of syntactic Case features must be triggered by overt morphology, but we assume that the evidence for these morphological distinctions does not have to be so transparent; the dative/accusative distinction can be fairly abstract in that as long as this distinction was maintained anywhere in the morphology, it was maintained as morphological features which could license dative Case even when it was not marked overtly. By this hypothesis, we expect to find DO IO order in the case-rich texts but not in the case-impoverished ones.

Hypothesis (3) is that purely *syntactic* evidence can be used for Case distinctions when morphological evidence is not available. By this hypothesis, language learners could use quite abstract evidence for Case, thereby perhaps maintaining DO IO order after the morphological dative/accusative distinction had disappeared completely.

To test our hypotheses, it is not enough simply to look at the beginning stage, OE, where both orders of DO and IO were possible and there was a clear dative/accusative distinction, and the end stage, the mid-to-late fourteenth century, when IO DO had become the only possibility for two bare NP/DPs and the dative/accusative distinction had been totally lost in the morphology. We must look at intermediate stages and determine whether there was any stage when the order was not fixed but the morphological distinction appears to have been lost. Furthermore, we must look at the evidence concerning the maintenance of the dative/accusative system in the pronominal system, and whether there is evidence that as long as this system was maintained overtly in the pronouns, it was maintained covertly in the nominal system.

9.4 The Loss of DO IO Order

Traditional handbooks such as Mustanoja (1960) and Jespersen (1909–49) give insufficient detail on the fixing of the order of two objects to be of much help in evaluating our hypotheses, but more recent theoretically oriented studies such as Allen (1995), McFadden (2002), and Polo (2002) offer a much better empirical base for examining this relationship between the loss of case morphology and the loss of DO IO order.

The first thing we can say is that hypothesis (1) is clearly not tenable: quite clearly, the order of two nominal objects was still variable in texts written in dialects in which nouns and their modifiers were no longer overtly marked for the dative/accusative distinction. It is particularly clear that the lack of overt marking on the nouns in a particular sentence was no bar to DO IO order without a preposition; in the *Ancrene Wisse* (*AW*), IO DO order is the most frequent, but we find examples like (3):

(3) Ha chepeð hire sawle þe chapmon of helle
she sells her soul the merchant of hell
'she sells her soul to the merchant of hell'
(*AW* 213.28)

And in *PC II* we have:

(4) and te king iaf ðat abbotrice an prior of Sanct Neod
and the king gave that abbacy a prior of Saint Neot
'and the king gave that abbacy to a prior of Saint Neot's'
(*PC II*, 1132)

Similarly, in the *Ormulum*, we find examples like (5):

(5) Gast ȝifeþþ witt & wille & mahht whatt mann swa him sellf god
Spirit gives wit and will and power what man so him self good
þinnkeþþ To spellen haliȝlike
seems to preach holily
'The Holy Spirit gives wit and desire and power to preach divinely to whatever man (it) seems good to Him'
(*Ormulum* 17280–2)

In all of these examples, there is no overt case marking, either on the DO or on the IO. It is easy to establish, then, that no overt marking or fixed word order was needed to distinguish the IO and DO in a given sentence. Furthermore, the period where no overt marking was necessary in DO IO order was apparently a long one, as examples like (3) through (5) are found as late as the early fourteenth century in works such as *Havelok the Dane* and the pieces in the Auchinleck manuscript.

Hypothesis (2) is harder to test because of the problems which were alluded to earlier in evaluating the evidence concerning the case-marking system reflected in each text. For example, it could be claimed that the DO IO examples found in the *Ancrene Wisse* work (e.g. (3) above) are archaic retentions which the scribe simply failed to change. It is also unfortunate that we lack prose texts from the mid-to-late thirteenth century and early fourteenth century in the crucial dialects in which case marking deteriorated early. The only published case-impoverished texts we have available to us from this period are poetry, with the exception of *The Earliest Prose Psalter* (first half of the fourteenth century). Unfortunately this text shows a strong preference for *to*-datives, and the fact that 100 percent of the double object examples have IO DO order is not significant, because there are only three relevant examples. So we are forced to rely on poetry, and it can hardly be doubted that some archaic orders continue to appear in verse long after they have disappeared from ordinary speech and prose. It might therefore be suggested that examples of DO IO order in verse should be discounted as not representative of the ordinary language of the time.

Despite these problems, it is apparent that such evidence as we can adduce all points in the same direction: DO IO order remained available after all overt dative/accusative distinctions had been lost, both in the nominal and pronominal systems. Examples (4) and (5) both come from case-impoverished texts which show no retention whatsoever of an overt dative/accusative distinction, even in the pronominal system. Furthermore, the period which goes against hypothesis (2) is a substantial one, as far as we can tell from the texts, since in the dialects of *Havelok* and the Auchinleck manuscript, the distinction had disappeared long before these texts were written.

We might want to dismiss most of this evidence because it comes from verse, but it should be noted that DO IO order seems to have disappeared from poetry by the late fourteenth century, suggesting that the retention of DO IO order in the thirteenth century and the earlier fourteenth century is probably not simply due to stylistic license. Furthermore, example (4) is from a prose text. While we could wish to have a larger corpus of ditransitive sentences from texts like this one, it is problematic for hypothesis (2) that the single example of a ditransitive construction with two bare objects which is found in this text has just the order which the hypothesis predicts should be impossible in that text.

Furthermore, there is no correlation between the robustness of the overt dative/accusative distinction in a given ME text and the frequency of DO IO order. DO IO becomes markedly less frequent in EME even in the case-rich texts. Indeed, we find, rather surprisingly, that the twelfth- and thirteenth-century texts with the most marking of the dative/accusative distinction have a very low frequency of DO IO order: it is not found in any of the five examples with two bare double objects in the twelfth-century *Kentish Homilies*, where NP/DPs still always have some overt marking of dative or accusative case. In the thirteenth-century texts where the category had clearly been retained but the marking was optional, it is also on the decline; all five relevant examples in the *Kentish Sermons* have IO DO order, and the selections from the *Vices and Virtues* in the *PPCME2* yield only eight examples of DO IO order, i.e. 40 percent of the twenty examples with two NP/DP objects. An investigation of the entire *Aȝenbite of Inwit* shows that only two of the eleven examples with two bare objects have DO IO order, giving a proportion of only 18.18 percent in this morphologically conservative text (when we reject some putative DO IO examples which are misparsed in the *PPCME2* selections). Similarly, DO IO order is found only twice in the six relevant examples in the case-rich *Owl and the Nightingale* (*O&N*), and, interestingly enough, one of these examples (namely (6)) completely lacks overt marking, suggesting that the author did not have to choose between case marking and position to mark the IO, even though he had dative case marking as an option:

(6) heo walde neoþeless ȝefe answere þe niȝtegale
she would nevertheless give answer the nightingale
'She would nevertheless give answer to the nightingale'
(*O&N* 1710)

Presumably, the complete absence of DO IO order in some of these texts is to be attributed to the small corpus size, rather than to a grammatical impossibility; nevertheless, the low cumulative frequency in these texts leads to the conclusion that the decline of DO IO order was not simply a reflection of the loss of the dative/accusative distinction, and this is an embarrassment for hypotheses (1) and (2), which predict a correlation between the robustness of the dative/accusative distinction in a dialect and the amount of DO IO order.

We might try to dismiss the infrequency of DO IO order in the case-rich texts as simply an artifact of the texts. But Faroese facts, as presented by Holmberg and Platzack (1995) indicate that it is quite possible for a language to develop fixed IO DO order without losing the morphological dative/accusative distinction. Holmberg and Platzack indicate that Faroese is a language with a well-maintained morphological dative/accusative distinction but say (1995: 218 n.6) that "inversion" (i.e. DO IO order) is not possible in this language. So although we might want to maintain, on theoretical grounds, that a dative/accusative Case distinction (whether overtly marked or completely abstract) is a *necessary* condition for DO IO order, it is not a sufficient one.

Since neither hypothesis (1) nor (2) holds up, if we want to preserve our idea that the loss of case distinctions was the trigger for the fixing of the order of two objects, we will have to move to hypothesis (3) and look for more abstract, syntactic, evidence for the retention of the dative/accusative distinction as one which was still present in the syntax, although it was never overtly marked. And there is in fact a piece of evidence that we might bring to bear. This is the retention of what I will refer to as "dative-fronted" passives, e.g. (7), into the fourteenth century:

(7) þat him was so hard grace y-ȝarked
that him was such hard grace prepared
'That such a hard fate had been prepared for him'
(*Sir Orfeo* 547)

Under widely held assumptions, the continued existence of passives of this sort indicates the continued ability of NP/DPs to have inherent Case which was not marked by a preposition (although whether this is taken to imply a dative/accusative distinction in the morphological features will depend on theoretical assumptions). We could suggest that language learners could learn of the existence of inherent Case from passives of this sort in their acquisition data even when overt marking of the dative/accusative distinction had become too infrequent to trigger the acquisition of this distinction. Because of this, they could continue to learn the old grammar with abstract Case features, which would allow them to generate DO IO order, as long as the frequency of dative-fronted passives was reasonably high in their acquisition data.

However, it should be noted that the connection between the loss of the dative-fronted passive and the loss of the dative/accusative distinction is not as straightforward as it might seem. For one thing, monotransitive verbs complicate this picture. In OE, a monotransitive verb could require an object in the dative Case, and this Case would be retained in a passive sentence, as is typical of inherent Case:

(8) ac him bið gedemed
but them(D) be judged
'but they will be judged'
(*ÆHom* 11 365)

Verbs which normally took objects with accusative Case, in contrast, had an unremarkable passive with a nominative subject, as we would expect. Now we might expect that these two types of passives would be maintained as long as the dative-fronted passives of ditransitive verbs (e.g. (7)) remained. That is, language learners would have evidence that certain verbs took indirect objects, rather than direct objects, or alternatively, that certain verbs were subcategorized for objects with dative Case while others were not. Interestingly, this is clearly not what happened; there is an enormous time lag between the replacement of passives like (8) by "personal" passives like *they are judged* and the loss of the dative-fronted passives like (7), which are still found in the fourteenth century. The distinction in the passives of the two classes of monotransitive verbs disappeared quite abruptly in the early thirteenth century (in both prose and poetry). This is the same time when the overt dative/accusative distinction disappeared in most dialects, but, interestingly, these passives also disappeared in the texts which maintained a robust dative/accusative distinction in active sentences at this time. That is, in texts like the *Vices and Virtues* we find some dative-fronted passives with ditransitive verbs and we find a clear dative/accusative distinction for the objects of monotransitive verbs in active sentences, but all objects of monotransitive verbs show up as nominative in the passive. It is intriguing that the author of this text had clearly acquired a dative/accusative distinction, but must have had a rather different case-marking system from earlier generations, because he did not maintain the distinction in the passives of monotransitive verbs.

It is interesting to note that Holmberg and Platzack (1995) outline facts for modern Faroese which appear to be exactly parallel to the situation in the *Vices and Virtues* regarding the asymmetries in case retention in monotransitive and ditransitive passives (although not in the variability found in active sentences; see below). They suggest that the asymmetry in Faroese is due to the "weakness" of morphological case in that language; while there is an overt dative/accusative distinction, dative Case is licensed only under very restricted circumstances. Essentially, it must be close to the verb which licenses it. They suggest that the reason why dative Case is allowed to be retained in the passives of ditransitive verbs is that with these verbs, this Case is linked to a thematic role. However this intriguing case marking system is to be accounted for, two basic facts stand out. First, the Faroese facts strongly suggest that the situation which is apparently found in texts like the *Vices and Virtues* is not a typologically impossible situation, as we might suggest if we did not find a similar situation in a living language. This supports our confidence in our findings from text-based studies. Second, the Faroese facts indicate how complex the relationship between morphological and syntactic Case is and how subtle the evidence for the exact nature of the Case system may be; clearly, we cannot simply correlate an overt morphological distinction with an abstract feature distinction which will allow DO IO order.

It remains debatable what role the dative-fronted passive might have played in the retention of DO IO order in English. For one thing, these passives were becoming infrequent already in EME texts, regardless of the state of case morphology in a given text. This is not because these passives were being replaced by "indirect passives" such as *I was given a gift*, as one might assume, since such passives do not appear until the last quarter of the fourteenth century (see Allen 1995: ch. 9). It appears that the decline in dative-fronted passives was part of a general increase in all dialects in the use of "unmarked" word orders, even though more marked orders such as passives with a fronted dative and DO IO order were still grammatical. For a discussion of some developments with respect to marked and unmarked orders in English, see Seoane's paper (chapter 15, this volume). Whatever the cause may be of the decline of dative-fronted passives, it is not certain that the low frequency of these passives (judging from the texts) in ME would have been sufficient to trigger the acquisition of a Case distinction on their own.

In fact, it is probably the wrong way to look at things to assume that the loss of one of these two constructions (DO IO order and the dative-fronted passive) must be the trigger for the loss of the other, since both seem to have disappeared around the same time. It is possible to maintain the assumption that DO IO order indicates the retention of Case distinctions and still see the eventual loss of both this order and the Case features which permitted it as the end result of performance factors. We can assume that both of these constructions provided evidence in the language learner's acquisitional data for the construction of a grammar with Case distinctions, but that this evidence became increasingly reduced as these constructions were used less, for various reasons. Once the frequency of the constructions dropped to a sufficient point, language learners failed to construct grammars with any sort of dative/accusative distinction, and DO IO order became not only marked, but ungrammatical.

It is not difficult to find reasons why these constructions should have become less frequent. It is important to remember that there had been competition between dative case and prepositions as Case markers even in the OE period. McFadden (2002) argues that the *to*-dative can be seen as a replacement of the IO with dative Case, and that there is a general overall correlation between the frequency of *to*-datives and a lack of overt case marking in the ME texts, although the correlation does not hold up for each text. But given that the *to*-dative was already found with some verbs in OE when it was not in any sense "necessary" to mark Case, there is no necessity to assume that the *to*-dative only became available once the morphological dative was not available. It is only natural that this way of marking Case should extend to other verbs as time wore on, regardless of the availability of the morphological dative. Nor does the (generally) higher frequency of the *to*-dative in the case-impoverished texts prove that the writers of these texts had to use either the *to*-dative or word order to mark Case features overtly in each sentence; while it does not seem to be true that languages always require an overt marking of thematic relations, it is nevertheless clearly true that languages do tend to use either word order, case morphology, or adpositions to mark these roles. It is reasonable to assume that processing factors underlie this tendency; an overt marker of Case allows for an instant calculation of these roles. This being so, it is not surprising that a case-impoverished language user would have a comparatively high frequency of *to*-datives even though they were not absolutely necessary to distinguish the Recipient from the Theme in the ordinary situation with a human Recipient and a non-human Theme.

At any rate, the spread of the *to*-dative would have led not only to a lesser need to maintain the dative/accusative distinction but also to a reduction in DO IO order. The reason for this is that both these constructions serve a similar pragmatic function: to focus on the Recipient by putting it sentence-finally.

It can be noted, finally, that we do not require deflexion as an explanation for the rapid increase in *to*-datives in ME. The influence of French, in which the marking of the IO by a preposition was already well advanced, appears to be the best way to explain such text-specific facts as the surprisingly high incidence of *to*-datives in the *Aȝenbite of Inwit*. As mentioned above, the dative/accusative distinction was well preserved in the *Aȝenbite*, which might lead us to expect that the *to*-dative would be infrequent because it was not needed to mark Case, but in fact we find that this work has a significantly higher frequency of this construction than do many texts in which the dative/accusative distinction has disappeared in overt morphology. The puzzle is explained, however, when we realize that the *Azenbite* was a rather slavish translation from French and shows some unmistakable signs of the influence of its French exemplar in its syntax. It is, of course, uncertain how important French influence was in the spoken language, but contact with French would surely have encouraged the use of the *to*-dative. It should also be remembered that an innovation such as the *to*-dative typically follows an S-curve, starting slowly and then rapidly increasing, so that no sudden change in another part of the grammar is required to explain the sudden increase of the *to*-dative.

To sum up, there is clearly a connection between the loss of the dative/accusative distinction and the loss of the DO IO construction, but this connection is not as simple as one might expect. Although we might want to say that the DO IO construction could only remain available as long as there was an abstract dative/accusative distinction, we certainly cannot conclude from the evidence of the texts that the syncretism of the dative and accusative forms was a direct trigger for the decline of DO IO order. Furthermore, it is reasonable to assume that the interaction between the decline of case marking and the fixing of word order is not a one-way street. Once there was a clearly unmarked order for two objects, language users could use a processing strategy by which they assumed that the first object was probably the IO, and this might make them less careful to use such case marking as was still available to them. In this way, the development of an unmarked order, which might have resulted to some extent from reduced reliability in the morphological system, in conjunction with the increase in the use of adpositions to mark Case distinctions, would lead to a (further) increase in syncretism of case forms, which would in turn lead to further reliance on word order as a way of processing thematic relations. At some point, any grammatical device which allows such constructions as the dative-fronted passive and DO IO order is no longer part of the grammar which language learners construct. Such a development can be accommodated by a version of Case licensing theory that assumes that the evidence for Case distinctions may be quite abstract.

It must also be kept in mind that other changes were going on in the grammar of English in the period when DO IO order was lost, and a truly satisfying explanation of how language learners were able to construct grammars with DO IO order even though the overt dative/accusative distinction had been lost (i.e. in terms of Case licensing, acquired an abstract dative/accusative distinction) is only likely to emerge when the grammar is looked at as a whole system.

I have been examining the facts from the perspective of Case licensing, but we should note that the assumption that all NPs must be licensed for Case is not universal. For example, Lexical Functional Grammar (LFG) treats grammatical relations as primitives and does not allow syntactic movements. In this framework, it is not assumed that all NPs must have Case licensed in some way. For an analysis within this framework which treats the fixing of the order of two objects as involving the loss of evidence for indirect objects and triggering the introduction of new passives such as *I was given a book*, see Allen (1995: ch. 9).

9.5 The Loss of Post-head Genitives

Now we turn to another development in which deflexion has been implicated in the fixing of word order, the loss of the post-head genitive. As has often been noted, in OE genitive modifiers are found both before their heads (9a) or after them (9b):

(9) a. & þær wæs Kola ðæs cyninges heahgereafa
and there was Kola the(G) king(G) high reeve
'and there was Kola, the king's high-reeve'
(ASC(A) 1001.21)

b. þæt wæron þa ærestan scipu deniscra monna þe . . .
that were the first ships Danish(GP) men(GP) which . . .
'those were the first ships of Danish men which . . .'
(ASC(A) 787.5)

Postposition was especially common when the head was a quantifier, as in (10):

(10) þæt manige þara selestena cynges þena þe . . .
that many the(GP) best(GP) king's thanes . . .
'that many of the best royal thanes who . . .
(ASC(A) 896.8)

It has been suggested that deflexion was directly responsible for the loss of the post-head genitive and its replacement by the *of*-genitive. This idea is easily incorporated into generative frameworks, whether we assume (as in earlier generative works) that case was *assigned* by an appropriate head, or make the more recent assumption that cases are *checked* against a feature of the appropriate sort.

For example, Lightfoot (1999: 117–25) assumes that by the thirteenth century, children were learning grammars without any morphological case, including genitive case. Lightfoot assumes that the collapse of the distinction between nominative, accusative, and dative case made it impossible to maintain the genitive as a morphological case despite its fairly distinctive marking. Under the widespread assumption that all nouns must have Case and the further assumption that without morphological case the abstract Case cannot be licensed, this development would have made it impossible for these children to generate postnominal genitives, and they would have to use the preposition *of* as an equivalent of genitive case.

We must pause here to consider how it can be claimed that genitive case disappeared in EME when strings such as *the cynges sunu* 'the king's son' continued to be generated. The answer is that once we no longer have agreement between things like determiners, adjectives, etc. and the "genitive" noun, it is possible to analyze the putative genitive case marking as a clitic which occurred at the edge of the possessive NP/DP. Some sort of clitic analysis is usually considered necessary for PDE, where "group genitives" such as *the king of France's daughter* (replacing the earlier *the king's daughter of France*) show that the possessive marker is no longer simply an inflection of the possessor N, as in OE. Following Abney (1987), it is usually assumed that the modern possessive marker is the functional head D which follows the possessor NP.

There is disagreement over exactly when and how the genitive inflection became reanalyzed as a clitic; for a discussion, see Allen (2003). Let us leave aside the issue of whether a clitic analysis is appropriate for the early stage where agreement between the modifiers and the possessor noun has pretty much disappeared but the most convincing evidence for a clitic analysis, i.e. the group genitives, had not yet appeared in the texts. We will simply make the uncontroversial assumption that in the case-rich dialects where we still do find (at least optional) agreement in case between genitive nouns and their modifiers as well as an overt dative/accusative distinction, the genitive case is still retained as a morphological case in EME. So the most straightforward analysis for an example like (11) is that everything in the possessor NP/DP is marked for genitive case:

(11) ʒe modi menn, ðes dieules folʒeres
ye proud men, the(G) devil(G) followers
'you proud people, the devil's followers'
(CMVICES1,41.480)

By the widely held assumption that there is a close connection between the loss of post-head genitives and the loss of the genitive as a morphological case, we would expect that in the case-rich texts like the *Vices and Virtues*, we would still find post-head genitives, while in the case-impoverished texts, they would have disappeared. In the few texts we have from the twelfth century, there does indeed seem to be a pretty good correlation between the state of case marking in general and the appearance of post-head genitives. In the case-impoverished *PCII*, we find no examples of post-head genitives, while they are still reasonably common in the case-rich *Kentish Homilies*, e.g. (12):

(12) næs se cæstel hire mægeðhades . . . gewæmmed
not-was the(N) castle(N) her maidenhood(G) defiled
'the castle of her maidenhood was not defiled'
(CMKENTHO,136.59)

Given the situation in the twelfth century, it is not surprising that the loss of the post-head genitive is generally assumed to correlate closely with the general collapse of case marking. But when we look at the texts of the late twelfth and early thirteenth centuries, we find a rather surprising fact: the situation with regard to post-head genitives seems to be essentially the same in the case-rich texts and the case-impoverished ones; that is, post-head genitives have become quite restricted.

Leaving aside the question of genitive complements to adjectival heads, we can make the following generalizations about the examples of post-head genitives from all texts composed later than c.1200.

First, all these examples have a form which is inflected for genitive case as the first (or only) element of the post-head genitive. In the case-rich texts, this may be an inflected determiner, as in (13):

(13) ne ðurh nan ðare þinge ðe hie baðe muȝen don
nor through none those(GPL) things(GPL) that they both may do
'nor through any of those things that they both may do'
(CMVICES1,29.314)

This inflection need not be unambiguously genitive, e.g. the form *ðare* in (13) is used for the dative and genitive feminine singular as well as for the genitive plural in this text; the important generalization is that the genitive phrase always begins with an element which can be considered to be marked for genitive case. It must be emphasized, however, that even in the *Vices and Virtues*, where a determiner is nearly always inflected for agreement with a genitive noun, such examples are quite unusual; there are only six in the selections from this text used in the *PPCME2*. The *of*-genitive is highly favored in this text in contexts in which the post-head genitive would have been used in OE. The difference with the much shorter twelfth-century *Kentish Homilies*, where *of*-genitives are found but are unusual compared with twenty post-head genitives, is striking.

Second, almost without exception, the examples are partitive (in a broad sense of the term which refers to relationships to sets, such as "all of the men" and "the tallest of the men"). These partitive examples are found both in the case-rich texts, e.g. (14) and the case-impoverished texts, e.g. (15):

(14) and hwaþer ȝunker hes tobrecð: *justicia dei* scall þar of don riht.
and which you(G) it breaks; justice God shall thereof do right
'and whichever of you (lit. 'whichever your') breaks it, the Justice of God (Latin) will make that right'
(CMVICES1,95.1131)

(15) Forr eȝȝþerr here ȝede swa
Because either they(G) went so
'Because either of them (lit. 'either their') went so'
(*Ormulum* 119)

Examples like (15), which have only a pronoun as the (partitive) post-head genitive, are in fact the only examples in the *Ormulum*, where inflected determiners are unavailable. However, this fact does not lead to a greater scarcity of post-head genitives in general in the *Ormulum* compared to the case-rich *Vices and Virtues*, the *Kentish Sermons*, and the *Azenbite of Inwit* because of the preference for *of*-genitives in the latter texts. There are certainly some *of*-partitives in the *Ormulum*, but genitives (whether prenominal or postnominal) seem to be preferred in this text.

The existence of examples like (15) clearly demonstrates that the collapse of the dative/accusative distinction did not make post-head genitives completely unavailable. Our first generalization suggests that overt case marking was indeed crucial in the licensing of postnominal genitives; the facts are by no means incompatible with the view that postnominal genitives needed to be licensed somehow. However, it is clear enough that the retention of a system of overt marking which distinguished accusative, dative, and genitive cases was not sufficient to prevent a sharp reduction in the number and range of post-head genitives. Deflexion cannot be the whole answer to the question of why the post-head genitive disappeared when it did.

Mitchell (1985: §1305) notes that "the change to complete pre-position of inflected genitives was under way in OE." That is, postnominal genitives were already becoming more restricted in OE (when we compare early OE texts to late OE ones) even before the *of*-genitive had really become available to "replace" the postnominal genitive. And even in those twelfth-century texts in which the post-head genitive is still reasonably common, we find that the semantic range of this construction has become more limited. Of the twenty examples in the *Kentish Homilies*, we find that none have a meaning of either possession or kinship, although post-head genitives are found expressing these relationships in late OE, in some texts at least. Whether or not we agree with Fischer (1992: 231) that "[t]he loss of the Old English postnominal possessive is explained by the fact that the Old English genitive functions which survived into Middle English most commonly occurred in prenominal position," it is important to keep in mind that pre-head and post-head genitives were not simply in free variation in OE; some types of genitives never appear post-head in OE, or at least are not found in all texts. It appears that by EME, we see the end stages of the progressive restriction of post-head genitives. While this restriction would have been exacerbated by deflexion, it does not seem to have been caused by it, at least in the initial stages. For a generative treatment which does not treat deflexion as a trigger for the loss of postnominal genitives, see Crisma (to appear).

One possible approach to the restrictions on post-head genitives in EME is to treat some genitives as involving *structural* Case marking/checking but others as involving *lexical* Case marking/checking. By such an approach, we could say that by the thirteenth century, the only post-head genitives which the grammar allowed were ones licensed by particular lexical heads (quantifiers and specific adjectives). Later, all these post-head functions were replaced by *of*-genitives.

9.6 Conclusions and Further Directions

The two case studies examined here do not support the view that the fixing of word order in English was driven solely by the loss of case inflections or the assumption that at every stage of English, there was a simple correlation between less inflection and more fixed word order. This is not to say that deflexion did not play an important role in the disappearance of some previously possible word orders. It is reasonable to suggest that although it may have been pragmatic considerations which gave the initial impetus to making certain word orders more dominant than others, deflexion played a role in making these orders increasingly dominant. It seems likely that the two developments worked hand in hand; more fixed word order allowed for less overt case marking, which in turn increased the reliance on word order.

Such a development is by no means incompatible with current Case licensing theory (although this is not the only possible approach); one possibility is that orders which had become highly marked, but were still grammatical, simply became impossible at the point when Case could no longer be licensed in certain positions. Such an approach would seem to have to allow for fairly abstract evidence for Case in the construction of grammars by language learners to explain the retention of DO IO order with bare objects even after the overt dative/accusative distinction had been lost. Possible candidates for the provision of such abstract evidence include the dative-fronted passives, but of course there may be other facts not considered in this chapter which turn out to be relevant. If abstract evidence is indeed used in this way, then it becomes particularly important to take a "whole grammar" approach.

It is of particular interest to note that though morphological case did not disappear in the case-rich dialects in EME, the system was not simply the same as the OE system. If it were, we would expect to find Case preservation in the passives of monotransitive verbs which selected dative objects, as in OE, but we do not. So it seems that there may have been a change in the "strength" of the morphology in some sense. If we looked only at EME, we might suggest that this change had to do with the optionality of case marking, which appears in even the case-rich texts, but when we look at Faroese, where such optionality is apparently lacking, this does not seem like a very fruitful avenue of investigation.

The light which Faroese sheds on the ME situation is an illustration of how important it is to keep cross-linguistic considerations in mind when formulating hypotheses about possible explanations for historical changes. But we must also remember that any explanation which is given for the impossibility of DO IO order in Faroese must also not rule the same order out in EME, where it is found in the case-impoverished texts lacking the morphological distinctions that Faroese retains. Any change to the morphological "strength" which may have taken place did not rule out DO IO order, although it may have encouraged the use of alternatives. Further investigation of the Faroese situation would be useful here in understanding how some word orders can become fixed even when there is substantial morphology. It also seems that more attention to considerations such as how language users process the sentences they hear could be helpful in understanding changes like the disappearance of DO IO order.

Cross-linguistic studies are also likely to prove helpful in understanding the development of genitives in English, since some strikingly similar developments have taken place in other Germanic languages, but it is important to sound a note of caution here: superficially similar changes may not appear so similar when we look more deeply (see e.g. Allen 2003). In the case of the postnominal genitive in English, we still need a good account of why this construction was already becoming more restricted during the OE period. Also, we need an explanation for why possessive pronouns were apparently sufficient to license postposed genitives in partitives even in case-impoverished dialects in EME, but became unable to do so in later ME. What seems clear, however, is that the obsolescence of the postnominal genitives is not explained simply as a result of the collapse of the nominative/accusative/dative distinctions.

A final general comment which can be made is that while a formal account of the systems which operated at different historical periods is essential, historical studies cannot ignore questions of usage. When speakers have more than one grammatical option at their disposal, extra-linguistic factors will be important in which option they use, and the resulting usage patterns will affect the input data that language learners have for constructing their grammars.

REFERENCES

Abney, S. (1987). The English noun phrase in its sentential aspect. Unpublished PhD thesis, Department of Linguistics, MIT.

Allen, C. L. (1995). *Case Marking and Reanalysis*. Oxford: Oxford University Press.

Allen, C. L. (2003). Deflexion and the development of the genitive in English. *English Language and Linguistics* 7.1: 1–28.

Chomsky, N. (1995). *The Minimalist Program*. Cambridge, MA: MIT Press.

Crisma, P. (to appear). Genitive constructions in the history of English. In G. Banti, P. Di Giovine, and P. Ramat (eds.), *Typological Change in the Morphosyntax of the Indo-European Languages*. Munich: Lincom Europa.

Fischer, O. (1992). Syntax. In N. Blake (ed.), *The Cambridge History of the English Language*, vol. 2: *1066–1476* (pp. 207–408). Cambridge: Cambridge University Press.

Holmberg, A. and C. Platzack (1995). *The Role of Inflection in Scandinavian Syntax*. New York: Oxford University Press.

Jespersen, O. (1894). *Progress in Language: With Special Reference to English*. London: Swan.

Jespersen, O. (1909–49). *A Modern English Grammar on Historical Principles*. London: Allen and Unwin.

Kellner, L. (1892). *Historical Outlines of English Syntax*. London: Macmillan.

Kroch, A. and A. Taylor (1999). *The Penn-Helsinki Parsed Corpus of Middle English 2*. Philadelphia: Department of Linguistics, University of Pennsylvania.

Lass, R. (1992). Phonology and morphology. In N. Blake (ed.), *The Cambridge History of the English Language*, vol. 2: *1066–1476* (pp. 23–155). Cambridge: Cambridge University Press.

Lightfoot, D. (1999). *The Development of Language: Acquisition, Change and Evolution*. Oxford: Blackwell.

Lightfoot, D. (2002). *Syntactic Effects of Morphological Change*. Oxford and New York: Oxford University Press.

McFadden, T. (2002). The rise of the to-dative in Middle English. In D. W. Lightfoot (ed.), *Syntactic Effects of Morphological Change* (pp. 107–23). Oxford and New York: Oxford University Press.

Meillet, A. (1949). *Caractères généraux des langues germaniques* (4th edn.). Paris: Librairie Hachette.

Mitchell, B. (1985). *Old English Syntax*. Oxford: Clarendon Press.

Mossé, F. (1952). *A Handbook of Middle English* (tr. James A. Walker). Baltimore: Johns Hopkins Press (*Manuel de l'anglais du moyen âge des origines au XIVème siècle*, published 1945).

Mustanoja, T. (1960). *A Middle English Syntax*. Helsinki: Société Néophilologique.

Polo, C. (2002). Double objects and morphological triggers for syntactic case. In D. W. Lightfoot (ed.), *Syntactic Effects of Morphological Change* (pp. 124–42). Oxford and New York: Oxford University Press.

Randall, B. (2000). *CorpusSearch: A Java Program for Searching Syntactically Annotated Corpora*. Philadelphia: Department of Linguistics, University of Philadelphia.

FURTHER READING

Allen, C. L. (1997). The origins of the "group genitive" in English. *Transactions of the Philological Society* 95: 111–31.

Allen, C. L. (2001). The development of a new passive in English. In M. Butt and T. H. King (eds.), *Time over Matter: Diachronic Perspectives on Morphosyntax* (pp. 43–72). Stanford, CA: CSLI Publications.

Bresnan, J. (2001). *Lexical-functional Syntax*. Oxford: Blackwell.

Carstairs, A. (1987). Diachronic evidence and the affix–clitic distinction. In A. G. Ramat, O. Carruba, and G. Bernini (eds.), *Papers from the 7th International Conference on Historical Linguistics* (pp. 151–62). Amsterdam and Philadelphia: John Benjamins.

Janda, R. D. (1981). A case of liberation from morphology into syntax: the fate of the English genitive-marker *-(e)s*. In B. B. Johns and D. R. Strong (eds.), *Syntactic Change* (pp. 60–114). Ann Arbor, MI: Department of Linguistics, University of Michigan.

Kemenade, A. van (1987). *Syntactic Case and Morphological Case in the History of English*. Dordrecht: Foris.

Koopman, W. (1993). The order of dative and accusative objects in Old English and scrambling. *Studia Anglica Posnaniensia* 25–27: 109–21.

Larson, R. K. (1988). On the double object construction. *Linguistic Inquiry* 19: 335–91.

Nunnally, T. E. (1992). Man's son/son of man: translation, textual conditioning and the history of the English genitive. In M. Rissanenen, O. Ihalainen, T. Nevalainen, and I. Taavitsainen (eds.), *History of Englishes: New Methods and Interpretations in Historical Linguistics* (pp. 359–72). Berlin and New York: Mouton de Gruyter.

Nunnally, T. E. (1991). Morphology and word order within the Old English noun phrase. *Neuphilologische Mitteilungen* 92: 421–31.

Seppänen, A. (1997). The genitive and the category of case in the history of English. In R. Hickey and S. Puppel (eds.), *Language History and Linguistic Modelling* (pp. 193–214). Berlin: Mouton de Gruyter.

Thomas, R. (1931). Statistical processes involved in the development of the adnominal periphrastic genitive in the English language. Unpublished PhD thesis, University of Michigan.

Weerman, F. (1997). On the relation between morphological and syntactic case. In A. van Kemenade and N. Vincent (eds.), *Parameters of Morphosyntactic Change* (pp. 427–59). Cambridge: Cambridge University Press.

Yerkes, D. (1982). *Syntax and Style in Old English*. Binghamton, NY: Center for Medieval and Renaissance Studies.

10 Discourse Adverbs and Clausal Syntax in Old and Middle English

ANS VAN KEMENADE AND BETTELOU LOS

In this chapter, we discuss the syntactic and discourse properties of a number of adverbs in Old and Middle English, concentrating on *þa* and *þonne*, which both have 'then' as their literal meaning. This may seem like a small topic, but in fact we will show that the syntactic and discourse properties of these adverbs reveal a good deal about the changing organization of clause structure and discourse during the Old English period and the transition to Middle English. Building our argument around the properties of these adverbs, we will address a number of core issues in the analysis of Old English clause structure, such as the shift from parataxis to hypotaxis, the underlying motivation for the Verb Second constraint, and the changing position of various types of subject. An important implication of our discussion will turn out to be that the syntactic organization of the clause, at least in Old English, is interwoven with discourse organization much more closely than has been thought so far, and that the transition to Middle English is one that results in a more strictly syntactic organization of the clause.

10.1 Adverbs and Clause Structure in Old English

Þa and *þonne* are the most consistent members of a rather elusive class of adverbs, which includes temporal adverbs such as *þa* 'then', *nu* 'now', *þonne* 'then'; the interjection *la* 'lo'; reinforcing negative adverbs, *eac* 'also'. Perhaps a better term for these adverbs is the one coined by Kuhn (1933), *Satzpartikeln*; we will come back to this below. Their elusiveness lies primarily in that it is hard to see them as a natural class. We will address this problem later; for the moment we anticipate that discussion with the observation that what ties these elements together is that they are often used as rhetorical devices, and thus serve an important discourse function.

In the literature it has been observed that our adverbs, when they occur in clause-internal position, tend to occupy a rather fixed position high in the clause, with pronominal subjects on their left and nominal subjects on their right. This observation suggests that these adverbs may serve as interesting word order diagnostics and has led to an excited quest for their role in a syntactically defined clause structure (van Kemenade 1999, 2000, 2002; Haeberli 2000; van Bergen 2000; Haeberli and Ingham 2003). At the same time, it is obvious that an analysis in terms of one fixed position in the clause is at present rather problematic in particular for subclauses, and it is embarrassingly unclear why this should be the case. This is one of the problems addressed by the analysis in this chapter.

Our strategy here is as follows: we will concentrate on our two adverbs *þa* and *þonne,* as they are the most frequent and consistent representatives in their class. The advantage of this is that we can base the discussion on a relatively extensive body of data. We will focus on their syntactic behavior and, given their rhetorical use, on their discourse behavior. The broad picture we suggest is that *þa* and *þonne* are temporary adverbs in origin, marking a sequence in time. In various contexts, they have become entrenched in differential strategies of clause typing and discourse marking, and in some of these contexts their meaning has become quite bleached. In the Old English prose of the ninth and tenth centuries, *þa* and *þonne* are used in two main "parts" of the clause: in the left periphery and clause-internally, as mentioned above. We will devote subsections to each of these uses.

Throughout the chapter, the data are based on extensive searches in the York Corpus of Old English (Taylor et al. 2003) and the Penn-Helsinki Parsed Corpus of Middle English 2 (Taylor 2000). The references follow the system of short titles as employed in Healey and Venezky (1985 [1980]) (in turn based on the system of Mitchell et al. 1975, 1979). Note that line numbers refer to the beginning of the sentence rather than the line in which the relevant structure occurs. The corpora used are specified in the Appendix to this volume.

10.2 Þa and Þonne in the Left Periphery

The first and probably most eye-catching use of *þa* and *þonne* is as a main clause introducer, as in the following examples:

(1) a. **Þa** wæs þæt folc þæs micclan welan ungemetlice brucende, . . .
Then was the people the great prosperity (G) excessively partaking
'Then the people were partaking excessively of the great prosperity'
(*Or* 1.23.3)

b. **Ðonne** todælað hi his feoh, þæt þær to lafe bið æfter þæm gedrynce and þæm plegan
then divides he his property, that there to leave is after the drinking and the games
'then he will divide his property, which is left there after the drinking and the games'
(*Or* 1.17.12)

This pattern is as frequent and well known as it is puzzling The generally accepted syntactic analysis for this word-order pattern, given that inversion of finite verb and subject takes place regardless of whether the subject is nominal or pronominal, is that *þa* is in the highest functional specifier position Spec,CP, whereas the finite verb has been fronted to C. This entails that *þa* is treated as a topic. The term "topic" here is one adopted from the syntactic literature, but is really a misnomer for "the constituent in first position." This may be misleading in the sense that in discourse terms, such first constituents may represent given information, but they may as easily represent focalized information.

The puzzling thing about the word order in (1) from a syntactic point of view is that it patterns, not with other preposed non-subject topics (where the finite verb is most typically fronted to a lower position, see van Kemenade 2000), but with *wh*-phrases and initial negative elements, as in (2):

(2) a. **for hwam** noldest þu ðe sylfe me gecyðan þæt . . .
for what not-wanted you yourself me make-known that . . .
'wherefore would you not want to make known to me yourself that'
(*LS* 7(Euphr) 305)
b. Ne sceal he naht unaliefedes don
Not shall he nothing unlawful do
'He shall not do anything unlawful'
(*CP* 10.61.14)

The trigger for front position of the finite verb in questions and negative-initial clauses has been standardly analyzed, for historical and Present-day English alike, as a syntactic one (cf. a spate of literature on this, e.g. Rizzi (1996), Haegeman (1995) and references cited there). The problem for Old English here is that *wh*-phrases and negative elements do not in any obvious way form a natural class with preposed temporal elements like *þa* and *þonne*. We suggest, following up further the ideas in van Kemenade and Milicev (2005), that in Old English discourse marking is tied up with morphosyntactic marking to a much larger extent than has so far been realized. This leads us to resume the much criticized idea in van Kemenade (1987) that in word orders such as (1), *þa*/*þonne* is a discourse operator which triggers movement of the finite verb to C in much the same way as a *wh*-operator or a negative operator. Given that the CP domain of the clause is typically where clause type and discourse linking is encoded, this is no cause for surprise.

(3)
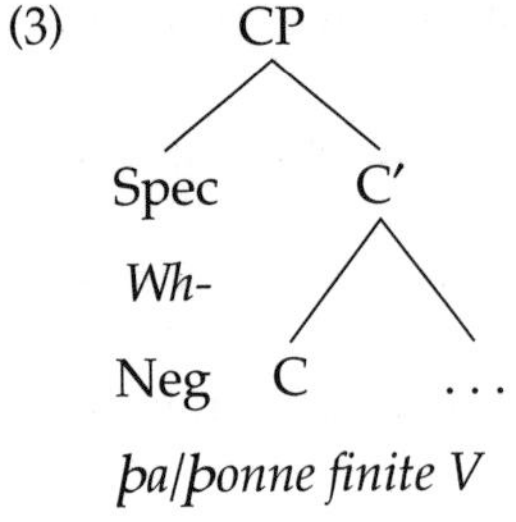

The word order in (1) typically encodes discourse sequence. This ties in with the analysis in Los (2000), who looks at various word orders with *onginnan/ beginnan* 'begin' as the finite verb in combination with types of infinitive in the prose of Ælfric (c.950). She observes two word-order patterns which are differentiated crucially by discourse considerations. Main clauses introduced by *þa* + finite *on/beginnan* take a bare infinitive and mark discourse continuity, as in the following examples:

(4) þa ongann se apostol hi ealle læran ofer twelf monað. ða deopan lare be drihtnes tocyme. to ðyssere woruld
then began the apostle them all teach for twelve months the deep lore about lord's coming to this world
'Then the apostle taught (*began to teach) them all for twelve months the profound doctrine of the Lord's coming to this world'
(ÆCHom II, 18 170.27)

This is contrasted with verb-initial main clauses (which tend to be typical of lively narrative style) which are followed by a *to*-infinitive, and Los argues that these introduce a new episode in the discourse:

(5) Begann ða to secgenne þam sceaðan geleafan. and mid boclicere lare hine læran ongann; Hwæt ða se sceaða sona gelyfde.on ðone lifigendan god. and tolysde ða benda
began then to say (to) the ruffian faith and with scriptural doctrine him teach began; lo then the ruffian at-once believed in the living god and released the bonds
'[he] began then to explain the faith to the ruffian and began to guide him with scriptural doctrine; Lo, then the ruffian at once believed in the living god and untied his bonds'
(ÆCHom II, 39.1 290.70–1)

While the construction with *on/beginnan* 'begin' as finite verb is special in that the choice of the following infinitive is of further consequence, it seems generally reasonable to analyze main clauses introduced by *þa*–finite verb in terms of discourse continuity. We come back to this below. The mapping between syntax and discourse function for main clauses introduced by *þa*–finite verb is then that discourse continuity is associated with a syntactic structure in which *þa* is what is usually called a topic (in Spec,CP position), whereas the finite verb is in C.

The use of *þa/þonne* as a main clause introducer as illustrated in (1) becomes even clearer when we contrast it with the second type of use in the left periphery. Before we go on discussing this, we give a few examples:

(6) a. Ða gelamp hit sarlicum gelimpe: **þa ða** se fæder **þohte** hwam he hi mihte healicost forgifan, **þa gefeol his agen mod** on hyre lufe mid

unrihtre gewilnunge, to ðam swiðe þæt he forgeat þa fæderlican arfæstnesse and gewilnode his agenre dohtor him to gemæccan.
then befell it a sorrowful event: **then when** the father **considered** whom he her might most loftily give, **then fell his own mood** in her love with wrong desire, so greatly that he forgot the fatherly virtue and desired his own daughter him to wife.
'Then a sad event happened: when the father considered to whom he might best give her hand in marriage, a wrongful love and desire came over him which was so strong that he forgot fatherly honor and desired his own daughter as his wife'
(coapollo, ApT:1.6.7)

b. **Mid þy þa** æfter swa monegum gearum hire lichoma **wæs** of byrgenne up **ahæfen, þa aþenedon heo** & aslogon geteld ofer,
with that when after so many years her body was from grave up lifted, **then stretched they** and spread tent over
'When after so many years her body was lifted out of the grave, they stretched and spread a tent over it'
(cobede, Bede_4:21.320.30.3223)

c. **þa** he þa ure Drihten his þæm halgum **sægde** þæt þæt heora gemet nære þæt hie þæt wiston, hwonne he ðisse worlde ende gesettan wolde, **þa cwæþ he** to him, Seþ accipietis uirtutem superuenientes Spiritus Sancti in uos;
when he then our Lord to his the holy said that that their capacity not-was that they that knew, when he this world's end set would, then said he to them
'When our Lord said [that] to his holy people that it was beyond their power to know when he would ordain the end of this world, then he said unto them'
(coblick, HomS_46_[BlHom_11]:119.49.1511)

(7) a. ond seo gesihð him wæs on swa micelre gemynde þæt he on ðæm miclan wintres cele, **þonne** he ymb þæt **þohte** oþþe spræc, **ðonne aswætte he** eall,
and the sight him was on so great memory that he in the great winter's cold, when he about that thought or spoke, then sweated he all
'and the sight was so vivid in his memory, that even in the sharp cold of winter, he broke out all in a sweat when he thought about it'
(comart3, Mart_5_[Kotzor]:Ja16,B.6.109)

b. forðæm, **ðonne** ðæt mod **sceamað** ðæt hit mon wite, **ðonne mæg hit** eaðe gesælan æt sumum cierre ðæt hine eac scamige ðæt he hit wyrce.
Because, when the mind shames that it men know, then may it easily happen at some time that him also shame that he it do.
'because when the mind is ashamed that men should know about it, it may at some point happen that it is also ashamed to do it'
(cocura, CP:55.427.22.3002)

In each of these sentences, we have a sequence of two clauses both introduced by *þa/þonne*. The first of the two clauses serves to locate the context in time/discourse, the second then relates the subsequent event. In the light of the previous discussion, it comes as no surprise that the second clause has *þa*–finite-subject order since it typically continues the discourse and follows on the previous clause. What is perhaps more surprising is that the first of the two clauses in each case behaves morphosyntactically as a subclause: while the finite verb is not fronted and *þa/þonne* seems to act as a subordinating conjunction, the fact that the clause locates the discourse in time seems to be more indicative of main clause behavior. Observe, however, that the idea that *þa/þonne* acts as a subordinating conjunction immediately accounts for the subclause behavior: since in a structure like (3) above, subordinating conjunctions are in the C-position, their presence would block fronting of the finite verb to C as in the second clause, since the C-position is already filled.

(8)

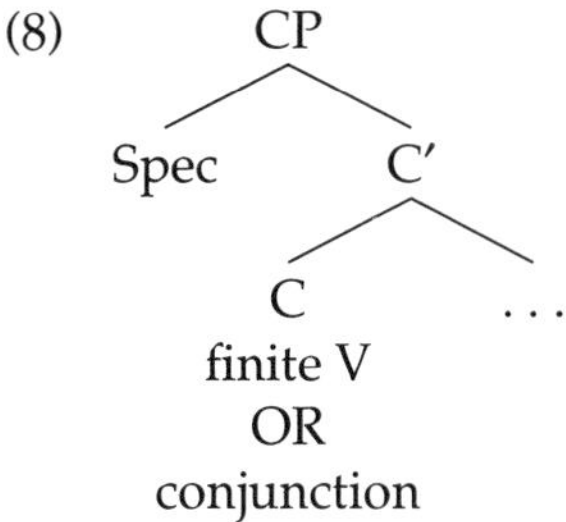

If this is correct, it has interesting implications for how *þa/þonne* as original temporal adverbs have become entrenched in marking discourse relations and syntactic functions.

The question how this complex of Old English facts came about is of some interest. We believe that our current state of insight into early Germanic syntax allows at least part of an answer to this question, even if this is in part (necessarily) a speculative one. The first ingredient in this scenario is drawn from Kiparsky (1995), who hypothesizes that in the historical development from Indo-European, movement of the finite verb to C in questions and negatives (with accompanying subject–finite inversion) arose as a strategy for marking main clauses in the development from dominant parataxis to dominant hypotaxis. The second ingredient is from Ferraresi's (1997) work on Gothic, in which she draws an interesting parallel between verbal inflections which mark the modality of the clause (indicative, subjunctive, imperative) and the clause particles which (still) exist in Gothic and which mark clause type (interrogative, negative, declarative). Let us look at a few examples: clause typing in Gothic is marked to an important extent by clause particles: questions are marked by the interrogative particle *-u*, enclicitized to the first word of a clause (as in (9)); coordination is marked by the coordinating particle *-uh*, which is likewise encliticized (as in (10)); relative clauses are marked by the particle

-ei (as in (11)), which may be encliticized to the antecedent of the relative clause. Verb fronting in Gothic certainly exists, but is highly variable. Here are examples of each of these contexts, taken from Eythórsson (1995):

(9) ga-*u*-laubjats þatei magjau þata taujan?
be-u-lieve that [I] can that do
'do you believe that I can do this?'
(Matt 9.28, Eythórsson 1995: 122)

(10) þata rodida Iesus uz-*uh*-hof augona seina du himina
thus spoke Jesus, and-up-lifted eyes his to heaven
'Thus spoke Jesus, and lifted up his eyes to heaven'
(John 17.1, Eythórsson 1995: 121)

(11) þo*ei* ni skulda sind
those which not permitted are
'those which are not permitted'
(1 Tim 5.13, Eythórsson 1995: 118)

Eythórsson (1995) and Ferraresi (1997) agree that these clause-typing particles, which in their use cut through the main/subclause distinction, are C-elements. The rather interesting historical scenario that Ferraresi surmises is that when these clause-typing particles were lost, presumably as the result of erosion of inflection, this gave rise to V-movement to C (in the absence of any other lexical filler), which should accordingly be viewed as a periphrastic strategy to mark clause type. Combining these ideas, the loss of clause-typing particles and the increase of hypotaxis called for new morphosyntactic strategies to differentiate clause modalities and clause embedding. This seems to us to be an interesting background scenario for how the behavior of *þa/þonne* in the left periphery of the clause may have become differentiated. We speculate that at some prehistorical moment, *þa* and *þonne* in clause-initial position were not so differentiated, but were clause-introducing adverbs in a sequence of similar clauses which were conjoined paratactically. Gothic is not exactly a direct ancestor of the West Germanic languages, but the presence of clause-typing particles which were C-elements seems a reasonable assumption for an earlier Germanic state. Let us suppose that, at the time when clause typing particles were getting lost, V-movement was highly variable. This is clearly supported even for questions in Gothic, and we may also note a similar scenario for negative-initial clauses in early Old English in van Kemenade (2000).

In contexts where V-movement did take place, *þa/þonne* in clause-initial position, followed by the finite verb, was reanalyzed as a main clause, parallel to questions and negative-initial clauses. Where V-movement did not take place, *þa/þonne* itself was reanalyzed as a subordinating conjunction.

This is admittedly a speculative scenario, but it is entirely in line with recent insight into the structure of early Germanic, and in our view makes very good sense of some core facts of Old English prose discourse. We now turn to the use of *þa/þonne* in clause-internal position.

10.3 *Þa* and *Þonne* in Clause-internal Position

The discussion in the literature on the clause-internal position of *þa/þonne* and other adverbs has played an important role in the recent debate about the finer points of Old and Middle English clause structure. Observing that in Old English multiple sentential negation, the reinforcing negative adverb occupies a fixed position in the clause, van Kemenade (1999, 2000) argues the cue status of such adverbs in clause structure. Van Kemenade (2002) extends this analysis to the role of *þa/þonne*. The core observation is that personal pronouns appear on the left of *þa/þonne* (object pronouns do so optionally), whereas nominal elements, including subjects, occur on the right. The examples in (12) and (13) illustrate this pattern:

(12) Pronominal subject + pronominal object preceding *þa/þonne*
He ne mihte swaþeah æfre libban, þeah ðe he hine *þa* ut alysde
He not-could nevertheless ever live, though that they him then released
'Nevertheless, he could not live forever, though they then released him'
(coælive, ÆLS[Ash_Wed]:119.2763)

(13) Pronominal object preceding *þa/þonne*, nominal subject following *þa/þonne*
Gif him *þonne* God ryhtlice & stræclice deman wile.
If him then God justly and strictly judge will
'if God will then justly and strictly judge him'
(cocura, CP.5.45.20)

Van Kemenade (2002) shows that this generalization holds very well for main clause questions. By way of illustration, table 10.1 has some statistics for *þonne* in main clause questions in one text, King Alfred's translation of *Cura Pastoralis*.

These facts have played a key role in the debate on clause structure, since they show quite clearly that it is the position of the adverb that seems to be

Table 10.1 Root questions: order of subject and *ðonne* in *Cura Pastoralis*

	Nominal subject	*Personal pronoun subject or object*
Subject left of *ðonne*	0	10
Subject right of *ðonne*	17	0

Table 10.2 *Þa/þonne* and pronominal subject in Old English

	Subclauses
Pro subject preceding *þa/þonne*	1,250
Pro subject following *þa/þonne*	5

Table 10.3 *Þa/þonne* and nominal subject in Old English

	Subclauses
Nominal subject follows *þa/þonne*	419
Nominal subject precedes *þa/þonne*	293

quite fixed. If this is correct, they also, importantly, show that personal pronouns occur in a position that is genuinely higher than that of nominal subjects. But, however clear these facts seem to be, the picture is more complicated. Haeberli and Ingham (2003), looking at the position of adverbs generally in the first period of Middle English (up to 1250), point out that in subclauses nominal subjects occur on the left of adverbs quite frequently in early Middle English. The following facts show that this is true in Old English as well, even if, unlike Haeberli and Ingham, we restrict the choice of adverb to *þa/þonne*: while the figures for pronominal subjects are clear enough, as can be seen in table 10.2, those for nominal subjects in table 10.3 are rather equivocal (the figures are based on exhaustive searches of the York Corpus of Old English (Taylor et al. 2003):

These facts thus pose a problem for a purely syntactic treatment of Old English clause structure: within the subclause, the differentiation of nominal subject positions is unclear; we can say, as we will see in more detail below, that the position on the left of *þa/þonne* tends to be reserved for definite subjects, but this is a one-way correlation: definite subjects can occur on the left of *þa/þonne* and indefinite subjects are quite rare there; on the other hand, definite as well as indefinite subjects are common on the right of *þa/þonne*. With respect to the differentiation between clause types, we can say that while the situation seems to be clear in main clauses, subclauses show a rather different picture, and it is unclear why this should be so: there is little reason to expect a syntactic difference between main clauses and subclauses apart from the realization of the CP-domain, as discussed in the previous section. This state of affairs poses a difficult task: while upholding the insights achieved within a syntactic approach, the challenge of accounting for the facts in subclauses remains open.

Our approach follows up that in van Kemenade and Milicev (2005). This approach entails that Old English morphosyntax encodes discourse relations. The central claim is that in its clause-internal use *þa/þonne* is a focus particle, i.e. a morphosyntactic marker which separates the topic domain of the clause from the focus domain. "Topic" domain is here understood as the portion of the clause that encodes given information, whereas the "focus" domain contains new information. This means broadly, and we will be more specific below, that the topic domain contains the material that refers back to a referent in the discourse: definite subjects and pronominal subjects and objects in the most typical case; less usually (certainly in the subclause) contrastive topics. The focus domain contains the new information in the clause.

The notion that Old English syntax encodes discourse relations and that *þa/þonne* play a role in marking off subdomains of the clause goes a lot further than saying that *þa/þonne* is a pragmatic marker, as in chapter 13 (this volume), where Brinton follows up Enkvist and Wårvik (1987) and Wårvik (1995). Our claim entails that discourse relations are entrenched in morphosyntactic marking, as is typical of what have come to be called discourse-configurational languages (see e.g. Kiss 1995). Bearing this in mind, let us consider the motivation for analyzing *þa/þonne* as a focus particle in some more detail.

Let us come back first of all to the question of what the property could be that puts elements like *þa/þonne* in a natural class with *nu* 'now', *eac* 'also', *la* 'lo' (see also Kato 1995). What unites these elements is that they are often used as rhetorical devices. This is particularly clearly the case when they are used in clause-internal position. We illustrate this with a few examples involving *þa/þonne*:

(14) Forðæm se se ðe ðonne sacerdhad onfehð, he onfehð friccan scire & foreryneles ða her iernað beforan kyningum, & bodigeað hira færelt & hiera willan hlydende. Sua sculun ða sacerdas **nu** faran hlydende & bodiende beforan ðæm egeslican deman ðe him suiðe andrysnlic æfter gæð. Gif **ðonne** se sacerd bið ungerad ðæs lareowdomes, hwæt forstent **ðonne** his gehlyd?
Because he who that then priesthood undertakes, he undertakes herald's office & footmen who here run before kings, & proclaim their journey and their will loudly. So shall the priests **now** run proclaiming and preaching before the awful judge who them very majestically after goes. If **then** the teacher is unskilled in instruction, what avails **then** his cry?
'For he who undertakes the priesthood undertakes the office of herald and footmen who run before kings, loudly proclaiming their journey and will. Thus priests ought to run and proclaim loudly before the awful judge, who follows them in great majesty. But if the priest is unskilled in instruction, what avails his cry?
(cocura, CP, 15,91,25)

There is no clear question of temporal reference in (14) for either *nu* or *ðonne*. Brinton (chapter 13, this volume) remarks that these elements serve to section off events, which may be a natural kind of grammaticalization path with temporal adverbs as its origin. We think they have a rhetorical use as well, and serve to underline the admonishing and exhorting effect in context, which is a very typical feature of *Cura Pastoralis*. The rhetorical effect of *þa* is particularly clear in exclamatory combinations like *hwæt þa* 'what lo':

(15) a. **Hwæt ða** la ongunnon **þa** godes cempan hnexian and heora mod awendon to hyre maga sarnysse.
what then lo began then God's champions yield and their mood turn to their kinsmen's anguish
'Well, then, behold! God's champions began to yield, and to turn their thought on their kinsmen's anguish'
(ÆLS (Sebastian) 48)

b. **Hwæt þa** se biscop hine bliþelice gefullode, and ealle his hiwan on þæs Hælendes naman.
What then the bishop him blithely baptized, and all his household in the Savior's name
'and indeed the bishop blithely baptized him and all his household in the Savior's name.'
(ÆLS (Basil) 167)

c. Ono **hwæt** he **þa** se ilca cyning Osweo æfter Pendan slege þreo winter ful Mercna þeode & swylce eac tham oðrum folcum þara suðmægða in aldordome ofer wæs.
Lo what he then the same king Oswio after Penda's death three winters whole Mercia's people and also the other nations of the southern provinces authority over was.
'Now this king Oswio after Penda's death for three whole years had authority over the Mercians and the other nations also of the southern provinces'
(Bede 3.18.238.27)

In (15), the exclamatory part of the clause in each case primarily serves to draw particular attention to the event following. The temporal effect of *þa* is minimal at best. The text in (15c) is of particular interest because the subject is expressed both as a personal pronoun (preceding *þa*) and as a definite subject (following *þa*), drawing particular attention to this same king Oswio. This particular use of *þa* illustrates very well the function of focus particles as we see them: the focus part of the clause is "introduced" by the focus particle in the sense that it immediately precedes the focus part.

Our claim is then that the separation of the topic and focus areas in the clause is marked morphosyntactically. Let us now take a look at the topic domain more closely, focusing on subclauses.

10.4 The Topic Domain in the Subclause

At the start of the discussion in this section, it may be useful to point out yet again that the term "topic domain" refers to the portion of the clause that contains given information. Topic for us then subsumes personal pronouns, definite nominal subjects, and contrastive topics (which are rare but not non-existent in the subclause). We discuss each of these types of topic in turn.

We regard personal pronouns as continued topics. They are (discourse) anaphoric expressions and as such are definite and specific; this is true for their semantics as well as for their morphology. Semantically, they are presuppositional; morphologically, we note their inflectional kinship to demonstrative pronouns and strong adjectives, as is also pointed out in chapter 12 (this volume). Table 10.2 shows that pronominal subjects occur overwhelmingly in a high position on the left of *þa/þonne*. This needs no further illustration beyond (16), in which the pronominal subject is in the highest position. We defer discussion of the remaining examples in which the subject pronoun is on the right of *þa/þonne*.

Object pronouns may appear in the high position as well, as we saw above in (13), where it occurs alone on the left of *þonne*; an object pronoun may also cluster with other pronouns:

(16) on Salomonnes bocum, hit is awrieten ðæt mon ne scyle cweðan to his frind: Ga, cum to morgen, ðonne selle ic ðe hwæthwugu, gif **he hit him ðonne** sellan mæge.
in Solomon's books, it is written that that one not shall say to one's friend: "Go, come tomorrow, then give I you something, if he it him then give may."
'in the books of Solomon, it is written that we are not to say to our friend: "Go, and come tomorrow, then I will give you something," if he can give it him then'
(cocura, CP.44.323.24)

The order of pronouns in such clusters is fixed: subject–direct object–indirect object, and we assume that this is due to a syntactic constraint. Such a sequence of pronouns on the left of *þa/þonne* indicates in discourse terms that the referents of the various pronouns are of equal prominence in the discourse. The high position for object pronouns is optional; they can stay on the right of *þa/þonne* as well, as is evident from table 10.4.

Given our hypothesis that *þa/þonne* is a focus particle, it is of some importance to understand which properties differentiate pronouns that occur left of

Table 10.4 *Þa/þonne* and pronominal object in Old English

	Subclauses
Pro object (alone)–*þa/þonne*	39
Pro subject–pro object–*þa/þonne*	74
Þa/þonne–pro object	86

þa/þonne from those on the right of *þa/þonne*. Object pronouns alone in the "high" position as in table 10.4 typically occur with a nominal subject on the right of *þa/þonne*: here is a typical example in context:

(17) Ond eft ðonne sume yfele menn swa gerade beoð ðæt hie ne magon godum monnum derian, ðeah hie willen, ðonne is betere ðeah ðæt mon eorðlice sibbe betwux ðæm fæstnige, oððæt hie mægen ongietan ða uplican sibbe; ðætte hie ðurh ða menniscan sibbe mægen astigan to ðære godcundan sibbe, ðeah hio him ðonne giet feorr sie, forðæm ðæt yfel hiera unryhtwisnesse hie hæfð ðonne giet ahierde, ðætte **hie ðonne** gemonnðwærige sio lufu & sio geferræden hiora niehstena, & hie to beteran gebrenge.

And again, when any evil men so disposed are that they not can good people harm, though they wish, then is better though that one earthly peace between them confirm, until they may appreciate the sublime peace; that they through the human peace may ascend to the divine peace, though they from-it still far may-be, because the evil of-their unrighteousness them has then still hardened, that **them then** may-humanize the love and the society of-their neighbors and them to better may-bring

'And again, when any bad men are so disposed as not to be able to harm the good, although they desire it, it is better to confirm earthly peace between them, until they can appreciate the sublime peace, although it is yet far from them, because the evil of their unrighteousness still hardens them, that love and the society of their neighbors may humanize them' (cocura,CP:47.363.15.2461)

This example shows that a high object pronoun has a referent that is prominent in the discourse: the whole passage is concerned with the description of the people that *them* refers to; it is the material following *þonne* that forms the focus of the clause. Let us now consider object pronouns below *þa/þonne*.

The main diagnostic for postulating a low position for pronouns is the possibility of separation from the subject pronoun, or the possibility of separation between two object pronouns, as in (18). Generally speaking, it is dative pronouns that show the strongest tendency towards a low pronoun position, whether they are indirect object pronouns or pronouns stranding P. Also, reflexive pronouns generally prefer to follow their antecedents, but such cases can be said to be determined by c-command. A possible explanation for the distribution of indirect object and P-stranding pronouns can be found in the fact that they are part of a more complex verb complementation structure and that their presence is required by this structure, i.e. double object structure, or a PP structure. But this does not account for a number of examples in which subject and object pronoun are separated, like the following:

(18) Ic wat þæt he hæfde ane dolhswaðe on his hneccan þæt him gelamp iu on gefeohte. Gyman we nu hwæðer he þæt taken þære wunde hæbbe. *þa* **hi þa hine** *geornlice* beheoldon, *þa* gesawon hi *þa* dolhswaðe on him,

I know that he had a scar on his neck which him happened once in fight. Look we now whether he the mark of the wound have. When **they then him** carefully beheld, then saw they the scars on him,
'I know he had a scar on his neck that happened to him in a fight; let us look now whether he has the mark of the wound. When they then carefully beheld him, they saw the scar on him'
(coeust,LS_8_[Eust]:270.286)

The position of object pronouns in the focus area, and its internal structure, is beyond the scope of the present discussion. At this stage, we concentrate on the generalizations that can be made about pronouns occurring in the topic area.

Before we discuss the remaining facts concerning high object pronouns, we will consider the discourse effects of nominal subjects in relation to their positioning with *þa/þonne*. As is evident from table 10.2, NP subjects can be found left and right of *þa/þonne*, in our terms, in the topic domain or in the focus area. One clear generalization can be made concerning the semantics of NP subjects left and right of *þa/þonne*: while definite NPs are found left and right of the focus particle, indefinite NPs are preferred on the right, in the focus area. The text in (19) gives an example of a definite subject preceding *þa/þonne*:

(19) Forðæm bið se sige micle mara ðe man mid geðylde gewinð, forðæm **sio gesceadwisnes ðonne** hæfð ofercumen ðæt mod & gewielð, swelce he self hæbbe hiene selfne gewildne, & sio geðyld hæbbe ðæt mod geðreatod & gecafstrod.
Therefore is the victory much greater which one with patience wins, because the wisdom then has overcome the mind and subdued, as if he self have himself conquered, and the patience have the mind intimidated and curbed.
'Therefore the victory which is won with patience is much greater, because in this case wisdom has overcome and subdued the mind, as if he himself had conquered himself, and patience had intimidated and curbed the mind'
(cocuraC,CP_[Cotton]:33.218.19.42)

These definite subjects are to be viewed as contrastive topics: in the context in (19) the NP *seo gesceadwisnes* 'wisdom' is contrasted in context with the impatience that wins lesser victories.

When the subject is an indefinite NP, only the personal pronoun object occupies the topic area (20), or the topic area remains empty, yielding the sequence complementizer–*þa/þonne* (21).

(20) a. Gif hine **þonne** [yfel mon] hæfð, *þonne* bið he yfel þurh þæs monnes yfel þe him yfel mid deð, & þurh dioful

if him then evil man has, then be he evil through the man's evil who him evil with does and through devil
'If an evil man has him, then he is evil through the evil of the man who does evil with him, and through the devil'
(coboeth,Bo:16.38.26.702)

b. Mid þy hine **þa** nænig mon ne gehabban ne gebindan meahte, *þa* orn sum þegn
when him then no man not capture nor tie-up, then ran some servant
'when no one then could capture him and tie him up, then a servant pursued him'
(cobede,Bede_3:9.184.27.1847)

(21) a. Gif **þonne** swiðra wind aras, *þonne* tynde he his bec
if then stronger wind arose, then closed he his books
'if a stronger wind then arose, then he closed his books'
(cobede,Bede_4:3.268.18.2727)

b. Gif **þonne** hwylc læsse þing sie to smeagenne, *þonne* hæbbe he þara yldestra manna geþeaht
if then any less thing be to think on then have he the oldest men's advice
'If there is any more minor thing to consider, then he shall take the advice of the oldest men'
(cobenrul,BenR:3.16.9.232)

This tendency of OE indefinites to occur low in the clause seems to support the semantic partition into the "given" and "new" part. Therefore, we may assume that a mapping principle associating NPs in particular syntactic positions with particular types of interpretation is operative in OE, at least for the topic area: a definite NP can occur in the topic area as a contrastive topic. Observe, however, that this is a one-way correlation: while indefinite NP seems to be restricted to the focus area, definite NP can occur there as well. We refrain from discussion of the internal structure of the focus area.

The observations made here about indefinite subject NPs do not hold for indefinite pronouns: *hwa* 'whoever' and *ænig* 'any' as pronouns may occur in the topic area, and the impersonal pronoun *man* 'one, people', overwhelmingly occurs in the topic area:

(22) a. Gif hwa **ðonne** of giernesse & gewealdes ofslea his þone nehstan þurh searwa
If any then out of importunity and of his own will slay his the nearest through treachery
'if any then importunely and willingly kills his next of kin through treachery'
(colawafint,LawAfEl:13.37)

b. & gif **ænig þonne** sy up ahafen & swa swiðe gredig þissere worulde
and if any then be up lifted and very greedy of-this-world
'and if anyone then is arrogant and so covetous of this world'
(Ch 1232.11; van Bergen 2000:119; (53a))

c. Swa se æþela lareow sægde, þæt se cyning & se bisceop sceoldan beon Cristenra folca hyrdas, & hi from eallum unrihtwisum ahweorfan; & gif **mon þonne** ne mihte hi to rihte gecyrron
As the eminent teacher has said, that the king and the bishop should be Christian folk's shepherds, and them from all unrighteous things turn; and if **one then** not might them to justice/equity turn
'As the eminent teacher has said, the king and the bishop ought to be shepherds of Christian people, and turn them from all unrighteousness; if one might then turn them to justice'
(coblick,HomS_14_[BlHom_4]:45.120.575)

We suggest that as pronouns, the indefinites may be interpreted as presuppositional like other pronouns: they can on occasion have a discourse referent. Note that in the case of *ænig* and *hwa*, this may easily refer to "any of a particular group" or "whoever in a particular group." *Man* in (22c) appears to refer to "the king and the bishop," which is a prominent discourse referent in this context (though a rather surprising one for *man* as this pronoun is typically discursively inert and an ultra-indefinite in the sense of Koenig (1999: 237) (see Los 2005: 285)).

We now turn to a set of facts in which NP subjects combine with object pronouns on the left of *þa/þonne*. Both patterns are relatively infrequent, as shown in table 10.5 – note that this reflects 24 examples in the complete York Corpus of Old English.

Table 10.5 Combinations of NP subject and pronominal object in the topic domain

	Non-root clauses
Pro object–NP subject–*þa/þonne*	12
NP subject–pro object–*þa/þonne*	12

These are rather unusual discourses, as we will illustrate. The first 12 examples with object pronoun–NP subject–*þa/þonne* include 6 cases in which the subject is impersonal *mon*, 4 in which the subject is emphatic indefinite *hwa*, and 2 cases in which the subject is a definite NP. The following examples illustrate this.

(23) a. ðonne he oferstæled bið, & him gereaht bið ðæt he oðrum mæg nytt bion on ðam ðe **him mon ðonne** bebeodeð

when he exalted is and him appointed is that he to-others may use be on that that him one then offers
'When he is exalted and appointed that he may be useful to others in that which is offered to him'
(cocura, CP 6.47.17; see also van Bergen 2000:108; (34a))

b. Se cwæð to þam, þe me tugon: gelædaþ hine eft ham, forþon Seuerus se mæssepreost cwyþeð & mæneþ his sawle & mid tearum biddeð, þæt **him Drihten þa** forgife.
He says to them, who me raised: lead him after home, because Severus the mass-priest bewails and laments his soul and with tears prays that him Lord then forgive
'he says to those who raised me: lead him home now, because the mass-priest Severus bewails and laments his soul, and begs the Lord in tears to forgive him'
(cogregd,C,GD_1_[C]:12.89.31.1036)

c. Gif **hit hwa þonne** deð, he unarwirðað God
if it whoever then does, he dishonors God
'If anyone were to do it, he would dishonor God (by doing it)'
(colwstan2,æLet_3_[Wulfstan_2]:96.124)

In (23a), *mon* has an implicit discourse referent as it occurs in a sequence of conjoined passives with implicit agents. The pronoun *him* then has the more prominent discourse referent – it refers back to *he* in both previous clauses.

The second set in table 10.5 consists of rather interesting cases in which we would argue that the NP subject is again a contrastive topic. We discuss two examples to illustrate this:

(24) Gif hwa fæmnan beswice unbeweddode & hire mid slæpo, **forgielde hie and hæbbe hie siððan him to wife**. Gif ðære fæmnan fæder **hie** ðonne sellan nelle, agife he ðæt feoh æfter þam weotuman
if anyone maid deceive unmarried and her with sleep, pay-for her and have her afterwards him to woman. if that maid father her then give not-will, give he the cattle after the dowry.
'If anyone deceives a maid unwedded and sleeps with her, he shall repay her and take her from then on as his wife. If the woman's father will then not give her in marriage, he shall give her cattle proportionate to the dowry'
(LAW2,38.29.1–2)

We believe that the pronoun *hie* follows the subject due to a discourse shift that renders the referent of the pronoun less prominent than required for the highest position in the topic domain. If we take a look at the preceding line, we see that this condition is indeed met. The clause with the pronoun following the NP subject expresses a shift to a new situation which is in contrast to the previous line (cf. the negative form of the verb, *sellan nelle*, which is in contrast with the verb *forgieldan* in the previous line). A similar example is (25) in which the clause *gif se hlaford him þonne wif sealde* is in a comparison/contrast relation to the similar law regulating the marital status of servants in the previous clause, *gif he wif self hæbbe*:

(25) *Gif he wif* **self** *hæbbe*, gange hio ut mid him. Gif se hlaford **him** þonne wif sealde, sie hio & hire bearn þæs hlafordes
if he woman self have, go she out with him. If the lord him then woman gave, be she and her children that lord
'If he will have the woman himself, she will go with him. Now if the lord gave him the woman, she and her children will belong to the lord' (LAW2,28.11.2–3)

We conclude that the nominal subject preceding the pronoun acts as a contrastive topic and assumes the position higher than the pronoun on that account.

We now turn to nominal objects. Table 10.6 gives the patterns that are attested. On the face of it, NP objects may appear in the topic domain alone or in combination with a subject. When a subject and a NP object together precede *þa/þonne*, the subject always precedes the object, as it does in similar sequences with object pronouns. We take it that a syntactic constraint is responsible for this.

Let us first consider the fifteen cases in which the NP object alone precedes the particle: these are dominated by cases like (26), in which the object consists of a single demonstrative pronoun, notably the neuter accusative demonstrative *þæt*. This is then either anaphoric or cataphoric to an event in the previous or following context, often expressed by a *that*-clause. Here are some examples:

(26) þa þæt **þa** Porsenna gehierde, he ðæt setl & þæt gewin mid ealle forlet, þe he ær þreo winter dreogende wæs.
when that then Porsenna heard, he the siege and the fight with all left, which he before three winters conducting was
'when Porsenna heard that, he immediately withdrew from the war he had been engaged in for three years'
(coorosiu,Or_2:3.41.9.778)

Table 10.6 NP objects preceding *þa/þonne* in Old English

NP subject–NP object–*þa/þonne*	7
Pro subject–NP object–*þa/þonne*	17
NP object–NP subject–*þa/þonne*	0
NP object–*þa/þonne*–NPsubject	15

The demonstrative pronoun here refers back to an event in the previous discourse; it does not have an individual as its referent. *Þæt* here can also be cataphoric, as in the following context:

(27) þa ðæt **þa** Wulfhere se cyning onget, & him gebodad wæs, þæt in þære mægðe Eastseaxna of dæle Cristes geleafa aidlad wære, þa sende he Gearaman þone biscop,
When then that then Wulfhere the king perceived, and him announced was, that in the province of the East-Saxons in part of-Christ's faith apostatized were, then sent he Jaruman the bishop,
'As soon as King Wulfhere perceived that, and it was announced to him, that part of the East-Saxon province had apostatized from the faith, he sent Bishop Jaruman'
(cobede,Bede_3:22.250.17.2554)

The same can be said for the word order NP subject–NP object–*þa/þonne*. These cases, like (26) and (27), have a demonstrative pronoun *þæt* as the object (though not necessarily anaphoric):

(28) Þa se broðor þæt **þa** gehyrde, sona þæs þe heo in þæt mynster eodon, þa cyðde he hit
When the brother that **then** heard, soon after that they in the monastery went, then made-known he it
'When the brother heard this, immediately after their arrival at the monastery, he made it known'
(cobede,Bede_4:26.352.26.3556)

The word order pronominal subject–NP object–*þa/þonne* comprises cases where the object is accusative demonstrative *þæt* and definite NPs.

(29) a. Ða he ðæt **þa** for his untrymnesse uneaðe þurhteah, þa cwom he to Lundenceastre bioscope . . .
When he that **then** for his disability with-difficulty carried out, then came he to London's bishop,
'When he had carried this out with some difficulty because of his infirmity, he came to the bishop of London'
(cobede,Bede_4:14.294.17.2967)

b. Gif he þæt broð **þonne** ær sypð ne meaht þu him þy dæge attor gesellan.
If he the broth **then** first sips, not may you him that day poison give
'After drinking the broth, you should give him no more venom the rest of the day'
(colaece,Lch_II_[3]:43.1.3.3958)

We have seen in this section that if we make the assumption that the position of *þa/þonne* is fixed and has the status of a focus particle, we get a novel view of the organization of the clause in which syntactic factors and discourse factors are closely interwoven. The topic area left of the focus marker is in very many cases quite simple and straightforward: subject pronouns are in that position in an impressive 1,250 cases. It is only when we take the position of *þa/þonne* as a starting point that we can reveal that, at a rather lower rate, the organization of this area may be more complex, as the figures in the various tables show. We have shown that the nature and order of constituents in the topic domain reveal possible generalizations about the discourse embedding of this domain: one generalization is that personal pronouns, if they are assumed to reflect continued topics in discourse terms, are positioned within the topic domain according to the prominence of their discourse referent. Other material such as a NP subject or NP object may take precedence over the pronoun within the topic domain and in that case they are interpreted as contrastive topics. A further generalization is that in the topic domain, indefinite NP subjects do not occur, although indefinite pronouns may do so. One trait that is shared by the topic domain material, then, is that it shows a strong tendency towards being definite and specific, including definite NPs, personal pronouns (and indefinite pronouns) which have a discourse referent, and demonstrative pronouns which are inherently definite and which in the cases we have discussed have a highly prominent discourse referent.

If the discourse system we have outlined is correct, this implies that it should rest on a system of text referential marking on NPs. In fact, Old English has such a system: the use of articulated paradigms for demonstrative pronouns showing agreement with definite marking on attributive adjectives and inflectional similarity between the paradigms for personal and demonstrative pronouns ensures this (see also chapter 12, this volume). In fact, demonstrative pronouns serve to mark discourse anaphoricity on NPs. It is well known that the paradigms for demonstrative pronouns were a relatively early victim of inflectional demise in the transition to Middle English. We will see below what the effects of this on the topic domain of the clause may have been.

A final point we should discuss is the development of the subclause. We hypothesize that the relatively small number of cases in which the topic area in the subclause is complex in Old English, as discussed in the foregoing section, reflect a language stage where clausal organization was more paratactic, i.e. a stage where the distinction between main clause and subclauses had emerged less clearly than by late Old English times. What we have seen then in this section are the relics of paratactic clause organization. We will for this case resist the temptation to speculate on the historical origin of this situation. We will pursue elsewhere the theoretical implications of the facts presented here, but refer to van Kemenade and Milicev (2005) for a contribution toward an analysis. Let us now turn to Middle English.

10.5 Middle English

The transition to Middle English marks a sharp contrast in several respects. The first contrast is that the use of *þa* and *þonne* in clause-internal position

Table 10.7 *Þa/þonne* and NP subject in Middle English

	Non-root clauses
NP subject follows *þa/þonne*	5
NP subject precedes *þa/þonne*	23

becomes a good deal less frequent in absolute numbers. Where the search file in Old English contains some 2,500 instances, the Middle English one includes 177. This in itself might indicate that *þa/þonne* were in the process of losing their discourse-marking properties, as it might suggest that the properties of *þa/þonne* were no longer represented robustly enough for the learner/speaker/writer to recognize the discourse system. But there are several further arguments as well. Within this data set for Middle English, it is clear that in comparison to Old English, the topic area has been drastically simplified, as is evident from table 10.7.

Table 10.7 shows that the relative number of NP subjects appearing on the left of *þa/þonne* has increased considerably since Old English times. NP subjects found on the left of *þa/þonne* include all the types discussed for Old English above (two examples are given in (30), but also indefinite subjects other than *hwa* or *man*, as in (31)):

(30) a. þt ænig hæfde þa geðincðe, þt heo mihte mæden beon & eac cildes moder.
that any had then thought that she might maiden be and also a child's mother
(CMKENTHO,135.54)
b. where Seynt Basilie was þo bishopp.
'where St. Basil was then bishop'
(CMROYAL,260.370)

(31) þatt tweȝȝenn burrȝhess wærenn þa / þa Crist comm her to manne, / An i þe land off Galile / I Zabuloness mæȝȝþe, / An oþerr i Juda nohht ferr / Fra ȝerrsalæmess chesstre,
That two citizens were then /when Christ came here to men/and in the land of Galilee/in the Zabulon's country/another in Juda not far from Jerusalem's city
(CMORM,I,242.1981)

Table 10.8 shows that the position of subject pronouns with respect to the adverb remains constant as compared to Old English. Table 10.9 shows up a significant change compared to the Old English situation. There is not a single example of an object pronoun in the highest position in the topic domain.

Table 10.8 *Þa/þonne* and pronominal subject in Middle English

	Non-root clauses
Pro subject preceding *þa/þonne*	51
Pro subject following *þa/þonne*	0

Table 10.9 *þa/þonne* and pro object in Middle English

	Non-root clauses
Pro object–*þa/þonne*–NP subject	0
Pro object–NP subject–*þa/þonne*	0
Pro subject–pro object–*þa/þonne*	1
NP subject–pro object–*þa/þonne*	1
Total pro object–*þa/þonne*	2

The two examples of an object pronoun following a pronominal subject and a NP subject are respectively:

(32) & tatt þeod wass hæþene þeod / þatt Crist ȝaff þa swillc takenn; / Forrþi þatt **he þeȝȝm** wollde þa / To rihhte læfe wendenn.
that people was heathen people / which Christ gave then such a sign / because that he them wanted then / the true faith lead
'they were heathen people, whom Christ gave such a sign, because he wanted to lead them to the true faith'
(CMORM,I,118.1027)

(33) Swa summ **þe Romanisshe king / Itt** haffde þanne dæledd, / þatt ta wass Kaserr oferr hemm / & oferr fele kingess.
As the Roman king / it had then divided / who then was emperor over them / and over many kings
(CMORM,I,289.2393)

Likewise, there are two cases in which a NP object is found following the subject in the topic domain:

(34) a. & ȝho wass þa swa winntredd wif / & off swa mikell elde, / þatt naffde ȝho nan kinde þa / Onn hire forr to tæmenn.
and she was then such aged woman / and of such great age / that not-had she no kindred then / in her to bring forth
'and she was then of such an age that she could not bring forth any kindred'
(CMORM,I,13.225)

b. þt tu þi mis-bileaue lete þenne, lanhure, & lihte to ure.
that you your unbelief leave then, at least, and descend to ours
'that thou wilt then, at least, forsake thy unbelief and descend to ours (our faith)'
(CMKATHE,31.191)

Note that all examples are from the relatively early *Ormulum*. The figures show then that in Middle English, the topic area has become virtually restricted to the subject pronoun or NP. One interesting qualification that should be made here is that in a good number of cases (14 out of 51 for pronominal subjects, and 13 out of 23 for NP subjects), we find the pattern: Subject–finite verb–*þa/þonne*.

We interpret this development as a final straightening out of the left periphery of the subclause to a fixed SVO order with a relatively straightforward functional structure in which the subject is licensed in an inflectional specifier position whose head attracts the finite verb. We should emphasize here that this is how we would characterize the Old English subclause – clearly the topic area in the main clause remains complex up until at least the end of the Middle English period. We leave the details of this for further research, but note that this accounts for the often-made observation that in some respects, the subclause is more innovative than the main clause. We have speculated that this situation is inherited from earlier stages in which the main clause/subclause distinction was not as clear-cut and clearly encoded as it came to be in the course of the Middle English period. We may then interpret the development from Old English to Middle English as a reanalysis from topic domain to subject domain. This is a development that is well known from the typological literature, and in this case it is, perhaps surprisingly, one in which the subclause is earlier than the main clause, as a spin-off from the establishment of hypotaxis. The question remains of why this happened. Let us begin by pointing out that subjects did occur in the topic domain in Old English: the pronominal subject occurs there virtually always, the NP subject in some 40 percent of the cases. Subjects were therefore robustly represented in this portion of the clause. But their occurrence there is triggered by discourse considerations and is strongly associated with definiteness/anaphoricity of the subject, as discussed above. The figures in table 10.7 show that NP subjects, whatever their character (definite/indefinite/impersonal . . .), encroach upon this area to some 80 percent in Middle English, and this happens early in the period. We suggest, therefore, that the characteristics associated with topic-hood: definiteness/anaphoricity, contrastive topic status, prominence of discourse referent, no longer provided the crucial clue for appearance in this area of the clause. It makes sense to relate this to the substantial loss of morphology to mark the definiteness/anaphoricity of the NP. Observe in this connection that the case paradigms for demonstrative pronouns were lost relatively early in Middle English, and that agreement between demonstrative pronouns and adjectives was drastically reduced, resulting in considerable loss of anaphoricity marking (Lass 1992). Further research will have to show whether this correlation can be upheld.

The two little adverbs discussed in this chapter, when considered in their various contexts and uses, reveal a great deal, we feel, about clausal organization in Old English against the backdrop of early Germanic, although there is also a lot of further work to be done on related discourse adverbs, on the general role of adverbs, on the diachronic development during the Old English period (is there one? It is a fact that our best examples tend to be from early texts), and on the clausal perspective during the developing hypotaxis.

REFERENCES

Bergen, L. van (2000). Pronouns and Word Order in Old English, with Particular Reference to the Indefinite Pronoun Man. Unpublished dissertation, University of Manchester.

Enkvist, N. E. and B. Wårvik (1987). Old English *þa*, temporal chains, and narrative structure. In Anna Giacalone Ramat, Onofrio Carruba, and Giuliano Bernini (eds.), *Papers from the 7th International Conference on Historical Linguistics* (pp. 221–37). Amsterdam and Philadelphia: John Benjamins.

Eythórsson, T. (1995). Verbal Syntax in the Early Germanic Languages. Unpublished PhD dissertation, Cornell University.

Ferraresi, G. (1997). Word Order and Phrase Structure in Gothic: A Comparative Study. Unpublished PhD dissertation, University of Stuttgart.

Haeberli, E. (2000). Adjuncts and the syntax of subjects in Old and Middle English. In S. Pintzuk, G. Tsoulas, and A. Warner (eds.), *Diachronic Syntax: Models and Mechanisms* (pp. 109–21). Oxford: Oxford University Press.

Haeberli, E. and R. Ingham (2003). The position of negation and adverbs in early Middle English. Paper presented at the 2nd York-Holland Symposium on English historical syntax, Leiden.

Haegeman, L. (1995). *The Syntax of Negation*. Cambridge: Cambridge University Press.

Healey, A. D. and R. L. Venezky (1985 [1980]). *A Microfiche Concordance to Old English*. Toronto: Pontifical Institute of Mediaeval Studies.

Kato, K. (1995). The interjection la and subject pronouns in Old English. In H. Nakano (ed.), *Linguistics and Philology* 15: 23–40.

Kemenade, A. van (1987). *Syntactic Case and Morphological Case in the History of English*. Dordrecht: Foris.

Kemenade, A. van (1999). Sentential negation and clause structure in Old English. In I. Tieken-Boon van Ostade, G. Tottie, and W. van der Wurff (eds.), *Negation in the History of English* (pp. 147–65). (Topics in English Linguistics 26). Berlin and New York: Mouton de Gruyter

Kemenade, A. van (2000). Jespersen's Cycle revisited: formal properties of grammaticalization. In S. Pintzuk, G. Tsoulas, and A. Warner (eds.), *Diachronic Syntax: Models and Mechanisms* (pp. 51–74). Oxford: Oxford University Press.

Kemenade, A. van (2002). Word order in Old English prose and poetry: the position of finite verbs and adverbs. In D. Minkova and R. Stockwell (eds.), *Studies in the History of the English Language: A Millennial Perspective* (pp. 355–73). Berlin: Mouton de Gruyter.

Kemenade, A. van and T. Milicev (2005). Syntax and discourse in Old and Middle English word order. In Stephen Anderson and Dianne Jonas (eds.), *Articles from the 8th Diachronic Generative Syntax Conference*. To appear with Oxford University Press.

Kiparsky, P. (1995). Indo-European origins of Germanic syntax. In Adrian Battye and Ian Roberts (eds.), *Clause Structure and Language Change* (pp. 140–70). Oxford: Oxford University Press.

Kiss, K. (1995). *Discourse Configurational Languages*. Oxford: Oxford University Press.

Koenig, J.-P. (1999). On a tué le président! The nature of passives and ultra-indefinites. In B. A. Fox, D. Jurafsky, and L. A. Michaelis (eds.), *Cognition and Function in Language*. Stanford: CSLI.

Kuhn, H. (1933). Zur Wortstellung und -betonung im Altgermanischen. *Beiträge zur Geschichte der deutschen Sprache und Literatur* 57: 1–109.

Lass, Roger (1992). Phonology and morphology. In Roger Lass (ed.), *The Cambridge History of the English Language*, vol. 2: *1066–1476*. Cambridge: Cambridge University Press.

Los, B. (2000). Onginnan/beginnan with bare and to-infinitive in Ælfric. In Olga Fischer, Anette Rosenbach, and Dieter Stein (eds.), *Pathways of Change: Grammaticalization in English* (pp. 251–74) (Studies in Language companion series). Amsterdam: John Benjamins.

Los, B. (2005). *The Rise of the* To-*Infinitive*. Oxford: Oxford University Press.

Mitchell, B., C. Ball, and A. Cameron (eds.) (1975). Short titles of Old English texts. *Anglo-Saxon England* 4: 207–21.

Mitchell, B., C. Ball, and A. Cameron (eds.) (1979). Addenda and corrigenda. *Anglo-Saxon England* 8: 331–3.

Rizzi, L. (1996). *Parameters and Functional Heads: Essays in Comparative Syntax*. Oxford: Oxford University Press.

Taylor, A. (2000). *The Penn-Helsinki Parsed Corpus of Middle English* 2. University of Pennsylvania, Department of Linguistics.

Taylor, A., A. Warner, S. Pintzuk, and F. Beths (2003). *The York–Toronto–Helsinki Parsed Corpus of Old English*. York: Department of Language and Linguistic Science, University of York. (Available through the Oxford Text Archive.)

Wårvik, Brita (1995). The ambiguous adverbial/conjunction *þa* and *þonne* in Middle English: a discourse-pragmatic study of *then* and *when* in early English saints' lives. In Jucker (ed.), *Historical Pragmatics: Pragmatic Developments in the History of English* (pp. 345–57). Amsterdam and Philadelphia: John Benjamins.

11 The Loss of OV Order in the History of English

SUSAN PINTZUK AND
ANN TAYLOR

It is well known that English in its history changed from predominantly object–verb (OV) in Old English to categorically verb–object (VO) in Modern English. It is also well known that this change was gradual: the position of objects varied in Old and Middle English texts, preverbal vs. postverbal, as shown in (1) and (2), where the object is underlined and the verb is in bold face.

(1) Verb–object order in Old English
  a. Ac he sceal <u>þa sacfullan</u> **gesibbian**
     But he must the quarrelsome reconcile
     'But he must reconcile the quarrelsome'
     (colwstan1,+ALet_2_[Wulfstan_1]:188.256)
  b. Se wolde **gelytlian** <u>þone lyfigendan hælend</u>
     He would diminish the living lord
     'He would diminish the living lord'
     (colwstan1,+ALet_2_[Wulfstan_1]:55.98)

(2) Verb–object order in Middle English
  a. ear he hefde <u>his ranceun</u> fulleliche **ipaiȝet**
     before he had his ransom fully paid
     'Before he had fully paid his ransom'
     (CMANCRIW,II.101.1228)
  b. ȝef þu wult **habben** <u>bricht sichðe</u> wid þine heorte echnen
     if you will have bright sight with your heart's eyes
     'If you will have bright sight with your heart's eyes'
     (CMANCRIW,II.73.839)

Like other major syntactic changes (for example, the loss of the verb-second constraint in French and English), the loss of OV order in the history of English involves a lengthy period of structured variation, in which two grammatical options (OV clauses and VO clauses) are used by individual speakers. The language of the historical written texts thus shows variation and optionality in the use of word orders and structures. Within a Principles and Parameters model of language, optionality of this type should be ruled out by economy constraints. There are in principle two ways of analyzing this type of variation: by setting up two or more equally economical derivations (see Wurff 1997), or by establishing competing parameter settings (see Kroch 1989, 1995). In this chapter we adopt the second approach. We interpret variation in the surface position of objects as the reflex of competition between internalized grammars with distinct options that are incompatible within a single grammar. The competition occurs within the individual speaker and can be understood as similar to code-switching or register-switching; speakers can be viewed as bidialectal or bilingual in their command of distinct grammars. The way in which the competing options are analyzed and described depends, of course, upon the syntactic framework being used. In a Government and Binding framework, competing options frequently correspond to contradictory parameter settings: for example, head-initial vs. head-final structure (that is, a directionality parameter). Within the Minimalist Program, competing options correspond to the presence in the lexicon of items with contradictory features. Thus it is not entire grammars that are in competition, but rather incompatible options within the grammars.

In this chapter we discuss the factors influencing the position of objects in Old and Middle English, and the time course of the change from OV to VO. We present the change in terms of grammatical competition in the headedness of the VP and thus in terms of variation in the setting of the VP directionality parameter; for arguments in favor of this analysis, see Pintzuk (2002). Our general approach is to use quantitative patterns and distributional facts as evidence for underlying structure and for syntactic variation and change. This approach has sometimes been called "variationist" and contrasted with a "structural" approach. But the terms are misnomers, for two reasons: first, any analysis of early English syntax must account for the variation in the data, and thus may in some sense be regarded as "variationist"; second, we use the patterns of variation as evidence for particular syntactic structures, and thus our account must also be regarded as "structural." In other words, our approach merges a formal structural account with an analysis of the patterns of variation found in the data.

We extend this approach by demonstrating that conclusions about grammar can be drawn from diachronic rates of change. Quantitative studies of syntactic variation over time have provided strong support for the "Constant Rate Effect" (Kroch 1989): during a period of change, when two linguistic options are in competition, the frequency of use of the two options may differ across contexts, but the rate of change for all contexts is the same. In other words, while some contexts may favor the innovating option and show a higher overall rate of use, the increase over time will be the same in all contexts. Conversely, in cases where the rates of change are different, the changes must be caused by different processes. In the case of the change from OV to VO, we demonstrate that the loss of OV order (or the increase in VO order) proceeds at different rates for quantified and non-quantified objects. We conclude that there are different processes affecting the position of quantified and non-quantified objects, and we support that conclusion with evidence of differences in derivation.

As background to the analyses that follow, we make the following two assumptions about early English syntax. First, verb seconding in early English is movement of the finite verb to a position lower than C, call it I, in both main and subordinate clauses. Verb movement to C occurs only in some exceptional clause types. The position of topicalized constituents, whether Spec, CP or somewhere lower in the clause, is irrelevant for our concerns here. This analysis of verb seconding, for Old English in particular, is by now widely accepted. Second, projections in early English, in particular IP and VP, can vary in headedness; in terms of grammatical competition, there is variation between head-initial and head-final IPs, and head-initial and head-final VPs. Since movement of the finite verb to I is obligatory (because verbal inflection is strong), the headedness of IP is indicated by the position of the finite auxiliary verb. For example, the clauses in (1) and (2) are I-initial clauses, while (3) is an I-final clause.

(3) he þæs **habban** sceal <u>ece</u> <u>edlean</u> on Godes rice
he of-that have must eternal reward in God's kingdom
'he must have eternal reward of that in God's kingdom'
(cowulf,WHom_7:161.501)

The data we use have been extracted from two syntactically annotated electronic corpora: the York-Toronto-Helsinki Parsed Corpus of Old English Prose (Taylor et al. 2003), henceforth the YCOE; and the Penn-Helsinki Parsed Corpus of Middle English (Kroch and Taylor 2000b), henceforth the PPCME2. See Appendix A for a brief description of the corpora and the texts used. Since we are concerned with the order of verbs and their objects, we limit the data under consideration to clauses with finite auxiliaries and nonfinite main verbs, and thus abstract away from movement of the finite verb to I. And since pronouns in Old and Middle English behave differently from full nominal phrases (see van Kemenade 1987; Koopman 1997; Kroch and Taylor 1997; Pintzuk 1996), we investigate the behavior of nominal objects only.

This chapter is organized as follows. First we present a detailed analysis of the position of nonquantified (henceforth "positive") objects in Old and Middle English. We show that the factors influencing their position are the same in both periods, and we analyze the variation in terms of grammatical competition. Then we demonstrate that quantified and negative objects are affected by the same factors as positive objects. Preverbal position, however, is lost at different rates for the three object types, a result which we show to be due to the different processes affecting their position. The last section presents conclusions.

11.1 Positive Objects: Data and Analysis

In this section we consider the factors that have an effect on the position of positive objects in I-initial clauses in Old and Middle English. We do not consider I-final clauses here: although they are frequent in Old English, there are almost no I-final clauses in Middle English, and therefore the two stages of English can be compared only for the I-initial type. We demonstrate that the overall frequency of OV order is higher in Old English than in Middle English, but that the effect of the factors is the same in the two periods. The factors to be discussed are the following: length of object, clause type, date of composition of text, and case and thematic role of object. Space constraints prevent a discussion of additional factors that have a significant effect on the position of objects (dialect and definiteness for Middle English, Latin influence for Old English), although these factors were included in the quantitative analysis.

Length of the object: The length of the object is measured in words, with objects that are modified by relative clauses given a separate category ("DP + relative clause"). Of course we are not interested in how length *per se* affects the position of the object, but in what the length represents. As we will see below, length was a significant factor for all object types, and may reflect a processing constraint against the center-embedding of long and complex material.

Clause type: Old English clauses are divided into four types: main clauses, conjoined main clauses, subordinate clauses, and conjoined subordinate clauses. Conjoined main clauses are main clauses that are conjoined to the preceding main clause by a conjunction; they are considered separately from non-conjoined main clauses because it has frequently been suggested that conjoined clauses in Old English behave syntactically more like subordinate clauses than like main clauses. Conjoined subordinate clauses are subordinate clauses that do not have overt complementizers or subordinating conjunctions and that are conjoined to a preceding subordinate clause which does have an overt complementizer or subordinator. For these as well, it is not always clear whether they are main or subordinate in their structure and behavior. As we will see below, the frequencies of preverbal objects in the two conjoined clause types in Old English fall consistently between the frequencies for main clauses and the frequencies for subordinate clauses. For Middle English, clauses are divided into main and subordinate clauses, not because we are convinced that conjoined clauses behave in the same way as non-conjoined clauses, but simply because the annotation scheme of the PPCME2 makes it difficult to isolate the conjoined clauses. As will be seen below, the Middle English patterns are comparable to the Old English ones, even though the divisions of the data are not quite the same.

Date of composition: The Old English texts are divided into two periods according to date of composition: early (OE1, before 950) and late (OE2, after 950). It would have been desirable to date the texts more precisely so that the chronology of the change over the Old English period could be examined in greater detail. To do this, a narrow date interval must be assigned to each text. This is straightforward in the case of some but not all Old English texts. We therefore decided to use only two Old English periods, early and late. The dividing point of 950 was chosen because it matched the Helsinki Corpus date divisions, and because almost none of the datable Old English texts were written in the middle of the tenth century. Even with this broad characterization of early vs. late, not enough is known about some Old English texts to date them early or late. The Middle English texts were divided into four periods (ME1 through ME4), using the date of composition assigned to the text by the Helsinki Corpus.

Case and thematic role of the object: Objects in the YCOE (Old English) are case-marked accusative, dative, or genitive if case marking is overt and unambiguous on any element of the DP; otherwise, objects are not marked for case. In the PPCME2 (Middle English), objects are categorized as first and second objects; these terms have nothing to do with order or position within the clause, but instead correspond roughly to theme (first object) and goal (second object). We will see below that Old English accusative objects behave much like first objects in Middle English, while obliquely case-marked objects in Old English behave like second objects in Middle English.

The results of quantitative analysis of the Old and Middle English data are presented below. All of the clauses in the tables that follow are I-initial with auxiliary verbs unless otherwise specified. We show frequencies and probabilistic weights (the output of multivariate analysis) for all factors within the independent factor groups (i.e. independent variables). Probabilistic weights center on .50: if a factor's weight is greater than .50, that factor favors preverbal objects; if a factor's weight is less than .50, that factor disfavors preverbal objects (and therefore favors postverbal objects). It is important to understand that favoring and disfavoring are concepts that reflect the relative ranking of the strength of the effect rather than the absolute frequency. Notice that the frequencies of preverbal objects are quite low for all of the Middle English data (see, for example, table 11.2); nevertheless, there is always at least one factor with a probabilistic weight above .50, indicating that the factor favors preverbal position. As is standard, probabilistic weights are shown in brackets if the independent variable is not statistically significant. Note that the ranking of weights does not always directly match the ranking of frequencies, since the effects of all of the independent variables, not just the one whose frequencies are shown in the individual table, are taken into account during the calculation of probabilistic weights. Tables 11.7 and 11.8 are particularly clear examples of ordering differences between frequencies and probabilistic weights. In these cases, the effect of each factor is reflected more accurately by the weight than by the frequency. While small numbers can affect frequencies and significance in quantitative studies, they are not a problem in our data: the number of possible occurrences of each factor (shown as *N* in the tables) is substantial for most factors, and the differences between *N*s is taken into account during the

Table 11.1 Effect of length on the position of positive nominal objects in Old English (statistically significant)

Length in words	*Preverbal*	N	*Preverbal (%)*	*Prob. weight*
1	589	787	74.8	.74
2	1,065	1,753	60.8	.59
3	290	656	44.2	.42
4 or more	120	428	28.0	.25
DP + relative clause	14	269	5.3	.05
Total	2,078	3,893	53.4	—

Table 11.2 Effect of length on the position of positive nominal objects in Middle English (statistically significant)

Length in words	*Preverbal*	N	*Preverbal (%)*	*Prob. weight*
1	75	1,150	6.5	.66
2	194	2,275	8.5	.66
3	30	570	5.3	.57
4 or more	22	1,052	2.1	.37
DP + relative clause	3	677	.4	.06
Total	324	5,724	5.7	—

calculation of probabilistic weights. In general, then, to understand the results presented in the tables, the reader should look first at the probabilistic weights, their order and their significance (as indicated by the presence or absence of brackets) to determine the favoring/disfavoring effect, and then at the frequencies.

The effect of length is shown in tables 11.1 and 11.2. Objects containing relative clauses are separated from the other data, since these objects are usually very heavy; their heaviness is reflected in their low preverbal frequency. The overall frequency of preverbal objects is lower in Middle English than in Old English. But for both periods, it is clear that the heavier the object, the less likely it is to appear preverbally, and we attribute this pattern to a processing constraint against the embedding of long and complex material. Notice that length grading is quite regular in Old English, while there is no significant difference between one- and two-word objects in the Middle English data; we currently have no explanation for this difference between the two periods.

The effect of clause type on the position of positive objects is shown in tables 11.3 and 11.4. In both Old and Middle English, main clauses exhibit a lower frequency of preverbal objects than subordinate clauses. And in Old English,

Table 11.3 Effect of clause type on the position of positive nominal objects in Old English (statistically significant)

Clause type	*Preverbal*	N	*Preverbal (%)*	*Prob. weight*
Main	353	879	40.2	.37
Conjoined main	338	694	48.7	.45
Subordinate	1,307	2,163	60.4	.57
Conjoined subordinate	80	157	51.0	.48
Total	2,078	3,893	53.4	—

Table 11.4 Effect of clause type on the position of positive nominal objects in Middle English (statistically significant)

Clause type	*Preverbal*	N	*Preverbal (%)*	*Prob. weight*
Main	99	2,503	4.0	.41
Subordinate	225	3,221	7.0	.57
Total	324	5,724	5.7	—

where conjoined clauses are separated from nonconjoined clauses, conjoined main and conjoined subordinate clauses fall between the other two types for both frequency and probabilistic weight. It has been demonstrated in other studies (Pintzuk 1999) that main clauses generally show higher frequencies of innovating structures than subordinate clauses; and it has often been observed that conjoined clauses in Old English sometimes behave like main clauses and sometimes like subordinate clauses. The numbers in tables 11.3 and 11.4 follow both of these trends.

The effect of date of composition of the text on the position of positive objects in Old and Middle English is shown in tables 11.5 and 11.6. As noted above,

Table 11.5 Effect of date of composition on the position of positive nominal objects in Old English (statistically significant)

Date of composition	*Preverbal*	N	*Preverbal (%)*	*Prob. weight*
OE1 (before 950)	803	1,416	56.7	.53
OE2 (after 950)	1,165	2,310	50.4	.48
Total	1,968	3,726	52.8	—

Table 11.6 Effect of date of composition on the position of positive nominal objects in Middle English (statistically significant)

Date of composition	*Preverbal*	N	*Preverbal (%)*	*Prob. weight*
ME1 (1150–1250)	253	892	28.4	.96
ME2 (1250–1350)	26	834	3.1	.36
ME3 (1350–1420)	35	2,612	1.3	.39
ME4 (1420–1500)	10	1,386	0.7	.28
Total	324	5,724	5.7	—

Table 11.7 Effect of case on the position of positive nominal objects in Old English (statistically significant)

Case	*Preverbal*	N	*Preverbal (%)*	*Prob. weight*
Accusative	1,230	2,302	53.4	.52
Genitive	100	185	54.1	.48
Dative	402	762	52.8	.45
Ambiguous	346	644	53.7	.47
Total	2,078	3,893	53.4	—

the date of composition could not be determined for some of the Old English texts, and therefore the total number of tokens in table 11.5 is not the same as in previous tables. Recall also that manuscript date is used for the Middle English texts in table 11.6. For both stages of the language, date of composition has a statistically significant effect: early texts show a higher frequency of preverbal objects than later texts, and the effect is regular in both the Old and the Middle English periods.

The effect of case on the position of positive objects in Old English is shown in table 11.7. Although the range of frequencies and probabilistic weights is small, the variable is statistically significant. Accusative objects favor preverbal position, while dative and genitive objects and objects not marked for case (in reality, a mixture of accusative, dative, and genitive objects) favor postverbal position. As noted above, the probabilistic weights reflect the effect of the factors more accurately than the frequencies in this case.

The effect of thematic role on the position of positive objects in Middle English is shown in table 11.8: second objects (often goals, as discussed above) clearly disfavor preverbal position, while first objects (often themes) neither favor nor disfavor preverbal position.

Table 11.8 Effect of object type on the position of positive nominal objects in Middle English (statistically significant)

Object type	*Preverbal*	N	*Preverbal (%)*	*Prob. weight*
First object	319	5,638	5.7	.50
Second object	5	81	5.8	.27
Total	305	4,420	5.7	—

It is not completely clear how to interpret the effect of case and thematic role, and at this point we can only suggest some possible lines of inquiry. One might want to link the effect of case marking in Old English to the difference between structural and inherent case, but it is not obvious why objects with inherent case should appear postverbally more frequently than objects with structural case. Given the similarities in Old English and Middle English of the other effects, a more plausible account involves thematic roles: accusative objects are most frequently themes in Old English, while dative and genitive objects (and therefore some of the objects that are marked "ambiguous" in the corpus) are most frequently goals or sources. The difference in thematic role reflects a difference in structure in most generative syntactic frameworks, and may also indicate a difference in focus, with focused objects more likely to appear preverbally than objects which are not focused. Another possibility is that goals and sources behave more like adjuncts than arguments; we know that adjuncts are much freer in their position than arguments in Old English (Pintzuk 1999), and the same may be true in Middle English. It is interesting and clearly significant that the effect of thematic role is seen in Middle English, after overt case marking has been lost. This suggests that the effect of thematic role on the position of objects should be investigated, to determine why an object that is more directly affected by the main verb is more likely to appear preverbally.

To summarize the results of this section, we have shown that positive objects in Old and Middle English behave in a remarkably similar manner: length, clause type, date of composition, and case and thematic role have the same significant effect in the same direction on the position of objects in the two stages. The major difference between Old English and Middle English is the overall frequency of preverbal position: more than half the objects in Old English are preverbal, compared to only 6 percent of the objects in Middle English. If we compare the later period in Old English with the first period in Middle English in tables 11.5 and 11.6, the difference is 50.4 percent vs. 28.4 percent. While this difference is not small, it reinforces the conclusion that there is not a qualitative difference between the two stages in the history of English.

11.2 Quantified and Negative Objects

We turn now to quantified and negative objects. As with positive objects, quantified and negative objects appear in both preverbal and postverbal position in Old and Middle English.

(4) Quantified objects in Old English
 a. hu heo ana mihte ealle þa gewytan **awægan** mid aðe
 how she alone could all the sages deceive with oath
 'how she alone could deceive all the sages with an oath'
 (coaelive,+ALS_[Eugenia]:223.324)
 b. þe hæfde **geinnod** ealle þas halgan
 who had lodged all the saints
 'who had lodged all the saints'
 (coaelive,+ALS_[Sebastian]:382.1442)

(5) Quantified objects in Middle English
 a. ȝef ȝe habbeð ani god **don**
 if you have any good done
 'if you have done any good'
 (CMANCRIW,I.76.310)
 b. fordon þe he scal aȝein **ȝeuen** awiht
 for he shall again give something
 'for he shall again give something'
 (CMLAMBX1,31.396)

(6) Negative objects in Old English
 a. þæt he ne mæge nan god **don**
 that he NEG can no good do
 'that he can do no good'
 (coaelive,+ALS_[Memory_of_Saints]:295.3490)
 b. ðæt he nolde **habban** nane gemodsumnesse wið da yfelan
 that he NEG-would have no agreement with the wicked
 'that he would have no agreement with the wicked'
 (cocura,CP:46.353.2.2378)

(7) Negative objects in Middle English
 a. þt he ne mai nan þing **don** us buten godes leaue
 that he NEG can no thing do us without God's leave
 'that he can do nothing to us without God's leave'
 (CMANCRIW,II.169.2346)
 b. swa þet ho ne scal of þere wunde **habbe** nan oðer uuel
 so that she NEG shall from her wound have no other evil
 'so that she shall have no other evil from her wound'
 (CMLAMB1,83.195)

Table 11.9 Frequency of preverbal position for three types of objects in Old and Middle English

	Positive		*Quantified*		*Negative*	
Period	N	*Preverbal (%)*	N	*Preverbal (%)*	N	*Preverbal (%)*
OE1	1,416	56.7	178	63.5	49	91.8
OE2	2,310	50.4	179	56.4	83	78.3
ME1	892	28.4	147	34.7	39	41.0
ME2	834	3.1	85	10.6	33	18.2
ME3	2,612	1.3	301	6.0	138	20.3
ME4	1,386	0.7	148	6.1	105	22.0

For the most part, the same factors that influence the position of positive objects are at work with quantified and negative objects as well, as the interested reader can confirm from the tables in Appendix B to this chapter. Despite these similarities, however, there are some crucial differences between the three types of objects. First, as shown in table 11.9, although the frequency of OV order is decreasing for all three types, it is always greater for quantified objects than for positives and, likewise, greater for negatives than for quantified objects. When the OV rate for positive objects is essentially zero, quantified and negative objects are still appearing preverbally at measurable rates.

Figure 11.1 shows the same data in graphic form. The loss of preverbal position for each type of object follows the familiar S-curve found in periods of language change involving competition between an old and a new variant. There are two possible explanations for the different frequencies of OV order shown by the three different types of objects. First, the derivation of preverbal position may be the same for all types of objects, but for reasons external to the syntax, the process applies differentially, resulting in higher rates for some types of objects than for others. If this were the case, we would expect preverbal position to be lost at the same rate for all types, since all are derived in the same way; the constant differential throughout the change simply results from the fact that quantified and negative objects started out with higher frequency of preverbal position than positives. The second possibility (as van der Wurff, 1999, suggests for late Middle English) is that preverbal position for the three types of objects is not derived in the same way. In this case, we take the different frequencies to represent different derivations, and thus the expectation is that the rate of change will also be different, as discussed earlier.

In order to decide between these two analyses, therefore, we need to compare the rate of change for each of the types of object. The same rate of change would suggest there is only one derivation at work, while different rates of change would indicate different derivations. To calculate the rate of change,

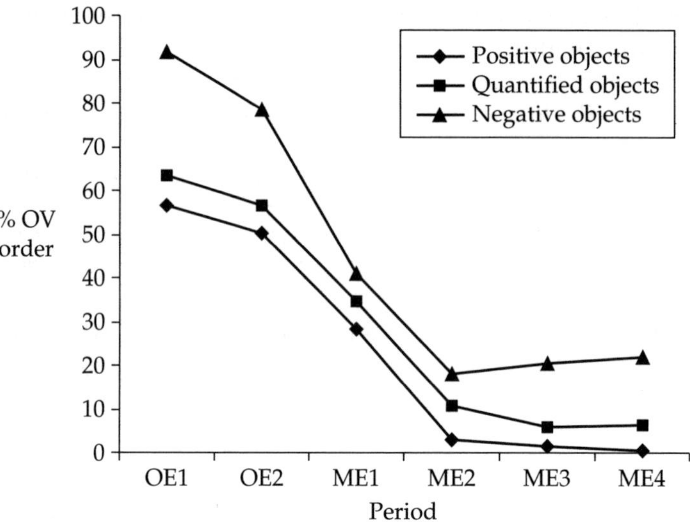

Figure 11.1 Loss of OV order in three types of object

we carry out a logistic regression analysis. The regression is done on the Middle English data only, since it requires specific dates to be assigned for each text; as discussed above, this is not possible for many of the Old English texts. The regression analysis allows us to measure the rate of change, at the same time taking into account the effect of the other factors that affect object position. In this way we can quantify the amount of change in the frequency of OV order that is attributable to time alone, abstracting away from all the other effects. The result of a regression analysis is a coefficient, called the β value, for each factor that affects object position. The β value indicates how much the dependent variable – that is, preverbal object order – changes for each unit change in the independent variable, in this case time; in other words, the β value is the rate of change. Table 11.10 gives the β value for time for each type of object. The unit of measurement in table 11.10 is logits per century, a result of the logistic transform used in the regression analysis. For our purposes the unit of

Table 11.10 Rate of change over time for three types of objects in Middle English, in logits per century

Object type	*β value*	*exp(β)*
Negative	0.5	0.60
Quantified	1.1	0.33
Positive	1.7	0.18

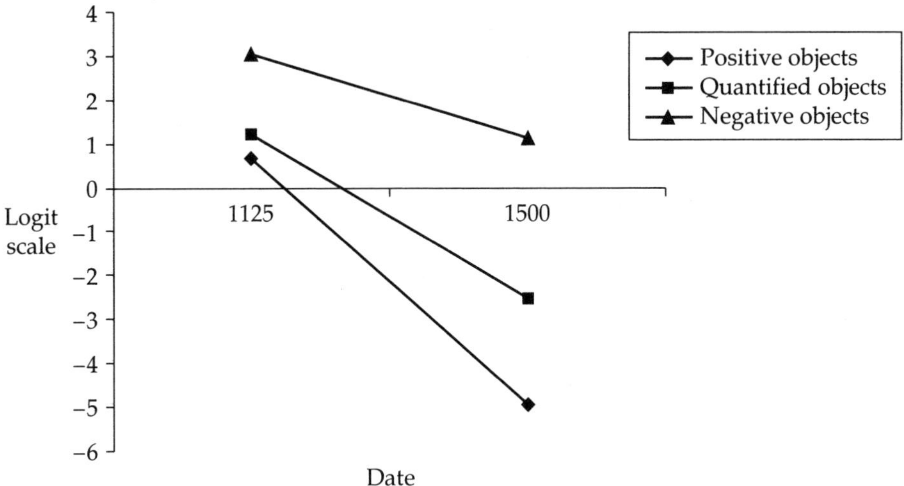

Figure 11.2 Regression lines for three types of objects

measurement is not important, since we simply want to know whether the β values are the same or different. As is clear from the table and from figure 11.2, which represents it graphically, the β values are different. The 95 percent confidence intervals of exp(β) (not shown in table 11.10) do not overlap, indicating that the difference in β values is significant.

The exp(β) (otherwise known as the odds ratio) in the second column of table 11.10 gives us another way to look at these data, one that is perhaps easier to understand: it quantifies the change in terms of the difference from one century to the next. Thus, the exp(β) in table 11.10 tells us that for each century that passes, negatives are between one-half and two-thirds (.60) as likely to be OV as they were in the previous century, quantified objects are about one-third (.33) as likely to be OV as they were in the previous century, while positives are just one-fifth (.18) as likely to be OV as in the previous century. From these results we can conclude that preverbal position is being lost at different rates for each type of object, and thus that different derivations are involved.

11.3. Derivation of Object Position in Old and Middle English

The regression analysis clearly indicates differences in the derivation of the three types of objects, but it does not indicate what these differences are. As discussed above, we assume grammatical competition in the headedness of the VP for both Old and Middle English, giving rise to both OV and VO orders in the base component. Each grammar has additional optional (stylistic) rules or processes associated with it that can alter the base-generated object position. In this section we will show that there are two processes affecting objects, postposing and preposing, each of which primarily affects two of the three object types. The effects of these processes, along with the ongoing loss of OV order in the base component, combine to give the surface distribution.

11.3.1 Postposing

The first of the processes we will look at is the postposing of a base-generated preverbal object to a position following the nonfinite verb. This process is the source of the length grading illustrated in tables 11.1 and 11.2, as it is primarily triggered by heaviness. Postposing can only be seen directly in I-final clauses in Old English, as in (3) above, repeated as (8), where the object cannot have been base-generated in this position. In I-initial clauses the results of postposition are indistinguishable on the surface from base-generated VO clauses.

(8) he þæs **habban** sceal <u>ece</u> <u>edlean</u> on Godes rice
he of-that have must eternal reward in God's kingdom
'he must have eternal reward of that in God's kingdom'
(cowulf, WHom_7:161.501)

Table 11.11 gives the percentage of postposed objects in I-final clauses in Old English, and shows that while positive and quantified objects postpose at the same rate of about 15 percent, negative objects do not postpose at all. The different behavior of negative objects arises because postposition creates islands and blocks negative concord, which is required in Old English.

Table 11.12 compares the rate of postposing over the Old English period. Although the frequencies of postposing are somewhat different, the probabilistic weights are not significantly different, indicating that there is no change over time. The difference in the frequencies is due to the different distribution of Latin-influenced texts in the two periods. We assume that the rate of postposition is the same for Middle English as well; however, since the rate of postposition can only be seen directly in I-final clauses, it is not possible to calculate it for Middle English, where I-final clauses are rare.

Table 11.11 Postposing in I-final clauses in Old English for three object types

Object type	*Postverbal*	N	*Postverbal (%)*
Positive	154	1,070	14.4
Quantified	25	167	15.0
Negative	0	81	0.0

Table 11.12 Rate of postposing in Old English I-final clauses over time

Date of composition	*Postverbal*	N	*Postverbal (%)*	*Prob. weight*
OE1 (before 950)	553	482	11.0	[.451]
OE2 (after 950)	98	527	18.6	[.545]
Total	151	1,009	15.0	—

11.3.2 *Preposing*

Data from Late Middle English (presented here and in van der Wurff 1999) show that when OV rates for positive objects are essentially zero, quantified and negative objects still appear in preverbal position at fairly high rates. The lack of positive objects in preverbal position indicates that underlying OV order (i.e. head-final VPs) has been lost, and therefore quantified and negative objects must be able to prepose from postverbal position to a position between the auxiliary and nonfinite verb. For our purposes it is immaterial what this preposing process is, as long as it can be defined so that it applies to the appropriate categories.

Interestingly, there is evidence that preposing is not just a property of Late Middle English, after underlying OV order has been lost. Looking at clauses from Old and Early Middle English which must be underlyingly VO because they contain a diagnostic element, such as a pronoun or particle, in postverbal position, we can see a clear difference in behavior between positive, quantified, and negative objects, as illustrated in tables 11.13 and 11.14. Quantified and negative objects, grouped together in tables 11.13 and 11.14 because of the small numbers, appear in preverbal position in these clauses at fairly high rates, while positives do not.

Although the data are sparse, the pattern is clear. Quantified and negative objects appear in preverbal position in VO clauses in Old and Middle English. Clearly, preposing is not just a Late Middle English process but has been in operation throughout the attested period. As the tables show, there are also two cases of a positive object in preverbal position in VO clauses, one in Old English and one in Middle English. The Middle English case is somewhat

Table 11.13 Distribution of objects in clauses with postverbal diagnostic elements in Old English

Object type	*Preverbal*	*Postverbal*	*Total*	*Preverbal (%)*
Positive	1	39	40	2.5
Quantified/negative	3	1	4	75.0

Table 11.14 Distribution of objects in clauses with postverbal pronouns in Early Middle English

Object type	*Preverbal*	*Postverbal*	*Total*	*Preverbal (%)*
Positive	1	19	20	5.0
Quantified/negative	4	9	13	30.8

Source: Kroch and Taylor (2000a: table 6.9).

dubious (see Kroch and Taylor, 2000a, for a discussion of this example) and might be dismissed as spurious. However, the Old English example, given in (9), appears solid, suggesting that positive objects may also prepose at a very low rate. There is no way to decide this issue based on the data to hand, and for the purposes of this chapter we will adopt the simpler approach and ignore the possibility of positive preposing. If this turns out to be the wrong assumption and positive objects do, in fact, prepose, the adjustment necessary to the model will be very small and will not affect the pattern presented by the data, which is our main interest.

(9) þæt ma ne mæge þæt drincgemett bringan forð
that one NEG can the measure-of-drink bring forth
'that one may not bring forth the measure of drink'
(cochdrul,ChrodR_1:6.28.167)

To summarize, the frequency data and rates of change obtained from the regression analysis show that the loss of OV order in the three types of objects is not proceeding at the same rate, suggesting that the derivation of preverbal position is not the same for the three types. Evidence from I-final clauses (see table 11.11) shows that while positive and quantified objects postpose, negative objects do not. Evidence of preverbal quantified and negative objects from Late Middle English postdating the loss of underlying OV order (see table 11.9) and from Old and Early Middle English in unambiguously VO clauses (see tables 11.13 and 11.14) demonstrates that a process of preposing is at work in all periods for these types, and that if positive objects do prepose, it is at a very low rate.

Our analysis of the derivation of surface object position is thus based on the following assumptions:

(10) a. In both Old English and Middle English, there is grammatical competition between head-initial and head-final VPs, giving rise to underlying OV and VO order.

b. The underlying rate of head-initial and head-final structure is the same for all objects (positive, quantified, and negative); this is the simplest assumption.

c. There is an optional postposing rule associated with the OV grammar that postposes positive and quantified objects from preverbal position to postverbal position. The rate of postposing is the same for both types and remains constant over time (tables 11.11 and 11.12). Since negative objects do not postpose, this means that all postverbal negative objects are base-generated in that position, within a head-initial VP.
d. There is an optional preposing rule associated with the VO grammar that preposes quantified and negative objects (tables 11.13 and 11.14) from postverbal position to preverbal position. Since positive objects do not generally prepose (but see (9)), this means that all preverbal positive objects are base-generated in that position, within a head-final VP. Note that preposing in this context refers to the movement of an object from postverbal position to preverbal position across the verb, not to scrambling within the preverbal field.

Given the assumptions in (10), the derivations of surface position (OV or VO) for the three types of objects in Old and Middle English are sketched in (11) through (13). The (a) and (b) examples have head-final VPs and head-initial VPs, respectively, with no movement of the object. The (c) and (d) examples show rightward and leftward object movement.

(11) Positive objects
a. SUBJ AUX [$_{VP}$ OBJ V]
b. SUBJ AUX [$_{VP}$ V OBJ]
c. SUBJ AUX [$_{VP}$ t_i V] OBJ_i

(12) Quantified objects
a. SUBJ AUX [$_{VP}$ OBJ V]
b. SUBJ AUX [$_{VP}$ V OBJ]
c. SUBJ AUX [$_{VP}$ t_i V] OBJ_i
d. SUBJ AUX OBJ_i [$_{VP}$ V t_i]

(13) Negative objects
a. SUBJ AUX [$_{VP}$ OBJ V]
b. SUBJ AUX [$_{VP}$ V OBJ]
c. SUBJ AUX OBJ_i [$_{VP}$ V t_i]

As (11–13) illustrate, our approach to the derivation of surface object position combines variation in underlying structure with optional movement rules. At first blush this approach seems to involve a fair amount of indeterminacy. There are two ways to derive Aux O V order with quantified and negative objects: head-final VP, as in (12a) and (13a), and leftward movement from a head-initial VP, as in (12d) and (13c). Similarly, there are two ways to derive Aux V O order with positive and quantified objects: head-initial VP, as in (11b) and (12b), and rightward movement from a head-final VP, as in (11c) and (12c).

But a closer examination of the assumptions shows that there is no indeterminacy once the VP directionality parameter is set to either head-initial or head-final. For example, if the VP is head-final, then the order Aux V O can be derived in only one way: by postposition of the object. Similarly, if the VP is head-initial, then the order Aux O V can be derived in only one way: by leftward movement of the object. This is equivalent to the notion that certain movement rules are associated with particular grammars. Head-initial grammars do not use rightward movement over the nonfinite verb, since there are no preverbal objects to be moved rightward; head-final grammars do not use leftward movement over the nonfinite verb, since there are no postverbal objects to be moved leftward. We can see, therefore, that indeterminacy is not a problem under this approach. Nevertheless, the grammatical system must incorporate optionality of two types: choice of grammar (head-initial vs. head-final), and then whether or not to apply the appropriate optional rule (leftward or rightward movement). Choice of grammar is readily understandable: for example, bilingual speakers select a grammar for each utterance. Optional movement may be viewed as a problem for current syntactic frameworks, but it is a widespread problem and one that is not limited to analyses that make use of grammatical competition.

11.4 Loss of OV Order

Given the assumptions outlined above in (10), it is clear that the loss of OV surface order in English is not a simple reflection of the loss of the base-generated OV grammar. We need to take into account both the underlying frequency of OV order and the effect of the postposing and preposing processes. The first step in modeling the loss of OV order, therefore, is to calculate the frequency of underlying OV order for each period so that we have a baseline to which the pre- and postposing processes may apply. Given that postposing applies at a constant rate, we can calculate the underlying frequency of OV order for positive objects in each period by adjusting for the proportion postposed. This is approximately 15 percent according to table 11.11. The formula for calculating the underlying rate of OV order for each period is shown in (14). As can be seen from (14b), the "before postposing" rate of OV order for positive objects is the surface OV rate, shown in table 11.9, divided by .85.

(14) a. $x - (x * .15)$ = surface OV rate of positives,
where x is the "before postposing" OV rate
b. solving for x, the "before preposing" OV rate:
x = surface OV rate of positives/.85.

In fact, this is the underlying rate of OV order for all objects (since we assume that the underlying rate is the same for all types); that is, it is the proportion of the data generated by the head-final grammar.

Table 11.15 Underlying rate of OV order by period

Period	*Underlying frequency of OV order (%)*
OE1	66.7
OE2	59.3
ME1	33.4
ME2	3.6
ME3	1.5
ME4	0.8

Table 11.16 Comparison of the underlying and surface orders of three object types

Period	*Underlying % OV*	*Surface positive % OV*	*Surface quantified % OV*	*Surface negative % OV*
OE1	66.7	56.7	63.5	91.8
OE2	59.3	50.4	56.4	78.3
ME1	33.4	28.4	34.7	41.0
ME2	3.6	3.1	10.6	18.2
ME3	1.5	1.3	6.0	20.3
ME4	0.8	0.7	6.1	22.0

Table 11.15 clearly shows the decrease in head-final VPs. Table 11.16 compares this underlying rate with the observed surface rates of the three types of objects (from table 11.9). The table is also represented graphically in figure 11.3. We can see that the surface frequency of preverbal position for positive objects is always lower than the underlying rate, and for negatives it is always higher. The surface distribution of quantified objects bears a more complicated relation to the underlying OV frequency, however: in the early periods, the surface rate is lower, as with the positives, but in the later periods it is higher, as with the negatives. Thus, in the graph in figure 11.3, the line representing surface OV rate for quantified objects starts out under the underlying rate, but then crosses over and finishes above it.

The reason that the OV rate of positive objects is lower than the underlying rate is clear: 15 percent of all underlying preverbal objects postpose, thereby lowering the observed rate. Similarly, we know from table 11.11 that negative objects do not postpose, but only prepose (tables 11.13 and 11.14), thereby raising the observed OV rate for this type in each period. The more complicated

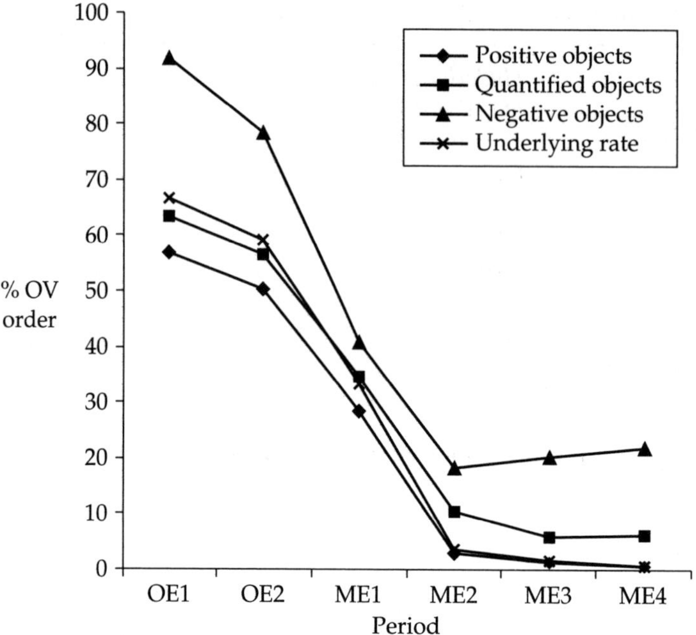

Figure 11.3 Comparison of underlying and surface rates of OV order

relationship between the underlying rate and the observed rate for quantified objects is related to the fact that quantified objects are affected by both postposing (when base-generated in preverbal position) and preposing (when base-generated in postverbal position). When the underlying OV rate is high (i.e. in the early periods), the effect of postposing is strongest, lowering the surface OV rate for quantified objects; but in later periods, as more and more of the data are underlyingly VO, the effect of preposing outweighs that of postposing and the surface OV rate for quantified objects is higher than the base rate.

11.5 Rate of Preposing

In the previous discussion, we have taken the rate of postposing as 15 percent (from table 11.11); and on the basis of table 11.12 we have assumed it to be constant over time. But what about the rates of quantified and negative object preposing? Are they also constant? Given that quantified and negative preverbal objects eventually disappear, it seems natural to assume that the rates are decreasing. However, it is possible that the loss of preverbal position for these two types of objects is caused by some other later change, and that during the period in question the preposing rates are constant. Both scenarios will result in a

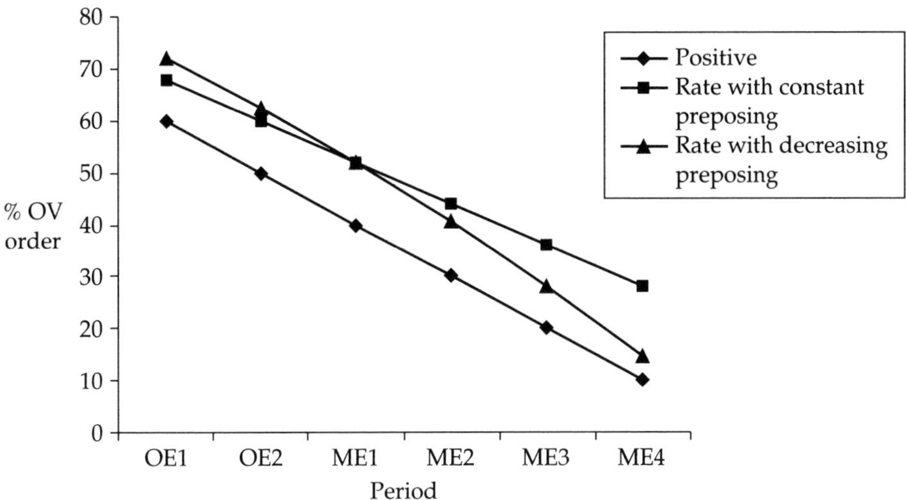

Figure 11.4 Comparison of a constant rate of preposing (20 percent) versus a decreasing rate (5 percent) per period

decrease in the surface OV rate of quantified and negative objects, since this rate is related to the underlying rate of positive objects, which is decreasing, although in the latter case the decrease will be steeper. This is illustrated in figure 11.4 using a constructed data set.

The rate of negative preposing can be calculated from the difference between the underlying distribution of all objects and the surface distribution of negative objects (from table 11.16) as shown in table 11.17, using the period OE1 as an example. The difference between the number of underlying VO tokens and the number of surface negative VO tokens (33.3 – 8.2) gives us the number of tokens that have preposed (25.1). This number divided by the number of underlying VO tokens (25.1/33.3) gives us the rate of preposing (75.4 percent).

As shown in table 11.18 below, calculating the rate of quantified preposing is a bit more complicated, because the surface rate includes postposing as well as preposing. Only objects in underlying VO tokens are affected by preposing,

Table 11.17 Calculating negative object preposing

Object–verb order	*OV*	*VO*
Underlying distribution of objects	66.7	33.3
Surface distribution of negative objects	91.8	8.2
Difference in VO rates = tokens preposed	33.3 – 8.2 = 25.1	
Frequency of preposing	25.1/33.3 = 75.4%	

Table 11.18 Calculating quantified object preposing

Object–verb order	*OV*	*VO*
Underlying distribution of objects	66.7	33.3
Surface distribution of positive objects (= distribution of quantified objects after postposing)	56.7	43.3
Surface distribution of quantified objects	63.5	36.5
Difference in surface VO rates = tokens preposed	43.3 – 36.5 = 6.8	
Frequency of preposing	6.8/33.3 = 20.4%	

since preposing is associated with the VO grammar. Tokens in which the object is in postverbal position due to postposing are part of the OV grammar and thus cannot be affected by preposing. In this case, therefore, we calculate the number of tokens that must prepose to achieve the surface distribution as the difference in the surface distribution of positive objects, which equals the distribution of quantified objects after postposing has taken place (because the two types postpose at the same rate) but before preposing (43.3 – 36.5 = 6.8). These 6.8 tokens then are taken as a percentage of the 33.3 underlying VO tokens (6.8/33.3 = 20.4 percent).

The rate of preposing for quantified objects, calculated by the method in table 11.18, is shown below in table 11.19 for all six periods. There is a clear decrease in the rate of preposing over time. We can conclude from this that preposing of quantified objects is being lost over time, and its eventual extinction is simply the end point of a long-term change.

Turning to the negative objects, the rate of preposing, calculated by the method in table 11.17, is shown below in table 11.20 for all six periods. We can see that the pattern in table 11.20 is nothing like as clear and consistent as that of the quantified objects. The first reason for this is undoubtedly that there are far fewer tokens with negative objects (sample sizes range from 33 to 138 for the

Table 11.19 Rate of preposing for quantified objects

Period	*Rate of preposing (%)*	*95% confidence intervals*
OE1	20.4	17.4–23.4
OE2	14.7	12.1–17.3
ME1	9.5	7.1–11.9
ME2	7.8	4.9–10.7
ME3	4.8	3.6–6.0
ME4	5.4	5.4–7.4

Table 11.20 Rate of preposing for negative objects

Period	*Rate of preposing (%)*	*95% confidence intervals*
OE1	75.4	69.1–81.5
OE2	46.7	41.2–52.2
ME1	11.4	6.3–16.5
ME2	15.1	8.9–21.3
ME3	19.1	15.8–22.4
ME4	21.3	17.3–25.3

six periods) and thus much more variability in the data. There is a clear decrease from OE1 to ME1, but then there appears to be a slight rise. The low rate for ME1, which appears to be distinct from OE1/2 and ME3/4 at least, is a mystery. What is clear is that the rate is decreasing within Old English, and the decrease continues into Middle English. The true pattern of behavior of the negatives in the Middle English period, however, remains something of an open question, which further data from the Early Modern English period may help to elucidate.

11.6 Conclusions

In this chapter we have analyzed in detail the distribution of three types of objects in order to reveal the complex interaction of underlying structure and movement which results in their surface position. We showed first that the positions of all types of objects (positive, quantified, and negative) in both Old and Middle English are influenced by the same factors (length, clause type, date of composition, and case/thematic role). Quantitative evidence, however, shows that the different types of objects appear in preverbal position at different frequencies, and, moreover, that preverbal position is lost at different rates for the three types. Assuming grammatical competition in the headedness of VPs, we showed that the derivation of objects in preverbal and postverbal position is dependent on the underlying structure of the clause (OV or VO) and is further affected by optional processes which are different for the three types. Thus, positive objects may postpose from preverbal position in OV clauses, negative objects may prepose from postverbal position in VO clauses, and quantified objects are subject to both types of movement, postposing in underlying OV clauses and preposing in underlying VO clauses. It is important to emphasize that rightward and leftward movement operate in different grammars; in other words, it is not the case that quantified objects move leftward from postverbal position and then rightward again within the same clause, since each clause is generated either by an OV grammar or a VO grammar, but not both. We used this analysis to estimate first the underlying frequency of OV order for each period and then the rates of preposing and postposing associated with each of the grammars. The results show that the rate of OV order is decreasing over time, and furthermore that the rates of preposing for quantified and negative objects associated with the VO grammar are also decreasing, although at different rates. The loss of OV order for all types of objects, therefore, is the final outcome of several long-term changes which begin in the Old English period and continue until after the end of the Middle English, rather than any abrupt change in late Middle English.

APPENDIX A: NOTES ON THE DATA

The Helsinki Corpus, the original diachronic corpus of early stages of the English language upon which many annotated corpora are based, is a compilation of balanced samples from Old, Middle, and Early Modern English texts, and includes information on date of composition and date of manuscript for each text. See Kytö (1996) for a complete description.

The Old English data used for this study consist of all the files in the YCOE, with the exception of duplicate manuscripts and Old English documents (charters, wills, etc.). For those YCOE texts that were included in the Helsinki Corpus, the texts are assigned to periods according to the earlier Helsinki date, i.e. the date of composition.

The Middle English data used for this study consist of all the texts included in the PPCME2, apart from the *Ormulum*. The texts are assigned to periods according to the earlier Helsinki date, i.e. the date of composition.

The second Middle English period (ME2) is not well represented, and the texts included are not a homogeneous lot. They include the *Ayenbite of Inwyt*, a translation from French, *The Earliest Prose Psalter* which, although a large text ($N = 371$), has no OV order at all, even with negatives, the most likely type to appear in preverbal position. The Kentish Sermons are represented by only 18 tokens, and the Rolle texts, although composed in the second period, are attested only in fourth-period manuscripts. The data from ME2 therefore should not be taken over-seriously.

There are two other large Middle English texts that have no OV order at all: the Wycliffite Sermons (c.1400), and Purvey's Prologue to the Bible (c.1388). It is not clear whether these texts should be considered part of the same speech community as texts which show variation, since they may only have one grammar, rather than the competing grammars of the other texts; they have, however, been included in the analysis.

APPENDIX B

Table 11.A.1 Multivariate analysis of the factors influencing the position of quantified objects in Old English clauses

Independent factor	*Preverbal*	N	*Preverbal (%)*	*Prob. weight*
Length in words				
1	47	56	83.9	.77
2	117	159	73.6	.66
3	38	73	52.1	.40
4 or more	18	40	45.0	.34
DP + relative clause	6	48	12.5	.08
Total	226	376	60.1	—
Clause type				
Main	39	78	50.0	[.39]
Conjoined main	40	72	55.6	[.42]
Subordinate	143	217	65.9	[.56]
Conjoined subordinate	4	9	44.4	[.60]
Total	226	376	60.1	—
Date of composition				
OE1 (before 950)	113	178	63.5	[.55]
OE2 (after 950)	101	179	56.4	[.45]
Total	214	357	59.9	—
Case				
Accusative	167	266	62.8	.55
Genitive	8	18	44.4	.26
Dative	34	64	53.1	.39
Ambiguous	17	28	60.7	.49
Total	226	376	60.1	—

Table 11.A.2 Factors influencing the position of negative objects in Old English clauses

Independent factor	*Preverbal*	N	*Preverbal (%)*
Length in words			
1	16	16	100.0
2	87	103	84.5
3	12	14	85.7
4 or more	2	4	50.0
DP + relative clause	1	6	16.7
Total	118	143	82.5
Clause type			
Main	30	33	90.9
Conjoined main	34	43	79.1
Subordinate	47	60	78.3
Conjoined subordinate	7	7	100.0
Total	118	143	82.5
Date of composition			
OE1 (before 950)	45	49	91.8
OE2 (after 950)	65	83	78.3
Total	110	132	83.3
Case			
Accusative	96	114	84.2
Genitive	2	5	40.0
Dative	19	23	82.6
Ambiguous	1	1	100.0
Total	118	143	82.5

Table 11.A.3 Factors influencing the position of quantified objects in Middle English clauses

Independent factor	*Preverbal*	N	*Preverbal (%)*	*Prob. weight*
Clause type				
Main	31	318	9.7	.38
Subordinate	56	363	15.4	.61
Total	87	681	12.8	—
Length in words				
1	32	72	44.4	.91
2	36	193	18.7	.75
3	13	146	8.9	.52
4 or more	3	114	2.6	.29
DP + relative clause	3	156	1.9	.14
Total	87	681	12.8	—
Object type				
Object 1	86	673	12.8	[.50]
Object 2	1	8	12.5	[.47]
Total	87	681	12.8	—
Period				
ME1	51	147	34.7	.87
ME2	9	85	10.6	.30
ME3	18	301	6.0	.42
ME4	9	148	6.1	.32
Total	87	681	12.8	—

Table 11.A.4 Factors influencing the position of negative objects in Middle English clauses

Independent factor	*Preverbal*	N	*Preverbal (%)*	*Prob. weight*
Clause type				
Main	33	169	19.5	.43
Subordinate	40	146	27.4	.58
Total	73	315	23.2	—
Length in words				
1	21	36	58.3	.84
2	42	173	24.3	.51
3	8	30	26.7	.55
4 or more	2	38	10.5	.14
DP + relative clause	0	38	0.0	
Total	73	315	23.2	—
Object type				
Object 1	72	313	23.0	[.50]
Object 2	1	2	50.0	[.56]
Total	73	315	23.2	—
Period				
ME1	16	39	41.0	.72
ME2	6	33	18.2	.42
ME3	28	138	20.3	.45
ME4	23	105	22.0	.50
Total	73	315	23.2	—

ACKNOWLEDGMENTS

Some of the material in this chapter has been presented before audiences at the Seventh Diachronic Generative Syntax Conference (University of Girona 2002), the Second York-Holland Symposium on the History of English Syntax (University of Leiden 2003), and NWAVE 32 (University of Pennsylvania 2003). We thank these audiences, the editors of this volume, and Anthony Warner for helpful comments and discussion. All errors and omissions remain our own responsibility. Pintzuk's work has been supported by AHRB Research Leave Grant 4727 APN 13199 and a matching grant from the Department of Language and Linguistic Science, University of York; this support is gratefully acknowledged. Finally, thanks are due to Beth Randall for Corpus Search, the software that makes it possible to search large annotated corpora.

REFERENCES

Kemenade, A. van (1987). *Syntactic Case and Morphological Case in the History of English*. Dordrecht: Foris.

Koopman, W. F. (1997). Another look at clitics in Old English. *Transactions of the Philological Society* 95: 73–93.

Kroch, A. S. (1989). Reflexes of grammar in patterns of language change. *Language Variation and Change* 1: 199–244.

Kroch, A. S. (1995). Morphosyntactic variation. In K. Beals, J. Denton, B. Knippen, L. Melnar, H. Suzuki, and E. Zeinfeld (eds.), *Proceedings of the Thirtieth Annual Meeting of the Chicago Linguistics Society* (vol. 2) (pp. 180–201). Chicago: Chicago Linguistic Society.

Kroch, A. S. and A. Taylor (1997). Verb movement in Old and Middle English: dialect variation and language contact. In A. van Kemenade and N. Vincent (eds.), *Parameters of Morphosyntactic Change* (pp. 297–325). Cambridge: Cambridge University Press.

Kroch, A. S. and A. Taylor (2000a). Verb–complement order in Middle English. In S. Pintzuk, G. Tsoulas, and A. Warner (eds.), *Diachronic Syntax: Models and Mechanisms* (pp. 132–63). Oxford: Oxford University Press.

Kroch, A. S. and A. Taylor (2000b). *The Penn-Helsinki Parsed Corpus of Middle English* (2nd edn.). Philadelphia: Department of Linguistics, University of Pennsylvania. (Accessible via: http://www.ling.upenn.edu/mideng)

Kytö, M. (1996). *Manual to the Diachronic Part of the Helsinki Corpus of English Texts* (3rd edn.). Helsinki: Department of English, University of Helsinki.

Pintzuk, S. (1996). Cliticization in Old English. In A. L. Halpern and A. M. Zwicky (eds.), *Approaching Second: Second Position Clitics and Related Phenomena* (pp. 375–409). Stanford, CA: CSLI Publications.

Pintzuk, S. (1999). *Phrase Structures in Competition: Variation and Change in Old English Word Order*. New York: Garland.

Pintzuk, S. (2002). Verb–object order in Old English: variation as grammatical competition. In D. W. Lightfoot (ed.), *Syntactic Effects of Morphological Change* (pp. 276–99). Oxford: Oxford University Press.

Taylor, A., A. Warner, S. Pintzuk, and F. Beths (2003). *The York-Toronto-Helsinki Parsed Corpus of Old English.* York, UK: Department of Language and Linguistic Science, University of York. (Available through the Oxford Text Archive.)

Wurff, W. van der (1997). Deriving object–verb order in Late Middle English. *Journal of Linguistics* 33: 485–509.

Wurff, W. van der (1999). Objects and verbs in modern Icelandic and fifteenth-century English: a word order parallel and its causes. *Lingua* 109: 237–65.

FURTHER READING

Fischer, O., A. van Kemenade, W. Koopman, and W. van der Wurff (2000). *The Syntax of Early English.* Cambridge: Cambridge University Press.

Foster, T. and W. van der Wurff (1995). The survival of object–verb order in Middle English: some data. *Neophilologus* 79: 309–27.

Foster, T. and W. van der Wurff (1997). From syntax to discourse: the function of the object–verb order in Later Middle English. In J. Fisiak (ed.), *Studies in Middle English Linguistics* (pp. 135–56). Berlin: Mouton de Gruyter.

Ingham, R. (2000). Negation and OV order in Late Middle English. *Journal of Linguistics* 36: 13–38.

Ingham, R. (2002). Negated subjects and objects in 15th century nonliterary English. *Language Variation and Change* 14: 291–322.

Pintzuk, S. (1996). Old English verb–complement word order and the change from OV to VO. *York Papers in Linguistics* 17: 241–64.

Roberts, I. (1997). Directionality and word order change in the history of English. In A. van Kemenade and N. Vincent (eds.), *Parameters of Morphosyntactic Change* (pp. 397–426). Cambridge: Cambridge University Press.

12 Category Change and Gradience in the Determiner System

DAVID DENISON

12.1 Introduction

In this chapter I will explore gradience between adjectives and determiners, part of an ongoing research program. I begin with some pre-theoretical background. The main thrust is as follows. An account of Present-day English (PDE) morphosyntax cannot easily be made to fit the facts if it insists on Aristotelian categories with necessary and sufficient conditions for membership and hard-and-fast boundaries. An alternative is to admit the idea of prototypes into morphosyntactic categorization, allowing for gradience within the category and perhaps degrees of membership. A special case arises when increasing distance in one direction from the prototype of one category corresponds to increasing closeness to the prototype of another, which can be the case where different values of the same parameter help to define each of the categories concerned: now we can have gradience *between* two categories. For several examples of this in English, notably across the Adjective ~ Noun boundary, see Denison (2001), and for further accounts along broadly similar lines see the survey in Aarts et al. (2004: 10–12) and works excerpted in Part III of that reader. Fuzzy boundaries between categories turn out to be helpful – in my opinion, necessary – in the description of the history of determiners in English (of which this chapter makes no attempt to be a full account).

Note that allowing for gradience within and between categories does not preclude the employment of categories either in the mental representations of language users or the grammars of linguists. It may well be the case that inter-category gradience is a marked option in the language system: certainly, intermediate forms are often unstable chronologically, as e.g. the transitive adjectives that hover between Adjective and Preposition (Denison 2001: 131–3). Furthermore, gradience need not involve strict adherence to prototype concepts. There are associated ideas, such as **schema-based prototypes** and the **cluster concept** – and indeed the earlier **family resemblance** – which do not require every category to possess at least one wholly prototypical member, since various combinations of condition may in some cases be sufficient for membership without any particular set of conditions being necessary. See the helpful discussions of the cluster concept and references in Jackendoff (2002: 352–6), there largely in relation to conceptual semantics rather than morphosyntax, and of prototypes in Croft (2001).

The consequences for syntax of categorial gradience are less clear, but one possible avenue, if category labels for individual words are no longer always clear-cut, is to abandon syntactic models which require both a unique category label and a single mother node for every single word in a sentence. Some version of Construction Grammar may be a more appropriate model.

I will motivate gradience a little further in the remainder of section 1, then, confining myself to PDE for the time being, look at the major categories involved in the NP in section 2 and their interrelationships in section 2.4. In section 3 I review some approaches to the Determiner category. After that we can turn to the history of determiners in English. Section 4 considers inflectional behavior, positional syntax, and co-occurrence, and in section 5 there is specific evidence for gradience, including a detailed corpus investigation. Section 6 forms a brief conclusion. There follows a list of corpora cited as sources of examples.

12.1.1 *Mainstream morphosyntax*

It is widely recognized that:

- any lexical category (N, A, V, etc.) is defined by a basket of properties;
- not all members of a category display every property of that category;
- some items are "better" (more prototypical) members than others.

Fat is a really "good" Adjective, whereas *mere, potential, ill, well, woolen* are for various reasons less good. *Mere,* for example, lacks gradability, a comparative (but not a superlative), and cannot occur in predicative function. *Boy* is a really "good" Noun, being concrete (indeed animate), countable, and morphologically regular, whereas *flour, ridicule, English* are less good exemplars of the category Noun.

12.1.2 *Mainstream syntax*

In most formal and many structuralist approaches we find:

- Aristotelian category membership of lexical items (e.g. no degrees of nouniness);
- no intermediate possibilities between, say, N and A;
- unique constituent analysis of a sentence (± derivational movement and reanalysis).

Tree diagrams, as for example a phrase formed by the adjective *mere* and the noun *ridicule*, do not have percentages or question marks against category labels, whether in constituent or dependency syntax, even if the lexical items concerned are not prototypical members of their category:

(1)

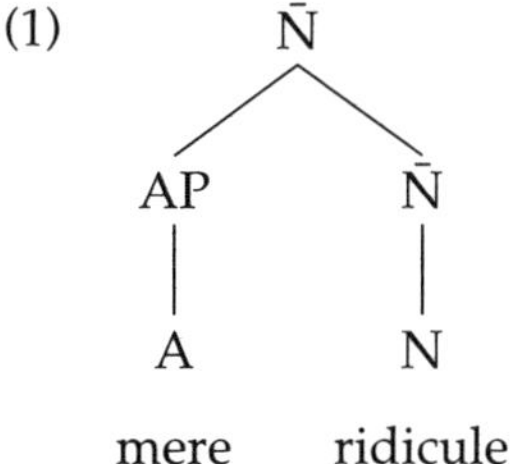

Nor does constituent structure involve degrees of motherhood (lines of variable thickness?) or multiple mothers for one daughter node (upward branching trees).

12.1.3 *Same river?*

Are these approaches, which I have cheerfully (but, I hope, fairly) characterized as "mainstream morphosyntax" and "mainstream syntax," actually consistent with each other? Here are two possible answers:

- **Yes**. Sentence patterns are stored and processed differently from lexis. For example, a general – if generally unstated – assumption seems to be that even poorer exemplars of a given category "snap into place" in a particular syntactic structure *as if* they were prototypical members of that category.
- **No**. Gradient category membership for words implies the possibility of constructional gradience for sentences. Consider those sentences where an alternative analysis of the category membership of a word would correspond to a difference in structural position (as with SKT-constructions: see section 12.5.3 below). If the alternative category membership is one of those cases which look like gradience between categories, then the structure ought to be treated as in some way intermediate or gradient as well.

It is the latter option that is implicit in what follows, though I will not explore the syntactic consequences here. A helpful survey of some relevant material on category membership appears in Aarts (2004), though Aarts himself discounts most claimed instances of inter-category gradience.

12.2 PDE Nominal Categories in Practice

Formal grammars and most modern descriptive grammars of English start with a fixed set of categories which includes D = Determiner. However, it is possible

– and desirable – to look at a language without preconceptions about its lexical categories. Ordinary, uneducated language users have no knowledge of non-inflectional categories, and it is not *a priori* obvious that categories are fundamental in language description (see, for example, Croft (2001: ch. 2)). What speakers experience is *usage*, from which they no doubt intuit patterns of various kinds. Most linguists attempting to generalize from usage find it a helpful economy to recognize that words generally pattern according to a relatively small number of syntactic categories, but categories are still a secondary phenomenon. Whether categories or constructions have more psychological reality is not clear.

12.2.1 Determiner

The structuralist tradition derives its categories by distributional means. Suppose it has been decided that the categories N = Noun and A = Adjective are justifiable or indeed necessary for English – and they are almost universally accepted. Where does D = Determiner come from? According to OED (the *Oxford English Dictionary*) the term is Bloomfield's (1933), but *article* as a category is much older. In English, the usual route to the postulation of a category D is to argue as follows, exemplified by the *Cambridge Grammar of the English Language*, henceforth *CGEL* (Huddleston and Pullum 2002: 538–40), where the category label used is "determinative":

- Like A, the articles *a* and *the* can serve as pre-modifiers of N.
- However, they are so different from prototypical A as to justify a separate category label of their own. (Note, however, that Bloomfield defines *determiner* as one kind of "limiting adjective.") For example, the articles cannot occur alone in predicative position, unlike pronouns and adjectives.
- *This, that, my, each,* etc. have a similar distribution to the articles and are mutually exclusive with each other and with the articles.
- Overall, *this, that, my, each,* etc. are much more like the articles than they are like A.
- These facts make it handy to put them all in one category, D.

Let me emphasize that this approach seems methodologically defensible and empirically quite successful, and there are many advantages in distinguishing the three categories D, A, N. In an earlier work, Huddleston had first pursued a similar line (1984: 97–8), then conceded that there was insufficient evidence to decide whether or not D is a subclass of A (1984: 304–5).

In the generative tradition, D can be a functional category rather than, or as well as, a lexical category. Its semantics are largely to do with definiteness or referentiality, and this provides much of its cross-linguistic justification in the grammatical model. Most determiners with lexical content are members of more specific categories, such as DEM = Demonstrative. However, functional projections serve no purpose outside Minimalism and related theories. The structuralist approach outlined in the previous paragraph only deals with items that have overt phonetic form, and it relies heavily, if not completely, on formal and distributional criteria for the identification of categories. In that approach, therefore, being the locus of definiteness would not be a primary criterion. For an excellent treatment of prenominal categories and the problems of demarcation in Swedish, interested readers are referred to Börjars (1998), whose methodology and indeed conclusions often carry over to English.

12.2.2 *The principal nominal categories*

The principal domain of the categories D, A, and N is the NP, whose other important possible constituent is Prn = Pronoun. Again we have a problem, because Prn may be a separate category in its own right or perhaps a subcategory of N, since it can – like a noun – act as head of NP (thus *CGEL*: 327). The latter point is not valid under the DP Hypothesis, where N is head of NP but D is head of a higher DP node. In fact there is strong distributional evidence both against treating D as a subcategory of A and against treating Prn as a subcategory of N, if I have made a good choice of parameters in table 12.1.

Here the first property is to do with openness of the class, though it has a semantic component, and it is probably related to the second, which is a syntactic property, as is the third. The last three are morphological, though comparison has a semantic component too.

12.2.3 *Rough edges to nominal categories*

But not a single one of the "facts" in table 12.1 is straightforward, even in PDE. For example,

- The contrast lexical ~ grammatical is not a clear-cut one.
- Within D some iteration is possible.
- Not all A can act as predicate.

Table 12.1 Categories in Present-day English

Property	*D*	*A*	*N*	*Prn*	*Kind of property*
Lexical rather than grammatical	–	+	+	–	open/closed class, semantic
Can iterate	–	+	(–)	–	syntactic
Can act as predicate	–	+	–	?	syntactic
Number marking	(–)	–	+	+	morphological
Subjective~objective case marking	–	–	–	+	morphological
Comparison	–	+	–	–	morphological, semantic

- Number marking is sporadic in D and lacking in some N and Prn.
- Case marking is sporadic in Prn.
- Comparison is not universal in A and conversely *is* possible with some quantificational and degree D.

Remember, too, that the original argumentation suggested that the articles were very distant from *prototypical* adjectives – and the very possibility of appealing to prototypical membership of a category concedes implicitly that membership of that category is gradient. (For some scholars, a gradient of prototypicality *within* a category is still compatible with an insistence on clear yes-or-no membership of the category [Aarts 2004].)

12.2.4 Subcategories of D

Co-occurrence with D should disqualify a word from being D itself, since part of the case for D was that it was a non-iterative category, like M = Modal in standard English. However, there are words which are semantically and syntactically more like D than A, which precede (other) adjectives in the NP, but which nevertheless can co-occur with D. One solution is to subcategorize D into Predeterminer, (central) Determiner, and Postdeterminer. Thus we get strings like *both the other movements* (Brown Corpus) and *all its many aspects* (LOB), which suggest that *both, all* are predeterminers and *other, many* postdeterminers.

However, there are well-known problems here. One of these is *such*. It is incompatible with many central determiners, which suggests that it is one itself. But it is frequent before *a* and after *any*, which implies respectively pre- or post-determiner. And with *(an)other* there are alternative orders, with a historical change in frequency:

(2) The risk of cancer from normal radiation exposure is simply insignificant compared to *such other causes* as smoking, industrial pollution, and life-style. (Frown)

(3) She was not alone for there were *three other such children* in the big city's special nursery. (Brown)

The conclusion of two recent works is that *such* is not a determiner at all, but an adjective (Huddleston and Pullum 2002; Spinillo 2003). Note, for example,

(4) *The latest such gratifying eye-popper* comes from Manhattan. (Frown)

where it comes between two adjectives. (We might also be tempted to group predeterminer *such a* with certain other originally multi-word forms like *don't, let's*, and *there's* – all of them tending to behave as invariant particles which signal phrase or clause type in initial position. Johanna Wood provides additional evidence of invariance from the frequent "error" *a such a* [2002: 109].)

There are similar problems with *every*. Is *every* a central determiner – because incompatible with *the* – or a postdeterminer? An apparent example of the latter is:

(5) The stock market leaps and tumbles at *Peking's every smile or frown*. (BNC)

Such postdeterminer usage is rather limited. *Every* in the (5) pattern is described in *CGEL* (2002: 379, 469) as having a modifier rather than a determiner function, but with no detail on the limited range of heads it occurs with, apart from the claim that they are "probably all abstract." Quirk et al. are similarly unspecific (1985: 257 n.[c]).

12.2.5 *D and Prn*

Another problem concerns whether particular members of the category D need to be used with a following noun. This is usually taken to be an either-or matter. Most of them can, which is part of the argument in favor of the DP Hypothesis, in which D and Prn effectively fall together. But the distinction may be gradient. On the basis of behavior with gerunds, as in

(6) *This being seduced continually* is kind of fun

Ross concludes (1973: 168–9 [= 2004: 372–3]):

> In my speech, there is a hierarchy of "noun-requiringness" of determiners, with those on the left end of the hierarchy occurring in a wider range of contexts than those on the right.

His hierarchy is as follows:

(7) $$\text{NPs} > {?}\begin{Bmatrix}\textit{this}\\ \textit{that}\end{Bmatrix} > \begin{Bmatrix}\textit{no}\\ \textit{some}\\ \textit{much}\\ \textit{little}\end{Bmatrix} > \begin{Bmatrix}\textit{the}\\ \textit{prior}\\ \textit{occasional}\\ \textit{frequent}\end{Bmatrix} > \begin{Bmatrix}\textit{careful}\\ \textit{reluctant}\\ \text{etc.}\end{Bmatrix} > \begin{Bmatrix}\textit{good}\\ \textit{bad}\end{Bmatrix} \mathrel{?}> \begin{Bmatrix}\textit{other}\\ \textit{mere}\end{Bmatrix}$$

We can recognize some support for the gradedness of the subcategorization facts without necessarily endorsing every detail of Ross's claims.

12.3 How to Handle Nominal Categories

12.3.1 *Category space*

The four categories D, A, N, and Prn, assuming we decide to retain them, all show gradient membership, and there is leakiness of boundary between

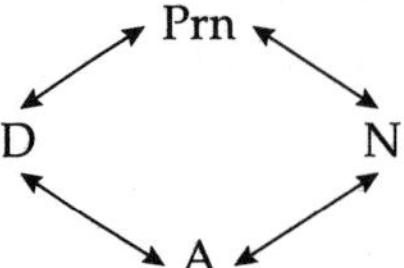

Figure 12.1 Category space

all four adjacent pairs in the diagram in figure 12.1. By contrast, there does not appear to be a fuzzy boundary between the categories represented as opposing vertices (D ~ N or Prn ~ A). The diagram simply represents my empirical knowledge of English, and I hesitate to claim any cross-linguistic validity for it.

12.3.2 *Does dependency grammar have a need for D?*

Hudson has suggested an analysis of determiners in which D is seen as a type of Prn, thus capturing the similarity of

(8) a. I don't like that.
  b. I don't like that pudding.

A range of arguments is given in Hudson (2000) and Spinillo (2000). *The* and *every* are categorized as pronouns that require common-noun complements, while *I* and *him* are pronouns that disallow them. Accepting this would solve some of the problems noted in section 12.2.3 above. Hudson goes on to argue that Prn, like common noun, is merely a kind of noun, thus collapsing three of our four nominal categories under a super-category, N. Although the analysis has some attractive features and offers genuine insights – note that common nouns, like some of Hudson's pronouns, can act as premodifiers of other nouns, as in *hilltop phone transmitters* – common noun and Prn remain distinct labels. And differences of distribution within the super-category still need to be captured.

12.3.3 *Do generative grammar or typology have a need for D?*

Working in the Principles and Parameters framework and using a modest sample of cross-linguistic evidence, Giusti (1997) suggests that the category D is too diverse to show uniform syntax across languages, and that a more successful analysis (both cross-linguistically and in the individual languages considered) would split the category up. She focuses on three types of element normally thought of as D: articles, demonstratives, and quantifiers. She argues that "only articles are extended heads of the noun phrase," i.e. truly D. Demonstratives "occupy specifier positions," while quantifiers are either adjectives or are lexical heads complemented by a full DP. The details would take us too far afield, but these conclusions are not dissimilar to those of scholars working in very different traditions, e.g. Spamer's work on OE (Old English), on which see sections 12.3.4 and 12.4.2 below. Several papers in Kemenade and Vincent (1997) examine accretion to the category D in particular languages (Romance or Germanic) without questioning its status as a linguistic universal. It would be useful to investigate whether there is widespread typological and cross-linguistic support for the category D.

12.3.4 *Category and function*

A recurrent concern of this chapter is the boundary between Determiner and Adjective, which leads us to a brief digression on the definition of the latter. Spamer (1979: 242–3) makes a distinction between **adjectives** and **adjuncts**, defined positionally. This seems to be a functional distinction rather than a categorical one, though he confusingly uses "adjective" as a category label as well and has no systematic distinction between functional and categorical facts. In PDE, for instance, he cites from Jespersen (1909–49: II 328):

(9) a. an eminent Shakespearean critic
    b. a learned Dante scholar

In (9), *eminent* and *learned* would be adjectives, while *Shakespearean* (= A) and *Dante* (= N) would be adjuncts. (The difference can also be captured by calling the latter type a **pre-head complement**, since *Shakespearean critic* = *critic of Shakespeare*.) In PDE both the adjective and the adjunct slots are recursive. Spamer's brief account fails to explain why within his adjunct slot (equivalent, I think, to what Quirk et al. (1985: 1338–40) call Zone IV, the prehead zone), A normally still precedes N:

(10) a. Gothic church towers
     b. Chinese jade idols

However, it brings out some interesting facts in Old English.

12.4 Inflection and Co-occurrence in History

12.4.1 *Determiner in history*

We have already noted some problems with the category D in PDE. The term **Determiner** is retained without comment by all four authors of "Syntax" chapters in the historical volumes of *The Cambridge History of the English Language* (Hogg 1992–2001), of whom I was one, but I now realize that the evidence for the existence of D is much shakier in earlier English. For example, it is generally agreed that "definite article" is a problematic term for the *se / þæt / seo* paradigm ('the, that') in OE. And if in Present-day English the articles, the core of D, are clearly different in their distribution from Prn, this is quite unclear for the apparent precursor of *the*, which has full pronominal function in Old English, and for the etymon of *a*, which is certainly a numeral in many instances and possibly an indefinite article in others (Mitchell 1985: 95–101; Traugott 1992: 176). So the very starting point used in the PDE argument (section 12.2.1 above) is much weaker. Furthermore, inflectional variation is common to the precursors of all four categories D, A, N, and Prn, which carry both number and case marking, while the precursors of central determiners permit iteration in ways that have become impossible in late ModE (Modern English). Thus the distributional evidence for separating off a category D is much less clear, or at the very least must be considerably different. Let us look more closely at some of the main NP categories in Old English.

12.4.2 *Inflection in Old English*

In Old English, adjectives share parts of their inflectional paradigms with both determiners and nouns. (For the time being, demonstratives and so on will be put under the category label Determiner for expository purposes, an analysis questioned below.) When D is present in the NP – and also in vocatives and when A is comparative – A is inflected according to the so-called weak or definite or *n*-declension, which is shared with a declension of nouns and is rather different from the kinds of inflectional paradigm found with D. Otherwise A follows the strong or indefinite declension, which is more similar morphologically to the pattern of D (as represented by *se / þæt / seo*) than to any noun pattern; details are given in any handbook of OE grammar. In fact this declensional pattern is virtually identical to the pattern of 3 person Prn. On the strength of this, one might be tempted to recognize three positional slots in NPs containing no more than one prenominal adjective (strings of prenominal adjectives not being especially common in OE [Fischer 2000: 172–4]). The examples in table 12.2 are from the Toronto Corpus, though it is surprisingly hard to find genuine minimal weak ~ strong pairs. This is not to argue

Table 12.2 The simple NP in Old English

1	*2*	*3*	
D	weak A	N	*þone soðan dryhten* 'the true lord' (ACC SG)
strong A		N	*soðne drihten* 'true lord' (ACC SG)
Prn			*þone* 'that one' (ACC SG)
Prn			*hine* 'him' (ACC SG)

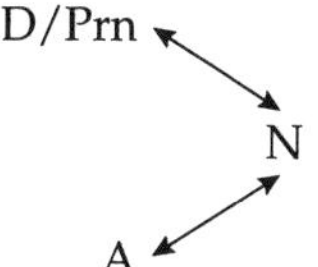

Figure 12.2 Simplified category space in Old English

that D = Prn = strong A in category terms, though such arguments have been put forward in the past. What it might represent is a functional similarity between them, however.

In Spamer's account of OE, only A with strong endings are adjectives in the functional sense, whereas A with weak endings are actually adjuncts; but cf. Fischer (2000: 165, 172). The distributional facts cited by Spamer support the classification made in table 12.2 on inflectional grounds. For him the adjective slot is non-recursive, unlike in PDE. He goes on from this to argue that weak adjectives in OE are substantivized, while demonstratives and strong adjectives – being mutually exclusive – belong to the same morphosyntactic category. Thus "the demonstrative was synchronically realized as an adjective" in OE, or "both belong to the same form class which I have here called 'modifiers'" (Spamer 1979: 247). One strong point of Spamer's analysis is that weak adjectives in OE do not appear to undergo degree modification (Fischer 2000: 169, 174).

Rather than equating D and A, it would be easier in distributional terms to justify lumping D and Prn together, suggesting a possible simplification of our category space (see figure 12.2). We might also retain some of Spamer's insights by enforcing a distinction between categorial and functional levels, so that his "modifier" would be seen as a functional slot which could be filled by items from the categories (weak) adjective or noun. However, collapsing the categories D and Prn is actually least convincing for what might be thought of as the central members of Prn. The personal pronouns (and even more so the indefinite pronoun *man*) do not generally co-occur with A or N, unless in apposition.

12.4.3 *Inflection in Middle and Modern English*

If there is any merit in the observations encapsulated in table 12.2, it is interesting to note that the break-up of the OE nominal inflectional system included the loss of any inflectional distinction between strong and weak adjectives, and the disappearance of non-clitic *the*, so that position 1 became less well supported. The development of articles is generally dated to the ME (Middle English) period, and the articles – as noted in section 12.2.1 above – provide the strongest justification for a category D. Arguably the newer dispensation is as shown in figure 12.3.

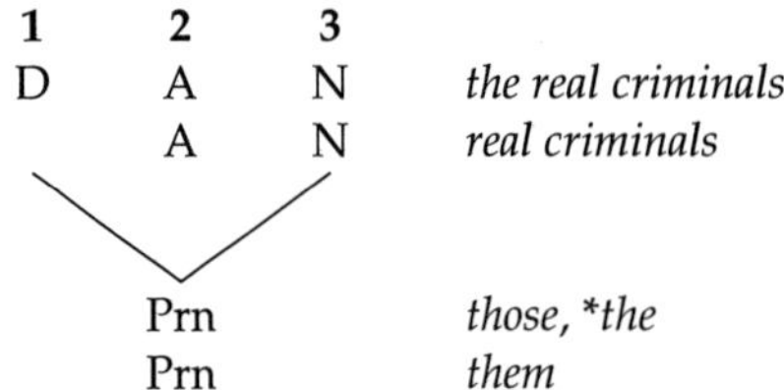

Figure 12.3 The simple NP in Middle and Modern English

12.4.4 Co-occurrence in earlier English

It will be recalled that the structuralist conception of D is of a non-iterative category that precedes (A and) N in the NP. Historically there is a great deal to say about the evidence of order and co-occurrence, but I have little space to go into detail. Adjectives occurred more freely post-nominally, but also, occasionally, even before D. Mitchell gives (11) as a rare example from Old English (1985: 70), while Fischer cites (12) as a nice contrast from the two MSS of Laȝamon's *Brut* in early Middle English (1992: 215–16).

(11) on wlancan þam wicge
on proud the horse
(*Mald* 240)

(12) a. mid godene heore worden
b. mid hire gode wordes
'with their good words'
(Lay. *Brut* 334)

Fischer treats co-occurrence as well, noting such ME combinations as the following (1992: 211–14):

- predeterminers *each, many, such, which, what* before *a;*
- *some, any* before *the;*
- *all* + *both* (suggesting that *all* is originally an intensifier, not a quantifier);
- two determiners together: *other* + *some, all, many, more.*

Similarly Mitchell (1985: 68–71) and Traugott (1992: 173) for Old English, Rissanen (1999: 195, 205–8) for early Modern English. Another alteration of co-occurrence restrictions is the loss of the *this my chapter* construction in late ModE (Denison 1998: 114–15; Fischer 1992: 213; Rissanen 1999: 206).

A cautionary note is needed here: frequency is an important consideration with all such possibilities. There are common patterns and there are patterns which are difficult to find, and they should not be given equal status – though a pattern may be infrequent for many reasons other than marginal grammaticality, including full grammaticality but restricted pragmatic usefulness, and relic status. On the place of frequency in historical change see, for instance, Bybee and Hopper (2001) and Krug (2003). All in all, though, the very different co-occurrence restrictions in earlier English make it unacceptable to use without question a set of categories mutually defined for PDE. Furthermore, the evidence of long-term change over many centuries does not support the idea of a sudden, "catastrophic" switch, whether in the inventory of categories or in the category of individual lexical items, at a single point between OE and late ModE. Rather there has been step-wise change, and part of the input for such diachronic changes has been synchronic gradience.

12.5 Gradience in History

I give four separate pieces of evidence that gradient categorization has played a part in the history of determiners.

12.5.1 Possessives as D or Prn

The first concerns the so-called possessive pronouns. In PDE, the possessive determiner *my* and the pronoun *mine* – and all other such pairs – belong to different categories in conventional (traditional) analysis. The forms like *my* are very similar to the definite article in distribution, acting only as proclitics. I will summarize their history; for a full and careful recent study see Allen (2002). OE had the 1 and 2 person pronouns shown in table 12.3 (ignoring dual forms, which only survived into early ME).

The genitives were formed from the Germanic suffixes *-īno-* in the singular, *-oro-* in the plural (Prokosch 1939: 285) and could function as normal case forms, as in (13) after the verb *andbidian* 'wait for', which is construed with a genitive object:

(13) We andbidodon *ðin* halga fæder þæt ðu . . .
we wait-for(PAST) you(GEN) Holy Father(NOM) that you . . .
(ÆCHom II)

Table 12.3 Deictic personal pronouns in Old English

	Singular		*Plural*	
	1 SG	*2 SG*	*1 PL*	*2 PL*
Nominative	*ic*	*þu*	*we*	*ge*
Dative (later also accusative)	*me*	*þe*	*us*	*eow*
Genitive	*min*	*þin*	*ure*	*eower*

But the 1 and 2 genitive forms could take additional adjectival inflections, as in (14):

(14) astrece *ðine* hand ofer ða sæ.
stretch your hand(ACC SG FEM) over the sea
(*ÆCHom* II)

By the end of the morphophonological reductions of the ME period, there were no case inflections left, and genitive was no longer a case used after verbs or prepositions, so that *min* and *þin* were now exclusively possessives. Gradually there developed a phonologically conditioned alternation between forms with and without *-n*, depending essentially on whether the next word began with a vowel or *h-*, or not, as in *thyne oure* 'your hour/time' vs. *thy grete batayle* 'your great battle' (Malory). The same alternation was seen with *one* and *none*, whose *-n* was of very different origin. And this phonological conditioning turned in the course of the EModE (Early Modern English) period into a grammatical conditioning for *my* ~ *mine*, *thy* ~ *thine*, and *no* ~ *none* (but not *a* ~ *an*). Meanwhile, other possessives like *our*, *your*, *her*, *their* had developed forms with *-s*; see Mustanoja (1960: 157, 164), Allen (2002: 202). These are historically double possessives, used exclusively as independent (= disjunctive) pronouns apart from brief, occasional interludes as possessive determiners in ME (*hers*), EModE (*ours*, *yours*) or both periods (*theirs*). The forms without *-s* had wholly lost pronominal function before the end of the EModE period, thus bringing about the same grammatical alternation, D ~ Prn, for *your* ~ *yours* as for *my* ~ *mine*. Only the possessives whose determiner form ends in *-s* already (*his*, *its*, *one's*, *whose*) have failed to develop this grammatical alternation.

Even if one's theory demanded sudden reanalyses, it would be very hard to pin one down in the historical data. The histories sketched above, especially the developments of a phonological conditioning and then of a grammatical conditioning of possessives, seem to me classic cases of a synchronic gradient leading eventually, though not necessarily in a unidirectional fashion, to a diachronic change.

12.5.2 D and A

The second piece of evidence concerns the D ~ A boundary. We have already looked at Spamer's attempt to group demonstratives and strong adjectives together (section 12.4.2 above). At the same time as Spamer, but apparently independently, Lightfoot attempted to show that quantifiers at least began life as adjectives in Old English but were reanalyzed as determiners in the sixteenth century (1979: 167–86).

It is a problem trying to find syntactic tests for distinguishing Determiner and Adjective in OE. An obvious starting-point is the major grammars of PDE. Curiously, Quirk et al. discuss adjectives in relation to various other word classes, but not Determiner (1985: 404–16). *CGEL*, however, offers three tests satisfied by D but not A (2002: 538–40), adding a fourth subsequently for gradable determiners:

(a) mutual exclusiveness with the articles (**the neither book*);
(b) admissibility of count singular NPs (*neither book*);
(c) the partitive construction (*neither of them*), also called a **fused-head construction** because a constituent is simultaneously a head and a determiner (in their nomenclature, determinative) or modifier;
(d) functioning as pre-head dependent in NP structure when modified by *so*, without having to be a predeterminer before the indefinite article (*so many mistakes*).

Of these tests, none apart possibly from (c) would be appropriate for OE. Lightfoot, however, does not regard headship of a partitive phrase as categorially significant, attributing to Kellner the claim that a number of categories, including adjectives, could govern partitive genitives in (unspecified) earlier English (1979: 170–1). But Kellner (1892: 108) had actually specified comparatives or superlatives as possible adjectival heads of a partitive (and illustrated neither), while Mitchell mentions only superlatives and a limited set of quantificational forms (1985: 545–7, 560). More generally, Dick Hudson finds it hard to imagine a plausible *use* for A as head of a partitive (personal communication, March 15, 2004).

So could an ordinary, positive adjective be head of a partitive in early English? I have tested this in the York-Toronto-Helsinki Parsed Corpus of Old English Prose (YCOE) (2003) and in the Penn-Helsinki Parsed Corpus of Middle English (PPCME2) (2003). Partitives can either be an NP marked with genitive case (the norm in OE) or an *of*-phrase (the norm from ME onwards), and they can precede or follow the head. I searched the 1.5-million-word YCOE for NPs consisting of a head which is tagged in the corpus as genitive NP plus quantifier, determiner, numeral, or adjective (lexical or phrasal). There were 3,634 hits, about 30 percent of them with genitive NP before head, and all are partitive structures bar at most a dozen. The doubtful cases include some like

(15) seo is ure ealra moder
'she is mother of us all/of all of us'

where the genitive *ealra* could be taken either as an adjective postmodifying genitive *ure* or as the head of a partitive. In OE the construction is naturally rarer with an *of*-phrase: up to 80 examples, some of which may involve *of* in a spatial sense. All in all, the heads of partitives are overwhelmingly the ancestors of what would later be determiners, where they survived. Here are the ones I found, ignoring most spelling and inflectional variants, and with very crude and often etymological glosses given for convenience:

(16) *Ægðer/æghwæðer/aðer* 'either', *ælc* 'each', *ænig* 'any', *nænig* 'not any, no(ne)', *an* 'one', *nan* 'none', *awiht* 'anything, "owt"', *nowiht* 'nothing, "nowt"', *eall* 'all', *efenfela/emfela* 'equally many', *fela* 'many', *fea* 'few', *ane feawa* 'a few', *genog* 'enough', *healfe* 'half', *hwa/hwæt* 'who, what', *æghwæt* 'each/any one', *gehwa/gehwæt* 'each/any one', *hwætwugu* 'something, somewhat', *hwæðer* 'which of two', *gehweðer* 'each of two', *naðer* = *nahwæðer* 'neither of two', *hwon* 'a little', *hwylc* 'which', *gehwylc* 'each', *hwylcehugu* 'some', *læsse* 'less', *lyt* 'little', *an lytel* 'a little', *unlytel* 'much', *ma* 'more', *monig* 'many', *efenmycel/emmicel* 'of equal size', *medmicel* 'small, unimportant', *oðer* 'other, second', *se* 'the, that', *sum* 'some', *swilc* 'such', *twæde* 'two-thirds', and numerals.

I did not find either *un(ge)rim* 'innumerable' or *þes* 'this'. The following examples could be regarded as having an adjectival head, though *frumcenned* 'first-born' in (19) is a kind of ordinal numeral (or superlative), *æges hwit* 'white of egg' in (18) is arguably quantifying in meaning, and the remainder certainly are:

(17) Wið eagna miste genim *cileþonian seawes cuclerfulne*
'for mistiness of eyes take a spoonful of juice of celandine'
(colaece,Lch_II_[1]:2.1.17.173)

(18) gedo *æges hwit* to
'add white of egg to it'
(colaece,Lch_II_[3]:59.1.1.4047)

(19) *þinra bearna frumcenned* þu scealt alysan
'firstborn of your sons you shall redeem'
(cootest,Exod:34.20.3595)

(20) *gehwæde arodes woses*
'a little juice of arum'
(colacnu,Med_3_[Grattan-Singer]:7.1.32)

Note in relation to *cuclerful* in (17) that OED gives *handful* as the only such compound found in OE (s.v. *-ful* suffix 2); in any event, such compounds have always been used either as determiners or as nouns in English.

A number of examples tagged in YCOE as adjectives involve *midd* or directional and locative forms ending in *-weard*, precisely the group of adjective-like words whose positional behavior and (in the case of *midd*) choice of weak or strong declension is quite different from any other adjective (Mitchell 1985: 70–1), for example:

(21) on *Israhela bearna middan*
'amidst the children of Israel'
(cootest,Deut:32.50.5139)

(22) eallswa we ær on *foreweardan þysre race* rehton.
'as we earlier told in the front part of this narrative'
(cosevensl,LS_34_[SevenSleepers]:721.571)

Although YCOE is only a proportion of the whole Toronto Corpus, the large number of partitives is sufficient to guarantee the rarity of truly adjectival partitive heads – unless, of course, the above forms can be taken as positive adjectives in OE, which would be a circular argument. This strongly suggests that adjectives and (pre-)determiners were already largely distinct in OE.

In the 1.3-million-word PPCME2 the results are as follows. Possessive phrases are rarely used as partitives, except in early ME, where they occur about 18 times in OE-like patterns of the type *ure ech* 'each of us', and in such phrases as *alre earst* 'first of all', *allre læste* 'last of all'. There are some 729 hits with an *of*-phrase, including the strings *last of all, wurst of al, most of alle.* I spotted 32 obvious non-partitives in this total, and in addition at least three difficult cases like:

(23) a man þat cowþe moch of wycchecraft
'a man who knew much about witchcraft'
(CMMIRK,106.2905)

where the *of*-phrase is probably a dependant of *cowþe* 'knew' rather than of *moch* 'much'. Otherwise I found very few non-superlative adjectives as possible head of a partitive:

(24) in *misliche of þeose fondinges*
'into various of these temptations'
(PPCME, CMANCRIW,II.144.1945)

(25) to *dyuers of hem*
'to divers/various of them'
(CMKEMPE,25.548)

(26) hwer he hefde wið þe cwen iwunet & iwiket *swa longe of þe niht*
'where he had with the queen dwelt and gone so long of the night'
(CMKATHE,41.348)

(27) þe gude herde, þat lefte in þe munte *ane wane of a hundrez sep*
'the good shepherd, who left in the mount one missing of a hundred sheep'
(CMBENRUL,22.762)

(28) Moni of þan floc manna þe earþon fulieden ure drihten and ec *ʒe-leafulle of þere burh* heo nomen heore claþes and þe beste þat heo hefde
'many of the flock of men who earlier followed our Lord and also believing of/from the city they took their clothes and the best that they had'
(CMLAMBX1,3.23)

(29) these weren *myȝti of the world* and famouse men.
'these were mighty of the world and famous men'
(CMOTEST,VI,1G.195)

Dyuers in (25) is one of the items discussed in section 12.5.4 below, and *mislich* 'diverse, various' in (24) is semantically very like them. The *of*-phrase in (27) is dependent on *ane* 'one', not the adjective *wane* 'lacking, absent'; that in (28) may be spatial; and that in (29) does not look like a partitive and may in any case depend on *men*. The other partitive heads were much more determiner-like; I give modern spellings where I can:

(30) *All, (ever) any, anything, both, each, each one, ei* 'any', *either, enough, every, everyone, fele* 'much, many', *(a) few, half, least, less, little, many, mo* 'more', *more, most, much(el), neither, none, nothing, one, other* [pl.], *another, ought* 'anything', *nought, some, somedeal* 'somewhat', *somewhat,* and numerals.

Once again, then, ordinary positive adjectives hardly seem to function as heads of partitives.

If D and A seem to behave differently in OE and ME, so far I have found maybe four examples in OE where *se / þæt / seo* is head of a possible partitive, which reduces the distance between D and Prn:

(31) Þonne þuhte eow þas tida beteran þonne þa, for þon eowre brocu nu læssan sindon þonne *heora þa* wære.
then would-seem to you these times better than those, because your afflictions now lesser are than of-them those were
(coorosiu,Or_3:7.66.1.1290)

In ME there were some 14 examples with demonstratives as heads, none with an article:

(32) & þei ben als harde as *þo of ynde.*
'and they [diamonds] are as hard as those of India'
(CMMANDEV,105.2559)

This corpus investigation set out to test the demarcation between D and A by means of the partitive head criterion. What came out was not an absolute boundary but a clear *statistical* distinction in both OE and ME. The same test also showed that the incipient distinction between D and Prn was growing stronger.

12.5.3 *Constructional gradience*

A third piece of evidence for the gradient boundary of D will be discussed in detail elsewhere (Denison 2002; Keizer and Denison 2002). It concerns

"SKT-constructions" involving *sort of*, *kind of*, and *type of*, some of which have determiner-like properties. The most relevant usages can be exemplified as follows:

(33) three *kinds of cheese* (binominal SKT)

(34) He made a *sort of* gesture of appeasement (qualifying SKT)

(35) *those sort of* people (postdeterminer SKT)

(36) She's *sort of* sexy; he *sort of* likes her (adverbial SKT)

(37) and I *sort of* opened the door, and looked out, and I *sort of* saw Richard (bleached SKT)

If we just compare the first three patterns mentioned, all of which contain the string D_1 N_1 *of* (D_2) N_2, we find that the post-determiner pattern, (35), shares some properties with the binominal, (33), such as primary stress falling on D_1 or N_2; N_2 being omissible; and occurrence with all of the SKT-nouns. It shares with the qualifying construction, (34), the facts that *of* is not in constituency with N_2; that 'N_1' cannot be plural and is hardly characterizable as a noun at all; and that the stylistic level is informal. I advocate a Construction Grammar analysis in which the synchronic properties of (35) have a dual inheritance from (33) and (34). Now in (33) *sort/kind* is clearly N, in (34) it is probably not an N, and in (35) it is arguably part of D. There is a complex mesh of interlinked constructions, both within and outside the NP/DP, involving among other categories D, N, A, and Adv.

12.5.4 Semantics and syntax of D and A

The fourth piece of evidence comes from some lexicological analyses in OED. In my view the difference between the morphosyntactic categories D and A is also a matter of semantics, and I consider now a small selection of rather similar words.

12.5.4.1 Divers(e)

In OED we find separate entries for *divers* and *diverse*, which started off as mere spelling variants but gradually diverged in pronunciation and usage. The meaning 'different or not alike . . .' occurs from the thirteenth century. It is a typically adjectival meaning, used attributively and predicatively. Developing out of it quite early on – from the early or late fourteenth century, depending whether the notion of variety or number is more prominent – is the meaning 'various, sundry, several; more than one, some number of'. OED regards this as a natural semantic change, '[r]eferring originally . . . to the variety of objects; but, as variety implies number, becoming an indefinite numeral word expressing multiplicity' (s.v. *divers* a. 3). In the newer meanings it is semantically a quantifier and syntactically is not used predicatively, and it develops the partitive 'fused-head' construction, as seen in (25) above; in other words, it looks like a determiner.

For some three centuries both spellings of *divers(e)* show both kinds of use. By about 1700 the forms are strongly divergent, and *diverse* reverts entirely to adjectival uses, while *divers* continues with determiner-like uses. Incidentally, I was surprised to find the following approximate figures for occurrence in OED quotations, allowing for <u/v> and <i/y> variation and subtracting obvious instances of *diver* 'one who dives'. For *divers* vs. *diverse* I count 2,317 : 860 up to the end of the seventeenth century, and 283 : 155 afterwards. This suggests that until quite recently the more determiner-like *divers* remained more frequent, as might be expected for a grammatical word. But now it is obsolescent; in the British National Corpus of the late twentieth century the figures are about 55 : 1,311.

12.5.4.2 *Several*

A somewhat similar semantic development occurs with this word. *Several* can mean 'existing apart, separate' from the fifteenth century in predicative use, and from the early sixteenth in attributive use as well. This adjective-like use spreads subsequently into such related senses as 'separate, distinct', 'distinctive, particular', and 'acting separately'. OED notes how from the mid-fifteenth century it occurs before plural nouns, where it means 'individually separate; different', at first preceded by a numeral, other quantifier, or definite determiner. By the beginning of the sixteenth century this usage occurs, as OED puts it, "without limiting word" in the sense 'a number of different, various, divers, sundry', which then by the beginning of the seventeenth century merges (OED's term) into what is called the chief current sense, 'as a vague numeral'. In this sense, of course, it is hardly used predicatively, and it is generally regarded as a determiner, not an adjective. The partitive construction occurs at least as early as 1598:

(38) hee and several of his fellows (OED)

12.5.4.3 *Certain*

OED's entry for *certain* shows a similar lexical-cum-categorical split between senses which are "hardly separable . . . in a large number of examples" (OED s.v. *certain* a. II.7a). The partitive construction occurs at least as early as 1484. Here is a slightly later example:

(39) certain of the most notable and arrant traitours recepted in Scotland (OED, 1542)

CGEL (2002: 392–3) regards *certain* as a marginal determiner in Present-day English because of its general semantics, non-generic semantics, occurrence in the fused-head construction, and its use with *a* in

(40) They must also have had *a certain* influence on my father's outlook. (LOB)

12.5.4.4 *Various*

This word is rather less far along the road toward determiner status. The lexical history is similar to some of the previously mentioned items. OED offers its sense 8, '[w]ith pl. n. Different from one another; of different kinds or sorts', from early-to-mid seventeenth century, while its sense 9, '[i]n weakened sense, as an enumerative term: Different, divers, several, many, more than one', is found by the end of the century. Once again OED comments: 'It is not always possible to distinguish absolutely between this sense and 8, as the meaning freq. merges into "many different": cf. divers *a.* 3'.

As for the partitive, examples are easy to find:

(41) *Various of the apartments* are of the terrace type (Brown)

This usage appears to date only from the mid-nineteenth century and in the twentieth century to be more American than British.

Sense 8 is a development of the historic meaning 'varied, variable' and is largely adjectival. Sense 9 is more typical of a quantifier and thus of D. In other words, there are two very different lexical senses of *various* which can be argued to be categorially different as well, yet there are many early examples which are equivocal. Similar facts have been pointed out for other words discussed above. It is striking how much of this kind of data is found to be equivocal by the lexicographers. Given that the gradual – or at least **graduated** – nature of semantic change is reasonably widely accepted, why not allow that syntactic change may proceed by small steps too?

12.5.5 *Sudden vs. graduated change*

How would this work? We need to discuss various models of change. The conventional mechanism is reanalysis. For the development of a determiner use of *various*, say, we must imagine an earlier grammatical state in which *various* is exclusively categorized as A. Later grammars would have a lexicon which included a D variant of *various* and which would permit at least some structures where *various* functioned as D. We could call this a diachronic reanalysis. It might have come about via an intermediate grammar which entailed synchronic reanalysis as part of the derivation of these new structural possibilities for *various*. In any case, *various* is always clearly either A or D, and any switch between categories is an all-or-nothing affair.

Kroch, Pintzuk, and others have developed an approach which retains the all-or-nothing categorization of conventional generative grammar while explaining the variation that is central to corpus linguistics. The solution for them is system competition: the availability of several grammars at any one time, usually with gradual diffusion of the newer grammar through a population; see e.g. Kroch et al. (2000) and Pintzuk (1995). The obvious problem with this approach is the burgeoning number of grammars needed to explain all the diverse linguistic changes going on at any moment in history, assuming that they cannot all be reduced to variation in a very small number of parameters.

Another approach which allows for gradual change is grammaticalization. For some proponents of grammaticalization, the coexistence of different stages of the process (**layering**) only implies that a given string can have different analyses in different utterances in the same epoch, not that an individual instance is subject to gradient analysis. In any case, grammaticalization only applies to that subset of syntactic, semantic, and morphological changes which move an item away from the lexicon and towards the grammar.

What I am suggesting is different from all of these. We have synchronic evidence that the boundaries between categories may be fuzzy. Categories may be cluster concepts, and it is possible for a given word to possess some subset of the properties associated with a particular category. Diachronically, then, category change may consist of the stepwise acquisition of properties, rather than the wholesale, simultaneous acquisition of "all-and-only" the definitional properties of the new category. This seems both a more plausible mechanism of change and a more economical account of intermediate stages. Thus *various* and *certain*, while still adjectives, have moved a small way toward acquiring properties more typical of determiners. Arguably their natural position in NPs is already toward the left-hand edge of the adjective sequence – Quirk et al.'s **precentral** position (1985: 436–7, 1337–41) – because they are nongradable and non-inherent, and what with their appropriate semantics, often they will be indistinguishable in a particular context from determiners; see Adamson's (2000) work on the relationship between word order and category. The point is that in the equivocal instances we do not have to insist either that they "are" still adjectives or that they "have become" determiners. (An alternative account would allow for multiple category membership, although this provides a less satisfying motivation for the development of equivocal examples.)

Note that this is not necessarily an argument for *slowness* of change, merely for graduatedness of at least some changes. One of the insights of Rosch's work on human categorization is that we tend where possible to strengthen perceived categories, so that hybrid or uncertain categorizations may be disfavored and hence of relatively short duration in the history of a language (unless exceptionally, like the donkey of Aesop's *Fables*, speakers find equally strong attractions in each direction and the intermediate status persists over time). Warner has discussed the development of the category Modal in terms of category strengthening (1990). That is overall a long-drawn-out process but one with arguably almost continual change from OE to the present.

12.6 Conclusion

I have tried to point out a number of problems with an excessively clean categorization of determiners in English. The evidence points rather to fuzzy boundaries between D and adjacent categories and sometimes to stepwise movement from one category to another.

As we have seen, there is at least a case for doing without a separate category Determiner in OE, though it would then have to fall in with Pronoun rather than Adjective, in my opinion. By the end of the ME period it is possible to distinguish Prn and D pretty much in the same way as for Present-day English. Individual items continue to redistribute themselves among the categories concerned. As Dick Hudson has observed (personal communication, March 24, 2004), the development of Aux besides V is analogous to (and largely simultaneous with) that of D besides N. How to represent an incipient morphological category in syntactic structure remains to be worked out. In any case you may get different answers if you insist on the primacy of categories or the primacy of constructions.

ACKNOWLEDGMENTS

This work has been in fitful progress for some time and owes improvements to Bas Aarts, Cindy Allen, Alison Cort, Willem Hollmann, Dick Hudson, Ans van Kemenade, Anette Rosenbach, and Johanna Wood. Earlier versions of different parts have been tried out on audiences at York, Kyoto, Nagoya, Bergerac, Santiago, Manchester, Stanford, Lille 3, and Helsinki. I am grateful too to Susan Pintzuk for her help with the CorpusSearch software (Randall 2000) and YCOE.

CORPORA MENTIONED

BNC: The British National Corpus (texts mostly 1985–93).

Brown Corpus: Francis, W. N. and Henry Kucera (1961). A standard corpus of present-day edited American English.

Frown: (1999). The Freiburg–Brown Corpus of American English (texts of 1992).

LOB: (1961). The Lancaster–Oslo/Bergen Corpus of British English, for use with digital computers.

OED: *The Oxford English Dictionary*, 2nd edn., online version.

PPCME2: Kroch, Anthony S. and Ann Taylor (2003). The Penn–Helsinki Parsed Corpus of Middle English, 2nd edn.

Toronto Corpus: Healey, Antonette diPaolo, Joan Holland, Ian McDougall, and Peter Mielke (2000). *The Dictionary of Old English Corpus in Electronic Form.*

YCOE: Taylor, Ann, Anthony Warner, Susan Pintzuk, and Frank Beths (2003). The York–Toronto–Helsinki Parsed Corpus of Old English Prose.

REFERENCES

Aarts, B. (2004). Modelling linguistic gradience. *Studies in Language* 28: 1–50.

Aarts, B., D. Denison, E. Keizer and G. Popova (eds.) (2004). *Fuzzy Grammar: A Reader*. Oxford: Oxford University Press.

Adamson, S. (2000). A lovely little example: word order options and category shift in the premodifying string. In O. Fischer, A. Rosenbach, and D. Stein (eds.), *Pathways of Change: Grammaticalization in English* (pp. 39–66) (Studies in Language Companion Series 53). Amsterdam and Philadelphia: John Benjamins.

Allen, C. L. (2002). The development of "strengthened" possessive pronouns in English. *Language Sciences* 24: 189–211.

Bloomfield, L. (1933). *Language*. New York: Henry Holt.

Börjars, K. (1998). *Feature Distribution in Swedish Noun Phrases* (Publications of the Philological Society 32). Oxford and Malden, MA: Blackwell.

Bybee, J. and P. Hopper (eds.) (2001). *Frequency and the Emergence of Linguistic Structure* (Typological Studies in Language 45). Amsterdam and Philadelphia: John Benjamins.

Croft, W. (2001). *Radical Construction Grammar: Syntactic Theory in Typological Perspective*. Oxford: Oxford University Press.

Denison, D. (1998). Syntax. In S. Romaine (ed.), *The Cambridge History of the English Language*, vol. 4: *1776–1997* (pp. 92–329). Cambridge: Cambridge University Press.

Denison, D. (2001). Gradience and linguistic change. In L. J. Brinton (ed.), *Historical Linguistics 1999: Selected Papers from the 14th International Conference on Historical Linguistics, Vancouver, 9–13 August 1999* (pp. 119–44) (Current Issues in Linguistic Theory 215). Amsterdam and Philadelphia: John Benjamins.

Denison, D. (2002). History of the *sort of* construction family. Paper presented at ICCG2: Second International Conference on Construction Grammar, Helsinki, September.

Fischer, O. (1992). Syntax. In N. Blake (ed.), *The Cambridge History of the English Language*, vol. 2: *1066–1476* (pp. 207–408). Cambridge: Cambridge University Press.

Fischer, O. (2000). The position of the adjective in Old English. In R. Bermúdez-Otero, D. Denison, R. M. Hogg, and C. B. McCully (eds.), *Generative Theory and Corpus Studies: A Dialogue from 10 ICEHL* (pp. 153–81) (Topics in English Linguistics 31). Berlin and New York: Mouton de Gruyter.

Giusti, G. (1997). The categorical status of determiners. In L. Haegeman (ed.), *The New Comparative Syntax* (pp. 95–123) (Longman Linguistics Library). London and New York: Longman.

Hogg, R. M. (ed.) (1992–2001). *The Cambridge History of the English Language* (6 vols.). Cambridge: Cambridge University Press.

Huddleston, R. (1984). *Introduction to the Grammar of English* (Cambridge Textbooks in Linguistics). Cambridge: Cambridge University Press.

Huddleston, R. and G. K. Pullum (2002). *The Cambridge Grammar of the English Language*. Cambridge: Cambridge University Press.

Hudson, R. (2000). Grammar without functional categories. In R. D. Borsley (ed.), *Syntax and Semantics*, vol. 32 (pp. 7–35). New York: Academic Press.

Jackendoff, R. (2002). *Foundations of Language: Brain, Meaning, Grammar, Evolution*. Oxford and New York: Oxford University Press.

Jespersen, O. (1909–49). *A Modern English Grammar on Historical Principles* (7 vols.). Heidelberg: Carl Winters Universitätsbuchhandlung.

Keizer, E. and D. Denison (2002). *Sort of* constructions: grammar and change. Ms.

Kellner, L. (1892). *Historical Outlines of English Syntax*. London and New York: Macmillan.

Kemenade, A. van and N. Vincent (eds.) (1997). *Parameters of Morphosyntactic Change*. Cambridge: Cambridge University Press.

Kroch, A., A. Taylor, and D. Ringe (2000). The Middle English verb-second constraint: a case study in language contact and language change. In S. Herring, P. van Reenen and L. Schøsler (eds.), *Textual Parameters in Older Languages* (pp. 353–91) (Current Issues in Linguistic Theory 195). Amsterdam and Philadelphia: John Benjamins.

Kroch, A. S. and A. Taylor (2003). The Penn-Helsinki Parsed Corpus of Middle English. See: http://www.ling.upenn. edu/hist-corpora

Krug, M. (2003). Frequency as a determinant in grammatical variation and change. In G. Rohdenburg and B. Mondorf (eds.), *Determinants of Grammatical Variation in English* (pp. 7–67) (Topics in English Linguistics 43). Berlin and New York: Mouton de Gruyter.

Lightfoot, D. W. (1979). *Principles of Diachronic Syntax* (Cambridge Studies in Linguistics 23). Cambridge: Cambridge University Press.

Mitchell, B. (1985). *Old English Syntax* (2 vols.). Oxford: Clarendon Press.

Mustanoja, T. F. (1960). *A Middle English Syntax*, vol. 1: *Parts of Speech* (Mémoires de la Société Néophilologique de Helsinki 23). Helsinki: Société Néophilologique.

Pintzuk, S. (1995). Variation and change in Old English clause structure. *Language Variation and Change* 7: 229–60.

Prokosch, E. (1939). *A Comparative Germanic Grammar* (William Dwight Whitney Linguistic Series). Philadelphia: Linguistic Society of America, University of Pennsylvania.

Quirk, R., S. Greenbaum, G. Leech, and J. Svartvik (1985). *A Comprehensive Grammar of the English Language*. London and New York: Longman.

Rissanen, M. (1999). Syntax. In R. Lass (ed.), *The Cambridge History of the English Language*, vol. 3: *1476–1776* (pp. 187–331). Cambridge: Cambridge University Press.

Ross, J. R. (1973). Nouniness. In O. Fujimura (ed.), *Three Dimensions of Linguistic Theory* (pp. 137–257). Tokyo: TEC for Tokyo Institute for Advanced Studies of Language.

Spamer, J. B. (1979). The development of the definite article in English: a case study of syntactic change. *Glossa* 13: 241–50.

Spinillo, M. (2000). Determiners: a class to be got rid of? *Arbeiten aus Anglistik und Amerikanistik* 25: 173–89.

Spinillo, M. (2003). On *such*. *English Language and Linguistics* 7: 195–210.

Taylor, A., A. Warner, S. Pintzuk, and F. Beths (2003). The York–Toronto–Helsinki Parsed Corpus of Old English Prose. York: Department of Language and Linguistic Science, University of York. (Available through the Oxford Text Archive: http://ota.ahds.ac.uk)

Traugott, E. C. (1992). Syntax. In R. M. Hogg (ed.), *The Cambridge History of the English Language*, vol. 1: *The Beginnings to 1066* (pp. 168–289). Cambridge: Cambridge University Press.

Warner, A. R. (1990). Reworking the history of English auxiliaries. In S. Adamson, V. A. Law, N. Vincent, and S. Wright (eds.), *Papers from the 5th International Conference on English Historical Linguistics: Cambridge, 6–9 April 1987* (pp. 537–58) (Current Issues in Linguistic Theory 65). Amsterdam and Philadelphia: John Benjamins.

Wood, J. L. (2002). Much about *such*. *Studia Linguistica* 56: 91–115.

IV Pragmatics

13 Pathways in the Development of Pragmatic Markers in English

LAUREL BRINTON

13.1 Introduction

In her ground-breaking article on the regularity of semantic change (1982), Elizabeth Traugott offered some initial observations concerning the historical development of discourse markers. She suggested that the "conversational routines" *well* and *right*, as in

(1) a. **Well**, don't you want to go?
    b. You'll do it tomorrow, **right**?

arise out of predicate adverbs and undergo a shift from the propositional to the textual and expressive components of language and from less to more personal meaning (1982: 251, 253). Traugott again took up this topic in her (1995) address to the International Conference on English Historical Linguistics, but here with a focus on the syntactic as well as semantic paths followed by discourse markers. More recently, she has explored the history of discourse markers as evidence of the regularity of semantic change:

> DMs [discourse markers] are highly language-specific in their distribution and function. But nevertheless there seem to be quite similar paths of development at the macro-level. When their histories are accessible to us, they typically arise out of conceptual meanings and uses constrained to the argument structure of the clause. Over time, they not only acquire pragmatic meanings (which typically coexist for some time with earlier, less pragmatic meanings) but also come to have scope over propositions. (Traugott and Dasher 2002: 156)

In the two decades since Traugott's initial work, publications on the development of discourse markers in English have become somewhat of a "growth industry," as evidenced by Jucker (1995) and Brinton (1996), among others.

It is perhaps not surprising, given the focus of much of Traugott's work, that most studies of discourse markers have been carried out within the framework of grammaticalization studies. For the purposes of this paper, grammaticalization will be defined as "the change whereby lexical items and constructions come in certain linguistic contexts to serve grammatical functions or grammatical items develop new grammatical functions" (Hopper and Traugott 1993 [2003]). Research (see e.g. Brinton 1996: 272–7; Traugott 1995: §4) has shown that discourse markers appear to undergo many of the morphosyntactic and semantic changes associated with grammaticalization (as set out, e.g., in Lehmann 1995: 122ff.), provided that the notion of "grammatical function" is allowed to encompass the pragmatic and procedural functions of discourse markers. Although discourse markers do not always show phonological reduction (Lehmann's "attrition") and morphological bonding (Lehmann's "coalescence") – nor can they be said to become part of a fixed grammatical paradigm (Lehmann's "paradigmaticalization") – they do undergo decategorialization, change from major (open) to minor (closed) class membership, freezing or ossification of form, desemanticization or generalization of meaning, shift from referential (propositional) to non-referential (procedural) meaning, subjectification, and conventionalization of invited inferences. They thus follow the unidirectional avenues of change typical of grammaticalization.

While there appears to be a consensus about the semantic/pragmatic and morphological development of discourse markers – to the extent that Traugott and Dasher feel confident in asserting (see above) that "there seem to be quite similar paths of development at the macro-level" – there is less agreement about whether their syntactic development is typical of grammaticalization. In contrast to other items undergoing grammaticalization, discourse markers apparently do not shrink in the scope of their modification (Lehmann's "condensation"). In fact, in their pragmatic functions, discourse markers relate not to smaller linguistic units but normally to larger stretches of discourse; that is, they come to function extra-sententially. However, Tabor and Traugott (1998) have challenged the notion of scope reduction (from "loose" to "tight" syntax) in the process of grammaticalization generally, arguing instead for scope expansion (under tightly controlled conditions). Moreover, evidence for the restriction of discourse markers to a particular syntactic slot (Lehmann's "fixation") is ambiguous. While many discourse markers become fixed in initial position, this position is not obligatory, and some forms, such as parentheticals, acquire increased mobility. Traugott (1995: §4) notes that decategorialization and phonological reduction entail loss of syntactic freedom, while the process of adjunction and increase in syntactic scope entail increase in syntactic freedom; thus, loss of syntactic freedom would not seem to be a necessary consequence of this type of grammaticalization.

More significantly for the purposes of this chapter, little attention has been paid to the syntactic origins of discourse markers, which come from a wide variety of sources, ranging from individual words, to phrasal collocations and clauses, and even less attention has been given to the syntactic processes (of reanalysis, etc.) by which discourse markers arise. The question of the ways in which, syntactically, discourse markers come to have scope over propositions

Table 13.1 Clines of grammaticality

(a)	content word > grammatical word > clitic > inflectional affix (> zero)
(b)	relational noun > secondary adposition > primary adposition > agglutinative affix > fusional affix
(c)	full verb > (vector verb) > auxiliary > clitic > affix

needs to be more fully addressed. A partial answer may be provided by focusing on the concept of "cline" of grammaticalization, or pathway along which items undergoing grammaticalization are understood as developing. A cline of grammaticality "has as its leftmost component a lexical, or content, item.... Each item to the right is more clearly grammatical and less lexical than its partner to the left" (Hopper and Traugott 1993: 7). One generalized cline of grammaticality has been proposed, as have two more specific clines (Hopper and Traugott 1993: 106, 108) (see table 13.1).

Note that an item undergoing grammaticalization may stop at any point upon the cline and need not progress to the end. A cline actually forms a continuum. Heine, Claudi, and Hünnemeyer (1991: 220–9) see grammaticalization clines, which they refer to as "grammaticalization chains," as consisting of overlapping conceptual and morphosyntactic structures. Although the points on the continuum are to some extent arbitrary and the boundaries between categories inexact, most scholars can agree upon the order of points along a cline of grammaticality (Hopper and Traugott 1993: 7).

The major focus of this chapter will be on a number of syntactic clines, or pathways, of grammaticalization that arise, either explicitly or implicitly, in the study of individual discourse markers. It would appear that many discourse markers arise from adverbs/prepositions, predicate adverbs, and matrix clauses. Other syntactic sources include imperative clauses, adverbial clauses, and relative clauses. The assumption here is that the syntactic development of discourse markers is equally important for our understanding of their grammaticalization as are the semantic changes involved. The chapter will conclude by discussing what the pathways of syntactic development for discourse markers tell us about their grammaticalization, and about grammaticalization in general.

Before beginning, it may be useful to set out what is typically encompassed by the term *discourse marker*, or what I prefer to call a *pragmatic marker*. In Modern English, frequently cited forms include *actually, anyway, I mean, now, so, then, well, you know*, and *you see*, though there are widely divergent views about the forms that belong to the category, ranging in number from a dozen to five hundred. In Modern English, pragmatic markers can be said to possess a number of formal features. They are marginal in word class, often being placed within the traditional class of "interjection" or otherwise seen as differing from the homophonous adverbial and conjunctive forms. They typically occur outside the core syntactic structure, often in sentence-initial position. They have an apparent lack of semantic content, and are not easily glossed or translated. Phonetically, they are often "short" or reduced and occur in a separate tone group. Their presence in a discourse is optional, with their absence rendering the discourse neither ungrammatical nor unintelligible. Finally, they are of high frequency, characteristic of the oral medium, and stylistically stigmatized (see Brinton 1996: 29–35).

In addition to formal similarities, pragmatic markers may be defined by their functional features. One early definition sees pragmatic markers as having both relational and structural roles, as "**sequentially dependent** elements which bracket units of talk" (Schiffrin 1987: 31). In a more recent definition, pragmatic markers "taken as distinct from the propositional content of the sentence, are linguistically encoded clues which signal the speaker's potential communicative intentions" (Fraser 1996: 169). It is possible to understand the function of pragmatic markers in respect to the functional–semantic components of language identified by Halliday (see Brinton 1996: 35–40). In function, pragmatic markers serve a "textual function" of language, which relates to the structuring of discourse as text, and/or an "interpersonal function" (or what Traugott 1982 calls "expressive"), which relates to the expression of speaker attitude and to the organization of the social exchange. Among the textual functions are those of claiming the attention of the hearer, initiating and ending discourse, sustaining discourse, marking boundaries, including topic shifts and episode boundaries, constraining the relevance of adjoining clauses, and repairing discourse. Among the interpersonal functions are subjective functions such as expressing responses, reactions, attitudes, understanding, tentativeness, or continued attention, as well as interactive functions such as expressing intimacy, cooperation, shared knowledge, deference, or face-saving (politeness). Together, the textual and interpersonal functions constitute "pragmatic" meaning.

The various functions of pragmatic markers have been seen as determining the semantic-pragmatic path of their evolution, namely from propositional > textual > expressive (as initially postulated by Traugott 1982). This evolution was formalized in a set of three "tendencies": (1) shift from meanings based in the external situation to those based in the internal situation; (2) change from meanings based in the external or internal situation to meanings based in the textual situation; and (3) progression towards meanings increasingly situated in the speaker's subjective believe-state or attitude (see Traugott and König 1991: 208–9). In more recent work, Traugott has queried this simple unidimensional development, and she now prefers a more complex conception of unidirectional change, in which meanings become increasingly pragmatic, procedural, and metatextual according to multiple trajectories (see Traugott and Dasher 2002: 40), including:

nonsubjective > subjective > intersubjective
truth-conditional > non-truth-conditional
content > content/procedural > procedural

13.2 Three Prototypical Pathways of Development for Pragmatic Markers

A question to be posed here is whether we find syntactic clines in the grammaticalization of pragmatic makers comparable to the semantic-pragmatic clines that have been discovered. Traugott (1995) has proposed one such path. The remainder of the chapter will examine a wide selection of studies of the development of pragmatic markers in English in order to determine whether they point to the existence of other syntactic clines of grammaticalization. A working hypothesis is that semantic-pragmatic change and syntactic change go hand-in-hand: that is, the shift from content meaning based in the argument structure at the clausal level to pragmatic procedural meaning at the discourse level will be accompanied by a syntactic shift of an item from having scope over phrasal and then clausal elements and ultimately to one having scope over more global elements of the discourse.

13.2.1 *Adverb/preposition > conjunction > pragmatic marker*

The first cline to be explored here is in fact implicit in Traugott's early work. In her (1982) article, she mentions the evolution of *why* from an interrogative to a complementizer to a pragmatic marker functioning as a "hearer-engaging" form (following the semantic-pragmatic development from propositional > textual > expressive) (1982: 255), as in:

(2) a. *adverb*: **Why** didn't John come?
b. *conjunction*: She couldn't understand **why** John hadn't come.
c. *pragmatic marker*: If you have any trouble reaching her, **why** just feel free to call me.
(Romaine and Lange 1991: 260)

Note that the pragmatic function of *why {so, then}* is already evident in Shakespeare's language (see Blake 1992). A similar course of development is suggested by Romaine and Lange (1991) for the synchronic grammaticalization of *like*: from a preposition (in the propositional component) to a conjunction (in the textual component) to a pragmatic marker (in the expressive component), as in:

(3) a. *preposition*: That sounded **like** a lecture. (Meehan 1991: 40)
b. *conjunction*: . . . it was **like** I was watching someone else do it. (Meehan 1991: 41)
c. *pragmatic marker*: And there were **like** people blocking, you know. (Romaine and Lange 1991: 244)

While the preposition is subcategorized to take a nominal or pronominal complement, in its shift to a conjunction, it is recategorized to take a sentential complement, and in its reanalysis as a pragmatic marker, it "shows syntactic detachability and positional mobility" (Romaine and Lange 1991: 261). Though there are different theories concerning the meaning of the pragmatic marker *like*, many scholars agree that it has a focusing function. Meehan (1991) discusses the grammaticalization of *like* historically from a comparative (meaning 'similar to') with narrow scope to a focus marker (having little or no lexical meaning) with wide scope. It should be noted that Romaine and Lange (1991) express some caution about this "simple linear model of grammaticalization," suggesting instead that the evolution of *like* may involve "a network of related meanings" (1991: 262). Note that an offshoot of the conjunctive function within the textual component is the "quasi-complementizer," or "quotative," use of *be like*, as in: And she's **like**, "Um . . . Well, that's cool" (Romaine and Lange 1991: 239).

The synchronic paths of *so* and *now* are suggestively parallel. Rather than expressing manner as does the adverb in (4a) or cause or result as does the conjunction in (4b), *so* in (4c) functions as a pragmatic marker denoting an inferential relation.

(4) a. *manner adverb*: Do not tap your fingers **so**.
intensifier: I am **so** happy.
b. *conjunction*: I was hungry, **so** I bought a sandwich. I left early **so** that I would not miss my flight.
c. *pragmatic marker*: John's lights are burning, **so** he is home. (Schiffrin 1987: 211)
There's $5 in my wallet. **So** I didn't spend all the money then. (Blakemore 1988: 188)

According to Blakemore (1988), pragmatic *so* assists the hearer to process new information in the context of old information and to understand the way in which two propositions are connected, namely, that the proposition introduced by *so* is a contextual implication of the preceding proposition (see Brinton 1996: 199ff., 280, for a comparison between pragmatic *so* and OE *hwæt þa*).

The temporal meaning of adverbial *now* yields a causal inference, which is conventionalized in the meaning of the conjunction (Traugott and König 1991: 197–8). The pragmatic function of *now*, in referring forward to something in the discourse context, can also be viewed as an extension of the temporal meaning.

(5) a. *adverb*: The doctor can see you **now**.
b. *conjunction*: **Now** (that) I have received a raise, I can afford a new house.
c. *pragmatic marker*: **Now** Italian people are very outgoing. (Schiffrin 1987: 233)

Schiffrin (1987: 230) argues that the pragmatic function of *now* in (5c) is to mark "a speaker's progression through discourse time [i.e. the temporal relation of utterances in a discourse] by displaying attention to an upcoming idea unit, orientation, and/or participation framework." Aijmer (1988: 16) considers *now* in this case to be a kind of "misplacement marker" intended as a signal for the hearer to reconstruct a coherent discourse; it is used to express evaluation, as a textual organizer guiding the hearer in the interpretation process, to shift topic, or to change footing. (See Brinton 1996: 101–3, 280, for a comparison between pragmatic *now* and ME *anon*.)

In all of these studies, however, determination of whether the pragmatic markers, *why, like, so,* and *now*, develop from the conjunctive use or directly from the adverbial use (or in some other way) will await fuller diachronic exploration.

A number of historical studies have underscored the general validity of the proposed cline, while at the same time pointing out potential complications. Brinton (1996: ch. 7) traces the evolution of OE *hwæt* 'what' (but often translated 'lo, alas, thus') as a pragmatic marker. It would appear to evolve from an interrogative pronoun/adverb/adjective introducing direct questions, to a complementizer introducing indirect questions, to a pragmatic marker. As a pragmatic marker, *hwæt* assumes fixed, initial position and always occurs with a first or second person pronoun. It functions as a marker which questions or assumes common knowledge (cf. modern *y'know*), expresses speaker surprise, and focuses attention (cf. modern *y'know what?*). It conventionalizes an invited inference, namely from a questioning of what the hearer knows is inferred an expression of the speaker's belief in what the hearer knows:

(6) a. *adverb*: **Hwæt** murcnast þu þonn[e] æfter þam þe þu forlure?
'why do you grieve then after that which you lost?'
(c.888 Ælfred, *Boethius* xiv. 2; OED: s.v. *what*, def. III 19)

b. *complementizer*: he . . . him getæhte **hwæt** hi on ðæm don sceolden, hwæt ne scolden.
'He them taught what they should do in respect to that and what they should not'
(c.897 Ælfred, *Gregory's Pastoral Care* lii. 405; OED: s.v. *what*, def. I 6b)

c. *pragmatic marker*: "**Hwæt**, þu worn fela, wine min Unferð, / beore druncen ymb Brecan spræce."
'What [you know]! you spoke many things, my friend Unferth, drunk with beer, about Breca'
(*Beowulf* 530–1)

It is not possible to say whether the pragmatic marker develops from the complementizer function, which is very old, or directly from the interrogative adverb. In Middle English, *what, what ho,* and *what a* function as somewhat different kinds of pragmatic markers: *what* denotes surprise or incredulity, which often turns to contempt or scorn (see Blake 1992), while *what ho* is used for attention-getting, and *what a* is used in exclamations. But again, *what ho* perhaps derives from the exclamatory *eala hwæt* in Old English and *what a* from the interrogative adjective, not from the conjunctive use of *what*.

An additional pragmatic marker that might also show the pattern of development from adverb/preposition > conjunction > pragmatic marker is Old English *þa* 'then'. In Old English *þa* may function as an adverb, as a conjunction meaning 'when' (especially in the correlated structure *þa . . . þa* 'then . . . when'), or, as has been extensively argued, as a pragmatic marker denoting foregrounded action, narrative segmentation, or discourse-level shifts (see, for example, Enkvist and Wårvik 1987; Kim 1992):

(7) a. *adverb*: **þa** gegaderade Ælfred cyning his fierd.
'then King Ælfred gathered his army'
(*Chron.A* 84.20 [894]; Mitchell 1985, I, 474)

b. *conjunction*: ⁊ on ðare nihte **ða** hi scolde an morgen togædere cuman se sylfa Ælfric scoc fram ðare fyrde.
'and on that night when they should in the morning come together, Ælfric himself fled from the army'
(*Chron.F* 126.24 [992]; Mitchell 1985, II, 316)

c. *pragmatic marker*: **þa** on sumere nihte hlosnode sum oðer munuc his færeldes . . . **Ða** dyde cuþberhtus swa his gewuna wæs . . . Efne **ða** comon twegen seolas of sælicum grunde . . . **þa** cuðberhtus ða sælican nytenu on sund asende.
'then one night another monk watched his going. . . . Then Cuthbert did as he was accustomed to. . . . Indeed, then there came two seals from the sea-bottom. . . . Then Cuthbert sent the blessed creatures back to the sea with a true blessing'
(Ælfric, *Catholic Homilies, second series* X, 76–86; Enkvist and Wårvik 1987, 228–9, 235)

However, little attention has focused on the evolution of the pragmatic marker and its syntactic relation to the adverbial and conjunctive forms. Wårvik (1995: 348) apparently considers the pragmatic use to be related to the adverbial form, not to the conjunctive form, as the adverb marks foregrounded action and the conjunction backgrounded action. She argues that in Middle English, adverbial *þa* is replaced by *þonne*, which originally marked backgrounded material, while conjunctive *þa*/*þonne* is replaced by *when*. The foregrounding functions of 'then' are lost in Middle English, and it becomes first a marker of episodic structure and then a mere sequencer; a variety of other pragmatic markers, *anon, as, so (that), hwæt þa, this,* and especially *when . . . then*, come to replace *þa* (Wårvik 1990: 568, 570; Fludernik 1995, 2000). However, Schiffrin (1988) points out that *then* can have various pragmatic functions in Modern English in sectioning off events or other kinds of sequentially ordered units and marking inferences that are warranted by another's prior talk. While she sees the latter as very similar to conditional (and conjunctive) *then* marking the apodosis of a condition (*if* X, *then* Y), she argues for the source of both in the temporal *then*, one via straightforward extension of the temporal meaning and the other via pragmatic inferencing from temporal succession to causal meaning. Although she is not explicit on this point, it would seem that she sees both pragmatic uses of *then* as deriving from the adverbial function.

13.2.2 *Predicate adverb > sentence adverb > pragmatic marker*

Traugott (1995) proposes the following cline as one possible avenue for the development of pragmatic markers:

(Full lexical noun >) adverbial phrase > sentence adverbial > pragmatic marker

She instances the trajectory of *indeed* from full noun to pragmatic marker:

(8) a. *predicate adverb*: for þe ende **in dede** schulde come aftur þat schulde be euen as þe furst siȝt
'for the end should come after, that should be like the first sight'
(c.1380 *English Wycliffite Sermons* 1, 589; HC)

b. *sentential adverb*: they [the teachers] somtyme purposely suffring [allowing] the more noble children to vainquysshe, and, as it were, gyuying to them place and soueraintie, thoughe **in dede** the inferiour chyldren haue more lernyng.
(1531 Thomas Elyot, *The Boke Named the Gouernour*, 21; HC)

c. *pragmatic marker*: thereby [the flea is] inabled to walk very securely both on the skin and hair; and **indeed** this contrivance of the feet is very curious . . . for performing both these requisite motions.
(1665 Robert Hooke, *Micrographia* 13.5, 212; HC)

The full lexical noun (*deed*) is found in a prepositional phrase (*in deed*) functioning adverbially. This adverbial phrase is located clause-internally, within the predicate of the sentence. It then moves to sentence-initial position with a disjunct function. In this extra-sentential position, it may then develop into a pragmatic marker with textual and/or interpersonal functions. Traugott describes the process as follows:

> The hypothesis is that an adverbial, say a manner adverb, will in English be dislocated from its typical adverb position within the predicate, where it has narrow scope and evaluates the predicated event, to whatever position is the site for wide-scope sentential adverbs, where it evaluates the content of the proposition. Here it initially retains semantic functions but also acquires new pragmatic functions and polysemies. Over time it may then come to acquire Discourse Marker functions either in this position or in a further dislocated position; this stage involves the acquisition of further polysemies by semanticization and also morphosyntactic and prosodic constraints. As a Discourse Marker it serves to evaluate the text, of which the proposition is only a component. (Traugott 1995: §3)

Importantly, this process involves a widening of scope, or as Traugott and Dasher (2002: 40) describe it, a trajectory from "scope within proposition" to "scope over proposition" to "scope over discourse."

In addition to *indeed*, Traugott and her colleagues have demonstrated that *actually, after all, anyway, as far as, besides,* and *in fact* follow a similar course of development. As pragmatic markers, these forms display a variety of functions: *as far as* is a topic-restrictor, *indeed* expresses elaboration or clarification of discourse content, *in fact* is also primarily elaborative, *actually* is additive, *besides* marks an afterthought, and *anyway* justifies what has been said (see Traugott 1995, 1997, 2003; Tabor and Traugott 1998; Schwenter and Traugott 2000; Traugott and Dasher 2002). While Traugott views the developments of all of these forms as instances of grammaticalization, she observes that contrary to the direction of change expected in this diachronic process, they undergo an increase rather than a decrease in both syntactic scope and syntactic freedom.

A number of other forms in the history of English can be seen as following an analogous trajectory. In the evolution of *only* (Brinton 1998), there has been a shift from the numeral *one* to the adjective/adverb *only* meaning 'solely, uniquely' (9a) to the focusing adverb *only* with exclusive meaning (9b). Then in Early Modern English, *only* begins to function as an "adversative" conjunction (9c):

(9) a. *adverb*:
Eliezer . . . brogt him a wif . . . He luuede hire **on-like** and wel.
'Elizer brought for himself a wife. He loved her solely and well'
(a.1325[c.1250] *The Middle English Genesis and Exodus* 1439–43; MED: s.v. *ōnlī* [adv.], def. 2d)
adjective:
Ich geleue . . . on halende crist, his **anliche** sune, ure lhaferd.
'I believe in the holy Christ, his only son, our lord'
(a.1250 *Creed* [Blick 6864] 138; MED: s.v. *ōnlī* [adj.], def. 2a)
b. *focusing adverb*:
þis **onelich** y knowe, þat I know not.
'this only I know, that I do not know'
(a.1382 *Wycliffite Bible(1), Prefatory Epistles of St. Jerome* 9[Bod 959] 7.145; MED; s.v. *ōnlī* [adv.])
c. *conjunction/pragmatic marker*: I am able to walke with a staff reasonable well, **only** my knee is not yet recovred . . .
(1628–32 John Barrington, *Letters* 96–7; HC)

The conjunction also expresses an "exceptive" sense (e.g. *I would've asked you; only my mother told me not to* [Quirk et al. 1985: 1103]). The conjunctive uses can be understood as pragmatic since they express the interpersonal meaning 'in spite of the roles we are playing, the state of the argument' and contribute to negative politeness.

A second form is *whilom*, the dative plural of *while*. *While* has been seen as an uncontrovertible case of grammaticalization, evolving from noun > adverb > conjunction and from propositional meaning ('at the time that') to textual meaning ('during') to expressive meaning ('although') (Traugott and König 1991: 200–1). In contrast, *whilom* shifts from a sentence-internal adverb meaning 'at times' that modifies an iterative or habitual event, to a sentential adverb meaning 'formerly' that modifies an entire proposition, to a pragmatic marker meaning 'once upon a time' that marks the initiation of a story, episode, or exemplum (see Brinton 1999):

(10) a. *predicate adverb*: **Hwilum** mæru cwen, / friðusibb folca, flet eall geondhwearf, / bædde byre geonge . . .
'at times the famous queen, the people's pledge of peace, went throughout the hall, urged on the young sons'
(*Beowulf* 2016–18)
b. *sentential adverb*: Đider com in gangan **hwilon** an meretrix.
'formerly a prostitute came walking in thither'
(1100 *History of the Holy Rood-tree* 26, ll. 11–12; HC)
c. *pragmatic marker*: **Whilom**, as olde stories tellen us, / Ther was a duc that highte Theseus.
'Once upon a time, as old stories tell us, there was a duke who was named Theseus'
(1396–1400 Geoffrey Chaucer, *The Canterbury Tales* Kn.A859–860)

It should be noted that the subsequent development of an adjectival form (as in *the whilom king of Crete*) poses a question for the hypothesis of unidirectionality in grammaticalization.

Brinton (1996: ch. 4) discusses *anon*, which originates in the Old English prepositional phrase *on an(e)*, and grammaticalizes as an adverb meaning 'at once, immediately' in Middle English. A conjunction, *anon as* 'as soon as', develops from the adverb. A further development in the ME period, motivated in part by the perfective semantics of *anon*, is its use as a pragmatic marker signaling salient action and emphasizing the sequence of events in an ongoing narrative (see further Fludernik 1995: 381, 386–7). *Anon* also has an internal evaluative function. In Early Modern English *anon* develops as a pragmatic marker serving as a sign of attentiveness in dialogue. The original sense of immediacy of the locative/temporal adverb gives rise first to invited inferences of saliency/importance/sequence and then of willingness/readiness, which conventionalize in the meaning of the pragmatic marker.

(11) a. *adverb*: Đider he wente him **anon**, / So suiþe so he miȝtte gon.
'thither he went at once as quickly as he could'
(*Dame Sirith* 8, ll. 155–6; HC)
b. *conjunction*: "ek men ben so untrewe, / That right **anon as** cessed is hire lest, / So cesseth love . . ."

'also men are so untrue that as soon as their (sexual) pleasure has ceased so too has their love . . .'
(1382–6 Geoffrey Chaucer, *Troilus and Criseyde* II 786–8; HC)

c. *pragmatic marker*: But streght into hire closet wente **anon**, / And set hire doun as stylle as any ston . . .
'But straight into her room she went at once, and set herself down as still as any stone'
(1382–6 Geoffrey Chaucer, *Troilus and Criseyde* II 599–600)

d. *pragmatic marker*: *Sir John*: Some sack, Francis. *Prince and Poins [coming forward]*: **Anon, anon**, sir.
(1597–8 William Shakespeare, *Henry the Fourth, Part Two* II, iv, 284–5)

On the surface, we would seem to have an instance of the shift from adverb > conjunction > pragmatic marker discussed in the previous section. However, the pragmatic marker appears not to develop from the conjunction but directly from the adverb along the route suggested by Traugott (1995).

A form that bears some similarity to *anon* is ME *for the nones*. This derives from the prepositional phrase *for þen anes* (with later false morphological division). While it may function as a clause-internal adverb meaning 'for that purpose', 'for the occasion', 'for that position', it is apparently more frequent as a so-called "intensive tag" with clausal scope meaning 'indeed, assuredly', and as fairly colorless "metrical tag" (presumably, some fashion of pragmatic marker). It would seem to follow the course of change set out by Traugott (1995), but more detailed study is required.

Another clear example of this course of development is the evolution of OE *witodlice* and *soþlice* discussed by Lenker (2000). These adverbs derive from the adjectives *witodlic* and *soþlic* (by the addition of adverbial *-e*), themselves derivations from the nouns *witod* and *soþ*. She shows how the adverbs evolve from manner adjuncts with scope within the predicate, or more often, truth-intensifying, speaker-oriented "emphasizers" (12a), to speaker comments with sentential scope which conveys the speaker's assertion that her words are true (12b), and finally to pragmatic markers serving as highlighters and markers of discourse discontinuity (12c). This change involves increased syntactic freedom and scope as well as heightened subjectivity (examples from Lenker 2000: 233–7).

(12) a. *predicate adverb*: Ic eam **soðlice** romanisc. and ic on hæftnyd hider gelæd wæs.
'I am truly a Roman, and I was brought hither in captivity' (Skeat's translation)
(Ælfric, *Lives of Saints*, Eustace 344)

b. *sentential adverb*: Wæs he **soðlice** on rightwisnysse weorcum . . . swiðe gefrætwod.
'Truly he was greatly adorned . . . with works of righteousness' (Skeat's translation)
(Ælfric, *Lives of Saints*, Eustace 4)

c. *pragmatic marker*: **Soðlice** on þam dagum wæs geworden gebod from þam casere augusto.
'Truly, in these days an order was given by the Emperor Augustus' (*The Old English Version of the Gospels*, Luke 2,2)

A somewhat less clear example of this trajectory is the development of the "interjection" *marry* (see Fischer 1998). Originating in the nominal phrase *by Mary*, this form evolves in the late fourteenth century into a pragmatic marker *marry*, which occurs frequently at the beginning of the second part of an adjacency pair and signals the speaker's emotional involvement. However, while Fischer documents the initial and final stages, he gives no evidence of the middle stage (as predicate adverb).

13.2.3 *Matrix clause > matrix clause/parenthetical disjunct > pragmatic marker*

Quirk et al. (1985: 1112–20) discuss a set of parenthetical disjuncts that they term "comment clauses." Comment clauses include forms such as *I believe*, which resemble matrix clauses otherwise requiring a *that*-clause complement, and forms such as *as you know*, which resemble finite adverbial or relative clauses. Given their function in expressing speaker tentativeness, certainty, or emotional attitude or in claiming the hearer's attention, comment clauses may be understood as a type of pragmatic marker. Focusing on *I think* and *I guess*, which they term "epistemic parentheticals," Thompson and Mulac (1991: 313) propose a synchronic cline of development for the matrix-clause type of comment clause, as shown in the sequence given in (13a–c):

(13) a. **I think that** we're definitely moving towards being more technological.
b. **I think** Ø exercise is really beneficial, to anybody.
c. It's just your point of view you know what you like to do in your spare time **I think**.

I think followed by *that* in (13a) is a matrix clause, *I think* without *that* in (13b) is ambiguous between a matrix clause and a parenthetical disjunct, and moveable *I think* in (13c) is clearly parenthetical, as it is no longer restricted to sentence-initial position.

Thompson and Mulac believe that there is a direct correlation between frequency / first person subjects / *that*-less complements and the grammaticalization of *I think* and *I guess* as epistemic parentheticals; the phrases undergo decategorialization of the complement-taking noun + verb sequence into a kind of unitary particle with different distributional properties. In essence, there is reversal of the matrix clause/complement clause structure, the original complement clause being reanalyzed as the matrix clause and the original matrix clause now serving as a parenthetical disjunct, as schematized below:

(14) S_1 *that* S_2 > S_1 Ø S_2 > PM*, S_2
* the pragmatic marker may be sentence-initial, -medial, or -final

In a diachronic study, Palandar-Collin (1999), using evidence such as increasing fixedness in first person, and occurrence sentence-initially without *that* or parenthetically, concludes that the matrix clause *I think* and the impersonal verb *methinks* have been grammaticalized – or what she calls "adverbialized" – as markers of evidentiality, opinion, or subjective truth. In comparison to *I think*, *methinks* (< *me þynceð*) is further fossilized, its verbal origins cease to be recognized, its positional mobility increases, and its scope expands. The three steps in the development of *methinks* can be seen in the following examples (without any attempt to establish chronological sequence):

(15) a. *matrix clause*: **Methynkyth** that knyght is muche bygger than ever was sir Kay.
'it seems to me that the knight is much bigger that Sir Kay ever was'
(a.1470 Sir Thomas Malory, *Le Morte dArthur* 06/13/277; HC)

b. *matrix clause/parenthetical*: And lathe **methinkeþ**, on þe todir seyde, / My wiff with any man to defame.
'and lately it seems to me, on the other side, my wife with any man to defame'
(a.1450 *The York Plays* 118, ll. 51–2; HC)

c. *pragmatic marker*: On lyve **methynkith** I lyffe to lange, / Allas þe whille.
'on life it seems to me I live too long / all the while'
(a.1450 *The York Plays* 72, ll. 103–4; HC)

Wischer (2000) views *methink*'s syntactic reanalysis, phonetic attrition, extension of scope, and restriction to certain clausal slots as, in part, a process of grammaticalization and as, in part, a process of lexicalization.

The courtesy markers *pray* (< *I pray you*) and *prithee* (< *I pray thee*) have disjunct-like qualities similar to comment clauses in Modern English; they serve as pragmatic markers of politeness, asserting the sincerity of the speaker (Busse 2002) or they convey "social deictic" meaning and reflect the speaker's negotiation of the addressee's needs (Traugott and Dasher 2002). Like *I think* forms, they begin as main clauses and develop into parentheticals. Akimoto (2000) shows that *pray* may be followed by *that*-complements in earlier English. Following Thompson and Mulac (1991), he argues that *that*-deletion promotes the change from syntactic main verb to "interjection." Traugott and Dasher (2002: 252–5) likewise trace the evolution of *pray, prithee* from a main clause performative *I pray you/thee* followed by a subordinate clause (a *that*-clause, an imperative, or an interrogative) to a pragmatic marker. Although *I pray* in initial position may be ambiguous between a matrix clause and a parenthetical, Busse (2002) sees *pray*-expressions as functioning primarily as parentheticals even in this position. The three stages are exemplified below:

(16) a. *matrix clause*: Seg. Do you approve their judgments Madam, which / Are grounded on your will? I may not do't. / Only **I pray, that** you may understand . . . the difference. (1657 Richard Brome, *The Queenes Exchange* I, 64–7; CH)

b. *matrix clause/parenthetical*: **I pray** you doe not stirre till my returne. (1632 Peter Hausted, *The Rivall Friends* V, ii, 32; CH)

c. *pragmatic marker*: Cram. What makes *Argyrius* **I pray you** fart as he goes / Up and down? (1659 H.H.B., *The Worlds Idol*, I, 214–15; CH)

The timing of these changes is not entirely clear. In Akimoto's data, *pray* begins to occur parenthetically in the sixteenth century; the object *you (thee)* may be deleted beginning in the sixteenth, and the subject *I* in the seventeenth century. However, in Kryk-Kastovsky's Early Modern English court data (1998: 50–1), truncated forms are used sparingly: *I* is present in the majority of cases and *(I) pray thee/pray you* forms are twice as common as *(I) prithee* forms. Moreover, while derivation from *I pray that* S is plausible, the data do not seem to support such a derivation: *that* complements are the minority form even in the earlier periods. In Akimoto's fifteenth-century data, *I pray* is more often followed by a *wh*-interrogative or an imperative, and by Shakespeare's time *pray*-forms are almost exclusively restricted to such complements (Busse 2002: 205–6), as shown in the following:

(17) a. **I pray you**, speake for me to master Doctor. (1616 Ben Jonson, *The Alchemist* I, iii, 29; CH)

b. Valen. **I pray you** sir is not your name *Onion*? (1609 Ben Jonson, *The Case is Altered* I, i, 111; CH)

Focusing on another epistemic parenthetical, Traugott and Dasher (2002: 206–9) discuss the development of performative (commissive) *I promise you* (followed by a *that*-clause) into a construction which is both subjective and modal in nature. Here they see a shift from content verb to procedural, "to increasingly pragmatic, discourse-based meanings, as well as to more subjective meanings" (2002: 209). The parenthetical not only expresses epistemic modality (the speaker's degree of certitude) but acknowledges that the addressee might have doubts about the speaker's message. The native *hatan* (*behatan*, *gehatan*) 'to promise' verbs followed a parallel course of development in Old English (2002: 211–14). Although Traugott and Dasher do not explicitly discuss the syntactic mechanisms of these developments (apart from suggesting that the parentheticals do not develop from *I Verb so* constructions), they presumably believe them to follow the course set out by Thompson and Mulac (1991).

The matrix clause *(I) say* follows a similar path of development into a parenthetical adjunct with three distinct pragmatic functions: as an expression of surprise or disbelief, as an attention-getting device, and metalinguistically with emphatic meaning (see Brinton forthcoming):

(18) a. "**I say**, hospital life certainly suits you!" (*Women's weekly* P27:24; FLOB)

b. "Old Lloydie, **I say**, let's take a walk . . ." (*Portrait: A West Coast Collection* K10:1; ACE)

c. All my life I never care what people thought about nothing I did, **I say**. (*The News* B15:1; ACE)

Furthermore, *I* may be deleted in some dialects (cf. the loss of *I* in *I pray* above). The derivation of this form in a scenario similar to the one suggested by Thompson and Mulac (1991) seems plausible:

(19) a. *matrix clause*: **I say well þ^{t}** I myht nat drawe .20 degres owt of .8. degres
'I say well that I might not draw 20 degrees out of 8 degrees'
(c.1392 *The Equatorie of the Planetis* 44, l. 4; HC)
b. *matrix clause/parenthetical*: **I say** thou art too presumptuous, and the officers shall schoole thee.
(1592 Robert Greene, *The Scottish Historie of James the Fourth* III, ii, 22–3; OED, s.v. *school*, def. 3b)
c. *pragmatic marker*: But till then, Money must be had, **I say**.
(1682 Aphra Behn, *The City Heiress* II, ii, 227)

Akimoto (2002), in a brief discussion, asserts that the development of *I'm afraid* parallels that of *I think* (examples from Akimoto 2002: 4–5):

(20) a. *matrix clause*: **I am afraid that** I have trespassed a little upon the patience of the Reader. (1652 Urquhart Jewel 274)
b. *matrix clause/parenthetical*: **I am afraid** some of these great mean countenance this bold and Heretical writer. (1709 Hearne Collect [Oxf. Hist. Soc.] II.252)
c. *pragmatic marker*: Affairs, **I am afraid**, are about to look squally on our Canada frontier. (1814 W. Irving in Life and Lett. [1864] I.315)

However, in Akimoto's data, *be afraid that* is always fairly rare and usually occurs with a third person subject; and while parenthetical *I am afraid* becomes more common over time, so does matrix *I am afraid* S (2002: 3, 6). This makes an evolution similar to *I think*, as proposed by Thompson and Mulac (1991), unlikely. Similarly, while the development of *I am sorry* (see Molina 2002) might appear to follow the Thompson and Mulac scenario, further research is necessary:

(21) a. *matrix clause*: Hor. Captaine, **I'm sorry that** you lay this wrong / So close vnto your heart (1602 Thomas Dekker, *Satiro-mastix* 1609–10; CH)
b. *matrix clause/parenthetical*: **I am sorry** the Bishopric of Fernes is so spurgalled (1635 Ab William Laud, *Works* [1860] VII.117; OED, s.v. *spur-galled*)
c. *pragmatic marker*: Melantius. Trust me, **I am sorry**; / Would thou hadst ta'ne her room (1679 Francis Beaumont, *The Maids Tragedy*, III; ii, 2–3; CH)

In addition to the first person forms discussed so far, there exist a number of second and third person comment clauses. The common pragmatic marker *you know*, whose function is to indicate (presumed or actual) shared knowledge, would seem to show a similar change from matrix clause to pragmatic marker (Brinton 1996: 206–9). The ME expression of epistemic certainty, *God woot*, likewise originates in a matrix clause. Interestingly it has progressed further along the grammaticalization path, as witnessed by univerbated and phonologically reduced forms such as *Goddot*, *Goddoth*, or *Goddote* (Brinton 1996: 255–61). Iyeiri (2002) discusses the function of the similar *God forbid*, which might likewise follow the path proposed by Thompson and Mulac (1991):

(22) a. *matrix clause*: **God for-bed þat** crewell ore vengaunce In ony woman founde shulde be
'God forbid that cruelty or vengeance should be found in any woman'
(c.1440 *Partonope of Blois* (Rawl. MS) 11281; MED, s.v. *illīcoun*)
b. *matrix clause/parenthetical*: **God forbid** I should from the poore withdrawe my hand (1578 Thomas Lupton, *All for Money* 755; CH)
c. *pragmatic marker*: I bade her come. What Lamb? What ladybird? / **God forbid**, where's this Girl? What Juliet? (1594–6 William Shakespeare, *Romeo and Juliet* I, iii, 3–4)

In general, the claim that all of these comment clauses develop from matrix clauses followed by *that*-clause complements would seem to be too limited. There appear to be a variety of possible complement clauses, including imperatives and interrogatives. It may even be the case that other types of (non-clausal) complements occur. Brinton (2002) explores the development of *I mean*. Historically *I mean* is followed rarely by a *that*-clause, and only slightly more often by a clause without *that*. The predominant structure is *I mean* followed by a phrasal complement {NP, AP, PP, VP, AdvP}, with the meaning 'in other words' (23a) or 'namely, that is' (23b). Parenthetical structures become common in the Early Modern English period (23c):

(23) a. The claper of his distouned bell . . . **I mene** his fals tunge
'the clapper of his discordant bell . . . I mean his false tongue'
(1450 [?1422] John Lydgate, *Life of our Lady* [Dur-U Cosin V.2.16] 9.222; MED, s.v. *claper*)
b. Shuldrys sharpe, **I mene** not reysed with slevys, Off evyl feith is lyklynesse
'Sharp shoulders, I mean, not raised with sleeves, is evidence of evil faith'
(1450 John Lydgate, *Secreta Secretorum* Ctn [Sln 2464] 2670; MED, s.v. *reisen*, def. 1d)
c. Duke: But she **I mean** is promised by her friends / Unto a youghful gentleman of worth, / And kept severly from resort of men, / That no man hath access by day to her (1593–4 William Shakespeare, *The Two Gentlemen of Verona* III, i, 106–9)

A proposed model for the syntactic development of *I mean* is as follows. Initially *I mean* occurs with a phrasal element as complement. The bonds between *I mean* and the phrasal element are weakened, and *I mean* can begin to be postposed to the phrasal element. The phrasal element is then reanalyzed as an independent element, and *I mean* as a syntactically free parenthetical. At this point, *I mean* is extended to the context of clauses and can be pre- or post-posed to clausal elements as well as phrasal elements.

13.3 Additional Pathways

13.3.1 Matrix imperative > matrix imperative/ parenthetical > pragmatic marker

A somewhat different verbal source for pragmatic parentheticals is imperative constructions. Brinton (2001) discusses the imperative verb construction *look (ye) (here)*, which develops into the pragmatic marker *(now) look (here)*, *lookee*, and *lookahere*; this serves as an appeal to the listener to pay attention to, accept the premise of, or perform the action requested in the following proposition:

(24) a. **Now look**, there's work to be done and lots of it (Brown Corpus)
b. "What is good enough for granfer is good enough for us, **look'ee**" (1930 *Daily Express* 10/3; OED: s.v. *grandfer*)
c. "**Look-a-here**, child what are you talking about?" (1912 Porter, *Pollyanna*)

The pragmatic marker originates in a matrix imperative clause meaning 'see to it (that)' followed by a subordinate clause introduced by a variety of subordinating conjunctions, including *that*, *what*, *how*, *what (that)*, *who (that)*, and *which* (25a). Grammaticalization of the pragmatic marker involves deletion of the subordinating conjunction (25b) and subsequent restructuring (25c):

(25) a. *matrix imperative*: **Looke wel that** ye unto no vice assente
'look well that you agree to no vice'
(1396–1400 Geoffrey Chaucer, *The Canterbury Tales* C.PH 87)
b. *matrix imperative/parenthetical*: **loke** ye take no discomforte!
'see you take no discomfort'
(1470 Sir Thomas Malory, *Le Morte dArthur* 20/05/1169)
c. *pragmatic marker*: **Look you**, she loved her kinsman Tybalt dearly, / And so did I
(1594–6 William Shakespeare, *Romeo and Juliet* III, iv, 3–4)

The change from matrix clause to parenthetical involves not only reversal of the status of the matrix and subordinate clauses, but also reanalysis, or rebracketing, as follows:

[look] [you be not late] > [look you] [be not late]

That is, the second-person pronoun, *you/ye*, originally the subject of the complement clause of *look* is reanalyzed as subject of *look*. Similar developments affect other sensory verbs, such as *see* (*sithee* and *seesta* in British dialects), *hark/hark'ee*, and *listen* as well as a cognitive verb such as *mind*:

(26) a. "**Mind that** you apply not your Traphine on the temporal Bones, Sutures, or Sinciput" (1686/9 John Moyle, *Abstractum Chirurgiae Marinae; or an Abstract of Sea Surgery* ii. vii; OED, s.v. *sinciput*)
b. "**Mind** you have a vent-peg at the top of the vessel." (1747–96 Mrs. Hannah Glasse, *The Art of Cookery: by a Lady* xxii. 349; OED, s.v. *vent-peg*)
c. "There's rummer things than women in this world though, **mind you**." (1837 Charles Dickens, *The Posthumous Papers of the Pickwick Club* xiv; OED, s.v. *rum*, [a. 2])
"**Mind**, you must never let the *sauté*. be too much done." (1813 [1822, 1827] Louis E. Ude, *The French Cook* (1827) 194; *OED*, s.v. *saute*, [a.] and [sb.])

Imperative *say* before questions may develop in a similar way (see Brinton forthcoming). Originating in a construction consisting of imperative *say* + (*to me/us*) + indirect question, the pragmatic marker arises through loss of the indirect object and switch in the status of the two clauses: *say* becomes a parenthetical disjunct and the indirect question becomes a direct question:

(27) a. **Say** maidens, how es þis? / Tels me þe soþe, rede I
'Say, maidens, how is this? Tell me the truth, I advise'
(a.1450 *The York Plays* 120, ll. 108–9; HC)
b. **Say**, wall-eyed slave, whither wouldst thou convey / This growing image of thy fiendlike face? (1592–94 William Shakespeare, *Titus Andronicus* V, i, 44–5)

Syntactically, the details of this change are somewhat less clear than the other changes discussed, but *say* clearly becomes a kind of pragmatic marker: it undergoes a change from a request by the speaker to the hearer for information to a subjective marker of speaker impatience or an intersubjective attention-getter.

Traugott and Dasher (2002: 176–8; see also Hopper and Traugott 1993: 10–14) discuss the syntactic development of hortatory *let's*, seeing a change from the biclausal imperative (28a) to the modalized single-clause hortatory (28b; note that tag questions differentiate these forms) to the single clause with pragmatic marker (28c):

(28) a. **Let us** go(, will you?)
b. **Let's** go(, shall we?)
c. **Let's** take our pills now, Johnny.

13.3.2 *Adverbial clause > pragmatic parenthetical*

Quirk et al. (1985: 1115–17) point to a second type of comment clause resembling a finite adverbial clause, e.g., *as you said, as you know, so I believe, as it happens*. While the details are complex and need yet to be fully explored, the politeness marker *please* would appear to originate in an adverbial clause. The OED (s.v. *please*, def. II6c) initially proposes a source for *please* in the impersonal *please it you* 'may it please you' > *please you* > *please* but allows that *please* is now usually seen as a shortened form of the personal conditional *if you please* (functioning as "a courteous qualification to a request") or of the passive of the personal verb, *be pleased*. Chen (1998: 25–7) suggests that the personal conditional *if you please*, not the optative *please it you*, should be seen as the source of the politeness marker *please*. Allen (1995) provides support for this claim. She argues that the personal construction with nominative experiencer subject (*if/when you please*), rather than resulting from a syntactic reanalysis of the impersonal construction, as traditionally argued (see e.g. OED, def. II6a), is an option added to the grammar. According to Allen, the two constructions differ pragmatically even in Shakespeare's usage, the personal occurring with actions over which the experiencer can exert some control, and they follow different courses of development: *if it please you* becomes increasingly deferential and finally recessive, and *if you please* becomes restricted to a polite formula.

There is also some controversy about the occurrence of clausal complements with *please*. The OED (s.v. *please*, def. I3) notes the existence of clausal subjects (either expressed or understood) with impersonal *please* (29a). While Akimoto (2000: 80) remarks upon the existence of personal *please* followed by an infinitive in his eighteenth-century data (29b), Allen (1995: 295) finds such constructions to be uncommon in conditionals (e.g. *if you please to take note*) (29c). The infrequency of clausal complements thus calls into doubt *please*'s development from a matrix clause. Rather, it would appear that *please* derives from an adjoined adverbial clause, as in (29d):

(29) a. **Please** it your full wyse discretions, to consider the matier (1423 *Rolls of Parliament* IV.249; OED, s.v. *please* [v.], def. 3b)
b. **Please** then my Lord to read this Epistle (1622 Francis Markham, *Five Decades of Epistles of Warre* v.vii.185; OED, s.v. *please* [v.], def. 6c)
c. If you **please** / To shoote another arrow that selfe way (1596–7 William Shakespeare, *Merchant of Venice* I, i,147–8; OED, s.v. *please* [v.], def. 6b)
d. But tary, I pray you all, **Yf ye please** (1530 *Jyl of Brentford's Test.* [Ballad Soc.] 15; OED, s.v. *please* [v.], def. 6b)

If you please becomes fixed and routinized by the nineteenth century (Allen 1995: 298) and is rare in contemporary English. *Please*, without either *if* or the subject-experiencer, comes to function as a pragmatic marker of politeness by the beginning of the twentieth century. Like *pray*, *please* shows a shift from "a construction with meaning at the propositional level to a pragmatic marker with functions at the sociodiscourse level" (Traugott and Dasher 2002: 257).

13.3.3 *Relative clause > pragmatic parenthetical*

Quirk et al. (1985: 1116) observe that a comment clause such as *as you know* is intermediate between an adverbial and a relative construction, and may be equivalent to a sentential relative *which you know.*

Brinton (1996: ch. 8) argues that in the case of *I gesse* parentheticals (including *believe, deem, doubt not, guess, know, leve, suppose, think, trow, understand, undertake, be aware, wene,* and *woot*), the data from Old and Middle English do not bear out Thompson and Mulac's (1991) synchronic findings (cf. Aijmer 1997: 8–10). There does not appear to be a correlation between forms occurring without *that* and epistemic parentheticals, nor the clear progression from a matrix clause shown in (14). Rather, *I gesse* parentheticals would seem to originate in an adjoined relativized structure "that/as/so ('which') I guess" in Old English (30a) and Middle English (30b), with gradual deletion of the relative pronoun (30c):

(30) a. "Habbað we to þæm mæran micel ærende, / Deniga frean, ne sceal þær dyrne sum / wesan, **þæs ic wene**
'We have for the famous lord of the Danes a great errand; nor shall anything there be secret, of this I think'
(*Beowulf* 270–2)

b. Thee were nede of hennes, **as I wene** / Ya, moo than seven tymes seventene
'You have need of hens, as I think, yes more than seven times seventeen'
(1396–1400 Geoffrey Chaucer, *The Canterbury Tales* B.NP 3453–54)

c. I wol with lusty herte, fressh and grene, / Seyn you a song to glade you, **I wene**
'I will with lusty heart, fresh and green / say to you a song to gladden you, I think'
(1396–1400 Geoffrey Chaucer, *The Canterbury Tales* E.Cl. 1173–74)

Loss of the relativizer leads to a change in status for the *I gesse* clause, from adjoined subordinate clause (introduced by a complementizer) to parenthetical disjunct; this reanalysis results in an increase in syntactic independence and positional mobility of the clause. The change can be schematized as follows:

(31) S_1 relative S_2 > S_1 Ø S_2 > S_1, *PM
* the pragmatic marker may occur sentence-initial, -medial, or -final

A similar origin (in a relativized structure) is suggested by Rickford et al. (1995) for the development of the topic-restrictor *as far as* (*insofar as, so far as*). In the early structures *as far as* seems to function as a relative:

(32) In sum, he hath the supreme power in all causes, as well as ecclesiastical as civil, *as far as concerneth* actions, and words . . . (1652 Thomas Hobbes, *Leviathan* 546; Rickford et al. 1995: 121)

This would seem to be equivalent to *He hath the supreme power in all causes . . . which concern actions and words*. However, the subsequent history of this form is different, as *as far as* seems to be reanalyzed as a preposition.

As far as {concerns, touches, regards} NP (earliest attestation 1652)
As far as NP {is concerned} (earliest attestation 1777)
As far as NP (rare before the 1960s)

13.4 Concluding Observations

Although this chapter has been limited to English data, we might conclude that there exist at least three distinct syntactic trajectories for pragmatic markers. The first cline can be represented as in figure 13.1. Synchronic studies of forms such as *why, like, so,* and *now* point to the existence of a cline as in (1a), in which decategorization from preposition/adverb > conjunction > pragmatic marker is accompanied by change in the scope of the unit modified or governed, from phrase > clause > discourse. However, diachronic studies, e.g. of OE *hwæt* and *þa,* do not show conclusively that pragmatic markers develop via conjunctions, but suggest instead that they may derive directly from adverbs. This I have shown with the arrow directly from adverb to pragmatic marker in figure 13.1. In the development of a wide variety of historical forms, including OE *witodlice,* and *soþlice,* ME *whilom, anon,* and *for the nones,* and ModE *only, indeed, in fact, besides, anyway,* and *after all,* there would appear to be more extensive, and more convincing, historical evidence for the cline from predicate adverb > sentence adverb > pragmatic marker as in (1b). What distinguishes (1b) crucially from (1a) is that in its initial step (1b) does not involve a categorial shift and decategorialization (from adverb > conjunction), but rather only a shift from narrow to wide scope (from scope within the proposition to scope over the proposition), with the category of the item (adverb) remaining the same.

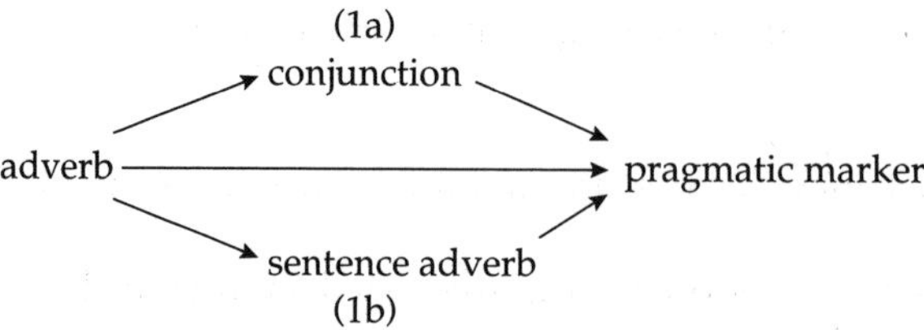

Figure 13.1

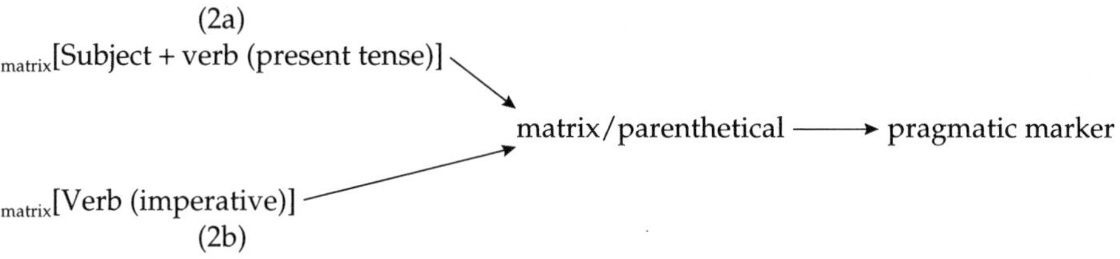

Figure 13.2

Stenström (1998) proposes a more general unidirectional cline:

Lexeme(s) > sentence connective > discourse marker

This path, although quite general, has the advantage of incorporating both of the paths shown in figure 13.1, providing one classifies both conjunctions and sentential adverbs (disjuncts) as types of sentence connectives.

The second cline accounts for the development of the matrix-clause type of comment clause. It can be represented as in figure 13.2. Here, the shift from matrix clause to parenthetical disjunct generally begins with deletion of the complementizer of the subordinate clause (which may be a *that*-clause, an interrogative clause, or an imperative clause, or, in some circumstances, a phrasal complement). Loss of the complementizer and occurrence of the present-tense or imperative verb in sentence-initial position leads to structural ambiguity. This ambiguity allows the original complement clause to be reanalyzed as the matrix clause, with the original matrix clause assuming parenthetical status and acquiring positional mobility. In this process the original matrix clause also undergoes a change in scope, from scope over a proposition to scope over discourse. The first person comment clauses, *I pray you/thee, I promise you, I say, I'm afraid, I'm sorry, I mean* as well as the second and third person expressions, *you know, God woot,* and *God forbid,* would seem to show the first path of development (2a). In addition to fixing and ossification, these phrases may undergo reduction, such as deletion of the subject and/or object (*I pray, pray, say*), or some degree of univerbation and phonological attrition (*prithee, y'know, Goddote*). A variant of this cline is the development of *methinks,* where the dative experiencer *me* coalesces with the impersonal verb *think.* Comment clauses exemplifying the second path of development (2b) include *(now) look (here), hark, listen, see, mind, say,* and *let's.* These forms may show bonding of verb and subject (*lookee, harkee, seesta, sithee, let's*) or more drastic forms of univerbation (*lookahere* < *look you here*). Note that path (2b) may require an additional rebracketing in which the subject of the subordinate clause becomes the subject of the parenthetical: [look] [you be not late] > [look you] [be not late].

$_{\text{matrix}}[S_1] + {}_{\text{subordinate}}[\text{adverbial/relative complementizer} + S_2] \longrightarrow {}_{\text{matrix}}[S_1] + {}_{\text{parenthetical}}[\varnothing\ S_2]$

Figure 13.3

The third cline accounts for the development of the adverbial/relative type of comment clause. It can be represented as in figure 13.3. Deletion of the complementizer yields a parenthetical disjunct, which then acquires positional mobility. Unlike the path (2), this one does not involve reversal of the matrix/subordinate hierarchical structure, though it does involve change in the status of the adjunct relative clause to a disjunct parenthetical, with accompanying increase in its positional freedom and change in its scope of modification, from scope within the proposition to scope over the discourse. I have suggested an origin for the first person epistemic parthenthicals (*I think, I guess, I know, I suppose,* etc.) in an adjoined relative construction *{as, so, which} I think,* etc. Similarly, there is some evidence that the politeness marker *please* derives from an adverbial (conditional) clause, *if you please,* where deletion of the complementizer and further deletion of the subject *you* yields the form *please.*

Study of the syntactic pathways of development of pragmatic markers thus provides evidence for a number of syntactic pathways, or clines, of development. Nor is this surprising, as numerous sources for pragmatic markers have been recognized. As Fraser points out (1996: 170–1): "Pragmatic markers are drawn from all segments of the grammar. Verbs, nouns, and adverbs as well as idioms such as *ok* are all pressed into service as pragmatic markers." Not only individual words but also phrases and clauses can be the source of pragmatic markers. Their syntactic pathways of development would seem to be directly related to their syntactic sources. Despite the variety of pathways, however, there is a unidirectionality of development from **scope within the proposition > scope over the proposition > scope over discourse**. Some pathways exhibit all three steps, as in the case of [preposition/adverb > conjunction > pragmatic marker] or of [predicate adverb > sentence adverb > pragmatic marker]. Just as frequently, however, one step may be skipped, as in the case of [adverb > pragmatic marker] or of [adverbial/relative clause > pragmatic marker], which skip the middle step, or of [Subject + present-tense verb > pragmatic marker] or [Imperative verb > pragmatic marker], which skip the initial step. But none exhibits an opposite direction of change. More importantly, the syntactic changes parallel, and work in tandem with, the observed semantic-pragmatic changes: that is, syntactic shifts from an item having scope within and over clausal elements and ultimately over more global elements of the discourse accompany the well-known shifts from content meaning based within the argument structure at the clausal level to pragmatic/procedural meaning at the discourse level. More work needs yet to be carried out on the other syntactic sources for pragmatic markers, such as tags and afterthoughts, but we may be quite confident that, despite their surface variety, these will follow the same general unidirectional syntactic and semantic/pragmatic paths.

DATA SOURCES

English Drama (1994–5). Chadwyck Healey Ltd. At: http://www.proquest.com/products_pq/descriptions/english_drama.shtml.

ICAME Collection of English Language Corpora (1999). 2nd edn. The HIT Centre, University of Bergen, Norway. [ACE = Australian Corpus of English, FLOB = Freiburg Lancaster–Oslo–Bergen, HC = The Helsinki Corpus of English Texts, Diachronic Part (see Kytö 1996)].

Middle English Dictionary (2001). Online, available at the Middle English Compendium. At: http://quod.lib.umich.edu/m/mec/.

Oxford English Dictionary (1989). J. Simpson and E. S. C. Weiner (eds.). 2nd edn. Oxford: Oxford University Press. 3rd edn. online. At: http://dictionary.oed.com / [OED].

REFERENCES

Aijmer, Karin (1988). "Now may we have a word on this": the use of *now* as a discourse particle. In Merja Kytö, Ossi Ihalainen, and Matti Rissanen (eds.), *Corpus Linguistics, Hard and Soft: Proceedings of the Eighth International Conference on English Language Research on Computerized Corpora* (15–34). Amsterdam: Rodopi.

Aijmer, Karin (1997). *I think* – an English modal particle. In Toril Swan and Olaf Jansen Westvik (eds.), *Modality in Germanic Languages: Historical and Comparative Perspective* (1–47). Berlin and New York: Mouton de Gruyter.

Akimoto, Minoji (2000). The grammaticalization of the verb "pray." In Fischer, Rosenbach, and Stein (eds.) (pp. 67–84).

Akimoto, Minoji (2002). On the grammaticalization of the parenthetical "I'm afraid." In Jacek Fisiak (ed.), *Studies in English Historical Linguistics and Philology: A Festschrift for Akio Oizumi* (pp. 1–9). Frankfurt am Main: Peter Lang.

Allen, Cynthia L. (1995). On doing as you please. In Jucker (ed.) (pp. 275–309).

Blake, Norman F. (1992). *Why* and *what* in Shakespeare. In Toshiyuki Takamiya and Richard Beadle (eds.), *Chaucer to Shakespeare: Essays in Honour of Shinsuke Ando* (pp. 179–93). Cambridge: D. S. Brewer.

Blakemore, Diane (1988). *So* as a constraint on relevance. In Ruth M. Kempson (ed.), *Mental Representations: The Interface between Language and Reality* (pp. 183–95). Cambridge: Cambridge University Press.

Borgmeier, Raimund, Herbert Grabes, and Andreas H. Jucker (eds.) (1998). *Anglistentag 1997 Giessen: Proceedings.* Trier: Wissenschaftlicher Verlag.

Brinton, Laurel J. (1996). *Pragmatic Markers in English: Grammaticalization and Discourse Functions.* Berlin and New York: Mouton de Gruyter.

Brinton, Laurel J. (1998). "The flowers are lovely; only, they have no scent": the evolution of a pragmatic marker. In Borgmeier, Grabes, and Jucker (eds.) (pp. 9–33).

Brinton, Laurel J. (1999). "Whilom, as olde stories tellen us": the discourse marker *whilom* in Middle English. In A. E. Christa Canitz and Gernot R.

Wieland (eds.), *From Arabye to Engelond: Medieval Studies in Honour of Mahmoud Manzalaoui on his 75th Birthday* (pp. 175–99). Ottawa: University of Ottawa Press.

Brinton, Laurel J. (2001). From matrix clause to pragmatic marker: the history of *look*-forms. *Journal of Historical Pragmatics* 2: 177–99.

Brinton, Laurel J. (2002). Historical pragmatics and the diachronic study of pragmatic markers: a reassessment. Workshop on Historical Pragmatics, 12th International Conference on English Historical Linguistics, August 2002, Glasgow, UK.

Brinton, Laurel J. (2005). Processes underlying the development of pragmatic markers: the case of *(I) say*. In Janne Skaffari, Matti Peikola, Ruth Carroll, Risto Hiltunen, and Brita Wårvik (eds.), *Opening Windows on Texts and Discourses of the Past* (pp. 279–99). Amsterdam and Philadelphia: John Benjamins.

Busse, Ulrich (2002). *Linguistic Variation in the Shakespeare Corpus: Morpho-syntactic Variability of Second Person Pronouns.* Amsterdam and Philadelphia: John Benjamins.

Chen, Guohua (1998). The degrammaticalization of addressee-satisfaction conditionals in Early Modern English. In Jacek Fisiak and Marcin Krygier (eds.), *Advances in English Historical Linguistics* (pp. 23–32). Berlin and New York: Mouton de Gruyter.

Enkvist, Nils Erik and Brita Wårvik (1987). Old English *þa*, temporal chains, and narrative structure. In Anna Giacalone Ramat, Onofrio Carruba, and Giuliano Bernini (eds.), *Papers from the 7th International Conference on Historical Linguistics* (pp. 221–37). Amsterdam and Philadelphia: Benjamins.

Fischer, Andreas (1998). *Marry*: from religious invocation to discourse marker. In Borgmeier, Grabes, and Jucker (eds.) (pp. 35–46).

Fischer, Olga, Anette Rosenbach, and Dieter Stein (eds.) (2000). *Pathways of Change: Grammaticalization in English.* Amsterdam and Philadelphia: John Benjamins.

Fludernik, Monika (1995). Middle English *þo* and other narrative discourse markers. In Jucker (ed.) (pp. 359–92).

Fludernik, Monika (2000). Narrative discourse markers in Malory's *Morte D'Arthur*. *Journal of Historical Pragmatics* 1: 231–62.

Fraser, Bruce (1996). Pragmatic markers. *Pragmatics* 6.2: 167–90.

Heine, Bernd, Ulrike Claudi, and Friederike Hünnemeyer (1991). *Grammaticalization: A Conceptual Framework*. Chicago and London: University of Chicago Press.

Hopper, Paul J. and Elizabeth Closs Traugott (1993 [2003]). *Grammaticalization* (2nd edn.). Cambridge: Cambridge University Press.

Iyeiri, Yoko (2002). "God forbid!" revisited: a historical analysis of the English verb *forbid*. Paper presented at the 12th International Conference on English Historical Linguistics, Glasgow, UK, August 2002.

Jucker, Andreas H. (ed.) (1995). *Historical Pragmatics: Pragmatic Developments in the History of English.* Amsterdam and Philadelphia: John Benjamins.

Kim, Taejin (1992). *The Particle* Þa *in the West-Saxon Gospels: A Discourse-level Analysis*. Bern: Peter Lang.

Kryk-Kastovsky, Barbara (1998). Pragmatic particles in Early Modern English court trials. In Borgmeier, Grabes, and Jucker (eds.) (pp. 47–56).

Kytö, Merja (1996). *Manual to the Diachronic Part of The Helsinki Corpus of English Texts: Coding Conventions and Lists of Source Texts* (3rd edn.).

Helsinki: Department of English, University of Helsinki.

Lehmann, Christian (1995). *Thoughts on Grammaticalization*. Munich: Lincom Europa.

Lenker, Ursula (2000). *Soþlice* and *witodlice*: discourse markers in Old English. In Fischer, Rosenbach, and Stein (eds.) (pp. 229–49).

Meehan, Teresa (1991). It's like, "what's happening in the evolution of like?" A theory of grammaticalization. *Kansas Working Papers in Linguistics* 16: 37–51.

Mitchell, Bruce (1985). *Old English Syntax* (2 vols.). Oxford: Clarendon Press.

Molina, Clara (2002). On the role of meaning in the historical development of discourse markers. Paper presented at the 12th International Conference on English Historical Linguistics, Glasgow, UK, August 2002.

Palander-Collin, Minna (1999). *Grammaticalization and Social Embedding: I THINK and METHINKS in Middle and Early Modern English*. Helsinki: Société Néophilologique.

Quirk, Randolph, Sidney Greenbaum, Geoffrey Leech, and Jan Svartvik (1985). *A Comprehensive Grammar of the English Language*. London and New York: Longman.

Rickford, John R., Thomas A. Wasow, Norma Mendoza-Denton, and Juli Espinoza (1995). Syntactic variation and change in progress: loss of the verbal coda in topic-restricting *as far as* constructions. *Language* 71: 102–31.

Romaine, Suzanne and Deborah Lange (1991). The use of *like* as a marker of reported speech and thought: a case of grammaticalization in progress. *American Speech* 66: 227–79.

Schiffrin, Deborah (1987). *Discourse Markers*. Cambridge: Cambridge University Press.

Schiffrin, Deborah (1988). Semantic and pragmatic sources of the discourse marker *then*. Paper presented at the Georgetown University Roundtable in Linguistics (GURT).

Schwenter, Scott A. and Elizabeth Closs Traugott (2000). Invoking scalarity: the development of *in fact*. *Journal of Historical Pragmatics* 1: 7–25.

Stenström, Anna-Brita (1998). From sentence to discourse: *cos* (because) in teenage talk. In Andreas H. Jucker and Yael Ziv (eds.), *Discourse Markers: Descriptions and Theory* (pp. 127–46). Amsterdam and Philadelphia: John Benjamins.

Tabor, Whitney and Elizabeth Closs Traugott (1998). Structural scope expansion and grammaticalization. In Anna Giacalone Ramat and Paul J. Hopper (eds.), *The Limits of Grammaticalization* (pp. 229–72). Amsterdam and Philadelphia: John Benjamins.

Thompson, Sandra A. and Anthony Mulac (1991). A quantitative perspective on the grammaticization of epistemic parentheticals in English. In Traugott and Heine (eds.), (vol. 2, pp. 313–29).

Traugott, Elizabeth Closs (1982). From propositional to textual and expressive meanings: some semantic-pragmatic aspects of grammaticalization. In Winfred Lehmann and Yakov Malkiel (eds.), *Perspectives on Historical Linguistics* (pp. 245–71). Amsterdam and Philadelphia: John Benjamins.

Traugott, Elizabeth Closs (1995). The role of the development of discourse markers in a theory of grammaticalization. Paper presented at the 12th International Conference on Historical Linguistics, Manchester, August 1995. Available at: http://www.stanford.edu/~traugott/ect-papersonline.html

Traugott, Elizabeth Closs (1997). The discourse connective *after all*: a historical pragmatic account. Paper presented at ICL, Paris, July 1997.

Traugott, Elizabeth Closs (2003). Constructions in grammaticalization. In Brian D. Joseph and Richard D. Janda (eds.), *The Handbook of Historical Linguistics* (pp. 624–47). Oxford: Blackwell.

Traugott, Elizabeth Closs and Richard B. Dasher (2002). *Regularity in Semantic Change*. Cambridge: Cambridge University Press.

Traugott, Elizabeth Closs and Bernd Heine (eds.) (1991). *Approaches to Grammaticalization*. Amsterdam and Philadelphia: John Benjamins.

Traugott, Elizabeth Closs and Ekkehard König (1991). The semantics-pragmatics of grammaticalization revisited. In Traugott and Heine (eds.) (vol. 1, pp. 189–218).

Wårvik, Brita (1990). On grounding in English narratives: a diachronic perspective. In Sylvia Adamson, Vivien Law, Nigel Vincent, and Susan Wright (eds.), *Papers from the 5th International Conference on English Historical Linguistics* (pp. 559–75). Amsterdam and Philadelphia: John Benjamins.

Wårvik, Brita (1995). The ambiguous adverbial/conjunction *þa* and *þonne* in Middle English: a discourse-pragmatic study of *then* and *when* in early English Saints' Lives. In Jucker (ed.) (pp. 345–57).

Wischer, Ilse (2000). Grammaticalization versus lexicalization: "*methinks*" there is some confusion. In Fischer, Rosenbach, and Stein (eds.) (pp. 355–70).

14 The Semantic Development of Scalar Focus Modifiers

ELIZABETH CLOSS TRAUGOTT

14.1 Introduction

In a book published over a hundred years ago, Stoffel (1901) drew attention to a class of adverbials which he called "intensives" (e.g. *very, purely, even*) and "downtoners" (e.g. *rather, pretty,* as in *rather/pretty good*). His main objectives were to show that:

(a) many of these were derived from adjectives (e.g. *even, pretty, very,* the latter borrowed in Middle English from French as *verrai* 'true' (cf. 1390–5 Chaucer, Canterbury Tales, Man of Law 167 *Hir herte is verray chambre of holiness* 'Her heart is a true chamber of holiness');

(b) intensives typically underwent semantic weakening from expressions of completeness of degree to high degree of quality, and occasionally low degree (e.g. *merely,* which is derived from French *mier* 'pure' and as an adverb meant 'completely', as in c.1600 Shakespeare, Hamlet I.ii.137. *Things rank and gross in nature possess it merely* ['entirely'], cf. also *purely*);

(c) some intensives were extended from word modifiers to phrasal modifiers (e.g. *quite,* borrowed in Middle English presumably from French and ultimately from Latin *quietus* 'clean, free'; according to Stoffel it was used until the eighteenth century exclusively in constructions like *quite clean,* but then extended to phrasal expressions like *quite a number* (a phrase said in 1862 *Punch,* to be "ridiculous");

(d) in these extended meanings the forms came to be weakly stressed (compare *a quíte educated person* with *quite an educated person*);

(e) in these extended meanings the forms usually occupied syntactically different slots from their word-modifying variants;

(f) in these extended meanings the forms were modalized, and subjectified, i.e. expressed speaker evaluation of the proposition.

For its time, this was a highly insightful study, but it now seems to touch only the surface of some additional, very complex issues, absent the kinds of theoretical distinctions that have been developed over the last hundred years in syntax, semantics, and pragmatics, absent extensive corpora, absent a tradition of studying semantic change in discourse context, and absent a theory of semantic change arising out of speakers implicating meanings rhetorically and hearers inferring (or failing to infer) these meanings.

My purpose here is to point to some of the theories currently available that allow us to investigate in greater depth adverbials of the type that concerned Stoffel. These comments are intended to complement Brinton's (chapter 13, this volume) broader-sweeping account of work on pragmatic markers. Section 14.2 outlines some of the current semantic distinctions among the kinds of adverbials Stoffel discusses, with particular attention to distinctions between "degree" and "focus" modifiers, and within the class of focus modifiers, a class of adverbials now often referred to as "scalar focus particles" (here called "scalar focus modifiers"). I will show that although there is significant overlap between degree and focus modifiers, they serve different purposes and should be distinguished, as is often implied, but not always made fully explicit (see König 1991; Nevalainen 1994). Section 14.3 outlines findings to date regarding the types of change that degree and focus modifiers undergo. In section 14.4 a brief sketch is given of two case studies of such adverbs, specifically *even* and *barely*. Section 14.5 suggests some questions for further study.

14.2 Distinctions among Adverbials

Historical work is best approached from a good grounding in synchronic analysis on the assumption that synchronic variation is both the result of historical change and a condition for further change. However, we must always remember that particular stages in the history of an individual word or construction may have been entirely lost (cf. *very* 'truly', though in Modern English *truly* 'truthfully' and *truly* 'to a great extent' coexist), or may be sedimented in frozen expressions (e.g. *break even*, with *even* in a sense now largely lost of 'in equal amount', *purblind* from 'purely/totally blind'). Therefore, we cannot use the present to investigate all of the past history of a form (here I am referring to language-specific form–meaning pairs; this comment has no bearing on the general proviso known as the uniformitarian principle, that one should not reconstruct an earlier stage of a language that has no known analogue in the languages of the world; see Labov 1974; Romaine 1982). Wherever we can, we must find evidence for synchronic variation at earlier times that can give us insight into stages and possible contexts now lost to us. Because originally dominant meanings can become obsolescent, we can also not assume that the synchronic organization of a set of variants matches their historical development (Michaelis 1993).

Historical development has been shown to proceed typically in very small incremental steps rather than in big leaps; thus *verrai* 'true' did not suddenly come to have degree meaning, but was attributed this meaning in a series of minor adjustments. It is our task as historical linguists to identify these adjustments and to develop testable hypotheses about how they were made. This means that we need a theory of linguistics that is conducive to discussion of change. This theory should account for the importance not only of abstract cognitive schemas, but also of patterns of use because it is only in use that we can observe language, and only in use that we can see change (see e.g. Milroy 1992; Croft 2000; Andersen 2001). This theory should also account for the fact that much change is directional, not random: there are major change schemas that have been shown to operate cross-linguistically in morphosyntax and semantics (see e.g. Bybee et al. 1994).

These change schemas are not individual changes, but generalizations over changes (Andersen 2001: 241). In the semantic area in particular, we need a theory that will allow us to consider new meanings as variants of older meanings, not unrelated homonyms. The approaches that have proved most fruitful so far are those that have combined elements of prototype theory (e.g. Geeraerts 1997), cognitive semantics (e.g. Sweetser 1990), and what is known as neo-Gricean pragmatics (e.g. Horn 1984; Traugott and Dasher 2002). These all privilege polysemy, the hypothesis that discrete meanings of a lexeme are related, and that later polysemies derive from earlier meanings in non-arbitrary ways, via implicatures and inferences that can be deduced from the uses of lexemes in specific constructions, not cited out of context, e.g. *fairly* 'honestly, justly, appropriately' comes to be used as a degree modifier meaning 'to a reasonable degree, pretty much' in preverbal position, especially with passives, such as:

(1) You will now give up your claim on me – I am *fairly* exonerated.
(1811 Holman The Gazette Extraordinary, LION drama; cited in Nevalainen and Rissanen 2002: 375)

None of this can be done, however, without a metalanguage for the kinds of meaning-differences we observe, or believe we observe, and some criteria for identifying them. For the set of meanings that Stoffel was interested in, and some of the differences in meaning and distribution that he grappled with, we now have some useful distinctions.

Syntactically, Stoffel was concerned with what he called "adverbs" (e.g. *quite*) and "adverbial phrases" (e.g. *as far as*). The syntactic characteristics of the kinds of adverbials he was concerned with have been the subject of extensive discussion. While a detailed account of semantic change cannot be made without due attention to syntax, the focus here will be on semantic distinctions. Nevertheless, it should be pointed out that the distinction Stoffel noted between what he called "word" and "phrasal" modifiers is an important one, and *grosso modo* correlates with the distinctions between "degree" and "focus" modifiers to be discussed below. In English the former are normally adjoined as constituents of AdjP (see e.g. Ernst 1984; Zwicky 1995). By contrast, the latter can be left-adjoined to a wide range of constituents, e.g. NP, VP, and even

S (see e.g. Jackendoff 1972; Ernst 1984, 2002; Quirk et al. 1985; Huddleston and Pullum 2002).

Semantically, Stoffel was concerned with what he called "high degree," "completeness," and "moderate, slight or just perceptible degree." The individual lexemes he discussed, and others with similar functions, are now considered to show specific properties related to one or more of two major related but independent conceptual categories: "degree" and "focus." As will be shown below, both involve "scale" in the sense that they imply alternatives within a set or partial set. I will discuss degree modifiers and focus modifiers first, and then scale.

14.2.1 *Degree modifiers*

Many concepts are semantically gradable in terms of extent, e.g. many adjectives (cf. *young*), verbs (especially statives, cf. *last*), adverbs (especially manner adverbs, cf. *willingly*), and a few nouns (cf. *baby* in *He's such a baby*; *villain* in *He's an utter villain* [Bolinger 1972]). Adverbs in English that express extent or intensity of this gradability are called "degree adverbs" or "degree modifiers" (also "intensifiers"), and can usually be paraphrased by *to a great/minimal extent, to a high/low degree, very much*, etc.

Those expressing positive degree, i.e. above a certain norm, may be called "boosters," "amplifiers," "maximizers," or "reinforcers" (e.g. *so* as in *That was so good!*; *very, purely, awfully, that* as in *It's not that bad*). Several have modal properties or are at the very least polysemous with modals, e.g. *really, truly* (see Ernst 1984; Gelderen 2001; Lorenz 2002). Most, but not all (e.g. *comparatively*) express speaker evaluation of the type "'*to a degree/extent that I consider X*', with X being the adjectival base of the respective modifier" (Lorenz 2002: 149). Those expressing a negative, slight or only perceptible degree may be called "downtoners," "diminishers," "minimizers," "approximators," or "attenuators" (e.g. *hardly* in *That's hardly likely, fairly*). (See Bäcklund 1973; Paradis 1997; Huddleston and Pullum 2002; Nevalainen and Rissanen 2002; Méndez-Naya 2002, for these and other distinctions). In English they typically originate in adjectives (e.g. *pretty*) or nominals (e.g. *sort/kind of*) as well as adverbs (e.g. *too*, cf. also the very recent *enough* as in *enough bad*, Paradis 2000).

A distinction cross-cutting positive and negative orientation is often made between those degree modifiers that do not imply boundary restrictions (e.g. *so*), and those that do (e.g. *completely*). This kind of distinction can also be found among adjectives and verbs; for example *green* and *run* do not have boundary restrictions, but *dead, full*, and *win* do. Such distinctions account for "harmony" between degree modifiers and adjectives, such as **completely green*, and *completely clean/full* (Quirk et al. 1985; Paradis 1997, on harmonic relations between degree adverbs and adjectives; Ernst 1984, on harmonic relations between degree adverbs and verbs).

A further important distinction that has been made is between degree and "quantitative" meanings (see Bolinger 1972), e.g. *much* is degree-intensifying in *much better*, and answers *To what extent?* Degree modifiers are indefinite and pertain to extent (from minimal *none*, to maximal *all*, cf. *all gone*, *all wet*). By contrast, *many* and numerals like *six* are not degree modifiers; they answer *How many?* not *How much?* Quantitative expressions in this sense are a subclass of "quantifiers," indefinite expressions of quantity, which include both *many* and *much*.

14.2.2 Focus modifiers

In his study of "degree words" Bolinger treats them as markers of intensification (with either positive or negative orientation) and says: "Intensification is the linguistic expression of exaggeration and depreciation" (Bolinger 1972: 20). Intensifying forms add "emphasis in some way to a sentence or some element within it" (Matthews 1997: 'intensifying'). In so far as degree modifiers express emphasis, their semantics intersects with a property of discourse that has drawn major attention in recent decades, that of "focus." A "focus-structure" is a discourse structure that partitions a clause into two parts: one that is focused or highlighted (the "focus"), and one that is backgrounded or assumed (the "focus-frame," or "background"). Focus is usually thought to be associated with information, and to be signaled by intonational prominence. It is typically identified with the intonationally prominent element in responses in question–answer pairs such as (2) (cf. Jackendoff 1972; Rooth 1996, among many others):

(2) a. Q. Who likes Mary?
    b. A. JOHN likes Mary
          Focus Focus-frame

In (2b) John is selected as the particular individual who likes Mary from the larger set of individuals who could be possible candidates.

In addition, there are a variety of other expressions ("focus-modifiers") which are said to be "focus-sensitive" because their interpretation correlates with the location of focus (Beaver and Clark 2002). Focus markers signal that the focus is to be understood as "addressee-new" material (i.e. material introduced into the discourse model) (see Kiss 1995, and the extensive bibliography therein). Typically, they do not add content meaning; in other words, the sentence without the adverbial is semantically identical (but the hearer is, of course, given fewer cues as to how the speaker evaluates the focus). Such focus markers may be expressed by word order, e.g. inversion as in *I walked into the kitchen. On a/the counter-top was a large book* (cf. Birner and Ward 1998), *it*-clefts as in *It was in the book store that I met her*, and elements like *-self* in *John himself left* (e.g. Primus 1992; Baker 1995; Siemund 2000, who call such elements "intensifiers"). Focus markers may also be expressed by a number of adverbs which are sometimes called "focus adverbs" (e.g. Nevalainen 1991), "focus particles" (e.g. König 1991; Hartmann 1994), or "focus modifiers" (e.g. Huddleston and Pullum 2002). I will use the latter term here.

At least the following English adverbs and adverbial phrases have been assigned to focus modifier status in some of their uses:

(3) also, alone, as well, at least, either, even, especially, exactly, exclusively, just, likewise, merely, only, precisely, purely, simply, solely, still, too, in addition, let alone, in particular, much less, so much as. (König 1991: 15; Huddleston and Pullum 2002: 587)

Some of these are polysemous with non-focus markers, e.g. *too*, which is a degree modifier in *That material is too pink for my taste*, and a focus modifier in *I want pink curtains too*.

Various subdistinctions have been proposed among focus modifiers. A two-way distinction is widely used, between additives that imply that the focused element is in addition to other elements, and restrictives that delimit the focused elements in some way (e.g. Quirk et al. 1985; Nevalainen 1991; Huddleston and Pullum 2002). This distinction is reminiscent of that between degree adverbs that imply boundary restrictions and those that do not. Nevalainen (1994: 254) splits the restrictive category into exclusives and particularizers to make a three-way distinction:

(i) exclusives such as *only, merely, just*, which "exclude all focus alternatives except the current one" (Nevalainen 1994: 254), e.g. (4):

(4) Only/just John likes Mary. (only John = no one other than John)

(ii) particularizers such as *exactly, particularly, just*, which "identify or specify the focus value under discussion" (ibid.), e.g. (5):

(5) I need exactly/just three envelopes. (not more nor less than three)

(iii) additives such as *also, too, even*, which "add a new focus value to a previous one" (ibid.), e.g. (6):

(6) Even/also John likes Mary. (John and someone other than John)

The three-way distinction is useful because particularizers play a special role in historical developments, as we will see below in section 14.3.

Additional types of focus have been identified. The number of distinctions may be dependent on the focus modifiers and the contexts in which they are used. What many types have in common is that the focus of the modifier "establishes a relation between the value of the focused expression and a set of alternatives (e.g. Jacobs 1983; . . . Rooth 1985)" (König 1991: 32). There is currently some debate whether all focus modifiers, e.g. *always, rarely*, etc., or all the uses of a typical focus modifier like *only* relate the value of the focused expression to a set of alternatives (cf. Beaver and Clark 2002); however, those to be discussed below do relate to such a set.

14.2.3 *The terminology of "scalars" and "intensifiers"*

As Nevalainen (1991) points out, confusion may arise because in recent years the term "scale" has been used in different, seemingly incompatible, senses. One refers to degree modifiers. Discussing adverbs of degree, which he calls "intensifiers," Bolinger says: "I use the term intensifier for any device that scales a quality" (1972: 17); "they intensify, scale upwards or downwards, the inherent properties of their heads (e.g. FULLY, HIGHLY, MILDLY X" (Nevalainen 1991: 86 fn.18), and the inherent properties of these heads are gradable. *Fully aware* is high on the scale of awareness, *mildly aware* is relatively low on it. More particularly, Allerton (1987) and Paradis (1997) identify a subset of gradable adjectives as "scalar," specifically those that can occur in comparative and superlative constructions (e.g. *good, long,* but typically not *huge* or *identical*).

"Scale" is also used to refer to alternative values (see the definition by Jacobs and Rooth cited by König, above). Focus modifiers do not intensify their heads – *John* and *envelope* are not gradable words. We do not understand *John* to be extended any way in (4) or (6); instead, focus modifiers invoke (activate) a scale or set for their heads. In *Also John likes Mary,* John is implied to be a member of a set of people who like Mary. We therefore need to distinguish items that have inherently scalar semantics (e.g. degree modifiers), and those that evoke scales (focus modifiers).

Much recent discussion of scales in the sense of alternatives has occurred in the context of the semantics and pragmatics of implicature (for a useful summary, see Schwenter 1999: 185–9).

(i) Some scales are "semantic" and "logical" in that they form lexical sets which involve logical entailment between expressions ordered by degrees of informativeness/strength, e.g. <*all, some*>, <*must, may*>, <*hot, warm*>. *All* entails *some,* but not vice versa, etc. These are widely known as "Horn scales" (e.g. Horn 1989). They are inherently scalar, like degree modifiers. They are not of concern in this chapter except in so far as *all* combines with other forms such as adjectives, participles, etc. to form expressions in which the degree modifier meaning predominates (cf. *all wet, all gone*).

(ii) Some scales are non-logical, pragmatic scales invoked by, among other things, (a) connectives, e.g. *in fact,* which rhetorically marks what follows as a better or more specific instance (cf. *bad, in fact terrible*); (b) temporals, e.g. *still* in *She is still talking about the party;* (c) part–whole, e.g. *finger–hand–arm* (see Fauconnier 1975; Hirschberg 1985; Kay 1990); and (d) focus modifiers. Here there are not logical entailments, but implicatures derived from speaker–addressee expectations about the world. These are not inherently scalar, but evoke scales.

(iii) Some scales are "argumentative"; utterances are presented as ranked with respect to the strength or force for a conclusion (see e.g. Anscombre and Ducrot 1989; Schwenter 1999).

It is the second type – non-logical, pragmatic scales – that is the focus of discussion here.

A similar confusion of terminology should be noted for the term "intensifier." As we have seen, degree words are often referred to as intensifiers (cf. Bolinger 1972; Greenbaum 1970), and so are many focus modifiers (cf. Primus 1992). Again, we can distinguish between inherent intensifiers (e.g. *very, dreadfully*), and those that invoke intensification (e.g. *-self*).

14.2.4 *Scalar focus modifiers*

A subset of focus modifiers is known as "scalar focus modifiers." Since, as we have seen, at least some, possibly all, focus modifiers involve alternatives, and therefore scales, this is not a good term. However, I will retain it since it is widely used in the linguistic literature (often in the form "scalar focus particle"). Crucially, scalar focus modifiers not only invoke alternatives on a scale but also rank the focus on that scale, usually with other elements of the same type (qualities, events, persons, etc.). This ranking often signals discourse evaluation such as expectation, e.g. *even, only*. Consider (6) *Even John likes Mary* again. Here *even* evokes alternatives: not only others who like Mary, but those who might not – it implies that there are very few, if any, who do not like Mary; furthermore, John might be expected to be one of those who do not like Mary but in fact he is not. In (4) *Only John likes Mary, only* identifies John as the single member of the possible set of alternatives, and denies that there are alternatives (in the discourse model, at least; there might be others unknown to the interlocutors).

The importance of expectations regarding alternatives for scalar focus adverbs can be seen by contrasting (7a) with (7b):

(7) a. John even reads SHAKESPEARE.
 b. John also reads SHAKESPEARE. (König 1991: 37)

In both, the focus is *read Shakespeare*, in both there is an additive adverb implying that John reads other authors as well, but only in (7a) is reading Shakespeare put on a scale of evaluation or expectation – the speaker regards Shakespeare as an unlikely author for John to read: "the values included by this particle are characterized as ranking lower than the one given" (König 1991: 38; see also Huddleston and Pullum 2002: 292, on *even* (scalar focus modifier) vs. *too* (focus modifier)).

In sum, where Stoffel (1901), and to some extent even Bolinger (1972), made only intuitive distinctions between degree modifiers and focus modifiers, we can now make the following observations. Within the macrodomain of gradable, inherently scalar expressions there is the subdomain of degree modifiers. Within the macrodomain of focus expressions, which include most basically intonational prominence, there is the subdomain of focus modifiers, many of which invoke scales. A subset of focus modifiers, known as scalar focus modifiers, evoke a ranking of the focus on the scale. When a degree modifier is associated with intonational prominence (focus), the two domains conflate, and so the distinction is blurred, as in:

(8) This is VERY good.

The distinction between degree modifier and focus expression is blurred even when the degree modifier does not carry intonational prominence, because it frequently occurs in predicate position, the position that is the default for focus, cf. (9):

(9) This is very GOOD.
Focus frame Focus

14.3 Some Generalizations about Historical Development

Historically, several generalizations have been made about the development of the classes of expressions under discussion here.

(i) Both degree and focus modifiers are subjective in the sense that they involve the speaker's assessment and evaluation of intensity, position on a scale, ordering of alternatives, etc. (Contrast uses of "subjective" to refer to "subject-oriented adverbs" like *cleverly* in *Cleverly, he lifted the cover off,* understood as 'He was clever in lifting the cover off', see Huddleston and Pullum 2002, and, on Early Modern English, Killie 1993). They typically derive from expressions that have more "objective" meaning, often quite concrete meaning like *purely, pretty, barely, even.* In other words, they exemplify the widely attested semantic–pragmatic change known as "subjectification." Subjectification is the mechanism whereby meanings come over time to encode or externalize the speaker or writer's perspectives and attitudes as constrained by the communicative world of the speech event, rather than by the so-called "real-world" characteristics of the event or situation referred to. It originates in conversational implicatures regarding the speaker or writer's attitudes to the ongoing discourse and its purposes that arise out of the strategic stances speakers and writers adopt in the speech event. These implicatures may become widely recognized in a community and may be reanalyzed as polysemies of a lexeme (Traugott 1989; Traugott and Dasher 2002).

Specifically, Peters (1994) identifies five main sources for the subset of degree adverbs known as boosters, many of which derive from adjectives:

(10) a. local/dimensional adverbs (*highly, extremely*);
b. quantitative adverbs (*much, vastly*);

c. qualitative adverbs (*terribly, violently*);
d. emphasizers (*really*);
e. taboo/swear words (*damned*, etc.). (Peters 1994: 269)

To this set may be added:

(10) f. identifiers (*sort of, kind of*). (Bolinger 1972: 92)

Many express scales from the beginning, e.g. types (a) and (b), which originally refer to relatively objectively definable extent and quantity, e.g. height and size. As degree modifiers they are located on a scale of subjectively assessed intensity.

(ii) Undecidability or ambiguity is to be expected and is indeed often noted between manner, degree, and focus adverbs (see Nevalainen and Rissanen 2002, on historical data; Bäcklund 1973 on synchronic data). Although written historical texts cannot reveal this directly, we may infer that this undecidability/ambiguity is in part a function of the coinciding of degree modifier with intonational focus.

(iii) While degree and focus adverbs are attested in earlier periods of English, their numbers increased dramatically in the EModE period. This is part of a major reorganization and expansion of adverbial resources at this period (Swan 1988; Nevalainen 1994).

According to Peters, most boosters prior to EModE derived from local, dimensional, or quantitative adverbs (10a, 10b); derivation from qualitative adverbs (10c) is largely an EModE phenomenon. The peak period for the development of boosters from native adverbs is around 1600; between 1650 and 1660 there was another peak when words of mainly foreign origin were introduced (1994: 272).

Peters regards the shift to degree adverb status as a case of abstraction, a "metaphorical meaning change" (1994: 269; see also Bolinger 1972). However, close inspection of the contexts in which the changes occur suggest that the metaphor is a result of gradual meaning-shifts in context and, as in many other cases, is the outcome of meaning-changes that start out as conversational implicatures; these conversational implicatures become generalized and may eventually be coded as semantic polysemies, though they may also retain their status as pragmatic polysemies. (See Traugott and Dasher 2002: 39; the importance of recognizing pragmatic as well as semantic polysemies is discussed in e.g. Horn 1985 and Sweetser 1990.)

Sources for focus modifiers are more diverse. Like degree modifiers, most originate in semantically concrete domains (e.g. *let alone*). König says of additive scalar focus particles that they are often of the same origins cross-linguistically: manner and/or degree (*so*), identity, equality of manner (*as well*), increase (French *non . . . plus*), inclusion (*so much as*, Italian *perfino*), emphatic reflexives (Dutch *zelfs*), and metalinguistic terms meaning 'truly' (French *voire* < Lat. *vero*). Exclusives, by contrast, typically derive from the numeral "one" (*only*, *alone*), restricted negation ('nothing except') (German *nur*, Dutch *maar*), and "privative notions" (*merely* < Latin *merus* 'unmixed') (König 1989: 322–3, 1991: 164–7). It should be noted that the "privative notions" all originate in the meaning 'pure, unmixed'. As in semantic change in general, the semantic properties of the source correlate directly with the later scalar meaning.

(iv) A particularly strong tendency that has frequently been noted in the domains of both degree modifiers and focus modifiers is a shift from restrictors to non-restrictors. Bolinger writes, with reference to the shift of *such* or *what* from the determiner domain to degree modifier domain, that "identification to intensification is typical of a kind of wholesale migration" (1972: 61). It occurs within degree modifiers (cf. Stoffel 1901, on *purely*, *quite*, and Paradis 2000, on contemporary developments of *quite*). Similarly it occurs within the focus domain: particularizers can become exclusives, as in the case of *even*, *just* (König 1989; Nevalainen 1994). Nevalainen shows that EModE was the time when these shifts were highly productive (as we have seen, particularizers are a subset of focus modifiers, and identify the focus value under discussion):

(11)

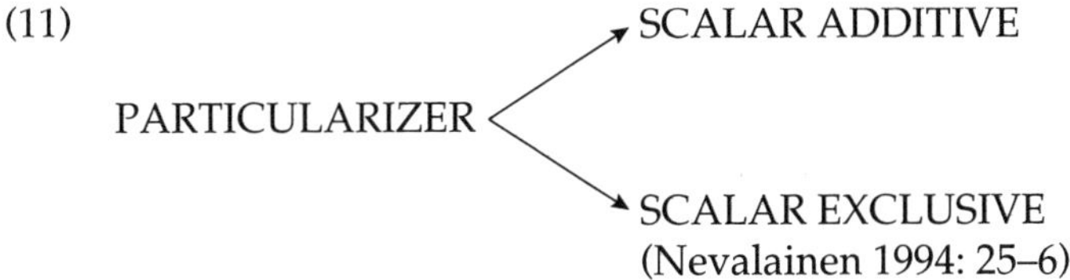

14.4 The Development of Two Scalar Focus Modifiers

The following necessarily brief sketches of the development of the scalar focus modifier meanings of *even* and *barely* are based primarily on discourse data in the Helsinki, Early English Correspondence (Ceecs), and Lampeter Corpora made available by ICAME, supplemented by the Chadwyck-Healey Corpus of Early English Prose Fiction (1500–1700). *Even* has been chosen as an example of the development of an additive modifier because its modern function and that of its (partial) equivalents in several other languages have been discussed at length, sometimes with comments on historical developments, but typically with constructed data. For English see e.g. Kay (1990), Kalokerinos (1995); for its (partial) equivalents in German see e.g. Eckardt (2001) and references therein on *selbst*; for Spanish see e.g. Schwenter (2002) on *hasta*, *incluso*; and for Hindi see e.g. Schwenter and Vasishth (2001) on *-tak*, *-bhii*. *Barely* has been chosen as an example of the development of a restrictor, to complement fuller histories of other restrictors such as *only* (Nevalainen 1991) and *fairly* (Nevalainen and Rissanen 2002).

14.4.1 *Even*

As is the case with many other lexemes, *even* already shows evidence of several polysemies in the Old and Middle English periods. This requires us to reconstruct developments as well as trace observable ones. Two main traceable stages can be identified in the historical record: adverb of manner and focus/ particularizer modifier > scalar focus modifier. The first stage will be illustrated primarily from Middle English for ease of interpretation, but the polysemies listed here all exist in Old English as well, as attested by the OED:

Stage I: At the first stage we find at least the following meanings:

(i) 'Evenly, smoothly'; this is an adverb of manner:

(12) Do past or cleye ther-upon al aboute as ytold bi-fore, caste Scaldynge hote hony **euene** ther-upon.
Put paste or mud thereon all-around as said before cast scalding hot honey evenly thereon.
(c.1450 *Horses*, p. 113 [Helsinki]).

'Smoothly' is a gradable concept and so is not totally devoid of scalar meaning, but the prime meaning is concrete and answers the question 'how', not 'to what extent'.

(ii) 'Similarly'; this meaning involves comparison, either of appearances as in (13), or of parts, as in (14):

(13) We shullen parten vs bitwen alle myne londes **euen** atwo.
We shall divide us between all my lands evenly in:two.
'We shall divide the land in two equally between us'.
(c.1300 *King Alexander*, p. 1, 217 [Helsinki]

(14) þer wende of him a lem þat toward þe norþ drou.
There came from it (comet) a light that toward the north turned
Euene as it were a launce red & cler inou.
Like as it was a lance red and bright enough.
(c.1325 *Robert of Gloucester*, p. 751 [Helsinki])

(iii) 'Particularizer'. This polysemy is syntactically different in that *even* is a modifying constituent of a phrase. In (15a) God is speaking to Noah. He instructs Noah to build an ark, and focuses on a particular measure (thirty) and also specifies (by using *even*) that this measure is a precise point of expectation; in (15b) Noah comments that he has met this delimitation (note the somewhat redundant *full strength*):

(15) a. Of lennth thi ship be Thre hundreth cubettys, warn I the; Of heght **euen** thirte; Of fyfty als in brede.
Of length thy ship should:be three hundred cubits, warn I thee; Of height exactly thirty; of fifty also in breadth.
(c.1500 Towneley Plays, p. 17 [Helsinki])
b. The heght is **euen** thyrty Cubettys full strenght.
The height is exactly thirty cubits full strength.
(Ibid. p. 21 [Helsinki])

We find *euene* in this particularizing sense in prepositional phrases of time at which and occasionally place at which (e.g. *even on St. Michaelmas Day, even this day, even now, even by* 'precisely close by') and of place or time from or to which (e.g. *even unto death*). In all these contexts alternatives are implied: 'exactly thirty' excludes possibilities of less or more, 'exactly on St. Michaelmas Day' excludes other days, 'as far as death' implies a set of possibilities, the most extreme of which is death. This is especially clear in contexts where gradable expressions are in focus: 'all the way to the end' entails stages that fall short of the endpoint, as we see clearly in (16a), 'all the way to the Star Chamber' entails stages that fall short of the Chamber (16b):

(16) a. Amides the torte slit the skyn **euene** doun to the erthe til the slitte come to the hole flesche & then clanse it well that is redi rotun.
In:the:middle:of the abscess slit the skin all:the:way down to the earth till the slit come to the whole flesh and then cleanse it well that is already rotten.
(c.1450 *Horses*, p. 115 [Helsinki])
b. His man carried it after hym *even* to the Sterre chamber and soddenly his man sterted away and tooke a boote.
'His man carried it (the money) after him right up to the Star Chamber, and suddenly ran away and took a boat'.
(1585 William Fleetwood, line 1796 [Ceecs, Original 2])

Faced with evidence for several synchronically available meanings, what can we conclude about the possible historical relationship among them? They probably developed in pre-OE in the order (i), (ii), (iii). The reasoning here is that we need to hypothesize plausible cognitive moves (pragmatic derivations) from one stage to the next. Smoothness (meaning (i)) implies similarity and uniformity across a surface that is accessible to sight or touch. Similarity in size or shape (meaning (ii)) implies uniformity/equivalence of extent when division of a single thing into a number of parts is at issue (13), or at least partial equivalence when two or more things are compared (14); in neither case is smoothness implied. The particularizer meaning (iii) presupposes that two items can be assessed as equal, whether it is height of a building and a specific measure (15) or extent of a cut and healthy flesh (16a). Being more abstract than either of the other meanings, and having rhetorical rather than literal meaning (indeed, it can be left out without significant loss of information), the particularizer sense can be hypothesized to have developed later than the more literal sense 'smooth' or 'equal'. It does not imply smoothness, and so the latter cannot be derived from it any more than from meaning (ii).

The data presented here do not take adjectival uses of *even* into account; there is no doubt that these influenced the meaning of the adverb; according to the OED, they seem to have patterned very much like the adverbial meanings outlined here, with the exception that the identity/particularizer meaning is absent, which is another reason to think of this as a later development.

At the beginning of the sixteenth century we find a significant increase in the number of instances with a particularizing meaning, often in the context of counter-expectation. A good example is:

(17) The king's highness himself, that hath bine so many waies my singuler good Lord and gracious soueraigne . . . **even** att my very first cominge into his noble service . . . vouchsafing to admit me and to offices of greate creditt and worshippe most liberally advanced me.
'The king's highness himself . . . that has loved and trusted me so dearly, from my very first coming into his noble service . . . deigning to admit me and most liberally promoted me'
(1556 Roper, *Life of More*, p. 90 [Helsinki])

In this passage Sir Thomas More is defending himself against charges of treason, rhetorically narrating how the King (Henry VIII) had been unusually gracious, going so far as to trust him from the first time they met (something one would not expect).

Even in (15–17) modifies overtly quantified contexts of measure, distance, and time; these imply scales or sets (all the way down, not part-way down; first meeting, not second or third). In (17) it modifies a PP that includes *very*, a degree modifier that at that time was still largely used in the sense now reserved for *truly*, i.e. in delimited contexts. There is a strong sense of particularizing harmony between *even*, *very*, and *first*. Especially interesting is (18), in which *evene* modifies *veray* and the latter modifies the gradable, not bounded adjective *glade*:

(18) when I remembre your ffavour and your sadde loffynge delynge to me wardes, ffor south ye make me **evene** veray glade and joyus in my hart: and on the tothersyde agayn whanne I remembre . . .
'When I remember your beauty and sober loving behavior toward me, truly you make me really very glad and joyous in my heart, and on the other hand again, when I remember . . .'
(1476 *Private Letters of John Shillingford*, II,7 [Helsinki])

Stage II. Particularizing focus modifier: It should be noted that typically *even* in the particularizer meaning (iii) does not invoke a scale by itself; its focus does that. By the beginning of the sixteenth century, however, *even* begins to appear in contexts where the head is neither delimited as a measure nor maximally modalized. Although in (19) *even* modifies a unique referent (Christ, in this case the speaker), this referent is not conceptually part of a natural set (of numbers, of epistemic attitudes, etc.).

(19) [The disciples speak] Is not this he that sate and begged? Some sayde: this is he. Other sayd: he is lyke him. But he him selfe sayde: I am **even** he.
'Is not this the man that sat and begged? Some said: This is he. Others said: He is like him. But he himself said, I am indeed he'
(1534 Tyndale, New Testament, IX, i [Helsinki])

In this scene from the Bible in which Christ's appearance to the disciples shortly after the Resurrection is recounted, *even* picks out the referent as exactly the individual the disciples are asking about, and excludes other possible individuals who might look like him. *Even* has here become a particularizing focus modifier. Note that while this can be translated as 'I am precisely he', the context of counter-expectation by no means excludes a modal meaning like 'truly, really' (B [myself] really is equal to/identical with A [whom you talk about]). The transition from contexts like (17) and (18) to contexts like (19) is easy to hypothesize: the restriction that the focus be explicitly a member of a set is relaxed, and now *even* serves to invoke the set by itself. *Even* appears to have absorbed the pragmatics of scalarity.

Stage III. Additive scalar focus modifier: At Stage II, *even* became a particularizing focus modifier, the prime function of which is to particularize or identify the focus under discussion, independently of the semantics of the focus. In the data consulted, the modern scalar focus modifier with additive meaning is first clearly seen in a new context, that of the "list construction" *and/but even* (for the importance of *and even* for a theory of modern *even*, see Kalokerinos 1995). Here it serves to highlight (focus) the added constituent; it is used to imply that what follows is to be taken not as just equal to its conjunct but as the entity that completes the list and is its most valued member for the purposes at hand. In other words, the scale is now ordered:

(20) It is a lamentable case to see how the deuill has bewitched thousands at this day to run after him: and **euen** to offer sacrifice vnto him. (1593 *Witches*, B2R [Helsinki])

A more elaborate example is (21), where correlative pairs of manner adverbs are scaled from negative to positive values:

(21) caused me, nether arrogantly nor contemptuouslye, but **even** merely ['without qualification'] and faythfully, to doe hir majesty the best servyce. (1586 Robert Dudley, line 3640 [Ceecs, Leyceste])

By the end of the seventeenth century additive *even* came to be generalized to non-list contexts. *Even* appears now not only to have absorbed the pragmatics of scalarity, but also that of counter-expectation; at the same time it has lost the limiting particularizer meaning, and adds new focus values to previous ones already mentioned. It implicates that the X it focuses is unexpected or increasingly improbable on some scale of values projected by the speaker:

(22) and was upon the way incountred and intertained in all places with such a concourse ('assembly') of people, with soe lively representations of love, joy and hope, that it far exceeded her expectatione. The people of all sorts (**even** such whose fortunes were unlike either to bee amended or impaired by change) went many myles out of the City to see her. (1627 *Annals of Elizabeth*, p. 6 [Helsinki]).

It is worth noting that in the Lampeter Corpus of Letters from 1640 to 1740, the most common use of *even* appears to be compatible with Present-day English (PDE) meanings, though sometimes, with our knowledge of the earlier meanings, now lost, we may need to enrich the possibilities of interpretation. For example in (23), *even* can be understood as evaluating land tax as an unlikely source of revenue (i.e. as an additive scalar focus modifier), especially given the conditional *if better Expedients be not offered*, but the meaning 'precisely' (i.e. a particularizer) cannot be ruled out:

(23) It will supply his Majesties present wants, **Even** by a Land Tax, if better Expedients be not offered, which both the Landlord and Tenant may afford once more to admit, being eased and recompensed another way. (1668 Abatement of Usury, line 10 [Lampeter, eca])

One of the rather notable things about the history of *even* is that the older meanings that existed at Stage I were replaced, especially in the EModE period:

(24) Manner adverb 'smoothly' (12) was replaced by *evenly*.
Manner adverb 'equally' (13, 14) was replaced by *equally, similarly*.
Particularizer (15–19) was replaced by *exactly, precisely*.

This may be part of the regularization of *-ly* adverbials in EModE and especially ModE and restriction of adverbs without *-ly* to specific semantic functions noted by Nevalainen (1994) and Nevalainen and Rissanen (2002). Whatever the reason for this replacement of older meanings of *even*, the links between them and the modern meanings have been lost. As a consequence, the adjective *even* and the adverb *even* appear to the present-day speaker to be totally unrelated, i.e. they have become homonyms. However, the polysemous relationships between the meanings exemplified in (12) through (18) seem quite apparent in Old and Middle English texts when they all coexisted. Likewise the relationship of these to (19–23) remain apparent in the EModE period, since they all coexisted then, although (12–18) were becoming recessive.

14.4.2 *Barely*

In PDE *barely* is an approximative (minimizing) scalar focus marker like *hardly*. *Barely*, like *hardly* collocates in PDE with quantifiers such as *any* and other expressions characteristic of negatives and questions, cf.

(25) a. She didn't have any apples (She didn't have some apples negates the expression *She had some apples*, not the fact that she had apples, i.e. it is metalinguistic)
b. She had barely any/*some apples.

In recent years expressions that collocate in this way have come to be known as licensors of Negative Polarity Items (NPIs). NPIs include not only *any* rather than *some*, but also such phrases as *lift a finger*, *sleep a wink*, *touch a drop*, *so much as a* (Ladusaw 1996: 325–37; Israel 1998). Exactly how to analyze forms of this sort in PDE has been a subject of debate (cf. Horn 2002; Beaver and Clark 2003). This is because approximatives like *barely* (an NPI licensor) and *almost* (which is not an NPI licensor) have the paradoxical properties of entailing one thing but being rhetorically oriented to the reverse. *Barely* entails the proposition *p*, but is rhetorically oriented to the negative ~*p*, whereas *almost* entails ~*p*, but is rhetorically positively oriented to *p*.

(26) a. She barely won (entails she did win, but rhetorically functions negatively)
b. She almost won (entails she did not win, but rhetorically functions positively)

As we will see, *barely* has always entailed *p*, but has not always been negatively oriented.

Stage I. Manner Adverb: In OE *bærlice* 'barely' was a manner adverb which meant "openly, without disguise, clearly, plainly" (OED). In this sense it was frequently used to describe manner of speaking, and this meaning survived well into the nineteenth century:

(27) Nu **bærlice** þu spreces
'Now you speak openly'
(c.950, Lindisfarne Gosp., John xvi.29 [OED])

In some contexts, unadorned speech can be considered to be simple, even inadequate speech:

(28) if we haue done wel, & as the cause required, it is that we desire, if we haue spoken slenderly ('poorly') and **barely** ('simply'), we haue done what we could. (1614, Hooker, *Two Sermons upon Part of S. Judes Epistle* Helsinki])

Stage II. Exclusive scalar focus modifier: During the fourteenth century this adverb appears occasionally as a focus modifier, adjoining to the following prepositional phrase. The MED lists (*barli*) as "(a) Solely, only, exclusively, absolutely; (b) without exception, without reserve, without fail; (c) completely, fully, to the utmost, utterly." None of the examples given seems to require a separate interpretation (c) from (a). The focus modifier use may have arisen in EModE out of the senses 'plainly' (hence 'unadornedly') and 'without disguise' (hence 'truly'):

(29) a. Hou be-come ðe godes kinne But **barelych** þorw þe wommones blod?
'How did you become god's kin except solely through the woman's blood?'
(c.1390 In worschupe 102 [MED])

b. þat no man be of the Kinges counsail but suche as be **barely** of his consail, and entendying upon noon oþers counsail.
'that noone be a member of the King's council but those who are members of it exclusively, and serve on no-one else's council'.
(1426 Proc. Privy C.3.219 [MED])

These have some of the characteristics of a particularizer, restricting the event to a specific time or situation, but appear to function primarily as exclusives.

While they imply alternatives, the early examples do not show them being used in explicitly scalar contexts. However, use of *barely* in such contexts was well established by the EModE period. Nevalainen (1991: 142) says that half of the cases in her corpus occur in contrastive constructions of the kind [NOT . . . BARELY . . . BUT] where the construction means 'not exclusively, not only', i.e. *barely* is here being used as an exclusive scalar focus modifier:

(30) Not **barely** in word, but truly in deed. (1577 Hanmer, *Anc. Eccl. Hist.* (1619) 526 [OED])

Here and elsewhere it marks the positive, but low end of a set of alternatives (cf. *just*).

Sometimes exclusive *barely* occurs in the context of exclusive *but*. Here the low value remains:

(31) For I remember where as Paule doth but **barely** alowe matrimonie, he commendeth virginite. (1555 *The Image of Idleness*, p. 58 [Chadwyck-Healey])

Sometimes *barely* is explicitly used without a negative or *but*, to identify a focus that is valued minimally by contrast to some other one:

(32) let me only ask the Usurer this sober Question . . . whether even lawful Interest, (exceeding this measure) be not a kind of Extortion, since it is clear, The Law doth **barely** tolerate, not warrant, or countenance Six per Cent. (1668 Abatement of Usury, line 112 [Lampeter, eca])

Note that in (32) neither *even* nor *barely* are semantically necessary. The rhetorical function of *even* is to order interest that is lawful, but exceeds a specified amount, as an unexpected member on a scale of extortions. The rhetorical function of *barely* is to order tolerance of 6 percent interest as the lowest member on a scale of attitudes.

Stage III. Approximative scalar focus modifier: Negative constructions of the type [NOT BARELY . . . BUT], such as (30), entail the existence of the focus. So do exclusive constructions of the type [BUT BARELY], such as (31). Because *but* signals exclusivity in (31) the main function of *barely* is to signal positive entailment (Paul did tolerate marriage) but also to signal low value on the scale ('just a little'). This may be the kind of context in which approximative meanings arose. There are two approximative meanings, one of which in PDE we may paraphrase as 'merely' as well as the more restrictive 'exclusively'. The second (and later) approximative meaning may be paraphrased by 'hardly'.

The first kind of approximative use is particularly clear in comparative contexts such as in (33); in both examples 'not just, merely' are reasonable paraphrases as well as 'exclusively':

(33) a. they had other designs then **barely** her converse ('conversation'), or they desired a nearer association with her Body, (1673 Kirkman, The Counterfeit Lady Unveiled, p. 111 [Chadwyck-Healey])
b. She thought there was something in it a little more serious, than to be **barely** Gallantry. (1692 Congreve, *Incognita*, pp. 74–5 [Chadwyck-Healey])

This 'merely' is cited as "archaic" in the OED, and the last example given dates from 1817.

The modern approximative paraphrasable by 'hardly' begins to be attested in the later seventeenth century. Although the OED has an entry "Only just; hence, not quite, hardly, scarcely, with difficulty" ('barely' 5) with examples from as early as 1494, (34) is the earliest that clearly has the scalar meaning 'hardly' in an affirmative context.

(34) My flocks are free from love, yet look so thin,
Their Bones are **barely** cover'ed with their Skin.
(1697 Dryden, *Virg. Eclog.* iii. 162 [OED])

Here 'exclusively' is not an appropriate reading, nor is 'merely'.

14.4.3 *Summary*

The histories of both *even* and *barely*, though different, illustrate several issues in the study of semantic change, most especially:

(a) Pragmatic implicatures arising in context are crucial for interpreting how each new meaning comes into being.
(b) Many semantic changes follow predictable paths (Traugott and Dasher 2002). *Even* exemplifies such well-known changes as:

   (i) Concrete > abstract. The manner adverbs meaning 'evenly', 'openly, clearly' are relatively objectively definable and concrete or at least testable (even though *barely* meaning 'openly' in the context of speech is clearly a metaphor, measures are in place to test how open or true what one says is). By contrast the scalar focus modifiers *even, barely* are abstract (Peters 1994).
   (ii) Less > more subjective. The scalar focus modifiers *even, barely* are construed in the mind of the Speaker/Writer, who establishes the scale and signals how he or she conceives the focus to be ordered with respect to the scale. This is a semantic change that Stoffel (1901) identified in the development of "intensives" and "downtoners," and Nevalainen (1991) for scalar modifiers; it is also illustrated by the development of modal verbs from obligation to epistemic meaning (Traugott 1989), and of discourse markers (Brinton 1996).
   (iii) Less > more language-based. The scalar focus modifiers *even, barely* depend on language, not on world knowledge, for their meaning. Shifts toward language-based meanings have been widely recognized, including in the development of illocutionary uses of speech act verbs (themselves derived from lexemes with no reference to language, e.g. *promise*, which is ultimately from Lat. *promittere* 'send forward' (Traugott 1987; Sweetser 1990).
   (iv) The changes undergone exemplify the cross-linguistic transition from particularizer > scalar focus particle that König (1991) noted and Nevalainen (1994) schematized in (11) above (section 14.3). *Barely* underwent a further change from exclusive scalar focus modifier to approximative scalar focus modifier, which is a weakening of the restriction, but not of scalar force.

14.5 Questions for Further Study

Many questions remain for later research. Among them the following may be of special interest:

(a) How were members of degree modifier and focus modifier domains semantically and syntactically differentiated over time in their various meanings, despite considerable overlap (see, for example, *barely, hardly, simply*)?

(b) Are there particular text types in which particular focus modifiers are favored over others? (See Nevalainen 1991, for discussion of (a)–(b) with respect to exclusives. She says that *barely* is "confined to sermons and educational treatises" in her EModE corpus.)
(c) Are there particular social factors that correlate with the distribution of focus modifiers, such as sex and age? (See Ito and Tagliamonte 2003, for a study of changing usage patterns for *very* and *really* in contemporary York, England.)
(d) What evidence can we find in recordings and other oral materials collected during the last hundred years or so of changes in stress, and of meaning-differentiations associated with them? Can poetic meter give us insights into stress changes in earlier English?
(e) How did the division of labor between the positive and negative entailments of such pairs as *barely* and *almost* develop?
(f) What constraints are there on the order of modifiers when they are stacked as in (18) where we find *even verray*? How are certain stacked collocations to be understood, e.g. *only barely* in (35)?

(35) I surrender'd to her all my Stock, with a Covenant however that it was only **barely** lent, and that I might call it in again at my pleasure, without any loss or diminution. (1692 Gildon, *The Post-boy rob'd of his Mail*, p. 360 [Chadwyck-Healey])

(g) What further paths of development are available for focus modifiers? Brinton (1998) has shown how *only* developed in EModE into a clause-initial adversative conjunctive as in:

(36) I am able to walk a staff reasonable well, *only* my knee is not yet recovered. (1629 John Barrington, *Letters* 97 [Helsinki], cited in Brinton 1998: 24)

In this function it introduces a clause that "denotes the opposite of the consequence or conclusion expected from the first" (Poutsma 1904–5: 385), and expresses "a limitation on what has just been said" (Jespersen 1949: 95) (both cited in Brinton 1998: 18). It would appear that *only* maintains some of its scalar focus modifier meaning here, with the scalar evaluation strengthened, and the range ("scope") extended to clausal relations. A further development, also attested in EModE, is to a clause-initial "conjunction/pragmatic marker":

(37) My former speeches have but hit your thoughts,
Which can interpret farther. **Only** I say
Things have been strangely borne.
(c.1607 Shakespeare, *Macbeth* III.vi.1–3, cited in Brinton 1998: 25)

In this respect *only* shares developmental characteristics with adverbs like VP-internal *indeed* and *actually* that came to modify clauses and comment on the speaker's evaluation of the discourse relation between the preceding and the following discourse (Traugott and Dasher 2002), and scale the following clause argumentatively higher than the preceding one (Schwenter and Traugott 2000). To what extent this sort of development has occurred with other degree and focus modifiers remains to be investigated.

(h) Is there historical evidence that can give insight into the question whether there are non-scalar focus expressions, e.g. *rarely*, *almost* as Beaver and Clark (2003) suggest, or whether there are non-scalar uses of typically focus scalar modifiers like *only* as Taglicht (1984) suggests? If the contexts for the development of focus expressions are scalar, as (16–18) and (30–32) suggest, the apparently non-scalar meanings may be later developments. Alternatively, they may be a function of constructed examples rather than of natural language.

ACKNOWLEDGMENTS

I have benefited greatly from comments by Brady Z. Clark, Laurence R. Horn, and Scott A. Schwenter on earlier drafts of this paper, and discussion of scales with David Beaver. The historical analysis of *even* has been presented in various contexts, including the Linguistic Society of America Summer Session at the University of California, Santa Barbara, in 2001; thanks to the audiences for discussion and comments.

REFERENCES

Allerton, D. J. (1987). English intensifiers and their idiosyncracies. In Ross Steele and Terry Threadgold (eds.), *Language Topics: Essays in Honour of Michael Halliday* (II, pp. 15–31). Amsterdam: Benjamins.

Andersen, Henning (2001). *Actualization: Linguistic Change in Progress* (Amsterdam Studies in the Theory and History of Linguistic Science 219). Amsterdam: Benjamins.

Anscombre, Jean-Claude and Oswald Ducrot (1989). Argumentivity and informativity. In Michael Meyer (ed.), *From Metaphysics to Rhetoric* (pp. 71–87). Dordrecht: Kluwer.

Bäcklund, Ulf (1973). *The Collocation of Adverbs of Degree in English* (Studia Anglistica Upsaliensia 13). Uppsala: Acta Universitatis Upsaliensis.

Baker, C. L. (1995). Contrast, discourse prominence, and intensification, with special reference to locally free reflexives in British English. *Language* 71: 63–101.

Beaver, David I. and Brady Z. Clark (2002). The proper treatment of focus sensitivity. In L. Mikkelsen and C. Potts (eds.), *WCCFL 21 Proceedings* (pp. 15–28). Somerville, MA: Cascadilla Press.

Beaver, David and Brady Clark (2003). "Always" and "Only": why not all focus sensitive operators are alike.

Natural Language Semantics 11.4: 323–62.

Birner, Betty J. and Gregory Ward (1998). *Information Status and Non-Canonical Word Order in English* (Studies in Language Companion Series 40). Amsterdam: Benjamins.

Bolinger, Dwight (1972). *Degree Words.* The Hague: Mouton.

Brinton, Laurel J. (1996). *Pragmatic Markers in English: Grammaticalization and Discourse Functions* (Topics in English Linguistics 19). Berlin and New York: Mouton de Gruyter.

Brinton, Laurel J. (1998). "The flowers are lovely; only, they have no scent": The evolution of a pragmatic marker. In Raimund Borgmeier, Herbert Grabes, and Andreas H, Jucker (eds.), *Anglistentag 1997 Giessen* (pp. 9–18) (Proceedings of the Conference of the German Association of University Teachers of English 19). Trier: Wissenschaftlicher Verlag Trier.

Bybee, Joan, Revere Perkins, and William Pagliuca (1994). *The Evolution of Grammar: Tense, Aspect, and Modality in the Languages of the World.* Chicago: University of Chicago Press.

Croft, William (2000). *Explaining Language Change: An Evolutionary Approach.* Harlow: Pearson Education.

Eckardt, Regine (2001). Renalysing *selbst. Natural Language Semantics* 9: 371–412.

Ernst, Thomas (1984). *Towards an Integrated Theory of Adverb Position in English.* Bloomington, IN: Indiana University Linguistics Club.

Ernst, Thomas (2002). *The Syntax of Adjuncts.* Cambridge: Cambridge University Press.

Fauconnier, Gilles (1975). Pragmatic scales and logical structure. *Linguistic Inquiry* 6: 353–75.

Geeraerts, Dirk (1997). *Diachronic Prototype Semantics: A Contribution to Historical Lexicology.* Oxford: Clarendon Press.

Gelderen, Elly van (2001). The syntax of mood particles in the history of English. *Folia Linguistica Historica* 22: 301–30.

Greenbaum, Sidney (1970). *Verb-intensifier Collocations in English: An Experimental Approach* (Janua Linguarum, Series Minor 86). The Hague: Mouton.

Hartmann, D. (1994). Particles. In R. E. Asher and J. M. Y. Simpson (eds.), *The Encyclopedia of Language and Linguistics* (VI, pp. 2953–8). Oxford: Pergamon Press.

Hirschberg, Julia Bell (1985). *A Theory of Scalar Implicature.* PhD dissertation, University of Pennsylvania.

Horn, Laurence R. (1984). Toward a new taxonomy for pragmatic inference: Q-based and R-based implicature. In Deborah Schiffrin (ed.), *Meaning, Form, and Use in Context: Linguistic Applications; Georgetown University Round Table '84* (pp. 11–42). Washington, DC: Georgetown University Press.

Horn, Laurence R. (1985). Metalinguistic negation and pragmatic ambiguity. *Language* 61: 121–74.

Horn, Laurence R. (1989). *A Natural History of Negation.* Chicago: University of Chicago Press.

Horn, Laurence R. (2002). Assertoric inertia and NPI licensing. In Mary Andronis, Erin Debenport, Anne Pycha, and Keiko Yoshimura (eds.), *Proceedings of the Chicago Linguistics Society* 38 (Part 2, pp. 55–82). Chicago: Chicago Linguistics Society

Huddleston, Rodney and Geoffrey K. Pullum (2002). *The Cambridge Grammar of the English Language.* Cambridge: Cambridge University Press.

Israel, Michael (1998). *Ever*: polysemy and polarity sensitivity. *Linguistic Notes from La Jolla* 19.

Ito, Rika and Sali Tagliamonte (2003). *Well* weird, *right* dodgy, *very* strange, *really* cool: layering and recycling in

English intensifiers. *Language in Society* 32: 257–79.

Jackendoff, Ray (1972). *Semantic Interpretation in Generative Grammar*. Cambridge, MA: MIT Press.

Jacobs, Joachim (1983). *Fokus und Skalen: Zur Syntax und Semantik der Gradpartikeln im Deutschen*. Tübingen: Niemeyer.

Jacobs, Joachim (ed.) (1992). *Informationsstruktur und Grammatik*. Linguistische Berichte, Special Issue, 4/1991–2.

Jespersen, Otto (1949). *A Grammar of Modern English on Historical Principles*. Part 7: *Syntax* (completed by Niels Haislund). Copenhagen: Munksgaard.

Kalokerinos, Alexis (1995). *Even*: how to make theories with a word. *Journal of Pragmatics* 24: 77–98.

Kastovsky, Dieter (ed.) (1994). *Studies in Early Modern English*. Berlin: Mouton de Gruyter.

Kay, Paul (1990). *Even*. *Linguistics and Philosophy* 13: 59–111.

Killie, Kristin (1993). *Early Modern English Subject Modifiers* (Tromsø Studies in Linguistics 13). Oslo: Novus.

Kiss, Katalin É. (ed.) (1995). *Discourse Configurational Languages*. New York: Oxford University Press.

König, Ekkehard (1989). On the historical development of focus particles. In Harald Weydt (ed.), *Sprechen mit Partikeln* (pp. 318–29). Berlin: Mouton de Gruyter.

König, Ekkehard (1991). *The Meaning of Focus Particles: A Comparative Perspective*. London: Routledge.

Labov, William (1974). On the use of the present to explain the past. In Luigi Heilman (ed.), *Proceedings of the 11th International Congress of Linguists* (pp. 825–52). Bologna: Mulino.

Ladusaw, William A. (1996). Negation and polarity items. In Lappin (ed.), pp. 321–41.

Lappin, Shalom (ed.) (1996). *The Handbook of Contemporary Semantic Theory*, Malden, MA: Blackwell.

Lorenz, Gunter (2002). *Really worthwhile* or *not really significant*? A corpus-based approach to the delexicalization and grammaticalization of intensifiers in Modern English. In Ilse Wischer and Gabriele Diewald (eds.), *New Reflections on Grammaticalization* (pp. 143–61). Amsterdam: Benjamins.

Matthews, Peter (1997). *The Concise Dictionary of Linguistics*. Oxford and New York: Oxford University Press.

Méndez-Naya, Belén (2003). On intensifiers and grammaticalization: the case of *swiþe*. *English Studies* 84: 372–91.

Michaelis, Laura A. (1993). "Continuity" within three scalar models: the polysemy of adverbial *still*. *Journal of Semantics* 10: 193–237.

Milroy, James (1992). *Linguistic Variation and Change: On the Historical Sociolinguistics of English*. Oxford: Blackwell.

Nevalainen, Terttu (1991). *BUT, ONLY, JUST: Focusing Adverbial Change in Modern English 1500–1900* (Mémoires de la Société Néophilologique de Helsinki 51). Helsinki: Société Néophilologique.

Nevalainen, Terttu (1994). Aspects of adverbial change in Early Modern English, In Kastovsky (ed.), pp. 243–59.

Nevalainen, Terttu and Matti Rissanen (2002). Fairly pretty or pretty fair? On the development and grammaticalization of English downtoners. *Language Sciences* 24: 359–80.

Paradis, Carita (1997). *Degree Modifiers of Adjectives in Spoken British English* (Lund Studies in English 92). Lund: Lund University Press.

Paradis, Carita (2000). *It's well weird*: Degree modifiers of adjectives revisited: the nineties. In John M. Kirk (ed.), *Corpora Galore: Analyses and Techniques in Describing English: Papers from the Nineteenth International Conference on English Language Research on Computational Corpora (ICAME 1998)* (pp. 146–60). Amsterdam: Rodopi.

Peters, Hans (1994). Degree adverbs in Early Modern English. In Kastovsky (ed.), pp. 269–88.

Poutsma, H. (1904–5). *A Grammar of Late Modern English.* Part I: *The Sentence.* Groningen: Noordhoff.

Primus, Beatrice (1992). Variants of a scalar adverb in German. In Jacobs (ed.), pp. 54–88.

Quirk, Randolph, Sidney Greenbaum, Geoffrey Leech, and Jan Svartvik (1985). *A Comprehensive Grammar of the English Language.* New York: Longman.

Romaine, Suzanne (1982). *Socio-Historical Linguistics: Its Status and Methodology* (Cambridge Studies in Linguistics 34). Cambridge: Cambridge University Press.

Rooth, Mats (1985). *Association with Focus.* Unpublished PhD dissertation, University of Massachusetts, Amherst.

Rooth, Mats (1996). Focus. In Lappin (ed.), pp. 271–97.

Schwenter, Scott A. (1999). *Pragmatics of Conditional Marking: Implicature, Scalarity and Exclusivity.* New York: Garland.

Schwenter, Scott A. (2002). Additive particles and scalar endpoint marking. *Belgian Journal of Linguistics* 16: 119–33.

Schwenter, Scott A. and Elizabeth Closs Traugott (2000). Invoking scalarity: the development of *in fact. Journal of Historical Pragmatics* 1: 7–25.

Schwenter, Scott A. and Shravan Vasishth (2001). Absolute and relative scalar particles in Spanish and Hindi. In *Proceedings of the Twenty-sixth Annual Meeting of the Berkeley Linguistics Society* (pp. 225–33). Berkeley, CA: Berkeley Linguistics Society.

Siemund, Peter (2000). *Intensifiers in English and German: A Comparison.* London and New York: Routledge.

Stoffel, C. (1901). *Intensives and Down-Toners: A Study in English Adverbs.* Heidelberg: Carl Winter.

Swan, Toril (1988). *Sentence Adverbials in English: A Synchronic and Diachronic Investigation.* Oslo: Novus.

Sweetser, Eve E. (1990). *From Etymology to Pragmatics: Metaphorical and Cultural Aspects of Semantic Structure.* Cambridge: Cambridge University Press.

Taglicht, Josef (1984). *Message and Emphasis.* London: Longman.

Traugott, Elizabeth Closs (1987). Literacy and language change: the special case of speech act verbs. In Judith Langer (ed.), *Language, Literacy, and Culture: Issues of Society and Schooling* (pp. 11–27). Norwood: Ablex.

Traugott, Elizabeth Closs (1989). On the rise of epistemic meanings in English: an example of subjectification in semantic change. *Language* 57: 33–65.

Traugott, Elizabeth Closs and Richard B. Dasher (2002). *Regularity in Semantic Change.* Cambridge: Cambridge University Press.

Zwicky, Arnold (1995). Exceptional degree markers: a puzzle in internal and external syntax. *Ohio State University Working Papers in Linguistics* 47: 111–23.

15 Information Structure and Word Order Change: The Passive as an Information-rearranging Strategy in the History of English

ELENA SEOANE

15.1 Introduction

In 1977 Li described word order change as "the most drastic and complex category of syntactic changes" (1977: xii). Indeed, the word order change which English underwent at some time between Old, Middle and Early Modern English has been ascribed to a whole myriad of determining factors. These have mostly been identified as of a syntactic nature, such as the leveling of inflections, the principle of end-weight or the integration and grammaticalization of afterthought material. More recently, a number of studies have shown the influence of communicative pragmatic parameters on word order change in English. Still, the pragmatic/discourse structure side of the coin has not yet been sufficiently explored.

Consequently, this study is sustained by the belief that a comprehensive account of diachronic developments such as word order change needs to take into consideration both syntactic and pragmatic factors. This seems to be Jucker's (1995: ix) view when he asserts, with regard to the recent upsurge of historical pragmatics, that

> It seems only natural that pragmatic and historical linguistics should be combined in order to pose and perhaps even answer questions concerning the use of language at different stages of its development.

I therefore intend to examine the interaction between syntax and pragmatics as reflected in the diachronic development of the passive construction. Accordingly, I will show that the substantial developments in the syntax of the passive in Middle and Early Modern English, as well as its increase in frequency, are strongly determined by pragmatic factors, namely the need to place pragmatically salient NPs in unmarked topic position.

In my argumentation I start with one of the most significant aftermaths of the structural change in English, namely the progressive rigidification of word order and the subsequent reduction of the number of alternative ways of organizing information in the sentence. As a consequence, the preverbal unmarked topic position becomes identified as the subject position, so that the former (relative) freedom to locate any constituent conveying old information in initial, unmarked topic position is lost. Therefore, new ordering strategies are implemented or, alternatively, old strategies that proved useful to rearrange information are promoted. One of these strategies is the passive construction, which has been described as an argument-reversing device whereby a non-agent can be made subject of a passive, that is, can be promoted to unmarked topic position.

I thus begin with outlining the word order change in English and its causes (section 15.2), with a greater emphasis on the relevance of pragmatic factors in the ordering of information (section 15.3). Subsequently, in section 15.4.1 I describe the identification between subject and unmarked topic in English. Finally, in 15.4.2 I analyze the role of the passive as an information-rearranging device in the critical period when the change is made visible.

15.2 Word Order in English: Changes and Causes

Word order change in the history of English has been the subject of extensive research. There seems to be a general consensus now that Old English (OE) had some kind of verb-second (V2) constraint by which the finite verb took second position in declarative main clauses, and that it was in the course of the Middle English (ME) period that the language acquired its present status as a verb-medial language. As to the post-ME developments, although Early Modern English (EModE) has received considerably less attention than earlier periods of the language, there is growing evidence to claim that EModE shows a strong tendency towards verb-medial order, but this tendency is not yet grammaticalized in the period, at least not in the sense of exhibiting the set patterns and fixed rules which characterize present-day English (cf. Jacobsson 1951; Görlach 1990, 1991; Breivik and Swan 1994; Stein 1995; Bech 1998, 2001; Bækken 1998, 2003; Van der Wurff 2001).

In accounting for this major word order change from V2 to verb-medial, scholars have mainly adduced syntactic explanations. The traditional view has been that the fixation of verb-medial word order derives from the leveling of inflections and the consequent need to signal syntactic functions through alternative means, namely word order. Thus, verb-medial order would be favored as a useful device to disambiguate between formally similar subject and object NPs (Sapir 1921; Fries 1940; Vennemann 1973, 1974; Kohonen 1978). Even if ambiguity avoidance may have played a role in the fixation of verb-medial order, the context itself would often be enough to distinguish the subject from the object, and therefore verb-medial word order does not appear necessary as a disambiguating device. Moreover, it has been shown that verb-medial word order was widely attested already in OE, which is before the case system actually collapsed. If the OE syntactic system relies on both word order and inflection, the word order restructuring must have taken place pretty independently of any change in the case system (cf. Carlton 1970; Breivik 1990; Faarlund 1990: 51).

Another factor that has been suggested as partially responsible for the fixation of verb-medial word order is the so-called "afterthought phenomenon" (Givón 1975; Hyman 1975; Vennemann 1975). Here, the speaker decides to add yet another element after the verb-final utterance, as if responding to a pragmatic and communicative need to complement what he has already said. This hypothesis is discussed in Faarlund (1990: 54ff.), who rejects it for a number of reasons, the most important being that it only justifies the addition of objects and adverbials, while it does not contemplate the possibility that subjects can be added as afterthoughts too (cf. also Kohonen 1978).

Constituent weight has also been discussed in connection with the word order change. Kohonen (1978), for example, found that the position of the vast majority of constituents in early ME correlates with the principle of end-weight. This factor alone, however, cannot have played a significant role in determining the change because there is a clear continuity from OE to DE in this respect.

A different explanation is provided by Kroch, Taylor, and Ringe (2000) and has more recently been pursued by Trips (2002). These authors argue that the loss of V2 is the result of language acquisition in a contact area. They demonstrate that in ME the northern and southern dialects differed in the way they implemented the V2 constraint, so that in the North the V2 constraint is similar to the one found in the language of the Viking settlers (and similar to the one operating in Dutch and German today), while in the South it is like the one found in OE. According to the authors, this difference is "a syntactic consequence of contact-induced simplification in the verbal agreement paradigm of the northern dialect" (Kroch et al. 2000: 354). Subsequent contact between northern and southern speakers led to a mixture of northern and southern features that resulted in the loss of V2.

However brief, the foregoing exposition of the issue shows that word order change cannot be seen otherwise than as a complex interplay of various factors and, therefore, does not appear amenable to an explanation in terms of one single perspective only, certainly not in terms of the hitherto prevailing autonomous systemic considerations. As this pronouncement has been voiced most clearly on the grounds of functionalism, I thus accordingly share the functionally grounded conviction that "language cannot be conceptualized or described separate from its functions in discourse" (Copeland 2000: xv). Most revealing of the spirit of the present research is the following remark that Givón (2001: xv) makes as an allusion to the form and/or function dilemma:

> [W]hile structures without functions are plainly senseless, functions without structures are downright lame. The hallmark of biological design is that organisms perform their adaptive functions with structured organs.

With this conviction in mind, I assume that neither isolated syntactic criteria nor appraised pragmatic considerations alone can prove infallible in explaining the change from V2 to verb-medial word order in English, as both kinds of considerations can be found monitoring and manipulating the use of language. As Abraham and Molnárfi (2003: 1) point out, the explanatory framework that would account for word order variation "seems to lie in the very conflict zone of two mainstreams of modern linguistic theorizing, viz. formalism and functionalism, which represent two different (and possibly incompatible) views on word order variation." However, while the general atmosphere in linguistics has been favorable for non-autonomous syntactic attempts for quite some time now, only a few studies have allowed for the possibility that pragmatic discourse features may at all have influenced the word order change that English once underwent, and these, as I will show below, have failed to offer a convincing functional explanation for the decline of V2. Faced with the scarcity of discourse-oriented analyses, I primarily intend to underline the importance of pragmatic discourse factors in word order variation. In the section that follows, I sketch the relationship between pragmatic factors and word order in the history of English.

15.3 Word Order in English: Pragmatic Considerations

Examination of an OE text immediately reveals that despite the fact that a large number of declarative main clauses do display V2 order, such as (1) below, OE is not as consistent a V2 language as Present-day Dutch or German. There can be found quite a few examples of main clauses in OE that run counter to the V2 constraint. This is the case of (2), which exhibits the order XSV:

(1) *Þa gelomp þætte Gregorius betwoh oðre eac þider cwom*
Then happened that Gregory among others also thither came
'Then it happened that Gregory, among others, also came there'
(*Bede*, 96: 8)

(2) *On ðæm gefeohte Poros 7 Alexander gefuhton anwig on horsum*
'In that fight Poros and Alexander fought a duel on horseback'
(*Orosius*, 72: 15)

Let us now consider examples (3), from *Blickling Homilies* (ed. Morris, p. 97, quoted in van Kemenade 1987: 127) and (4), from Bech (2001: 62).

(3) *Forðon we sceolan mid ealle mod and mægene to Gode gecyrran*
Therefore we must with all mind and power to God turn
'Therefore we must turn to God with all our mind and power'

(4) *Heold he 7 rehte þa cyricean on þara casera tidum Maurici 7 Uocati*
Ruled he and directed the church in of-the emperors time Mauricius and Phocas
'He ruled and directed the church in the time of the emperors Mauricius and Phocas'
(*Bede*, 94: 6)

Examples like (3), which exhibit the order XSV and, therefore, seem to contravene the V2 rule, are frequent in OE. They show a pronominal subject preceding the finite verb and following a topicalized constituent (not an operator, i.e. a *wh*-word, the negator *ne* or an adverb like *þa*). The standard accounts for these clauses are that the verb is indeed in second position (V2) but has taken along the pronoun as a clitic (Kemenade 1987; Koopman 1997; Pintzuk 1999) or that the verb is fronted, but to a lower position (Kemenade 2000).

Example (4) illustrates V1, another word order pattern attested in OE which is also characteristic of modern West Germanic V2 languages. V1, which has a clear stylistic function in narrative prose, is generally interpreted as V being also in second position underlyingly with a non-overt narrative operator in the first position (cf. Diesing 1990). In any case, it is a stylistic word order deviation typical of V2 languages which cannot be taken as counter-evidence for the V2 nature of OE.

The disparity of word order patterns in OE main declarative clauses has brought scholars to justify the extent to which OE can be described as a V2 language at all. To mention one example, Haiman (1974) holds the view that OE is a V2 language on account of the development of dummy subjects in English, which, as is well known, is typical of languages which either are or have been subject to the V2 constraint, their function being that of filling the initial position in clauses where no other element occupies it (cf. also Breivik 1991).

In general, the strength of the verb-second restriction induces most scholars to classify OE as a V2 language. That, on the other hand, there are alternative word order patterns, such as that illustrated in (2) above, would simply indicate that V2 in OE is a word order norm that is not fully grammaticalized (Haiman 1974; Stockwell 1977, 1984; Vennemann 1974, 1984; Breivik 1990; Lightfoot 1991; Van Hoorick 1994; Ehala 1998; Los 2002; Miller 2002).

The fact that V2 word order is not categorical in OE is possibly highly significant in view of the fact that V2 was subsequently lost. It could indicate that the loss of V2 is already under way in OE, and that therefore some of the driving forces behind the change might be identified in that period. In order to ascertain whether any of these driving forces are pragmatic in nature, it would be necessary to demonstrate that the word order variation observed in OE is a sign that it was possible to modify word order so as to meet pragmatic constraints in the language. It is in this line that Bech (1998, 2001) conducts a study in which she examines the information structure of OE and ME clauses with an initial element other than the subject (X) followed by inversion (XVS, a typical V2 pattern) or non-inversion (XSV, a typical verb-medial pattern), whereas Bækken (1998, 2003) supplements her study by examining the same structures in a large EModE corpus.

A quick look at Bech's and Bækken's data immediately allows for two major generalizations. Firstly, the V2 constraint is by no means obligatory in OE; secondly, the rate of non-inverted patterns (XSV) increases markedly all the way from OE to EModE at the expense of inverted patterns (XVS). Unfortunately, however, their data cannot be given indiscriminately as evidence for the use of V2 in OE or for its subsequent decay and loss, since (i) they do not make a distinction between pronominal and full NP subjects; as shown in example (3), preverbal pronouns occurring after an initial topicalized element are regarded as clitics, so that the V2 order is not disrupted in these examples. In other words, many of the examples that these two authors classify as XSV (verb-medial) are in fact V2.

Another factor that undoubtedly alters the incidence of V2 in their account is that (ii) they fail to filter out clauses introduced by coordinating conjunctions (also called *conjunct clauses*), which, as is well known, often exhibit subclause rather than main clause orders. It must be noted that Bech (2001: 93–4) shows the distribution of word order patterns in Old and Middle English when clitics are taken into account and conjunct clauses are disregarded. However, she does not incorporate these data into her general account of the loss of V2 on the grounds that the clitic hypothesis "serves to obscure the picture when it comes to the question of word order development" (2001: 94). For this reason, the data provided by Bech and Bækken on word order variation in OE and on the decline of V2 are not useful; consequently, when it comes to determining the factors responsible for the use of V2 their analysis cannot be relied on either.

What their work does demonstrate, however, is that the distribution of information in XSV and XVS constructions, independently of whether the subject is a pronoun or a full NP, testifies to a tendency to structure the discourse in such a way that given information precedes new information in the sentence in all the periods examined, that is from Old to Early Modern English (cf. also Kohonen 1978, for this attestation in ME material). There is, therefore, a subtle association between pragmatic discourse factors, such as the arrangement of information in a given–new sequence, and word order arrangements. This does not mean, however, that the all-embracing determinant of the word order change under consideration can hope to be found among pragmatic discourse principles alone, since the arrangement of sentential constituents in terms of given–new information observed in the three periods examined was never challenged in the history of English. As was mentioned before, it will be necessary to incorporate both syntactic and pragmatic factors in a comprehensive account of word order change. The decline of V2, therefore, remains a puzzle still to be accounted for.

A new question, however, emerges at this point. On the one hand, the tendency to arrange information in a given–new sequence remained constant in the history of English. On the other hand, word order changed and, moreover, it became less variable, which is an indication of the well-known gradual grammaticalization of the ordering of constituents at clause level which took place in English (Bernárdez and Tejada 1995; Bech 1998). Consequently, the language must have implemented new ways of making it possible for the distribution of information to be structured along the given–new sequence. In other words, the decline of V2 must have had repercussions elsewhere in the grammar so that the pragmatic ordering of information could still be maintained despite the changes and fixation of word order. Section 15.4 below is an attempt to illustrate this interplay between syntax and pragmatics; it examines the role of pragmatic factors in the use and development of the passive construction, a syntactic device with an argument-reversing function.

15.4 The Passive as an Information-rearranging Strategy in the History of English

So far, I have described the pragmatic import of main declarative sentences exclusively in terms of the given–new structuring of information. However, initial position in PE does not correlate merely with given information, but also with a whole array of syntactic, semantic, and pragmatic features which make up the notion of "topic." These features will be discussed in some detail in connection with the passive in section 15.4.2.

At this point, nevertheless, it may prove desirable to provide a working definition of "topic." From the syntactic angle, topic seems to be the first propositional constituent of the clause, and, hence, is identified with initial position (Hinds 1975; Hutchins 1975; Chafe 1976; Li and Thompson 1976; Halliday 1985; Pérez Guerra 1999). When it comes to a purely semantic conception of topic, the notion tends to be defined as the constituent which states what the clause is about (Foley 1994; Kuppevel, 1994; Lambrech, 1994; Kis, 1998). Finally, at the pragmatic level, topic has mainly been viewed as the sentence element providing given (old) information, which is the element with the lowest degree of communicative dynamism defined by Firbas as "the extent to which the sentence element contributes to the development of the communication" (1966: 270; cf. Lyons 1968; Dahl 1974; Chafe 1976; Dik 1980; Prince 1985).

In thematically unmarked declarative clauses in English, it is the subject which encodes the unmarked topic. This association between subject and unmarked topic is relevant in any study of passivization since passives create new subjects; that is, they can rearrange clause constituents in such a way that a NP other than the agent is turned into the unmarked topic/subject of the sentence.

For this reason, an explanation of the association between subject and topic seems in order here.

15.4.1 Subjects as unmarked topics in English

The three definitions of topic outlined above are useful to describe a well-established correspondence between subject and topic in English. To be specific, English subjects are unmarked topics in declarative sentences. The subject–topic correlation is, in fact, so strong that it is at times claimed to be a universal feature of natural language. The subject of a sentence in any given language will then be interpreted as its topic, unless such a sentence is marked from a morphological, syntactic, prosodic, or semantic perspective. For example, in his cross-linguistic analysis, Sornicola (1994: 4346) provides the following Hierarchy of Accessibility to topic position: "Subject > indirect object > direct object > locative complement > manner complement." Notice that the prime candidate for the position of topic is precisely the subject.

The reason most commonly adduced to explain this universal tendency to encode the topic as the grammatical subject is the fact that subjects usually convey easily accessible language data. Firstly, subjects normally have human referents, and this reflects the "unqualified interest of humans in the ego, their conversational partners and other humans" (Siewierska 1994: 4996). Secondly, subjects most often play the semantic role of agent. That the agent role is pragmatically prominent is because, as the Principle of Iconicity predicts, languages tend to reflect the natural progression of actions and events in the real world, and these normally start with the agent (Givón 1985; Siewierska, 1994; Hori, 2000). These two features of subjects, animacy and agentivity, correlate with a high degree of accessibility of the language material, which, in turn, involves an easy and automatic processing mode on the part of the hearer. The co-occurrence of animacy and agentivity appears to be confirmed by psycholinguistic research (cf. the summary in Bock 1982, and also Halliday 2000: 224).

From a pragmatic perspective topic is equated with information that is given and, thus, available for quick retrieval. This explains why subjects are the prime candidates to become topics: they are high in accessibility and easy to process. Similarly, in the semantically driven definition, topic indicates the position of the referent about which something is predicated. The notion of "aboutness" relates directly also to pragmatic salience and prominence, and, as already noted, the animacy and agentivity features of subjects make them salient (central) in the sense that the former reflects the tendency of humans to talk about themselves and other humans, while the latter captures the iconic ordering of constituents in line with the actual temporal succession of events.

Finally, it would also be of interest to justify why topics tend to be placed in initial position cross-linguistically. The starting point could be Prince's (1981b: 224) famous view that

> [P]erhaps this is not only universal, but also distinctive of human language – the crucial factor appears to be the tailoring of an utterance by a sender to meet the particular assumed needs of the intended receiver. That is, information-packaging in natural language reflects the sender's hypotheses about the receiver's assumptions and beliefs and strategies.

According to her, a characteristic feature of human language is that it is addressee-oriented, which means that the speaker will shape his discourse taking into account the addressee's need for clarity and distinctiveness. The addressee-oriented language is claimed to be the optimal communicative system because it is more difficult for the listener to decode the message than for the speaker to encode it. Placing topical material in initial position is an addressee-oriented strategy, since it provides the addressee with an easily accessible and familiar referent that can serve both as the perspective from which to interpret the new information in the sentence and/or as a link with previous discourse. In Sornicola's (1994: 4639) words:

> [I]t seems a fairly general property of human communication under nonemphatic conditions, to organize the information flow in the utterance according to a strategy of centering attention on specific information units first, and then giving prominence to others. This might well be a universal tendency across natural languages, which accounts for semantic or structural configurations such as topic-comment, subject-predicate, NP-VP, etc.

Both the universal strength of the subject–topic correlation and topic-initial position as well as its relevance in an addressee-oriented system, are supported by the widely attested preference for subject–object ordering in the basic constituent orders of the world's languages (Greenberg 1966). Further evidence that topical subjects in initial position are listener-friendly is that Creoles usually prefer SV-based order, as this has been related to the fact that speakers are likely to adopt a listener-oriented form of speech in situations where accessibility of speech to its listener is not easily predictable (Bernárdez and Tejada 1995: 232).

Whereas the subject is the only unmarked topic in PDE, OE (as a V2 language) imposes no restriction upon the syntactic category that can encode an unmarked topic. So, for example, an object or an adverbial can be used as topics without implying a contrast; cf. (5), from Los (2002: 187), where the topic is an adverbial:

(5) *Be ðisum lytlan man mæg understandan*
By this little one may understand
'By means of this little thing can be understood . . .'
(ÆGenPref 72)

After the loss of V2, encoding given–new information structure becomes constrained by the fact that the initial position is reserved, in thematically unmarked clauses, for nominal subjects. The loss of V2, therefore, involves a drastic reduction in the possibilities so far available to place any constituent in unmarked topic position. The only way of expressing alternatives of topic choice came to be the selection of different subjects, as can be seen, for example, in the pair *Tears* (= topic) *streamed down her face* vs. *Her face* (= topic) *streamed with tears* (from Foley 1994: 1679).

According to Los (2002: 189) it is not coincidental that from the early fifteenth century the language produces a number of innovative devices which can turn topical constituents into subjects, such as the prepositional passive, as in *The doctor was sent for*, and subject-to-object raising, as in *Those towns were thought to be empty*; the latter construction tends to occur in the passive (cf. Noël 1998; Los 2002), because the passive construction turns the patient of an active transitive clause into the subject, thus enabling it to be fronted without becoming a marked topic.

Given the substantial developments in the syntax of the passive that were still under way in EModE (e.g. the consolidation of the indirect and prepositional passives, the establishment of the *by*-phrase; cf. in this connection Seoane 1993: 199–212; 1999; Moessner 1994: 218–24), it is tempting to hypothesize that such developments may have semantic and discoursal correlates. In the light of the discussion so far, the following hypothesis seems tenable: the loss of V2, and the resulting restriction that only subjects can be unmarked topics, brought about the promotion of the passive as a word order-rearranging strategy which can, in addition, create subjects/unmarked topics. Such a stratagem would not have been necessary before the loss of V2, since at that stage there was no ban on any constituent to become an unmarked theme. See (6a), from Bech (2001: 64), where V2 makes it possible to topicalize the non-agent pronoun *us*:

(6) a. *And ðy us deriað 7 ðearle dyrfað fela ungelimpa*
And then us harm and severely injure many misfortunes
'And then many misfortunes will severely harm and injure us'
(*WHom*, 124:20)

The arrangement of constituents found in (6a), i.e. a patient in unmarked topic position (*us*) followed by an agent in focus position (*fela ungelimpa*) can only be attained, after the loss of V2, through the use of the passive voice (6b):

(6) b. *And then we will be severely harmed and injured by many misfortunes*

If my hypothesis is correct, what we should expect from the fifteenth century onwards is a steady increase in the frequency of passives with topical subjects, the tendency that would qualify as the speaker's response to the need to subjectivize constituents other than the agent.

15.4.2 *The passive as an argument-reversing strategy in the history of English*

This section tries to ascertain whether the hypothesis advanced in the previous section can be confirmed, namely that the loss of V2 brought about the promotion of passives as an argument-reversing strategy capable of creating unmarked topics/subjects. I will proceed to establish to what extent, if any at all, my assertion can be evidenced on empirical grounds. As what I expect of the passive is some kind of structure–use correlation, I will in the first place briefly outline the functional dimension of the passive.

As a member of the thematic system of voice, the passive involves two related phenomena: firstly, *subject backgrounding*, whereby the subject/topic of an active transitive clause is removed from the forefront of the clause, the prototypical topic position. Secondly, *object foregrounding* or *topicalization* (Givón 1981, 1982), which involves promotion of a non-agent to subject and topic position. As a topicalizing device, the passive serves essentially a two-pronged purpose; on the one hand, it restores the unmarked given/new order of information within the clause (7); on the other hand, it places an inherently topical NP in topic position (8–9):

(7) [I spoke to John last Tuesday.] He said he had been betrayed by Peter only a week earlier.

(8) John was chased by this car

(9) The roots of my saplings were ruined by a mole

In (7) the passive serves the purpose of topicalizing a patient NP conveying given information; the referent of *he*, namely *John*, is given information by virtue of being present in the previous linguistic context. As will be explained later in this section, sentence (8) is more likely to occur than its active counterpart because the patient is higher on the animacy hierarchy than the original subject. Similarly, in example (9) the function of the passive is to topicalize a patient which is more definite and, therefore, inherently more topical than the agent.

Although they are two distinct functions, subject backgrounding and object foregrounding can often be identified in one and the same passive construction. However, the subject backgrounding function is undoubtedly the primary motivation for the use of passives lacking an overt *by*-phrase, i.e. the so-called short passives. These serve the purpose of demoting the agent completely by omitting it, and, as is well known, the most effective way of backgrounding a constituent is not to encode it syntactically. Long passives, on the contrary, background the agent to a lesser extent, since this remains present in the form of a *by*-phrase, and object foregrounding factors seem to be more prominent. What is more, only long passives constitute argument-reversing strategies, which are triggered by the imbalance between subject and object in terms of topicality.

Table 15.1 Number of words examined, with indication of actives and passives and of relative frequency of passives with respect to actives

	Words	*Actives*	*Percent active*	*Passives*	*Percent passive*
M4 (1420–1500)	44,000	2,928	81.9	647	18.0
E1 (1500–1570)	50,000	2,236	78.5	612	21.4
E2 (1570–1640)	48,000	2,550	77.9	722	22.0
E3 (1640–1710)	55,000	2,893	75.8	922	24.1
Total	197,000	10,607	78.5	2,903	21.3

In Givón's words, "the pragmatics of voice involves the *relative topicality* of the agent and patient participants of the event" (1993: 47; emphasis in the original).

In order to examine the role of the passive as an argument-reversing device after the loss of V2, it is necessary to analyze, therefore, the topicality features of the subject and agent NPs in passive constructions. My research is based on data retrieved from the computerized *Helsinki Corpus*. The sample used covers the period from the early fifteenth to the early eighteenth centuries. Table 15.1 shows the number of words examined and the ratio of passives with respect to actives in each chronological subperiod. The count of active constructions was restricted to those for which a passive counterpart would be available, that is, to those active transitive constructions with an overt object eligible to become passive subject.

Table 15.1 shows that the proportion of passives with respect to actives steadily increases from the fifteenth century onwards. It will be interesting to ascertain whether this general increase in the frequency of the passive correlates with an increase in its use as an argument-reversing strategy determined by pragmatic factors.

As for the textual composition of the corpus, I selected a balanced proportion of typically formal and informal text types (in the compilers' terminology, cf. Nevalainen and Raumolin-Brunberg 1993), since stylistic factors intervene in the choice of passive vs. active. I singled out three text types classified as formal, namely *Law*, *Science*, and *Sermons*, and three informal text types, *Private Letters*, *Fiction*, and *Drama*, which represent a language which is closer to the oral style. These two groups of text types are also representative of, respectively, informative vs. imaginative registers, another variable that is claimed to play a role in the choice of passives (cf. Svartvik 1966; Francis and Kucera 1982; Bernárdez and Tejada 1995; Kennedy 2001).

As can be seen in table 15.2, no text belonging to *Science* has been included in the late ME period. The only *Science* text available in the *Helsinki Corpus* for the period 1420–1500 (M4) is *The Cyrurgie of Guy de Chauliac* (Kytö 1991: 12–13). This text exhibits an unusually high frequency of passives as well as

Table 15.2 Distribution of short and long passives by text type

	Middle English		*Early Modern English*		
	Short	*Long*	*Short*	*Long*	*Total*
Law	217 (76.4%)	67 (23.5%)	804 (78.0%)	226 (21.9%)	1,314/52.0%
Science	—	—	368 (88.6%)	47 (11.3%)	—/31.6%
Sermons	72 (90%)	8 (10%)	154 (80.2%)	38 (19.7%)	272/22.5%
Private letters	102 (91.0%)	10 (8.9%)	340 (93.4%)	24 (6.5%)	476/13.0%
Drama	72 (92.3%)	6 (7.6%)	126 (96.1%)	5 (3.8%)	209/10.4%
Fiction	93 (100%)	0	115 (92.7%)	9 (7.2%)	217/7.1%
Total	Short = 2,463	(84.8%)	Long = 440	(15.1%)	

an unusual passive–active proportion: 228–161. In other words, in this text passives are, surprisingly enough, more numerous than actives. The reason is that it is a translation from Latin (Kytö 1991: 12–13); moreover, its style has been shown to be highly unidiomatic and far removed from the normal English idiom of the time (Donner 1986: 398). This text would undoubtedly bias my results, which has led me to disregard it.

We mentioned earlier that the study of the passive as an order-rearranging device concerns only long passives, i.e. passives with the demoted agent in a *by*-phrase, for they are most likely to have been triggered by pragmatic factors as an argument-reversal strategy (cf. Birner and Ward 1998: 155ff.). Table 15.2 isolates short and long passives in the different text types and periods; as in other quantitative studies the proportion of long passives (15.1 percent) was found to be much lower than that of short passives (84.8 percent) (cf. Svartvik 1966 and Dusková 1971, on PDE passives; Bækken 1998, on EModE).

The percentages underlined in the right-hand column show the proportion of passives with respect to actives in each text type. As was expected, the passive is greatly favored in the formal text types examined, namely *Law*, *Science*, and *Sermons*. More interesting is the association observed between such formal text types and long passives in particular. As mentioned, a number of scholars provide evidence that one of the most significant factors conditioning the textual distribution of the passive is whether the text is informative, where long passives abound, or imaginative, with lower frequencies for long passives. The reason adduced is that the passive "may reflect perhaps a stronger rheme-focus in informative prose" (Kennedy 2001: 41). From the data expounded in table 15.2 we can gather that the passive as an argument-reversing strategy is more relevant in formal, informative texts, while the use of the passive as a means of eliding a non-topical agent seems to be more prominent in imaginative text types. Aside from the formal/informal and informative/imaginative variables, it is important to bear in mind the written/oral style characteristic of texts. Ellipsis is more common in speech-based texts, which may well determine the higher proportion of short passives in informal texts. In prototypically written styles, on the contrary, given information is repeated and must, therefore, be integrated in clause structure. In contexts where the patient is given information the passive will be resorted to.

In what follows I will examine the topicality features of passive subjects as compared to those of *by*-phrases in order to find out whether the use of the passive as an argument-reversing strategy in the corpus is controlled by such features. Some of the hypotheses concerning the diachrony of the passive as an information-rearranging device are also presented in Seoane (2000).

Statistical data gleaned from cross-language investigations show that the eligibility of nominal topics depends on an array of syntactic, semantic, and pragmatic factors. Several ordering hierarchies have been discussed in the literature. Following Allan (1987), discussed in Siewierska (1988: 29ff.), I have classified the most relevant of such hierarchies into the three following groups, based on, respectively, syntactic, semantic, and pragmatic criteria. NPs with features figuring at the left of these hierarchies are more likely candidates to become topics than those displaying the features on the right of the hierarchies.

These are not the only variables available in the literature. Boucher and Osgood (1969), for example, have put forward the Pollyanna hypothesis, according to which the speaker should place affectively positive information earlier in sentences than affectively negative information. Stein (1995: 133) also recognizes the "left-shifted element to have some sort of affective meaning in addition to propositional meaning." Another well-known hierarchy is that distinguishing between referential vs. non-referential material. However, the term is far from clear; while for Foley (1994: 1682), for example, "A nominal is referential if the speaker intends that it refer to a particular entity in the world", for Givón (1992: 16–17) *referential accessibility* is the "referential distance" (number of clauses from the last occurrence of the NP in the preceding discourse; cf. also Svoboda 1981:178ff.; Bækken 1998: 301). Referentiality in Foley's view overlaps, in my opinion, with another pragmatic hierarchy, that between definite and indefinite. As for the referential distance explained in Givón, there is no agreement as to the extent of the span of discourse during which an element will remain present in the consciousness of the interlocutor, and this factor may well be context/text type-dependent.

The Formal Hierarchies
structurally simpler > structurally complex
short > long

The Dominance Hierarchies

The personal hierarchy:	1st p. > 2nd p. > 3rd p. human > higher animals > other organisms > inorganic matter > abstract

The semantic role hierarchy: agent > recipient/benefactive > patient > instrumental > spatial > temporal

The Familiarity Hierarchies
given > new
definite > indefinite

The remainder of this section outlines the results of the examination of my data as regards the topicality features described in the above-mentioned hierarchies.

The Formal Hierarchies: length and complexity: It has long been assumed that the principle of end-weight, which refers to the tendency of syntactically heavy phrases to occupy clause-final position, has always been operative in the history of English. There is also compelling evidence that such a tendency is cross-linguistic, and that the weight of an element, i.e. its length and complexity, co-varies inversely with the accessibility of its referent. Therefore, at least some word order rearrangements may have their basis in the weight of the constituents involved (Siewierska 1994: 4997; Birner and Ward 1998: 24). In fact, authors such as Hawkins (1994: 240–1) are of the opinion that syntactic weight is the major determinant of word order, pragmatic factors being only epiphenomenal.

As an argument-reversing strategy, the passive voice serves the purpose of rearranging clause constituents in order to comply with the principle of end-weight. In the corpus, subjects and *by*-phrases have been analyzed as regards their length (number of words) and syntactic complexity. *By*-phrases have proved to be longer and more complex than passive subjects in 335 (76.1 percent) out of the 440 long passives in the corpus; this tendency is reversed in 58 examples, while in 47 the subject and *by*-phrase are similar as regards their length and complexity. Therefore, end-weight has been found to constitute an important principle in the overall structuring of information in the passive sentences in the corpus.

The Dominance Hierarchies (i): the personal hierarchy: The personal hierarchy predicts that in PDE those NPs whose referent is human, [+H], are more likely candidates to become topics than those whose referent is non-human [–H]. Among non-human referents, those being animate, [+A], are more likely to be selected as topics than inanimate ones [–A]. Therefore, it is NPs whose referents bear the [+H+A] features which tend to occupy topic position (cf. Silverstein 1976; the Animated First Principle in Tomlin 1987; Croft 1990). As mentioned in section 15.4.1, the personal hierarchy reflects the tendency to talk about humans, a preference which is consistently adhered to on a cross-linguistic basis. In fact, the effects of the animacy hierarchy are categorical in some languages, such as Lummi, which have person-driven passives (Bresnan et al. 2001). Situations arise in which the patient NP of an active clause is human and animate, while the agent NP is [–H–A]. Passivization, by fronting and subjectivizing the patient, topicalizes that NP whose characteristics make it more

Table 15.3 Human and animacy features of the subject and agent

Subject/Agent		
[+H+A]/[–H–A]	38	(28.1%)
[–H–A]/[+H+A]	97	(71.8%)

eligible to become topic. In order to ascertain the extent to which the passives in the corpus serve this purpose, the human and animacy features of the subject and *by*-phrase were examined and compared. Table 15.3 shows the results; it includes only the data relative to passives in which the subject and the *by*-phrase differ as regards their human and animacy features, which total 135 out of 440. In the remaining 305 long passives in the corpus, the features under study are irrelevant as regards triggering the use of the passive, for the following reasons: (i) the subject and agent share the same human and animacy features (125 examples); (ii) 23 long passives occur in comment clauses introduced by relative *as* (e.g. *she left the country, as was expected*; Quirk et al. 1985: 1112–17); (iii) 157 long passives have a clause as subject

Table 15.3 reveals that only 28.1 percent of passives topicalize a patient NP whose referent is higher than the agent in the animacy hierarchy. The reverse case, that in which a [–H–A] patient is promoted to topic position despite the fact that the agent is [+H+A], and should, therefore, have become topic, takes place in more than 70 percent of the passives. This is illustrated in (10):

(10) But as the Earth, the Mother of all Creatures here below, sends up all its Vapours and proper emissions at the command of the Sun, and yet requires them again to refresh her own Needs, and they are deposited between them both in the bosome of a Cloud as a common receptacle, that they may cool his Flames, and yet descend to make her Fruitful: So are **the proprieties of a Wife** to be dispos'd of by **her Lord**; (|QE3_IR_SERM_JETAYLO: 12)

In the vast majority of cases, therefore, the passive subject is lower on the animacy hierarchy than the *by*-phrase.

Within human referents, speech-act participants (SAPs), that is, NPs with first and second person referents, outrank human third person referents (cf. the Empathy Hierarchy in Kuno and Kaburaki 1977; DeLancey 1981; Foley 1994). Among the 440 agent passives in the corpus, only 19 involve SAPs, and most of them (16 out of 19) are patient NPs which have been topicalized via passivization, and thus conform to the tendency for SAPs to occupy subject/topic position. There are, however, three instances, as that illustrated in (11), in which this tendency is reversed, since an agent SAP is relegated to final position and to the status of oblique adjunct.

(11) I may hope to see you at Easter, which time will be much longed for by **me**. (|QE2_XX_CORP_HARLEY: 90)

This example would hardly be possible today (in this connection, see further section ii (Definite > indefinite), below). PDE would definitely prefer an active construction with the SAP in subject position (e.g. *a time I will much long for*).

We must, then, conclude that, contrary to PDE, the personal hierarchy does not trigger the use of the passive as an argument-reversing strategy in our period, since only 28.1 percent of the examples comply with it. Such a conclusion seems to go against the cross-linguistic tendency to talk about human and, specially, first person subjects, and appears to confirm the data adduced by Strang (1970) and Söderlind (1951–8) for earlier periods of the language.

The Dominance Hierarchies (ii): the semantic role hierarchy: A second semantic factor that determines the eligibility of a NP to become topic, and, may, therefore, lead to the use of long passives in the corpus, is the semantic role of the NP in question. According to the semantic role hierarchy, the most likely candidates to become topics are NPs with the role of agent, followed by those with the role of recipient/benefactive, patient, and oblique. As already mentioned, the ordering of elements in line with this hierarchy can be said to constitute one of the strongest manifestations of the iconic character of language, since it is consistent with the perceived directionality of events (Siewierska 1994: 4996–7). This hierarchy accounts, *inter alia,* for the higher frequency of actives over passives in English, since the former have agents as subjects/topics; secondly, it also accounts for the preference for indirect over direct passives in PDE (Huddleston 1984: 440–1), since the former topicalize NPs whose semantic role is that of recipient/benefactive while the latter topicalize NPs with the role of patients.

In order to ascertain whether the semantic role of NPs is a determining factor for the topicalization of such NPs via passivization in the corpus, I analyzed the semantic role of the topicalized NP in the passives of ditransitive clauses. As is obvious, passives from monotransitive clauses were not examined, since they only have the possibility of topicalizing the patient NP. As for passives from ditransitive actives, the only two possible semantic roles that the NP subject of the passive can have are that of patient, if it is the DO that is promoted to subject, or, in the case of IOs promoted to passive subjects, that of recipient/benefactive.

Table 15.4 shows that it is the passive with the DO as subject which prevails, since it occurs in 77.2 percent of the long passives from ditransitive actives,

Table 15.4 Passives from ditransitive actives in EModE

	Long passives	*Short passives*	*Total*
IO as subject (24.2%)	5 (22.7%)	36 (24.4%)	41
DO as subject (75.7%)	17 (77.2%)	111 (75.5%)	128

while the IO/benefactive is promoted to subject only in 22.7 percent of the cases. That the passive of ditransitives with the direct object as subject is more in favor in late ME and EModE than nowadays is observed in (12), where the verb *allow* is used in the direct passive, a construction that would be highly unlikely in PDE.

(12) and the other halfe to such person or p~sons as shall sue or informe for the same in any Court of Recorde, by Action of Debte Bill Plainte or Information, wherein **no Essoyne Protection or Wager of Lawe shall be allowed to the Defendant.** (|QE2_STA_LAW_STAT4: 19).

Therefore, the PDE tendency to topicalize NPs with roles high up on the semantic hierarchy is not observed in my EModE corpus. It must be borne in mind that passivization of IOs is greatly restricted in late ME and EModE not only because of semantic factors, but also because the indirect passive was still undergoing a process of consolidation (cf. Söderlind 1951–8; Kisbye 1972; Visser 1963–73; Strang 1970; Denison 1993; Moessner 1994).

To end this section, let us recall the strong association between human referent – agent role – topic discourse function, which was described in section 15.4.1 and captured in the two Dominance Hierarchies just analyzed. For some authors, this association goes as far as to entail a cause–effect relationship: "The grammatical subject (usually an agent or an experiencer) is the most common topic because it is the argument most likely to have the feature [+human]" (Kiss 1998: 683). Such strong influence of semantic factors on the choice of voice is not attested in the corpus, so it cannot account for the increase in passives (cf. table 15.2). If neither the person nor the semantic hierarchy is responsible for this increase, this only leaves the two familiarity hierarchies.

The Familiarity Hierarchy (i): given > new: In the previous section the corpus data showed that the semantic import of patient NPs fails to explain the use of the passive as a topicalizing device in late ME and EModE. This section will try to find out whether the increase in frequency of the use of a constituent ordering pattern such as the passive qualifies as a response to the need to meet pragmatic requirements posed by communicative situations.

Of the three notions of topic outlined in section 15.4.1, one was pragmatic, with topic defined as the clausal constituent with the lowest degree of communicative dynamism (CD), i.e. the one providing old or given information. Briefly, a constituent has been said to convey "given" or "old" information if it is predictable (the hearer can predict its presence), recoverable (the hearer will be able to recover it from the preceding context), salient (present in the consciousness of the interlocutor) or familiar (it represents shared knowledge between speaker and hearer). Obviously, we are dealing with a set of interrelated features here (Halliday 1967; Chafe 1976; Kuno 1978; Prince 1981a, 1985; Birner and Ward 1998).

The givenness or novelty of the passive subject and *by*-phrase, then, can be largely determined on the basis of their being bound deictically by the situation or anaphorically by the context; otherwise, it is derived from the hearer's general knowledge store. In order to ascertain the extent to which the passive has the function of maintaining the given/new distribution of information within the clause in the corpus, I examined the degree of CD of the subject and *by*-phrase in the long passives in the corpus. This was established by analyzing both the extralinguistic and the linguistic context; extralinguistically, deictic pronouns which were found to point at entities in the situational context were judged to encode given information, since they are within the perception and consciousness of both interlocutors. When prior mention of the referent of the NP occurred in the linguistic context, the NP was also regarded as conveying given information. Lambrecht (1994: 165) measures the type of information conveyed by a NP depending on the position of its referent in the Topic Acceptability Scale, which includes the following categories, from most to least salient: active, accessible, unused, brand-new anchored, and brand-new unanchored. Chafe (1987: 36, 1994: 72) also proposes a scale from given to new, applying the labels "already active," "previously semi-active," and "previously inactive." The crucial question in debating the passive as an information-rearranging device, however, is the difference between subject and *by*-phrase as regards CD, and not so much the degrees of novelty or givenness of each NP individually. For this reason, the givenness scale is disregarded in this study and only the binary distinction given vs. new is taken into account. Table 15.5 provides the results.

As shown in table 15.5, most long passives (64.3 percent) contain given patients and new agents, while the reverse order, new/given, is observed in only 3.6 percent of passives. These data reveal that, in the corpus, contexts in which the agent is new and the patient is given information favor the use of long passives, since only by rendering the clause in the passive voice can the unmarked given/new order be achieved. Therefore, the type of information that the NPs involved convey is confirmed as a factor triggering the use of the passive in late ME and EModE.

Table 15.5 Information conveyed by the subject and agent in passive clauses

Order of information	*Number*	*Percentage*
Given/new	283	64.3
New/given	16	3.6
New/new	105	23.8
Given/given	36	8.1
Total	440	100.0

Earlier in this section I mentioned that the higher percentage of long passives found in formal texts could possibly be conditioned by the need to position old information, which is not normally elided in formal texts, in initial position. Obvious reasons of space make it impossible to expound the data concerning the informational structure of passive clauses in each text type individually; suffice it to say that the distribution of passives by text type is indeed suggestive of some association between formal texts and the passive as an order-rearranging device.

The significance of this parameter for EModE passives is further corroborated by comparison with another argument-reversing construction available in the period under study, namely inversion (cf. Pérez Guerra 1999: 235–81), as exemplified in (13):

(13) Down in the cellar there is a new tool.

This construction, like the passive, places the subject of the corresponding canonical (non-inverted) clause (*a new tool*) in postverbal position, and a constituent other than the agent (*Down in the cellar*) in preverbal position. According to Birner and Ward (1998: 156ff.), both passives and inversions are triggered by the same discourse factors, namely the discrepancy between the subject and the postverbal NP as regards information. Since inversions serve the same purpose in the language and are readily available in the period under consideration, one would expect passives not to be so prominent as order-rearranging devices. However, inversion and passivization operate in different syntactic environments: passivization applies to transitive verbs whereas inversion applies to intransitive and copular clauses. Empirical studies (Bækken 1998: 248–9; Bech 2001: 109–19) have made manifest that the tendency of inversion to apply to intransitive clauses was already observed in OE, ME, and EModE, when intransitive verbs dominate in the inverted (XVS) order, while there is a predominance of transitive verbs in the non-inverted order (XSV, probably determined by the need to maintain the cohesion between V and O; cf. Tomlin's 1987 Bonding Principle). As argument-reversing constructions, therefore, passivization and inversion were in a nearly complementary distribution and passives were almost the only order-rearranging pattern available for transitive clauses.

However, the most significant difference between the two argument-reversing devices is that, even if they satisfy the same discourse constraints, inversion produces marked topics, while passivization is the only strategy reversing the order of clausal constituents and creating unmarked topics/subjects. Hence the relevance of passivization in this period.

Another finding in the corpus comes to underline the relevance of the passive as a strategy that creates unmarked topic/subjects. Consider (14)

(14) *By hure þe dewell is putt in gret drede.*
(QM3/4_IR_SERM_ROYAL:176).

Here the patient-subject ("the devil") is new and the agent *by*-phrase ("her"), is given; the distribution of information is unmarked because the order of constituents has been reversed, the agent appearing before the subject. In other words, the example above has the order given agent + new patient, an order which could also be attained by means of an active clause. Even if such an arrangement of passive constituents is natural in other languages (as in Dutch, cf. Cornelis 1997: 26ff.), it is extremely rare in PDE; Svartvik (1966), for example, did not find a single example comparable to (14) in his 323,000-word corpus of PDE.

Examples of this type, which amount to 81 in the corpus, reveal that the passive in earlier periods was not used exclusively to restore the unmarked informational structure. Rather, this alternative arrangement of constituents responds to (i) the wish to locate an agent in marked topic position, in order to give it emphasis or to use it as a cohesive device with the previous context (the pronominal nature of the agent corroborates this), and (ii) the need to place an inherently topical patient in unmarked topic position (the devil, even if not mentioned previously, is definite and inferable on the basis of knowledge of the world). Such an arrangement of constituents is only possible through the passive, which again reveals itself as a useful information-structuring device in this period.

The Familiarity Hierarchy (ii): definite > indefinite: The choice of a NP as topic is also conditioned by its degree of definiteness, which constitutes an important grammatical correlate of the distinction between identifiable and unidentifiable referents, so that the most common instantiations of topic constituents include highly definite elements such as pronouns, proper names, and definite NPs (Lambrecht 1994: 79; Kiss 1998: 683). With the aim of ascertaining whether passivization in the corpus was or was not determined by a higher degree of definiteness of the patient NP with respect to the *by*-phrase, the degree of definiteness of both constituents was examined in each passive example. The NPs involved in the passives in the corpus were found to fall into the following classes, ordered, according to their degree of definiteness, from most to least definite: pronouns > proper nouns/proper names > definite NPs > indefinite NPs (cf. Chafe 1976; Prince 1985: 66; Croft 1990: 127). As was the case with the animacy parameter, the following examples were excluded from the analysis: (i) the 99 cases where subject and agent are on a par as regards the degree of definiteness; (ii) the 23 passive *as*-comment clauses, and (iii) passives in which either the agent or the subject was realized by means of a clause (157 examples in all). Table 15.6 shows the results.

Table 15.6 Degree of definiteness of the subject and agent NPs

Subject more definite than agent	113	70.0%
Subject less definite than agent	48	29.8%

As can be seen in the table, more than 70 percent of the long passives in the corpus have a subject which is more definite than the agent. In sum, therefore, my findings reveal that the degree of definiteness is an important determining factor for passivization in my data.

Examination of the factors which make patient NPs topical and that, therefore, might determine their promotion to unmarked topic position through passivization reveals that only syntactic and pragmatic factors play a significant role in late ME and EModE passives, namely the principle of end-weight, the given–new ordering of information, and the degree of definiteness of the subject and the *by*-phrase. In contrast with PDE and most of the world's languages, the animacy and human features of the subject and agent do not trigger passivization in the corpus, for 71.8 percent of the passives showing discrepancy in this variable exhibit the marked combination [–H–A] subject and [+H+A] *by*-phrase. Therefore, the data retrieved from the corpus confirm the hypothesis that the increase in frequency of the passive as an information-rearranging strategy is triggered mainly by pragmatic factors.

15.5 Conclusions

In the foregoing pages, I have attempted to show that the seemingly bewildering endeavor to explain word order developments might be eased if pragmatic discourse factors are taken into account. I have first tried to lay bare the insufficiency of all-syntactic considerations, and have exposed a subtle relationship between word order change and the pragmatic monitoring of information. The interaction between syntactic and pragmatic factors was illustrated with the use of the passive as an order-rearranging device determined by pragmatic discourse factors. The hypothesis that the increase in frequency of the passive from the early fifteenth century onwards was largely determined by pragmatic factors as a response to the loss of V2 seems to be supported by the analysis of the information structure of passives in a late ME and EModE corpus. Thus, highly prominent and cross-linguistic semantic factors which make a NP inherently topical and therefore eligible to become subject, such as its animacy and agentivity, have been proved to be absolutely irrelevant in the choice of passive in the corpus. The data demonstrate that it is syntactic factors, namely the principle of end-weight, and essentially pragmatic factors, namely the distribution of given–new information and of definite and indefinite referents, that determined the use of this word order arrangement pattern.

I hope to have shown that syntax and pragmatic considerations must go hand in hand in the analysis of word order phenomena.

ACKNOWLEDGMENTS

This research has been supported by the University of Santiago project *Variation and Linguistic Change*, funded by the Spanish Ministry of Education (grant number BFF2001-2914) and the Xunta de Galicia (grant number PGIDT01PXI20404PR). I am indebted to Professor Teresa Fanego, leader of the research project, who has contributed a great many insightful comments. I would like to record my debt to Dr. Przemyslaw Lozowski for his valuable suggestions and support. I am also grateful to the editors of this volume for their comments on an earlier version. I retain full responsibility for the final contents of this chapter.

REFERENCES

The abbreviation *ELL* stands for *The Encyclopedia of Language and Linguistics*, ed. R. E. Asher and J. M. Y. Simpson. Oxford: Pergamon (1994).

Allen, C. (1995). *Case Marking and Reanalysis: Grammatical Relations from Old to Early Modern English*. Oxford: Clarendon Press.

Bækken, B. (1998). *Word Order Patterns in Early Modern English with Special Reference to the Position of the Subject and the Finite Verb* (Studia anglistica norvegica 9). Oslo: Novus Press.

Bækken, B. (2003). *Word Order in 17th Century English: A Study of the Stabilisation of the XSV Pattern* (Studia Anglistica Norvegica 12). Oslo: Novus Press.

Bean, M. C. (1983). *The Development of Word-order Patterns in Relation to Theories of Word Order Change*. London and Canberra: Croom Helm.

Bech, K. (1998). Pragmatic factors in language change: XVS and XSV clauses in Old and Middle English. *Folia Linguistica Historica*, 19.1–2: 79–102.

Bech, K. (2001). *Word Order Patterns in Old and Middle English: A Syntactic and Pragmatic Study*. Bergen: University of Bergen.

Bernárdez, E. and Tejada, P. (1995). Pragmatic constraints to word order, and word-order change in English. In A. H. Jucker (ed.), *Historical Pragmatics: Pragmatic Developments in the History of English* (pp. 217–41). Amsterdam and Philadelphia: John Benjamins.

Birner, B. J. and Ward, G. (1998). *Information Status and Noncanonical Word Order in English* (Studies in Language Companion Series 40). Amsterdam and Philadelphia: John Benjamins.

Bock, J. K. (1982). Toward a cognitive psychology of syntax information processing contributions to sentence formulation. *Psychological Review* 89.1: 1–47.

Boucher, J., and Osgood, C. E. (1969). The Pollyanna hypothesis. *Journal of Verbal Learning and Verbal Behavior* 8: 1–8.

Breivik, L. E. (1989). On the causes of syntactic change in English. In L. E. Breivik and E. H. Jahr (eds.), *Language Change: Contributions to the Study of its Causes*. (Trends in linguistics. Studies and monographs 43) (pp. 29–70). Berlin and New York: Mouton de Gruyter.

Breivik, L. E. (1990). *Existential* There: *A Synchronic and Diachronic Study*. Oslo: Novus Press.
Breivik, L. E. (1991). On the typological status of Old English. In D. Kastovsky (ed.), *Historical English Syntax* (Topics in English Linguistics 2) (pp. 31–50). Berlin and New York: Mouton de Gruyter.
Breivik, L. E. and Swan, T. (1994). Initial adverbials and word order in English with special reference to the Early Modern English period. In D. Kastovsky (ed.), *Studies in Early Modern English* (Topics in English Linguistics 13) (pp. 11–43). Berlin and New York: Mouton de Gruyter.
Bresnan, J., Dingare, S., and Manning, C. D. (2001). Soft constraints mirror hard constraints: voice and person in English and Lummi. In M. Butt and T. H. King (eds.), *Proceedings of the LFG01 Conference*. Stanford: CSLI Publications. Draft on-line, Stanford University: http://csli-publications.stanford.edu/.
Carlton, C. (1970). *Descriptive Syntax of the Old English Charters*. The Hague: Mouton.
Chafe, W. L. (1976). Givenness, contrastiveness, definiteness, subjects, topics and points of view. In C. N. Li (ed.), *Subject and Topic* (pp. 25–55). New York: Academic Press.
Chafe, W. L. (1987). Cognitive constraints on information. In R. S. Tomlin (ed.), *Coherence and Grounding in Discourse: Outcome of a Symposium, Eugene, Oregon 1984* (Typological Studies in Language 11) (pp. 21–51). Amsterdam: Benjamins.
Chafe, W. L. (1994). *Discourse, Consciousness, and Time*. Chicago and London: University of Chicago Press.
Copeland, J. E. (2000). Introduction. In D. G. Lockwood, P. H. Fries, and J. E. Copeland (eds.), *Functional Approach to Language, Culture and Cognition: Papers in Honor of Sydney M. Lamb*. (Current Issues in Linguistic Theory 163) (pp. xiii–xviii). Amsterdam and Philadelphia: John Benjamins.
Cornelis, L. H. (1997). *Passive and Perspective* (Utrecht Studies in Language and Communication 10). Amsterdam: Rodopi.
Croft, W. (1990). *Typology and Universals*. Cambridge: Cambridge University Press.
Dahl, Ö. (1974). Topic-comment structure revisited. In Ö. Dahl (ed.), *Topic and Comment, Contextual Boundness and Focus* (pp. 1–24). Hamburg: Helmut Buske Verlag.
Davies, W. D. and Dubinsky, S. (2001). Functional architecture and the distribution of subject properties. In W. D. Davies and S. Dubinsky (eds.), *Objects and Other Subjects. Grammatical Functions, Functional Categories and Configurationality* (Studies in Natural Language and Linguistic Theory 52) (pp. 247–79). Dordrecht: Kluwer Academic Publishers.
DeLancey, S. (1981). An interpretation of split ergativity and related patterns. *Language* 57: 627–57.
Denison, D. (1986). On word order in Old English. *Dutch Quarterly Review* 16: 277–95.
Denison, D. (1993). *English Historical Syntax*. London: Longman.
Diesing, M. (1990). Verb movement and the subject position in Yiddish. *Natural Language and Linguistic Theory* 8.1: 41–81.
Dik, S. C. (1980). *Studies in Functional Grammar*. London: Academic Press.
Doherty, M. (1996). Passive perspectives: different preferences in English and German: a result of parameterized processing. *Linguistics* 34.3: 591–643.
Donner, Morton (1986). The gerund in Middle English. *English Studies* 67: 394–400.
Downing, P. and Noonan, M. (1995). *Word-order in Discourse*. Amsterdam and Philadelphia: John Benjamins.
Drubig, H. B. (1988). On the discourse

function of subject verb inversion. In J. Klegraf and D. Nehls (eds.), *Essays on the English Language and Applied Linguistics on the Occasion of Gerhard Nickel's 60th Birthday* (pp. 83–95). Heidelberg: Julius Groos Verlag.

Dusková, L. (1971). On some functional and stylistic aspects of the passive voice in Present-day English. *Philologica Pragensia* 14: 117–43.

Ehala, M. (1998). How a man changed a parameter value: the loss of SOV in Estonian subclauses. In R. M. Hogg and L. van Bergen (eds.), *Historical Linguistics 1995*. Vol. 2: *Germanic Linguistics* (Current Issues in Linguistic Theory 162). (pp. 73–88). Amsterdam and Philadelphia: John Benjamins.

Faarlund, J. T. (1990). *Syntactic Change: Toward a Theory of Historical Syntax* (Trends in Linguistics. Studies and Monographs 50). Berlin and New York: Mouton de Gruyter.

Fawcett, R. (2000). *A Theory of Syntax for Systemic Functional Linguistics*. (Current Issues in Linguistic Theory 206). Amsterdam/Philadelphia: John Benjamins.

Firbas, J. (1966). On defining the theme in functional sentence analysis. *Travaux Linguistiques de Prague* 1: 267–80.

Firbas, J. (1988). On the role of the parts of speech in functional sentence perspective. In J. Klegraf and D. Nehls (eds.), *Essays on the English Language and Applied Linguistics on the Occasion of Gerhard Nickel's 60th Birthday* (pp. 96–109). Heidelberg: Julius Groos Verlag.

Firbas, J. (1992). *Functional Sentence Perspective in Written and Spoken Communication*. Cambridge: Cambridge University Press.

Fischer, O. (1992). Syntax. In N. Blake (ed.), *The Cambridge History of the English Language*. Vol. 2: *1066–1476* (pp. 207–408). Cambridge: Cambridge University Press.

Fischer, O., Kemenade, A. van, Koopman, W., and Wurff, W. van der (2000). *The Syntax of Early English*. Cambridge: Cambridge University Press.

Foley, A., and van Valin, R. D. (1985). Information packaging in the clause. In T. Shopen (ed.), *Language Typology and Syntactic Description* (pp. 299–347). Cambridge: Cambridge University Press.

Foley, W. (1994). Information structure. *ELL* 3: 1678–85.

Frajzyngier, Z. (1982). Indefinite agent, passive and impersonal passive: a functional study. *Lingua* 58: 267–90.

Francis, W. N. and Kucera, H. (1982). *Frequency Analysis of English Usage*. New York: Houghton Mifflin.

Fries, C. C. (1940). On the development of the structural use of word-order in Modern English. *Language* 16: 102–64.

Givón, T. (1975). Serial verbs and syntactic change: Niger-Congo. In C. N. Li (ed.), *Word Order and Word Order Change* (pp. 47–112). Austin: University of Texas Press.

Givón, T. (1977). The drift from VSO to SVO in biblical Hebrew: the pragmatics of tense-aspect. In C. Li (ed.) (pp. 181–254).

Givón, T. (1979). *On Understanding Grammar*. New York: Academic Press.

Givón, T. (1981). Typology and functional domains. *Studies in Language* 5: 163–93.

Givón, T. (1982). Transitivity, topicality and the Ute impersonal passive. In P. Hopper and S. A. Thompson (eds.), *Studies in Transitivity* (Syntax and Semantics 15) (pp. 143–60). New York: Academic Press.

Givón, T. (1983). Topic continuity in discourse: an introduction. In T. Givón (ed.), *Topic Continuity in Discourse: A Quantitive Cross-language Study* (Typological Studies in Language 3) (pp. 1–41). Amsterdam and Philadelphia: John Benjamins.

Givón, T. (1985). Iconicity, isomorphism and non-arbitrary coding in syntax. In John Haiman (ed.), *Iconicity in Syntax* (pp. 187–219). Amsterdam: John Benjamins.

Givón, T. (1990). *Syntax: A Functional Typological Introduction* (2 vols.). Amsterdam and Philadelphia: John Benjamins.

Givon, T. (1992). The grammar of referential coherence as mental processing instructions. *Linguistics* 30: 5–55.

Givón, T. (1993). *English Grammar: A Function-based Introduction* (vol. 2). Amsterdam and Philadelphia: John Benjamins.

Givón, T. (1995). *Functionalism and Grammar*. Amsterdam/Philadelphia: John Benjamins.

Givón, T. (1994). The pragmatics of de-transitive voice: functional and typological aspects of inversion. In T. Givón (ed.), *Voice and Inversion* (Typological Studies in Language 28) (pp. 3–44). Amsterdam and Philadelphia: John Benjamins.

Givón, T. (2001). *Syntax: An Introduction* (vol. 1). Amsterdam and Philidelphia: John Benjamins.

Görlach, M. (1990). Chaucer's English: what remains to be done. In M. Görlach (ed.), *Studies in the History of the English Language* (pp. 79–94). Heidelberg: Carl Winter Universitätsverlag.

Görlach, M. (1991). *Introduction to Early Modern English*. Cambridge: Cambridge University Press.

Greenberg, J. H. (1966). *Language Universals*. The Hague and Paris: Mouton.

Haiman, J. (1974). *Targets and Syntactic Change* (Janua Linguarum, Series Minor 186). The Hague and Paris: Mouton.

Halliday, M. A. K. (1967). Notes on transitivity and theme in English, part 2. *Journal of Linguistics* 4: 179–215.

Halliday, M. A. K. (1985). *An Introduction to Functional Grammar*. London: Edward Arnold.

Halliday, M. A. K. (2000). Grammar and daily life: concurrence and complementarity. In D. G. Lockwood, P. H. Fries, and J. E. Copeland (eds.), *Functional Approach to Language, Culture and Cognition: Papers in Honor of Sydney M. Lamb* (Current Issues in Linguistic Theory 163) (pp. 221–37). Amsterdam/Philadelphia: John Benjamins.

Hartvigson, H. H. and Jakobsen, L. K. (1974). *Inversion in Present-day English* (Odense University studies in English 2). Odense: Odense University Press.

Hawkins, J. A. (1994). *A Performance Theory of Order and Constituency*. Cambridge: Cambridge University Press.

Hinds, J. (1975). Passives, pronouns and themes and rhemes. *Glossa* 9.1: 79–106.

Horie, K. (2000). Glossary. In K. Horie (ed.), *Complementation: Cognitive and Functional Perspectives* (Converging Evidence in Language and Communication research 1) (pp. 227–33) Amsterdam/Philadelphia: John Benjamins.

Huddleston, R. (1984). *Introduction to the Grammar of English*. Cambridge: Cambridge University Press.

Huddleston, R. and Pullum, G. K. (2002). *The Cambridge Grammar of the English Language*. Cambridge: Cambridge University Press.

Hutchins, W. J. (1975). Subjects, themes, and case grammars. *Lingua* 35.2: 101–33.

Hyman, L. (1975). On the change from SOV to SVO: evidence from Niger-Congo. In C. N. Li (ed.), *Word Order and Word Order Change* (pp. 113–47). Austin: University of Texas Press.

Jacobsson, B. (1951). *Inversion in English with Special Reference to the Early Modern English Period*. Uppsala: Almqvist and Wiksell.

Jucker, Andreas H. (ed.) (1995). *Historical Pragmatics: Pragmatic Developments in the History of English*. Amsterdam and Philadelphia: John Benjamins.

Keenan, E. L. (1985). Passive in the world's language. In T. Shopen (ed.), *Language Typology and Syntactic Description* (pp. 243–81). Cambridge: Cambridge University Press.

Kemenade, A. van (1987). *Syntactic Case and Morphological Case in the History of English*. Dordrecht: Foris.

Kemenade, A. van (2000). The syntax and use of some light elements in OE. Paper delivered at the 11th ICEHL, Santiago de Compostela.

Kennedy, G. (2001). The distribution of agent marking and finiteness as possible contributors to the difficulty of passive voice structures. In K. Aijmer (ed.), *A Wealth of English: Studies in Honour of Göran Kjellmer* (Gothenburg Studies in English 81) (pp. 39–46). Göteborg: Acta Universitatis Gothoburgensis.

Kisbye, T. (1972). *An Historical Outline of English Syntax* (2 vols.). Aarhus: Akademisk Boghandel.

Kiss, K. É. (1998). Discourse-configurationality in the languages of Europe. In A. Siewierska (ed.), *Constituent Order in the Languages of Europe* (pp. 681–727). Berlin and New York: Mouton de Gruyter.

Kohonen, V. (1978). *On the Development of English Religious Prose around 1000 and 1200 A.D. A Quantitative Study of Word Order in Context* (Meddelanen från Stifelsens för Åbo Akademi Forskningsinstitut, Nr 38). Åbo: Publications of the Research Institute of the Åbo Akademi Foundation.

Koopman, W. F. (1997). Another look at clitics in Old English. *Transactions of the Philological Society* 95.1: 73–93.

Kroch, A. and Taylor, A. (1997). Verb movement in Old and Middle English: dialect variation and language contact. In A. van Kemenade and N. Vincent (eds.), *Paramenters of Morphosyntactic Change* (pp. 297–325). Cambridge: Cambridge University Press.

Kroch, A., Taylor, A., and Ringe, D. (2000). The Middle English Verb-Second constraint: a case study in language contact and language change. In S. C. Herring, P. van Reenen, and L. Schøsler (eds.), *Textual Parameters in Older Languages* (pp. 353–91). Amsterdam and Philadelphia: John Benjamins.

Kuno, S. (1978). Generative discourse analysis in America. In W. U. Dressler (ed.), *Current Trends in Text Linguistics* (pp. 275–94). Berlin: Walter de Gruyter.

Kuno, S. and Kaburaki, E. (1977). Empathy and syntax. *Linguistic Enquiry* 8: 627–73.

Kuppevelt, J. van (1994). Topic and comment. *ELL* 9: 4629–33.

Kytö, M. (1991). *Manual to the Diachronic Part of the Helsinki Corpus of English Texts*. Helsinki: Helsinki University Press.

Kytö, M. and Rissanen, M. (1993). "By and by enters [this] my artificiall foole . . . who, when Jack beheld, sodainely he flew at him": searching for syntactic constructions in the Helsinki Corpus. In M. Rissanen, M. Kytö, and M. Palander-Collin (eds.), *Early English in the Computer Age: Explorations through the Helsinki Corpus* (Topics in English Linguistics 11) (pp. 253–66). Berlin and New York: Mouton de Gruyter.

Lambrecht, K. (1994). *Information Structure and Sentence Form: Topic, Focus, and the Mental Representations of Discourse Referents*. Cambridge: Cambridge University Press.

Langacker, R. W. and Munro, P. (1975). Passives and their meaning. *Language* 51.4: 789–830.

Li, C. N. (ed.) (1977). *Mechanisms of Syntactic Change*. Austin: University of Texas Press.

Li, C. N. and Thompson, S. A. (1976). Subject and topic: a new typology of language. In C. N. Li (ed.), *Subject and Topic* (pp. 445–91). New York: Academic Press.

Lightfoot, D. (1991). *How to Set Parameters: Arguments for Language Change*. Cambridge, MA: MIT Press.

Los, B. (2002). The loss of the indefinite pronoun *man*: syntactic change and information structure. In T. Fanego, M. J. López-Couso, and J. Pérez-Guerra (eds.), *English Historical Syntax and Morphology* (Current Issues in Linguistic Theory 223) (pp. 181–202). Amsterdam and Philadelphia: John Benjamins.

Lyons, J. (1968). *Introduction to Theoretical Linguistics*. London: Cambridge University Press.

Miller, D. G. (2002). *Nonfinite Structures in Theory and Change*. Oxford: Oxford University Press.

Moessner, L. (1994). Early Modern English passive constructions. In D. Kastovsky (ed.), *Studies in Early Modern English* (Topics in English Linguistics 13) (pp. 217–32). Berlin and New York: Mouton de Gruyter.

Nevalainen, T. and Raumolin-Brunberg, H. (1993). Early Modern British English. In M. Rissanen, M. Kytö, and M. Palander-Collin (eds.), *Early English in the Computer Age: Explorations through the Helsinki Corpus* (pp. 53–73). Berlin/New York: Mouton de Gruyter.

Noël, D. (1998). Infinitival complement clauses in Modern English: explaining the predominance of passive matrix verbs. *Linguistics* 36.6: 1045–63.

Pérez Guerra, J. (1999). *Historical English Syntax: A Statistical Corpus-based Study on the Organization of Early Modern English Sentences* (LINCOM Studies in Germanic Linguistics 11). München: LINCOM Europa.

Pintzuk, S. (1999). *Phrase Structures in Competition: Variation and Change in Old English Word Order*. New York and London: Garland.

Prince, E. F. (1981a). Topicalization, focus-movement, and Yiddish-movement: a pragmatic differentiation. In *Proceedings of the Annual Meeting of the Berkeley Linguistics Society. February 14–16, 1981* (pp. 249–64). Berkeley: Berkeley Linguistics Society.

Prince, E. F. (1981b). Toward a taxonomy of given–new information. In P. Cole (ed.), *Radical Pragmatics* (pp. 223–55). New York: Academic Press.

Prince, E. F. (1985). Fancy syntax and "shared knowledge." *Journal of Pragmatics* 9: 65–81.

Prince, E. F. (1997). On the functions of left-dislocation in English discourse. In A. Kamio (ed.), *Directions in Functional Linguistics* (Studies in Language Companion Series 36) (pp. 117–43). Amsterdam and Philadelphia: John Benjamins.

Quirk, R., S. Greenbaum, G. Leech, and J. Svartvik (1985). *A Comprehensive Grammar of the English Language*. London and New York: Longman.

Rissanen, M. (1999a). Syntax. In R. Lass (ed.), *The Cambridge History of the English Language*. Vol. 3: *1476–1776* (pp. 187–331). Cambridge: Cambridge University Press.

Rissanen, M. (1999b). Isn't it? Or is it not? On the order of postverbal subject and negative particle in the history of English. In I. Tieken-Boon van Ostade, G. Tottie, and W. van der Wurff (eds.), *Negation in the History of English* (Topics in English linguistics 26) (pp. 189–205). Berlin and New York: Mouton de Gruyter.

Rissanen, M., Ihalainen, O., and Kytö, M. (compilers) (1991). *Helsinki Corpus of English Texts: Diachronic and Dialectal*. Helsinki: University of Helsinki.

Roberts, I. (1997). Directionality and word order change in the history of English. In A. van Kemenade and N. Vincent (eds.) (pp. 397–426).

Sapir, E. (1921). *Language: An Introduction to the Study of Speech*. New York: Harcourt, Brace.

Seoane, E. (1993). The passive in early Modern English. *Atlantis* 15: 191–213.

Seoane, E. (1999). The consolidation of the indirect and prepositional passive in Early Modern English: evidence from the Helsinki Corpus. *Estudios Ingleses de la Universidad Complutense* 7: 119–39.

Seoane, E. (2000). The passive as an information-rearranging device in Early Modern English. *Studia Neophilologica* 72: 24–33.

Shibatani, M. (1985). Passives and related constructions: a prototype analysis. *Language* 61.4: 821–48.

Siewierska, A. (1984). *The Passive: A Comparative Linguistic Analysis*. London: Croom Helm.

Siewierska, A. (1988). *Word Order Rules*. London: Croom Helm.

Siewierska, A. (1994). Word order and linearization. *ELL* 9: 4993–99.

Silverstein, M. (1976). Hierarchy of features and ergativity. In R. M. W. Dixon (ed.), *Grammatical Categories in Australian Languages* (pp. 112–71). Canberra: Australian Institute of Aboriginal Studies.

Söderlind, J. (1951–8). *Verb Syntax in John Dryden's Prose* (2 vols.). Uppsala: Lundequistska Bokhandeln.

Sornicola, R. (1994). Topic, focus, and word order. *ELL* 9: 4633–40.

Sornicola, R. (1998). The interpretation of historical sources as a problem for diachronic typology: word-order in English rhetorical and grammatical treatises of the XVIth and early XVIIth centuries. In D. Stein and R. Sornicola (eds.), *The Virtues of Language. History in Language, Linguistics and Texts* (Studies in the History of the Language Sciences 87) (pp. 81–128). Amsterdam and Philadelphia: John Benjamins.

Stein, D. (1995). Subjective meaning and the history of inversions in English. In D. Stein and S. Wright (eds.), *Subjectivity and Subjectivisation* (pp. 129–50). Cambridge: Cambridge University Press.

Stein, G. (1979). *Studies in the Function of the Passive*. Tübingen: Gunter Narr Verlag.

Stockwell, R. P. (1977). Motivations for exbraciation in Old English. In C. N. Li (ed.), *Mechanisms of Syntactic Change* (pp. 291–314). Austin: University of Texas Press.

Stockwell, R. P. (1984). On the history of the verb-second rule in English. In J. Fisiak (ed.), *Historical Syntax* (pp. 575–92). Berlin: Mouton.

Stockwell, R. P. and Minkova, D. (1991). Subordination and word order change in the history of English. In D. Kastovsky (ed.), *Historical English Syntax* (Topics in English Linguistics 2) (pp. 367–408). Berlin: Mouton de Gruyter.

Strang, B. M. H. (1970). *A History of English*. London: Methuen.

Svartvik, J. (1966). *On Voice in the English Verb*. The Hague: Mouton.

Svoboda, A. (1981). *Diatheme*. Brno: Masaryk University.

Tomlin, R. S. (ed.) (1987). *Coherence and Grounding in Discourse* (Typological Studies in Language 11). Amsterdam: John Benjamins.

Traugott, E. C. (1972). *The History of English Syntax*. New York: Holt, Rinehart and Winston.

Traugott, E. C. (1992). Syntax. In R. M. Hogg (ed.), *The Cambridge History of the English Language*. Vol. 1: *The Beginnings to 1066* (pp. 168–289). Cambridge: Cambridge University Press.

Travis, L. (2001). Derived objects in Malagasy. In W. D. Davies and S. Dubinsky (eds.), *Objects and Other Subjects: Grammatical Functions, Functional Categories and Configurationality* (Studies in Natural

Language and Linguistic Theory 52) (pp. 123–55). Dordrecht: Kluwer Academic Publishers.
Trips, C. (2002). *From OV to VO in Early Middle English* (Linguistik Aktuell). Amsterdam and Philadelphia: John Benjamins.
Vallduví, E. and Engdahl, E. (1996). The linguistic realization of information packaging. *Linguistics* 34.3: 459–519.
Van der Wurff, W. (2001). Review of "Word Order Patterns in Early Modern English, with Special Reference to the Position of the Subject and the Finite Verb" by Bjørg Bækken. *Studies in Language* 25.3: 685–91.
Van Hoorick, B. (1994). *Pragmatic Positions and the History of English Word Order: A Functional Grammar Perspective* (pp. 1–96) (Working Papers in Functional Grammar 56). Amsterdam: University of Amsterdam.
Van Valin, R. D. (1980). On the distribution of passive and antipassive constructions in universal grammar. *Lingua* 50: 303–27.
Vennemann, T. (1973). Explanation in syntax. In J. P. Kimball (ed.), *Syntax and Semantics* (vol. 2) (pp. 1–50). New York: Seminar Press.
Vennemann, T. (1974). Topics, subjects, and word order: from SXV to SVX via TVX. In J. M. Anderson and C. Jones (eds.), *Historical Linguistics I: Syntax, Morphology, Internal and Comparative Reconstruction* (pp. 339–76). Amsterdam and Oxford: North-Holland Publishing.
Vennemann, T. (1975). An explanation of drift. In C. Li (ed.) (pp. 269–306).
Vennemann, T. (1984). Verb-second, verb late, and the brace construction in Germanic: a discussion. In J. Fisiak (ed.), *Historical Syntax* (Trends in Linguistics. Studies and Monographs 23) (pp. 627–36). Berlin, New York and Amsterdam: Mouton.
Visser, F. Th. (1963–73). *An Historical Syntax of the English Language* (4 vols.). Leiden: E. J. Brill.
Werth, P. (1984). *Focus, Coherence and Emphasis*. London: Croom Helm.

FURTHER READING

Andrew, S. O. (1940). *Syntax and Style in Old English*. Cambridge: Cambridge University Press.
Andrew, S. O. (1934). Some principles of Old English word-order. *Medium Aevum* 3: 167–88.
Drubig, H. B. (1988). On the discourse function of subject verb inversion. In J. Klegraf and D. Nehls (eds.), *Essays on the English Language and Applied Linguistics on the Occasion of Gerhard Nickel's 60th Birthday* (pp. 83–95). Heidelberg: Julius Groos Verlag.
Firbas, J. (1964). From comparative word-order studies. *BRNO Studies in English* 4: 111–26.
Kemenade, A. van (1997a). Topics in Old and Middle English negative sentences. In R. Hickey and S. Puppel (eds.), *Language History and Language Modelling* (pp. 293–306). Berlin and New York: Mouton de Gruyter.
Kemenade, A. van (1997b). Negative-initial sentences in Old and Middle English. In J. Fisiak (ed.), *Festschrift for Roger Lass on his Sixtieth Birthday* (Studia Anglica Posnaniensia 31) (pp. 91–104). Poznan: Uniwersytet im. A. Mickiewicza.
Kemenade, A. van (2000). The syntax and use of some light elements in OE. Paper delivered at the 11th ICEHL, Santiago de Compostela.

Kemenade, A. van (2001). Jespersen's cycle revisited: formal properties of grammaticalization. In S. Pintzuk, G. Tsoulas, and A. Warner (eds.), *Diachronic Syntax: Models and Mechanisms*. Oxford: Oxford University Press.

Koktova, E. (1997). Towards a new theory of syntax. Part I: basic ideas. *Theoretical Linguistics* 23.1–2: 21–48.

Koktova, E. (1999). *Word-order Based Grammar* (Trends in Linguistics. Studies and Monographs 121). Berlin and New York: Mouton de Gruyter.

Koopman, W. F. (1990). *Word Order in Old English, with Special Reference to the Verb Phrase* (Amsterdam Studies in Generative Grammar 1). Amsterdam: The Faculty of Arts, University of Amsterdam.

Li, C. N. and Thompson, S. A. (1975). The semantic function of word-order: a case study in Mandarin. In C. N. Li (ed.), *Word Order and Word Order Change* (pp. 163–96). Austin: University of Texas Press.

Marín Arrese, J. (1997). Cognitive and discourse-pragmatic factors in passivization. *Atlantis* 19.1: 203–18.

Ohkado, M. (1999). On MV/VM order in Old English. *Folia Linguistica Historica* 20.1–2: 79–106.

Reszkiewicz, A. (1966). *Main Sentence Elements in* The book of Margery Kempe*: A Study in Major Syntax*. Warsaw: Komitet Neofilologiczny Polskiej Akademii Nauk.

Rissanen, M. (1999b). Isn't it? Or is it not? On the order of postverbal subject and negative particle in the history of English. In I. T.-B. van Ostade, G. Tottie, and W. van der Wurff (eds.), *Negation in the History of English* (Topics in English linguistics 26) (pp. 189–205). Berlin and New York: Mouton de Gruyter.

Seoane, E. (1999). Inherent topicality and object foregrounding in Early Modern English. *ICAME Journal* 23: 117–40.

Seoane, E. (2000a). Impersonalising strategies in Early Modern English. *English Studies* 81.2: 102–16.

Seoane, E. (2000b). The passive as an object foregrounding device in Early Modern English. In R. Bermúdez, R. Hogg, D. Denison, and C. B. McCully (eds.), *Generative Theory and Corpus Studies: A Dialogue from 10 ICEHL* (Topics in English linguistics 31) (pp. 211–32). Berlin and New York: Mouton de Gruyter.

Sgall, P., Hajicová, E., and Panenová, J. (1986). *The Meaning of the Sentence in its Semantic and Pragmatic Aspects*. Dordrecht: D. Reidel.

Sornicola, R. (1998). The interpretation of historical sources as a problem for diachronic typology: word-order in English rhetorical and grammatical treatises of the XVIth and early XVIIth centuries. In D. Stein and R. Sornicola (eds.), *The Virtues of Language: History in Language, Linguistics and Texts* (Studies in the History of the Language Sciences 87) (pp. 81–128). Amsterdam and Philadelphia: John Benjamins.

Svenonius, P. (ed.) (2000). *The Derivation of VO and OV*. Amsterdam and Philadelphia: John Benjamins.

Swan, T. (1994). A note on Old English and Old Norse initial adverbials and word order with special reference to sentence adverbials. In T. Swan, E. Mørck, and O. J. Westvik (eds.), *Language Change and Language Structure* (pp. 233–70). Berlin and New York: Mouton de Gruyter.

Swieczkowski, W. (1962). *Word Order Patterning in Middle English* (Janua Linguarum. Series Minor 19). 'S-Gravenhage: Mouton.

Thompson, S. A. (1978). Modern English from a typological point of view: some implications of the function of word order. *Linguistische Berichte* 54: 19–35.

Van der Wurff, W. (1999). Objects and verbs in Modern Icelandic and fifteenth-century English: a word order parallel and its causes. *Lingua* 109: 237–65.

Warner, A. (1997). The structure of parametric change and V-movement in the history of English. In A. van Kemenade and N. Vincent (eds.), *Parameters of Morphosyntactic Change* (pp. 380–93). Cambridge: Cambridge University Press.

Warner, Anthony (2001). *Interpreting Variation: Verb Second Order in Late Middle English.* University of York: UKLVC3.

V Pre- and Post-colonial Varieties

16 Old English Dialectology

RICHARD HOGG

16.1 Introduction

As for any period in the distant past, the study of the dialects of the Old English period brings its own special problems. Some of these problems are quite obvious: for example we have no access to the actual speech of the period; we have to rely on scattered manuscripts which can range from extensive collections of sermons or poetry to mere scraps with no more than a few words. Furthermore, from our present-day point of reference it is too easy to allow ourselves to be fooled into seeing Old English as a homogeneous and stable entity, even though we are dealing with a time-span of about 700 years, from its beginnings in the fifth century to shortly after the Norman Conquest, i.e. a time-span which is equivalent to that from the time of Chaucer to the present day. That leads to further difficulties. Note, for example, that the actual texts which we have do not start to appear in substantial quantities until the mid-ninth century, and by far the greatest proportion of texts are actually from between the end of the tenth century and the loss of new material which begins to occur shortly after the Norman Conquest.

There are other difficulties which face us. For example, no present-day analysis of dialect variation could be conducted without reference to social variation. This will include the kinds of variation which are induced by, for example, class features or gender, or age. For Old English little of this makes much sense, even though we would like it to. The texts we do have are all the result of a tiny literate proportion of society – we can have no idea of how the average farm worker or traveling merchant spoke. Such persons remain, for ever, a hidden majority. The literate community, furthermore, were, for the most part, members of religious communities, and this necessarily further limits the type of language which was written down. Those who wrote down our texts, although not necessarily those who composed the thoughts that were written down, were from a highly restricted stratum of society. They were also likely to be from only a restricted age group, and virtually none of them was female.

It is quite difficult to comprehend how restricted the literate section of Old English society was. These remarks from a letter by Alfred may elucidate the problem:

> Swæ clæne hio wæs oðfeallenu on Angelcynne ðæt swiðe feawa wæron behionan Humbre ðe hiora ðeninga cuðen understondan on Englisc oððe furðuman ærendgewrit of Lædene on Englisc areccean; ond ic wene ðætte noht monige begiondan Humbre næren. Swæ feawa hiora wæron ðæt ic furðum anne anlepne ne mæg geðencean be suðan Temese ða ða ic to rice feng. (Whitelock 1967)

'So completely had it [learning] declined in England that there were very few this side of the Humber who could understand their services in English or even translate a letter from Latin into English; and I think that there were not many beyond the Humber either. There were so few of them, that I cannot even think of a single one south of the Thames when I came to the throne.'

All the above suggests a council of despair. Certainly, I could not advise a spirit of mindless optimism, but it has to be recognized that over the last 150 years or so there have been striking advances in the study of Old English dialects. In the next part of this chapter my aim will be to demonstrate how Old English dialectology has evolved over time so that we can then examine the issues that now face us.

16.2 The Evolution of Old English Dialectology

By the mid-nineteenth century there was already an appreciation that there was a distinction between northern and southern dialects of Old English, the former usually described as Anglian, the latter as Saxon, reflecting distinctions first made by Bede in his *Historia Ecclesiastica Gentis Anglorum* of the early eighth century. The first real breakthrough, however, came with Sweet's 1876 paper presented to the Philological Society, entitled "Dialects and prehistoric forms of Old English" (Sweet 1876). In this paper Sweet recognized four dialect areas: Northumbrian, Mercian, Kentish, and West Saxon. The recognition of these dialect areas is one that remains until the present day, with only a few minor changes and only one of substance, namely Sweet's own reattribution of the *Vespasian Psalter* to Mercian rather than Kentish (Sweet 1885).

To the modern reader the recognition of Old English as consisting of four discrete dialect areas must seem unusual. After all, we are used to concepts such as dialect overlap, of features which are shared unequally between informants from different parts of the country, of relic areas and innovations. But the picture which appears to be drawn by Sweet suggests stability and lack of change, with each dialect sharply differentiated from each of the others. I do not believe, even for a moment, that this was Sweet's view, but it certainly was one which came to dominate the field.

In order to understand how this came about and then to understand how it was eventually replaced by a more sophisticated view, it is necessary to

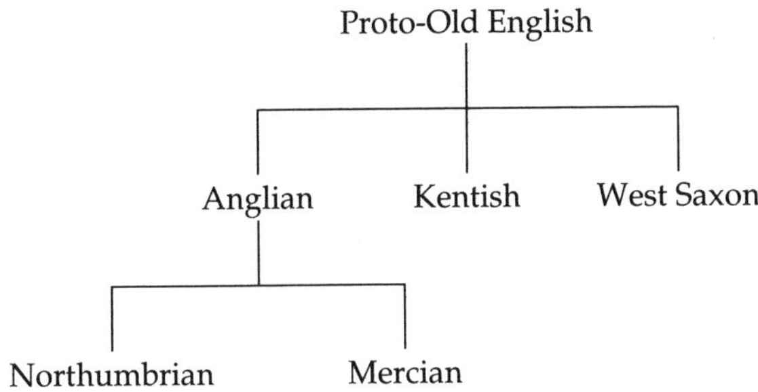

Figure 16.1 Old English *Stammbaum*

understand that Sweet's description of these four dialects was reinforced by two quite different strands of thought. One of these was linguistic in origin, namely the rise of the Neogrammarian movement associated with Leipzig, and in particular the further development of *Stammbaum* theory, in which the development of a language into dialects can be represented by branching nodes. Thus we can view the major dialects of Old English as shown in figure 16.1.

Alongside this we must recall that this age was one of high Victorianism and the ideological concerns of the period both reflect the new concept of the nation state, and furthermore, albeit anachronistically, attempt to invest much earlier ages with that same concept. In our context this led, for example, to the concept of an Anglo-Saxon heptarchy which could be transformed, despite the caveats of the editors of the OED, into a nation state of its own.

Despite the fact that Sweet's work was very much of its time and that Neogrammarianism was replaced or, rather, substantially amended by later linguistic theories and the concept of a nation state was equally subject to change, for eighty years or more Old English dialectology remained essentially unaltered. This is not to deny the work done during that time, which, for the most part, has easily withstood the ravages of time. But the framework had been set.

And it was only with the appearance of Campbell's *Old English Grammar* (Campbell 1959) that a different framework became possible. At first sight this seems an implausible claim. Perhaps the most obvious feature of that work is how deeply conservative it appears to be. As Bazell (1960) remarked in his review of the book, it ignores any of the advances in linguistic theory of the preceding fifty years: for example, from reading the book one would begin to believe that the phoneme had still to be invented, and there is not a single phonemic element invoked at any stage. And in the first chapter of the work the only sign of disaffection with the traditional view of Old English dialectology comes in a section on Mercian (Campbell 1959: §11). And that, like much else, is written in a form which, deliberately or not, conceals the views being expressed. It is only much later in the book that Campbell begins to reveal his actual views. The passage is worth quoting in detail (Campbell 1959: §256).

> It must first be emphasized that the dialectal names are in this book used practically without territorial significance. Northumbrian means the agreement of *Lindisfarne Gospels, Durham Ritual, Ru.*[2] [*Rushworth Gospels*[2]], and the early names and fragments.... Mercian means similarly the agreement of *Vespasian Psalter, Corpus Glossary, Epinal Glossary*, and the majority forms of *Ru.*[1][*Rushworth Gospels*[1]], or of such of these as afford evidence. Anglian means the agreement of Northumbrian so defined with Mercian so defined. Kent means such forms in the charters of Kentish origin as are shown to be genuinely Kentish by their reappearance in *Kentish Glosses*, or the appearance of their obvious reflexes ... there. Non-West-Saxon is the agreement of Anglian so defined with Kentish so defined. West-Saxon means the agreement of the majority forms of the four generally accepted early West Saxon manuscripts ... with a large body of later West-Saxon. [L]ate West-Saxon means forms prevailing in a considerable body of the later West-Saxon manuscripts, but not prevailing in the four manuscripts accepted as early West Saxon. [Note that I have silently expanded the abbreviations of the original text, for the purposes of clarity: RMH]

Why have I quoted at such length? What makes this passage so striking? In many respects Campbell appears to be repeating what had been said before. Note, for example, that essentially he assigns texts to the same dialects as Sweet eventually did. The dialect names themselves are the traditional ones. So what makes Campbell's account different? It contains, I believe, two new, but very salient, features. Firstly there is the denial that the dialect names have, except in the broadest of terms, territorial significance. Thus, for example, Campbell is denying that Mercian necessarily equates with the whole of England south of the Mersey and Humber and north of the Thames. All previous work, as far as I can gather, had assumed that Anglo-Saxon England was, dialectally, divisible into four parts. There is, with Campbell, no sense of total inclusion. The second feature is the way in which Campbell defines the dialects negatively. Essentially, each is defined in terms of the absence of forms found in other dialects. It may seem strange that Campbell should employ such a strictly structuralist approach to dialect study when in other areas, as I have mentioned, he avoids such an approach. The explanation for this may be that he has taken his structuralist approach from other fields than linguistics, most probably, I would guess, from logical philosophy. However, there is another explanation, at least as plausible. As a scholar steeped in classical philology, Campbell may well have been thinking of the stemmata codicum of that discipline and have introduced that into his thought processes. As it happens, there is little substantial difference between Neogrammarian thinking and that of classical philology in this respect (see, for example, Davies 1998: 186).

Whatever the rights and wrongs of those last remarks, the effects are radical. What Campbell is presenting is a group of dialect clusters without claiming that these clusters represent all the dialects of the country. Furthermore, it is clear these clusters can themselves contain internal variation (note, for example, the repetition of phrases such as "the majority forms"). The emergence of dialect clusters which are determined, not by pre-existing political divisions, whether tribal (Angles vs. Saxons) or pseudo-political (the Heptarchy), but only by the agreement of individual linguistic features is, although it has not always been recognized, genuinely ground-breaking.

I have devoted considerable space to this account of the past history of Old English dialectology, not merely because it is intrinsically interesting (as it is!), but because it remains the foundation for study, even, perhaps especially, when it is not easily recognized, as in Campbell's work. The rest of this chapter will attempt to move us forward from this point to consider the status of recent and current work in Old English dialectology. In doing this I want to proceed by way of four case studies, which will look at, respectively, West Saxon, Mercian, Northumbrian, Kentish, and, to broaden the horizon, syntactic features and lexical features.

16.3 West Saxon and "Standard Old English"

In a seminal article, C. L. Wrenn (1933) demonstrated that Early West Saxon, or, rather, the language of Alfred and his circle did not, as had been supposed by Sweet (1871) and others following him, have the character of a normalized standard language which in some, perhaps mystical, way prefigured the later alleged emergence of a standard language. If Old English did acquire a standard language, then it is to be found, not in the works of Alfred, but in those of Ælfric, a century later (see also Quirk and Wrenn 1957: §5).

Wrenn's argument was subsequently amplified and strengthened in an equally important article, Gneuss (1972). Gneuss's substantial contribution was to identify the source of what he, like Wrenn, calls Standard Old English with the scriptorium at the Old Minster in Winchester, where Æthelwold was bishop, and where Ælfric was one of his pupils, perhaps his best pupil. Together, perhaps, or by the former and subsequently the latter, Standard Old English emerged. There can be no doubt that many of the details of Gneuss's account are right. It also has the advantage of exploring in particular what Gneuss calls "Winchester words," that is to say, unlike most studies of the period, Gneuss concentrates on vocabulary rather than phonology, a topic I shall explore later. For all that, there are underlying and serious problems with Gneuss's article. As often in Old English dialectology these problems resolve themselves into issues of nomenclature. The two terms which cause the most difficulty in this context are "West Saxon" and "Standard Old English." For neither of these is either happy or appropriate.

Let me start with the former. Recall now my earlier quotation from Campbell (1959). He makes it quite clear that there are important differences between two varieties of West Saxon, Early and Late. And it so happens that some of these differences crucially affect the argument and relate to issues of territorial integrity. Let us examine one of these, the best known. In doing so, let us also talk of Alfredian Old English and Ælfrician Old English, rather than

Table 16.1 <ie> in West Saxon

	"Normal"	*Labials*	*Palatals*
Alfredian WS	hīran	wyrsa	miht
Ælfrician WS	hȳran	wyrsa	miht

early West Saxon and late West Saxon. The example concerns the digraph <ie> which is only commonly found in Alfredian English and not at all in Ælfrician English. Phonologically there are three sources for this digraph, see Hogg (1992: §5.163): (1) palatalization of earlier */e:/; (2) the *i*-umlaut of earlier diphthongs; (3) hiatus resolution between /i/ and /e/. Therefore, we should find results such as *hīeran* 'hear' and *wiersa* 'worse' in West Saxon. The usual situation is rather different. In Alfredian West Saxon the apparently original diphthongs represented by <ie> are most frequently represented by <i>, except between a labial consonant and /r/; in Ælfrician West Saxon the usual representation is <y>, except before palatal consonants, where <y> is the regular spelling. The distribution of the relevant types is shown in table 16.1.

There have been various attempts to provide a purely phonological explanation of this phenomenon. For example, both Girvan (1931: §§132–4) and Quirk and Wrenn (1957) concentrate on various processes of labialization and unrounding in an attempt to follow Neogrammarian practice. On the other hand, Campbell (1959: §301) is quite clear that the solution is dialectal:

> The picture obtained from later West Saxon texts is different. It is plain that the type of language found in the manuscripts accepted as eWS differed considerably from that which contributed most to the formation of lWS.

It surely follows from this that the differences between Alfredian and Ælfrician West Saxon cannot be reduced to mere chronology. There is also underlying dialectal variation. This brings us back to the dialect clusters which are observable in Campbell's work. The Alfredian texts form one cluster; the Ælfrician texts another, different, cluster. As Campbell states above "[L]ate West-Saxon means forms prevailing in a considerable body of the later West-Saxon manuscripts, but not prevailing in the four manuscripts accepted as early West Saxon." Under these circumstances the so-called "purity" of West Saxon which Gneuss, following most earlier scholars, sees is in fact a mirage. It works only on the assumption that the above varieties of West Saxon form a single indivisible cluster. Once that assumption is first questioned and then demolished, "purity" vanishes too.

The issue of "purity" leads us directly to the second problem I have highlighted, namely the meaning or appropriateness of the term Standard Old

English. Essentially, Gneuss shifts the locus of Standard Old English, if not to Ælfric, then certainly to his teacher, Æthelwold. There are good reasons for this, which Gneuss clearly sets out. But the claim that Gneuss makes for that variety of Old English being a standard language is not itself established. Let me explain why I believe this to be the case, particularly for Ælfrician Old English.

Haugen (1966) laid out the essential prerequisites for a standard language. Firstly, it must be *selected*, i.e. it must be used in an important political or commercial center. If we allow that to include Anglo-Saxon scriptoria, then the Old Minster at Winchester fits the bill. Secondly, it must be *codified* by some external authority. Even though Ælfric's language is often remarkably regular, it is well known that in some respects it changes over time, and his usages are by no means all adopted by others. Consider the following quotation from Gneuss (1972: 79):

> What seems particularly important for our argument is the fact that those contemporaries of Ælfric who otherwise kept to Standard Old English felt themselves at liberty, in their choice of words, to follow their own inclinations or other models.

It is quite difficult to understand what Gneuss means, other than the obvious point that Ælfric's language was neither selected nor codified by others. Thirdly, it must be *elaborated*, that is to say, extended into new areas, such as government documents and literature. But Ælfric's language remained essentially that of the religious and scholarly community in which he lived. Fourthly, it has to be *accepted* nationally. Although it can be argued that Ælfric's language was, at least to some extent, accepted in large parts of the south, it is equally clear that elsewhere the forms of language could be quite different.

No matter how much we modify Haugen's criteria to accommodate a different age, it is difficult to see how we can describe Ælfrician Old English as a standard language. This is not to deny the validity of Gneuss's remarks in general, but it does seem as if he misunderstood their import. There is a viable alternative. This is to claim, following Smith (1996: 65–7), that we are dealing, in the case of Ælfric, with a focused language, rather than a standard language. The mark of a focused language is that rather than having fixed, codified forms, it contains a small amount of internal variation and as such it attracts other varieties which have further variations of their own. But these other varieties then tend to adopt at least some of the forms of the focused and more prestigious language. This is precisely what seems to be happening in the case of Ælfrician English and explains some of Gneuss's difficulties. If, for example, Wulfstan, alongside and despite "Standard Old English," chooses to use a model of his own, as Gneuss states, this means that for Wulfstan, other things being equal, Ælfrician Old English is a focused variety which he can, if he wishes, ignore.

16.4 Mercian

We have now seen that it is doubtful that there ever existed a variety of West Saxon which could properly be described as forming a "Standard Old English." Rather, there existed one or more focused varieties of the kind which Smith (1996: 67) believes to have been quite common in the medieval period as a whole. It may be, for example, that Alfredian Old English was itself an earlier, but ultimately less successful, focused language, just as Ælfrician Old English was successful less than a century later. It is important to note that the existence of a focused language is not an either/or question, nor is the mutual existence of two or more focused languages in any way excluded. This is well illustrated by the situation in the dialect area normally called Mercian, to which I now turn.

Mercian, in Campbell's terms, is defined, essentially, by the shared properties of four major texts. From the eighth and ninth centuries there are three texts, the *Épinal Glossary* (Ep), the *Corpus Glossary* (Corp), and the *Vespasian Psalter Gloss* (VP); finally, there is the late tenth-century *Rushworth Gloss* (Ru^1). It is important to remember that, as Campbell says, the name Mercian is "practically without territorial significance." For of these texts only VP is, for most writers, directly associated with Lichfield in Staffordshire. Both Ep and Corp, which are linked texts, may have their original sources in Malmesbury in Wiltshire. There is a further problem with Ru^1. The actual manuscript contains parts written by two scribes, Farman and Owun. The Mercian part is that written down by Farman. On the other hand, the other part, called Ru^2, is recognized by everyone as essentially Northumbrian. For a long time now it has been thought to have been written at Harewood, between Leeds and York, obviously part of Northumbria. Since, during the Old English period, Harewood was a place without significance, this raises a problem.

Quite recently Coates (1997) has suggested that the Rushworth manuscript was actually written at Lichfield. The issue turns on the location of the place described in the manuscript as *æt harawuda* 'at Harewood'. Without going into details here, Coates suggests that the phrase is a loan-translation of a Romano-British place name *letoceto* 'gray- (hoar-) wood', which can only plausibly be *Wall*, which is about three miles south of Lichfield. If Coates is correct, then there are also plausible explanations of how the two very different scribes could have come to cooperate in the production of their joint text.

All well and good, but still the problem remains of what Mercian might be. In terms of geography the situation is not helped by the reassignment of Ru^1 to Lichfield, for that means that the two texts supposed to be from there, Ru^1 and VP, are the texts described by Campbell (1959: §11) as "highly divergent." It is worth examining the reasons for this claim, and here I shall restrict myself to one particular feature, by way of exemplification. The feature I shall examine is the effects of the sound change known as Second Fronting (see, for example, Hogg 1992: §5.87ff.) but also Kristensson (1986, 1987) and Hogg

(1997). I choose this feature because it is well known as a mark of Mercian English, one, as I shall show below, which has a history extending not merely through the Old English period, but right up to the present or near-present.

The simplest account of Second Fronting is to say that it was a change which caused short front vowels to front and raise so that original /æ/ and /ɑ/ changed to [ɛ] and [æ] respectively (the best phonemic analysis is hazardous), with the corresponding new spellings <e> and <æ>. How does the sound change appear in the four major texts? The following list demonstrates the situation in each:

Épinal:	5–30%
Corpus:	5–20%
Vespasian:	100%
Rushworth[1]:	10%

The figures for Ep and Corp, and to a much lesser extent Ru[1], are necessarily approximate because of confusions introduced by other interacting sound changes: in practice we are probably talking about a proportion of 15–20 percent in the former, and 10–15 percent in the latter.

If we start with the earliest of these texts, Ep, and draw a line between it and VP, then the differences can easily be accounted for by assuming chronological change: the change had hardly started at the time of Ep. Then a straight line of development can be drawn. Yet the other two texts contradict this. Corp is much later than Ep, it is also much less conservative in its language. But, as can been seen, it has, at best, no more examples of Second Fronting than Ep, and by no means the completeness of VP, which is at best only a few decades later. And Ru[1], which is about 150 years later than VP, has the fewest examples of all. This accounts, in part, for Campbell's "highly divergent" dialects.

One obvious explanation would be to assume that VP represents merely a peak and that later, perhaps as the result of dialect contact, the change begins to disappear from Mercia. But there is good reason to suppose that that is false. The early Middle English evidence tells against it. Thus *The Life of St. Chad*, which we have in an early twelfth-century text most probably associated with Worcester, shows a fundamental (albeit not complete) preference for Second Fronting (see Vleeskruyer 1953: §7). And later, in the early thirteenth century, the so-called AB dialect shows the same. Furthermore, both the *Linguistic Atlas of Late Medieval English* (LALME; McIntosh et al. 1986), for later Middle English, see LALME item map WAS (2), and even the *SED* for the twentieth century (see Kolb et al. 1979: 200) show distinct traces of Second Fronting. Thus the differences between VP and Ru[1] cannot be explained as the result of mere chronology.

There is an alternative explanation available. Note that the odd text out, as it were, is VP, with its unvarying presentation of Second Fronting. This type of behavior is unusual in any text of the period. The only work that is similar is the core group of Ælfrician texts. And that may provide us with a clue to what is happening in VP. It will be recalled that I suggested that Ælfrician Old English provides an example of Smith's (1996) focused language. Now one other thing of which we are aware, especially since Vleeskruyer's (1953) edition of *Chad,* is that there existed a Mercian literary tradition which started much earlier than anything in West Saxon and continued for much longer too, as evidenced by the Middle English AB dialect. This type of literary language seems to be precisely what Smith means by a focused language. One feature of such a language seems to have been that in the scriptoria in which it was used (which may have been a single scriptorium) there was an attempt to rationalize spelling traditions to a much greater extent than elsewhere. We may therefore be able to assume that the regularity of VP is one that was normal in this scriptorium at that time. On the other hand, the remaining texts, for reasons of either chronology or localization, did not require such regularity. Indeed, as Laing and Lass (2003; and chapter 17, this volume) show, in early Middle English regularization of orthography is apparently not usually seen as a necessary objective.

But that tells us nothing about their localization of our Mercian texts. For example, in the case of Ru[1], it could have been written at a different scriptorium in or near Lichfield, or, given that there is a gap of 150 years, at the same scriptorium but where the habits of the scriptorium itself had changed. And in any case, for none of the texts do we have any direct information of where the scribe himself came from apart from the tantalizing mention of *harawuda*.

Does this mean that we have, at this stage, to give up? Is it the case that, as Campbell says, Old English dialect names are practically without territorial significance, or that, as the title of Hogg (1988) might appear to imply, Old English dialectology is impossible? By no means. Recall the methods by which Campbell determines dialects: what he does is define each dialect in terms of features shared by a number of texts. What this actually means is that Mercian, for example, simply equates to a cluster of texts. Hence Campbell's reluctance to discuss questions of territorial significance. Yet it is possible to say a little more than Campbell allows. If we assume that both VP and Ru[1] demonstrate, albeit in different ways, dialects which must have been current in areas reasonably near the Lichfield area, and if we assume, as I suggested earlier, that both Ep and Corp are most likely to show dialects from, perhaps, Worcestershire or Warwickshire, as has been implied by Kitson (1990: 219; see also Pheifer 1974: §89), then the cluster we are dealing with is essentially one which covers the central West Midlands area.

This is of importance not merely for the study of Old English, but for the whole history of our language. There is a general belief that "Standard English," whatever that concept might refer to, has its origins, not in London English, but rather in various dialects of the Midlands and East Anglia (see Samuels 1963). This is undoubtedly an entirely proper view to take, but unfortunately it is too often transformed into a claim that this can be referred back to Old English Mercian. However, it should now be clear that Old Mercian relates to the cluster of texts I have been discussing, and these texts all have an origin in the West Midlands and therefore are not implicated in the emergence of Standard English, whose ancient origins remain unknown to us.

16.5 Northumbrian

The existence of a distinctive northern variety of Old English has been known almost since the beginning of the linguistic study of the language. It is of the utmost importance for the later history of the language, for there we see a variety of effects which are, during the Middle English period, to spread throughout the country. For example, it is in the late tenth-century Northumbrian texts that we find the widespread use of forms such as *aron* 'they are' supplanting earlier *synd(on)*, and it is in Northumbrian that the first clear signs of loss of grammatical gender can be observed (see Jones 1988).

Yet, for all that, Northumbrian Old English is, relatively speaking, the poor relation of Old English dialectal study. There are several reasons for this. Firstly, there are few texts, only some scattered relics from the eighth and ninth centuries together with some major interlinear glosses from near the end of the tenth century. Secondly, a series of studies done around 1900 by, especially, Uno Lindelöf and Karl Bülbring remain the standard work on the dialect, and rightly so (see Bülbring 1902; Lindelöf 1890, 1901). Thirdly, later work has concentrated on the admittedly complex glossarial practices of the best-known Northumbrian scribe, Aldred.

Despite Lindelöf's excellence, he leaves us with at least one dialectological puzzle. For both Lindelöf and his contemporary Bülbring saw a division between "North Northumbrian" and "South Northumbrian." Although this division is often supposed to include both the earlier texts and the late tenth-century texts, it is probably safe only to see a distinction in the later group. Here the principal northern text is *The Lindisfarne Gospels* (Li) and the principal southern text is *The Rushworth Gospels* (Ru^2), that is to say, the parts of *Rushworth* written by the Northumbrian scribe Owun. There can be no dispute that there are differences between Li and Ru^2, even if they are quite small, the best known being the development of the Gmc diphthong **au*, which in Ru^2 is mostly spelled <eo> whereas in Li the usual spelling is, as elsewhere in the country, <ea>.

It is not particularly easy to ascertain the implications of such variation, and I shall not attempt any explanation here, for there is a more general issue which must be explored; see, however, Hogg (2004a). This revolves around the question of what might be meant by the terms "North" and "South" in the context of Northumbrian. What is known for certain is that the glossator of Li was a priest called Aldred from Chester-le-Street close to Durham. No doubt, the long-standing belief that Owun, the scribe of Ru^2, was based at Harewood in Yorkshire led to the description of that text as South Northumbrian, contrasting with the North Northumbrian of Aldred and Chester-le-Street. But if Coates's arguments are even in part accepted, this looks more and more mistaken. It is far more probable that Owun, like Aldred, was based at Chester-le-Street and that he took *Lindisfarne* to Lichfield for safekeeping and for, together with Farman, glossing the Latin bible there with *Lindisfarne* as an aid.

Under that scenario, of course, Ru^2 is no more South Northumbrian than Li is North Northumbrian. Even if Aldred and Owun used different dialects, the differences between the two must have been minimal. It is most probable that the differences between the two are the result of different scribal habits rather than dialect. In other words, both varieties of Northumbrian are likely to be showing, in slightly different ways, the dialect of present-day County Durham.

16.6 Kentish

Although Kentish shares some of the difficulties which we have noted with the other traditional dialect areas, it also has some difficulties of its own. Thus, as with the other dialect clusters I have discussed, the majority of Kentish texts come from one single locality, namely Canterbury. On the other hand, there is evidence, particularly from Middle English, that we are dealing with a set of features which are more generally south-eastern, including areas just to the north of the Thames. On the other hand, the relatively few texts we have, although they are mostly charters, have a decidedly heterogeneous linguistic character.

The explanation of this is not, at least in broad outline, particularly difficult. The establishment of the Church in Anglo-Saxon England, after various early difficulties, was firmly based at Canterbury, with its archbishop. But, in contrast to ecclesiastical domains, political structures were, for most of the time, much more fluid. Furthermore, the political centers always lay elsewhere. Crudely speaking, we may suggest that until the second quarter of the ninth century the major political centers lay in Mercia, with its capital at Lichfield, and to some extent in Northumbria, especially at Durham and York. But from then on Wessex became the dominant force, with its capital at Winchester.

If any major leader, such as Offa, who reigned in Mercia from 756 to 796, or Cenwulf who followed him and reigned until 821, was to assert supremacy over the majority of the country, then it was imperative that they control Canterbury and its archbishopric. And indeed, the early Kentish charters, all those up to, I believe, 851, when Canterbury was sacked by the Vikings, show distinct traces of Mercian influence and teaching (see Brooks 1984). For the next quarter of a century the few extant charters show a very different character, one which we may assume to be the result of a loss of Mercian influence and a concomitant assertion of local speech patterns. But then what is found is the growing influence of Wessex, so that we find West Saxon forms alongside the native Kentish forms, just as previously Mercian forms had appeared beside Kentish ones.

The results of such dialect contact are most starkly demonstrated in the history of the sounds known as ǣ^{1} and ǣ^{2}. The first of these sounds develops in the earliest Old English to /æ:/ whereas the latter developed as the result of the monophthongization of earlier */ai/ to /ɑ:/ and its subsequent fronting by *i*-umlaut to /æ:/. The traditional view is that these sound changes carry through into a varying dialect situation, the most important point of which is that ǣ^{1} remains as /æ:/ only in West Saxon and that everywhere else it develops as /e:/, while in all dialects ǣ^{2} remains as /æ:/. As, for example, in Campbell (1959: §257):

> The Germanic invaders of Britain already most probably possessed one clear dialect distinction: the dialects from which W[est] S[axon] was to descend had *æ* from Prim. Gmc *æ*, but those from which are descended all other known OE dialects had *ē*.

And this is the general view.

Although it is undoubtedly the case that this is what happens eventually, it is doubtful that the end results are the outcome of the story which Campbell's account tells. And the reason for saying this lies in the history of Kentish. As I have shown elsewhere (see Hogg 1988), the differences between the histories of ǣ^{1} and ǣ^{2} in Kentish are no more than trivial. Both vowels are in the earliest texts represented by either <æ> or <e> but without a strong preference for either spelling. Yet in the late ninth century they both become spelled with <e> only, while in the tenth century both vowels can be spelled, mostly, as <e> although <æ> is also possible for both.

The relatively free variation seen in the later texts may well be result of West Saxon influence, as explained earlier. It certainly points to the view that the two sounds were indeed identical and all the evidence suggests that this identity reflects the vowel /e:/. That, however, is less important than the suggestion that in Kentish, apparently unlike any area of the country, ǣ^{1} and ǣ^{2} merged, as something like /æ:/ at an early stage of Old English and that shortly afterwards the merged sounds were raised to /e:/. This is contrary to received opinion, as we have seen, which claims that ǣ^{1} from Germanic **æ* becomes /e:/ in all non-West Saxon dialects but remains as /æ:/ in West Saxon, while ǣ^{2}, when subject to *i*-umlaut, changes from /ɑ:/ to /æ:/.

This present account claims that ǣ^{1} persisted as /æ:/ throughout the south of the century until the eighth century, by which time ǣ^{2} had merged with it in those areas (but, it follows, only in those areas). Then in the south-east the merged sounds were raised to /e:/. That this makes Kentish look like Anglian in terms of ǣ^{1} is a chronological misnomer. The end result may be the same, or, more precisely, similar. This can be best understood in terms of what is called *Pogatscher's Line* (Pogatscher 1900). This line, which is based primarily on place-name evidence from Old English demonstrates that the area south of a line from the Wash to the Severn estuary was one where ǣ^{1} remained as /æ:/. But nothing that I have said above disputes that.

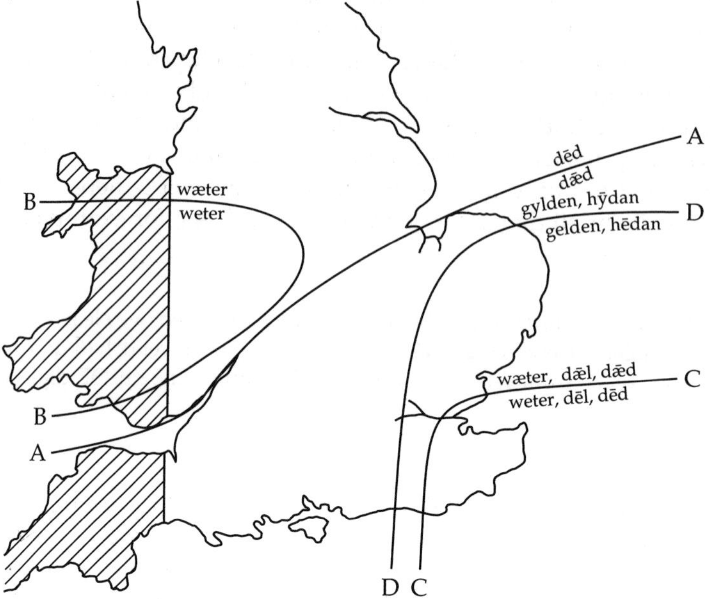

Map 16.1 Map from DeCamp (1958)

One important study which attempts to resolve these issues is DeCamp (1958). He presents the map reproduced as map 16.1. The critical isoglosses are *A*, which represents Pogatscher's Line, and hence the northern limits of $\bar{æ}^1$, and *C*, which represents the south-eastern limits of $\bar{æ}^2$. This, of course, goes precisely against the hypothesis suggested above, since it keeps $\bar{æ}^1$ and $\bar{æ}^2$ apart.

The interest in DeCamp's paper lies in how he explains what he sees as the changing patterns of Old English isoglosses during the period. His fundamental claim is that there were a series of Frisian developments which were brought across to Kent, whence they spread north and west. Thus, he claims, the shift of $\bar{æ}^1$ to /e:/ originated in Kent and then spread everywhere except the south-west (i.e. the West Saxon heartland). The obvious problem with DeCamp's hypothesis is that the above simply fails to explain a phenomenon such as Pogatscher's Line. But he has a solution to that too, which he describes as sociolinguistic. What he suggests is that after the initial surge of Kentish forms, up to about 650 for DeCamp, other areas, both in Mercia and Northumbria, came to predominate. At this point DeCamp's argument becomes rather unclear. For example, if he is correct in claiming that the spread of /e:/ was from Kent towards the north but that cultural supremacy has equally shifted to more northern areas, which should originally, in this thesis, have had /ǣ:/, how was it that the spread of /e:/ was not halted in its tracks? Of that there is no sign, except possibly in the dialect of Rushworth[1], where, moreover, there are alternative explanations available. Then DeCamp suggests a third stage in which

West Saxon becomes the dominant variety throughout the south, parts of the East Midlands and East Anglia. In this process various conservative features, such as the retention of ǣ^{1}, were, DeCamp claims, reintroduced into the East Midlands and East Anglia.

No doubt some of DeCamp's suggestions are correct, but there is also much to which we can object. Some of these issues can be ignored in the present context. For it is the fundamental context which is important. Some of the complexities in DeCamp's account can be removed if we accept, as I argued above, that the early shift of ǣ^{1} to /e:/ was only found north of Pogatscher's Line. This, of course, entails the view that the raising of ǣ^{1} was an innovation found only in the north and west.

This can quite easily be squared with the claims I made earlier concerning Kentish Raising of /æ:/ to /e:/, in terms both of ǣ^{1} and ǣ^{2}. For this change now appears to be a rather late Kentish innovation, unconnected with the early development of ǣ^{1} in the north. This leaves Pogatscher's Line intact but yet allows there to be new instances of /e:/ in the far south-east, perhaps not only in Kent but also, given later evidence, in the estuarial areas of Essex too. Although the evidence is uncertain, and fraught with difficulty (see Clark 1970: xlix), it does appear that the twelfth-century *Peterborough Chronicle* suggests the possibility that even as far north as that area there was considerable confusion concerning the values of both ǣ^{1} and ǣ^{2} and that they must have been, at least, close in pronunciation.

16.7 Syntax

There has been relatively little work done on dialect variation in terms of syntax. There are good explanations for why this is so. Firstly, syntax usually requires extensive data which are not easily available. Secondly, in terms of our dialect texts, in both Mercian and Northumbrian almost all the material is found in interlinear glosses which, because they are both Latin-based and word-for-word glosses, are quite resistant to the kind of analysis required. This makes the suggestions of, for example, Crowley (1980: 291 fn.1) doubtful, although interesting, and the same may hold for Koopman's (1990: 44) discussion of Bede's glossarial practice.

Perhaps the most enduring study is that reported on in Levin (1958), based on his PhD. In this paper Levin reports on the relative frequency of contracted and uncontracted forms of negation in various texts, that is to say, forms such as *nis* as opposed to *ne is* – 'isn't' vs. 'is not'. Levin studied both Old and Middle English texts, and in order to assess his work I shall have to look at both here. But let us start with his Old English material.

Levin looks at a variety of West Saxon texts and his results may be tabulated as in table 16.2. The corresponding figures for Anglian (i.e. Mercian and Northumbrian) are shown in table 16.3. The differences are striking. Contraction is all but canonical in West Saxon, whereas in Anglian, although

Table 16.2 Negative contraction in West Saxon

West Saxon	*+contract*	*−contract*	*%*
Cura Pastoralis	82	3	4
Orosius	145	3	2
Gospels: Corpus	79	3	4
Ælfric	477	4	1
Wulfstan	281	14	5
Gospels: Hatton	78	4	5

Table 16.3 Negative contraction in Anglian

Anglian	*+contract*	*−contract*	*%*
Vespasian	88	33	27
Lindisfarne	66	43	39
Rushworth[1]	39	23	37
Peterborough	61	28	31

it is predominant, there is always a substantial minority of uncontracted forms.

The problem with Levin's analysis lies not so much in his analysis of Old English, as in that of his Middle English material. Of contraction in Middle English he writes as follows:

> In Middle English the area of contraction comprises the Southern and West Midland dialects (these two dialects in Middle English carry on the West Saxon literary and linguistic traditions); on the other side of this isogloss are texts of East Midland and Northern provenience (1958: 498).

There is a clear contradiction here, which should be clear from what was said earlier about Mercian. If we take a text such as the *Vespasian Psalter*, then in terms of contraction it falls, as Levin says, on the side of Anglian. However, if we move on to Middle English, then a text such as *Ancrene Riwle* (AR) falls equally clearly on the side of the contracted variant (all but one out of its 118 examples show contraction). For what we saw earlier is that VP demonstrates canonical West Midlands forms. The same is true for Middle English in respect of AR, but with the opposite effect.

Levin misleads himself in this context by virtue of an interesting failure to pay sufficient attention to the historical context. Because VP, in Old English terms, is Mercian, and because AR, in Middle English terms, is West Midlands, the fact that we are dealing with essentially the same dialect area, centering on the dioceses of Lichfield and Worcester (including Hereford), is simply unnoticed by Levin. However, once that is acknowledged the different behaviors of the two texts become a matter of serious debate. For Levin offers no explanation of how West Midlands dialects show relatively little contraction in the Old English period but canonical contraction in Middle English.

I have argued elsewhere (see Hogg 2004b), that an explanation is available. Essentially this supposes that originally contraction was variably implemented throughout the country, but that, as Levin shows, it became canonical in parts of Wessex. Then it spread along the Thames Valley to the east and also along the Severn Valley to the north-west. Its spread along the Thames Valley to London was relatively unhindered, but along the Severn there were alternative writing centers which only slowly, if at all, came under West Saxon influence and were certainly not under such influence at the time of the *Vespasian Psalter*. The eventual spread of contraction to the West Midlands is only confirmed in the early Middle English period. What Levin sees as a continuation of older traditions is in fact a result, rather, of innovations from more prestigious writing centers.

Interesting as the phenomenon of negative contraction is, it must be admitted that it is a scarce haul in terms of syntactic dialect variation. There is the temptation, therefore, to believe that Old English was relatively uniform in terms of syntactic variation. This may be true, but it always has to be remembered, as I said at the beginning of this section, that the available evidence is simply not forthcoming because of the nature of our texts. It would, therefore, be dangerous to presuppose.

16.8 Lexis

Although the study of Old English dialect vocabulary has a long history, it is fair to observe that the first truly systematic modern study, particularly in its use of an extensive corpus, was that of Schabram (1965). For present purposes, one of the most interesting of all such studies is Wenisch's (1979), of the Anglian vocabulary of the language of the gospel of Luke in the *Lindisfarne Gospels*. Wenisch was able, by comparison of that text with other interlinear glosses of the same Latin text, to identify far more precisely than before the extent of forms identifiably Anglian or even Northumbrian, as well as vocabulary which was actually general Old English, but previously thought to be Anglian. Furthermore, Wenisch was also able to identify a number of other texts which are most probably of Anglian origin. Of necessity such identification is rather unspecific, yet it helps us get nearer an understanding of the dialectal spread of material.

I have already spent considerable time on one of the most important lexical studies of the last thirty years or so, namely Gneuss (1972). Since that paper is particularly interested in the vocabulary, which Gneuss shows to be associated with Æthelwold and hence with Ælfric too, what it is alleged that we are seeing is the formation of a Standard Old English vocabulary. As we have observed, Gneuss believes that this is the result of a conscious attempt at standardization by Æthelwold, and promoted further by Ælfric. Yet there is an alternative view, put forward firstly in Seebold (1974) and expanded in Hofstetter (1987). In this view, the preference for the so-called "Winchester" words is the result of local usage rather than a deliberate attempt to standardize. If the term "focused" language which I adopted earlier has any significance, then surely it is just such usage, which would involve a kind of dialect leveling of the type found in later Middle English, that would be involved.

Yet there are problems with both Gneuss's analysis and the modifications of that as proposed by Seebold and Hofstetter. The theories proposed in all these accounts are essentially the same, that there are specific "Winchester" lexical items which are replacements of other ordinary Old English items. For example, whereas Alfredian texts use either *cræft* or *mægen* for "(heavenly) powers," Winchester texts use, virtually exclusively, *miht* (see also Kastovsky 1992: 346–9). Whether this change is the result of standardization or simply a reflection of local usage is the type of issue which the above views reflect in their different ways.

Yet there is a further possibility which needs to be explored. It is possible that the source of the differences is neither the result of standardization nor the influence of local dialects. Or, rather, the source is neither necessarily nor exclusively either or both of those. The most obvious feature of the "Winchester" texts is that, in comparison with even the most religious of the Alfredian texts, they are much better defined in theological terms. We may, therefore, be dealing with language in a special theological register. In such a register concepts such as "heavenly powers" are likely to be appropriated from day-to-day language but in very particular usages and choices. When Gneuss (1972: 76) writes:

> In the main, however, the words are taken from a great variety of spheres. . . . Verbal concepts . . . are also to be found. So we see that it was not a case of some sort of new "technical" vocabulary being laid down; stylistic considerations, rather, must have been the chief concern in choosing individual words

I find it rather difficult to understand what his exact claim might be. Firstly, it is difficult to understand the distinction between "technical" and "stylistic." Secondly "technical" language need not be new, it need only be old words used in a different or more restricted contexts. Furthermore, it is undoubtedly the case that in many instances these are new words coined, or rather, most often, borrowed from Latin.

If it is the case that Ælfric and others were often using a new vocabulary (either genuinely new or adaptations of existing language), this is less helpful than at first might seem the case in terms of understanding the dialect geography of Old English vocabulary. The reason for this may be twofold. Firstly, the kinds of vocabulary being investigated may not be totally helpful. All the above studies are concerned, above all, with concepts and abstract language (or the use of ordinary words in conceptual frameworks). Secondly, the texts being used for these studies are by and large what may be called "literary" manuscripts, which, of course, predominate in the extant data.

These problems are well laid out in a series of papers by Peter Kitson, the most relevant for present purposes being Kitson (1993). The essential innovation in Kitson's paper is that he concentrates his study on the distribution, not of literary or conceptual words, but of function words or high-frequency items, and that the study is based on charter material rather than on the usual literary texts. In this 1993 paper, which is by no means easy to assimilate, he looks at the geography of Ælfric's and, to a lesser extent, Alfred's dialect features in the context of prepositional usage in his charter material.

A proper assessment of Kitson's work is not possible within the confines of this chapter, but it is clear that the analysis of charter material is vital to a proper understanding of variation in Old English. On more particular issues Kitson provides interesting clues to the dialect features of three key players. Firstly, there is more than enough external evidence to suggest that Æthelwold was a native of Winchester. Secondly, if Kitson is correct, the likelihood is that Ælfric was a native of the area around Abingdon and Witney (almost 50 miles north of Winchester and near Oxford), and here there is some suggestion that this might be correct, given his history. Thirdly, Kitson argues that it is most likely that Alfred was a native of Wilton, which is not impossible.

But more important than all of this is Kitson's demonstration that there was certainly a wide dialectal variation in this large area of the South and the South Midlands and that the phenomenon which has come to be known as "Standard Old English" was by no means unitary but found expression in a variety of local forms. There can be some objection to Kitson's work, which is certainly hypothesis-laden and which suffers from some unclear maps from which appropriate deductions are difficult to make. Nevertheless, his work offers a significant advance which should prove of lasting value.

16.9 Conclusion

Over the last few decades there has been a renewed interest in the study of Old English dialects. Much of the impetus for this has arisen from a source external to Old English, namely the work of McIntosh, Samuels, and Benskin on later Middle English, culminating in the production of LALME. The effects of that project have been seen in several ways. For example, we can note the quite general dissatisfaction with traditional methodology expressed in works such Benskin (1994) or Hogg (1988, 1998). This, of course, has resulted in a reappraisal of some fundamental work which, previously, had not been fully understood, notably Campbell (1959).

Other earlier work is in the process of being reevaluated, and here we might think, above all, of Wrenn's (1933) paper on Standard Old English, for this has resulted in a still ongoing debate about the usefulness of the concept of standardization in the Old English context, a debate inititiated by Gneuss's (1972) paper. As we have seen, it is quite possible that what we are witnessing in the West Saxon area during the tenth century is something more complex but also more interesting than has been previously thought. And, as we have also seen, the rise of what we may call focused languages, following Smith (1996), is not merely the privilege of one area of Anglo-Saxon England alone.

Much of the current interest in Old English dialectology is certainly due to the work of Peter Kitson and his study of Old English charter material. He has certainly taken the methodologies of LALME into the study of Old English, and already this has produced considerable results as well as much discussion. And a very new development which I have touched upon above is the progress made by Margaret Laing, Keith Williamson, and Roger Lass at the Institute of Historical Dialectology at Edinburgh University, where they have made considerable progress on adapting LALME for the study of early Middle English dialectology (see again Laing and Lass 2003, and chapter 17, this volume, and also a forthcoming paper of my own which attempts to show how this might be applied to some Old English texts – Hogg 2004b).

It may be that we can never have the kind of detailed analysis of Old English dialects that we can have for rather later periods, but it is slowly becoming clear that the opportunities for real progress are now far more promising than they have been, dare I say it, for almost a century.

REFERENCES

Bazell, C. E. (1960). Review of A. Campbell, An Old English Grammar. *Medium Aevum* 29: 27–30.

Benskin, M. (1994). Descriptions of dialect and areal distributions. In M. Laing and K. Williamson (eds.), *Speaking in Our Tongues* (pp. 169–87). Woodbridge: D. S. Brewer.

Brooks, N. (1984). *The Early History of the Church at Canterbury*. Leicester: Leicester University Press.

Bülbring, K. D. (1902). *Altenglisches Elementarbuch*. Heidelberg: Carl Winter.

Campbell, A. (1959). *An Old English Grammar*. Oxford: Clarendon Press.

Clark, C. (1970). *The Peterborough Chronicle 1070–1154* (2nd edn.). Oxford: Clarendon Press.

Coates, R. (1997). The scriptorium of the Mercian Rushworth Gloss: a bilingual perspective. *Notes and Queries* 242: 453–8.

Crowley, J. P. (1980). The study of Old English dialect. PhD dissertation, University of Michigan. Ann Arbor: University Microfilms International.

Davies, A. M. (1998). *History of Linguistics: Nineteenth-century Linguistics* (vol. 4). Harlow: Longman.

DeCamp, D. (1958). The genesis of the Old English dialects: a new hypothesis. *Language* 34: 232–44.

Girvan, R. (1931). *Angelsaksisch Handboek*. Haarlem: Tjeenk Willink.

Gneuss, H. (1972). The origin of standard Old English and Æthelwold's school at

Winchester. *Anglo-Saxon England* 1: 63–83.
Haugen, E. (1966). Dialect, language, nation. *American Anthropologist* 68: 922–35.
Hoffstetter, W. (1987). *Winchester und der spätaltenglische Sprachgebrauch: Untersuchungen zur geographischen und zeitlichen Verbreitung altenglische Synonyme.* Munich: Wilhelm Fink.
Hogg, R. M. (1988). On the impossibility of Old English dialectology. In D. Kastovsky and G. Bauer (eds.), *Luick Revisited* (pp. 183–203). Tübingen: Gunter Narr.
Hogg, R. M. (1992). *A Grammar of Old English.* Oxford: Basil Blackwell.
Hogg, R. M. (1997). Using the future to predict the past: Old English dialectology in the light of Middle English place-names. In J. Fisiak (ed.), *Studies in Middle English Linguistics* (pp. 207–20). Berlin: Mouton de Gruyter.
Hogg, R. M. (1998). On the ideological boundaries of Old English dialects. In J. Fisiak and M. Krygier (eds.), *Advances in English Historical Linguistics* (pp. 107–18). Berlin: Mouton de Gruyter.
Hogg, R. M. (2004a). North Northumbrian and South Northumbrian: a geographical question? In M. Dossena (ed.), *English Historical Dialectology* (pp. 241–55). München: Peter Lang.
Hogg, R. M. (2004b). The spread of negative contraction in early English. In A. Curzan and K. Emmons (eds.), *Studies in the History of the English Language II: Unfolding Conversations.* Berlin: Mouton de Gruyter.
Hogg, R. M. (in preparation). *A History of English Dialectology.*
Jones, C. (1988). *Grammatical Gender in English: 950–1250.* London: Croom Helm.
Kastovsky, D. (1992). Semantics and vocabulary. In R. M. Hogg (ed.), *The Cambridge History of the English Language* (pp. 290–408). Cambridge: Cambridge University Press.
Kitson, P. (1990). On Old English nouns of more than one gender. *English Studies* 71: 185–221.
Kitson, P. (1993). Geographical variation in Old English prepositions and the location of Ælfric's and other literary dialects. *English Studies* 74: 1–50.
Kolb, E., B. Glauser, W. Elmer, and R. Stamm (1979). *Atlas of English Sounds.* Bern: Francke Verlag.
Koopman, W. F. (1990). Word order in Old English with special reference to the verb phrase. PhD dissertation, University of Amsterdam.
Kristensson, G. (1986). A Middle English dialect boundary. In D. Kastovsky and A. Szwedek (eds.), *Linguistics Across Historical and Geographical Boundaries* (pp. 443–57). Berlin: Mouton de Gruyter.
Kristensson, G. (1987). *A Survey of Middle English Dialects 1290–1350: the West Midland Counties.* Lund: Lund University Press.
Laing, M. and R. Lass (2003). Tales of the 1000 Nists: the phonological implications of literal substitution sets in 13th-century south-west midlands texts. *English Language and Linguistics* 7: 257–78.
Levin, S. R. (1958). Negative contraction: an Old and Middle English dialect criterion. *Journal of English and Germanic Philology* 57: 492–501.
Lindelöf, U. (1890). *Die Sprache des Rituals von Durham.* Helsingfors: J. C. Frenckell.
Lindelöf, U. (1901). *Die Südnorthumbrische Mundart des 10. Jahrhunderts.* Bonn: P. Hansteins Verlag.
McIntosh, A., M. L. Samuels, and M. Benskin (1986). *A Linguistic Atlas of Late Medieval English.* Aberdeen: Aberdeen University Press.

Murray, J. A. H. et al. (1888–). *Oxford English Dictionary*. Oxford: Oxford University Press.
Pheifer, J. D. (1974). *Old English Glosses in the Épinal-Erfurt Glossary*. Oxford: Clarendon Press.
Pogatscher, A. (1900). Die ae. æ/ e-Grenze. *Anglia* 23: 302–9.
Quirk, R. and C. L. Wrenn (1957). *An Old English Grammar* (2nd edn.). London: Methuen.
Samuels, M. L. (1963). Some applications of Middle English dialectology. *English Studies* 44: 81–94.
Schabram, H. (1965). *Superbia: Studium zum altenglischen Wortschatz.* I: *Die dialektale und zeitliche Verbeitung des Wortschatz.* Munich: Wilhelm Fink.
Seebold, E. (1974). Die ae. Entsprechungen von lat. *sapiens* und *prudens*: Eine Untersuchung über die mundartliche Gliederung der ae. Literatur. *Anglia* 92: 291–333.
Smith, J. J. (1996). *An Historical Study of English.* London: Routledge.
Sweet, H. (1871). *King Alfred's West-Saxon Version of Gregory's Pastoral Care* (Early English Text Society, o.s. 45, 50). London: Oxford University Press.
Sweet, H. (1876). Dialects and prehistoric forms of Old English. *Transactions of the Philological Society* 16: 543–69.
Sweet, H. (1885). *The Oldest English Texts* (Early English Text Society, o.s. 83). London: Oxford University Press.
Vleeskruyer, R. (1953). *The Life of St. Chad: An Old English Homily.* Amsterdam: North-Holland.
Wenisch, F. (1979). *Spezifisch anglisches Wortgut in den nordhumbrischen Interlinearglossierungen des Lukasevangeliums* (Anglistische Forschungen, 132). Heidelberg: Carl Winter.
Whitelock, D. (1967). *Sweet's Anglo-Saxon Reader*. Oxford: Clarendon Press.
Wrenn, C. L. (1933). "Standard" Old English. *Transactions of the Philological Society* 32: 65–88.

Dispatch to:

Anthony D. Clover
Le Pic du Trèfle, Southbrook
Mere
Warminster
Wiltshire
BA12 6BG
United Kingdom

Order ID: 203-6763918-2820333

Thank you for buying from BethBradley on Amazon Marketplace.

Delivery address:
Anthony D. Clover
Le Pic du Trèfle, Southbrook
Mere
Warminster
Wiltshire
BA12 6BG
United Kingdom

Order Date: 15 Jan 2017
Delivery Service: Standard
Buyer Name: A.D.Clover
Seller Name: BethBradley

Quantity	Product Details	Price	Total

...ook of the History of English (Blackwell Handbooks in Linguistics) [Paperback] [2009] van Kemenade, Ans **SKU:** 73-L92F-Q8VC **ASIN:** 1405187867 **Listing ID:** 0817PLQK8PG **Order Item ID:** 18372041371971 **Condition:** New **Comments:** Never used		Shipping: £2.80 Total: £21.75
		ORDER TOTAL: £21.75

Thanks for buying on Amazon Marketplace. To provide feedback for the seller please visit www.amazon.co.uk/feedback. To contact the seller, go to Your Orders in Your Account. Click the seller's name under the appropriate product. Then, in the "Further Information" section, click "Contact the Seller."

17 Early Middle English Dialectology: Problems and Prospects

MARGARET LAING AND
ROGER LASS

17.1 On Dialectology

There are no such things as dialects. Or rather, "a dialect" does not exist as a discrete entity. Attempts to delimit a dialect by topographical, political, or administrative boundaries ignore the obvious fact that within any such boundaries there will be variation for some features, while other variants will cross the borders. Similar oversimplification arises from those purely linguistic definitions that adopt a single feature to characterize a large regional complex, e.g. [f] for <wh-> in present day Northeast Scotland or [e(:)] in "Old Kentish" for what elsewhere in Old English was represented as [y(:)]. Such definitions merely reify taxonomic conventions. A dialect atlas in fact displays a continuum of overlapping distributions in which the "isoglosses" delimiting dialectal features vary from map to map and "the areal transition between one dialect type and another is graded, not discrete" (Benskin 1994: 169–73).

To the non-dialectologist, the term "dialectology" usually suggests static displays of dots on regional maps, indicating the distribution of phonological, morphological, or lexical features. The dialectology considered here will, of course, include such items; but this is just a small part of our subject matter. Space is only one dimension of dialectology. Spatial distribution is normally a function of change over time projected on a geographical landscape. But change over time involves operations within speech communities; this introduces a third dimension – human interactions and the intricacies of language use. Dialectology therefore operates on three planes: space, time, and social milieu.

17.1.1 *On historical dialectology*

If this is "dialectology," how is it different from either historical linguistics or sociolinguistics? In principle it is not. The differences are matters of emphasis rather than of theoretical underpinning. Historical dialectology is simply historical linguistics with a spatial emphasis; in the same sense, historical linguistics is simply linguistics with a temporal emphasis. However, there are three major problems faced by those making a study of any past stage of a language. The first is that our samples depend on the contingent survival of text witnesses, and are therefore not expandable: all of our informants are dead. The second is the increasing opacity of social milieu with the passing of time. As a general rule, the further back we go, the more decontextualized and enigmatic our witnesses become. The third difference is that our witnesses are samples of written rather than of spoken language. The "native speakers" of past stages of a language are writers and copying scribes. Their output is our only source material; there is no recourse to language data of any other kind. These "text languages" must take the place of informants who can be questioned directly. One crucial limitation this imposes is that we cannot ask the same question more than once of a given informant. Nor can we ask our witnesses for anything that they have not already provided.

In modern dialect studies, the social dimension may involve variables such as age, sex, class, religion, occupation, economic status, education, and ethnicity. In the context of historical dialectology "social milieu" must be taken more generally to refer to the whole historical background. It is rarely possible to achieve the fineness of resolution typical of studies of contemporary language states. Variables will differ according to which historical vernacular is under scrutiny and at what period.

17.1.2 *Time, space, and historical context*

The input to any form of dialectology is language variation. Historical dialectology in particular is concerned with:

(a) how linguistic forms and structures change through time;
(b) how they vary across space – that is, the country or region where they were spoken and written;
(c) how the situation and intentions of the speakers and writers of the language engender this variation.

This chapter is concerned with the historical dialectology of "early Middle English": that is, all written English from about 1150 to 1325, after which the language is termed "late Middle English". For the process of creating, from the source texts of the period, A Linguistic Atlas of Early Middle English (LAEME), the "early"/"late" division was largely arbitrary and a matter of convenience. The language of the twelfth century and that of the fifteenth are different enough to justify separate identifying names. But language differences in time, like those in space, form continua: there are no sharp temporal boundaries. With respect to "archaism" and "modernness" Middle English before 1300 is certainly "early" and that after 1350 "late"; the language written between is perhaps "transitional," but this property exists only by virtue of the strong differences at both ends.

The *terminus a quo* for early Middle English sources is the historical accident (linguistically speaking) of the Norman Conquest, which set a political and cultural boundary between two stages of the history of England. To a much greater extent than their conquerors, the Anglo-Saxons used the vernacular (alongside Latin) to record their legal and administrative documents, as well as for religious, historical, and literary works. The post-Conquest practice of using primarily Latin, and to a lesser extent French, for the purposes for which English had previously been used, gradually ousted English as a written medium. Some post-Conquest documents were written wholly or partly in English (Pelteret 1990) but their language is largely based on earlier documentary models, while surviving literary works in English are almost entirely confined to copies of texts originally composed pre-Conquest. This means that for a century or more there was virtually no new writing in English. Only from the later part of the twelfth century does English start to be used again in written form. For LAEME and in this chapter, we take the work of the scribe of the second continuation of the Peterborough Chronicle, writing in 1154/5, to represent the earliest surviving text in truly Middle English language – that is, language that reflects how the spoken language of his region had developed in the preceding century.

The range of sociolinguistic variables we can access for the early Middle English period is limited; but because our materials come from a small, closed, and socially homogeneous milieu the standard variables of modern dialectology are largely irrelevant. Since all our sources are written, we are concerned only with the literate – a small subset of the population in twelfth- and thirteenth-century England. This sub-population would have been ethnically relatively homogeneous – descendants of native English, immigrant French, and mixtures of the two. (We do not, however, know in detail to what extent "native English" pre-Conquest included mixed Celtic and/or Scandinavian elements, whether there were still culturally distinct groups of English, Celtic, and Scandinavian ancestry, or what their relative statuses might have been.) The literate population was also religiously homogeneous and very largely (but not exclusively) male. So the number of variables out of the classic set is small: we are dealing with the output of literate, adult, English Catholics largely inhabiting closed institutions (monasteries, professions) where class stratification would be of little importance. Textual scholars, palaeographers, and codicologists can sometimes recover other variables, such as whether the author of a text was, say, a Franciscan or a Benedictine; whether a copyist worked in a particular scriptorium, or was expert in different kinds of script, format, or diplomatic. Such variables may have affected a writer's choice of written form, style, or content and thereby the kind of English he employed. The complexities of historical context and the relevant variables are thus tied directly to the sources and include: the intricate relations between the scribes' native varieties and their transcribing of languages other than English, the text genres, the provenance of exemplars and the different modes of copying. These complexities, and a much more sophisticated picture of the milieu, have emerged during the course of the twenty-year duration of the LAEME project. It may be that once the variables are clearly outlined, the sociolinguistic texture will become denser and more rich than it now is. Text type and scribal provenance (e.g. secular vs. religious text, prose vs. verse, monastic vs. freelance, or church-trained vs. school-trained scribes) may become, as our knowledge increases, indicative variables to substitute for some of the more conventional ones.

17.1.3 *Coverage*

A properly historical dialectology is narrative and dynamic as well as purely cartographic: it tells stories as well as showing pictures. But this desired goal is often thwarted by the geographic and temporal skewing of our surviving witnesses. The ideal database for displaying the story of a language in time and space is illustrated in figure 17.1. Here we have a set of attested "dialects" D_1–D_3 (shorthand for assemblages of regional features), each of which survives as a chronological sequence of text-corpora t_1–t_4. Let the spatial frame of the diagram represent the geographical region over which the language is spoken; in this case we have a continuous regional and temporal coverage.

Unfortunately, the survival-pattern of both Old English and earlier Middle English texts is typically rather more like figure 17.2. That is, some regional

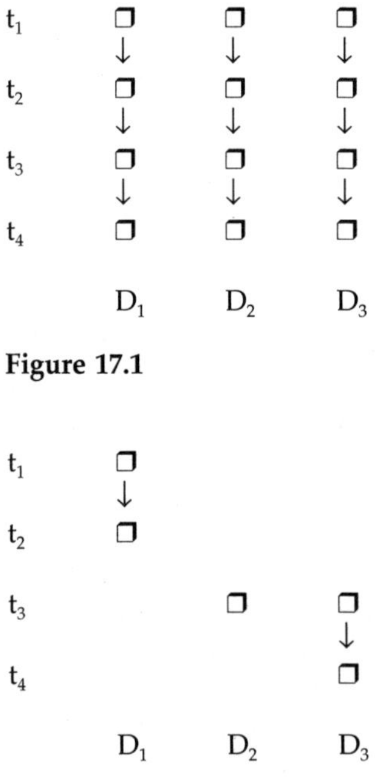

Figure 17.1

Figure 17.2

varieties are attested early, have a few descendants, and then vanish; some appear only at one period, apparently leaving no offspring; and others appear in sequence, but late, without visible ancestry. This means that at no point in the history is there a full t_1–t_4 sequence for any region. An attempt at a "vertical" history becomes *de facto* "diagonal" when the attestation is skewed or defective.

As an example, any handbook of Old English will tell us that the masculine/neuter genitive singular developed along the pathway **-os-* > **-as* > *-æs* > *-es*. But the *-æs* forms are attested only in older Anglian texts, and most of our surviving material is West Saxon. The early Anglian texts show forms which are taken as "ancestral" to the West Saxon ones; but since they come from a different dialect cluster, they are merely cognate, no more ancestral than their equivalents in Gothic or Old High German. Yet since they are archaic-looking and older, the handbooks allow the implication that "archaic" *-æs* in some sense "turns into" the later *-es*. Of course, it almost certainly did in the ancestor of West Saxon, but the evidence does not survive. If D_1 is Northumbrian and D_3 is West Saxon, then the "change" or "evolution" of these forms is in fact being plotted diagonally on the pseudo-geographical map, and projected on a manufactured time line which expunges the diagonality and appears vertical. This verticalization of skewed lineages is a typical presentation of the history of English. We hope that the approach to early Middle English dialectology and its sources described in this chapter will discourage misleading interpretations.

For LAEME, the situation is something between the two schemata presented in figures 17.1 and 17.2 above. Very little written Middle English survives from before the last quarter of the twelfth century. The West Midlands and to a lesser extent the East Midlands and the Southeast are reasonably well represented by texts from the thirteenth century. But almost nothing survives from the North or North Midlands from before 1300, nor from the extreme Southwest. The coverage in the South is also sparse, and a lack of texts from the Central Midlands makes it difficult to establish a dialectal continuum even between the well-attested areas to the West and East (Laing 2000a: 100). We therefore have to reconcile ourselves to a more patchy coverage for LAEME, both through time and across space, than that which it was possible to present in *A Linguistic Atlas of Late Medieval English* (LALME; see McIntosh et al. 1986). However, we do not have to contend in our period with the problem of supraregionalization. There is at this time no single, more prestigious form of the vernacular exercising undue influence on the linguistic usage of other regions, as late West Saxon did in the pre-Conquest period, and as the emerging national standard was beginning to do in the latter part of the Middle English period. For the end of our period, materials may be supplemented to a certain extent with the data collected by Gillis Kristensson (1967, 1987, 1995, 2001, 2002) gleaned from the Lay Subsidy Rolls of 1290–1350. This material, however, is purely onomastic; for the problems raised by the use of names in historical dialectology, see Lass and Laing forthcoming, fn.9).

17.2 Sources for Early Middle English Dialectology

17.2.1 *Text types*

There are three types of potential source material for a dialect atlas of early Middle English: local documents, glosses, and literary texts (Laing 1993).

17.2.1.1 Local documents

Local documents between 1150 and 1325 are mostly writs, charters, and wills, originating pre-Conquest (or from only shortly after), copied during our period into the cartularies of religious houses. Of these twelfth- and thirteenth-century copies very few have been updated by the copying scribe into contemporary local language; they remain in Old English or appear as some garbled version of what the copying scribe thought was intended in his exemplar. This makes it impossible to set up for LAEME the matrix of local documentary "anchor texts" that formed the basis of LALME and into which the material from the unlocalized literary texts was ultimately "fitted". Indeed, this paucity of documentary material in English from before the last quarter of the fourteenth century was one reason why the LALME editors chose the later Middle English period for their pioneering investigation. For early Middle English there are, however, a few usable documentary texts, and occasionally a literary text may also serve as an "anchor" if the manuscript containing it is known to have particular local associations. Comparison with the much denser dialect continuum available for late Middle English may also help us to localize earlier scribal dialects.

The terms "anchor" and "fitted" texts raise a major conceptual question. If an anchor text exists in real geographical space, how do we interpret the space in which we localize a fitted text? The Canterbury in which Dan Michel completed the *Ayenbyte of Inwyt* in 1340 is a place we know existed, just as modern Canterbury does. We can physically visit its descendant. But there is also a "linguistic" Canterbury – the more abstract place where a fitted Kentish text might have its existence. Linguistic space is a semi-independent dimension imposed on physical geographical space (Williamson 2000).

17.2.1.2 Glosses

Glosses furnish even less English source material. They reflect the immediate post-Conquest linguistic situation: most writing is in Latin and where vernacular is used it is as often French as English (Hunt 1991). Glosses may themselves be in Latin, as annotations to the main text, or they may be interlinear or marginal "Englishings" or "Frenchings" of the words of a Latin text. If they are only scattered examples in the text they will, of course, provide only fragmentary linguistic evidence with little potential for comparison with other language types. Continuous interlinear glosses would be of greater value, but in our period only one such survives, that of Eadwine's *Psalter* in Cambridge, Trinity College 987 (R.17.1) written in the mid-twelfth century. However, the language of the gloss is more Old English in character than Middle English.

17.2.1.3 Literary texts

The great bulk of source texts for early Middle English is literary works. These are very varied in type and in usefulness, ranging from extended narrative or instructive works that afford large quantities of linguistic data, through short lyrics of just a few stanzas, down to tiny tags or proverbial saws embedded in Latin texts. Literary texts (religious or secular) may be in verse or prose; if in verse, meter and/or rhyme will impose certain constraints on linguistic form.

17.2.2 Orthography

This is the inventory of our linguistic witnesses. But before we can assess what texts *can* tell us about the language in which they are written we must acknowledge what they *cannot* tell us. The *prima facie* evidence is the orthography of the text. Before we can interpret its significance we have to remember that of the three written languages in twelfth- and thirteenth-century England, English was the least commonly used. There was as yet no established approach to designing orthographies for contemporary spoken English. The writing of English in this period shows a great deal of experimentation: scribes' attempts to represent their native language include the entire historical repertoire (Anglo-French and Anglo-Latin as well as Old English traditions) adapted with varying degrees of individual inventiveness. The spelling and choice of lexis, and perhaps also syntax, will be affected by such variables as whether the text was originally composed in English or whether it is a translation from Latin, French, or from a version in an earlier form of English. Moreover, most written texts are not original works but copies made by scribes other than their authors. The entire feasibility of Middle English dialectology, however, relies on the fact that it is nevertheless possible to isolate examples of genuine individual and local linguistic usage.

17.2.3 Copying strategies

It has long been established (McIntosh [1973] 1989: 92) that although almost all Middle English witnesses are "copied" texts, they by no means all display linguistic mixture. In the course of copying, some scribes translated texts in other varieties of English into the local usage with which they and their readership were most familiar. Others, either by training or personal preference, simply copied as accurately as they could the text forms of their exemplar(s). In the former case the resulting output is an internally consistent witness of the translating scribe's local usage. In the latter case the result *could* be an internally consistent witness of the usage of the scribe of the exemplar – or indeed of an earlier scribe if there were a succession of such *literatim* copyists. If the scribe was responsible for copying more than one text in more than one scribal language, his strategy as a *literatim* copyist is revealed: each text will represent the language of some previous stage of transmission. Depending on the local origins of the exemplar for each text, one and the same scribe may provide text languages representing a number of different locations (e.g. the scribe of the Cotton version of *The Owl and the Nightingale*; Breier 1910: 49–51; Atkins 1922: xxix–xxxi) or different times (e.g. the scribe of the Lambeth Homilies; Sisam 1951).

17.2.4 Mischsprachen

Sometimes, however, a scribe would neither consistently translate nor copy accurately from his exemplar but would do something in between. Where this happens, or where a *literatim* copyist has such a text as his exemplar, the output will not represent an internally consistent scribal dialect but a mixture of two or more language types – that of the copying scribe and whatever he is copying from. In LALME, genuine *Mischsprachen* were noted but not used as sources for dialect mapping. Some apparent mixtures are, however, not inextricably mixed. Sometimes a translating scribe takes a few folios to get into his "translation stride." Then the first few folios of his version will contain some "relict" forms that belong rather to the dialect of his exemplar than to his own. But after this initial working-in period, his own usage becomes established. Or, a scribe may translate forms that are completely alien to his own usage, while leaving unchanged words whose spellings are familiar as part of his passive repertoire (Benskin and Laing 1981) – even if he himself would not normally spell them that way. This is known as "constrained selection." For LAEME, we have so little surviving source material we cannot afford to discard linguistically composite texts without at least attempting to analyze them and to isolate their different linguistic elements. In some cases it has proved possible to extrapolate from different linguistic layers inventories of forms that may be taken to represent genuine regional usage (Laing and McIntosh 1995a, 1995b; Laing 2000b).

17.3 Methodology

17.3.1 The questionnaire

The traditional dialectological tool is the questionnaire: a list of preselected items designed to elicit characteristically regional forms from the survey informants. The elicitation targets may be presented as words, phrases, or objects or pictures to be named, and depending on the aims of the survey, may elicit local usage at any linguistic level. The advantage of a questionnaire is that the same list of items is used for every informant. This enables the dialectologist to address the key desiderata of dialectology: description and comparison. The questionnaire's weakness is that its function as a linguistic net only ever results in a limited catch (Williamson 1992/3: 139).

Nevertheless, if it is large and varied enough in its scope, the questionnaire can provide a valuable conspectus of the language under investigation. LALME is witness to the effectiveness of the traditional questionnaire for the investigation of a medieval vernacular.

Questionnaire items must provide a good yield of dialectal discriminants: i.e. formal variation between witnesses and wide attestation across the population surveyed. It requires considerable prior knowledge of the language, or else a great deal of trial and error, before an effective questionnaire can be finalized. For this and other reasons we have elected to use a different analytical tool for the investigation of early Middle English linguistic variation.

17.3.2 *Reasons for abandoning the questionnaire for LAEME*

A questionnaire for English of 1150–1325 would need to take account of three period-specific variables: (a) versions of Old English texts, both documentary and literary, alongside original early Middle English works reflecting contemporary spoken regional varieties; (b) rapid ongoing linguistic change; (c) other points of comparison that might have regional or diachronic significance – e.g. idiosyncratic spelling, phonology, and morphology; the proportion in a text of Scandinavian or French lexis. In addition it would have to have enough overlap with the LALME questionnaire to facilitate comparison between the two periods.

A theoretically "ideal" questionnaire for early Middle English would have to register so many variables that in practice it would be unmanageable. At some point it is necessary to make a rigorous and often ruthless selection, from a large variety of potentially important phenomena, for the purposes of comparison and dialectal mapping. But a questionnaire is itself a highly selective tool. The more tractable we make it, the more likely we are to miss valuable information: the simpler the questionnaire the coarser the net. We have therefore adopted a different approach.

17.3.3 *Corpus-based dialectology*

Instead of using a questionnaire, we transcribe and key on to disk entire texts – or large samples of very long texts. This corpus forms a database that can be sorted and analyzed, and any pair or *n*-tuple of texts compared electronically (using software written for the purpose by Keith Williamson). The methodological advantage is that *all* the linguistic data in the text corpus can be subjected to analysis or manipulated without commitment to a preselected set of dialectal discriminants. This strategy allows the inductive emergence of significant categories whose existence we might not otherwise have expected. Computationally, it resembles the cluster analysis that has provided rich yields in synchronic sociolinguistics. Moreover, material not useful for dialectal analysis remains available for a wide range of other studies: historical phonology, morphology, syntax, or semantics.

There are various stages in the corpus-based approach.

17.3.3.1 Original manuscripts

Texts are transcribed from original manuscripts or from facsimiles like the small sample illustrated in figure 17.3. It is crucial that the corpus input is diplomatic transcription from originals or facsimiles, and not editions. Printed editions can be very useful for reference, but editorial practice varies considerably and for rigorous comparison all corpus texts must be treated consistently. While some editors present a more or less diplomatic version of a text, it is often the case that the original is modified in a number of ways, any of which may render it suspect for linguistic study.

Overtly "normalized" or "modernized" editions of medieval texts are obviously to be avoided by language scholars. But even scholarly single text editions have their pitfalls. Most editors silently expand manuscript abbreviations, taking as the form of the expansion the scribe's "usual" unabbreviated spelling. This practice may seriously skew numbers as well as suppressing valid distinct spellings. Though few editors of scholarly texts substitute modern "equivalents" for <þ>, <ð>, or <ȝ>, most nowadays change <ƿ> to <w>. These *litterae* are not always direct functional equivalents and the interchanges of their use with <u>, <v>, <uu>, and <vv> in both consonantal and vocalic functions is an important part of the story of early Middle English (Benskin 1982: 19–20; Laing 1999: 255–60).

Textual emendation is arguably an important part of an editor's remit. This is fine as long as any emendation is clearly marked and the manuscript reading is retrievable from the notes by the alert language scholar. Scribes did make mistakes and some emendations would no doubt have been approved by the errant scribes themselves, but the linguist's job is to study actual linguistic objects,

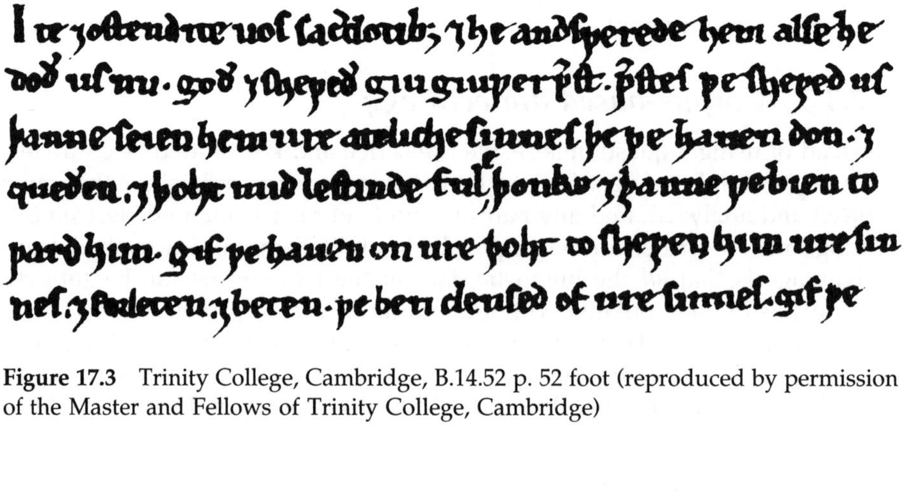

Figure 17.3 Trinity College, Cambridge, B.14.52 p. 52 foot (reproduced by permission of the Master and Fellows of Trinity College, Cambridge)

not what an informant is supposed to have "really meant." Some emendations are themselves erroneous and turn out to have removed a form that is a genuine part of the record (Laing 1998, 2001).

Finally, it is vital for linguistic study that each scribal contribution be treated separately. Conscientious compilers of single text editions will notice any changes of hand in their manuscript. But scholars trawling an edition for linguistic evidence may not always succeed in maintaining the distinction. Corrections and deletions must also be noted. A correction or deletion may not be by the scribe who wrote the main text and the reader should therefore be alerted to a possibly extraneous element in the scribal system or to loss of valid data.

17.3.3.2 Transcription and flagging

We transcribe texts using a special format with no non-ASCII characters. The advantage is twofold: (a) very large quantities of data can be manipulated on a mainframe computer without recourse to any code characters; (b) upgrade from one system to another, or transfer of data to others, even on quite different systems, can be done seamlessly. This "internal" format may look unusual at first, but it is quite transparent. In the web-mounted version of LAEME, we intend in the future to provide a re-encoding into a more familiar typography, though this will retain all the distinctions made in the internal format. In this section we use internal format for our illustrative examples. (For a key and description of the internal format see Appendix 17.1, below).

17.3.3.3 Tagging

Each form in a text is then assigned a tag representing its meaning and/or grammatical function. A form, as in LALME, refers to a word or grammatical morph as it appears in the text. The result is a "tagged text" illustrated in figure 17.5. The tags appear to the left of the text which is still readable down the right-hand side of each column. Each tagged text begins with an index number, title, date, and (if it is localized) Ordance Survey National Grid reference and ends with |.

A tag comprises two elements: (a) a lemma which is usually the modern English equivalent of the Middle English word, or (where this is lacking or

{(*ITE & OSTENDITE UOS SACerDOTIBus(} & HE ANDSwER+EDE HEM ALSE HE {\} DO+d US NU {.} GO+d & SHEw+Ed GIU GIUwER PreST {.} PreST+ES wE SHEw+ED US {\} yANNE {[we[} SEI+EN HEM URE ATE:LICH+E SINN+ES yE wE HAU+EN DO+N {.} & {\} QU Ed+EN {.} & yOHT MID LEST+INDE FUL>E> yONKE & yANNE wE BIEN TO\wARD {="in a state of submission to" – see MED s.v. toward prep. sense 6, or "for" sense 8(b)=} HIM {.} GIF wE HAU+EN ON URE yOHT TO SHEw+EN HIM URE SIN\N+ES {.} & @FOR:LET+EN {.} & BET+EN {.} wE BEN CLENS+ED OF URE SINN+ES {.} GIF wE {\} {~p53~}

Figure 17.4 Transcript from Trinity College, Cambridge, B.14.52 p. 52 (Trinity Homily XII) in hand B

```
# 1300
{Cambridge, Trinity College B.14.52, hand B,
  p. 52 sample}
C12b2
571 267
{(*ITE & OSTENDITE UOS SACerDOTIBus()}
$&/cj_&
$/P13NM_HE
$answer/vpt13_ANDSwER+EDE
  $/vpt13R_+EDE
$/P23Oi_HEM
$as/cj_ALSE
$/P13NM_HE
{\}
$do/vps13_DO+d $/vps13V_+d
$/P21Oi_US
$now/av_NU
{.}
$go/v-imp22_GO+d $/v-imp22V_+d
$&/cj_&
$show/v-imp22K2_SHEw+Ed
  $/v-imp22K2_+Ed
$/P22OdX_GIU
$/P22G_GIUwER
$priest/nOi_PreST
{.}
$priest/nplOi_PreST+ES $/plnOi_+ES
$/P21N_wE
$show/vps21K2_SHEw+ED $/vps21K2_+ED
$/P21OdX_US
{\}
$when/cj_yANNE
{[we[}
$say/vps21_SEI+EN $/vps21_+EN
$/P23Oi_HEM
$/P21G_URE
$ateli:c/ajplOd_ATE+LICH+E
            $-ly/xs-ajplOd_+LICH+E $/plajOd_+E
$sin/nplOd_SINN+ES $/plnOd_+ES
$/RTIplOd_yE
$/P21N_wE
$have/vps21_HAU+EN $/vps21_+EN
$do/vSpp_DO+N $/vSppV_+N
{.}
$&/cj_&
{\}
$cweYan/vSpp_QUEd+EN $/vSpp_+EN
{.}
$&/cj_&
$think/vpp_yOHT
$mid{w}/pr_MID
$last/vpsp-aj<pr_LEST+INDE
  $/vpsp-aj<pr_+INDE
$foul/aj<pr_FUL>E>
$thank{c}/n<pr_yONKE
$&/cj_&
$then/av_yANNE
$/P21N_wE
$be/vps21_BIEN
$toward/pr_TO\wARD
{="in a state of submission to" – see MED
  s.v. toward prep. sense 6, or "for" sense
  8(b) =}
$/P13<prM_HIM
{.}
$if/cj_GIF
$/P21N_wE
$have/vps21_HAU+EN $/vps21_+EN
$in{p}/pr_ON
$/P21G_URE
$thought/n<pr_yOHT
$to/im+C_TO
$show/viK2-m_SHEw+EN $/viK2-m_+EN
$/P13OiM_HIM
$/P21G_URE
$sin/nplOd_SIN\N+ES $/plnOd_+ES
{.}
$&/cj_&
$forlae:tan/vi_FOR+LET+EN
            $for-/xp-v_FOR+ $/vi_+EN
{.}
$&/cj_&
$be:tan/vi_BET+EN $/vi_+EN
{.}
$/P21N_wE
$be/vps21_BEN
$cleanse/vpp-pl_CLENS+ED $/
  vpp-pl_+ED
$of/pr_OF
$/P21G_URE
$sin/npl<pr_SINN+ES $/pln<pr_+ES
{.}
$if/cj_GIF
$/P21N_wE
{~p53~}
|
```

Figure 17.5

ambiguous) a form of its etymon; (b) a grammatical element indicating its function. Each tag is introduced by $ and elements (a) and (b) are separated by /. Some words have no need of element (a) because element (b) is sufficient to describe them fully, e.g. $/P13NM in line 8 of figure 17.5, where P stands for personal pronoun, 1 for singular, 3 for third person, N for nominative and M for masculine, i.e. 'he'. The tagged texts can be seen to carry a great deal of information of potential use in the study of historical syntax as well as in lexicography, phonology, and dialectology itself.

Each newly tagged text is added to the corpus. The tagging creates a taxonomy of the linguistic material in the texts and permits systematic comparison of their dialects by means of text dictionaries.

17.3.3.4 Text dictionaries

Text dictionaries, or text profiles, are generated from the tagged texts. These text dictionaries are the equivalent of LALME's linguistic profiles from questionnaires, but they record all words in the text and their frequencies. Figure 17.6 shows the text dictionary created from our small Trinity Homily sample.

Text dictionaries are the input for other programs that analyze the degree of variation in words and morphemes within and across texts. Information on particular "items" (defined by one or more tags) may be abstracted from the

```
# 1300
{Cambridge, Trinity
College B.14.52, hand B,
p. 52 sample}
C12b2
571 267
$&/cj & 7
$-ly/xs-ajplOd +LICHE 1
$/P13<prM HIM 1
$/P13NM HE 2
$/P13OiM HIM 1
$/P21G URE 4
$/P21N wE 6
$/P21OdX US 1
$/P21Oi US 1
$/P22G GIUwER 1
$/P22OdX GIU 1
$/P23Oi HEM 2
$/RTIplOd yE 1
$/plajOd +E 1
$/pln<pr +ES 1
$/plnOd +ES 2
$/plnOi +ES 1
$/v-imp22K2 +Ed 1
$/v-imp22V +d 1
$/vSpp +EN 1
$/vSppV +N 1
$/vi +EN 2
$/viK2-m +EN 1
$/vpp-pl +ED 1
$/vps13V +d 1
$/vps21 +EN 3
$/vps21K2 +ED 1
$/vpsp-aj<pr +INDE 1
$/vpt13R +EDE 1
$answer/vpt13 ANDSwEREDE 1
$as/cj ALSE 1
$ateli:c/ajplOd ATELICHE 1
$be/vps21 BEN 1 BIEN 1
$be:tan/vi BETEN 1
$cleanse/vpp-pl CLENSED 1
$cweYan/vSpp QUEdEN 1
$do/vSpp DON 1
$do/vps13 DOd 1
$for-/xp-v FOR+ 1
$forlae:tan/vi FORLETEN 1
$foul/aj<pr FUL>E> 1
$go/v-imp22 GOd 1
$have/vps21 HAUEN 2
$if/cj GIF 2
$in{p}/pr ON 1
$last/vpsp-aj<pr LESTINDE 1
$mid{w}/pr MID 1
$now/av NU 1
$of/pr OF 1
$priest/nOi PreST 1
$priest/nplOi PreSTES 1
$say/vps21 SEIEN 1
$show/v-imp22K2 SHEwEd 1
$show/viK2-m SHEwEN 1
$show/vps21K2 SHEwED 1
$sin/npl<pr SINNES 1
$sin/nplOd SINNES 2
$thank{c}/n<pr yONKE 1
$then/av yANNE 1
$think/vpp yOHT 1
$thought/n<pr yOHT 1
$to/im+C TO 1
$toward/pr TOwARD 1
$when/cj yANNE 1
|
```

Figure 17.6

corpus to identify spatial and/or temporal distributions of the forms associated with the item. Programs can also generate concordances, chronological charts, and input files to mapping software.

17.4 Interpretation: Letters and Sounds

17.4.1 What does LAEME map?

The LAEME agenda appears unproblematic: mapping the history of early Middle English through time and across space. But what are we actually saying when we include in our corpus (and subsequently map) the written forms from our manuscript sources? Here are the forms listed under the lemma $night in a number of Southwest Midland text languages:

Cambridge, Trinity College MS B.14.39 (323), Hand A: *nicst(e), nict, nist(e)*
London, British Library, Cotton Caligula A.ix, Layamon A, hand A: *niht(e), nith*
London, British Library, Cotton Cleopatra C.vi, *Ancrene Riwle*, hand A: *nicht, nihcte*
Oxford, Bodleian Library, Digby 86: *niȝt(e), niȝtt(e)*
Oxford, Bodleian Library, Laud Misc 108, Part 1, hand A: *niȝht(e), nyȝht, niȝte*

In some uncontroversial sense these are surely all representations of "the same thing," e.g. a "word." But a word is not a pure abstraction: there must be some reason we call these by the same name. Obviously, to shift metalanguage, they are "tokens of word forms of the same lexeme." The maps in LALME constitute "a dialect atlas of written Middle English" (vol. I: 6), and texts are "treated as examples of a system of written language operating in its own right." The emphasis on the independent value of written evidence was particularly apposite two decades ago, given the post-Bloomfieldian view then (and to a large extent still) that writing is of no independent linguistic interest, but merely "parasitic on" speech. But this emphasis has been frequently misunderstood and taken to imply that phonological interpretation is *per se* unnecessary. The LALME editors take no such line. They were fully aware of the potential phonological implications of their data. LALME is rich in phonological commentary, while the series of dot maps (vol. 1) depends on acknowledging the relationship between sound and symbol.

The history of a language cannot be restricted to its orthography. We take spelling with the utmost seriousness, in no sense "merely" as indicative of phonology; but we take phonology equally seriously. LAEME is not an atlas of early Middle English orthographic forms, but an atlas of both first-order data and the second-order but equally important information deducible or otherwise arguable from it. The history it portrays is that of orthography, phonology (*sensu lato*: see section 17.4.4), and their interactions. The inclusion of both is logically necessary: we could not assume that any two orthographic objects represented "the same" anything unless we assumed a system-level rather than utterance-level entity lying behind them, and tying them together as sames. The very identification of <nist, niȝt, niht . . . > as "forms of $night" recognizes an "invisible" abstract level of representation running across all the text languages. In the simplest cases we presuppose a truth-conditional identity such that the statement "nist, niȝt, niht . . . > is the name for what comes after <dai, day, dei, . . . >" is true in all possible text languages. In other words, every orthographic string is paired with a lexical identity and therefore also a semantic representation.

But in written languages using alphabetic or alphabet-like scripts, this pairing is mediated by another: sound to symbol. Orthography is certainly an independent historical variable, but it exists only because it is designed to represent some kind of "phonetic substance." (This is necessarily true unless all speakers of early Middle English were deaf and used written English as a purely visual system, which would be ruled out by the over 200 forms of the verb 'hear' in our corpus so far.) So we need to assign, at least conjecturally, some kind of phonetic interpretation to the graphs in each system. However, graphs may not always have phonological interpretations; sometimes they are merely "decorative" – e.g. the otiose final <e> on <huse> 'house' nom sg < OE *hūs*. "The history of $night" or "the geographical distribution of forms of $night" is ultimately the distribution of strings of segmental representations at some stipulated level of delicacy.

17.4.2 *The value of medieval taxonomy in the interpretation of medieval writing systems*

17.4.2.1 *The doctrine of* littera

For commentary on the LAEME corpus and the writing systems of its scribal texts, we adopt a form of citation from the late antique and medieval doctrine of *littera*. *Littera* is a tripartite taxonomic complex that ties together coherently both the written and the spoken representations of language: *nomen* (the name of the letter), *figura* (the written symbol representing it), and *potestas* (its sound-value) (see Donatus *Ars Maior*, book 1).

In this section we adopt (for the most part) the conventions established by Michael Benskin (2001: 194 fn.4). When we refer to *litterae* independently of manuscript citation, we enclose them in single inverted commas. Particular manuscript *figurae* are enclosed in angle brackets (or italicized if more extended citations are used). *Potestates* are represented by International Phonetic Alphabet (IPA) symbols in phonetic brackets.

17.4.2.2 *Litteral and "potestatic" substitution sets*

Some designers of early Middle English writing systems had an economical attitude towards the mapping of sound to symbol that approaches the "one word, one spelling" of many modern written standards. But most did not. The complex interactions of sound-change, persistence of tradition, orthographic developments, and the processes of decoding and re-encoding adopted for the translation of an exemplar's text from one writing system into another, give rise in the medieval period to "extensive grammars of interchange" (Benskin 1991: 226). The complexity displayed by some early Middle English writing systems arises from the availability of large numbers of orthographic variants to realize some sounds. We call these litteral substitution sets (Laing 1999).

We have already come across a litteral substitution set (LSS) in the 'night' examples cited in section 17.4.1 above. The graphic set {*-icst, -ict, -ist, -iht, -ith, -icht, -ihct, -iȝt, -iȝht*} constitutes (part of) an LSS. When we map the orthographic systems of early Middle English scribes who adopt contrasting LSSs, we find a high degree of apparent mismatch or surface discontinuity (see map 17.3, below, and the discussion in section 17.5.1). In order to reveal, at least in part, the spoken dialect continuum we believe to have existed, we must interpret the underlying sound substance behind the orthography and reduce the appearance of complexity to a simpler orderliness.

The existence of an LSS implies an associated set which we call a potestatic substitution set (PSS) (Laing and Lass 2003). The content of our putative PSS derived from the spellings for 'night' in section 17.4.1 above could be specified as { [nixt] }: it is perfectly possible for a PSS (or an LSS) to have only one member. The set {*-icst, -ict, -ist, -iht*, etc.} might also be taken to include the possibilities { [-içt], [-iht] } but the orthography does not give us enough information to allow such delicacy, and we take the [x] in [nixt] as a cover term to represent "some non-anterior fricative." But the set could well also include { [niθ] } if the <th> in <nith> is taken to represent a dental rather than a velar. If we add from other Southwest Midland text languages the spelling <nit> we arrive at an early Middle English PSS for the vowel and final consonant (cluster) in 'night' consisting of the following: { [-ixt], [-iθ], [-i:t] }.

For LAEME, orthographic maps of the kind familiar in LALME will present the primary data. But for at least some items we intend also to present potestatic maps derived from them to offer a representation of the early Middle English spoken dialect continuum.

17.4.3 Phonetic interpretation: "narrowness"

There are standard protocols for assigning phonic interpretations to written forms (for an exposition see Lass 1992: 27–32). But there are two Hard Questions: (a) how sharply resolved are the phonetic values we assign? and (b) what (if any) systemic or "structural" reference are they intended to have? We take up the first of these questions in this section, and the second in section 17.4.4.

The further back in time we go, the harder it is to specify phonetic values with any precision. The interpretation we use in LAEME might best be called "poorly resolved broad transcription." We think this is the right way to represent most historical sound substance. That is, we hope that our reconstructions are well enough supported so that if a responsible phonetician equipped with a time machine were able to hear the items represented, the symbol in question would be a reasonable transcriptional response. This is not just wishful thinking, but is based on our assessment of the results of work in comparative and historical linguistics over the past two centuries.

For instance, the graphic string <niȝt>, as we suggested above, is likely to represent a segmental string something like [nixt]. If it were possible to hear a Middle English speaker say the word, we would be very much surprised to encounter anything other than a coronal nasal in first position, followed by a high front vowel, then some kind of non-anterior fricative plus a voiceless coronal stop. Of course we cannot specify whether [n, t] are dental or alveolar (or even both dental or both alveolar), how high and how front [i] is, how palatal or velar [x] is. Each segmental representation is equivalent to a range or "smear" of values with roughly the coordinates that the symbol in question would occupy in a modern phonetic transcription. Therefore, our phonetic interpretation is essentially typological: a representation of sound substance at an unspecified but coarse level.

17.4.3.1 Phonetic values and inventories

In phonetic interpretation in LAEME, we utilize the following segmental inventories, which appear to us to represent the limit of possible discrimination. Certain distinctions, perhaps arguably relevant for our period, are simply not recoverable: [i] vs [ɪ], [u] vs [ʊ] are prime examples. The inventory of sound types we work with is shown in tables 17.1 and 17.2. Note that this is an inventory of segment types; diphthongs and other combinatorial structures are therefore not listed separately.

We restrict ourselves to front vs. back because we do not think there is any evidence for "central" as a distinctive category at our period. Two other choices should be noted: (a) rather than specifically having its IPA value, [a] = that low vowel which is not [æ]; and (b) the choice of [œ] is arbitrary; Old English had only one mid front rounded vowel, and there is no way of knowing if in any given dialect it was high mid or low mid. (The high mid and low mid front unrounded and back rounded vowels are a different matter: the "long close *e, o*" / "long open *e, o*" contrasts are patent.)

In pairs of symbols separated by a comma, the first is voiceless and the second voiced. We group labials and labiodentals as "labials," and "true" palatals

Table 17.1 Vowels

	Front		*Back*	
	Unround	*Round*	*Unround*	*Round*
High	i	y		u
High mid	e			o
Low mid	ɛ	œ		ɔ
Low	æ		a	

Table 17.2 Consonants

	Labial	*Dental/alveolar*	*Palatal*	*Velar*	*Glottal*
Stop	p, b	t, d	tʃ, ʤ	k, g	
Fricative	f, v	θ, ð; s, z	ʃ, ʒ	x, ɣ	h
Nasal	m	n		ŋ	
Liquid		r, l			
Semivowel	w		j		

and palatoalveolars as "palatals," on grounds of behavioral similarities. (The palatal series may have to be more finely graded if we decide that [ç] is reconstructible: for now we will take it as a fronter variety of [x].) The so-called "affricates" are simply the palatal congeners of the other stops; the category "affricate" does not require separate recognition at any point in the history of English except as a low-level phonetic differentiator.

17.4.4 Substance and "structure"

Given our database and aims, we can make no commitment to any particular theory of "system structure"; evidence from individual text languages will always skew the picture. (Whether there are "overall systems" for continua made up of overlapping distributions from individual systems is not decidable. Any general agreement on the "status" of particular items would be difficult to find.) This looks at first retrogressive: we appear to be going back to the "prestructural" atomism of the nineteenth-century handbooks, where issues like phonemic status or underlying forms or distinctiveness were not treated – largely because the conceptual framework in which they were to become important had not yet been developed. But lip service to later conventions simply evades our main point and involves us in subsidiary and irrelevant ones. Language history in our sense, and using the data we do, is (and must be) *surface narrative and description.* Our concern is with forms within individual systems, their shapes and distributions in time and space – not with operations on systems as conceived in any kind of "structuralist" framework. For LAEME, the existence (or not) of systems "où tout se tient," or any structures more abstract than segmental strings, is irrelevant. Characterization of a given symbol as representing something "emic" or "etic" belongs to a different kind of discourse.

17.4.4.1 Non-structuralist spatial and temporal variation

We are not convinced that distinctiveness and redundancy are always a significant issue, or even that it is possible for most language states to draw up inventories that distinguish between the distinctive and the non-distinctive. This kind of analysis would certainly be obtuse for most of the text languages represented in the LAEME corpus. The option for producing a "structural" analysis of any kind will always be open to the user; indeed, if such analyses turn out to be possible or useful, our corpus provides precisely the kind of material one could use to make them.

Such an apparently contentious (if traditional) position needs some justification. Most of the text languages that form our data have writing systems that display two distinctly non-"structuralist" properties: (a) their creators are often not concerned with anything resembling biunique grapheme/phoneme mapping; and (b) the orthographies (and frequently the languages they represent) are highly variable. The evidence for structuralist "eme" systems or generativist "underlying-to-surface" pairings is too weak to allow us to use this kind of modeling. Such categories have no relevance to our task. Here is one example of the conceptual morass we would get into if we decided to attempt "classical" grapheme/phoneme mappings in a specific variable and "prodigal" text language. Consider the following forms from Cambridge, Trinity College B.14.39 (323), Hand A (Southwest Midlands, C13b2):

$/P13NF ['she']: HOE, HO, HEO, HE
$be/v: BOE-, BEO-, BE-
$boar/n: BOER-
$heart/n: HOERTE, HERTE, HORTE
$knee/n: CNOE
$kneel/v: CNEL-
$to/inf marker: TOE, TO

There is no way that we can make either historical or synchronic sense at any level but the orthographic from "inside" the data. Orthographically, we have a number of LSSs for the nuclear vowels of particular lexemes, and nothing else:

'she': {OE, O, EO, E}
'be': {OE, EO, E}
'heart': {OE, E, O}
'to': {OE, O}
'boar', 'knee': {OE}
'kneel': {E}

From the Modern English point of view the items group as follows:

[i:]: 'she', 'be', 'knee', 'kneel'
[a:] : 'heart'
[ɔ:]: 'boar'
[u:]: 'to'

If we project back, on the basis of our knowledge of Old English and the supporting argumentation that allows us to interpret *that* language, we find:

[e:o]: 'she', 'be', 'knee', 'kneel'
[eo]: 'heart'
[a:]: 'boar'
[o:]: 'to'

So there are two four-way groupings that coincide – because we chose examples where they would; we could have extracted much more complex cases from the same text language. Yet neither of these is suggested by the actual data, which even ("perversely," from the structural viewpoint) separates two forms with the same root, 'knee' and 'kneel' (OE *cnēow, cnēowlian*).

Looking further at the same hand, we find that the graphs <e> and <o> are used for the following etymological categories:

<e>: OE *e, ē, æ, ǣ, eo, ēo*
<o>: OE *o, ō, eo, ēo, u, ū, a, ā*

And each of these categories will yield multiple LSSs, not unlike the picture above. So this orthography is not based on a "structural" analysis of a lect (writing is not transcription: see Coulmas 2003: 31). Rather, it is a complex system whose inventor has interests other than those he apparently "ought to have," and writes a language that, with some effort and a bit of historical knowledge, we can understand perfectly well. But on orthographic evidence, which is our primary data, it is not clear what the internal structure of the sound system is. We cannot tell how many of the LSSs conceal potential phonetic (or phonemic) variation, or how much inverse spelling there is, bringing into question the existence of historically expected contrasts. It should be clear at this point why we are interested in the histories of forms, not "systems." The notion "phonological system" is not directly relevant to the task of providing a cartographically tractable surface representation of forms, and mapping early forms into subsequent ones: this is the business of LAEME.

17.5 The Notion of a Protean Corpus

Corpus-based dialectology makes it possible to envisage an entirely different kind of historical linguistic atlas, one that is dynamic and interactive. The base of both the corpus and the atlas is the tagged texts. These may be altered and adapted in a number of different ways to suit different purposes.

17.5.1 Different formats for presentation of comparative data

We have already illustrated in section 17.3 how the "base" data from the tagged texts may be processed in different ways to produce different formats.

The text dictionaries or text profiles (see figure 17.5) derived from the tagged texts are the equivalent of LALME's linguistic profiles derived from the questionnaire analysis. They provide a complete inventory of the surviving work of each individual scribal witness or text language for comparison with others.

Information on particular "items" (defined by one or more tags) may be abstracted from the text dictionaries to create "form dictionaries" of variant spellings, equivalent to those in the County Dictionary of LALME. Figure 17.7 illustrates the form dictionary for $/P23N 'they' for the LAEME corpus to date. Indications as to frequency of attestation are given for each text language by text number.

Figure 17.8 shows the "item list" for $/P23N 'they' which provides the input for the mapping software. The text identification number is on the left of the column, followed by the forms for 'they' found in that text. A non-bracketed form indicates that it is a majority form in that text language, occurring in more than 50 percent of attestations. A single bracketed form is one occurring in between 20 and 50 percent of attestations, and double brackets indicate a form is rare and occurs in fewer than 20 percent of attestations. Each localized text has a set of Ordnance Survey National Grid coordinates for a point on the map. The mapping software then prints the relevant forms for each text next to its point, thus producing a map for early ME forms of 'they'.

Maps are the final stage of presentation derived from the text dictionaries. Map 17.1 shows the item map for $/P23N 'they' for the East Midlands. Map 17.2 is a "feature map," the equivalent of two combined dot maps in LALME, showing the distributions of spellings with initial <þ-/y-> against those with initial <h->. As a further illustration of the possibilities we return to our example OE *-iht* in section 17.4 above. We illustrate, this time for the Southwest Midlands, an "item map" for the sequence OE *-iht* (map 17.3 – note that this includes data for all words containing OE *-iht*, not just 'night'). Map 17.4 is a phonetic map derived from the data in map 17.3, which involves a further level of extrapolation as described in section 17.4.3 above. With the evolving electronic version of LAEME, users will be able to choose and predefine items of interest and generate their own maps.

17.5.2 *Textual comparison*

The different formats described in section 17.5.1 are products of the initial primary objective of LAEME – comparison and mapping of different language types through time and across space. But the corpus of tagged texts enables us to do much more than this. It allows detailed and sophisticated textual comparison. Where two or more versions of a text survive in early Middle English, the text dictionaries of the different versions may be electronically compared to highlight their degree of dialectal difference from each other item by item. It is also possible to produce their tagged texts in parallel so that textual variation and differences in choice of lexis and syntactic structures are at once revealed beside

A	246x 247′ 248x 260x 271x 276x
A+	246′ 247′ 248x 278x
AA	260x
H	2002x
H+	260x
HA	118″ 122″ 189x 245′ 246′ 247′ 248x 260^ 261^ 262^ 272^ 273^ 275^ 276^ 278′ 1000^ 2000′ 2002x
HA+	260′ 273′
HAY	159x
HE	4′ 7′ 64′ 149x 150^ 155^ 161^ 162x 163x 175^ 234^ 246″ 247′ 248x 260x 261x 271x 273x 277′ 278′ 280′ 282^ 285^ 286′ 1100′ 1200′ 1300′ 1400^ 1500″ 1600′ 1700″ 1900x 2000′ 2002x 2003″
HE+	155x 234x
HEI	271′
HEM	155x
HEO	3^ 7x 11^ 12x 118x 163x 170^ 189x 245^ 246^ 247′ 260″ 261′ 262′ 271x 272x 273″ 276x 277^ 278^ 280′ 1000′ 1100^ 1500^ 1600″ 1800^ 1900^ 2000^ 2001^
HEOM	278′
HEY	234x 271x 2002x
HI	2^ 3″ 5″ 6^ 7^ 8^ 10^ 64′ 131x 140x 142^ 143^ 149^ 158^ 277x 278′ 280′ 286^ 291^ 1100″ 1300x 1400x 1900′ 2000′ 2002′ 2003″
HI+	286′
HIE	4^ 63x 64^ 65^ 67x 142x 184x 1200^ 1300^
HII	271′ 280^
HIJ	271x
HIT	2x 64′ 65′ 161x 260′ 271x 278′ 280′ 291x 1000x 1100x 1600x
HO	2′ 5^ 118^ 136^ 246x 247″ 1100′ 1900x 2001″
HOE	125x 246′ 247″ 1900x 2002″
HUI	271′
HUY	271′ 1600^
HY	6′ 7x 10x 271x 286″ 291″ 2002^
HY+	291x
H^IE	64′
Hx	246x
I	142′ 277x 280′
I+	278′ 280′ 286x
IT	150′ 155′ 246x 249^ 269x 285′ 286′ 1300′ 1400x 1600′ 2003x
TAI	122′
TEI	1700″
Y+	286x
YAI	159x 169^ 188^ 230x 295^
YAI+	295x
YAY	159x 188x 230x 256x
YE	182′
YEI	169″ 182^
dEI	155x
yA	248x
yAI	122″ 231x 280x
yE	137x 282x 285′ 1300′
yEI	122x 158′ 282″ 285′ 1300′ 1600′ 1700″
yEY	282x 285′ 2002′
zE	160^ 161x

Key: ^ = majority form (more than 50%)
′ = between 20% and 50% of attestations
″ = fewer than 20% of attestations
x = single occurrence

Note: There are other options for representing frequencies and proportions, see e.g. figure 17.8 below.

Figure 17.7 Item list

2 HI ((HO HIT))
3 HEO (HI)
4 HIE ((HE))
5 HO (HI)
6 HI ((HY))
7 HI ((HE HEO HY))
8 HI
10 HI ((HY))
11 HEO
12 HEO
63 HIE
64 HIE ((HE HI H^IE HIT))
65 HIE ((HIT))
67 HIE
118 HO (HA) ((HEO))
122 (HA yAI) ((TAI yEI))
125 HOE
131 HI
136 HO
137 yE
140 HI
142 HI ((I HIE))
143 HI
149 HI ((HE))
150 HE ((IT))
155 HE ((IT HE+ HEM dEI))
158 HI ((yEI))
159 HAY YAI YAY
160 zE
161 HE ((HIT zE))
162 HE
163 HE HEO
169 YAI (YEI)
170 HEO
175 HE
182 YEI ((YE))
184 HIE
188 YAI ((YAY))
189 HA HEO
230 YAI YAY
231 yAI
234 HE ((HE+ HEY))
245 HEO ((HA))
246 HEO (HE) ((A+ HA HOE A HO Hx IT))
247 (HO HOE) ((HEO HE HA A A+))
248 ((A A+ HA HE yA))
249 IT
256 YAY
260 HA (HEO) ((HA+ HIT A AA H+ HAREN HE))
261 HA ((HEO HE))
262 HA ((HEO))
269 IT
271 ((HII HEI HUI HUY A HE HEO HEY HIJ HIT HY))
272 HA ((HEO))
273 HA (HEO) ((HA+ HE))
275 HA
276 HA ((A HEO))
277 HEO ((HE HI I))
278 HEO ((HA HE HEOM HI HIT I+ A+))
280 HII ((HI I+ I HE HIT HEO yAI))
282 HE (yEI) ((yE yEY))
285 HE ((yEI yEY IT yE))
286 HI (HY) ((HI+ HE IT I+ Y+))
291 HI (HY) ((HIT HY+))
295 YAI ((YAI+))
1000 HA ((HEO HIT))
1100 HEO (HI) ((HE HO HIT))
1200 HIE ((HE))
1300 HIE ((HE IT yE yEI HI))
1400 HE ((HI IT))
1500 HEO (HE)
1600 HUY (HEO) ((HE yEI IT HIT))
1700 (HE TEI yEI)
1800 HEO
1900 HEO ((HI HE HO HOE))
2000 HEO ((HI HA HE))
2001 HEO (HO)
2002 HY (HOE) ((yEY HI H HA HE HEY))
2003 (HE HI) ((IT))

Figure 17.8 Form dictionary for $/P23N

any dialectal spelling variants. A concordance program, using tags as keys, can pull out from the corpus particular forms associated with particular items within a designated length of textual context for more detailed textual or linguistic investigations.

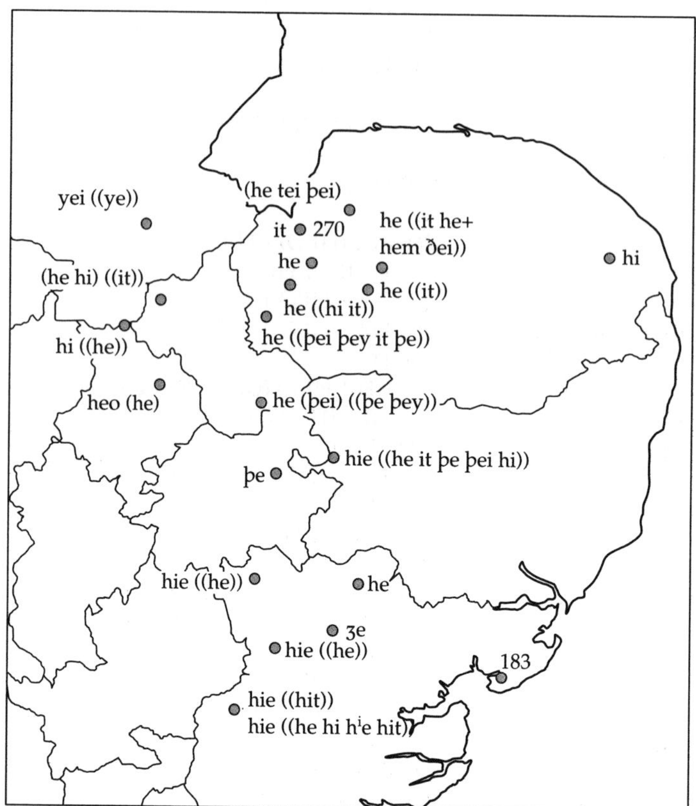

Map 17.1 Spellings of *they* in East Anglia and Essex attested in LAEME texts

17.5.3 Corpus-based "editions"

For those interested in the detail of individual texts, it is possible to recreate from any tagged text the original diplomatic transcript. Software then re-encodes the internal format into more familiar typography, stripping out the code flags, italicizing abbreviations and restoring manuscript capitals, "special" letters, and superscripts. The various categories of notes embedded in braces in the tagged text can be extracted in the form of textual and editorial notes and commentary.

17.5.4 The protean nature of the tags themselves

The editors have chosen particular tags for manuscript forms, on the basis of their experience, judgment, and interests. The choice is agnostic with respect to particular schools of modern formal syntactic theory. Users of the corpus may have different experience, judgment and interests. But the "base" tags are

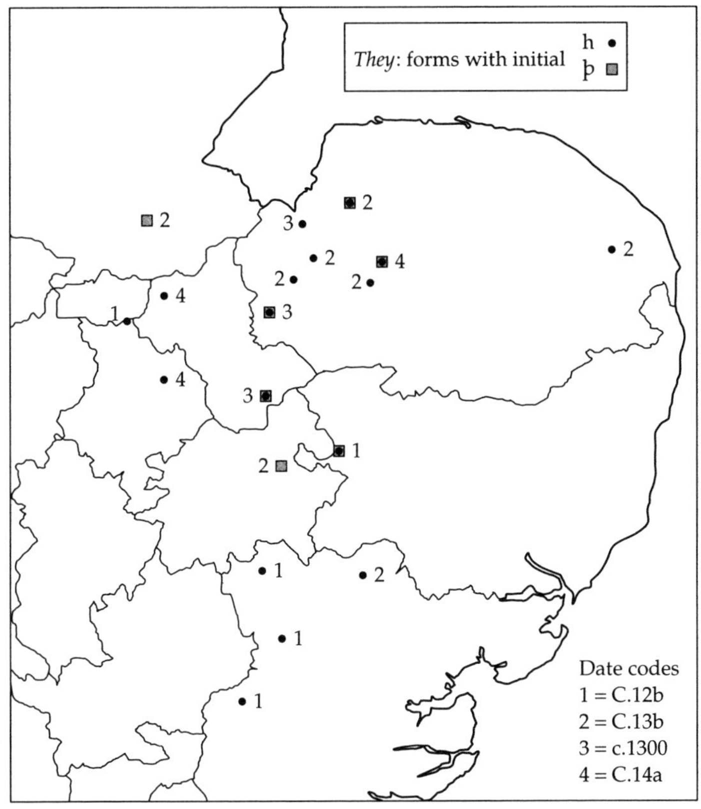

Map 17.2 *They*: initial <h> versus initial <þ>

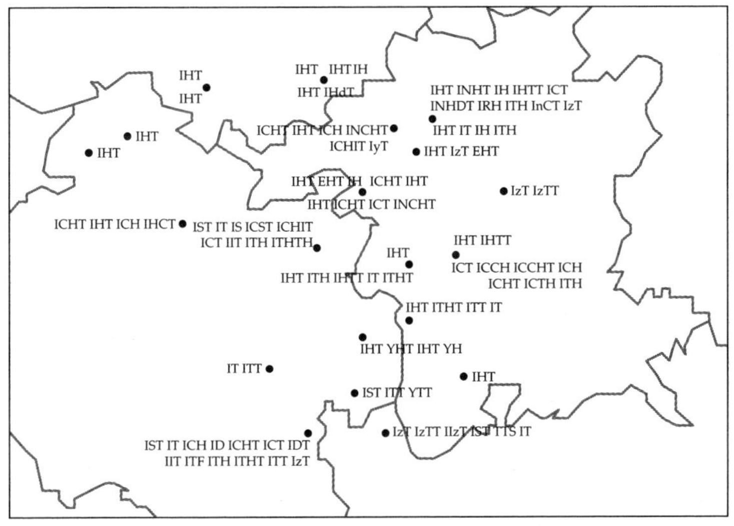

Map 17.3 LSS map of *-iht*

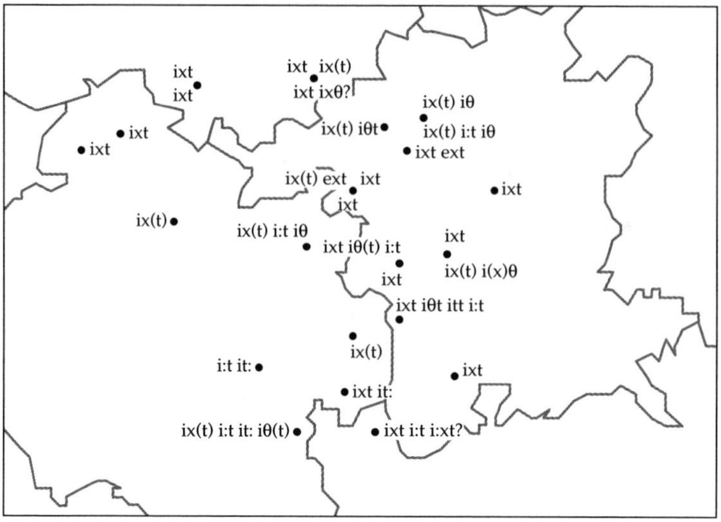

Map 17.4 PSS map of *-iht*

not immutable. Any tag or series of tags may be altered or adapted for specialized enquiry. For instance, the forms tagged "Oi" = "indirect object" could be subdivided by a user into "canonical indirect objects," "benefactives," or "allatives" by flagging the "Oi" tags accordingly.

17.6 The Corpus of Etymologies

LAEME is protean and dynamic in another more radical way. We are building into it a narrative dimension. Every lemma in the corpus is provided with an etymology, giving its history from a notional entry point of c.600 AD (when English could be said to be clearly differentiated from Continental West Germanic). This enables the history of any form in the LAEME corpus to be traced from an "ultimate" etymon through the various "dialects" of Old English.

Unlike typical dictionary etymologies, ours are genuine stories, in which the phonological and morphological changes producing the corpus forms can be retrieved in sequence. The corpus of etymologies consists of two subcorpora: a set of etymological entries and a list of the changes (formalized or not), which build the etymologies. Each entry has three parts:

(a) The lemma and presumed etymon (or etyma if there is no unique original).
(b) The sequence of changes (if any) leading to the attested Old English form(s) presumed to be ancestral to the LAEME corpus forms. These are retrievable by links from the etymological entry itself.

(c) The LAEME corpus forms themselves, with any post-Old English changes that affected them. For a sample etymological entry with links, see Appendix 17.2, below.

17.7 A Protean Prospect: Setting Topics for the Future Research Agenda

Numerous papers have already been published during the making of LAEME, illustrating the power of the corpus methodology for sorting out composite textual traditions and complex dialectal strata and for displaying the diversity of early Middle English spelling systems. But its use goes far beyond the concerns of the historical dialectologist alone. We have already drawn attention (section 17.5.4 above) to the flexibility of the tagging method. Now that the LAEME corpus is published, users will be able to make their own copies and devise their own tags, or parse the existing ones, to facilitate whatever linguistic investigation they wish to make. We offer here three examples as illustrations.

17.7.1 *Negation in Early Middle English*

Tags devised for identification and comparison of lexical and morphological variation may also serve as flags for syntactic investigation. Here again there is a danger in using printed editions rather than diplomatic transcriptions from originals. Most editors of medieval texts add modern punctuation and capitalization, and suppress such manuscript punctuation as exists. Manuscript word division is frequently "regularized" along modern lines. This enables medieval texts to be subjected to the same types of syntactic analysis as modern ones and all too easily allows the unchallenged assumption that medieval scribes had attitudes towards phrase and clause structure similar to our own.

An extra layer of detail was added to the LAEME tags for a study on negation in early Middle English (Laing 2002). This study shows how microtagging enables us to isolate and enumerate for comparison the three main types of negation found in Middle English: *ne* alone preceding the finite verb, *ne . . . not* (braced negation) and *not* alone following the finite verb. It also makes it possible to flag the use of other negators and confirms that *ne . . . not* negation does not normally occur with multiple negation from negative concord. Further, it has brought to light a number of rarer negative constructions present in early Middle English and indicates some possible constraints on their use.

17.7.2 *What is a part of speech?*

The level of grammatical tagging adopted for the LAEME corpus differentiates as a matter of course between nouns ($/n) and adjectives ($/aj). But it has proved necessary to adopt two further refinements: (a) adjectives used substantivally ($/ajn – e.g. 'the quick', 'the dead', 'the rich', 'the poor', 'the wise [man]'); and (b) (less commonly observed in early Middle English) nouns used adjectivally (S/naj – e.g. 'fox', 'head', 'master'). There is some fuzziness between this latter category and compound nouns, which are comparatively common at this period. Because the suffixes indicating genitive and plural are tagged as separable morphological elements, it will be possible to see to what extent "expected" nominal or adjectival endings are found in these categories. Further insights into what constitutes such categories as "noun," "adjective," and "compound noun" may then emerge.

Some words may represent a number of different parts of speech. Consider the following examples, all from *Ancrene Wisse* in Cambridge, Corpus Christi College 402.

(i) [fol. 13r] is hit nu se \ ouer uuel [$evil/aj] forte totin utƿart ? ȝe hit leoue suster . foR \ uuel [$evil/n<pr] þe þer kimeð of.'
'Is it now so overly evil to peep outwards? Yes it is, dear sister, because of the evil that comes of it'

(ii) [fol. 13v] an ald ancre mei \ do wel .' ꝥ te þu dest uuele [$evil/av]. ah totin ut ƿiðuten uuel [$evil/n<pr].' ne \ mei oþer noƿðer.
'An old anchoress may do well what thou dost evilly; but to peep out without evil, neither of you may do'

(iii) [fol. 21r] ant þis is þah ꝥ leaste uuel [$evil/n] of þe þreo uueles [$evil/npl<pr]
'and this is yet the smallest evil of the three evils'

(iv) [fol. 22r] he \ preiseð þe uuel [$evil/ajnOd] & his uuele [$evil/ajplOd] dede
'he praises the evil [man] and his evil deeds'

(v) [fol. 34v] Godd deð in his tresor þe unþre\aste & te uuele [$evil/ajnplOd]. Forte hure ƿið ham as me deð ƿið ger\sum þeo þe ƿel fehteð.
'God puts into his treasure house the feeble and the evil, to hire with them, as one does with money, those who fight well'

We have shown the LAEME tagging for the various instances of the word 'evil' used in the examples. In whatever other ways one might want to tag these instances, the act of tagging itself draws attention to data that prompt further analysis.

17.7.3 *Where do forms come from? The Corpus of Etymologies*

The Corpus of Etymologies (CE) assigns to each form in the corpus an ultimate etymon of "Primitive OE" date along with a narrative history listing all the changes the form has undergone to produce the individual spellings represented in the main corpus. Thus $old/aj is given the etymon **ald* and a set of subsequent stories including First Fronting, Breaking or Retraction and, for relevant forms, Homorganic Lengthening and Rounding of lengthened **a*. All changes are listed in a separate subcorpus, with commentary where appropriate, and individual forms may also be commented on (for an example see Appendix 17.2). Not only the root morphemes, but inflexional and derivational affixes and ablaut grades of strong verbs are separately etymologized.

The CE is designed to enrich the historicity of LAEME. It will enable the user to ask questions about the history of English for which the answers require larger and more tightly specified data inputs than were available to the writers of the standard handbooks. This allows the handbook accounts of phonological and morphological history to be tested and in some cases revised. It will now be possible to obtain more precise answers to questions like "what happened to the OE diphthongs spelled <eo> or the segment spelled <y>?" or "when and how did grammatical gender disappear in early ME?" The first of these questions has been treated in a paper that was a pilot study for the CE (Lass and Laing 2005), and the answer appears not to be what the handbooks tell us. The *communis opinio*, going back to Sweet (1888: §§ 644ff.) is that in the Southwest Midlands (SWML) long and short *eo* monophthongized to front rounded vowels [œ(:)], which were retained, spelled <eo, o, oe, ue, u>, and long and short *y* remained [y(:)] spelled <u> "after the French fashion." On the basis of over 2,500 examples of etymologically tagged tokens of these categories in SWML texts from the early Middle English period, we were able to show that there is in fact no strong supporting evidence in our materials for any of the three claims. There is no clearly univocal use of <eo>; the classical "three-region" split of [y(:)] into <i, e, u> regions is fuzzy; and there is no evidence of any particular spellings uniquely associated with the reflexes of any of the four Old English categories involved. Even in texts as supposedly "regular" as those in AB language we found as many as six different spellings for OE [e(:)o] alone, and five etymological categories overlapping in the spelling <eo>, including in AB the reflex of OE *e* in the stressed open syllables of strong verbs of classes IV and V, which nobody would want to characterize as front rounded.

In short, we can now ask a wide range of linguistic questions and get solid answers in a way that was not possible before electronic corpora with this detail of tagging and accompanying commentary were available. This may enable us to clarify historical claims about Middle English, and perhaps even feed back into Old English "dialect" distributions. For instance, by asking questions of the early Middle English data we may gain further insight into the generally accepted sound change "Second Fronting," which is normally assigned in Old English to the problematic and geographically poorly localized text cluster called "Mercian." We can determine the spread of that phenomenon in Middle English by asking the CE to provide all reflexes of OE *ǣ̆*, either by region or overall or both. The performance of this one task will also enable us to separate out changes that are probably different in origin. It would be clear from mapping, for instance, that the very frequent <e> for OE ǣ̆ in *Cursor Mundi* does not represent "the same change" as whatever results in <e, ea> in the SWML for the same category, and is distinct also from what results from it in Kent. That is, mapping of discontinuous distributions of etymological categories allows us to sort out single widespread changes from discontinuous convergences, and enables us to plot both in space-time. Even from so-far unmapped texts we can see that there are at least three independent [æ] > [e] changes: Second Fronting, "Kentish Collapse," and what we call in the change corpus "Northern Raising." A $be/vpt1 spelling <wes> is not a <wes> *simpliciter*, but one of three possible kinds.

17.7.4 *Proteanism is heuristic*

The project described in this chapter was originally conceived as being completely in the tradition of LALME, except for certain computational advances. But while it provides the database for LAEME, it is evident that the text corpus is also an independent research resource. The new methodology has enabled an expanded view of both dialectology and the possibilities of corpus-based historical linguistics. The project follows LALME in respecting the historical source witnesses, but has resulted in a corpus that can support investigations far beyond anything that its creators originally conceived.

It should by now be apparent why we refer to the LAEME corpus as "protean." Protean is a heuristic notion; the kind of corpus we have designed is a shape-shifter, and the number of ways it can be shaped is open-ended. This is equally true of LAEME's sister project A Linguistic Atlas of Older Scots (in combination with the Edinburgh Corpus of Older Scots) being created by Keith Williamson in collaboration with Anneli Meurman-Solin of the University of Helsinki, compiler of the Helsinki Corpus of Older Scots and related text corpora. Each project has its own subtly individual variations in what is meant by "protean," but interconnectedness and flexibility are the key concepts.

APPENDIX 17.1: EXPLANATION OF INTERNAL FORMAT USED IN THE ILLUSTRATIONS FROM THE LAEME CORPUS

The transcriptions use upper case for manuscript "plain text" letters. Majuscule letters or *litterae notabiliores* in the manuscript are differentiated by a preceding *. Lower case is reserved for the expansion of abbreviations and for the Old English and "special" letters: y = thorn <þ>, d = edh <ð>, ae = aesc <æ>, z = yogh <ʒ>, w = wynn <ƿ>, g = "insular g" <ᵹ>. Superscripts, including those that are in effect abbreviations, are not expanded but are preceded by ^, e.g. y^T = MS þ^{t} = 'that'; G^ENE = MS g^{e}ne = 'green'. Accents on vowels (other than the oblique stroke very commonly given to <i> to differentiate it from other *litterae* made up of minims) are indicated by lower case x following the vowel: e.g. FOxN = MS fón = 'foes'. Lower case x is also used to indicate the stroke through <þ> for abbreviated 'that', i.e. yx = MS ꝥ. & indicates any realization in manuscript of a conventional symbol for 'and', whether the Tironian sign or ampersand itself. Ampersand is much rarer than the Tironian sign, and is noted when it occurs. Scribal additions in the manuscript are placed within > > and deletions within < <. Some manuscripts have suffered damage affecting the legibility of the text. Partially legible letters are supplied and enclosed within []. Totally illegible text is not surmised, but its presence is flagged by empty [] and a note made on the probable number of missing letters or words.

A number of codes or flags are incorporated to mark word division, prefixes, suffixes, and other grammatical indicators. Figure 17.4 is a flagged transcription of the text in Figure 17.3 and illustrates the codes, which serve as signals to the tagging program: @ indicates prefix; : divides derivational suffixes from stems; + divides inflexions from stems.

Manuscript punctuation is recorded: . = punctus (whether on the base line or raised); .' = punctus elevatus; : = colon; , = virgule; ? = punctus interrogativus. Punctuation and other elements that are not to receive tags are placed within {}. Other elements to be skipped by the tagging program but retained in the tagged text are: line ends – marked \; folio or page references – placed within ~~; non-English words – placed within ((; English in a hand different from that of the rest of the scribal text – placed within)); conjectural readings, supplied in modern English and in lower case, for possibly missing words – placed within [[; glosses – placed within ""; headings – placed within ''; linguistic comments – placed within **; and general explanatory notes – placed within ==.

APPENDIX 17.2: A SAMPLE ENTRY IN THE LAEME ETYMOLOGICAL CORPUS – STILL BEING DEVELOPED

A sample etymological entry with links: $&/cj 'and'.

Conventions:

(a) Material in 12pt is the actual entry, with section descriptions in small caps;

(b) Material following => in 10pt italic is what would result from following the changes in (()) as links to the change corpus;

(c) Flags for changes %a = analogical; %l = lexically sensitive; %m = morphologically conditioned; %n = changes named in this corpus; %p = pre-attestation; %r = regionally restricted; {} enclose regional abbreviations; % v = variable or sporadic change.

I. LEMMA AND ULTIMATE ETYMOLOGY
$&/cj (see also $gE/cj) *and-i/*and-a

II. PRE-MIDDLE ENGLISH HISTORY; SEPARATE TRAJECTORIES FOR MORE THAN ONE ETYMON
Trajectory 1
*and-i ((IU)) > *end-i ((HVD)) > end

=>((IU))%p: i-Umlaut [OE]
{u, o, a, ae} > {y, oe, ae, e} / _C(C)i/j
{=IU produces the first front rounded vowels in English, as well as increasing the incidence of [ae, e]. [y, oe] are phonologized when the umlaut triggers are deleted or otherwise neutralized=}

=>((HVD)): High Vowel Deletion [OE]
{i, u} > 0/{VV, VCC}_#
{=Final high vowels delete after a heavy syllable=}

Trajectory 2
*and-a ((WSD)) > and ((PNR)) > ond

=> ((WSD))%n,v: Weak Syllable Deletion [OE, ME]
{=A catchall term for a host of disparate processes involving the loss of atonic syllables in any word position=}

=> ((PNR))%p,r,v: Pre-nasal Rounding [OE]
a > o/_N
{=Supposedly diagnostic for Mercian, but occurs in West Saxon as well. The more westerly LAEME texts tend to show it more extensively, sometimes exclusively, sometimes variably=}

III. FORM-TYPES OCCURRING IN CORPUS + POST-OLD ENGLISH HISTORY AND COMMENT; POST-OLD ENGLISH CHANGES IN LEFT MARGIN IN (())
AND, HAND
{=HAND inverse spelling due to h-deletion: see ((IHD))=}

=> ((IHD))%v,l: Initial h-Dropping [OE, ME]
[h] > 0/#_
{=This change is well established in the LAEME corpus and there is extensive inverse spelling, e.g. initial <h> in historically vowel initial words, like HAND for 'and'=}

OND
END
((FD2)) > ANT

=> ((FD2))%v,r{SWML}: Final Devoicing 2 [ME]
{b, d, g} > {p, t, k}/_#

{=Voiced stops devoice in final position. Relatively uncommon except in the SWML=}

((MPR)) > A

=> ((MPR))%n, v: Miscellaneous Prosodic Reductions [ME]
{=This is a catchall for various deletions and reductions in items that normally would be expected to carry low phrase stress, e.g. conjunctions or clitic pronouns. Often there is simple segmental loss, e.g. A for $&/cj; at other times there is also vowel change, as in A for $/P13NM 'he', which is not derivable in any regular way from [he:], but must represent it=}

((FCD)) > AN

=>((FCD))%v: Final Coronal Deletion
{t, d} > 0/C_{#, C}
{=Final coronal stops delete variably. Scattered throughout the texts, never constant. Deletion is promoted by the presence of an initial consonant in the following word or absolute finality in the phrase. More or less the same process operates in casual speech in most modern English dialects. See Chambers and Trudgill (1998 section 9.9.2)=}

IV. FORMS REQUIRING SPECIAL COMMENT
Varia:
AANT, ANDD
{=Probably dittography; certainly not lengthening in the first or gemination in the second=}
AD, aeD, ADN
{=Loss of expected N probably a simple graphic mistake, either omission of a letter or, more likely, a mark of abbreviation. In reduction of forms in -[n]C loss of the final stop ((FCD)) is more plausible. The apparent metathesis in ADN would be phonotactically impossible=}
ANDE
{=The <e> is probably not a survival of the original ending *-a, but a case of phonetically uninterpreted, "purely orthographic" <e>=}

ACKNOWLEDGMENTS

We thank the Arts and Humanities Research Board for supporting the work at the Institute of Historical Dialectology, University of Edinburgh, which provided the basis for this chapter. We also thank the Faculty of Humanities of the University of Cape Town for generous leave provision and financial support. We are grateful to Keith Williamson for useful suggestions on an early version and for producing the maps. Figure 17.3 is reproduced by kind permission of the Master and Fellows of Trinity College, Cambridge.

REFERENCES

Atkins, J. W. H. (ed.) (1922). *The Owl and the Nightingale*. Cambridge: Cambridge University Press.

Benskin, M. (1982). The letters <þ> and <y> in later Middle English, and some related matters. *Journal of the Society of Archivists* 7: 13–20.

Benskin, M. (1991). In reply to Dr Burton. *Leeds Studies in English* n.s. 22: 209–62.

Benskin, M. (1994). Descriptions of dialect and areal distributions. In M. Laing and K. Williamson (eds.), *Speaking in our Tongues: Medieval Dialectology and Related Disciplines* (pp. 169–87). Cambridge: D. S. Brewer.

Benskin, M. (2001). The language of the English texts. In T. Hunt (ed.), *Three Receptaria from Medieval England* (pp. 193–230) (Medium Ævum Monographs NS 21). Oxford: Society for the Study of Medieval Languages and Literature.

Benskin, M. and M. Laing (1981). Translations and *Mischsprachen* in Middle English manuscripts. In M. Benskin and M. L. Samuels (eds.), *So Meny People Longages and Tonges: Philological Essays in Scots and Mediœval English Presented to Angus McIntosh* (pp. 55–106). Edinburgh: The Editors.

Breier, W. (1910). *Eule und Nachtigall: eine Untersuchung der Überlieferung und der Sprache, der örtlichen und der zeitlichen Entstehung des me. Gedichts*. Halle a. S.: M. Niemeyer.

Chambers, J. K. and P. Trudgill (1998). *Dialectology* (2nd edn.). Cambridge: Cambridge University Press.

Coulmas, F. (2003). *Writing Systems: An Introduction to their Linguistic Analysis*. Cambridge: Cambridge University Press.

Hunt, T. (1991). *Teaching and Learning Latin in Thirteenth-century England* (3 vols.). Cambridge: D. S. Brewer.

Kristensson, G. (1967). *A Survey of Middle English Dialects 1290–1350: The Six Northern Counties and Lincolnshire*. Lund: Gleerup.

Kristensson, G. (1987). *A Survey of Middle English Dialects 1290–1350: The West Midland Counties*. Lund: Lund University Press.

Kristensson, G. (1995). *A Survey of Middle English Dialects 1290–1350: The East Midland Counties*. Lund: Lund University Press.

Kristensson, G. (2001). *A Survey of Middle English Dialects 1290–1350: The Southern Counties*. I: *Vowels (Except Diphthongs)*. Lund: Lund University Press.

Kristensson, G. (2002). *A Survey of Middle English Dialects 1290–1350: The Southern Counties*. II: *Diphthongs and Consonants*. Lund: Lund University Press.

Laing, M. (1993). *Catalogue of Sources for a Linguistic Atlas of Early Medieval English*. Cambridge: D. S. Brewer.

Laing, M. (1998). Raising a stink in *The Owl and the Nightingale*: a new reading at line 115. *Notes and Queries* 243: 276–84.

Laing, M. (1999). Confusion *wrs* confounded: litteral substitution sets in early Middle English writing systems. *Neuphilologische Mitteilungen* 100: 251–70.

Laing, M. (2000a). "Never the Twain Shall Meet"; early Middle English – the east–west divide. In I. Taavitsainen, T. Nevalainen, P. Pahta, and M. Rissanen (eds.), *Placing Middle English in Context* (pp. 97–124) (Topics in English Linguistics 35). Berlin, New York: Mouton de Gruyter.

Laing, M. (2000b). The linguistic stratification of the Middle English texts in Oxford, Bodleian Library, MS Digby 86. *Neuphilologische Mitteilungen* 101: 523–69.

Laing, M. (2001). Words reread: Middle English writing systems and the dictionary. *Linguistica e Filologia* 13: 87–129.

Laing, M. (2002). Corpus-provoked questions about negation in early Middle English. *Language Sciences* 24: 297–321.

Laing, M. and R. Lass (2003). Tales of the 1001 Nists: the phonological implications of litteral substitution sets in 13th-century south-west-midland texts. *English Language and Linguistics* 7.2.

Laing, M. and Lass, R. (2007). *A Linguistic Atlas of Early Middle English*, http://www.lel.ed.ac.uk/ind/laemel/laemel.html.

Laing, M. and A. McIntosh (1995a). Cambridge, Trinity College MS 335: its texts and their transmission. In R. Beadle and A. J. Piper (eds.), *New Science out of Old Books: Studies in Honour of A. I. Doyle* (pp. 14–52). Aldershot: Scolar Press.

Laing, M. and A. McIntosh (1995b). The language of *Ancrene Riwle*, the Katherine Group texts and *þe Wohunge of ure Lauerd* in BL Cotton Titus D xviii. *Neuphilologische Mitteilungen* 96: 235–63.

Lass, R. (1992). Phonology and morphology. In N. F. Blake (ed.), *The Cambridge History of the English Language*. vol. II: *1066–1476* (pp. 23–155). Cambridge: Cambridge University Press.

Lass, R. and M. Laing (2005). Are front rounded vowels retained in West Midland Middle English? In N. Ritt and H. Schendl (eds.), *Rethinking Middle English: Linguistic and Literary Approaches* (pp. 280–90). Frankfurt: Peter Lang.

McIntosh, A. (1989). Word geography in the lexicography of Middle English. In M. Laing (ed.), *Middle English Dialectology: Essays on Some Principles and Problems* (pp. 86–97). Aberdeen: Aberdeen University Press. (First published in *Annals of the New York Academy of Sciences* 211: 55–66 [1973].)

McIntosh, M., M. L. Samuels, and M. Benskin (eds.) (1986). *A Linguistic Atlas of Late Mediaeval English* (4 vols.). Aberdeen: Aberdeen University Press.

Pelteret, D. A. E. (1990). *Catalogue of English Post-Conquest Vernacular Documents*. Woodbridge: Boydell Press.

Sisam, C. (1951). The scribal tradition of the *Lambeth Homilies*. *Review of English Studies* NS 6: 105–13.

Sweet, H. (1888). *A History of English Sounds from the Earliest Period, with Full Word-lists*. Oxford: Clarendon Press.

Williamson, K. (1992/3). A computer-aided method for making a linguistic atlas of Older Scots. *Scottish Language* 11/12: 138–57.

Williamson, K. (2000). Changing spaces: linguistic relationships and the dialect continuum. In I. Taavitsainen, T. Nevalainen, P. Pahta, and M. Rissanen (eds.), *Placing Middle English in Context* (pp. 141–79) (Topics in English Linguistics 35). Berlin and New York: Mouton de Gruyter.

18 How English Became African American English

SHANA POPLACK

An abiding problem in the history of any language concerns the trajectories by which it developed into its descendant varieties. The ancestral forms of English are enviably well documented, at least those deriving from the written and/or standard registers. Yet there is relatively little useful information about ordinary *spoken* vernaculars of earlier times, which would offer the most pertinent direct evidence for the structure of contemporary offshoots. The dearth of information on the development of the spoken language is no doubt responsible for the widespread belief that many salient and stigmatized features of contemporary dialects are recent innovations. *African American Vernacular English* (AAVE), a variety with which a wide range of nonstandard forms have come to be identified, is a case in point.

The origins and development of contemporary AAVE are controversial. Despite decades of study, there is still little consensus over whether its emblematic features – copula deletion, negative concord, and variable marking of the plural, present, and past, to name but a few – are "bad" English (as most language professionals maintain), or simply *not* English, as would be the case if contemporary AAVE had descended from a relexified West African language or a prior creole. Proponents of the latter scenario claim that despite inevitable convergence with mainstream North American English over the last few centuries, the ultimate source of most of these features is an underlying creole grammar, traces of which AAVE purportedly still preserves. Another possibility, which I develop in this chapter, is that the varieties of English originally acquired by the ancestors of AAVE speakers, though admittedly very different from the contemporary mainstream standards typically used as benchmarks, may well have been much like those spoken by the British who colonized the United States.

Understanding of how AAVE developed cannot be achieved independent of historical context. Each of the competing scenarios involves change, and the study of change requires reference not only to current reflexes but, crucially, to an earlier stage of the language. Little is known about earlier stages of AAVE. Few useful textual records exist, and in any event, since the key features derive from the spoken language, the utility of most written texts in reconstructing their ancestry is unclear (but see Van Herk 2002; Van Herk and Poplack 2003). Records of older spoken varieties, though not entirely absent (e.g. Bailey et al. 1991), are even more sparse. Nor is much known about the nature and extent of differences between the English transported to the American colonies and contemporary standards, beyond the commonsense observation that the former could not possibly have consisted only of prestige forms.

In this chapter, I draw on a long-term research project, carried out in conjunction with Sali Tagliamonte and a number of our associates (e.g. Poplack 2000; Poplack and Tagliamonte 2001), aimed at providing an empirical answer to the question of how English became African American English (AAE). In the absence of sufficient pertinent diachronic data, we combine methods of historical comparative linguistics and variationist sociolinguistics to *reconstruct* an earlier stage of AAE. We then situate this stage with respect to Colonial (and on occasion, Middle) English, English-based Creoles, and contemporary AAVE (though only the first line of inquiry will be presented here). In so doing, we rely crucially on a variety of constructs outlined below.

18.1 Relic Area

A key concept in reconstructing earlier stages of a language is the *relic area*. In the diffusion of linguistic change, some areas, traditionally referred to as relic, or *peripheral*, may be missed. Because of their resistance to change and concomitant tendency to preserve older features, relic areas provide prime evidence about an earlier stage of the language. The relic areas we examined here are communities formed during the African American diaspora of the late eighteenth and early nineteenth centuries, when tens of thousands of African Americans fled the United States to resettle in the Caribbean, Canada, Liberia, and elsewhere. Small enclaves of their descendants maintained their language, culture, and religion for centuries. The geographic and social isolation in which these communities developed enabled them to successfully resist contact-induced change postdating the dispersal, and maintain their vernaculars for at least two centuries. Admitting internal evolution, such circumstances should qualify their language varieties as bona fide descendants of the African American English spoken in the early nineteenth century, thereby furnishing the older stage necessary to reconstruct the ancestor of AAVE. I refer to these varieties collectively as *Early* African American English (reserving the acronym AAVE for contemporary vernaculars). A test of the hypothesis that Early AAE may in fact be taken to represent such an older stage is a key component of the research reported here (see also Poplack 2000; Poplack and Tagliamonte 2001).

18.2 Research Framework

The approach taken here is essentially variationist, comparative, and historical. By *variationist* I refer to a specific focus on the recurrent choices speakers make in expressing the same referential value. The cohort of variant expressions of a given meaning or grammatical function constitutes the *linguistic variable*, the key theoretical construct of this paradigm. The goal is to discover the constraints governing the choice among variants, which may be construed as the grammar underlying the variability. Once the contexts in which the variants of a linguistic variable may occur are established, we attempt to determine which aspects of those contexts (phonological, morphological, syntactic, semantic, discourse, etc.) contribute to the choice process. Innovative here is the "operationalization" of competing hypotheses about the origin and development of variant forms (derived from the relevant theoretical, descriptive, synchronic, and historical literature) as factors in a multivariate analysis. The multiple regression procedure incorporated in the variable rule program (Rand and Sankoff 1990) reveals which factors contribute significant effects to variant choice when all are considered simultaneously, as well as the relative magnitude of each.

18.3 The Comparative Method

Identification of the distinctive features of AAVE as the legacy of an earlier widespread creole or as reflexes of the contemporaneous dialects of English to which its speakers were first exposed, is a diachronic question. Accordingly, we adopt the *Comparative Method* of historical linguistics to ascertain genetic relationships, by reconstructing proto-forms from the attested evidence of the descendant (i.e. diaspora) varieties. If two or more independent languages share a non-universal feature unlikely to have developed by chance or through borrowing, it is assumed to have been transmitted from a common ancestral source. Once we establish the nature of that source, we may begin to validate claims about the origins of AAVE. But assessing the behavior of spoken-language features is complicated by the ubiquitous property of inherent variability. Variability gives rise to competing realizations of the *same* meaning or function, and these may surface in identical form (often zero) in each of the putative ancestors (here, creoles, African languages, English). This vitiates attempts to assess relations among them on the basis of form-matching alone. Thus, for example, both English and English-based creoles share a zero realization of past tense, and it is impossible to determine, from surface inspection alone, whether the stem forms of *return*, *work*, or *come*, italicized in (1), convey the specific meaning of non-punctual or habitual past, as some creolists have claimed (e.g. Bickerton 1975; Winford 1992), result from deletion of past-tense *-ed*, as frequently occurs in other varieties of English (Guy 1980; Santa Ana 1996), or was never acquired to begin with. Likewise, a form like *ain't*, as in (2), which has become a stereotype of AAVE grammar, is widely attested in older English, most varieties of contemporary (nonstandard) English, and English-based creoles.

(1) As they *return*, the doctor went. And when the doctor went, she *come*, and she *work*, she *work*, she *work*. (SE/002/1176)[1]

(2) They *ain't* like they is now. (NPR/030/76)

This type of situation has important repercussions for reconstructing the ancestor of spoken languages. It shows that the provenance of a form cannot be ascertained simply by comparing the existence of cognates, as is traditional in historical linguistics, but only by examining their patterning in discourse.

We address this problem by incorporating into the Comparative Method the variationist construct of *constraint hierarchy* and use this as a basis for our correspondence sets. The constraint hierarchy, or the order with which the components of the context contribute to variant choice, represents the detailed structure of the relationship between form and context of occurrence. Thus the results of the variable rule analyses in table 18.1, for example, reveal not only that phonological, aspectual, and priming considerations all contribute to the choice of the stem form of weak verbs, but also the specific *direction* of these effects: habitual/durative aspect favors selection of the stem more than punctual aspect; a preceding consonant or consonant cluster favors the stem form more than a preceding vowel, etc. These patterns, or constraint hierarchies, interact to yield the probability that the verb will be instantiated as a given variant in a given context. As such, they may be construed as the "grammar" giving rise to the variable surface manifestations.

Our comparison points are variant expressions (e.g *-ed* and Ø in example (1)). Our *cognates* are linguistic functions or variable contexts. *Correspondences* emerge from parallel conditioning, instantiated as constraint hierarchies, or like patterns of favoring and disfavoring effects. To assess whether a correspondence is valid, we determine whether it occurs in other sets; this is effected through comparison with cognate varieties and controls, described below. When a correspondence recurs frequently among comparison varieties, the assumption is that it is real. A striking example of a robust correspondence is the aspectual effect mentioned above. Habitual aspect will be seen (tables 18.1, 18.2, 18.7) to favor stem forms of both weak and strong past-tense verbs, and marked forms of present-tense verbs, in virtually every variety studied here.

18.4 Diagnosticity

Cross-variety comparison is revealing to the extent that the element compared entertains a unique association with a source variety. As noted above, however, with few exceptions, the relevant variants are not only attested, but also frequent in all of the putative ancestors. For the comparison to be *diagnostic*, we require deeper correspondences than those afforded by surface similarity of form. The complex structural picture afforded by the constraint hierarchy serves as a tool in assessing the relationship and provenance of forms, as well as a check in controlling for universals. If two or more varieties share the same highly structured hierarchy of constraints on the variable occurrence of a morphosyntactic element, it is unlikely that they could have arisen independently. If, on the other hand, the pattern is not shared by one or more of the varieties, universals have effectively been ruled out.

18.5 Varieties and Controls

The data on which the analyses below are based, documented in detail in Poplack and Tagliamonte (2001), come from tape-recorded conversations with residents of three diaspora communities depicted in map 18.1. One is located on the Samaná peninsula of the Dominican Republic, settled by former slaves and their descendants in the early 1820s (Poplack and Sankoff 1987). Two others, Guysborough Enclave and North Preston, are located some 250 kilometers apart

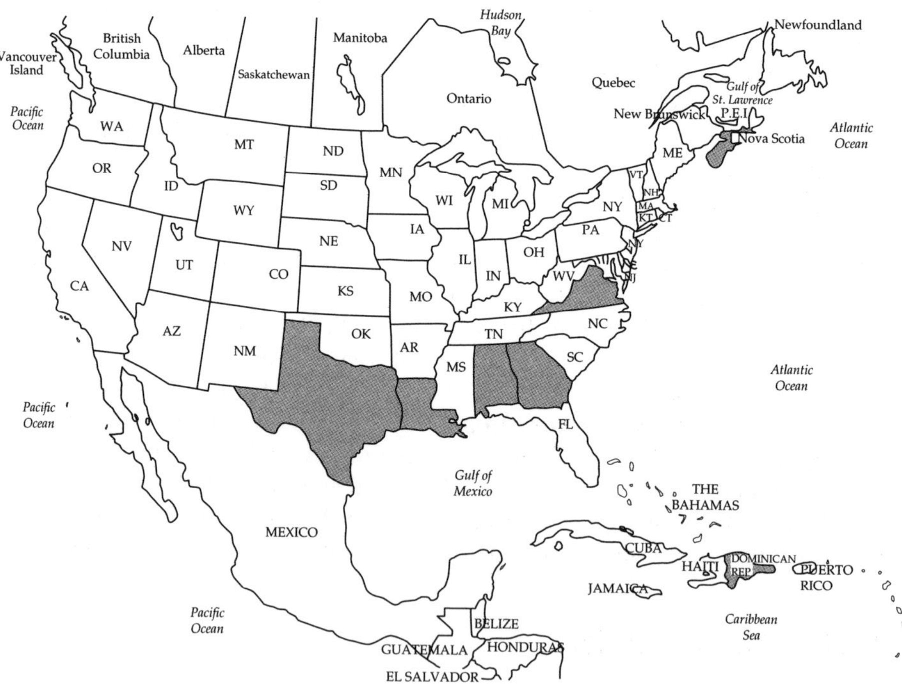

Map 18.1
The shaded areas indicate the diaspora communities examined in Nova Scotia and the Dominican Republic, and the states represented in the *Ex-Slave Recordings*.

on the eastern coast of Nova Scotia, Canada (Poplack and Tagliamonte 1991). They were settled by Black Loyalists after the American Revolutionary War (c.1783–5) and refugee slaves following the War of 1812. Community members at the time of data collection (1980s to 1990s) still spoke an apparently archaic form of English; many of the elderly individuals who participated in the original research projects are now deceased.

Consistent with the comparative method, we validate the diaspora varieties as evidence of Early AAE through detailed comparison of their grammatical structure, first among each other, and then with a number of controls. The *Ex-slave Recordings* is a benchmark variety of AAE which, in contrast to Samaná English and African Nova Scotian English, remained *in situ* in the southern United States. These are mechanically recorded interviews with former slaves born between 1844 and 1861, who would have acquired their language within three to five decades of the input settlers to Samaná. To control for the possibility of areal diffusion and convergence posterior to the dispersal, we supplement the African Nova Scotian materials with a small corpus of Nova Scotian Vernacular English (NSVE) spoken in a rural British-origin settlement adjacent to Guysborough Enclave. We refer to this community in what follows as Guysborough Village. Another check is provided by the dialect of English spoken in an insular rural community in the county of Devon, in southwest England. (For comparison with what is known of the structure of English-based creoles and contemporary AAVE, I refer the reader to Poplack and Tagliamonte 2001). Many older vernacular features which have since disappeared from mainstream standards are still robust in these dialects, making them particularly well suited for comparative reconstruction. The African-origin enclaves have evolved independently from each other for approximately two centuries. Taken together, they differ vastly from the British-origin communities along racial, cultural, and geographic lines. Yet despite these differences, they all share the defining features of peripheral communities (Anderson 1988: 60): spatial isolation, low density of inter-group communication, and language loyalty to vernacular norms. Such communities are known to retain conservative features. As we shall see, this fact will prove to be an invaluable adjunct to the reconstructive endeavor.

A final control is diachronic, tracing the variables identified as AAVE throughout the prescriptive history of English, as instantiated in the *Ottawa Grammar Resource on Early Variability in English, 1577–1898* (Poplack et al. 2001). We mined this collection of nearly 100 English grammars and usage manuals for description, prescription, and censure of the uses of interest, shedding light on the historical, social, and geographical trajectory of the variants. More revealing, hints as to the conditioning of their occurrence over time can be *operationalized* as factors in our analyses, enabling us to ascertain the extent, if any, to which older constraints remain operative. As illustrated in ensuing sections, this exercise reveals that many of the features stereotypically associated with AAVE (and English-based creoles) in fact have a robust precedent in the history of English.

In the remainder of this chapter I illustrate the variationist contribution to the Comparative Method with analyses of two well-documented features of the AAVE tense/aspect system: the variable expression of (simple) past and present temporal reference. The tense/aspect system is particularly amenable to comparative reconstruction, since this is the area in which creoles are considered most distinct from English. The plethora of aspectual distinctions in creoles seems to be associated with the dearth of inflectional morphology. Stem forms are routinely associated with a variety of aspectual readings in such languages, whereas in English they are more often analyzed as resulting from deletion of an underlying morpheme. This fundamental grammatical difference between the two putative ancestral sources of AAVE becomes the basis of the comparative endeavor.

The analyses of the next section are based on more than 11,000 uses of the past and present tenses in Early AAE, and compared with nearly 2,000 in the peripheral British-origin control varieties. These were extracted from informal conversations with over 100 elderly speakers of Early AAE, and 18 speakers of British-origin vernaculars, matched in age and other sociodemographic characteristics.

18.6 Marking the Simple Past

The first illustration involves marking of past time, a variable which has figured prominently in the origins debate. The main research focus has been on the alternation of the "regular" *-ed* affix and the verb stem, as in example (3). Far less attention has been paid to the parallel alternation of stem forms with strong or "irregular" verb morphology, as in (4).

(3) And I *looked* in that door and I *look* back in the corner, I seen them great big eye! (NPR/030/820)

(4) I *run* away from home and *went* to work in the lumber woods. (GYE/066/19)

As noted above, unmarked pasts have long been associated with creole or African origins, particularly when strong verbs like *run*, which could not have resulted from phonologically motivated deletion, are involved. In fact, stem forms (of both strong and weak verbs) are reportedly so common in English-based creoles that some researchers have suggested that their overtly marked counterparts are insertions from, or code-switches to, another system. Interestingly, although this seems to have been a little-known fact prior to the research I report here, variation between overtly marked preterites with stem forms has also been amply attested in the English grammatical tradition for nearly 500 years. We first encounter the *enallage*, or alternation, of marked and unmarked forms with past temporal reference in Peacham's *Garden of Elegance*, published in 1577, reproduced in (5).

(5) Enallage of tyme, when we put one tyme for another, thus. *Terence.* I *come* to the maydens, I *aske* who she *is*, they *say*, the sister of *Chrisis*, for, I *came* to the maydens, I *asked* who she *was*, they *sayd* the sister of *Chrisis*, the Presentence for the Preterperfectence . . . (Peacham 1577 [1971]: no page numbers)

Over a century later Miège (1688: 70) observed that the unmarked (or present) tense was "sometimes [i.e. variably] used for the Preter Imperfect. As, *having met with him, he brings him to his House, and gives him very good Intertainment.* There we say *brings* for *brought*, and *gives* for *gave*." Indeed, the English grammatical tradition shows a long, if not particularly harmonious, history of reporting such variation in past-tense marking. Most attempts to account for it involved efforts to classify the irregular verbs remaining from the several hundred extant in Old English according to perceived correspondences between present, preterite, and participle forms. Actually, the number, membership, and very existence of such verb classes have been contested since at least the early seventeenth century. Some grammarians (e.g. Fenning 1771 [1967]: 65) considered that the rules were "so numerous and intricate, that they rather perplex the judgement than assist the memory of the learner"; whence his long taxonomies of verb conjugations. Some of Fenning's contemporaries (e.g. Bayly 1772 [1969]; Fogg 1792 [1970]) arrived at twelve irregular verb class distinctions; still others posited four. Not only could grammarians not agree on how many kinds or classes of verb conjugation to posit, they also disputed which verbs belonged in which class. Witness Gill's characterization of his own third "conjugation," or class, in (6):

(6) The third conjugation comprises verbs which change the stem-vowel of the present both in the imperfect and the perfect, as spëk <loquor>, J späk <loquebar>, J häv spön <loquutus sum>; . . . In this conjugation also belong almost all the common verbs of the second conjugation (not because of any peculiarity in our language, but because common usage attempts anything) . . . (Gill 1619 [1972]: 121)

Clearly, variability between *-ed* and zero (as well as a variety of other forms) in the marking of past time has had a long history in the development of English. This is a first suggestion that the variable marking in examples (3) and (4) above was not an innovation of Early AAE. But what determines which mark will be selected? We first examine the class of regular or weak verbs (3). Multivariate analysis of the factors contributing to the selection of the stem form in past-tense weak verbs (table 18.1) shows that the same four are operative in each of the four Early AAE varieties. Even more striking, the hierarchy of constraints, which captures the underlying grammar of past-time marking, is virtually identical. This means that they share a grammar of past-tense formation.

One component of this grammar is aspectual: habitual aspect favors the stem form, as in (7). We also observe a priming effect. Contrary to any functionalist view of marker variability, speakers are more likely to select a stem form if

Table 18.1 Five independent variable rule analyses of the contribution of factors to the probability that *weak* verbs will surface as *stems* in Early AAE and Nova Scotian Vernacular English

	Early AAE				*British-origin adstrate*
	Diaspora varieties			*Benchmark*	
Variety	SE	NPR	GYE	ESR	NSVE
Corrected mean	.45	.31	.59	.29	.14
Total *N*	1,236	360	503	281	282
	Prob	*Prob*	*Prob*	*Prob*	*Prob*
Verbal aspect					
Habitual/durative	.63	.63	.56	.51	.53
Punctual	.47	.47	.39	.49	.47
Range	*16*	*16*	*17*	*2*	*6*
Priming					
Preceding verb unmarked	.68	.74	.75	.50	.84
Preceding verb marked	.45	.45	.44	.50	.47
Range	*23*	*29*	*31*		*37*
Preceding phonological segment					
Consonant cluster	.81	.73	.62	.73	.76
Single consonant	.60	.55	.55	.51	.70
Vowel	.26	.35	.35	.32	.11
Range	*55*	*38*	*27*	*41*	*65*
Following phonological segment					
Pause	.74	.91	.60	.81	.44
Consonant	.58	.68	.72	.65	.81
Vowel	.38	.31	.29	.32	.30
Range	*20*	*37*	*43*	*33*	*51*

Note: Results obtained from Goldvarb 2.0 (Rand and Sankoff 1990). Factor weights vary between zero and 1. The higher the figure, the greater the contribution of the factor in question to the probability that the (weak) verb will surface in stem form. The higher the range, the greater the relative magnitude of the factor group.

Not all factor effects presented in tables 18.1, 18.2, and 18.7 are statistically significant, largely due to sparse data in some contexts. However, statistical significance does not affect constraint hierarchies, on which we focus here. Ranges provided only for factors selected as statistically significant.

Source: Adapted from Poplack and Tagliamonte (2001: 124 (table 6.2)).

they have already uttered a stem form (8a), and a marked form following another marked one (8b).

(7) a. No. I got a few spankings when I shouldn't have- supposed to do. And they *spankø* me for that, but, nothing serious. (GYE/077/71)
 b. Sometime you *meltø* snow to wash with. (NPR/015/341)

(8) a. Now, I was around the fifteenth- fifteen or sixteen, all my people *workø* out- Mama *workø* all her day. (NPR/030/299)
 b. And I went to the door, and I *opened* the door and they *jumped* in there. (SE/003/543)

But the most important predictor of bare past temporal verbs is phonological. The stem form is favored in the context of a consonant, while a marked form tends to be retained in prevocalic position (9). The magnitude of the phonological effect (as assessed by the *range*) means that the bare form of regular past temporal reference verbs in Early AAE is first and foremost a result of consonant cluster simplification.

(9) I look*ed a*t it. It *look j*ust like Corney. (NPR/039/148)

Now although cluster simplification is widespread enough across languages and linguistic contexts to qualify as universal, there happens to be a specific precursor for it in the history of past-tense formation in English. This is the tendency, in both speech and poetry, to reduce the formerly syllabic *-ed*. By 1688, Miège had already observed "'tis usual to pronounce and write, for example, *esteem'd* for *esteemed*, *bang'd* for *banged*, . . ." (1688: 70). This was reiterated by Fenning a century later (10).

(10) When a soft letter, liquid, or vowel comes before *-ed*, the *e* is generally omitted in the pronunciation. Thus *robbed, rubbed, raged, begged, breathed, ruled, pulled, aimed, crammed, rained, stunned, pitied, cried, destroyed*, are all read as if they had been wrote *robb'd, rubb'd, rag'd, begg'd, breath'd, rul'd, pull'd, aim'd, cramm'd, rain'd*, . . . (Fenning 1771 [1967]: 65)

The anonymous author of *The English Accidence* complained that the tendency "has very much disfigured the tongue, and turned a tenth part of our smoothest words into so many clusters of consonants." From there it was but a short step to "losing in one syllable the terminations or ending of the preter or past time of our verbs" (Anonymous 1733 [1967]: 76–7).

The robust precedent for consonant cluster simplification in English past-tense weak verbs is no doubt responsible, if only in part, for the appearance of the same phonological effect in the NSVE spoken in the British-origin community adjacent to Guysborough Enclave (as well as in many other varieties of English studied elsewhere). Indeed, all of the variable patterning characteristic of Early AAE is mirrored in NSVE, as can be seen by comparing constraint hierarchies across the varieties in table 18.1. Overall rates of *-ed* deletion (as inferred from the *corrected means* in tables 18.1, 18.2, and 18.7) appear reduced in comparison to those of the Early AAE varieties but, crucially, the hierarchy of constraints conditioning its occurrence is the same. This suggests that there is essentially no grammatical difference between black and white vernacular English in the inflection for past tense in weak verbs.

18.7 Strong Verbs

We next examine the propensity of *strong verbs* to appear bare in Early AAE. With the exception of phonological conditioning, which is of course not relevant here, the factors examined are the same as those considered for the weak verbs. In addition, given its importance in the development of English, we consider the factor of verb class as well, though here we distinguish only the three commonly invoked for contemporary English: I: verb stem = participle (e.g. ***come****/came/****come***); II: preterite = participle (e.g. *say/****said****/****said***); III: verb stem ≠ preterite ≠ participle (e.g. *take/took/taken*).

Table 18.2 displays the results of five independent variable rule analyses of the contributions of these factors to the probability that strong verbs will surface as stems. As with weak verbs, we note first that sentential aspect also contributes to the choice process here: past habituals favor the stem form, as in (11), an effect which is evident in all varieties.

(11) *Interviewer*: Well uh, didn't you say you used to sing that in the field too?
Informant: Yeah I *sing* that in the field too. Yes, sir. (ESR/001/49)

There is also a priming effect, again reminiscent of what was observed for weak verbs: stem forms tend to cluster with stem forms, as in (12a), and marked forms with marks (12b). This is as would be expected of a general processing effect (and shows how little the actual morphological form is relied on to convey the temporal information of past).

(12) a. Aunt Hattie and the people used to work in town. We *come* out and *meet* them, *carry* the clothes home for them. (GYE/074/155)
b. And Dad *took* the twenty dollars and *bought* two young pigs. And Mother *took* her twenty dollars and *went* and *bought- bought* a young cow. (GYE/066/53)

By far the greatest effect on the selection of the stem in strong verbs is contributed by the factor we have labeled *verb class*. In all Early AAE varieties, class I verbs (i.e. in which verb stem = participle) highly favor zero marking. And as previously, all of these effects are paralleled in the NSVE spoken in adjacent Guysborough Village, regardless of the much lower overall rates

Table 18.2 Five independent variable rule analyses of the contribution of factors to the probability that *strong* verbs will surface as *stems* in Early AAE and Nova Scotian Vernacular English

	Early AAE				*British-origin adstrate*
	Diaspora varieties			*Benchmark*	
Variety	SE	NPR	GYE	ESR	NSVE
Corrected mean	.21	.15	.22	.29	.02
Total *N*	2,488	535	574	537	367
	Prob	*Prob*	*Prob*	*Prob*	*Prob*
Verbal aspect					
Habitual/durative	.66	.76	.73	.67	.73
Punctual	.18	.40	.23	.41	.25
Range	*48*	*36*	*50*	*26*	*48*
Priming					
Preceding verb unmarked	.72	.87	.81	.75	.90
Preceding verb marked	.44	.38	.45	.45	.47
Range	*28*	*49*	*36*	*30*	*43*
Verb class					
I Verb stem = participle	.72	.96	.91	.97	.98
II Preterite = participle	.59	.50	.39	.35	.32
III Verb stem ≠ preterite ≠ participle	.27	.33	.40	.42	.40
Range	*45*	*63*	*52*	*62*	*73*

Source: Adapted from Poplack and Tagliamonte (2001: 133 (table 6.3)).

(evidenced by the *corrected mean*) of stem forms in the latter. However, the effect of the other two classes is not so consistent. Strong verbs by definition have irregular past tense forms (e.g. *spoke, took, came, ran,* etc.); all presumably present some difficulty in acquisition, production, etc. Why then are some verbs so resistant to standard marking while others are not? It is reasonable to assume that the number of different morphological forms in a class might be inversely correlated with a speaker's ability to access them all, resulting in the type of variation we have observed. But comparison of the behavior of class I and II verbs (table 18.2), which both feature the same number of forms, reveals that this cannot be the source of the variation. Clearly, the tradition of confusion over the existence, number, and constitution of verb "classes" detailed above has not abated noticeably. In this context we examine the makeup of these classes more closely.

Table 18.3 Constitution of class I lexical verbs

	Early AAE				*British-origin adstrate*
	Diaspora varieties			*Benchmark*	
	SE	*NPR*	*GYE*	*ESR*	*NSVE*
Proportion class I represented by *come*	96%	88%	90%	88%	94%
% stem forms of come	37	76	50	95	38
% stem forms of other strong verbs	22	17	23	21	3

Table 18.3 reveals that a disproportionate number of "class I" verbs consists of the verb *come*, as in (13), and *come* has a greater propensity to surface bare than almost any other verb in the language. The disproportionate behavior of *come* is equally evident in NSVE (14). This is what explains the apparent propensity of class I verbs to surface as stems.

(13) Their turn *come* to clean the- the board. (GYE/040/319)

(14) And then when we were all through, before I *come* home, he *come* over to the [inc] – the infirmary to see me. (NSVE/107/939)

An important proportion of "class II" verbs is similarly made up of *say*. *Say* also tends to surface bare in most of the Early AAE varieties, giving rise to utterances such as that in (15). Indeed, closer inspection reveals that all the classes are made up of verbs with associated marking preferences, regardless of the structural definition of the class (preterite = participle, etc.) This explains the fluctuation of class II and III factor weights across communities. What is the source of these lexically determined preferences?

(15) And she took and she throwed me that baby there and she *say*, "I'm going." (SE/002/309)

Table 18.4 displays the prescriptive treatment over four centuries of English grammatical tradition of a number of preterite forms currently regarded as nonstandard. Note that the Early AAE tendency to select preterite *come* and *say* (as well as *give* and *run*),[2] has a robust precedent in English. Other verbs, however, notably *have*, *go*, and *be*, are never attested bare in the past tense.

Most compelling here is the *relative* treatment of these verbs (illustrated graphically in figure 18.1): some (*come*, *run*, *give*, and *say*) have a long history

Table 18.4 Attestation of selected bare preterite forms in the *Ottawa Grammar Resource on Early Variability in English*.

Date of publication	*Past-tense form*							
	eat	run	come	say(s)	give	have	go	be
1577			√	√				
1619		√	√					
1640	√	√						
1653	√	√	√					
1654		√						
1671	√		√					
1674		√						
1685					√			
1688	√				√			
1700		√	√					
1711	√	√	√					
1723	√	√	√					
1733	√							
1746	√							
1750	√							
1762	√							
1765	√							
1771		X						
1772		√						
1785		X						
1786	√							
1788	√	X		√				
1797	√							
1802	√							
1803	X	X	X					
1803	√							
1830				X				
1834	√	X						
1846	√							
1851	√	√						
1855		X		X				
1855	X							
1863	X	X	X					
1866	√	X						
1870	X							
1874	X	X						
1880	√	√						
1893	X							

Note: Vertical axis = date of publication of the grammar; horizontal axis = verb form cited. X indicates that the form was censured in the grammar in question; a check mark represents an uncritical attestation.
Source: Reproduced from Poplack et al. (2001: 97 (table 5.1)).

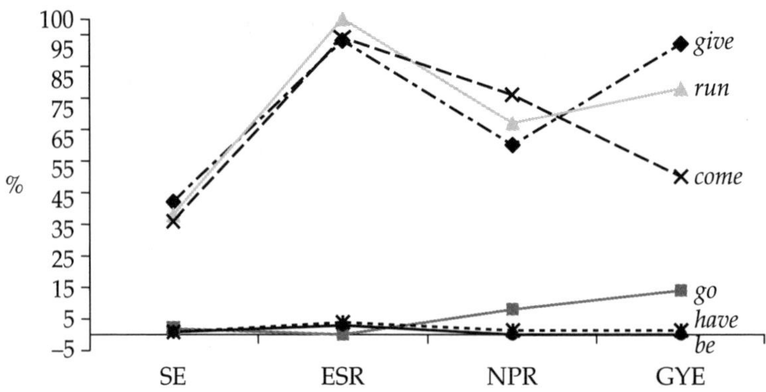

Figure 18.1 Relative marking of strong verbs according to lexical identity, Early AAE

of attestation in stem form; others (*had*, *was/were*, and *went*) in contrast, are virtually always marked. This inflectional profile mirrors exactly the patterns of Early AAE (*and* NSVE), arguing that the different forms do not represent distinct tense/aspect markers, as many creolists have claimed. Rather, the alternation between stem and marked forms of past-tense strong verbs is the lexically determined residue of patterns extant at an earlier stage of the English language, but which have since disappeared from mainstream standards. The trajectory leading to their disappearance can be inferred from table 18.4, which illustrates the widening gap between prescription and praxis with regard to the stem form of past-reference verbs. Acceptance of the (currently) nonstandard variant decreases over time, as evidenced by fewer checks toward the bottom of the table. With the entrenchment of the standard (post-1800), the tendency to stigmatize bare preterites as vulgar, provincial, or dialectal increases. This is no doubt a harbinger of their eventual expulsion from the inventory of Standard English, though not from the vernaculars of many speakers, including those studied here. Their disappearance from contemporary mainstream speech, coupled with the synchronic perspective prevalent in the field, explains why these variants are so often characterized as innovations, rather than the retentions our analysis has shown them to be.

To summarize, the results of this section show that despite the variable absence of an overt past-tense mark (at rates approximating 50 percent in some of the varieties studied), the morphological expression of simple past in Early AAE was inherited from English. Its surface manifestation continues to be regularly conditioned by the same type and hierarchy of constraints as in vernacular varieties of English, early and contemporary, and may be expressed as the output of the variable operation of phonological constraints in weak verbs, and the residue of (historically determined) alternation of morphologically strong forms with their bare stem counterparts in strong verbs. The aspectual effect on the morphological expression of past in both strong and weak verbs has not been attested in the English grammatical tradition, though it has been cited as a creole legacy. Its presence in NSVE, however, requires an alternative explanation. Further analysis (not shown here) reveals that stem forms in past habitual contexts prevail specifically where *would* and its contracted variant *'d* are admitted. This, coupled with the strong phonological effects detailed above, suggests that these bare preterites result from phonological deletion of contracted *would* in habitual contexts rather than any privative association with habitual aspect.

18.8 Marking the Simple Present

The legacy of English to Early AAE is also evidenced by the variable marking with *-s* of (simple) present tense, regardless of person and number of the subject, as in (16).

(16) a. Because when I drink the coffee it *keepø* me, you see. (SE/003/538)
b. And they all treating me mighty nice, all the white folks that *knowø* me, they *treats* me nice. (ESR/003/26)

Though this is a well-documented feature of contemporary AAVE, linguists have long been at odds over how best to characterize it. At first it was simply considered a hypercorrection, (somewhat arbitrarily) described as "tacking on a morpheme which [the speaker] knows is not characteristic of the standard language, but which he has not yet learned to use correctly" (Bickerton 1975), or "adoption of a Standard English form without the Standard English grammatical component" (Pitts 1981: 304). So closely was this usage associated with AAVE, and so alien was it considered to the grammar of Standard English, that many scholars concluded that *-s* must be a creole aspect marker. Other theories were also advanced, without, however, leading to consensus on its origins or current function(s). In tracking the trajectory of *-s* throughout the English grammatical tradition, we discovered that variable inflection across the present-tense paradigm had a long and venerable history. Indeed, the contemporary Standard English requirement that subject and verb must agree in 3rd person sing. (achieved via inflection with *-s*) is actually a fairly recent development, dating only from the Early Modern English period. Prior to that time, agreement was not categorical, nor was *-s* restricted to 3rd person sing., as can be seen from table 18.5, which displays the distribution of *-s* across grammatical persons in Middle English.

There is ample attestation of this phenomenon in English grammars. The citation from Beattie (1788 [1968]: 175) reproduced in (17) invokes not only the variability (a singular verb *sometimes* follows a plural noun), but also its social and geographic context. Given current associations of nonconcord *-s* with nonstandard and/or regional varieties of English, the fact that it was already attributed to "vulgar dialect" and "the common people" in the eighteenth

Table 18.5 Regional distribution of verbal inflections in Middle English

Grammatical person	*North*	*Midlands*	*South*
Singular			
1st	*hēr(e) (s)*	*hēr(e) (s)*	*hēre*
2nd	*hēres*	*hēres(t)*	*hēr(e) st*
3rd	*hēres*	*hēres, hēreþ*	*hēreþ*
Plural	*hēres*	*hēres, hēreþ, hēre (n)*	*hēreþ*

Source: Adapted from Mossé (1952: 78).

century comes as no surprise. Beattie also remarked on the (still) rather opaque nature of the standard agreement rule (18):

(17) in old [i.e. Early Modern] English, a verb singular *sometimes* follows a plural nominative; as in the following couplet from Shakespeare's Venus and Adonis, She lifts the *coffer-lids* that *close* his eyes, Where lo, *two lamps* burnt out in darkness *lies*. The same idiom prevails in the Scotch acts of parliament, in the vernacular writings of Scotch men prior to the last century *and in the vulgar dialect of North Britain to this day: and, even in England, the common people frequently speak in this manner*, without being misunderstood. (Beattie 1788 [1968]: 192–3, emphasis added)

(18) Custom has made this third person plural necessary, by determining, that the verb shall agree in number with its nominative. But if custom had determined otherwise, we might have done without it . . . if custom had not subjoined a plural verb to a plural nominative, or to two or more singular nominatives, there would have been no fault in the syntax. (Beattie 1788 [1968]: 192–3)

Indeed, grammarians of the past had little more success in explaining variable *-s* inflection than contemporary linguists. Most invoked doubts over the properties of the subject noun – whether it should be considered singular or plural, whether, when conjoined, it counts as one or two, and whether agreement applies to the grammatical subject or the noun closest to the verb. But few among the wealth of explanations we uncovered are relevant to contemporary behavior, since the elements of interest to grammarians turn out to be extremely rare in speech. The one important exception is a pattern, first described by Murray in 1873 for Northern (Scots and Northumbrian) dialects of English, which has come to be known as the *Northern Subject Rule*. This "rule," reproduced in (19), relates the alternation of *-s* and zero to type of subject and adjacency to the verb.

(19) In the PRESENT TENSE *aa leyke, wey leyke, you leyke, thay leyke,* are used only when the verb is accompanied by its proper pronoun; when the subject is a noun, adjective, interrogative or relative pronoun, or when the verb and subject are separated by a clause, the verb takes the termination *-s* in all persons. Thus *"aa cum first; yt's mey at cums first . . . thay cum and teake them; the burds cums an' paecks them."* (Murray 1873: 212)

We operationalized the Northern Subject Rule, along with phonological and aspectual factors suggested to constrain *-s* variability, as factors in a multivariate analysis, and analyzed the contribution of each to the probability that *-s* would be selected in present temporal reference contexts. As previously, we compare results, first among the Early AAE varieties, and then with a British-origin control. Because NSVE features too little nonconcord *-s* to permit quantitative analysis, for purposes of comparison we investigate *-s* usage in Devon, England. As may be seen in table 18.6, rates of verbal *-s* across the present-tense paradigm are in fact higher in this insular British community than in Early AAE, not only in 3rd person sing., but across the board.

It is also apparent from table 18.6 that verbal *-s* is far too frequent, in both concord and nonconcord contexts, and distributed too systematically across grammatical persons, to sustain an explanation of hypercorrect insertion.

Table 18.6 Distribution of verbal *-s* by grammatical person in Early AAE and Devon English

	Early AAE								*British-origin*	
	Diaspora varieties						*Benchmark*			
	SE		NPR		GYE		ESR		DVN	
	%	N	%	N	%	N	%	N	%	N
Grammatical person										
Singular										
1st	14	683	5	434	2	639	3	149	22	326
2nd	6	396	1	307	0	345	0	69	17	175
3rd	**42**	585	**41**	195	**55**	251	**50**	34	**85**	295
Plural										
1st	18	157	5	22	3	34	44	9	26	84
2nd	—	—	—	—	—	—	—	—	20	5
3rd	**28**	674	**14**	174	**9**	249	**8**	72	**37**	288
Total *N*		2,495		1,132		1,518		333		1,173

Table 18.7 Five independent variable rule analyses of the contribution of factors to the presence of verbal *-s* in 3rd person plural in Early AAE and Devon English

	Early AAE				*British-origin*
	Diaspora varieties			*Benchmark*	
Variety	SE	NPR	GYE	ESR	Devon
Corrected mean	.260	.114	.068	.064	.358
Total *N*	699	173	244	72	288
	Prob	*Prob*	*Prob*	*Prob*	*Prob*
Preceding phonological segment					
Vowel	.61	.37	.45	.75	.45
Consonant	.48	.56	.52	.39	.53
Range	*13*				
Following phonological segment					
Vowel	.56	.62	.57	.78	.49
Consonant	.47	.44	.47	.38	.51
Range	*9*			*40*	
Aspect					
Habitual	.57	.64	.50	.51	.53
Continuous	.37	.23	.50	.47	.46
Punctual	—	—	—	—	.38
Range	*20*	*41*			
Subject type/adjacency					
Non-adjacent pro or NP	.59	.41	.78	.70	.60
Adjacent personal pro	.47	.56	.35	.39	.48
Range	*11*		*43*		

Source: Adapted from Poplack and Tagliamonte (2001: 189 (table 7.6)).

Almost without exception, *-s* occurs most often in 3rd person sing., followed by 3rd person pl., then 1st person. Which factors underlie the selection of *-s* in these contexts? Table 18.7 displays the results for 3rd person pl., which in most particulars parallel those for the other grammatical persons (Poplack and Tagliamonte 2001).

The regular phonological effect on the occurrence of *-s* displayed in table 18.7 provides further evidence against a hypercorrection analysis. It is not entirely consistent across grammatical persons, nor is it of the same magnitude in each variety; nonetheless, in most varieties, vowels favor inflection with -*s*, as in (20), while consonants tend to disfavor it (21).

(20) 'Cause I *knows* it and I *sees* it now. (SE/002/211)

(21) Well, my niece and, uh, granddaughter here, she *takeø* care of baby. (ESR/013/156)

As with past-tense marking, we again observe a moderate aspectual effect in the present, which recurs regularly in all grammatical persons. Here, -*s* is preferred when the aspectual reading of the verb is habitual (22), in contrast to past habituals, which favored the stem form.

(22) But you never *gets* none now hardly for Natal day. You never *gets* none 'til after Natal day. (NPR/003/79)

I noted earlier that such aspectual uses of morphological elements by speakers of African origin are typically construed as the legacy of a prior creole grammar. But as with past-marking, the parallel contribution of habitual aspect to -*s* inflection in the British-origin control variety suggests that an English source is equally plausible. In fact, although English grammarians are silent with respect to aspectual distinctions until late in the eighteenth century, the link between the simple present tense and habitual aspect is clear. Pickbourn (1789 [1968]) recommends the simple present to denote *habits*, or repeated actions; Bullions (1869: 39) prescribes it "to express what is habitual or always true." Indeed, habituality is the default reading of the simple present tense when it has present temporal reference. In -*s*-conserving varieties like Early AAE, the simple present tense has two exponents, and as shown by Walker (2000), the aspectual readings of the present tense have been divided among them: -*s* is preferred in habitual contexts, and zero tends to be associated with durative readings. This same association between verbal -*s* and habitual aspect has also been reported in a number of British dialects, and has been confirmed quantitatively in such distant -*s*-preserving varieties as Newfoundland Vernacular English (Clarke 1997) and Devon English (Godfrey and Tagliamonte 1999), though it has of course disappeared from contemporary standards.

But perhaps the clearest effect is the one we have referred to as the Northern Subject Rule, instantiated in table 18.7 as the factor of Subject Type/Adjacency. With only one exception, all the varieties, whether of African or British origin, tend to avoid verbal -*s* after adjacent personal pronominal subjects, and to favor it with longer subjects, exactly as described by Murray in 1873. This gives rise to utterances like those in (23).

(23) a. Oh, *I liveø* my life. I and Emma, and Aunt Bridgie all- *we all lives* our life. (NPR/014/323)
b. That's why *you knowø, they celebrateø* that day. Colored folks *celebrates* that day. (ESR/013/201)

c. *You goø* off for the day, and *gives* 'em fish and chips on the way home. (DVN/6/386)

To summarize, despite the difficulty in reconstructing the conditioning of a variable process which has since gone to completion in most varieties of English, these results suggest that the variant forms of the simple present tense, as well as the constraints on their occurrence, are the reflexes of an older English model. This is evidenced by the trajectory of verbal *-s* throughout the English grammatical tradition, as well as the behavior of a peripheral British variety in which *-s* remains productive. Detailed cross-variety comparison showed that on the core grammatical measures, the constraint hierarchy underlying the selection of *-s* in Devon paralleled that of Early AAE. These facts suggest that verbal *-s* marking in Early AAE reflects the variability characteristic of the English language transported to the American colonies.

18.9 Discussion

The research reported here has combined the variationist approach to language variation and change with the reconstructive power of the Comparative Method, and used them to triangulate from several peripheral sister varieties. This provides an ideal opportunity to reconstruct the parent. We first compared the diaspora varieties among themselves and found striking parallels, bolstering the inference of a shared common ancestor. To ascertain the identity of that ancestor, we had recourse to a series of external controls. We compared the diaspora varieties with a benchmark variety of African American English, acquired some two to three generations later. In view of the sociolinguistic and geographic disparities between residents of the diaspora settlements on the one hand, and the southern blacks represented in the *Ex-slave Recordings* corpus on the other, the parallels we uncovered in both rate and conditioning of variability are little short of remarkable. But because innovations are often motivated through adstratal features in areal diffusion, we also examined the respective adstrates. In the Samaná context we established that the majority language, Spanish, had contributed little to local English. We also compared African- and British-origin vernaculars wherever shared variant forms permitted. NSVE was in fact found to display many parallels with the African Nova Scotian variety spoken in the adjacent Guysborough Village, but these are also present in the geographically remote settlements of North Preston, Samaná, and the southern United States. Further comparison shows that Devon English, a peripheral British variety, shares with Early AAE virtually all details of nonstandard present-tense usage. Such findings are inexplicable under the explanation of areal diffusion; they are best understood as common retentions typical of peripheral dialect areas.

The specific comparisons effected in this research also comply with core notions in the reconstruction of ancestral forms. Since morphosyntactic criteria are particularly relevant to the establishment of continuity between an ancestor and a later stage (Meillet 1921: 39), as is the focus on "irregular" (here, nonstandard) forms, we examined features related to the expression of tense and aspect, a core area of the grammar. Retentions of irregular morphosyntactic forms are more likely to represent historical residue than innovations introduced in the process of language change (Baldi 1990; Campbell-Kibler 1998). The correspondences we have established rest not on coincidental likenesses of form but on highly structured similarities in constraint hierarchies. Thus the conclusion that the diaspora varieties represent lineal descendants of a shared earlier stage is based on detailed and systematic cross-variety comparison of their variable linguistic behavior, coupled with the principle that a systematic pattern of correspondences between two or more independently evolving varieties is unlikely to have resulted from coincidental innovations. Again, the most credible explanation is that these are shared retentions from a common ancestor.

The conclusion that that ancestor was Colonial English, and conjectures about its likely constitution, were drawn from triangulating Early AAE structures with those of British-origin varieties which developed in similar circumstances of sociolinguistic peripherality. These were bolstered by the discovery of a centuries-old tradition of attestation, throughout the history of English, of the variants now deemed nonstandard. Results show that it is the peripherality of the speech community that best explains the variable patterns, since they recur in all of them regardless of speaker race or ethnicity. This, coupled with the many independent findings linking specific constraint hierarchies with patterns extant throughout the development of English, is proof that the differences between the peripheral varieties and contemporary Standard English are related more to the lack of participation of the former in current mainstream developments than to descent from an underlying creole grammar.

That the British-origin varieties are just as distinct from contemporary Standard English as Early AAE can be attributed to the retention, by *all* the sociolinguistically peripheral varieties (African- and British-origin), of reflexes which have since disappeared. Verbal *-s* is now localized to 3rd person sing. contexts, *-ed* has become the only productive affix for past-tense regular verbs, and the number of prescriptively accepted strong pasts has decreased markedly. The question of how and why contemporary *Standard* English was selected as a benchmark against which to compare African American English merits a research program of its own. But once older, regional, and nonstandard varieties of English are factored into the comparison, the similarities among them are revealed to be numerous and non-trivial. The English history of these variables has not figured in previous treatments, which have tended to opt for a resolutely synchronic approach. The synchronic focus has served to highlight the differences between AAVE and mainstream English. These, coupled with the disappearance of many of the key forms, have led linguists down the garden path of seeking and elaborating complicated external explanations for their development, in an (otherwise laudable) attempt to legitimate features they had previously claimed were incompletely or incorrectly acquired. The evidence presented here suggests that many of the features today considered nonstandard were not *created*, as would be expected if they had resulted from prior creolization or incomplete acquisition. On the contrary, they were retained from an older stage of English. The results of this research rightly legitimate Early AAE as a conservative rather than an incorrect variety of English – one whose core grammatical differences appear to reside largely in its resistance to ongoing mainstream change.

ACKNOWLEDGMENTS

The research on which this chapter is based was generously supported by the Social Science and Humanities Research Council of Canada (1990, 1994, 1995, 1999), the Institute for Social and Economic Research, Memorial University of Newfoundland (1990), and University and Faculty of Arts Research Funds from the University of Ottawa (1992, 1998).

NOTES

1 Codes in parentheses identify (1) the corpus: Samaná English (SE), Ex-slave Recordings (ESR), North Preston, Nova Scotia (NPR), Guysborough Enclave, NS (GYE), Guysborough Village, NS (GYV), and Devon, UK (DVN); (2) the speaker; and (3) the location of the example on recording, transcript or data file. All corpora are housed at the University of Ottawa Sociolinguistics Laboratory. Examples are reproduced verbatim from speaker utterances. Hyphens represent false starts, [inc] refers to incomprehensible material.
2 The verb *eat*, whose stem form predominated in past temporal reference contexts until the late nineteenth century, rarely occurred in our Early AAE data.

REFERENCES

Anderson, H. (1988). Center and periphery: adoption, diffusion, and spread. In J. Fisiak (ed.), *Historical Dialectology: Regional and Social* (pp. 39–83). Berlin: Mouton de Gruyter.

Anonymous (1733 [1967]). *The English Accidence*. Leeds: Scholar Press.

Bailey, G., Maynor, N., and Cukor-Avila, P. (1991). *The Emergence of Black English: Texts and Commentary*. Amsterdam and Philadelphia: John Benjamins.

Baldi, P. (1990). Introduction: the comparative method. In P. Baldi (ed.), *Linguistic Change and Reconstruction*

Methodology (pp. 1–13). Berlin: Mouton de Gruyter.

Bayly, A. (1772 [1969]). *A Plain and Complete Grammar with the English Accidence.* Menston, England: Scholar Press.

Beattie, J. (1788 [1968]). *The Theory of Language.* Menston, England: Scholar Press.

Bickerton, D. (1975). *Dynamics of a Creole System.* Cambridge: Cambridge University Press.

Bullions, P. (1869). *The Principles of English Grammar: Comprising the Substance of the Most Approved English Grammar Extant.* New York: Sheldon.

Campbell-Kibler, K. (1998). History in the making of language: a critique of the literature on the development of African-American English. MA thesis, University of Chicago.

Clarke, S. (1997). English verbal -*s* revisited: the evidence from Newfoundland. *American Speech* 72.3: 227–59.

Fenning, D. (1771 [1967]). *A New Grammar of the English Language.* Menston, England: Scholar Press.

Fogg, P. W. (1792 [1970]). *Elementa Anglicana.* Menston, England: Scholar Press.

Gill, A. (1619 [1972]). *Logonomia Anglica.* Stockholm: Almqvist and Wiksell.

Godfrey, E. and S. Tagliamonte (1999). Another piece for the verbal -*s* story: evidence from Devon in Southwest England. *Language Variation and Change* 11.1: 87–121.

Guy, G. R. (1980). Variation in the group and the individual: the case of final stop deletion. In W. Labov, *Locating Language in Time and Space* (pp. 1–36). New York: Academic Press.

Meillet, A. (1921). *Linguistique historique et linguistique générale.* Paris: Champion.

Miège, G. (1688). *The English Grammar.* Menston, England: Scholar Press.

Mossé, F. (1952). *A Handbook of Middle English.* Baltimore: Johns Hopkins University Press.

Murray, J. A. H. (1873). *The Dialect of the Southern Counties of Scotland: Its Pronunciation, Grammar and Historical Relations.* London: Philological Society.

Peacham, H. (1577 [1971]). *The Garden of Eloquence.* Menston, England: Scholar Press.

Pickbourn, J. (1789 [1968]). *A Dissertation on the English Verb.* Menston, England: Scholar Press.

Pitts, W. (1981). Beyond hypercorrection: the use of emphatic -*z* in BEV. *CLS* 17: 303–10.

Poplack, S. (ed.) (2000). *The English History of African American English.* Oxford: Blackwell.

Poplack, S. and D. Sankoff (1987). The Philadelphia story in the Spanish Caribbean. *American Speech* 62.4: 291–314.

Poplack, S. and S. Tagliamonte (1991). African American English in the diaspora: the case of old-line Nova Scotians. *Language Variation and Change* 3: 301–39.

Poplack, S. and S. Tagliamonte (2001). *African American English in the Diaspora.* Oxford: Blackwell.

Poplack, S., G. Van Herk, and D. Harvie (2001). "Deformed in the dialects": an alternative history of nonstandard English. In P. Trudgill and R. Watts (eds.), *Alternative Histories of English* (pp. 87–110). London: Routledge.

Rand, D. and D. Sankoff (1990). GoldVarb: a variable rule application for the Macintosh. Montreal: Centre de recherches mathématiques, Université de Montréal.

Santa Ana, O. (1996). Sonority and syllable structure in Chicano English. *Language Variation and Change* 8.1: 63–90.

Van Herk, G. (2002). A message from the past: past temporal reference in Early

African American letters. PhD dissertation, University of Ottawa, Canada.

Van Herk, G. and S. Poplack (2003). Rewriting the past: bare verbs in the *Ottawa Repository of Early African American Correspondence*. *Journal of Pidgin and Creole Languages* 18.2: 1–36.

Walker, J. A. (2000). Present accounted for: prosody and aspect in Early African American English. PhD dissertation, University of Ottawa, Canada.

Winford, D. (1992). Back to the past: the BEV/Creole connection revisited. *Language Variation and Change* 4: 311–57.

19 Historical Change in Synchronic Perspective: The Legacy of British Dialects

SALI A. TAGLIAMONTE

19.1 Introduction

A number of areas of English grammar have been the locus of extensive longitudinal reorganization in the last several hundred years, including deontic modality, the encoding of stative possessive meaning, relativization, and adverbialization with *-ly*. Contemporary British dialects are replete with variation of forms in each of these subsystems of grammar – use of *must/have to/have got to* for deontic modality, as in (1), variable *wh*-words, *that*, and zero marking relative clauses, as in (2), *have/have got* or *got* for stative possessive meaning, as in (3), *-ly* or zero for certain adverbs, as in (4).

(1) I'*ve got to* cycle all the way back and then this afternoon I'll be cycling back up again! You *have to* keep those thoughts er thoughts to yourself. (YRK/X)[1]

(2) It was a job *that* I always wanted . . . It was a job Ø I've always enjoyed. (CMK/x)

(3) He'*s got* bad breath; he *has* smelly feet. (YRK/I)

(4) I mean, you go to Leeds and Castleford, they take it so much more *seriously* . . . they take it so *serious*. (YRK/T)

This variability is often attributed to external factors, particularly as distinguishing major varieties of English (e.g. British vs. North American). Other explanations have been grounded in dialect origins, social class, age, etc. However, the variability may also be viewed as the product of grammatical change and reflecting the characteristics of grammaticalization (Hopper 1991).

Indeed, each of these represents a scenario of long-term evolution of forms for the same function, presenting interesting cases to study for a number of reasons. First, because the forms (variants) competing in each subsystem entered the language at different points in time – *must* for deontic modality; Old English, *have to*: 1579, *have got to*: nineteenth century – their distribution across dialects may shed light on the stages of development of the system itself and thus the nature of linguistic change in this area of English grammar (Bybee et al. 1994). Second, because the evolution of these subsystems often involves cases in which a vernacular feature – *gotta* for deontic modality; *'ve got* for possession; the zero adverb marker, etc. – has won out over erstwhile standard competitors, the developments in these areas may be useful in tracking the lag between written and spoken data in language change. On the other hand some changes are precisely the opposite, involving the evolution of forms from formal registers into the vernacular, e.g. the *wh*-relative markers *which* and *who*. Comparison of these different trajectories of change across features will further elucidate the forces driving them. Finally, information on linguistic patterns of variability, trends, constraints, etc. extrapolated from the historical and synchronic literature can be used for comparative study to track the varying trends across dialects and thus to tap into the evolving linguistic processes of the language.

Using a series of previous research studies as a foundation to explore various approaches to these problems, and to set issues for future research, I consider, first, the value of synchronic dialect study to the study of such language changes in English, in particular in British dialects. I will argue that systematically collected community-based samples of spoken vernacular language data from British regional dialects provide an important picture of varying stages in the (recent) development of the English language. Moreover, the information that can be gleaned from nonstandard vernacular data sheds light not only on community-based, regional norms, but also situate linguistic change at a particular point on its trajectory.

Second, I explore the utility of grammaticalization theory for the study of morpho-syntactic developments in English, in particular by providing relevant details of the results of four large-scale studies from an intra- and inter-community perspective. For example, synchronic British dialects sometimes differ in their favored variant for a particular subsystem of grammar; however, the internal linguistic factors that constrain the variability are often shared across all. In many cases, these can be traced to variable constraints attested in the history of the English language, and thus can be interpreted as "persistence" (Hopper and Traugott 1993). This provides some insights into what earlier points in the trajectory of development of these areas of grammar may have been like. Similarly, as forms take on new grammatical functions, we may observe shifts and reweighting of contextual effects pointing to "specialization" (Hopper 1991). On the other hand, differences in inter-variety distributions across generations as well as cross-dialectal anomalies reveal that the changes are not progressing at the same rate. Indeed, these results suggest that each community represents its own "slice in time," reflected, not only in the varying distribution of forms, but more strikingly in their patterns of use. Such findings illuminate how internal grammatical constraints, ongoing changes in other areas of the grammar, and external factors conspire to affect the ebb and flow of linguistic change. As I will argue, the critical contribution of synchronic dialect data is to illuminate these processes.

Third, I demonstrate the utility of variationist sociolinguistic methods in the analysis and interpretation of linguistic patterns and the critical role it serves in their evaluation (Poplack and Tagliamonte 2001: 88–102). In order to assess the grammatical function(s) of forms and their status in each community, I test the effects of linguistic features associated with the linguistic changes in each subsystem. I then correlate these parameters with the different variants in the data using quantitative techniques such as distributional analysis to assess their frequency and patterns.[2] The comparative method is then used to assess similarities and differences both within and across communities.[3]

19.2 Background

In historical linguistics, the study of peripheral dialects is considered to be one of the most informative means to shed light on the origins and development of languages (Anttila 1989: 294; Hock 1986: 442). Because of their geographic location or isolated social and/or political circumstances, dialects tend not to be affected by some of the changes that their cohorts in mainstream communities undergo.

Conventionally however, data from regional dialects have been the province of the dialectologist, and traditional practice has been heavily descriptivist, with a focus on word choice and traditional vocabulary items. In contrast, historical and comparative linguists have typically resorted to historical written sources and formal theories for their interpretation, while focusing on syntactical phenomena. However, recent research suggests that dialect data can contribute fruitful evidence for many types of linguistic inquiry – the study of language structure and meaning (e.g. Henry 1995; Wilson and Henry 1998), language contact (e.g. Chaudenson 1992; Mufwene 1996), and language endangerment (Mufwene 2001: 145–66; Wolfram and Schilling-Estes 1995), in addition to the more common studies relating to linguistic change over time and space (e.g. Labov 1994; Trudgill 1983). Moreover, researchers have shown that dialect phenomena provide ideal evidence for viewing intra-language variation in universal grammar (Trudgill and Chambers 1991: 294), the effects of competing linguistic systems (Labov 1998), and can reveal important insights into the links between diachronic and synchronic linguistic inquiry (Labov 1989; Trudgill 1986, 1996).

All these studies highlight the important contribution that dialects can make to ongoing developments in a number of diverse fields of linguistics. Such materials can be useful to much current research whose ability to address many of the new questions (more) adequately has been handicapped by its absence.

19.3 The Data

A well-known fact of historical and socio-linguistics is that certain dialects tend to be more conservative and do not participate in ongoing linguistic change at the same rate as others. Indeed, Meillet (1967) observes that "very often it is sufficient to arrange facts geographically to understand their history." Although synchronic dialects cannot exactly replicate varieties of English as they were spoken in earlier days, many communities still exist that are geographically peripheral and socially and/or politically isolated. Such communities often preserve features of seventeenth- and eighteenth-century nonstandard English vernaculars (e.g. Godfrey and Tagliamonte 1999; Tagliamonte and Smith 1998). Thus, they provide at least a partial "snapshot" of earlier stages in the history of the language.

19.3.1 Dialects in the British heartland

The data on which this study is based comprise a rich compendium of British dialects totaling 3 million words of natural speech, as outlined in table 19.1 and illustrated in map 19.1.[4] Each of these corpora comes from communities that exist in varying situations of contact with mainstream norms.

19.3.2 Nature of the data

These materials are replete with linguistic features worthy of investigation. Many are common to vernacular dialects across Britain. These include the ubiquitous lack of agreement with preterite *be*, as in (5), particularly in existential constructions (6), with simple present *be*, as in (7), verbal *-s* variation in

Table 19.1 British dialect data

	Male	*Female*	*Total speakers*	*Total words*
Buckie, Scotland [BCK]	4	5	9	198,086
Cumnock [CMK]	17	22	39	349,428
Cullybacky [CLB]	15	5	20	223,693
Henfield, Sussex [HEN]	4	4	8	128,421
Maryport [MPT]	20	23	43	401,376
Portavogie [PVG]	7	2	9	92,803
Tiverton, Devon [TIV]	7	2	9	96,472
Wheatley Hill [WHL]	12	13	25	206,320
Wincanton, Somerset [SMT]	17	17	34	205,783
York [YRK]	43	54	97	1.2 m

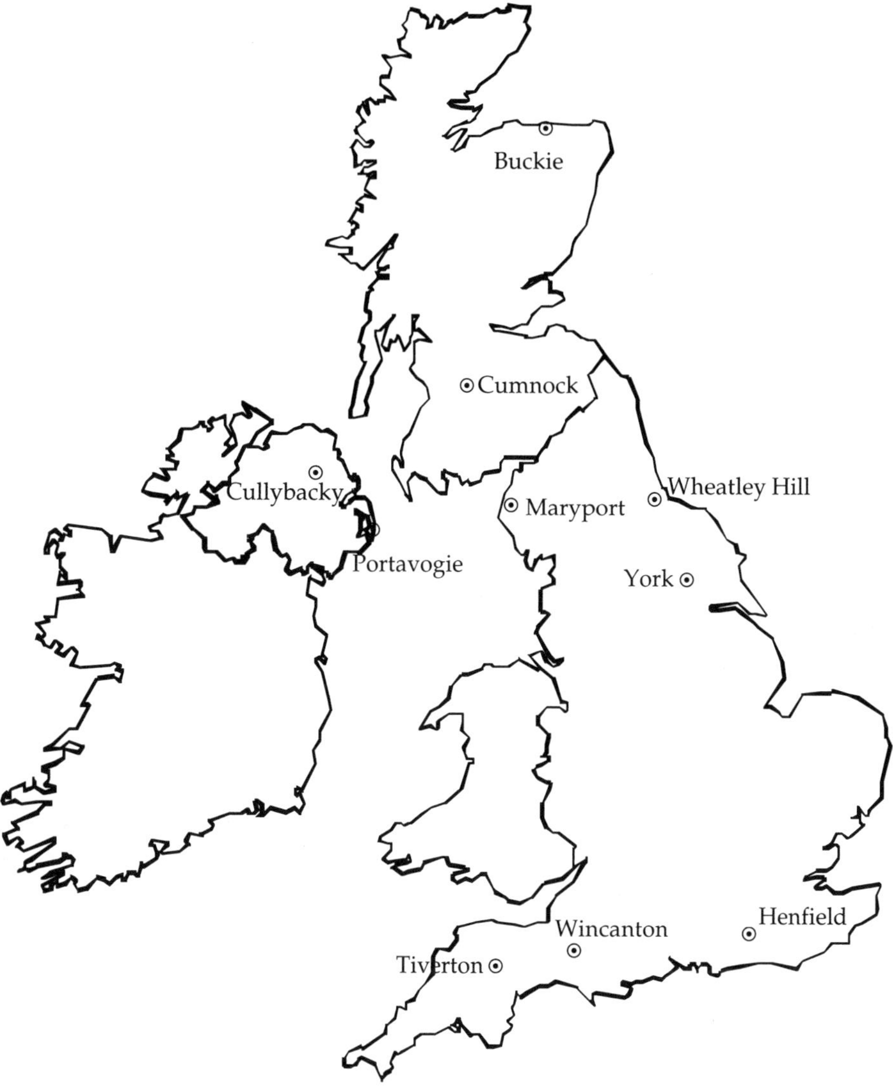

Map 19.1 The communities in Britain

the simple present-tense paradigm, as in (8), a variety of different complement markers, e.g. *for to*, as in (9), regularized *don't*, as in (10), and many others.

(5) a. In that picture of me with those cats, they *was* all ginger ones. (TIV/07)
b. And then, but we *was* going out through there um, with the donkey the first time. (WHL/002)
c. When we *was* kids it was good, really good fun. (HEN/004)

(6) a. There *was* railway cottages up on the bank. (HEN/005)
b. There *was* two of them (WHL/007)
c. There *was* a lot of good players there. (SMT/036)

(7) a. There'*s* not many round here. (HEN/008)
b. During the week, she comes now because weekends *is* no good because that's out for her you-see. (HEN/001)

(8) a. We don't call them Old Aged Pensioners, we *calls* 'em Senior Citizens. (TIV/2)
b. So I *goes* down to Mr.- M which was the welfare-officer. (WHL/002)

(9) a. We had about a dozen hens, just enough *for to get* eggs for, you-know, your own use. (GYV/100)
b. They used to run special trains up from Brighton to Henfield, but – yeah, when the station was still there and then er *for to go* there skating. (HEN/008)

(10) a. She *don't* know what a hoop is, do you? (HEN/005)
b. He *don't* have everything. (SMT/009)

Another important advantage of this archive is the perspective it affords of numerous dialects simultaneously. Unlike research which focuses on specific features in individual dialects, the breadth of these corpora enables exploration of dialect parallels and contrasts across a wide range of British dialects. In so doing, it is possible to answer questions above and beyond those that are particular to individual communities. For example, are the types of change found in one community also found in others? Can they be situated more broadly as part of ongoing grammatical change in Britain? Are the external influences on grammatical change in one community similar to those in another? If so, why? If not, why not? Further, if the grammatical changes observed across British dialects are similar, will they also be similar to what can be found in other dialects of English, for example in North America?

19.4 The Targeted Features

I now examine each of the linguistic subsystems identified above, both from an intra-community perspective, and across a number of the dialects. Each analysis provides a different perspective, building from an in-depth cross-section of age groups in one community (York), to a broad picture of the oldest generation across dialects from up to six localities in Britain (York, Buckie, Cumnock, Maryport, Cullybacky, Portavogie, Tiverton).

19.4.1 *Deontic modality*

According to Bolinger (1980) the modal auxiliary system of English is undergoing "wholesale reorganization." Indeed, in a recent study, Krug (1998) observes that *have got to* for the expression of necessity and/or obligation is one of the biggest success stories in English grammar of the last century. Such claims suggest that synchronic data spanning several generations in apparent time may provide insight into the mechanisms underlying ongoing change in this area of grammar.

Of the corpora available, the York English corpus is particularly well suited to such an analysis for a number of reasons. It spans four generations (ages 19–95) and comes from a small, relatively self-contained city (York) where the majority of local inhabitants have come from the immediate surroundings for at least the last century. Despite its relatively urban context (compared to the other dialect data), its insular history until recent times and particularly northern population base have led to the retention of conservative features (Tagliamonte 1998, 1999).

These data exhibit robust variation of a number of different forms used for the expression of necessity and/or obligation, as in (11).

(11) a. I'*ve got to* cycle all the way back and then this afternoon I'll be cycling back up again! You *have to* keep those thoughts er thoughts to yourself. (YRK/X/474,83)

b. If you have a school you *have to* have a team and you *have to* have the best ones in it. But the others mustn't feel as if they're not wanted. So you'*ve got to* steer a very close line. (YRK/§/154,47)

c. It's an old custom or something that they *must*- one day *has to* be kept for putting stalls all down. (YRK/o/267,90)

19.4.1.1 *Historical trajectory*

The historical trajectory of changes in the deontic modality system can help explain this variability. *Must* was the Old English means to express permission and possibility (Warner 1993: 160–1),[5] but by the Middle English period a wider range of meanings had developed, including both *deontic* readings, as in (12a), and *epistemic* readings, as in (12b), which developed from the late fourteenth century (Warner 1993: 180). This developmental trajectory of *epistemic modality* out of an original *deontic modality* is a common path in grammatical change, both in English and cross-linguistically (Bybee et al. 1994; Krug 1998; Traugott 1997).

According to the OED the use of *have to* in the sense of "obligation" is first attested in 1579, although it may have been even earlier (Crowell 1955). From this time onwards variation with *have to* and *must* was present. The construction *have got to* or with *got* by itself entered the English language much later – not until the nineteenth century (OED s.v. get, no 24; Visser 1963–73: 479). Both Visser and the OED label the forms with *got* as colloquial, even vulgar. In fact, prescriptive grammars have long regarded it as somewhat stigmatized and present-day English grammars usually consider it informal.

However, in a recent large-scale analysis of the British National Corpus of English, Krug demonstrated that referring to *have got to* or *gotta* as simply "informal" is quite an understatement. He found that in British English of the 1990s, *have got to* and *gotta* were one and a half times as frequent as the older forms *must* or *have to.* According to this general trajectory, it would seem that the construction with *got* is taking over as the marker of *deontic modality* in English.

19.4.1.2 *The synchronic picture*

What information can be gleaned from synchronic dialects? In contemporary English the form *must* has two main functions. *Epistemic modality* makes judgments about the possibility, probability, or belief that something is, or is not, the case (Palmer 1979: 50), as in (12).

(12) a. As soon as I saw Auntie-Janet, I said "You *must* be Auntie-Janet." (YRK/1)
 b. 'Cos they say, "Oh, it's less painful." I was like, "You *must* be joking!" (YRK/W)
 c. He *must* be getting ready for retirement now. (YRK/j)

Deontic modality on the other hand (which has also been referred to as *root modality*, among other terms) refers to a continuum of meanings, including obligation, permission, and necessity, as in (13).

(13) a. I *have to* have a bath whether I want one or not. (YRK/>)
 b. You*'ve got to* be very careful with kids. (YRK/¢)
 c. You *must* take these sweeties. (YRK/I)

Table 19.2 presents the overall distribution of forms in York.[6] Consistent with the historical trajectory, which suggests that *got(ta)* is a late development in this area of grammar, this northern variety of British English is extremely conservative. *Gotta* represents only 3 percent of the data. *Must* is much more frequent, occurring 15 percent of the time. However, the most interesting result is the extent of variability between *have to* and *have got to.* The rates of use are identical (41 percent).

Table 19.2 Overall distribution of variants of deontic modality in York English

must		have to		've/'s got to		got to/gotta	
%	N	%	N	%	N	%	N
15	67	**41**	187	**41**	189	3	15

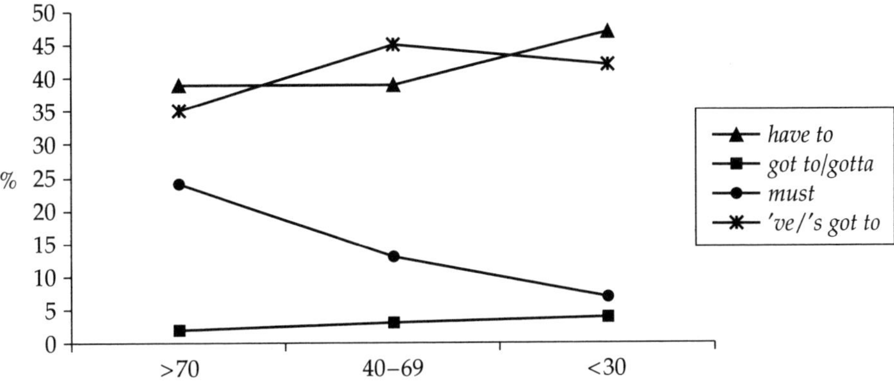

Figure 19.1 Overall distribution of variants of deontic modality (obligation/necessity)

However, the overall distribution of variants in table 19.1 combines all the speakers in the community. Because this is an area of grammar known to be undergoing change, we might expect to find a correlation between the incoming (and outgoing) variants and speaker age, i.e. change in apparent time.

Figure 19.1 provides an overall distribution of forms once again, however this time separating the same data into three broad age groupings of the speakers over 70 years, 31–69 years, and under 30 years.

First, consider the oldest variant in this system – *must*. This form is thought to be declining rapidly, and considered to be old and somewhat archaic. Here, we see a graphic confirmation of this. The greatest frequency of use is in the speakers over 70, with a smaller proportion among the middle-aged generation. The under-30-year-olds, on the other hand, hardly ever use it. *Must* clearly exhibits the trajectory of an obsolescing feature. Consider the next layer of development, the construction with *have to*. This form is used very frequently, and appears to be increasing in use among the younger generation, where it is the most common form used to express *deontic modality*. The construction with *have got to*, however, is nearly as frequent. Finally, the most recent layer in the development of *deontic modality* – *got to* or *gotta* with no corresponding auxiliary.[7] This form is hardly ever used and is restricted to the middle and younger age groups.

The extent to which *deontic modality* is expressed by variable use of *have to* and *have got to* across the generations in this community is noteworthy. Table 19.1 suggested that these two forms are competing in this area of the grammar. Figure 19.1 now reveals this to be consistent for all age groups. Nothing in the literature would lead one to expect such robust and stable variability between these two constructions. Taken together, these results suggests that *have got to* is not entirely taking over as the central modal of obligation, at least not in this variety of northern British English. Indeed, Krug (1998) reported quite a dramatic split between southern and northern British dialects with respect to the use of *have got to*.

Thus, the frequency of use of *have to* and *have got to* in York is a demonstration – on morphosyntactic grounds – of one of the most important dialect boundaries in Britain: that between north and south. As Trudgill (1990: 65–78) and others have argued, northern British dialects are generally more conservative than southern ones. In this case, the robust use of *have to* in York is consistent with the fact that northern dialects in general are relatively conservative.

19.4.1.3 Tracks of change: grammatical layering

In the context of a changing grammatical subsystem this synchronic dialect data may be interpreted as retention of an earlier layer in the grammaticalizing system of deontic modality. The following characteristics are relevant (Tagliamonte in press):

- *Must* is present, but decreases dramatically in apparent time.
- Use of *got to* or *gotta* is rare.
- *Epistemic* uses of *have to* or *have got to* are rare.
- Use of *have to* is robust across all generations of speakers in the community.
- Little or no extension to inanimate subjects.
- No modal-like uses of *got to/gotta.*
- Specialization of *have to* and *have got to* according to *type of verb* and *type of subject*.

These characteristics of York English in particular can now be used as a base line to compare and contrast the variability between *have to* and *have got to* from a comparative perspective. More generally, these results also suggest that further study of the system of deontic modality will present a unique opportunity to track the developments of grammar in this subsystem at a time when different present-day varieties still preserve varying stages in its development.

19.4.2 Possessive have and have got

Another feature which has been undergoing change over the last few centuries is the use of *have, have got,* or *got* for stative/possessive meaning. In contemporary English *have got* is considered the favored variant (Rice 1932: 288) despite widespread condemnation of its use in earlier times (Gwynne 1855; see also citation in Rice 1932: 292; White 1927; Wooley 1907). This feature is also thought to distinguish varieties of English, particularly British vs. American dialects (Biber et al. 1999: 159–63, 466; Quirk et al. 1985: 131–2), presenting another opportunity to examine language variation and change which is ongoing at the present moment. Moreover, Kroch's (1989) research has revealed that there are contextual effects (internal grammatical factors) on the competition among forms which are consistent over time, corroborating the *constant rate effect.*[8] However, little further attention has been devoted to a consideration of the grammatical determinants of this linguistic change, nor whether the historically attested effects for written corpora can be confirmed on contemporary dialect data.

As the examples in (14) attest, robust variation of forms are found in every synchronic British dialect we have studied so far, indicating grammatical layering.

(14) a. He'*s got* it but he hasn't got the will to force himself. (WHL/c/506,46)
  b. She'*s got* such a coarse tongue in her. (BCK/s/498,0)
  c. We *got* eight wooden swords. (YRK/#/276,69)
  d. I *have* my moments where I have my doubts. (WHL/e/204,11)
  e. I'*ve* arthritis of the spine. (WHL/e/868,52)
  f. What a bonny face she *has*. (BCK/Z/1249,10)
  g. And they *haven't – don't have* any roots to cling to. (YRK/h/535,11)

If we now extend the synchronic dialect perspective from a single community (York) to encompass a broader range of northern localities we might expect to find the "tracks" of earlier developments in this area of grammar by comparing across them. To the York data, I now add two supplementary data sets. Buckie, a northern fishing village on the far northeast shore of Scotland (Smith 2000; Smith and Tagliamonte 1998) provides a highly conservative, remote perspective. Wheatley Hill, a small but suburban village near Durham, provides an additional northern variety, but one which has had a greater amount of contact with the mainstream (Martin and Tagliamonte 1999).[9]

19.4.2.1 Historical trajectory

From the perspective of historical development, the construction with main verb *have* is the oldest of the variants. Around the sixteenth century *got* was added, which formed the construction *have got* (Crowell 1959: 280; Jespersen 1961b: 47; Visser 1963–73: 2202). The origins of the *have got* construction are controversial. Its earlier meaning 'to have acquired', can be traced back to early Middle English (Visser 1963–73: 2202). In the sixteenth century, however, it came to mean simply 'possess' (Jespersen 1961b: 47–48). Reasons for the rise of the *have got* construction for possessive meaning are attributed to: (a) the need for an alternative form to express possession since *have* was being used as an auxiliary (Jespersen 1961b: 47–48); and (b) the need for a more overt expression due to the fact that *have* often contracted to *'ve* (e.g. *I've blue eyes*) from the sixteenth century onwards (Crowell 1959: 283).

The last variant to appear on the scene is the construction with *got* alone (Quirk et al. 1985: 132; Visser 1963–73: 2206). According to this trajectory, here, as with deontic modality, we might expect to find an incremental development of forms reflected in the frequency of use of different variants across age groups in a single community. Further, different varieties, depending on their stage of development, may reflect different stages in this change.

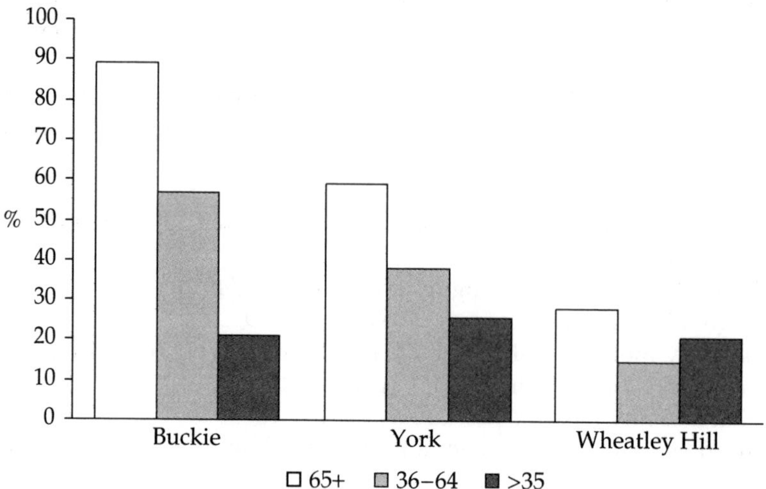

Figure 19.2 Distribution of possessive *have* by age groups across communities

19.4.2.2 *The synchronic picture*

As with the variant forms in the deontic modal system, we can view this feature too according to its trajectory in apparent time by viewing the distribution of different forms according to the age of the individuals in a community. An added dimension is to compare such a distribution across different dialects which can be differentiated according to their participation in mainstream developments in English and thus can be taken to represent different stages in its development: remote rural Buckie; suburban Wheatley Hill, and conservative (albeit urban) York. Figure 19.2 shows the distribution of possessive *have* by age across these three communities, separating the data into three broad age groups, over 65 years, 31–69 years, and under 35 years.[10]

Figure 19.2 reveals that there is a consistent patterning in apparent time, which is mirrored in each community. The oldest generation of speakers uses *have* most often. In Buckie and York, however, there is a striking gradient shift in apparent time – the over-65-year-olds, then the middle generation (36–46), then the younger speakers (35 and under). This pattern mirrors the historical trajectory of forms. Thus, the shifting patterns of variability across these communities can be interpreted as reflecting the progression of change from *have* to *have got* in British English. Where once *have* was the primary means to encode stative/possessive meaning, it is clearly receding and *have got* is clearly winning out.

Notice, however, that in Wheatley Hill the effect of generation is much attenuated. There is a relatively even distribution of *have* across generations. Moreover, in comparing the rates of *have* for only the youngest speakers of each community, notice that there is little difference in the frequency of *have* among them. This generation of speakers all uses *have* at about the same rate. This perspective shows that although *have got* may well be gradually taking over to mark stative/possessive meaning, *have* decreases to a certain threshold and then levels out. The older variant *have* is holding its own. Why would this be so?

As I mentioned earlier, stative/possessive *have* has been reported to be subject to a number of internal grammatical constraints. One of these involves the inherent nature of the object. Jespersen (1961b: 47) observed that *have got* probably entered the language for use with objects denoting physical concrete "things," then gradually spread to those denoting non-concrete, abstract objects. This is not surprising since *got* is historically, and in British dialects to this day, the past participle of *get*, whose original meaning, as mentioned earlier, is 'to acquire', hence acquisition of objects. This is in accordance with the principle of persistence in grammatical change, which says that traces of the original lexical meanings of forms may be reflected in constraints on their grammatical distribution (Hopper 1991). Thus, we may still be able to observe this tendency in the distribution of *have* and *have got* such that *have got* may exhibit a higher tendency toward collocation with concrete objects and *have* with abstract objects. Indeed, Kroch (1989: 207–9) reports consistent operation of such a constraint on the competition between *have* and *have got* in written corpora from 1750 to 1935.

Figure 19.3 tests for this conditioning effect in the data as well as its application across varieties using the comparative method. Operation of this constraint is only visible in two communities, York and Wheatley Hill. When the object is abstract *have* occurs more often than when the object is concrete. Thus, contexts such as in (15) are more likely to be lexicalized with *have*, than those in (16).

(15) Abstract:
   a. They *have* the Baptist beliefs. (BCK/H/380,0)
   b. I'*ve* a feeling that they don't know. (YRK/™/526,86)
   c. I *have* my doubts whether I should be doing it. (WHL/e/249,71)

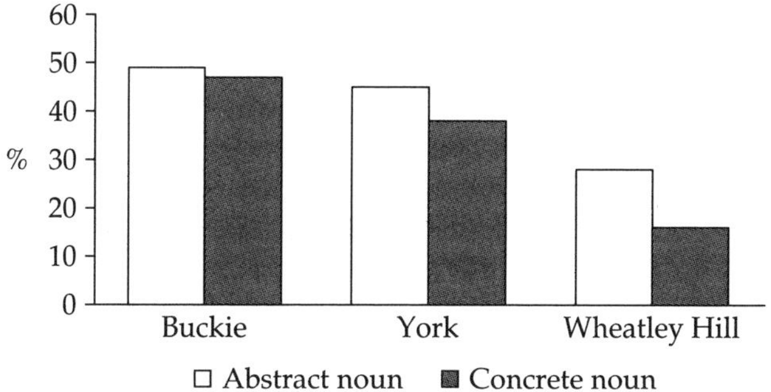

Figure 19.3 Distribution of *have* by abstract versus concrete NP by community

(16) Concrete:
  a. I'*ve got* a bump [on my head]. (WHL/g/440,80)
  b. You'*ve got* a great big dan pole. (BCK/v/229,31)
  c. Me sister'*s got* two and my mate'*s got* one [kitten]. (WHL/s/550,50)

However, put in cross-variety perspective, an interesting patterning can be observed across varieties. First, in Buckie there is barely any effect. Then, in York abstract nouns have more of a propensity to be encoded with *have*. Finally, in Wheatley Hill the same tendency is even more pronounced. Moreover, consistent with Kroch's data in Wheatley Hill and York, *have got* clearly exhibits its early/original meaning, and association with 'acquired', whereas *have* tends to be used for abstract concepts. The dialects differ in terms of how strong this effect is. In Buckie, where there is least *have got* (52 percent), there is no effect. In York, which has a little more *have got* (57 percent), there is a slight effect. In Wheatley Hill, which has the most *have got* (75 percent), the effect is visible, and this is where it is statistically significant, as we shall see below. This appears to correspond with the varying rates of *have got* overall. It is only where the proportion of use of *have got* is greater (and *have* lesser) that the constraint operates with any degree of strength.

Consider another conditioning factor that has been observed in the literature. Jespersen (1961b: 51) also noted that in certain contexts *have* tends to appear for general as opposed to specific reference. However, the effect of generic/non-generic is intertwined with the distinction between full NPs and pronouns. As we shall see, the use of *have* with pronoun vs. full NP subjects (whether generic or not), is quite distinct in some varieties.

I now examine the varieties again, this time showing the distribution of *have* according to these intersecting characteristics of the subject NP, as in figure 19.4. In Buckie the frequencies of *have* across these varying subject types hover near 45 percent. Thus, neither genericness of the subject nor the type of NP plays a role in the choice between *have* and *have got* in Buckie. In York and Wheatley Hill, however, there is a visible tendency towards the use of *have* in certain types of NPs. In York, full NPs that are generic have a far greater propensity for *have* than any other context (~80 percent). In Wheatley Hill the favoring effect is found for all generic subjects whether full NPs or pronouns, suggesting a generalizing trend.

Such a trajectory suggests that *have got* is not entirely ousting *have*. Instead, it appears that as *have got* increases, *have* may be gradually becoming specialized for a much more highly circumscribed function within the general domain of stative/possessive meaning. That meaning, when viewed in terms of type of subject, is first and foremost genericness. This can be observed in York, as encoded by NPs, but also generic subjects more generally, as can be observed in Wheatley Hill, perhaps as a later stage in the process.

This has the effect of making sentences such as in (17) all nondescript in these dialects, despite the fact that possessive *have* may be somewhat old-fashioned

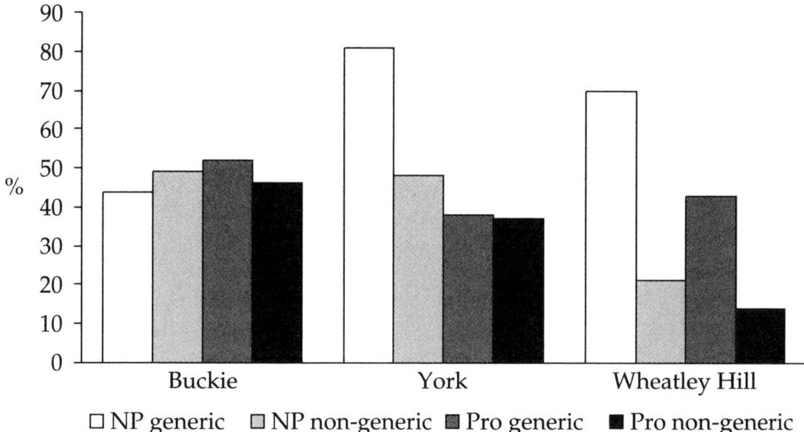

Figure 19.4 Distribution of *have* by type of subject across communities

in stative/possessive contexts more generally. *Have got*, on the other hand, is relegated to specific subjects, as in (18).

(17) a. Most people *have* dreams. (WHL/k)
b. Each sort of region *has* a different sort of accent. (BCK/m)
c. You still *have* your problems even when you're not married. (WHL/n)

(18) a. She'*s got* really blonde hair. (BCK/p)
b. I'*ve* still *got* all my lego. (YRK/N)
c. Me sister'*s got* two and my mate'*s got* one [kitten]. (WHL/s)

19.4.2.3 Tracks of change: constraints that change

In the context of this changing grammatical subsystem, the perspective of three dialects differentiated according to their participation in mainstream developments confirms the robust layering of forms. However, the broader inter-community perspective provided by comparative analysis reveals that this grammatical layering is not consistent across varieties, and hints at the trajectory of change in progress. While the contrast between abstract and concrete meaning showed constancy of constraints over time, further analysis uncovered specialization as well. At least some of the constraints which operate on the distribution of variants (*have* vs. *have got*) reveal ongoing specialization in the function of *have*, the older variant, while *have got* gradually takes over all other meanings. However, instead of ongoing *specialization* of function in which one form would be expected to take over the entire functional domain, here we have observed coexistence with concomitant divergence. As the two forms coexist, they appear to be developing divergent collocation patterns

(Hopper and Traugott 1993: 120). Thus, it appears that when the development of a form involves specialization, then a consequence will be that grammatical constraints on its distribution will strengthen as the change progresses.

It will be important to pursue this possibility by examining this feature in other varieties. More generally, however, these findings reveal that language drift proceeds in the same way, but not at the same rate in all communities. This can, in turn, be related to the varying participation of different dialects in mainstream developments. The cross-variety comparison has given us a critical bird's eye view of how the change is progressing, at least in British English. Those varieties which have evolved in peripheral as well as culturally cohesive regions – like Buckie – preserve obsolescing forms from earlier stages in the history of the change, while those which have come into contact with more mainstream developments – like Wheatley Hill – are moving at a much faster rate.

19.4.3 Relativization

Perhaps one of the most studied areas of recent grammatical change is the process by which English developed its contemporary relativization system.

The inventory of current markers across these corpora is robust, featuring *wh*-forms, *who, which, whose,* and *whom,* as in (19a–c), *that,* as in (19d) and no marker at all (commonly referred to as the "zero" form), as in (19e):

(19) a. The gentleman *who* started this archery-club was Major-Archer. (SMT/t)
b. We're doing things then *which* aren't viable today. (TIV/h)
c. I'd helped an old friend *whose* mother had died to clear the house out. (YRK/c)
d. He was the man *that* first set off the oil industry. (CMK/c)
e. Well you know a young lad Ø never says no for pigeons like. (MPT/h)

Most grammar books report a clear pattern of forms such that *who* is used for animate subject relatives, as in (19a), and *which* and *that* for inanimates, as in (19b). However, Romaine (1982b) reports that "the infiltration of *wh* into the relative system can be seen as completed in the modern written language . . . but it has not really affected the spoken language." This is supported in a study of the British National Corpus (Tottie 1997: 471) which reports there is actually a "paucity of *wh*-forms" in these materials too.[11] Yet other researchers (e.g. Ball 1996: 261) maintain that "the *wh*-strategy has affected not only standard British English and American English, but nonstandard varieties as well." Such claims position synchronic data from nonstandard dialects all over Britain in an important position for understanding linguistic change in this area of grammar.

The combined efforts of several research projects and student fieldwork (see note 3, below) provide a cross-section of a number of dialect corpora for consideration. This archive includes the three varieties discussed earlier as well as four additional dialects: two from areas considered "northern" (Cumnock in Lowland Scotland, Maryport in Northwest England) and another two from the south of England (Tiverton in Devon and Wincanton in Somerset, both in the Southwest). These additional data sets are ideal for the study of the spoken vernacular, as they provide representation of the oldest living generation in each community. Moreover, samples of synchronic dialects from widely dispersed geographic locales to contrast with Romaine's (1982b) research on Scots, and also the perspective of a wide variety of synchronic dialects to serve as a backdrop for the more formal, educated British National Corpus data targeted by Tottie (1997).

19.4.3.1 Historical trajectory

The original relative marker in English was *that*, which had earlier developed from a demonstrative pronoun (e.g. Romaine 1982a: 58; Wardale 1937: 95). However, from early on the zero relative pronoun can also be found, both as object and commonly as subject of the relative clause (Fischer 1992: 306). The *wh*-forms began to be used as relative pronouns in Middle English.

Most researchers agree that the *wh*-forms arose as a change from above (Nevalainen and Raumolin-Brunberg 2001; Romaine 1980; Tottie 1997: 465). When they were first used as relative pronouns they were confined to formal use. This is supported by Ball's (1996) data, where she observes "a clear lag between the more literary texts and spoken usage."[12] This suggests that there was sociolinguistic conditioning from the very beginning. The form *who* was the last to develop (Romaine 1982a: 223) with early examples reported in 1426 (Rydén 1983: 127).

Gradually, the frequency of *who* for human subjects increases and the marker *that* begins to appear more and more for non-human subjects. According to Ball (1996: 246–7), "these two changes – the replacement of *which* by *who* and the assignment of *that* to nonpersonal antecedents" – laid the foundation for the modern dominance of *who* for personal subject restrictive relatives. Fowler and Fowler (1973) write that by the late nineteenth century "there was formerly a tendency to use 'that' for everything: the tendency now is to use 'who' and 'which' for everything." According to this general trajectory, one might hypothesize that the *wh*-forms would have taken over as the markers of relative clauses in English by the twenty-first century.

Such a scenario of long-term evolution of forms, yet entirely contrastive claims in the literature, presents an interesting case to study. First, because systematically collected community-based samples of spoken vernacular language data from British regional dialects are not generally available. Any spoken data that do exist, like the British National Corpus, are not rigorously stratified according to sex or socioeconomic class, and the specific sociolinguistic profiles of the speakers are often not recoupable. Moreover, their geographic origins are not well stratified, making differences across dialects difficult to uncover as well (Tottie 1997: 469). Thus, further information from nonstandard vernacular data may shed light on community-based regional norms.

19.4.3.2 *The synchronic picture*

In the British dialect corpora described above variation among relative markers, as in (20) is extensive.

(20) a. It was a job *that* I always wanted . . . It was a job <u>Ø</u> I've always enjoyed. (CMK/x)
b. Or a cockney git *which* is someone from- like a Scouse git. It's someone *who's* from there. (YRK/%)
c. There's a certain amount of people *what* just stay but generations ago. . . . And then there's people *who*'s out for like the bank-holiday. (TIV/b)

However, given the conflicting claims in the literature, to what extent has grammatical change progressed? Can the synchronic dialects put the grammatical history of the *wh*-forms in perspective?

Table 19.3 shows the distribution of relative markers in the most critical grammatical context of subject function relative clauses. The amalgamated data from six synchronic varieties of British English (York, Wheatley Hill, Cumnock, Maryport, Devon, and Somerset) are categorized according to the critical semantic distinction of animacy of the antecedent NP. The table shows that the prescribed effect of animacy *does* constrain the choice of marker. While it is true that *that* is used more often to relativize subject antecedents that are things (78 percent), animals pattern along with them (80 percent), as in (21). This shows that the constraint is clearly human vs. non-human.

(21) a. Used to get *the fish* **that** fell off the boat. (CMK/l)
b. *This blackbird* **that** sung and sung and sung and has the one perch in this tree . . . (CMK/n)

Table 19.3 Distribution of relative markers by animacy of the antecedent NP (subject only)

	that		who		which		what		Ø		
	%	N	%	N	%	N	%	N	%	N	*Total*
Human	**52**	408	**31**	244	**1**	6	**1**	10	**14**	112	780
people	**49**	56	**39**	45	—	0	**2**	2	**10**	11	114
Collectives (Human)	**78**	25	13	4	**3**	1	—	0	**6**	2	32
Animals	**78**	18	—	0	**4**	1	—	0	**17**	4	23
Things	**80**	343	**1**	0.2	**9**	38	**1**	4	**10**	41	427
Total		850		294		46		16		170	1,376

However, even the human/thing contrast is not nearly as polarized as we might have expected it to be. In the most favored place for the relative marker *who*, subject function human antecedents, as in (22), it appears only 31 percent of the time. When the human antecedent is the noun *people*, as in (23), there is a slightly higher frequency, 39 percent.

(22) a. You know *that ginger haired fellow* ***who*** was there. (CMK/q)
 b. I just lost *a sister* ***who*** lived at Yeovil. (SMT/d)
 c. I married *a wife* ***who***'s also musical. (TIV/d)

(23) a. *People* ***who*** was nice said "Please" and "Thank you." (WHL/e)
 b. I think *people* ***who*** are crying are crying for theirself. (TIV/d)

Unexpectedly, given prescriptive grammars, human subjects are marked with *that* the majority of the time (52 percent), as in (24).

(24) a. *The old chap* ***that*** used to dig graves was t' bad fettle. (MPT/h)
 b. He was *a fella* ***that*** could booze a lot. (YRK/¥)
 c. She was *the one* ***that*** went off with your Uncle Tom. (WHL/d)
 d. But luckily *a woman* ***that*** was a nurse lived next but one. (TIV/d)

However, is this collocation pattern true of every dialect? Figure 19.5 shows the distribution of *that*, *who*, and zero forms in subject function human antecedent restrictive relative clauses, this time separating out the six communities individually. The same pattern can be observed across every dialect we have examined for this feature so far. The overall frequency of *who* varies across communities. Further, the striking result is the extent of use of *that* in every instance, well beyond the frequency of *who* in each case, but one. York is set apart by its higher use of *who*.

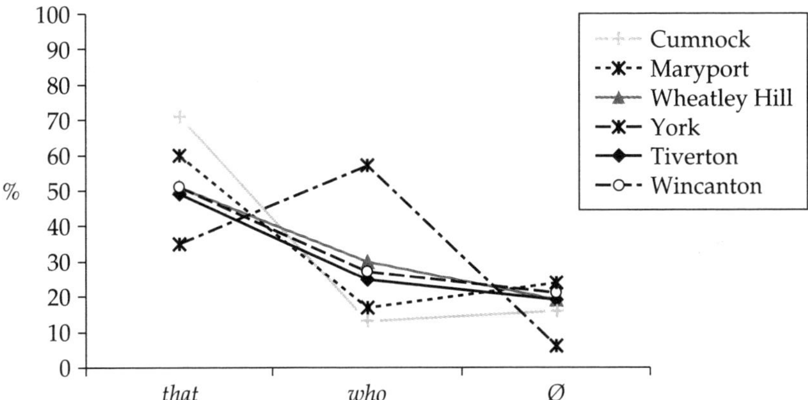

Figure 19.5 Distribution of relative markers in human subjects in subject function by community

What can explain the overwhelming use of *that* as a relative marker in these data when all indications in the literature point to the fact that the *wh*-words should have taken over, particularly for human antecedents? Further, why is York markedly different from all the other dialects in its higher frequency of *who*?

Recall that *who* came into English grammar as a change from above, associated with formal language and written styles. In these materials, the one striking difference between York and the other dialects is their remoteness from mainstream developments. York is a small city. Moreover, the data represent a cross-section of speakers from different social classes and educational backgrounds in a context of longitudinal conservatism, economic, social, and cultural. The other corpora come from small rural hamlets and villages, purposefully sought out for their peripheral characteristics. Here, the data analyzed for this study come from only the very oldest and most insular speakers. By definition, these speakers tend to be much less educated and have typically spent their lives in traditional jobs and close-knit social networks. Thus, what we may be viewing here is a marked contrast between peripheral vs. mainstream dialects, with dimensions such as urban vs. rural, educated vs. less educated, conservative vs. traditional, each playing a role in maintaining a community's linguistic preferences. In this case, the *wh*-relative markers, despite their prestigious associations (or perhaps because of them), have not usurped the traditional variant, *that*.

19.4.3.3 Tracks of change: vernacular lag?

Such results provoke yet another question. In which direction is the English relative marker system going in the twenty-first century? Has the infiltration of the *wh*-forms into the English relative marker system really gone to completion? These results confirm that it has not, at least not in the dialects of English studied here. In fact, there is a general lack of *wh*-forms in the data, even in York, the most conservative of them. Such an explanation also provides confirmation of Romaine's (1982a: 12) claim that "the infiltration of *wh* into the relative system can be seen as completed in the modern written language . . . but . . . has not really affected the spoken language." These findings, coupled with Tottie's (1997) research on the British National Corpus demonstrate that the use of *wh*-forms in British English has not entirely permeated the standard spoken language either, not simply in Scots, but in every nonstandard variety we have examined. If so, then perhaps the vernacular has been lagging behind mainstream developments in this area of grammar for quite a long time.

Once again distributional analysis of the layering of forms in apparent time may provide further insight. The best location where such an analysis is possible is the York English corpus. Figure 19.6 plots the use of *that* according to the critical human vs. non-human distinction in apparent time in this corpus. The figure clearly shows that the use of non-human *that* is stable across age groups in these data. Human *that*, however, is moderate among the older speakers and increases substantially among the youngest generation.

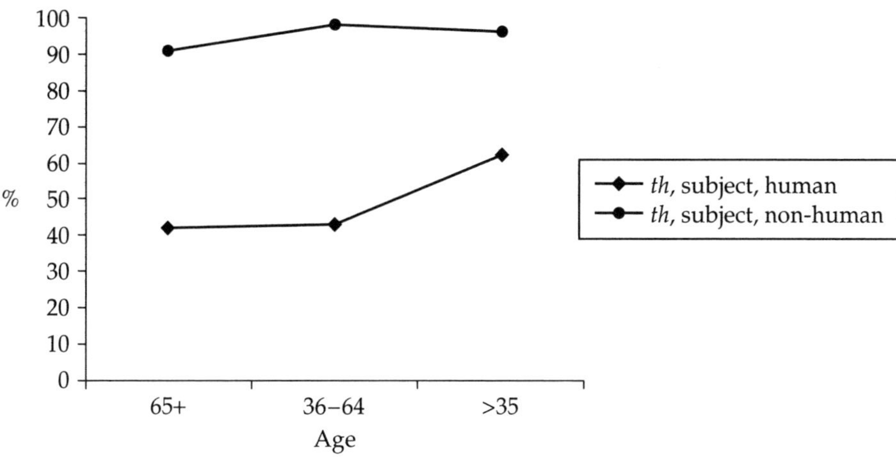

Figure 19.6 *That* in subject restrictive relatives according to type of antecedent across age groups in York English

Given the historical trajectory of this area of grammar where *that* is the older form and the *wh*-forms are incomers taking over the system, this result is puzzling. If the *wh*-forms are later developments which have been increasing over time an apparent time analysis might be expected to show that they are still getting more frequent, or have leveled out at a fairly high frequency. However, neither is the case. The use of *who* is actually decreasing in this community. If these data are any indication, perhaps we are witnessing a "shift in the tide" – the trajectory of development in the relativization system may be going in the opposite direction – towards *less* use of the *wh*-words. Further study of both southern British dialect data and for all age ranges across a range of dialects will provide the necessary data to test this possibility.

More generally, however, these findings confirm that language drift does not proceed in the vernacular as it does in the mainstream. Indeed, if these results are any indication there may be even more dramatic differences between vernacular and mainstream norms than previously thought. Such differences may become particularly pronounced in the case of linguistic innovations which involve change from above, as with the *wh*-relative markers in English. Further exploration of the dichotomy between change from above and change from below across different synchronic dialect situations will provide much further insight into the social mechanisms of language change and their interaction with the layering and specialization of linguistic forms.

19.4.4 Zero form adverbs

The last feature I will consider is variation between *-ly* and zero in manner adverbs (Tagliamonte and Smith in preparation). The zero variant is said to be widespread in many different varieties of English ranging from Estuary English (Crystal 1995: 347), to pidgin and creole varieties (Arends et al. 1995: 31), to American English (Görlach 1991; Wolfram and Schilling-Estes 1998: 338). In addition it is also associated with nonstandard (Quirk et al. 1985) and colloquial language (Poutsma 1926: 634), and is widely cited as particular to American English (Crystal 1995). Thus, all indications are that the zero adverb is geographically and socially diffused (Mencken 1961: 388). However, variation between the zero and *-ly* forms has not yet been quantitatively investigated in dialect data (but see Tagliamonte and Ito 2002). Thus, our archive of regional dialects provides an excellent opportunity to assess the synchronic situation in Britain.

19.4.4.1 Historical trajectory

As far as the historical record is concerned, variation between *-ly* and zero on adverbs is the result of longitudinal change in which zero is the earlier form which gradually gives rise to *-ly* – a process which has been described as "adverbialization" (e.g. Nevalainen 1994a).

The zero form was "common" throughout the Elizabethan period (1558–1603), in Shakespeare in particular (Abbott 1879; Emma 1964) and gradually decreased in the Early Modern English period (Nevalainen 1997). By the eighteenth century it had became heavily stigmatized (Lowth 1762 [1775]; Poutsma 1926). Thus, adverb formation in general can be viewed as a gradual process of increasing use of *-ly*, and most adverbs are thought to have "reached this final stage" (Schibsbye 1965: 151). This historical perspective is provocative since it presents an antithetic trajectory of change to that which more contemporary observations suggest, i.e. that the zero form in some contemporary dialects is an innovative form replacing the *-ly* form. Is this another cyclical change, in this case where adverbialization moves first toward *-ly* and then back again toward more use of zero? Without further analysis, it is impossible to determine which explanation best fits the facts. Once again, what perspective can synchronic dialects provide?

19.4.4.2 The synchronic picture

The zero variant of dual-form manner adverbs is widely reported in British dialects (e.g. Milroy and Milroy 1993; Tagliamonte and Ito 2002; Trudgill 1990: 86). Given its productivity at earlier stages in the history of English, as well as more recently, we would expect our corpora to have a high frequency of this feature. And indeed, they do. Dual-form manner adverbs often surface as zero, resulting in robust alternation with *-ly*. This is highlighted by the examples in (26) and (27), where the variants illustrated come from the same speakers, and in (28) from the same speaker in the same stretch of discourse.

(25) a. He wanted to get as many finished as he could that night as *quick* as he could. (WHL/c)
b. Be able to think twice as *quickly* as your customer. (WHL/c)

Table 19.4 Overall distribution of zero adverbs by individual community

YRK		*TIV*		*WHL*		*MPT*		*CMK*		*BCK*		*CLB*	
%	N	%	N	%	N	%	N	%	N	%	N	%	N
42	43	**56**	16	**62**	13	**35**	49	**36**	39	**77**	22	**85**	39

(26) a. Aye- I could've passed it quite *easily*, you-know. (CMK/A)
b. Oh I could've had a job quite *easy* with him. (CMK/A)

(27) We get our pension on a Monday and pension day comes around so *quickly* doesn't it? . . . It does come round *quick*, you-know, you can't believe it. (YRK/E)

However, what kind of layering of variant forms might we expect across dialects? Table 19.4 shows the overall distribution of the zero form across communities. Despite relatively vague observations in the literature that the use of zero adverbs is frequent in nonstandard usage (e.g. Edwards et al. 1984: 24), its rate of occurrence is actually highly diverse across these corpora. Proportions of zero range from a high of 85 percent in Cullybacky and 77 percent in Buckie, the most geographically remote communities, to a relatively low frequency of use, 15 percent, in York, where, as we have already seen, the data represent a more formal spectrum of the population. This perhaps reflects the trajectory of change from older zero forms to more *-ly* forms in the adverbialization process.

As we found with stative/possessive *have*, an examination of the internal constraints may provide a further perspective. In the trajectory of change from zero marking to *-ly*, concrete adverbs, as in (28), were said to occur more with the zero form than abstract adverbs, as in (29) (Donner 1991; Nevalainen 1994a, 1994b, 1997; Schibsbye 1965). An illustration of this can be found in Swift, quoted by Jespersen (1961a: 371–2): "in the contrast in *'tis **terrible** cold . . . it has snowed **terribly** all night.*"

(28) a. Food-wise people ate so *simple* in them days. (WHL/c)
b. They weren't just peas and you could *easy* get a handful. (MPT/s)
c. Well my mother, she went quite *quick*. (CMK/M)

(29) a. He's involved *heavily* in that one. (TIV/h)
b. I was never loved *properly*. (WHL/l)
c. They were all very *closely* connected. (CMK/A)

Table 19.5 separates the data according to this contextual factor. While the dearth of abstract adverbs in these data is notable, where there is sufficient data

Table 19.5 Overall distribution of zero adverbs by concrete vs. abstract and community

	YRK		*TIV*		*WHL*		*MPT*		*CMK*		*BCK*		*CLB*	
	%	N	%	N	%	N	%	N	%	N	%	N	%	N
Concrete	**50**	32	**60**	15	**64**	11	**36**	39	**50**	26	**88**	16	**84**	37
Abstract	**18**	11	—	1	—	2	**30**	10	**8**	13	**50**	5	—	2

to tell, the zero adverb is more frequent with concrete readings. Abstract readings, as in (29) above, tend towards *-ly*, Thus, synchronic dialects clearly retain this older constraint.

19.4.4.3 Tracks of change: stability of constraints?

From the overall distribution of zero adverbs across communities, one might have reasonably concluded that zero adverbs were simply part of "general nonstandard English grammar" (Schneider forthcoming: 23). However, once the well-known historical constraint on manner adverbs is taken into account we are able to observe that instead of simply being a nonstandard feature, the zero adverb participates in form/function asymmetry which reflects longitudinal linguistic variation in the adverbialization trajectory (Nevalainen 1994a, 1994b). Once again, these findings must be put in context with other dialects as well as compared across varying degrees of a variety's association with, or isolation from, mainstream norms. However, the inter-community stability of this constraint regardless of overall frequency and across six centuries of change provides another confirmation of Kroch's (1989) *constant rate effect*, this time for morphological suffixation processes.

19.5 Discussion

19.5.1 Diachrony in dialect

The studies I have summarized throughout this chapter apply a comparative sociolinguistic approach to the study of language variation and change in English. Each one demonstrates patterned variation in synchronic dialect data. This layering of functionally equivalent forms which may be specialized for different lexical items, constructions, or meanings is typical of grammaticalization – a longitudinal process which may go on for centuries. The variability actually provides a vivid snapshot of the different degrees of grammaticalization attained by the different forms which can be viewed as grammatical layering (Hopper 1991: 23).

Howevever, grammaticalization is conceived of as a series of transitions, forming a path or trajectory over time in which the number of choices gradually gets smaller and the survivors assume more general grammatical meanings or specialize for particular semantic functions. Indeed, underlying the overall frequency of forms in each of the studies are revealed remarkable patterns of linguistic change, not only across generations within a single community (where we have generational data to examine this) but also across (multiple) communities. These changes appear to be proceeding incrementally through systematic processes (e.g. extension, specialization) deriving from earlier patterns of use and/or ongoing grammaticalization. In such situations the fallout of grammaticalization involves shifts and reweighting of constraints as grammaticalizing morphemes take on revised functions in the grammar and can be interpreted as specialization (Hopper 1991: 23).

At the same time, I have also demonstrated the extent to which traces of the original lexical meaning of the forms continue, which can be explained using the principle of persistence (Hopper 1991: 23). Indeed, for some features, such as the abstract vs. concrete effect for stative/possessive *have got* or the abstract vs. concrete distinction for dual-form adverbs, the constancy of constraints across generations and the extent to which these parallel historically attested variation, is remarkable. Such findings strongly support Kroch's constant rate effect in demonstrating how the mix of two opposed settings of a single grammatical parameter may change drastically over time, but maintain the same constraints.

Further, all of these aspects of grammatical change are put in perspective by comparing and contrasting the details of linguistic and sociolinguistic conditioning which operate on linguistic variables in one community or *across* communities. In this regard, the consistent finding of these studies show that grammatical change can be profitably viewed from a synchronic cross-variety perspective. Variable inter-variety distributions across generations as well as cross-dialectal differences suggest that linguistic change is not progressing at the same rate in all speech communities. However, these different rates of change make the incremental stages of linguistic development visible and, as such, reveal the underlying mechanism guiding the change itself. These patterns tell the story of shifting norms and practices at the community level while at the same time preserving the pathways of language change. While the complexity of this situation bears much further investigation, I hope to have demonstrated the promising new research potential that exists for tracking grammatical change in synchronic data, particularly when viewed from a cross-variety perspective.

A provocative question that is also raised is: what are the implications of these cross-variety differences for language structure? Are they the result of grammatical change alone, or can they be interpreted as parametric variation (see e.g. Henry 1995)? Further exploration of these types of questions is critical not only for informing grammaticalization theory, but also for bridging the gap between formal theories of grammar, historical linguistics, and sociolinguistics.

NOTES

1 Codes in parentheses reference the community. BCK stands for Buckie, CMK for Cumnock, MPT for Maryport, CLB for Cullybacky, PVG for Portavogie, SMT for Wincanton in Somerset, TIV for Tiverton in Devon, WHL for Wheatley Hill, YRK for York, and HEN for Henfield in Sussex. The single-digit codes identify the speaker in each community. A hyphen after a word is a transcription convention representing a false start (i.e. hesitation) in the speech of the informant.

2 Further analysis using multiple regression techniques can assess the direction of effect of these patterns, their significance, and the relative importance of underlying constraints when all factors are considered simultaneously (Tagliamonte 2001b, 2002, to appear).

3 For further discussion of the comparative method as applied to sociolinguistics, see Poplack and Tagliamonte (2001) and Tagliamonte (2001a).

4 Some of the corpora were collected under the auspices of specific research projects: York (Tagliamonte 1996–8), Maryport, Cumnock, Cullybacky, Portavogie (Tagliamonte 2001–3). However, many were collected by graduate students: Buckie (Smith 2000), Tiverton (Godfrey 1997), Wheatley Hill (Martin 1999), Wincanton (Jones in preparation), Henfield (Ashcroft 1997). These materials are housed in the Sociolinguistics Laboratories of the University of Toronto, Canada, and the University of York, UK.

5 In late Old English it developed the modal meaning of subjective deontic necessity, which is the meaning that some authority grants permission for an action.

6 For further discussion and analysis of this feature in the York data, see Tagliamonte (in press).

7 The two surface forms, *got to* and *gotta*, were coded separately; however, there were so few instances of *gotta* that these were collapsed with the infrequent *got to* tokens.

8 The *constant rate effect* refers to "a change that spreads at the same rate in all contexts" (Kroch 1989: 205). In such an analysis differences in frequency "could be either due to differences in time of actuation or to an initial difference across contexts established when a change starts which *remain constant through time*" (Kroch 1989: 205; emphasis mine).

9 For further discussion and analysis, see Tagliamonte (2003).

10 The age groupings differ slightly from those presented in figure 19.1 due to the varying distribution of speakers by age in the different communities.

11 The British National Corpus (BNC) was collected between 1991 and 1994 (http://www.hcu.ox.ac.uk/BNC/index.html). From these materials Tottie (1997) selected eight conversations. The overall frequency of *who* was only 9 percent and of *which*, 8 percent – $N = 575$.

12 In the early stages, some researchers argue that *þæt/that* continued to predominate. Later, however, there arose a tendency to confine *þæt* to restrictive clauses (Romaine 1980: 222).

REFERENCES

Abbott, E. A. (1879). *A Shakespearian Grammar*. London: Macmillan.

Anttila, R. (1989). *An Introduction to Historical and Comparative Linguistics*. Amsterdam and New York: John Benjamins.

Arends, J., P. Muysken, and N. Smith (1995). *Pidgins and Creoles: An Introduction*. Amsterdam and Philadelphia: John Benjamins.

Ashcroft, E. (1997). A Study of the Copula in Sussex. Undergraduate dissertation, University of York.

Ball, C. (1996). A diachronic study of relative markers in spoken and written English. *Language Variation and Change* 8.2: 227–58.

Biber, D., S. Johansson, G. Leech, et al. (1999). *Longman Grammar of Spoken and Written English*. Harlow: Longman.

Bolinger, D. (1980). *Language: The Loaded Weapon*. London: Longman.

Bybee, J. L., R. D. Perkins, and W. Pagliuca (1994). *The Evolution of Grammar: Tense, Aspect, and Modality in the Languages of the World*. Chicago: University of Chicago Press.

Chaudenson, R. (1992). *Des îles, des hommes, des langues: essais sur la créolisation linguistique et culturelle*. Paris: L'Harmattan.

Crowell, T. L. (1955). Predating "have to," "must"? *American Speech* 30.1: 68–9.

Crowell, T. L. (1959). "Have got," a pattern preserver. *American Speech* 34.2: 280–6.

Crystal, D. (1995). *The Cambridge Encyclopedia of the English Language*. Cambridge: Cambridge University Press.

Donner, M. (1991). Adverb form in Middle English. *English Studies* 72: 1–11.

Edwards, Viv and Bert Weltens (1984). Research on non-standard dialects of British English: progress and prospects. Focus on England and Wales. In Wolfgang Viereck (ed.) (pp. 97–139). Amsterdam and Philadelphia: John Benjamins.

Emma, R. D. (1964). *Milton's grammar*. The Hague: Mouton.

Fischer, O. (1992). Syntax. In N. Blake (ed.), *The Cambridge History of the English Language*. Vol. II: *1066–1476* (pp. 207–408). Cambridge: Cambridge University Press.

Fowler, H. W. and F. G. Fowler (1973). *The King's English*. Oxford: Oxford University Press.

Godfrey, E. (1997). An analysis of verbal -s marking in Devon English. MA thesis, University of York.

Godfrey, E. and S. Tagliamonte (1999). Another piece for the verbal *-s* story: evidence from Devon in Southwest England. *Language Variation and Change* 11.1: 87–121.

Görlach, M. (1991). Colonial lag? The alleged conservative character of American English and other "colonial" varieties. In M. Görlach (ed.), *Englishes: Studies in Varieties of English 1984–1988* (pp. 90–107). Amsterdam and Philadelphia: John Benjamins.

Gwynne, P. (1855). *A Word to the Wise, or: Hints on the Current Improprieties of Expression in Writing and Speaking*. London: Griffith and Farran.

Henry, A. (1995). *Belfast English and Standard English: Dialect Variation and Parameter Setting*. New York/Oxford: Oxford University Press.

Hock, H. H. (1986). *Principles of Historical Linguistics*. Amsterdam: Mouton de Gruyter.

Hopper, P. J. (1991). On some principles of grammaticization. In E. C. Traugott and B. Heine (eds.), *Approaches to Grammaticalization*. Vol. 1: *Focus on Theoretical and Methodological Issues*

(pp. 17–35). Amsterdam and Philadelphia: John Benjamins.
Hopper, P. J. and E. C. Traugott (1993). *Grammaticalization*. Cambridge: Cambridge University Press.
Jespersen, O. H. (1961a). *A Modern English Grammar on Historical Principles*. Part II: *Syntax*, VII. London: George Allen and Unwin.
Jespersen, O. H. (1961b). *A Modern English Grammar on Historical Principles*. Part IV: *Syntax*, 3. London: George Allen and Unwin.
Jones, M. (in preparation). Roots of English in rural Somerset: putting the southwest into the picture. DPhil, University of York.
Kroch, A. S. (1989). Reflexes of grammar in patterns of language change. *Language Variation and Change* 1.3: 199–244.
Krug, M. (1998). *Gotta* – the tenth central modal in English? Social, stylistic and regional variation in the British National Corpus as evidence of ongoing grammaticalization. In H. Lindquist, S. Klintborg, M. Levin, and M. Estling (eds.), *The Major Varieties of English, 1* (pp. 177–91). Växjö: Växjö University.
Labov, W. (1989). The child as linguistic historian. *Language Variation and Change* 1.1: 85–97.
Labov, W. (1994). *Principles of Linguistic Change: Internal Factors*, 1. Oxford: Blackwell.
Labov, W. (1998). Coexistent systems in African-American English: structure, history and use. In S. Mufwene (ed.), *Coexistent Systems in African-American English: Structure, History and Use* (pp. 110–53). London: Routledge.
Lowth, R. (1762 [1775]). *A Short Introduction to English Grammar*. London: Printed by J. Hughs for A. Millar and J. Dodsley.
Martin, D. (1999). Copula variability in a northern British dialect: contraction, deletion and inherent variability. Unfinished MA thesis, University of York.
Martin, D. and S. Tagliamonte (1999). "Oh, it beautiful." Copula variability in Britain. Paper presented at NWAV (New Ways of Analyzing Variation) Conference, Toronto, Canada, October.
Meillet, A. (1967). *The Comparative Method in Historical Linguistics*. Paris: Librairie Honoré Champion.
Mencken, H. L. (1961). *The American Language: Supplement II*. New York: Alfred A. Knopf.
Milroy, J. and L. Milroy (1993). *Real English: The Grammar of English Dialects in the British Isles*. New York: Longman.
Mufwene, S. S. (1996). The founder principle in creole genesis. *Diachronica* 13.1: 83–134.
Mufwene, S. S. (2001). *The Ecology of Language Evolution*. Cambridge: Cambridge University Press.
Nevalainen, T. (1994a). Aspects of adverbial change in Early Modern English. In D. Kastovsky (ed.), *Studies in Early Modern English* (pp. 243–59). Berlin and New York: Mouton de Gruyter.
Nevalainen, T. (1994b). Diachronic issues in English adverb derivation. In U. Fries, G. Tottie, and P. Schneider (eds.), *Creating and Using English Language Corpora: Papers from the Fourteenth International Conference on English Language on Computerized Corpora, Zürich 1993* (pp. 139–47). Amsterdam and Atlanta: Rodopi B.V.
Nevalainen, T. (1997). The processes of adverb derivation in Late Middle and Early Modern English. In M. Rissanen, M. Kytö, and K. Heikkonen (eds.), *Grammaticalization at Work: Studies of Long Term Developments in English* (pp. 145–89). Berlin and New York: Mouton de Gruyter.
Nevalainen, T. and H. Raumolin-Brunberg (2001). The rise of relative *who* in early Modern English. In

P. Poussa (ed.), *Relativisation on the North Sea Littoral: Proceedings of the North Sea Littoral Conference.* Müchen/Newcastle: Lincom.
Palmer, F. R. (1979). *Modality and the English Modals.* New York: Longman.
Poplack, S. and S. Tagliamonte (2001). *African American English in the Diaspora: Tense and Aspect.* Malden, MA: Blackwell.
Poutsma, H. (1926). *A Grammar of Late Modern English,* II. Groningen: P. Noordhoff.
Quirk, R., S. Greenbaum, G. Leech, et al. (1985). *A Comprehensive Grammar of the English Language.* New York: Longman.
Rice, W. (1932). Get and got. *American Speech* 7.2: 280–96.
Romaine, S. (1980). The relative clause marker in Scots English: diffusion, complexity and style as dimensions of syntactic change. *Language in Society* 9.2: 221–47.
Romaine, S. (1982a). *Socio-historical Linguistics: Its Status and Methodology.* Cambridge: Cambridge University Press.
Romaine, S. (ed.) (1982b). *Sociolinguistic Variation in Speech Communities.* London: Edward Arnold.
Rydén, M. (1983). The emergence of *who* as a relativizer. *Studia Linguistica* 37: 126–34.
Schibsbye, K. (1965). *A Modern English Grammar.* London: Oxford University Press.
Schneider, E. W. (forthcoming). The English dialect heritage of the southern United States. In R. Hickey (ed.), *Transported Dialects: The Legacy of Nonstandard Colonial English.* Cambridge: Cambridge University Press.
Smith, J. (2000). Synchrony and Diachrony in the Evolution of English: Evidence from Scotland. DPhil dissertation, University of York.
Smith, J. and S. A. Tagliamonte (1998). "We were *all thegither* . . . *I think we* was *all thegither*": *was* regularization in Buckie English. *World Englishes* 17.2: 105–26.
Tagliamonte, S. A. (1996–8). *Roots of Identity: Variation and Grammaticization in Contemporary British English.* Research grant. Economic and Social Sciences Research Council (ESRC) of Great Britain. Reference #R000221842.
Tagliamonte, S. A. (1998). *Was/were* variation across the generations: view from the city of York. *Language Variation and Change* 10.2: 153–91.
Tagliamonte, S. A. (1999). Come/came variation in English: where did it come from and which way is it going? Paper presented at American Dialect Society, Los Angeles, California, January 7–9.
Tagliamonte, S. A. (2001a). English dialects . . . *and them*: form and function in comparative perspective. *American Speech* 75.4: 405–9.
Tagliamonte, S. A. (2001b). Variation and change in the relativiser system in British English dialects. Plenary lecture at the symposium on Relativisation on the North Sea Littoral. Paper presented at Ummeå, Sweden.
Tagliamonte, S. A. (2001–3). *Back to the Roots: The Legacy of British Dialects.* Research Grant. Economic and Social Research Council of the United Kingdom (ESRC).
Tagliamonte, S. A. (2002). Variation and change in the British relative marker system. In P. Poussa (ed.), *Relativisation on the North Sea Littoral.* Munich: Lincom Europa.
Tagliamonte, S. A. (2003). "Every place has a different toll": determinants of grammatical variation in cross-variety perspective. In G. Rhodenberg and B. Mondorf (eds.), *Determinants of Grammatical Variation in English.* Berlin and New York: Mouton de Gruyter.
Tagliamonte, S. A. (in press). Have to, gotta, must: grammaticalization,

variation and specialization in English deontic modality. In H. Lindquist and C. Mair (eds.), *Corpus Research on Grammaticalization in English.* Amsterdam: John Benjamins.

Tagliamonte, S. A. and R. Ito (2002). Think *really* different: continuity and specialization in the English adverbs. *Journal of Sociolinguistics* 6.2: 236–66.

Tagliamonte, S. A. and J. Smith (1998). Old was; new ecology: viewing English through the sociolinguistic filter. Paper presented at London, UK.

Tagliamonte, S. A. and J. Smith (in preparation). Talking broad(ly): dual form adverbs in the history of English.

Tagliamonte, S. A., J. Smith, and H. Lawrence (to appear). Disentangling the roots: the legacy of British dialects in cross-variety perspective. Paper presented at METHODS XI.

Tottie, G. (1997). Relatively speaking: relative marker usage in the British National Corpus. In T. Nevalainen and L. Kahlas-Tarkka (eds.), *To Explain the Present: Studies in the Changing English Language in Honour of Matti Rissanen* (pp. 465–81. Helsinki: Société Néophilologique.

Traugott, E. C. (1997). Subjectification and the development of epistemic meaning: the case of *promise* and *threaten*. In Toril Swan and Olaf Westvik (eds.), *Modality in Germanic Languages: Historical and Comparative Perspectives* (pp. 185–210). Berlin: Mouton de Gruyter.

Trudgill, P. (1986). *Dialects in Contact*. Oxford: Blackwell.

Trudgill, P. (1990). *The Dialects of England*. Oxford: Blackwell.

Trudgill, P. (1996). Dialect typology: isolation, social network and phonological structure. In G. Guy, C. Feagin, D. Schiffrin, and J. Baugh (eds.), *Towards a Social Science of Language: Papers in Honor of William Labov* (pp. 3–22). Amsterdam and Philadelphia: John Benjamins.

Trudgill, P. and J. Chambers (eds.) (1991). *Dialects of English: Studies in Grammatical Variation*. London/New York: Longman.

Trudgill, P. J. (1983). *On Dialect: Social and Geographical Perspectives*. Oxford: Basil Blackwell.

Visser, F. T. (1963–73). *An Historical Syntax of the English Language*. Leiden: E. J. Brill.

Wardale, E. E. (1937). *An Introduction to Middle English*. London: Routledge and Kegan Paul.

Warner, A. (1993). *English Auxiliaries: Structure and History*. Cambridge: Cambridge University Press.

White, R. G. (1927). *Words and their Uses, Past and Present: A Study of the English Language* (rev. edn.). Boston: Houghton.

Wilson, J. and A. Henry (1998). Parameter setting within a socially realistic linguistics. *Language in society* 27.1: 1–21.

Wolfram, W. and N. Schilling-Estes (1995). Moribund dialects and the endangerment canon: the case of the Ocracoke Brogue. *Language* 71.4: 696–721.

Wolfram, W. and N. Schilling–Estes (1998). *American English*. Malden, MA, and Oxford: Blackwell.

Wooley, E. C. (1907). *Handbook of Composition*. Boston: D. C. Heath.

20 The Making of Hiberno-English and Other "Celtic Englishes"

MARKKU FILPPULA

20.1 The Emergence of "Celtic English(es)"

Among the "Englishes" which have emerged from behind the unitary notion of Standard English (StE) and the "mainstream" varieties such as British English (BrE) or American English (AmE) are the dialects spoken on the western edges of the British Isles, in areas which until fairly recently were – and to some extent, still are – the territory of the Celtic languages: Irish English or "Hiberno-English" (HE) in Ireland, Welsh English (WE) in Wales, and some Scottish varieties of English spoken in the (north)western parts of Scotland. Also in this category, but perhaps less well known because of the lack of detailed descriptions, are Manx English (MxE), spoken in the Isle of Man, and Cornish English (CnE), the traditional dialect of English spoken in Cornwall. Although it is common knowledge that the English dialects in the Celtic areas share some phonological and syntactic features, it is only lately that the term "Celtic English(es)" (CEs for short) has come to the fore as a cover term for these varieties (see, especially, Tristram 1997). I hasten to emphasize that this term has yet to win the approval of those working on one or the other of these dialects, let alone other linguists or the general public (for a critical stand, see e.g. Görlach 1997). Differences of opinion aside, the largely similar conditions of emergence of these dialects, combined with a number of shared linguistic features which have close Celtic parallels, lend enough support to the term Celtic English as a useful "working concept" or cover term, without necessarily implying a common Celtic substratum in all the mentioned varieties of English or the existence of a common Celtic English.

This chapter will first briefly survey the historical background of the spread of English to the formerly (and in some cases, also presently) Celtic-speaking areas. This will pave the way for a discussion of the linguistic outcomes of the contacts between English and Celtic in these areas, with special emphasis on some of the most striking similarities in the phonology and syntax of the CEs. Hiberno-English will be given the most attention, as it is the clearest example here of what could be called a "contact English." This part will also contain a discussion of the various types of rival explanations which suggest themselves, or have been offered in the literature, to explain the similarities between the CEs. Some of the most obvious divergent developments and their implications for the notion of CEs are treated in the next section, and finally, in the concluding section, I will summarize the principal evidence speaking for or against the notion of CEs, and try to outline an agenda for further research on HE and the other CEs.

20.2 The Spread of English to the Formerly Celtic-speaking Areas

20.2.1 Early contacts between English and Celtic

It was soon after the Anglo-Saxons had settled in Britain from the mid-fifth century onwards that the process of Anglicization got under way among the indigenous British Celtic population. The traditional account holds that the British Celts were either extirpated in most of the southern and eastern parts of Britain by the invading Anglo-Saxon armies or completely pushed out from their homes and lands (see e.g. Freeman 1888). However, modern scholarship has adduced various kinds of historical and archaeological evidence to show that a large part of the indigenous Celtic population remained in their former territories and, after a period of extensive bilingualism, eventually assimilated linguistically and culturally to the conquering Germanic peoples, while other sections of the population gradually withdrew to the mountainous areas in the west (i.e. to present-day Wales and the adjoining areas) and northwest of the British Isles (see e.g. Chadwick 1963; Laing and Laing 1990; Higham 1992). After about one and a half millennia, the battle between the two linguistic cultures, English and Celtic, still goes on, albeit on a very small scale as compared with the earlier centuries of contact when the Celtic languages were still vigorous and spoken by the majority of the populations in Wales, Ireland, and Scotland.

In Scotland, too, English started to make inroads into the Celtic-speaking areas very early on. Thus, McClure (1994: 24) writes that the Angles obtained a permanent foothold in some southeastern parts of Lowland Scotland as early as the latter half of the sixth century. Having defeated the Celtic Britons and Scots residing in the northern parts of Britain, they established their Anglian speech in areas which had earlier been dominated by Celtic language and culture. The Anglian advance was restrained in the north by the fierce resistance offered by the Picts. These were the inhabitants of the far north, of whom we have but scant knowledge; according to some sources, they were the descendants of the pre-Celtic population who spoke an Indo-European language formerly widespread in western Europe (McClure 1994: 25). In the (north)west, the linguistic boundary between Celtic and Anglian English was gradually pushed northwestwards, and by the end of the medieval period it was close to the so-called "Highland Line," a linguistic boundary which cuts across Scotland from around present-day Glasgow in the southwest to an area east of Inverness in the northeast. The wave-like nature of the spread of English over the centuries can be seen in map 20.1.

It took considerably longer for English to reach the shores of Ireland. The year 1169 is usually mentioned as the first date for the introduction of English into Ireland, although some contacts between English speakers and the Irish Gaels must have occurred even earlier (see e.g. Kallen 1994). In any case, the arrival of the Anglo-Normans, the then rulers of England, marked the beginning of the history of English in Ireland. At first English had to compete not only with Irish, the indigenous language of Ireland, but with Latin and French. The latter was the language of the Anglo-Norman nobility, whereas the majority of the common soldiers spoke English. Latin and French were in fact long used as the languages of administration and education in Ireland as well as in England. However, surprising as it may seem from the present-day perspective, it was Irish which emerged victorious from this first round of battle with English and the other languages: there is historical evidence which shows that the English speakers in medieval Ireland were almost entirely assimilated to the Irish language and culture, and that by 1600 English survived only in some of the major towns like Dublin and in a few scattered rural areas in the east and southeast of Ireland (see e.g. Bliss 1979). In some of the most recent scholarship, the lack of continuity between the "Old (medieval) English" of Ireland and that of the later centuries from the early Modern period onwards has been called in question. For example, Kallen (1994) concludes on the basis of some contemporary reports that medieval English survived to a much greater extent, especially in the so-called English Pale in the eastern coastal regions around Dublin, than Bliss and some other scholars had assumed.

In Wales, as Thomas (1994: 94) writes, English started to encroach upon the position of Welsh (or "Cymric") somewhat later than in Ireland, namely in the fourteenth century, through the settlement of English colonies in some major towns or "townships." They then formed the power bases from which the English language gradually began to diffuse into the surrounding rural areas in the subsequent centuries. The Acts of Union of 1536 and 1546 gave a further impetus to the English language by promoting it to the status of the language of law and administration, while depriving Welsh of any official position. Yet, the vast majority of especially the rural population in the Welsh heartlands continued to speak Welsh well into the nineteenth century (Thomas 1994: 95).

20.2.2 *The advance of English in the modern era*

In the modern era, the progress of English has been steady but relatively slow in Scotland and especially in Wales, despite various administrative and other measures aimed at promoting the use of English in both areas. In Scotland, the so-called Statutes of Iona, signed in 1609, were explicitly directed against the use of Gaelic as a medium of education, and were thereby instrumental in

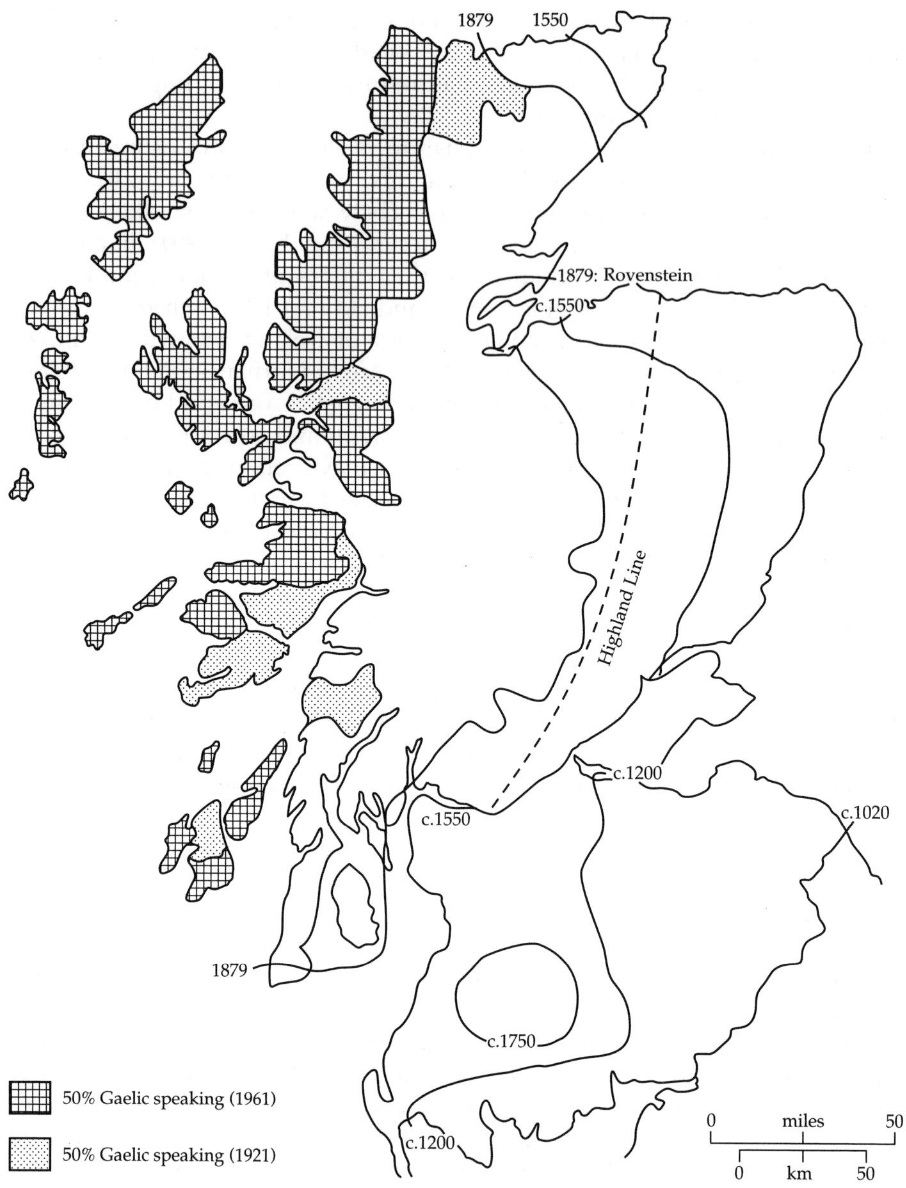

Map 20.1 The decline of Gaelic as a wave process, 1020–1961 (From Withers (1979: 51). Reproduced by permission of Professor Charles W. J. Withers and the Association for Scottish Literary Studies.)

making English the language of literacy in all parts of Scotland. As Withers (1979: 45) points out, it was educational policies like these which sent Gaelic into not only a spatial but also social decline, with English replacing it first as the language of the upper levels of society and then gradually creeping into other contexts involving other strata of society such as trade and later even religious services. Map 20.1 shows the gradual decline of Gaelic in spatial terms. The Gaelic language is now holding out in the northwest and in the islands off the northwest coast of Scotland. All other areas have long been almost completely English-speaking. The dialects of English spoken in Scotland retain some archaic features from the old Anglian dialect of English, which had towards the end of the Middle Ages developed into a distinct variety usually referred to by the term "Scots." For a time, Scots occupied the position of a standard literary language in Scotland, but from the sixteenth century onwards it began to absorb more and more influences from southern English and was eventually replaced by what is now called "Scottish English" (ScE) with its many subvarieties (for further discussion, see McClure 1994; Macafee and Ó Baoill 1997). Yet another type of English in the complex linguistic set-up of Scotland is the variety which has evolved in the Gaelic-speaking areas of the northwest and the Western Isles: the terms used for this variety, or varieties rather, are "Highland English" and "Island English." The most Gaelic-influenced subvariety of the latter is the one spoken in the Hebrides, known as "Hebridean English" (HebE). It is these Gaelic-influenced Englishes which are of the greatest interest to us here. It is true that Scots, and ScE too, contain some traces of the influence from Gaelic, but the majority of scholarly opinion considers the Celtic input rather minimal as compared with the Highland and Island Englishes, in which the presence of the Gaelic "substratum," i.e. features originating in Gaelic, is much more noticeable (see e.g. Sabban 1982; Shuken 1984; Macafee and Ó Baoill 1997).

Like Scotland, Wales is characterized by a gradual spread of English at the expense of the indigenous Welsh language. As mentioned above, the Acts of Union in 1536 and 1546 marked a turning point in the relative status of the two languages: besides substituting English laws and customs for the Welsh ones, English was from now on imposed as the only official language of Wales. In subsequent centuries, a special feature of the Welsh situation has been the sharp divide between the predominantly Welsh-speaking peasantry and the English-speaking townspeople. Indeed, even as late as the end of the eighteenth century the peasantry had been Anglicized only in the eastern parts of Wales, with the mass of the country remaining Welsh-speaking (Thomas 1994: 98). The situation changed in the nineteenth century along with the rapid industrialization of especially the southeastern parts of Wales. This was the period when the working class became increasingly Anglicized. The heavy demand for labor first drew large numbers of Welsh speakers from the north and west of Wales to the new industrial centers in the southeast. They were soon followed by increasing numbers of English-speaking immigrants from outside Wales. As a consequence, the social prestige of English rose sharply, while Welsh became increasingly restricted to the "hearth and chapel." This process was greatly aggravated by the Education Act of 1888, which made English the sole medium of instruction in schools and led to an almost complete neglect of Welsh. Map 20.2 shows the present-day language situation in Wales. Welsh is confined mainly to some western and northwestern areas, with some

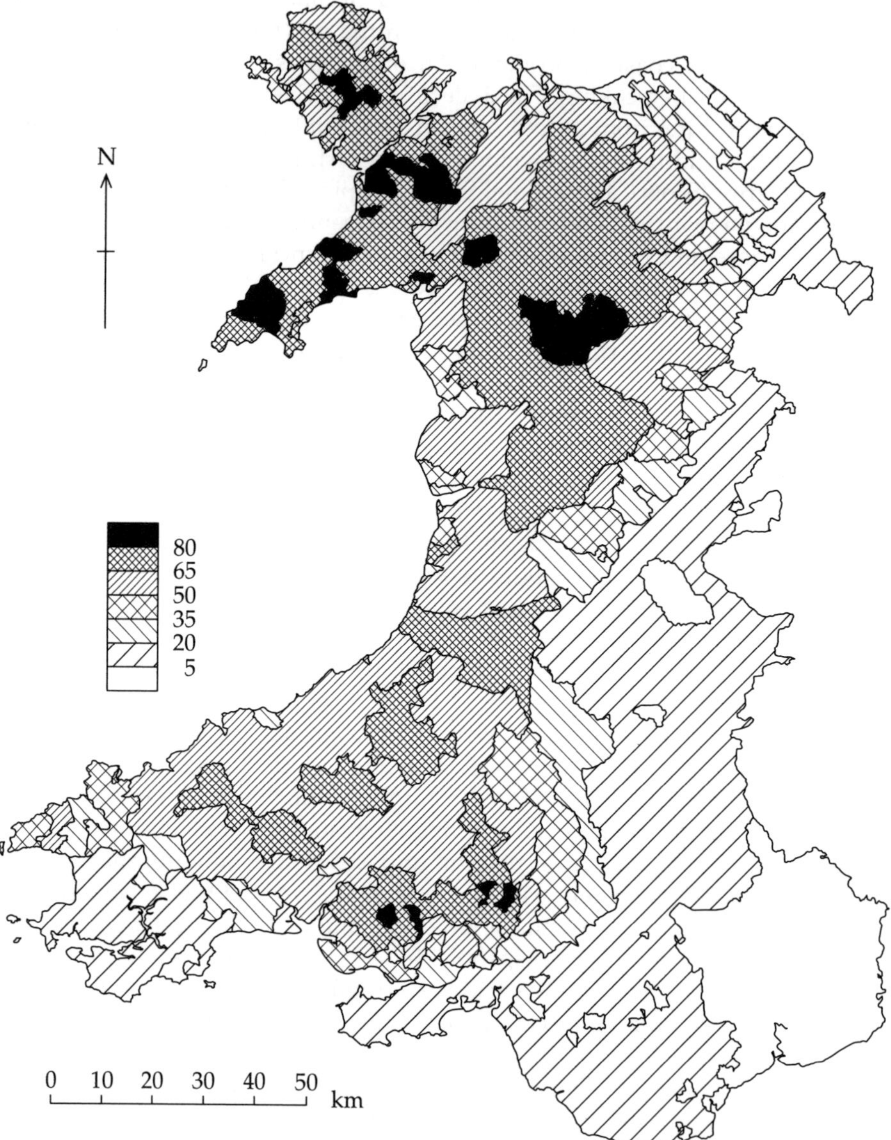

Map 20.2 Percentage of population able to speak Welsh, 1991 (From Aitchison and Carter (1994: 94). Reproduced by permission of Professors Harold Carter and John A. Aitchison.)

pockets holding out in the southern parts; the rest of Wales is predominantly, and in the east, almost completely monolingually English-speaking. The type of English spoken in the bilingual areas is somewhat different from that of the other areas, because it contains many features which derive from the indigenous Welsh language. By contrast, the speech in the southern parts of Wales reflects the historical influence from the neighboring, especially southwestern, English dialects (for further discussion, see Thomas 1994).

The fortunes of English in Ireland present a very different picture as compared with its steady advance in Scotland or Wales. The (near-)demise of medieval English in Ireland gave Irish only a very short respite: a new phase in the battle began with the late-sixteenth-century plantations of Ulster and parts of Munster, these being followed by the large-scale plantations under Cromwell in the mid-seventeenth century. Yet Irish was able to hold on to most of its positions right up to the end of the eighteenth century. It was the early part of the nineteenth century which then saw the tipping of the scales in favor of English. The process of language shift, once it had got under way, proceeded at a pace hardly paralleled in linguistic history, and by the middle of the century English had made deep inroads into the Irish-speaking communities throughout the country excepting the coastal areas in the west of Ireland and some rather isolated pockets inland. The setting up of National Schools in 1831 with English as the medium of instruction, the choice of English as the main vehicle of the Catholic Emancipation movement, followed by the Great Famine of the 1840s and the subsequent emigration of about 1 million Irish people, many of them Irish-speaking, were among the major factors which led to a "mass flight" from Irish and a drastic drop in the numbers of, especially, monoglot speakers of Irish. As Fréine (1977) and Hindley (1990), among others, have pointed out, it is remarkable that, once set in motion, this process was not so much enforced on the Irish people from above or outside, but rather occurred in the home: parents began to see English as an indispensable way to social and economic success for their children, as "the key to the golden door of America," to use Fréine's eloquent expression (1977: 86). This led them to actively discourage their children from using Irish, even in the home.

The present-day situation and the boundaries of the so-called *Gaeltacht* (i.e. Irish-speaking) areas are shown in map 20.3. As in Scotland, Irish survives only on the fringes and is most probably destined to die out as a living community language within the next few decades. The English language in Ireland, often called "Hiberno-English" (sometimes also "Anglo-Irish" or "Irish English") in the linguistic literature, reflects the influence of the Irish substratum in many areas of its pronunciation, grammar, and vocabulary. However, this influence varies a great deal from one place to another. It is at its strongest in the rural areas, especially in the west of Ireland, whereas the urban varieties show more influences coming from British and even American English. The dialects spoken in the northern historical province of Ulster form linguistically a group of their own because of the extensive input from the Scottish dialects introduced into these parts by the sixteenth- and seventeenth-century Scottish

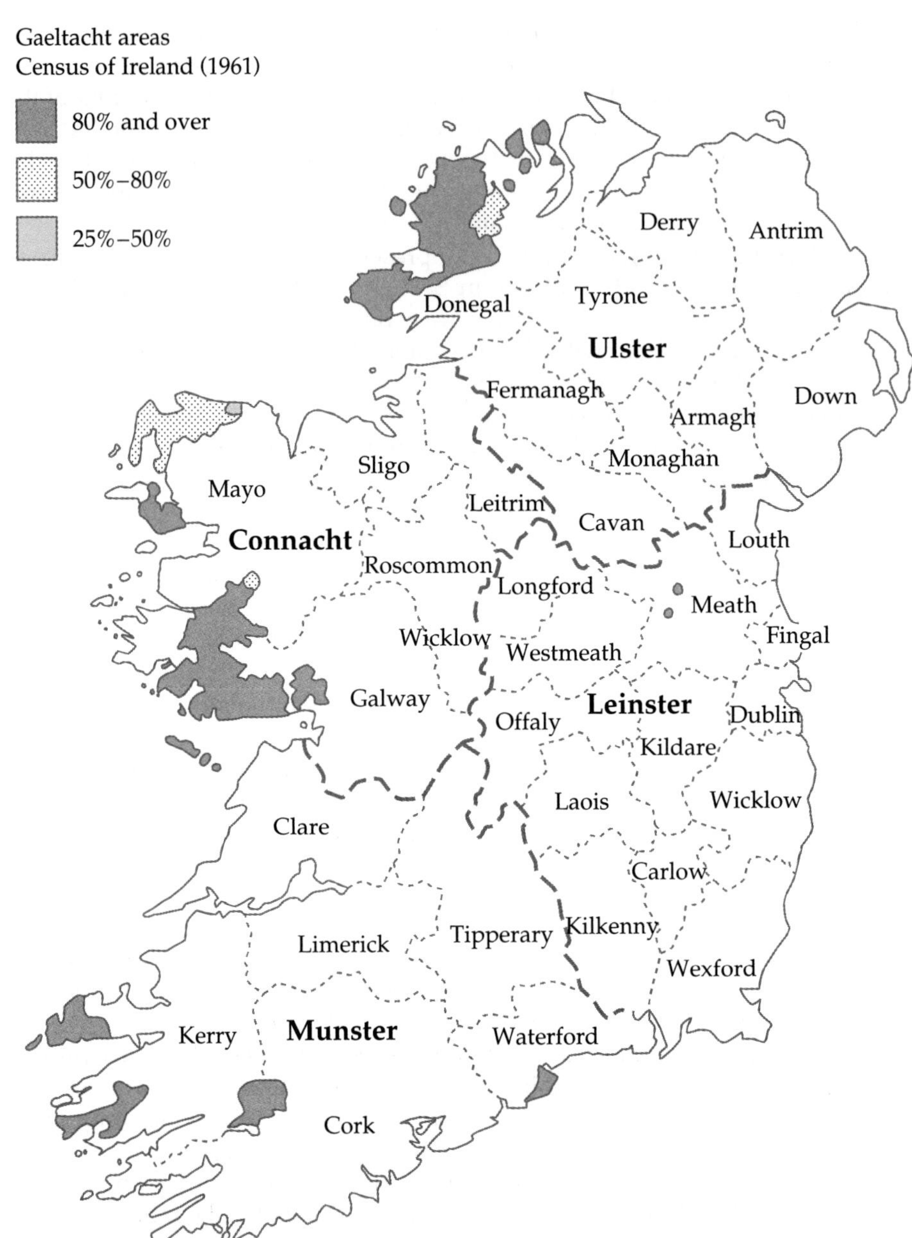

Map 20.3 The Gaeltacht areas and percentages of Irish speakers on the basis of the Census of Ireland, 1961 (after Filppula 1999: xvii)

settlers. The term "Ulster Scots"(or "Ullans") is now used to refer to the most Scots-influenced variety, while the other forms of English in Ulster are rather variably termed either "Ulster English(es)," "northern Irish English," or "northern Hiberno-English" (see e.g. Harris 1984; Hickey forthcoming).

The developments in the much more confined areas of Cornwall and the Isle of Man have been rather predictable, given the smallness of the indigenous Celtic populations. Once the ancient links between the Cornish and Welsh (earlier "Brythonic") languages had been severed, it was only a matter of time before the pressure of English became too overwhelming for Cornish to survive. As Thomas (1984: 278) notes, the last known native speaker of Cornish died in 1777, and with her died the Cornish language. However, from the beginning of the twentieth century onwards there have been various attempts to revive Cornish. Though it is as yet mainly used for some ceremonial functions, there are now small communities of enthusiasts in Cornwall who try to promote the teaching and use of "Revived Cornish" in schools and on all kinds of social occasions. The English dialect of Cornwall, Cornish English, is generally considered to show but few traces of the Cornish substratum; these are mainly to be found in its vocabulary. In fact, some scholars argue that the main influence on Cornish English has come from sixteenth- and seventeenth-century StE rather than Cornish (see e.g. Wakelin 1984: 195), but there are others who would like to see the traditional dialect of the westernmost areas of Cornwall, in particular, as a repository of features going back to the old Cornish substratum (for discussion, see Payton 1997).

The story of Manx is very similar to that of Cornish, although in this case the indigenous Celtic language survived much longer: tradition has it that the last native speaker of Manx, a man by the name of Ned Maddrell, died in 1974, but Manx as a living community language did not survive beyond the beginning of the twentieth century (Broderick 1997: 123). As in Cornwall, the once defunct language has been brought back to life through the efforts of enthusiasts. Manx is now being taught in schools and evening classes, and it continues to live as a medium of communication for a notable number of people in Man. The traditional dialect of English spoken in Man, called Manx English or "Anglo-Manx" (in some of the early works), exhibits a large number of features derived from the Manx substratum and is in many ways similar to the Hiberno-English of Ireland (see e.g. Gill 1934; Barry 1984; Broderick 1997; Preuß 1999).

20.3 Linguistic Characteristics of Hiberno-English and the Other "Celtic Englishes"

20.3.1 The contact-linguistic background to the "Celtic Englishes"

Despite disagreements about the appropriateness of the general term "Celtic English," one can easily point out several linguistic features of HE which are modeled on those of Irish. As will be seen below, many of these are shared by other putative CEs, such as WE, HebE, and MxE. Commonalities can be found especially in the syntax of the CEs and, to a somewhat lesser extent, in their phonology. By contrast, they are much harder to find in their lexicon. This is more or less what can be expected on the basis of evidence from other language contact situations: in conditions of language shift, phonological and syntactic features are the most likely to be transferred to the dominant language whenever the shifting population is large enough, access to the target language is restricted by lack of schooling, bilingualism is widespread, and the rate of language shift is relatively rapid (see especially Thomason and Kaufman 1988). This was the situation especially in the Ireland of the late eighteenth and nineteenth centuries, though not to the same extent, as we have seen above, in Wales or Scotland where the pace of the language shift has, by and large, been slower than in the Irish setting.

The role of schooling is another differentiating factor: while in Ireland the principal mode of transmission of English was "naturalistic" up until the establishment of the National Schools in the 1830s and even decades after it, the introduction of English to the Highlands of Scotland and to most parts of Wales took place mainly through schools. The poor educational opportunities in Ireland and their impact on the language learning process is best understood when one considers the large numbers of illiterate bilingual speakers of Irish and English as late as the 1850s. On the basis of the figures from the first official Census of 1851, Odlin (1997a: 5–6) has calculated that in many counties with large *Gaeltacht* areas, such as Mayo, Clare, Kerry, Cork, Waterford, and Donegal, the proportion of illiterate bilinguals could be as high as 70 percent. This he takes to refute the view held by some scholars, according to which schooling played a major role in the acquisition of English in mid-nineteenth-century Ireland. From the contact-linguistic perspective, then, the nineteenth century can be considered the most crucial from the point of view of the emergence of the Irish dialects of English. This is confirmed, among others, by Garvin (1977), who states that HE ("Anglo-Irish" in his terminology)

> owes its peculiarities to borrowings from the Irish language which took place mainly in the nineteenth century, when both Irish and English were in common use by a large proportion of the population. (1977: 100)

The naturalistic mode of transmission also makes it easier to understand why HE displays so many phonological and syntactic features which can plausibly be derived from the Irish substratum. Some of these have, indeed, become widely known hallmarks of the Irish dialects of English. The most extreme manifestations are the parodying uses found especially in earlier literature. "Stage Irish" is the familiar term for the kind of mock-Hiberno-English speech which used to be common in English plays from the seventeenth and eighteenth centuries (see especially Bliss 1979, for a detailed discussion), and which was also the subject of Jonathan Swift's two pieces of satirical writing entitled *Dialogue in*

Hybernian Style and *Irish Eloquence* (see Bliss 1977, for an edition of these). To some extent, the same type of caricatures have been devised for the English of the Welsh. It has become customary to refer to Shakespeare's attempts at representing the Irish and Welsh forms of English, e.g. through the characters of Captains Macmorris and Fluellen in his play *Henry V*. The following brief extract from act III (scene II) serves as an illustration of Shakespeare's use of modified spelling:

> *Mac[morris]*. By Chrish [Christ] la, tish [it is] ill done: the work ish [is] give[n] over, the trumpet sound the retreat. By my hand, I swear, and by my father's soul, the work ish ill done; it ish give over: I would have blowed up the town, so Chrish save me, la, in an hour: O, tish ill done, tish ill done; by my hand, tish ill done!
> *Flu(ellen)*. Captain Macmorris, I peseech [beseech] you, now, will you voutsafe [vouchsafe] me, look you, a few disputations with you, as partly touching or concerning the disciplines of the war, the Roman wars, . . .
>
> (Shakespeare, *Henry V*)

Shakespeare's use of *sh* for *s* in Macmorris's speech is explained by the Irish tendency to substitute a "slender" (palatalized) /s/, closely resembling the sound associated with the spelling *sh*, for the "broad"(alveolar) /s/ typical of British RP, e.g. in the word *Christ*. The slender /s/ of HE speech has its background in the consonant system of the Irish language, which involves a general distinction between slender and broad consonants. Shakespeare's use of *p* instead of *b* in Fluellen's speech, then, is a feature usually associated with Welsh English, in which plosive consonants such as /b/ and /p/ are accompanied by much stronger aspiration than those of RP. To an English English (EngE) ear, the WE pronunciations of /b/ and /p/ sound more or less alike, hence the typical caricature. As can be expected, the consonant system of Welsh looms behind this WE feature. Note further that Fluellen's use of the phrase *look you* can also be considered to derive from Welsh, in which (as in Irish and Scottish Gaelic) the sentence always starts with a verb.

Though particularly common in Elizabethan drama, the tradition of linguistic caricature has by no means died out, although it may have changed in content and in its cultural implications, which have shed at least some of their originally rather negative import. This is particularly true of HE, and seems to be associated with the economic and cultural successes which Ireland and the Irish people have enjoyed in the last couple of decades. In Wales, the modern counterpart of the old tradition is the "Wenglish" used in popular literature, radio and television soaps, tourist brochures, and other similar contexts (see Penhallurick 1993 and Williams 2000, for further discussion). In Scotland, the same kind of tradition lives on, e.g. in Lillian Beckwith's fictional works set in the context of the Hebridean Islands, in which she attempts to depict the dialect of English spoken in the Hebrides in a humorous light (see e.g. Beckwith 1959). Besides the caricatures, there is, of course, a wealth of literature written by Irish,

Welsh, and Scottish authors which aims to give more or less accurate representations of these regional varieties without a hint of parody.

20.3.2 *Shared phonological features and their origins*

From the purely linguistic perspective, perhaps the most striking phonological feature shared by the CEs is the retention of syllable-final /r/, including (in many CE varieties) in word-final position (as in *car*) where RP has a "silent" /r/. The CEs thus belong to so-called "rhotic" or "*r*-pronouncing" dialects, although the articulation of /r/ varies from one CE variety to another. Hickey (forthcoming) characterizes the /r/ of "traditional" southern HE as a velarized alveolar continuant, as opposed to the Scottish-style retroflex /r/, which is a feature of northern HE dialects and Ulster Scots. Writing on the southwestern and northern WE dialects, Thomas (1994: 128) states that the occurrence of postvocalic /r/ in words like *part* and *cord* "is clearly a feature of pronunciation which is carried over from the phonetic and phonological schema of the Welsh language." For HE dialects, a similar substratal account has been proposed, e.g. by Ó Baoill (1997). However, despite the existence of a parallel feature in the Celtic languages, it is debatable whether this feature can be ascribed to Celtic influence alone, as it is also found in some dialects of EngE and universally in earlier stages of English. Thus, writing on the origins of postvocalic /r/ in HE, Lass (1990: 145–6) points out that "no orthoepists before the mid-eighteenth century describe /r/ -loss as a general feature of the southern [EngE] standard." His conclusion therefore is that, instead of looking to the Celtic languages as a source of this feature, rhotic dialects such as HE retain it from seventeenth-century (and earlier) "Mainland English" (Lass 1990: 146). Yet, putting the matter in the wider CE perspective, it should be borne in mind that there are dialects of English spoken in the Celtic areas which have not evolved until relatively recent times, and consequently, they cannot be expected to display reflexes of seventeenth-century English. Even in the Irish setting, where English has had a strong presence since the beginning of the early modern period, the phonological system of Irish must have exercised at least a reinforcing influence upon that of the emerging new variety of English (cf. Hickey forthcoming).

Another striking consonantal feature shared by HE and most other CEs is word-final "clear" /l/, which is a robust feature of HE (Bliss 1984), Highland and Island English (Shuken 1984) and WE (Thomas 1984). There is again a close counterpart in the relevant Celtic substrate languages. It is noteworthy that, on the question of the origin of this feature in HE, Lass too is willing to accept the role of the Irish substratum (Lass 1990: 139). Hickey (forthcoming) also ascribes the HE use of what he terms "alveolar /l/" to the model of the non-velar, non-palatal /l/ of Irish.

Turning next to vowels, perhaps the most striking commonality between HE and other CEs is the "straight" long vowels which appear in lieu of the diphthongs in words like *face, name, great, boat, home, stone*. These are pronounced with [e:] and [o:], respectively, in most CEs (see e.g. Bliss 1984, Harris 1984, and Hickey forthcoming, on HE; Shuken 1984, on Highland and Island English; Thomas 1994 and Parry 1999, on WE). There are some variations based on spelling, though (see e.g. Thomas 1994: 107–8 on WE, in this respect). Although parallels to the CE usages exist in the Celtic languages, similar pronunciations are typical of the northern dialects of EngE and of earlier English, which complicates the issue of the origins. As in the case of rhoticity, the timing of the diphthongization of these two vowels in EngE dialects is rather late, which Lass (1990: 144–5) takes to be proof of their archaic rather than substratal nature in HE. In a similar vein, Bliss (1984: 139) assigns HE /e:/ to the class of seventeenth-century survivals in HE. In this case, then, any influence from the Celtic languages on the varieties in question must have been of the reinforcing rather than direct type.

Insertion of an epenthetic vowel between certain pairs of consonants is yet another characteristic shared by most CE varieties, with the notable exception of WE. Thus, a word like *film* is pronounced as [fɪləm], [fɪlɪm] or [fɪlʌm], depending on the variety. As for HE, Ó Baoill (1997: 84) states that the epenthetic vowel "has been borrowed from Irish where it is obligatory." Shuken (1984: 160) records this feature for "some speakers" in Highland and Island English (with some phonetic variations in the unstressed vowel). Macafee and Ó Baoill (1997: 266) note the same phenomenon in Scots and (relying on Wright 1896–1905: §234) in most of the counties of England, but also point out the widespread use of this type of epenthesis in Scottish Gaelic, Irish and Manx. However, they leave open the question of the influence of Gaelic on Scots.

Intonation or "accent" is another potentially interesting area where similarities between the CEs may exist, but little research has so far been done to document them. Thomas (1994: 122) draws attention to the WE tendency for an unstressed syllable to have prominence equal to, or even greater than, that of a preceding stressed one. This he considers to be a result of transfer from the Welsh system of intonation, which may explain the "high-pitch" impression of WE, as Thomas, following Pilch (1983/4), points out. Shuken (1984: 164) notes a somewhat similar phenomenon in some varieties of Highland and Island English, and it is also known to be characteristic of some dialects of HE, though no systematic investigations are available (see Hickey 2002, and forthcoming, for some comments).

To sum up so far, there are a number of obvious commonalities between the CEs with respect to phonological features, but there are many differences as well. The absence of the epenthetic vowel from WE is but one example; other phonological dissimilarities will be discussed in section 20.4, below. Some of these are explained by the differences between the Celtic languages themselves and especially by their internal historical division into so-called "Q-Celtic" (Irish, Scottish Gaelic, and Manx) and "P-Celtic" dialects (Welsh and Cornish). For others, explanations have to be sought in independent linguistic developments or in extralinguistic factors such as the differing conditions of emergence of the varieties at issue and differing amounts of input from other, "superstratal" varieties of English.

20.3.3 *Explaining syntactic parallels between the Celtic Englishes*

On the whole, Celticisms are much easier to point out in the syntax of HE and of the other CEs than in any other domain of language. Some of the most important of these are described and explained in contact-linguistic terms below. All have close parallels in the relevant Celtic substrata, which do not significantly differ from each other with respect to these features. In many cases, however, the question of substratal influences from Celtic is complicated by other possible explanations or divergent developments. Examples of the latter will be discussed in section 20.4.

20.3.3.1 *Prominence of the definite specification of nouns*

HE, WE, HebE, and MxE, too, have been observed to make much freer use of the definite article than other regional varieties spoken in the British Isles or StE (for documentation, see e.g. Wright 1896–1905; Joyce 1910 [1988]; Sabban 1982; Bliss 1984; Filppula 1999; Parry 1999; Preuß 1999). Contexts in which nonstandard usages of the definite article occur in these varieties include, most notably:

- names of social institutions: *be at the school/in the hospital; go to the church;*
- names of ailments and (unpleasant) physical sensations or states: *have the toothache/the headache;*
- quantifying expressions involving *most* or *both*, followed by a postmodifying *of*-phrase: *the most/both of them;*
- names of languages: *learn the English/the Gaelic.*

All are strikingly similar to the corresponding Celtic usages, but parallels can, to varying degrees, be found in other dialects of English, especially in ScE and Scots (see e.g. Miller 1993). The Scottish varieties may, however, have adopted at least part of these usages from Scottish Gaelic, as is suggested, for example, in the *Scottish National Dictionary* with respect to names of languages (*SND* s.v. *the* 5.(3); see also Filppula 1999: section 5.2). Apart from the usages illustrated above, there are others which have a slightly more restricted geographical distribution. For example, the following have been found to be characteristic of the Irish and Scottish dialects, but not (to the same extent at least) of the Welsh English dialects:

- names of feasts, e.g. *over the Christmas;*
- concrete mass and collective nouns, e.g. *I don' know when the coffee came;*
- abstract nouns, e.g. *turn to the drink; starve with the hunger;*
- expressions denoting emotive emphasis, especially eulogy and admiration (or their opposites), e.g. *That's the grand morning; You are the pig!;*
- quantifying expressions involving *half*, e.g. *the half of it.*

One of the first scholars to pay attention to the geographical distribution of the nonstandard usages of the definite article is Annette Sabban, who in her thorough description of the English of the Hebrides (Sabban 1982: 381) notes the tendency for "contact-English" (i.e. Hebridean English) to insert the definite article in contexts in which it would not be used in StE. She also points out parallel usages in ScE, in some northern EngE dialects, and in "Anglo-Irish" (i.e. HE). Sabban's statement is supported by *The Survey of English Dialects* (*SED*) data, which show that some of these usages extend to a number of the northernmost dialects of EngE, but either are not found or are much scarcer in the southern dialects. For example, the geographical distribution of the variants for Item S 5: VIII.5.1 *They go to church* makes it clear that the definite expression . . . *to the church* is limited to the northern counties of Lancashire, Yorkshire, Northumberland, Cumberland, and Westmorland (Orton et al. 1962–71). The map for Item S 6: VIII.6.1: *They go to school* shows an almost identical distribution for the variant with definite article. This confirms the mainly northern and western (including Wales, Ireland, and Scotland) provenance of these usages and thus lends indirect support to the Celtic substrate hypothesis.

Matters are not, however, so straightforward when the usages of the definite article are considered from a wider, "global," perspective. Recent work on other varieties of English spoken in widely different settings all over the world has brought to light more or less similar uses of the definite article, e.g. in Indian English, Singapore English, Jamaican English, and in some cases, in American English, too. This had led some researchers (see, especially, Sand 2003) to question the role of Celtic substratal influences in HE (and presumably, by the same token, in the other CEs as well). Instead, the nonstandard usages are explained as being due to either the application of universal features of definiteness, inherent variation in article use, or the extension of the standard English rules (Sand 2003: 430). The fact that many of the abovementioned usages are found in other varieties lends some support to this line of argumentation but hardly suffices to eliminate the role of substratal influences. If, indeed, these usages are universal in nature, why should they occur in just some varieties and not in others, and why do we not have the same set of usages in all varieties of English? There must have been some factors in each situation determining the choice of, or preference for, one or another variant. In the context of the British Isles, it is hard to escape the conclusion that the close parallels in the Celtic substrate languages must have constituted one of those factors. This is shown by the geographical distribution of the usages discussed above, which is such that it cannot be satisfactorily explained as a reflex of some universal properties of definiteness any more than as a result of mere inherent variation in article usage or as extensions of the StE rules. Furthermore, as the following discussion will show, the CEs share many other syntactic features, not all of which are found in other varieties of English.

20.3.3.2 *Free use of the "expanded form" of verbs*

A second feature shared by HE and other CE varieties is the general use of the "expanded" or *-ing* form of verbs (henceforth EF) in contexts where StE and other mainstream varieties would use the simple present-tense or past-tense form. Thus, the EF can occur with stative verbs (or, more precisely, verbs used in the stative sense) and with dynamic verbs which are used to express a habitual activity. Examples from HE, WE, and HebE are given in (1–6):

(1) There was a lot about fairies long ago . . . but I'*m thinkin'* that most of 'em are vanished.
'. . . but I think that most of them have vanished'
(HE; cited in Filppula 1999: 89)

(2) I think two of the lads was lost at sea during the War. They *were belonging* to the, them men here. (HE; cited in Filppula 2003: 162)

(3) I'*m not thinking* much of it.
'I'm not impressed by it'
(WE; cited in Parry 1999: 111)

(4) They'*re keeping* hens. (WE; cited in Parry 1999: 111)

(5) No, people don't need the weather like what they did then – they *were depending* on the weather.
'. . . they depended on the weather'
(HebE; cited in Sabban 1982: 276)

(6) And the people then *were having* plenty of potatoes and meal of their own.
(HebE; cited in Sabban 1982: 275)

It is interesting to note that similar uses have been recorded in the traditional dialect of Man, as is shown by the following examples from Preuß's (1999) study:

(7) It *was meaning* right the opposite. (MxE; cited in Preuß 1999: 111)

(8) I remember my grandfather and old people that lived down the road here, they *be* all *walking* over to the chapel of a Sunday afternoon and they *be going* again at night. (MxE; cited in Preuß 1999: 112)

Although similar nonstandard usages have long been recognized in the literature on CEs and some other varieties too, no agreement on their origin(s) has as yet been reached. A complicating factor is the general increase in the rates of use of the EF even in StE from the early Modern English period onwards and a concomitant relaxing of some of the semantic constraints on its use (see e.g. Elsness 1994; Mair and Hundt 1995). In AmE, this tendency appears to be even more pronounced than in BrE (see e.g. Śmiecińska 2002/3). Yet it seems clear that the CEs have been leading the way in this development, although they are joined here by some English-based creoles and various African and Asian varieties of English, as Gachelin (1997) points out. This adds an interesting universalist perspective to the problem at hand. In fact, Gachelin suggests that the high incidence of the EF in all these varieties has turned it semantically into a "general imperfective," which will probably lead to a further "devaluation" of the EF, making it less and less sensitive to contextual constraints. Indeed, it is his prediction that the generalization of the EF will be one of the characteristics of future "World English" (Gachelin 1997: 43–4).

In the context of the British Isles Englishes, however, the most likely background to the free use of the EF in the CEs is to be found in the corresponding Celtic systems, which favor the so-called "verbal noun construction" (similar in function to the English *-ing* form) in these kinds of context. One of the first to advocate the Celtic hypothesis is Mossé (1938), who is otherwise very critical towards the idea of Celtic influences in English grammar. Having discarded the Celtic hypothesis with regard to the earliest, medieval, forms of the English EF, he states that the abundant use of the EF in the English of Ireland, Scotland, and Wales in the modern period probably derives from the parallel tendency in Insular Celtic (Mossé 1938, II §106).

In more recent research, the same view is defended by Braaten (1967), who has been followed by several writers on one or other of the CEs. Thus, Filppula (2003) discusses the Irish roots of the HE usages of the EF. For WE, the Cymric parallels are documented by e.g. Parry (1999); he points out that examples like (3) and (4) are modeled on the Welsh "uninflected present tense," which consists of YR + BOD 'be' + subject + YN 'in' + verb-noun, e.g. *Y mae ef yn canu pob dydd* 'He sings [literally: is in sing/singing] every day' (Parry 1999: 111; see also Thomas 1994; Penhallurick 1996; Pitkänen 2003). HebE and its Gaelic heritage in this respect are treated in Sabban (1982) and Macafee and Ó Baoill (1997), while Barry (1984), Broderick (1997), and Preuß (1999) find evidence of reflexes of Manx syntax in the MxE usages of the EF.

20.3.3.3 *Prepositional usage*

Prepositions are known to be an area which is particularly susceptible to contact influences, and this is also confirmed by data from HE and the other CEs. Expressions denoting possession of some property or object and related notions can be mentioned as a good example of prepositional usages which are shared by the CEs. Consider first the examples in (9–14) from HE, WE, and HebE:

(9) . . . ah, if it's in a dog he'll train himself, if the goodness is *in 'im*.
'. . . if he's good'
(HE; cited in Filppula 1999: 229)

(10) The health isn't great *with her*.
'Her health . . .'
(HE; cited in Moylan 1996: 352)

(11) There's no horns *with the sheep* about this way. (WE; cited in Parry 1999: 117)

(12) There's no luck *with the rich*.
'The rich have no luck'
(WE; cited in Thomas 1994: 139)

(13) . . . sheep are so daring when the hunger is *on them*.
'. . . when they are hungry'
(HebE; cited in Sabban 1982: 448)

(14) The money was *in the family of these Campbells*.
'These Campbells had plenty of money'
(HebE; cited in Filppula 1999: 237)

As in the case of the EF, MxE shares this feature with the other CE varieties:

(15) They'd money *at them*.
'They possessed (plenty) of money'
(MxE; cited in Barry 1984: 176)

(16) There's a nice car *at him*.
'He has a nice car'
(MxE; cited in Preuß 1999: 63)

Despite variation in the prepositions used, all the examples cited above are similar in that the "possessor" (or "experiencer", as in (13)) is indicated by means of a prepositional phrase placed at the end of the clause or sentence rather than by making it the subject or "theme" of the clause, which is generally the case in StE. Again, there can be little doubt about the Celtic origin of these usages. A special feature of all the relevant Celtic languages is that they have no equivalent of the verb *have*; possession and other related notions must therefore be expressed by means of the verb 'be' followed by the thing or property "possessed" in subject position and, finally, the "possessor" cast in the form of a prepositional phrase, just as in the CE examples above. Examples (17–19) from Irish, Manx, and Welsh, respectively, illustrate the typical Celtic constructions:

(17) Tá ocras orthu.
Is hunger on-them
'They are hungry'

(18) Ta gleashtan mie echey.
Is nice car at-him
'He has a nice car'
(Preuß 1999: 63)

(19) Mae car gyda ni.
Is [a] car with us
'We have a car'
(Parry 1999: 117)

Besides expressions of possession, the CEs share a fair number of other prepositional idioms, which are discussed in some detail in the sources mentioned above. Though clearly recessive in most of the varieties at issue, these usages provide compelling evidence of the direct syntactic input from the Celtic substrata to the earliest, "basilectal," forms of the CEs, in particular.

20.3.3.4 Expression of thematic prominence and emphasis

A fourth syntactic feature shared by the CEs has to do with the expression of emphasis or some other type of prominence assigned to some element of the sentence. Here the CEs show a clear predilection for the use of word order or special syntactic constructions at the expense of prosodic means. Again, this is a well-known characteristic of all the Celtic languages, which use either the so-called copula construction (equivalent to the English cleft construction or "clefting" for short) or word order arrangements for purposes of thematic prominence. Thus, it comes as no surprise that word order, or more precisely "fronting," is a frequently employed focusing device in WE, where the word to be highlighted is placed at the beginning of the clause or sentence, as in (20). Another commonly used linguistic term for this is "topicalization," although it suffers from the widely differing meanings attached to it in various functional or generative frameworks. Further examples from WE are given in (21–23):

(20) *Singing* they were.
'They were singing [i.e. not doing something else]'
(WE; cited in Thomas 1994: 37)

(21) *Coal* they are getting out mostly. (WE; cited in Parry 1999: 120)

(22) . . . we were sitting up there just the two of us an' the dog was lying on the – on the floor by the settee where my husband was lying down, and er, *chatting* we were and I said well we'd better – might as well go to bed, it's getting late now I said. (Pitkänen 2002)

(23) That's Cynthia's kitchen, that is, and my two grandchildren. *Great, great* those are, yeah. (Pitkänen 2002)

The frontings used in (20–23) directly echo the corresponding Welsh structures, which rely "universally," as Thomas (1994: 37) writes, on fronting of a constituent rather than clefting. The last two examples, drawn from Heli Pitkänen's corpus of WE collected from a bilingual area in Llandybie, South Wales, make it particularly clear that fronting in WE does not necessarily follow the contextual constraints typical of StE. What is presented as "new" or otherwise prominent information by the speaker can readily be put in clause-initial position, a practice which is characteristic of Welsh and the other Celtic languages (see also Williams 2000).

In HE, as well as in HebE, the preferred means of emphasis is the cleft construction, which closely resembles WE fronting in that the item to be highlighted is the first stressed element in the sentence; the introductory *it is* or *it's* never receives stress. The examples in (24–29), drawn from earlier written and present-day spoken HE and HebE, illustrate the uses of clefting in these two varieties. Note especially the lack of some of the syntactic constraints of StE and of most other varieties of English, for that matter; thus, a part of a VP, an adverb of manner or a reflexive pronoun can occur in the focus position of clefts in HE and HebE.

(24) Dear Catolicks, you shee here de cause dat is after bringing you to dis plaace: 'tis *come bourying* you are de corp, de cadaver, of a verie good woman, . . . (John Dunton, *Report of a Sermon*, 1698; quoted here from Bliss 1979: 133)

(25) Don't blame me for Robert's not going out lastyear [last year]. It was *himself* that would not go and the reason he gave was . . . (*The Oldham Papers*, no. 8, 1854; Trinity College MS 10,435/8; cited in Filppula 1999: 256)

(26) 'Tis *joking* you are, I suppose. (HE; cited in Ó hÚrdail 1997: 190)

(27) 'Tis *well* you looked. (HE; cited in Ó hÚrdail 1997: 190)

(28) And this day I happened to be doing something, I think it was *painting* I was. (HebE; cited in Odlin 1997b: 40)

(29) Och, it's *myself* that's glad to see you . . . (HebE; cited in Sabban 1982: 374)

Although there is a clear preference for clefting in both HE and HebE speech, simple frontings also occur in contexts which are very similar to those observed in WE. Again, many of these would be contextually unusual or odd, if not ungrammatical as such, in EngE. Consider, for example, (30–31) recorded from HE and HebE, respectively:

(30) My brother that's over in England, . . . when he was young, *a story* now he told me, when he was young. (HE; cited in Filppula 1997: 194)

(31) [Interviewer: And there would be no care for people like that at this time?] [Informant:] Aye, there was. *Very, very little* they were getting but they were cared for all the same. (HebE; cited in Filppula 1997: 194)

Although both clefting and, especially, fronting have long been part of StE grammar, their uses are functionally and syntactically more restricted than those of their Celtic counterparts. Therefore, the prominent use and the syntactic and functional liberties of these focusing devices in the CEs can hardly be a coincidence but must be attributed to Celtic substratum influence (see Filppula 1997, 1999, for further discussion). The evidence is especially clear in the case of clefting, but fronting, too, owes a lot to substratal influence, as is shown by the WE evidence, in particular. It seems reasonable to argue that WE provides here indirect support to the claim that frontings in HE and HebE have also been influenced by the Celtic substratum. This is not to deny the possibility of earlier English superstratal input in the Irish context, in particular, because of the existence of parallels for most structural types of clefting and topicalization in earlier forms of English. The safest conclusion here is that the contact influences on the two constructions in the varieties at issue have been of two types: both reinforcing (i.e. consolidating already-existing structural parallels in varieties of English) and direct (coming exclusively from the substrate languages, as in certain types of clefting).

20.4 Divergent Developments

Just as one can point out linguistic similarities between the CEs, there are several clear differences between them at all levels of language. As was mentioned above, some of these can be plausibly explained by differences in the Celtic substrata, while others reflect genuinely divergent developments due to, for example, historical contacts with different dialects of English or to different sociolinguistic and historical circumstances surrounding the language contact and shift situations. These can lead to different linguistic outcomes, as has been shown by cross-linguistic evidence from other contact situations.

20.4.1 Phonological differences

Anyone with even scant knowledge of HE is bound to be struck by the absence of the voiceless and voiced interdental fricatives /θ/ and /ð/ from most varieties of especially southern HE, where they are replaced by the dental stops /t̪/ and /d̪/, respectively. For example, the words *thin* and *then* are pronounced as [t̪ɪn] and [d̪ɪn]. In some varieties of HE, the distinction between dental and alveolar stops is lost, which means that words like *thin* and *tin* sound alike (see Bliss 1984: 138; Ó Baoill 1997: 80–1). However, the dental realization of the interdental fricatives is not a feature of WE or HebE, or even of the northern varieties of HE, except in certain consonant clusters and in areas of Co. Donegal where Irish is still in living contact with English (Harris 1984; Hickey forthcoming). As regards WE, the non-occurrence of dental stops is easily explained by the Welsh consonant system, which contains both /θ/ and /ð/, unlike Irish, in which these consonants changed to /h/ and /ɣ/ in the course of the twelfth and thirteenth centuries (see Thurneysen 1946 [1975]: 76–7). In HebE and northern HE varieties, the situation is not so simple: dental stops do occur in both in clusters like /tr/ and /dr/ just as in southern varieties of HE, though not in lieu of interdental fricatives generally, as in southern HE (Shuken 1984: 156; Harris 1984: 130). This latter feature of the northern HE varieties can be explained by the strong historical influence from ScE (Ó Baoill 1997: 82). The same explanation probably accounts for the non-occurrence of dental stops outside the mentioned clusters in HebE, too.

20.4.2 *Syntactic differences*

One of the most striking examples from the domain of syntax is the type of perfect known as the "hot news" or *after*-perfect, as in (32) recorded from an Irishman. Besides HE, it is common enough in HebE; witness the example in (33). But somewhat surprisingly, there is no *after*-perfect in WE, although Welsh has a structural parallel for it.

(32) I was in the market, and I *was after buyin'* a load of strawberries.
'... and I had just bought ...'
(Filppula 1999: 99)

(33) He'*s after coming* from the Mackenzies.
'He has just come ...'
(Sabban 1982: 157)

An explanation for the absence of the *after*-perfect from WE syntax can be found in the aspectual system of Welsh. Greene (1979) writes that Welsh has no direct equivalent of the Irish and Scottish Gaelic *tréis/air* constructions, which provide the model for the HE and HebE *after*-perfects. Instead, Welsh expresses the notion of a recent event by adding *newydd* 'just' to the periphrastic construction involving the preposition *wedi* 'after', used (alongside the preterite) for the "ordinary" present perfect (i.e. with no particular emphasis on the recentness of the event or activity referred to). This leads to a contrast between *yr wyf wedi ei weld ef* 'I have seen him' and *yr wyf newydd ei weld ef* 'I have just seen him' (Greene 1979: 126). Thus, despite the apparent similarity with the Irish and Scottish Gaelic constructions, the Welsh periphrastic perfect requires the presence of the adverb (*newydd*) to underline the recentness of the event or activity, just like Standard English does. This probably explains the fact that WE has no *after*-perfect.

Another interesting divergence is the syntactic pattern known as "subordinating *and*." It is amply documented in its various syntactic and semantic subtypes in earlier and present-day HE and in HebE speech, and is exemplified in (34–36) below.

(34) If I should see Derry House *and he not living* there I would Surely shed tears for it . . . (*The Normile Letters*, no. 14, 1863; quoted from Fitzpatrick 1994: 92–3)

(35) [I] seen farms selling *and I young lad*.
'. . . when I was . . .'
(HE; cited in Filppula 1999: 196)

(36) And though he was blind I was the only one he was calling on . . . And he would come, *and him blind*, to the house. (HebE; cited in Filppula 1999: 205)

The same feature is also used to some extent in Scots (see Macafee and Ó Baoill 1997), but not commented on in the studies of WE. Yet, examples can be found in Anglo-Welsh literature, e.g. in the prose of Richard Llewellyn (as pointed out to me by Heli Pitkänen, personal communication). Consider the following three from his novel *How Green Was My Valley*. It is noteworthy that this feature appears to be confined to the narrative sections.

(37) That night I was in bed in this room when I woke up and heard my father talking to Davy, *and my mother crying*. (Llewellyn 1939 [1976]: 26)

(38) "It is true, Mama," Angharad said, *and tears coming to sparkle in the fire-light*. (Llewellyn 1939 [1976]: 50)

(39) I was on my mother's lap and she was sitting in the drift with her bonnet off *and her hair all covered with snow*, and looking down at me. (Llewellyn 1939 [1976]: 62)

As said above, studies of the spoken varieties do not recognize subordinating *and* as a characteristic feature of WE today or in the past, despite the existence of a Welsh parallel (see e.g. King 1993: 317). Why this should be so can only be conjectured here, pending further research. Possibilities worth exploring include the role of formal language instruction in schools and the possible stigma associated with this feature. In the Irish context, too, subordinating *and* is clearly recessive and confined to the most conservative rural dialects (see Filppula 1999: section 8.3). In HebE it also appears to be rather sporadic (ibid.). Writing on the possible influence of Gaelic on Scots, Macafee and Ó Baoill (1997) note the widespread nature and early attestation of the Celtic *agus* constructions and suggest that the corresponding Scots (and HE) constructions are early calques on them (cf., however, Häcker 1994, who argues for a Scots origin of this feature).

The existence of these and other dissimilarities between the CEs raises the question of whether the divergences are significant enough to undermine the notion of CE altogether? Indeed, this is the stand advocated by scholars like Görlach (1997), who does not consider the similarities to be extensive enough to justify the notion of CE. It should be noted, however, that he understands the term differently from the approach adopted in this chapter. For Görlach, the essential condition is the existence of a "common Celtic English" with its subvarieties, involving a maximally large number of shared features deriving from the Celtic substrata; furthermore, there ought to be popular awareness of this "pan-Celtic" form of English leading to a new norm (Görlach 1997: 45–6). By contrast, the present approach starts from the observation that there is a body of syntactic and phonological features shared by varieties of English spoken in the (formerly or currently) Celtic-speaking areas, and that a significant number of these commonalities have plausible origins in the Celtic relevant languages (which may, however, differ with respect to one or another of these features). In other words, the term "Celtic English" is here understood as being short for "Celtic-influenced variety of English," be this influence direct or merely indirect and reinforcing. Viewed from this perspective, there is clearly enough evidence to show that the Celtic substrate languages have had a significant molding effect on the varieties of English spoken in Ireland, Wales, and (some parts of) Scotland.

20.5 Conclusion and Directions for Future Research

In this chapter I have discussed several features which are shared by varieties of English which have evolved in (earlier or present-day) Celtic-speaking areas in Ireland, Scotland, Wales, and the Isle of Man. These features are most prominent on the level of syntax, although some phonological commonalities are also found.

As noted on several occasions above, many of the shared features have controversial origins, and it is by no means clear that even those which have parallels in the respective Celtic substrate languages derive from Celtic alone. It is sound wisdom always to consider first the nature and extent of the superstratal input from earlier and other varieties of English before turning to other possible sources such as contact with other languages. As the discussion on, for instance, the long vowels instead of diphthongs has shown, the possible input from earlier English provides a more plausible explanation for this feature of the CEs than the parallel feature of the Celtic languages, which may, however, have helped preserve it in these varieties. In addition to the superstratal input, one has to reckon with the possibility of independent developments in one or the other of the varieties at issue. A good example is provided by some aspects of the *after*-perfect in HE. Though clearly modeled on the corresponding Irish perfect, it has extended its functional and semantic range beyond those of its Irish counterpart.

On the other hand, the existence of a mere structural syntactic parallel in earlier English does not suffice to exclude contact influence. In addition, one has to consider the full syntactic, semantic, and functional range of the construction at issue. Some uses of the focusing devices such as clefting or topicalization in HE and WE serve as a good illustration here.

It is often forgotten that *dis*similarities in the substrata can also be used as evidence for substratal influences. Recall, for example, the Welsh system of perfects which differs in some respects from those of Irish and Scottish Gaelic, and may well explain some of the characteristics of WE, most notably the lack of the so-called *after*-perfect. In Filppula (1999) I have discussed another similar case, namely the absence of the type of perfect known as "PII" from the Scottish Gaelic system of perfects, which may then have led to the lack of the corresponding feature in HebE. In a similar vein, Filppula (1997) offers a detailed discussion of some differences in habitual aspect marking in the CEs, including the varied constructions involving the so-called periphrastic *do*; again, some of these can be explained by divergences among the Celtic languages.

Finally, two dimensions of study are hitherto relatively unexplored but will undoubtedly offer interesting insights into the kind of problems at hand. The first of these is (various kinds of) *contact universals* or *universals of language acquisition* which emerge in language contact situations. It should be remembered that, historically speaking, the varieties under discussion have all evolved as results of language contact and shift, involving essentially a second-language acquisition situation for the speakers shifting to English in different periods and in different types of sociohistorical settings. This dimension was touched on in our discussion on the free uses of the expanded form of verbs, which have been found to occur in English-based creoles and other varieties which have emerged in widely differing geographical contexts. Another candidate for a similar status is a syntactic feature known as "embedded inversion." Also shared by the CEs, it occurs in indirect (embedded) yes/no or *wh*-questions, such as *I wouldn't know would there be any there now* (cited in Thomas 1994: 138) and *I don' know what is it at all* (cited in Filppula 1999: 168). Again, this feature has been observed to occur in "learner-English" in different settings and could therefore be seen as some kind of contact universal. In the context of the CEs, however, an equally powerful, and in my view, more plausible explanatory factor is transfer from the Celtic substrate languages in which similar word order is fully grammaticalized. What also speaks for a historical contact effect rather than a second-language acquisition (SLA) universal is the presence of the same feature in Scots and ScE and the overall geographical distribution of this feature. Furthermore, English-based creoles do not typically exhibit this feature, as they could be expected to do if embedded inversion phenomena were to be explained as a universal feature (see Filppula 1999, 2000, for further discussion).

The second dimension focuses on areal and typological *Sprachbund* phenomena. The concept of *Sprachbund* has established itself in historical linguistics as a household term for situations in which two or more languages (or language-groups) spoken in the same geographical area share typological features regardless of their genetic background. In a *Sprachbund* situation the languages involved exercise, or have exercised, influence on each other in such a way that it is usually not possible to establish the direction of influence. In this kind of situation, the languages are said to stand in an "adstratal" relationship to each other (see e.g. Lehiste 1988: 61). It is important to notice that a *Sprachbund* situation may arise not only between different languages but between dialects or varieties of one language, such as the CEs. A suitable term for this type of adstratal situation would be *Dialektbund*; the English of this could be *dialect federation* or *dialect (convergence) area.*

Whatever term is chosen, adstratal influences should be considered as yet another possible factor explaining at least part of the observed similarities not only between the CEs but between all the languages involved in contact relationships in the "linguistic area" embracing the British Isles and Ireland, and extending even to the continent. Though largely neglected in research so far, this line of inquiry has some eminent early proponents such as the Celticist Heinrich Wagner (see Wagner 1959), who argues for what he calls the "North European" linguistic area, embracing the Celtic languages, Germanic, and even the Baltic Finnic languages. Another like-minded scholar is the Anglicist J. R. R. Tolkien, who in his O'Donnell Lecture on "English and Welsh," delivered in Oxford in the mid-1950s, urged scholars to see the British Isles and, indeed, the wider area of the northwest of Europe, as a "single philological province" (see Tolkien 1963: 33). While Tolkien's focus was on the earliest, medieval, contacts between English and Celtic, the same kind of areal and typological perspective will perhaps provide the most significant addition to our existing knowledge about the evolution of the Celtic Englishes in more recent times. As the foregoing discussion has shown, some of the features shared by the CEs can be plausibly explained as being due to substratum influence from the respective Celtic languages, but there are others for which it is very hard to pin down an exact source because of parallels in both English (or some of its present-day or earlier varieties, including Older Scots) and the Celtic languages. Of the features examined above, some uses of the definite article (e.g. with names of seasons and some ailments), and the expanded form of verbs provide good examples of possible adstratal developments shared by the CEs, and to some extent by other dialects of English in the British Isles. A third example could be subordinating *and*, which also has controversial origins. As noted above, Häcker (1994) has argued for a Middle Scots rather than a Gaelic source for the present-day ScE and Scots uses, which she also wants to keep distinct from the corresponding feature of HE dialects. Yet there is a certain amount of structural and functional overlap between the ScE and Scots uses, on one hand, and the HE uses, on the other, which indicates the existence of some kind of an adstratal relationship between these varieties. Notice, however, that the existence of a *Dialektbund* between the varieties at issue does not exclude the possibility of adstratal relationships between different languages (and not just dialects of one language); indeed, it is more than likely that the dialect convergence areas discussed here could not have come into existence without some degree of adstratal influences between English and the Celtic languages. It is to be hoped that even the simple gesture of treating the varieties of English in the Celtic areas under the same heading of Celtic Englishes will make a small contribution toward promoting the areal and typological dimension of research, too.

ACKNOWLEDGMENTS

The writing of this article was supported by the Research Council for Culture and Society, Academy of Finland (Project no. 47424). I would also like to thank Professor Charles W. J. Withers and Professors Harold Carter and John Aitchison for their kind permission to reproduce linguistic maps of Scotland and Wales from their published works.

REFERENCES

Aitchison, J. and H. Carter (1994). *A Geography of the Welsh Language 1961–1991*. Cardiff: University of Wales Press.

Barry, M. V. (1984). Manx English. In Trudgill, P. (ed.), pp. 167–77.

Beckwith, L. (1959). *The Hills Is Lonely*. London: Hutchinson/Arrow Books.

Bliss, A. J. (1977). *A Dialogue in Hybernian Stile between A&B and Irish Eloquence by Jonathan Swift*. Dublin: Cadenus Press.

Bliss, A. J. (1979). *Spoken English in Ireland 1600–1740*. Dublin: Dolmen Press.

Bliss, A. J. (1984). English in the south of Ireland. In P. Trudgill (ed.), *Language in the British Isles* (pp. 135–51). Cambridge: Cambridge University Press.

Braaten, Bjørn (1967). Notes on continuous tenses in English, *Norsk Tidsskrift for Sprogvidenskap* 21: 167–80.

Broderick, G. (1997). Manx English: an overview. In H. L. C. Tristram (ed.) (1997), pp. 123–34.

Burchfield, R. W. (ed.) (1994). *English in Britain and Overseas: Origins and Development*. Vol. V of *The Cambridge History of the English Language*. Cambridge: Cambridge University Press.

Chadwick, N. K. (1963). The British or Celtic part in the population of England. In *Angles and Britons* (O'Donnell Lectures) (pp. 111–47). Cardiff: University of Wales Press.

Elsness, J. (1994). On the progression of the progressive in early Modern English, *ICAME Journal* 18 (April): 5–25.

Filppula, M. (1997). Grammatical parallels in "Celtic Englishes." In A. R. Thomas (ed.), *Issues and Methods in Dialectology* (pp. 192–9). Bangor: Department of Linguistics, University of Wales Bangor.

Filppula, M. (1999). *The Grammar of Irish English: Language in Hibernian Style*. London and New York: Routledge.

Filppula, M. (2000). Inversion in embedded questions in some regional varieties of English. In R. Bermúdez-Otero, D. Denison, R. M. Hogg, and C. B. McCully (eds.), *Generative Theory and Corpus Studies: A Dialogue from 10ICEHL* (pp. 409–53). Berlin: de Gruyter.

Filppula, M. (2003). More on the English progressive and the Celtic connection. In H. L. C. Tristram (ed.) (2003), pp. 150–68.

Fitzpatrick, D. (1994). *Oceans of Consolation: Personal Accounts of Irish Migration to Australia*. Cork: Cork University Press.

Freeman, E. (1888). *Four Oxford Lectures: Fifty Years of European History. Teutonic Conquest in Gaul and Britain*. London: Macmillan.

Fréine, S. de (1977). The dominance of the English language in the 19th century. In D. Ó Muirithe (ed.), *The English Language in Ireland* (pp. 71–87). Dublin: Mercier Press.

Gachelin, J.-M. (1997). The Progressive and Habitual Aspects in Non-standard Englishes. In E. Schneider (ed.), *Englishes Around the World*. Vol. 1: *General Studies, British Isles, North America* (pp. 33–46). Amsterdam and Philadelphia: John Benjamins.

Garvin, J. (1977). The Anglo-Irish Idiom in the Works of Major Irish Writers. In D. Ó Muirithe (ed.), *The English Language in Ireland* (pp. 100–14) (The Thomas Davis Lecture Series). Dublin and Cork: Mercier Press.

Gill, W. W. (1934). *Manx Dialect: Words and Phrases*. London and Bristol: Arrowsmith.

Görlach, M. (1997). Celtic Englishes? In H. L. C. Tristram (ed.) (1997), pp. 27–54.

Greene, D. (1979). Perfects and perfectives in Modern Irish, *Ériu* 30: 122–41.

Häcker, M. (1994). Subordinate and-clauses in Scots and Hiberno-English: origins and development, *Scottish Language* 13: 34–50.

Harris, J. (1984). English in the north of Ireland. In P. Trudgill (ed.), pp. 115–34.

Hickey, R. (2002). *A Source Book for Irish English*. Amsterdam/Philadelphia: John Benjamins.

Hickey, R. (forthcoming). The phonology of Irish English. To appear in C. Upton (ed.), *Handbook of Varieties of English. British Isles: Phonology*. Berlin: Mouton.

Higham, N. (1992). *Rome, Britain and the Anglo-Saxons*. London: Seaby.

Hindley, R. (1990). *The Death of the Irish Language*. London: Routledge.

Joyce, P. W. (1910 [1988]). *English as We Speak It in Ireland* (3rd edn.). Dublin: Wolfhound Press.

Kallen, J. L. (1994). English in Ireland. In R. W. Burchfield (ed.), pp. 148–96.

King, G. (1993). *Modern Welsh: A Comprehensive Grammar*. London: Routledge.

Laing, L. and J. Laing (1990). *Celtic Britain and Ireland, AD 200–800: The Myth of the Dark Ages*. Dublin: Irish Academic Press.

Lass, R. (1990). Early mainland residues in southern Hiberno-English, *Irish University Review* 20: 137–48.

Lehiste, I. (1988). *Lectures on Language Contact*. Cambridge, MA: MIT Press.

Llewellyn, R. (1939 [1976]). *How Green Was My Valley*. London: Michael Joseph.

Macafee, C. I. and C. Ó Baoill (1997). Why Scots is not a Celtic English. In H. L. C. Tristram (ed.), pp. 245–86.

McClure, J. (1994). English in Scotland. In R. W. Burchfield (ed.), pp. 23–93.

Mair, C. and M. Hundt (1995). Why is the progressive becoming more frequent in English? A corpus-based investigation of language change in progress, *Zeitschrift für Anglistik und Amerikanistik* 43.2: 111–22.

Miller, J. (1993). The grammar of Scottish English. In J. Milroy and L. Milroy (eds.), *Real English: The Grammar of English Dialects in the British Isles* (pp. 99–138). London: Longman.

Mossé, F. (1938). *Histoire de la forme périphrastique être + participe présent en germanique*. Deuxième Partie: *Moyen-Anglais et Anglais Moderne*. Paris: Librairie C. Klincksieck.

Moylan, S. (1996). *The Language of Kilkenny: Lexicon, Semantics, Structures.* Dublin: Geography Publications.

Ó Baoill, D. P. (1997). The emerging Irish phonological substratum in Irish English. In J. L. Kallen (ed.), *Focus on Ireland* (pp. 73–87). Amsterdam/Philadelphia: John Benjamins.

Odlin, T. (1997a). Hiberno-English: pidgin, creole, or neither? *CLCS Occasional Paper* 49. Dublin: Trinity College.

Odlin, T. (1997b). Bilingualism and substrate influence: a look at clefts and reflexives. In J. L. Kallen (ed.), *Focus on Ireland* (pp. 35–50). Amsterdam: Benjamins.

Ó hÚrdail, R. (1997). Hiberno-English: historical background and synchronic features and variation. In H. L. C. Tristram (ed.), *The Celtic Englishes* (180–99). Heidelberg: Universitätsverlag C. Winter.

Orton, H., M. V. Barry, W. J. Halliday, P. M. Tilling, and M. F. Wakelin (eds.) (1962–71). *Survey of English Dialects* (4 vols.). Leeds: E. J. Arnold.

Parry, D. (ed.) (1999). *A Grammar and Glossary of the Conservative Anglo-Welsh Dialects of Rural Wales*. NATCECT Occasional Publications 8. University of Sheffield.

Payton, P. (1997). Identity, ideology and language in modern Cornwall. In H. L. C. Tristram (ed.) (1997), pp. 100–22.

Penhallurick, R. (1993). Welsh English: a national language? *Dialectologia et Geolinguistica* 1: 28–46.

Penhallurick, R. (1996). The grammar of Northern Welsh English. In J. Klemola M. Kytö, and M. Rissanen (eds.), *Speech Past and Present: Studies in English Philology in Memory of Ossi Ihalainen* (pp. 308–42). Frankfurt am Main: Peter Lang.

Pilch, H. (1983/4). The structure of Welsh tonality, *Studia Celtica* 18/19: 234–52.

Pitkänen, H. (2002). English in Wales or Welsh English? Investigating the identity of a dialect. Paper read at the Eleventh International Conference on Methods in Dialectology, August 5–9, 2002, University of Joensuu.

Pitkänen, H. (2003). Non-standard uses of the progressive form in Welsh English: an apparent time study. In H. L. C. Tristram (ed.) (2003), pp. 111–28.

Preuß, M. (1999). *Remaining Lexical and Syntactic Borrowings from Manx Gaelic in Present Day Manx English.* MPh thesis, University of Liverpool.

Sabban, A. (1982). *Gälisch-Englischer Sprachkontakt.* Heidelberg: Julius Groos.

Sand, A. (2003). The definite article in Irish English and other contact varieties of English. In H. L. C. Tristram (ed.) (2003), pp. 413–30.

The Scottish National Dictionary (SND) (1931–76). Ed. by W. Grant and D. D. Murison. Edinburgh: The Scottish National Dictionary Association.

Shuken, C. R. (1984). Highland and Island English. In P. Trudgill (ed.), pp. 152–66.

Śmiecińska, J. (2002/3). Stative verbs and the progressive aspect in English, *Poznań Studies in Contemporary Linguistics* 38: 187–95.

Thomas, A. R. (1984). Cornish. In P. Trudgill (ed.), pp. 278–88.

Thomas, A. R. (1994). English in Wales. In R. Burchfield (ed.), pp. 94–147.

Thomason, S. and T. Kaufman. (1988). *Language Contact, Creolization, and Genetic Linguistics*. Berkeley, CA: University of California Press.

Thurneysen, R. (1946 [1975]). *A Grammar of Old Irish* (rev. and enlarged edn.). Dublin: Dublin Institute for Advanced Studies.

Tolkien, J. R. R. (1963). English and Welsh. In *Angles and Britons* (pp. 1–41) (O'Donnell Lectures). Cardiff: University of Wales Press.

Tristram, H. L. C. (ed.) (1997). *The Celtic Englishes*. Heidelberg: Universitätsverlag C. Winter.

Tristram, H. L. C. (ed.) (2003). *The Celtic Englishes III*. Heidelberg: Universitätsverlag C. Winter.

Trudgill, P. (ed.) (1984). *Language in the British Isles*. Cambridge: Cambridge University Press.

Wagner, H. (1959). *Das Verbum in den Sprachen der Britischen Inseln: Ein Beitrag zur Geographischen Typologie des Verbums*. Tübingen: Max Niemeyer.

Wakelin, M. (1984). Cornish English. In P. Trudgill (ed.), pp. 195–8.

Williams, M. (2000). The pragmatics of predicate fronting in Welsh English. In H. L. C. Tristram (ed.), *The Celtic Englishes II* (210–30). Heidelberg: Universitätsverlag C. Winter.

Withers, C. W. J. (1979). The language geography of Scottish Gaelic, *Scottish Literary Journal* 9 (Supplement): 40–53.

Wright, J. (ed.) (1896–1905). *English Dialect Dictionary (EDD)* (6 vols.). Oxford: Oxford University Press.

Wright, J. (ed.) (1905). *The English Dialect Grammar (EDG)*. Oxford: Henry Frowde.

VI Standardization and Globalization

21 Eighteenth-century Prescriptivism and the Norm of Correctness

INGRID TIEKEN-BOON VAN OSTADE

21.1 Introduction

In *The Grammatical Art Improved: In Which the Errors of Grammarians and Lexicographers Are Exposed* (1795), Richard Postlethwaite (c.1759–1819) wrote: "Dr. Lowth, than *who* no better English Grammarian has existed, was an excellent Poet, a great Latinist, a famous Grecian, and a good Hebrician" (1795: 218). This sentence occurs in a section called "Exercises of Bad English," a feature of eighteenth-century grammars of English which was introduced by Ann Fisher in her *New Grammar* ([1745] 2nd edn. 1750), and which proved very popular after her grammar was first published (Rodríguez Gil 2002). With this example, Postlethwaite mocks the phenomenon, and with it eighteenth-century normative grammar as such. This is clear from the fact that he couples the name of Robert Lowth (1710–87), the author of one of the most popular grammars of the period, with a sentence containing a so-called grammatical solecism, i.e. *who* instead of *whom*, which the reader of the grammar had to correct. Another example from Postlethwaite's "Exercises of Bad English" is the following sentence, which plays on the well-known eighteenth-century stricture against the use of double negation:

> But, as I must *not never* imitate those, who, by their Ignorance and Vulgarity, are distinguishable from others, it *cannot not* be supposed, that I shall fall into their Errors; and therefore need *not* say *no* more on this Subject. (1795: 216)

Not only is this sentence unusual in the number of double negatives it contains, but also because the types of double negation illustrated, *not never*, . . . *not not* and *not* . . . *no*, did not to my knowledge occur at the time (Tieken-Boon van Ostade 1982: 281–2). Hence, it cannot have been intended to illustrate actual usage.

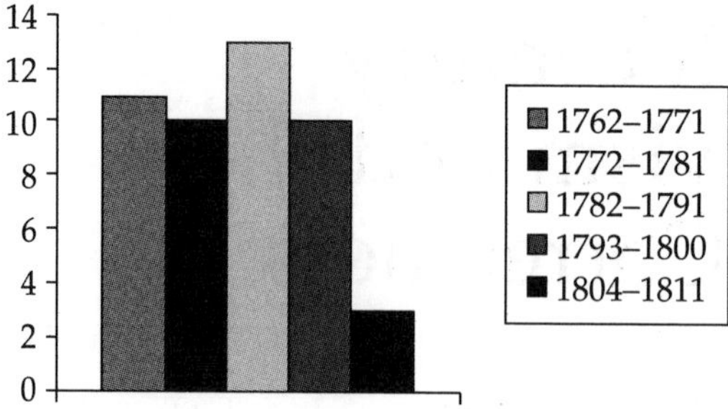

Figure 21.1 Editions and reprints of Lowth's grammar

Lowth's grammar, which is called *A Short Introduction to English Grammar* (1762), is a normative grammar which, to judge by the number of editions and reprints that have come down to us (see figure 21.1), became very popular immediately upon its publication, and remained so until well after the author's death (see Alston 1965: 42–8; see also Tieken-Boon van Ostade 2000a, 2001).

The strictures alluded to by Postlethwaite do not occur in the first edition of Lowth's grammar: this edition had been intended as a kind of trial version, that was to be augmented by additions from the reading public, thus getting a more definitive shape (see also below). Lowth evidently received a large number of suggestions for improvement (see the manuscript additions in Alston's facsimile edition of the grammar), and these were all incorporated into the second edition, along with the strictures referred to above:

> But the Relative *who*, having reference to no Verb or Preposition understood, but only to its Antecedent, when it follows *than*, is always in the objective Case; even tho' the Pronoun, if substituted in its place, would be in the Nominative: as
>
> "Beelzebub, *than whom*,
> Satan except, none higher sate."
> Milton, P.L. ii.299
>
> Which, if we substitute the Pronoun would be,
>
> "None higher sat, than *he*."
> (Lowth 1763: 159–60)

> Two Negatives in English destroy one another, or are equivalent to an Affirmative . . . : as,
>
> "*Nor* did they *not* perceive the evil plight
> In which they were, or the fierce pains *not* feel."
> Milton, P. L. i.335
> (Lowth 1763: 139–40)

21.2 The Prescriptivists and the Structuralists

Lowth's grammar was so popular that his name, according to the *Oxford Companion to the English Language*, came to be "synonymous with prescriptive grammar" (McArthur 1992, s.v. "Lowth"), and along with Lindley Murray, who based part of his grammar on Lowth's (Vorlat 1959) and who earned himself the epithet of "Father of English grammar" (Nietz 1961: 110), they can be considered as icons of English prescriptive grammar. Prescriptive grammars are not very popular with modern linguists – this unpopularity is already anticipated by Postlethwaite – and Pullum (1974: 66) lists their alleged shortcomings as

(a) a tendency to confuse the synchronic and the diachronic and to mistakenly offer historical explanations instead of the descriptions of the facts;
(b) an almost exclusive concentration on written language to the exclusion of spoken;
(c) an uncritical acceptance of Latin grammatical categories that are "not appropriate to English";
(d) a prescriptive, as opposed to descriptive, bias.

An illustration of this unpopularity may be found in Aitchison (1981: 23–4), who condemns Lowth for his prescriptive attitude to language, rather than analyzing his grammar in the context of the time in which it was written. Thus, she writes that "the most notable" eighteenth-century purist

> was Robert Lowth, Bishop of London. A prominent Hebraist and theologian, with fixed and eccentric opinions about language, he wrote *A Short Introduction to English Grammar* (1762) which had a surprising influence, perhaps because of his own high status . . . His grammar is bespattered with pompous notes in which he deplores the lamentable English of great writers. He set out to put matters right by laying down "rules," which were often based on currently fashionable or even personal stylistic preferences.

The aim of Pullum's article was to analyze Lowth's grammar on its own merits rather than from a structuralist perspective, and he concludes that the book "is basically a good, reliable, normative grammar of the English of his time" (1974: 78). Around the same time, a similar attempt was made by Subbiondo (1975) in relation to another eighteenth-century grammar, i.e. William Ward's (1708–72) *Essay on Grammar*, which was first published in 1765 and which was reprinted three times down to 1788 (Alston 1965: 50–1). Subbiondo also argues that Ward's grammar "should not be associated with the pejorative characteristics usually attributed to 'prescriptive' grammar," and like Pullum he believes that the work "is an interesting and well-conceived grammar in its own right, even by the criteria of present syntactic theory" (1975: 36).

Despite well-argued cases such as these, the unpopularity of eighteenth-century grammars among structural linguists continued to give rise to preconceptions and prejudice about the grammars themselves and the authors who wrote them. Thus, Ann Fisher, the first female English grammarian, would not originally

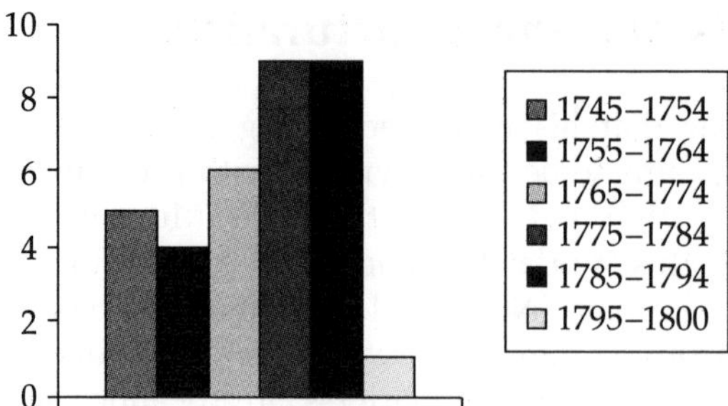

Figure 21.2 Editions and reprints of Fisher's grammar (Alston 1965)

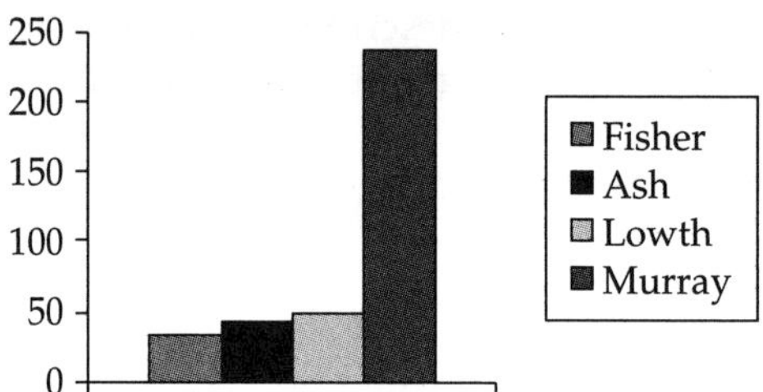

Figure 21.3 The most popular eighteenth-century grammarians (Alston 1965)

have been included in the *Lexicon Grammaticorum* (Stammerjohann 1996) on the grounds that, because "Fisher is said to have been the first to introduce into English textbooks the idea of teaching by mistake . . . it would not be particularly flattering to women linguists to have her remembered as the person who introduced such a pernicious method of language-teaching!" (personal communication with the editors; see Tieken-Boon van Ostade 2000b). The grammar, first published in 1745, was, however, very popular (see figure 21.2), and it rated fourth in popularity among eighteenth-century grammarians, after Murray (1795), Ash (1760), and Lowth (1762) (Rodríguez Gil 2002) (see figure 21.3).

Rodríguez Gil, moreover, argues that Fisher was more than merely the first female grammarian, whose main contribution to the English grammatical tradition was the invention of exercises of false syntax. Fisher showed an interest in the English language for its own sake, developing a native terminology rather than adopting the traditional terms of Latin grammar. Furthermore, she believed that English might be considered superior to Latin precisely for the reason that it was commonly considered inferior to it, i.e. its lack of inflectional endings.

21.3 The Case of Robert Lowth

Lowth has likewise been the subject of much prejudice, and the modern reputation of his grammar has unduly suffered from it (cf. Sledd 1959: 2–3); I have already quoted Aitchison, who concludes her discussion of Lowth as follows:

> In brief, Lowth's influence was profound and pernicious because so many of his strictures were based on his own preconceived notions. In retrospect, it is quite astonishing that he should have felt so confident about his prescriptions. Did he believe that, as a bishop, he was divinely inspired? It is also curious that his dogmatic statements were so widely accepted among educated Englishmen. It seems that, as a prominent religious leader, no one questioned his authority. (1981: 25)

Without evidently taking Lowth's personal background into consideration, Aitchison assumes that Lowth wrote his grammar as Bishop of London (see also Sledd 1959: 2; Freeborn 1992: 186; Finegan 1998: 546; Görlach 2001: 37). This was, indeed, the most prestigious post in his ecclesiastical career, but one which he reached only at the end of it, in 1777. He had been a bishop previously, first, though only briefly, of St. David's and subsequently of Oxford. But these appointments did not take place until 1766, when his grammar had already reached its fifth edition. In other words, the grammar owed its success not to Lowth's prominent position in the Church but to other reasons. There is, moreover, no indication that Lowth would have felt "confident about his prescriptions," as Aitchison suggests, for the first version had been corrected by William Melmoth (1710–99), an eighteenth-century author whose work was published by Robert Dodsley (1703–63), who was also Lowth's publisher (see Tieken-Boon van Ostade 2000a). Furthermore, Lowth had announced in the preface to his grammar that he would appreciate suggestions for improvement from his readers:

> If those, who are qualified to judge of such matters, and do not look upon them as beneath their notice, shall so far approve of it, as to think it worth a revisal, and capable of being improved into something really useful; their remarks and assistance, communicated through the hands of the Bookseller, shall be received with all proper deference and acknowledgement. (1762: xv)

The bookseller, Robert Dodsley, evidently did receive comments, and these were duly incorporated into the second edition, published in 1763. Two examples of such additions have already been quoted above.

Aitchison furthermore suggests that that Lowth's "strictures were based on his own preconceived notions"; Finegan (1992: 125) attributes Lowth's prescriptivism to a different source, i.e. to influence from "conservative writers like Swift and Johnson." In his preface, Lowth does indeed observe that Swift "is one of our most correct, and perhaps our very best prose writer" (1762: ii), but Swift does not appear to have been Lowth's model of correctness, and Johnson wasn't either. Lowth appears to have had a kind of corpus of example sentences at his disposal when he wrote his grammar, which consisted of grammatical errors committed by "our best Authors . . . [who] have sometimes fallen into mistakes, and been guilty of palpable errors in point of Grammar" (1762: ix). These errors are discussed in the notes to the grammar, and the following, randomly selected, example illustrates Lowth's working method:

> [Main text] In English [adverbs] admit of no Variation; except some few of them, which have the degrees of Comparison: as "often, oftener, oftenest;" "soon, sooner, soonest."
>
> "Was the *easilier* persuaded." – Raleigh, "The things *highliest* important to the growing age." Lord Shaftesbury, Letter to Lord Molesworth. Improperly, for *more easily, most highly.* (1762: 91–2)

About forty or fifty similar grammatical items are discussed in the footnotes (see Appendix 21.1). The index of names which I compiled in order to find out which authors were most criticized by Lowth in the first edition of his grammar (see Tieken-Boon van Ostade 1997: 461–3) shows that Swift features most prominently among those who were put to the pillory in the grammar (1997: 452). This provoked the following comment from Melmoth in a letter to Dodsley, dated November 20, 1759: "I was pleased to find [i.e. in the manuscript of Lowth's grammar which Melmoth had been asked to read critically] several instances of gross inaccuracies produced from Swift: a writer w^{m}. I have always looked upon as enjoying a reputation much higher than he deserves, in many respects" (Tierney 1988: 429). Despite Lowth's comment in the Preface relating to Swift's alleged excellence, close scrutiny of Swift's actual usage apparently proved otherwise, and Swift came to feature in the grammar itself as a negative example, who was not to be imitated in many points of usage. As for Johnson serving as Lowth's model of correctness as Finegan suggests, the index shows that Johnson is only referred to twice in the grammar, and in neither case to illustrate a grammatical mistake. This does not, however, put him into Lowth's category of "best Authors," for Lowth refers to Johnson only as a source to back up his own condemnation of a particular usage (1762: 43, 147). According to Percy (1997: 134), by the time the grammar was published, all Lowth's "best Authors" were dead. Perhaps Lowth decided not to expose living writers such as Johnson out of delicacy; but he doesn't praise his language as an example worth following either. Johnson, then, was used only as a scholarly source.

21.4 Normative Grammar Writing

Lowth's approach was essentially proscriptive, and it is this approach to grammar which, according to Hussey (1995: 154), the modern reader appears to find most offensive in him. The opposite of this approach, prescriptivism, is, as I have indicated above, usually leveled against the early grammarians as the main point of criticism, as these days the only acceptable approach in linguistics is considered to be a descriptive one. Consequently, Biber et al. (1998: 55) note that "unlike lexicography, grammar does not have a long tradition of empirical study." This quotation refers to the fact that "as early as 1755 . . . Johnson used a corpus of texts to gather authentic uses of words, which he then included as examples in his dictionary of English" (Biber et al. 1998: 21–2). I have already shown that Lowth, too, "gathered authentic uses of words": they were examples of grammatical mistakes, and perhaps all the more authentic for being so. These examples were evidently collected at random, for in his preface, he wrote: "The examples . . . given are such as occurred in reading, without any very curious or methodical examination: and they might easily have been much increased in number by any one, who had leisure or phlegm enough to have gone through a regular course of reading with this particular view" (1762: ix). Lowth evidently believed his corpus to be representative of actual usage. He was, moreover, by no means the only or even the first eighteenth-century grammarian who worked with a corpus: there are at least four other grammarians after the year 1760 who did so, too: White (1761), Ward (1765) (Tieken-Boon van Ostade 2000c), Baker (1770), and Fogg (1792/1796) (Tieken-Boon van Ostade 1990: 486–7; see also Wright 1994: 244). Taking an empirical, corpus-based approach appears to have been an eighteenth-century innovation, which arose around the middle of the period, and this idea possibly originated from the example of Johnson's dictionary. Contrary to what Biber et al. suggest, therefore, grammars have as long an empirical tradition as dictionaries, but this is obscured by the fact that eighteenth-century grammars are usually characterized as prescriptive, which presupposes the opposite.

Both a prescriptive and a proscriptive approach, in contrast to a purely descriptive one, characterize a grammar as normative, and eighteenth-century grammars may consequently be characterized as such. But even normative grammars are rarely entirely pre- or proscriptive in nature: as a result of my analysis of periphrastic *do* in eighteenth-century English, I found that most grammarians in one way or another are concerned with actual usage, though it is not always contemporary usage. Rodríguez Gil (2002) similarly describes Ann Fisher's grammar as "a blend of prescriptive and descriptive language analysis." The only criticism that might still legitimately be leveled at the grammarians from a structuralist perspective is that their approach was not systematically descriptive, and that their primary aim was normative. But the latter was expected of them by their reading public.

If normative grammarians were also to some extent descriptive in their approach to grammar, the question arises as to whose norm of usage they based themselves on. According to Leonard (1929: 169), the grammarians and rhetoricians of the eighteenth century focused on the language of gentlemen in order to decide what was grammatically correct and what was not, but the case of Lowth suggests that the situation must have been more complicated that that. Swift's language, for instance, apparently did not serve as an example to him. The author most criticized after Swift in the grammar is Addison (Tieken-Boon van Ostade 1997: 452): according to Wright (1994), Addison set a norm of correctness during much of the eighteenth century, but Lowth did not uphold him as an example of good usage either. Furthermore, it is argued by Finegan (1992: 124) that Lowth's own usage conflicted with the rule in his grammar according to which a preposition should not be "separated from the Relative which it governs, and joined to the Verb at the end of the Sentence, or of some member of it: as, 'Horace is an author, whom I am much delighted with.' 'The world is too well bred to shock authors with a truth, which generally their booksellers are the first that inform them of' " (1762: 127–8). But, Finegan adds, evidently surprised by the fact, "in the very sentence in which he says, 'This is an idiom which our language is strongly inclined to,' he uses the colloquial idiom himself, not the pied-piping he is recommending in [his grammar]."

Lowth's own usage is thus in conflict with the grammatical rules in his own grammar, and this appears to be confirmed by similar examples found in his private letters, such as (italics added):

(1) as I shall refer him to you for the Business above treated *of* (copy of a letter to Chapman, not in Lowth's own hand, September 11, 1756; BL Add. MS. 4297, ff. 66–7)

(2) I shall otherwise have no Copy to correct *by* (to R. Dodsley; February 24, 1758; Tierney 1988: 346)

(3) The uncertainty M^r^. Spence was *under* ab^t^. publishing the Drawings (letter to J. Dodsley, December 9, 1767; BL Add. MSS 35,339, f. 37)

(4) & what y^e^. Purchase of her Annuity will come *to* (Lowth to Ridley, September 17, 1768; Joseph Spence Papers, OSB MSS 4, Box 1, Folder 20, letter 4)

(5) such as You have given me a specimen *of* (letter to Woide, December 9, 1776; BL Add. MS. 48707, f. 66)

This is also true for other grammatical constructions, such as the use of forms like *wrote* as a past participle, *you was* rather than *you were,* and of *be* for *have* with mutative intransitive verbs (Tieken-Boon van Ostade 2002a, 2002b, 2002c). See, for instance (italics added):

(6) Old William, after having happily *drove* us to Town with great spirit, sett us down at . . . (Lowth to his wife, 1755, Bodleian Library, MS Eng. Lett. C572 f. 1)

(7) till I knew *you was* acquainted with the present situation of our affairs (Lowth to his wife, July 6, 1755, Bodleian Library, MS Eng. Lett. C572 f. 54)

(8) Your Letter of the 26th. *is* just *come* to my hands (Lowth to his wife, October 31, 1755; Bodleian, MS Eng. Lett. C572 f. 120^r^)

All these examples speak against Aitchison's claim that Lowth's "strictures were based on his own preconceived notions" (1981: 25; see above): Lowth evidently based his grammatical norm neither on his own language, nor on that of writers like Swift and Addison or any of those he criticized in his grammar.

21.5 Lowth's Linguistic Norm

What, then, did Lowth base his norm on? To find an answer to this question, we may begin by looking at his correspondence with Robert Dodsley, his publisher, which contains several instances of hypercorrection, such as (italics added):

(9) The Appendix I suppose you will print on a *less* Letter (Lowth to Robert Dodsley, February 24, 1758; Tierney 1988: 346)

(10) We have lost our good Friend D^{r}. Chapman, *than whom no man had better pretensions to long life* (Lowth to Robert Dodsley, June 19, 1760; Tierney 1988: 440).

In the first sentence Lowth used *less* instead of *lesser*, because he knew from Johnson's dictionary that *lesser*, as a double comparative, was wrong (Johnson 1755, s.v. *less*). He even quoted Johnson on this stricture in his grammar: "*Lesser*, says Mr. Johnson, is a barbarous corruption of *Less*, formed by the vulgar from the habit of terminating comparisons in *er*" (1762: 43, note). *Lesser*, however, as the opposite of *greater*, has a different meaning as well, in which case the word would have been correct in the context of example (9). As for the second sentence, grammatically speaking it is entirely correct, but at the same time it is so formal, due to its extreme grammatical correctness, that it seems out of place in the informal language of the correspondence between Lowth and Dodsley. That Postlethwaite ridiculed precisely this construction in the sentence quoted at the beginning of this chapter confirms that the construction was probably not in common use at the time. So we have here one example of grammatical hypercorrection and one of style-shift, which might be regarded as a kind of stylistic hypercorrection.

The sentences date from 1758 and 1760, the time when Lowth was working on his grammar. It seems as if in these letters he was doing his very best to produce grammatically correct sentences, even when writing to a close friend like Dodsley. Perhaps he was trying to show off linguistically to Dodsley, who had commissioned him to write the grammar (see Tieken-Boon van Ostade 2000a). At the same time, an over-careful usage such as that illustrated by examples (9) and (10) is characteristic of people who are sociolinguistically self-conscious, social climbers for instance (see Cameron and Coates 1985: 144). Lowth's career in the church was indeed characterized by a strong social mobility (see Hepworth 1978: 15), and the movements which were the consequence of his mobility in the church made him geographically mobile, too: after he had been Archdeacon of Winchester, he became Chaplain to the Lord Lieutenant of Ireland, Canon at Durham, Bishop of St. David's (though he never went to stay there), Bishop of Oxford, and, finally, Bishop of London. People who are socially and geographically mobile are of great interest from the perspective of social network analysis, because they usually abound in weak ties and may therefore function as bridges between different social networks along which linguistic change may travel. According to the model presented in Milroy (1987), Lowth therefore may have been a linguistic innovator, and he may consequently have been instrumental in introducing linguistic changes into the social networks he belonged to. This makes Lowth an interesting object for analysis in his own right, i.e. as a speaker and writer who was also a normative grammarian, and this is how I will discuss him in the remainder of this chapter. By looking at his own language I will try to answer the question of what kind of people served as the linguistic model for his grammar, and in order to do so I will first look at the social networks he belonged to.

21.6 Lowth's Social Networks

Lowth's social networks can be reconstructed by analyzing his private correspondence with a view to discovering who he wrote to, how well acquainted he was with his correspondents and what they wrote about. Unfortunately, there is no edition of his letters yet: only his correspondence with Robert Dodsley has appeared in print so far (Tierney 1988) as well as some of letters to his brother and successor James Dodsley (Tieken-Boon van Ostade 2001). The Dodsleys, who were running a publishing business, evidently kept files of the correspondence with their authors, so that quite a few letters by Lowth addressed to either of them, and some vice versa, have come down to us. Besides these, there are many more letters, and so far I have located 265 letters, 197 written by Lowth and 68 addressed to him; in addition, there is his correspondence in Latin with Johann David Michaelis (1717–91) from Göttingen, who published a German edition of his *De sacra poesie Hebraeorum* (1763), as well as some other letters in Latin and some in French. These letters will not concern me any further here.

Collecting the letters is an ongoing process, and the research for the present chapter is based on my transcription of about two-thirds of the letters I have located. The letters transcribed are listed in table 21.1. Apart from the Dodsleys and Mary Jackson, Lowth's wife, most of these people are either members of the aristocracy or people connected with the church. After he became a bishop, Lowth would have come into contact with a lot of people from the higher social classes; and the letters already analyzed suggest that Lowth had a strong social consciousness.

Lowth's circle of acquaintances thus consisted of highly placed people, whom he addressed very politely, as in (11):

(11) I beg Your Grace to be assured, that in all times & seasons I shall always embrace with the greatest pleasure every occasion of testifying the Respect & Gratitude, with which I am most sincerely & ardently, / My Lord, / Your Grace's / Most Obliged & / Obedient humble Servt. / R. St. Davids (Lowth to the Duke of Newcastle, July 31, 1766; BL Add. MS. 32,976, ff. 358–9)

Table 21.1 Lowth's correspondents

Correspondent	*Out-letters*	*In-letters*
Beattie, James		1
Carmarthen, Lord	1	
Chapman, Thomas (this letter is not in Lowth's own hand)	1	
Dalrymple, Sir David	14	
Dodsley, James	13	
Dodsley, Robert	17	1
Hardwicke, second Lord	1	
Jackson, Mary (Mrs Lowth)	63	
Jenkinson, C.		1
Johnson, Samuel		1
Liverpool, first Earl of	2	
Morant, P.	2	2
Newcastle, Duke of	3	2
Percy, Bishop	2	
Ridley, Gloster	23	
Warburton, William	8	6
Warton, Thomas	1	1
Woide, W.	4	
Unknown correspondents	2	
Total	*157*	*15*

but also of people like Robert Dodsley, with whom he stood on a more intimate footing:

(12) My Wife is, I thank God, perfectly well, & desires her Comp[ts]. to You. / Believe me ever, / Dear S[r]. / Your most affectionate / humble serv[t]. / R. Lowth. (Lowth to Robert Dodsley, June 19, 1760; Tierney 1988: 440).

On the basis of the forms of address he adopted in his letters and the personal comments he made in them (cf. Tieken-Boon van Ostade 1999, 2003), the people he was most intimate with can be identified as Robert Dodsley (but not James Dodsley), Gloster Ridley, Thomas Chapman, and Bishop Percy. Some distinguishing features of a close relationship are his passing on his wife's greetings to the correspondent in question and the use of the word *affectionate(ly)* as part of the closing formula, as in example (12). On the basis of the contents of the letters, a closed network cluster can be identified consisting of Robert Dodsley, Lowth, Joseph Spence (1699–1768), and (possibly) William Shenstone (1714–63). Lowth also appears to have been friendly with James Harris (1709–80), the author of *Hermes* (1751) (though I have not yet come across any letters between them). With neither Beattie nor Johnson did Lowth form a closed network cluster: in the only letter I have found from James Beattie, the author formally introduced himself to Lowth, and the one from Dr. Johnson, which dates from 1780, is a formal request for mediation in the preferment of an acquaintance. In the reply to the letter, according to the editor of Johnson's correspondence, Lowth "courteously, but emphatically rejected this . . . plea for ordination" (Redford 1992–4: 287n.). In his capacity of Bishop of London, Lowth must have received a lot of letters like this.

All this suggests that Lowth did indeed have many loose ties with people from a variety of social networks; many of these people were highly placed, but he also belonged to at least one closed network cluster consisting of less highly placed people such as Robert Dodsley. The letters also suggest that there was at the time no network, however loosely knit, consisting of what might be called linguists – lexicographers and grammarians. Johnson and Lowth knew of each other's work and referred to it in their own (Nagashima 1968), but they do not seem to have known each other personally, despite the fact that both men were friends of Robert Dodsley's and that both regularly visited his shop. Lowth's networks were scholarly and ecclesiastical in nature, while Johnson's were more literary. In Dodsley the networks touched, but they evidently did not overlap.

21.7 Lowth's Own Language

As shown, Lowth's private writings did not always follow his own prescriptions; what is more, his language also came in for criticism from other eighteenth-century grammarians, as appears from a list drawn up by Sundby et al. (1991: 35–7): interestingly, the list is headed by Swift (see above) with 224 citations, and it includes Johnson (26 citations), Melmoth (23), Harris (21), Warburton (11), Shenstone (9), and Dodsley (5), just to mention some authors who belonged to Lowth's social network. Lowth occupies fifty-third position among the authors who were most criticized, with six citations. To find out how Lowth's usage would have rated in his own eyes, I have selected one of his own strictures, the one which for some reason or other has been the focus of attack from modern linguists, i.e. the preposition at the end of the sentence (e.g. Finegan 1992: 124; Crystal 1995: 79). The full stricture reads as follows:

> The Preposition is often separated from the Relative which it governs, and joined to the Verb at the end of the Sentence, or of some member of it: as, "Horace is an author, *whom* I am much delighted *with*." "The world is too well bred to shock authors with a truth, *which* generally their booksellers are the first that inform them *of*." This is an Idiom which our language is strongly inclined to; it prevails in common conversation, and suits very well with the familiar style in writing; but the placing of the Preposition before the Relative is more graceful, as well as more perspicuous; and agrees much better with the solemn and elevated Style. (1762: 127–8)

I have already mentioned that in referring to this rule Finegan appeared quite surprised that Lowth "offended" against his own rule. But stranded prepositions also occur in his private letters, as examples (1–5) have already illustrated. These instances, and others like them, however, only occur in letters to less highly placed persons and to people he was friendly with. In the light of Biber's factor analysis (1988), such instances should not be regarded as grammatical mistakes but as characteristic of a more "involved" style, Lowth's "familiar style in writing" as he called it himself (see above). An analysis of his spelling has likewise shown that his use of nonstandard forms of spelling correlated with the nature of his relationship with the addressee: the closer the relationship, the more nonstandard spellings were found (Tieken-Boon van Ostade 2003). That stranded prepositions – and nonstandard spellings – do not appear in his formal letters shows that Lowth knew perfectly well how to distinguish between formal and informal styles of writing. Consequently, I believe that the alleged "error" in the grammar relating to his use of a stranded preposition to illustrate his stricture against it, i.e. "This is an Idiom which our language is strongly inclined to" (see above), must be reinterpreted as a joke! It is the kind of joke purists enjoy making, such as "a preposition is a word you cannot end a sentence with," or "this is something up with which I will not put." These days, such jokes are no longer considered funny, perhaps because they are too forced or because of the dubious reputation of prescriptive grammar in the eyes of modern linguists. But Lowth comes at the beginning of the prescriptive tradition, and he must have taken a huge delight in his joke. Postlethwaite's parody of the "Exercises of Bad English" suggests that he would have appreciated the joke, despite his criticism of grammarians like Lowth.

What I found with respect to a number of other rules when I checked them against Lowth's own language, i.e. the use of past-tense forms such as *wrote* for past participles, the use of the *be/have* periphrasis with mutative intransitive verbs, and the use of *you was* rather than *you were* (Tieken-Boon van Ostade 2002a, 2002b, 2002c), confirms this picture: Lowth "offends" against the rules only in letters to less highly placed persons, or, in other words, in his more informal, "involved" styles. His letters to more elevated members of society are characterized by a very formal style, and their language, by his own norms in particular, is always scrupulously correct. I therefore want to propose that the linguistic norm which lies at the basis of his grammar was not intended to reflect the language of eighteenth-century gentlemen, as Leonard suggested, but what Lowth, being a member of the middle classes himself, perceived to be the language of the social class above him. In other words, Lowth's norm of correctness is not a middle-class but an upper-class norm, such as he perceived that norm to be. I have encountered the same phenomenon in the language of Richardson (1689–1761), whose use of periphrastic *do* in his novels was unusual for its time and seems to reflect the way in which he believed the higher social classes spoke (Tieken-Boon van Ostade 1991a: 52–3). The same thing is found with two other eighteenth-century authors, the poet John Gay (1685–1732) and the playwright Richard Sheridan (1751–1816) (Tieken-Boon van Ostade 1999, 1991b). All three men wished to associate with the aristocracy, and seem to have tried to do so by adopting the aristocracy's linguistic norm.

What these men, Lowth included, have in common is that they were all socially ambitious: they all wished to belong to the highest regions of society. In the terms of social network analysis, they were outsiders with respect to the social network to which they aspired; they were people with many loose ties, and as such they were possible candidates for the role of linguistic innovator. Lowth, as a grammarian, was a linguistic innovator *par excellence*: he adopted a norm – alien to his own private usage, but one which carried social prestige, in his own eyes as well as in those of his social peers – which he put down in his grammar, and which subsequently had an enormous influence. The impact of his grammar, therefore, was not due to his position in society as Aitchison suggests, but to the fact that the grammar supplied a particular demand. Its reading public consisted of those who wished to have a firm or firmer footing among the upper gentry, and one way of doing so was by adopting the linguistic norm of its members. To be associated with the common people, or "the vulgar" as they were referred to (see above), by using a stigmatized form like *lesser* was to be avoided at all costs, even by Lowth himself, as example (9) shows. There was nothing similar to Lowth's grammar on the London market at the time, though the book was very likely also pushed by the publishers, the Dodsley brothers and Andrew Millar. The grammar was their project to begin with, and they had most to gain by good sales.

21.8 Conclusion

Prescriptive grammarians and their grammars have generally suffered from a lack of scholarly interest. Primarily, this is due to their linguistic approach, which differs fundamentally from that of modern, structural linguists. These differences in approach have been responsible for persistent prejudice and preconceptions concerning the aims and intentions of the normative grammarians. In this chapter I have focused on Lowth and his grammar, and I have shown that by studying the grammar in the light of its author's personal background a better insight is obtained into, particularly, the norm that formed the basis of his grammar. Lowth's approach is primarily proscriptive. By comparing his rules with his own usage, especially that found in his private correspondence, it has moreover been possible to identify the norm he put forward in his grammar as one which represented neither his own language nor that of his peers, but that of the social classes higher up on the social scale. Lowth was socially ambitious, and this is reflected in his letters to people who represented his social superiors: the language in these letters closely conforms to the rules he had presented in his own grammar. Lowth's grammar was so popular because it gave its readers exactly what they were looking for, a respected norm to imitate if they wished to improve their position in society.

In this chapter I have concentrated on Lowth and his search for a linguistic norm, but other prescriptive grammarians deserve closer attention, too, such as Ash, already referred to, Buchanan, who wrote three grammars (1753, 1762, and 1767) and Lady Eleanor Fenn, author of *The Child's Grammar* (1799) and *The Mother's Grammar* (1798?), to name but a few (see, further, Alston 1965). Fenn's grammars were enormously popular, and they must have influenced the language of many people. Further analysis of grammars such as these as well as of the phenomenal number of grammars published in the century afterwards (cf. Michael 1991) will enable us to acquire greater insight into the principles which lay at the basis of the prescriptive grammatical tradition, and to understand why the grammatical rules formulated at the time have continued to be at odds with actual practice. For despite what Lowth and others after him prescribed or proscribed, a sentence like

(13) The dream-lit world they provided her a glimpse *of* was magical. (Donna Tartt, *The Little Friend* (2002). New York: Alfred A. Knopf, p. 41; italics added)

is nowadays more common and generally considered more appropriate – except by inveterate purists – than its pied-piping counterpart *of which they provided her a glimpse*. The same applies to the "than whom" construction associated with Lowth by Postlethwaite, of which the entire British National Corpus (consulted in November 2002) contains no more than five instances. What we will end up with as a result is a clearer picture of how and why actual usage continued to differ from the norm which was imposed upon the language by the prescriptive grammarians of the eighteenth century and beyond.

APPENDIX 21.1: LOWTH'S NORMATIVE STRICTURES

The following is an alphabetical list of Lowth's proscriptive comments as they occur in the footnotes in the first edition of his grammar (1762).

- Adjectives used as adverbs (pp. 124–5)
- *As*
  instead of relative *that* or *which* (pp. 151–2)
  improperly omitted, e.g. *so bold to pronounce* (p. 152)
- *Be* for *have* with mutative intransitive verbs (p. 63)
- *Because* expressing motive or end (instead of *that*) (pp. 93–4)
- *Do*: scope in the sentence, e.g. *Did he not fear and besought . . .* (p. 117)
- *His* for *its* (pp. 34–5)
- Double comparatives
  Lesser (p. 43)
  Worser (p. 43)

- Wrong degrees of comparison (*easilier, highliest*) (p. 91)
- *Fly* for *flee* (p. 77)
- *-ing* form
  him descending vs. *he descending* (pp. 107–8)
  the sending to them the light (pp. 111–13)
- *It is I*
  Whom for *who* (p. 106)
- *Lay* for *lie* (p. 76)
- *Let* with subject pronoun, e.g. *let thee and I* (p. 117)
- Mood: consistent use (pp. 119–20)
- *Neither* sometimes included in *nor* (pp. 149–50)
- *Never so* (p. 147)
- *Not* before finite (p. 116)
- Nouns of multitude with plural finite (p. 104)
- Past participle forms (pp. 86–8)
  Sitten (pp. 75–6)
  Chosed (p. 76)
- Pronominalization/relativization problems (pp. 138–41)
- Relative clause dangling (p. 124)
- Relative and preposition omitted, e.g. *in the posture I lay* (p. 137)
- *So . . ., as* for *so . . ., that* (pp. 150–1)
- Subject
  lacking, e.g. *which it is not lawful to eat* (pp. 110; 122–4)
  superfluous after *who* (p. 135)
- Tense: consistent use (pp. 117–19)
- *Than* with pronoun following (pp. 144–7)
- *That* including *which*: *of that [which] is moved* (p. 134)
- *That* (conj.)
  improperly accompanied by the subjunctive (p. 143)
  omitted (p. 147)
- *This means/these means/this mean* (p. 120)
- *To* superfluous, e.g. *to see him to do it* (p. 109)
- Verb forms
  Subjunctive verbs in the Indicative (*wert* for *wast*) (p. 52)
  Thou might for *thou mightest* (pp. 97, 136)
  I am the Lord that maketh . . . : first person subject with third person finite in relative clause (p. 136)
- *Thou* for *you* (p. 49)
- *Who*
  Whom for *who* in subject position (p. 97)
  Who for *whom* in object position (pp. 99, 127)
  Whose as the possessive of *which* (p. 38)
  Who used for *as*, e.g. *no man so sanguine who did not apprehend* (*. . . so sanguine as to . . .*) (p. 152)
- *Woe is me* (p. 132); *ah me* (p. 153)

- *Ye* for *you* in object position (pp. 33–4)
- *You was* (pp. 48–9)
- Various:
  "Improper use of the Infinitive" (p. 111)
  Sentences "abounding" with adverbs (p. 127)
  "Improper" use of prepositions (pp. 129–31)
  "Disused in common discourse": *whereunto, whereby, thereof, therewith* (p. 131)
  Improperly used: *too . . . , that, too . . . , than, so . . . , but* (pp. 152–3).

REFERENCES

Primary sources

Ash, John (1760). *Grammatical Institutes: Or, Grammar Adapted to the Genius of the English Tongue*. Worcester. 4th edn. repr. in facs. by Alston (1974); EL 9.

Baker, Robert (1770). *Reflections on the English Language*. London. Repr. in facs. by Alston (1974); EL 87.

Buchanan, James (1753). *The Complete English Scholar*. London.

Buchanan, James (1762). *The British Grammar*. London.

Buchanan, James (1767). *A Regular English Syntax*. London.

Fenn, Lady Eleanor (1798?). *The Mother's Grammar*. London.

Fenn, Lady Eleanor (1799). *The Child's Grammar*. London.

Fisher, Ann ([1745] 1750). *A New Grammar*. Newcastle upon Tyne. 2nd edn. Repr. in facs. by Alston (1974); EL 130.

Fogg, Peter Walkden (1792/1796). *Elementa Anglicana*. Stockport. Repr. in facs. by Alston (1974); EL 251.

Johnson, Samuel (1755). *A Dictionary of the English Language*. London. Repr. in facs. Hildesheim: Georg Olms Verlagsbuchhandlung.

Lowth, Robert (1762 [1763]). *A Short Introduction to English Grammar*. London. Repr. in facs. by Alston (1974); EL 18; 2nd edn. 1763.

Murray, Lindley (1795). *English Grammar*. York. Repr. in facs. by Alston (1974); EL 106.

Postlethwaite, Richard (1795). *The Grammatical Art Improved: In Which the Errors of Grammarians and Lexicographers Are Exposed*. London.

Ward, William (1765). *Essay on Grammar*. London. Repr. in facs. by Alston (1974); EL 15.

White, James (1761). *The English Verb*. London. Repr. in facs. by Alston (1974); EL 135.

Secondary sources

Aitchison, Jean (1981). *Language Change: Progress or Decay?* (repr. 1984). Bungay, Suffolk: Richard Clay (The Chaucer Press).

Alston, R. C. (1965). *A Bibliography of the English Language from the Invention of Printing to the Year 1800* (vol. 1). Leeds: Arnold and Son.

Alston, R. C. (1974). *English Linguistics 1500–1800*. Menston: Scolar Press.

Biber, Douglas (1988). *Variation Across Speech and Writing* (repr. 1991). Cambridge: Cambridge University Press.

Biber, Douglas, Susan Conrad, and Randi Reppen (1998). *Corpus Linguistics: Investigating Language*

Structure and Use. Cambridge: Cambridge University Press.

Cameron, Deborah and Jennifer Coates (1985). Some problems in the sociolinguistic explanation of sex differences. *Language and Communication* 5: 143–51.

Crystal, David (1995). *The Cambridge Encyclopedia of the English Language*. Cambridge: Cambridge University Press.

Finegan, Edward (1992). Style and standardization in England: 1700–1900. In Tim William Machan and Charles T. Scott (eds.), *English in its Social Contexts* (pp. 103–30). New York and Oxford: Oxford University Press.

Finegan, Edward (1998). English grammar and usage. In Suzanne Romaine (ed.), *The Cambridge History of the English Language*. Vol. IV: *1776–1997*. Cambridge: Cambridge University Press.

Freeborn, Dennis (1992). *From Old English to Standard English*. Basingstoke: Macmillan.

Görlach, Manfred (2001). *Eighteenth-century English*. Heidelberg: Universitätsverlag C. Winter.

Hepworth, Brian (1978). *Robert Lowth*. Boston: Twayne.

Hussey, Stanley (1995). *The English Language: Structure and Development*. London and New York: Longman.

Leonard, S. A. (1929). *The Doctrine of Correctness in English Usage, 1700–1800*. Madison: University of Wisconsin Press.

McArthur, Tom (1992). *Oxford Companion to the English Language*. Oxford: Oxford University Press.

Michael, Ian (1991). More than enough English grammars. In Gerhard Leitner (ed.), *English Traditional Grammars* (pp. 11–26). Amsterdam: Benjamins.

Milroy, Lesley (1987). *Language and Social Networks* (2nd edn.; repr. 1989). Oxford: Blackwell.

Nagashima, Daisuke (1968). Mutual debt between Johnson and Lowth: a contribution to the history of English grammar. *Studies in English Literature* (Japan) 44: 221–32.

Nietz, John A. (1961). *Old Textbooks*. Pittsburgh: University of Pittsburgh Press.

Percy, Carol (1997). Paradigms lost: Bishop Lowth and the "poetic dialect" in his English Grammar. *Neophilologus* 81: 129–44.

Pullum, Geoffrey (1974). Lowth's grammar: a re-evaluation. *Linguistics* 137: 63–78.

Redford, Bruce (ed.) (1992–4). *The Letters of Samuel Johnson* (5 vols., vol. 3). Oxford: Clarendon Press.

Rodríguez Gil, María (2002). Ann Fisher: first female grammarian. *Historical Sociolinguistics and Sociohistorical Linguistics* 2. Available at: http://www.let.leidenuniv.nl/hsl_shl/ (→ contents → articles).

Sledd, James (1959). *A Short Introduction to English Grammar*. Chicago: Scott, Foresman.

Subbiondo, Joseph L. (1975). William Ward and the Doctrine of Correctness. *Journal of English Linguistics* 9: 36–46.

Stammerjohann, Harro (gen. ed.) (1996). *Lexicon Grammaticorum: Who's Who in the History of World Linguistics*. Tübingen: Niemeyer.

Sundby, Bertil, Anne Kari Bjørge, and Kari E. Haugland (1991). *A Dictionary of English Normative Grammar*. Amsterdam: Benjamins.

Tieken-Boon van Ostade, Ingrid (1982). Double negation and eighteenth-century English grammars. *Neophilologus* 66: 278–85.

Tieken-Boon van Ostade, Ingrid (1987). *The Auxiliary Do in Eighteenth-century English: A Sociohistorical Linguistic Approach*. Dordrecht: Foris.

Tieken-Boon van Ostade, Ingrid (1990). Exemplification in eighteenth-century English grammars. In Sylvia Adamson,

Vivien Law, Nigel Vincent, and Susan Wright (eds.), *Papers from the 5th International Conference on English Historical Linguistics* (pp. 481–96). Amsterdam: Benjamins.

Tieken-Boon van Ostade, Ingrid (1991a). Samuel Richardson's role as linguistic innovator: a sociolinguistic analysis. In Ingrid Tieken-Boon van Ostade and John Frankis (eds.), *Language, Usage and Description* (pp. 47–57). Amsterdam and Atlanta, GA: Rodopi.

Tieken-Boon van Ostade, Ingrid (1991b). Social ambition reflected in the language of Betsy and Richard Sheridan. *Neuphilologische Mitteilungen* 92: 237–46.

Tieken-Boon van Ostade, Ingrid (1997). Lowth's corpus of prescriptivism. In Terttu Nevalainen and Leena Kahlas-Tarkka (eds.), *To Explain the Present* (pp. 451–63). Helsinki: Société Néophilologique.

Tieken-Boon van Ostade, Ingrid (1999). Of formulas and friends: expressions of politeness in John Gay's letters. In Guy A. J. Tops, Betty Devriendt and Steven Geukens (eds.), *Thinking English Grammar: To Honour Xavier Dekeyser, Professor Emeritus* (pp. 99–112). Leuven and Paris: Peeters.

Tieken-Boon van Ostade, Ingrid (2000a). Robert Dodsley and the genesis of Lowth's *Short Introduction to English Grammar. Historiographia Linguistica* 27: 21–36.

Tieken-Boon van Ostade, Ingrid (2000b). Female grammarians of the eighteenth century. *Historical Sociolinguistics and Sociohistorical Linguistics* 1. Available at: http://www.let.leidenuniv.nl/hsl_shl/ (→ contents → articles).

Tieken-Boon van Ostade, Ingrid (2000c). Normative studies in England. In Sylvain Auroux, E. F. K. Koerner, Hans-Josef Niederehe, and Kees Versteegh (eds.), *History of the Language Sciences/Geschichte der Sprachwissenschaften/Histoire des sciences du langage* (pp. 876–87). Berlin and New York: Walter de Gruyter.

Tieken-Boon van Ostade, Ingrid (2001). Lowth's *Short Introduction to English Grammar* reprinted. *Publishing History* 49: 5–17.

Tieken-Boon van Ostade, Ingrid (2002a). Robert Lowth and the strong verb system. *Language Sciences* 24: 459–69.

Tieken-Boon van Ostade, Ingrid (2002b). *You was* and eighteenth-century normative grammar. In Katja Lenz and Ruth Möhlig (eds.), *Of Dyuersite & Chaunge of Langage: Essays Presented to Manfred Görlach on the Occasion of his 65th Birthday* (pp. 88–102). Heidelberg: C. Winter Universitätsverlag.

Tieken-Boon van Ostade, Ingrid (2002c). Robert Lowth and the Corpus of Early English Correspondence. In Helena Raumolin-Brunberg, Minna Nevala, Arja Nurmi, and Matti Rissanen (eds.), *Variation Past and Present. VARIENG Studies on English for Terttu Nevalainen* (pp. 161–72). Helsinki: Société Néophilologique.

Tieken-Boon van Ostade, Ingrid (2003). Lowth's language. In Marina Dossena and Charles Jones (eds.), *Insights into Late Modern English* (pp. 241–64). Bem: Peter Lang.

Tierney, James E. (1988). *The Correspondence of Robert Dodsley 1733–1764*. Cambridge: Cambridge University Press.

Vorlat, Emma (1959). The sources of Lindley Murray's "The English Grammar." *Leuvense Bijdragen* 48: 108–25.

Wright, Susan (1994). The critic and the grammarians: Joseph Addison and the prescriptivists. In Dieter Stein and Ingrid Tieken-Boon van Ostade (eds.), *Towards a Standard Language 1600–1800* (pp. 243–84). Berlin and New York: Mouton de Gruyter.

22 Historical Sociolinguistics and Language Change

TERTTU NEVALAINEN

22.1 Introduction: An Interdisciplinary Approach

Sociolinguistics was introduced into English historical linguistics in the early 1980s. The foundations for the new field of research were laid by Suzanne Romaine, who in her *Socio-historical Linguistics* (1982) applied sociolinguistic techniques to the study of relativization in mid-sixteenth-century Scots. She found that this methodology could be successfully extended to correlate linguistic variation with external factors in historical data. In Romaine's study, stylistic stratification emerged as a major factor in language maintenance and shift. In the 1990s, historical sociolinguists' research agenda diversified to comprise a wide range of issues including social and regional embedding in linguistic change. Connecting linguistic and external variation, historical sociolinguistics now works in tandem with historical dialectology.

What historical sociolinguistics adds to the study of English historical dialectology is systematic attention paid to the role of speaker variables in linguistic variation and change. These include factors such as the social status, education, gender, and age of the individuals and groups of people whose language is being investigated. The work naturally extends to the study of register variation and social networks, taking account of patterns of migration, regional variation, and dialect contact. Just as in studies of present speech communities, the domains of historical sociolinguistics and dialectology often overlap to the extent that it is not always meaningful to pigeonhole them by introducing strict disciplinary labels.

After introducing the material and methods used to study the changing English language in its social context (section 22.2), this chapter will focus on some basic historical sociolinguistic issues, including variation in the time courses, and register and social embedding of language changes in earlier English (section 22.3). The discussion will then move on to questions that may also be of more direct concern to those historical linguists who focus on linguistic change from a language-internal point of view, with transmission of language change across successive generations as one of the key issues (section 22.4.1). In sociolinguistic terms, this "transmission problem" can be formulated as a question of generational as opposed to communal change. Section 22.4 concludes by addressing two topic areas of interest to both English historical linguists and sociolinguists: gender differentiation in language change (22.4.2) and the status of English "vernacular universals" (22.4.3).

22.2 Empirical Foundations

22.2.1 Labov's paradoxes

William Labov (1972: 100; 1994: 11) identifies two particular problem areas for historical sociolinguistics. One is the **bad-data problem**, the fact that there is no spoken data available from earlier periods, and that even the written material that has come down to us has been preserved only sporadically. The other problem Labov calls the **historical paradox**: we know that the past was different from the present but we do not know how different. Both assertions are, of course, valid as such, but the first one is appropriate only if we expect sociolinguistic variation to manifest solely in speech and not in writing, and the second only if we completely ignore the long tradition of historical scholarship.

Romaine (1988: 1454) notes that the lack of spoken data does not prevent the reconstruction of language in its social context. Written material can and should be studied in its own right. Recent corpus-based research into English register variation has provided ways in which written and spoken texts can be compared in linguistic terms across time (Biber and Finegan 1989, 1997; Biber 2001). That personal letters, for instance, pattern more like conversation and drama than other written genres (such as fiction, essays, and medical and legal prose) is of direct relevance to historical sociolinguistic research.[1]

The historical paradox cannot be resolved without crossing discipline boundaries. Just like modern sociolinguists, who have close links with sociology, historical sociolinguists are informed by the research findings of other history disciplines, including social, cultural, demographic, and economic history (Nevalainen and Raumolin-Brunberg 1989, 2003: 30–43). Taking a relativist view of the social world, however, we may argue that studying the present also involves reconstructing vastly different speech communities. There is no one analysis, say, of social status differences that could be applied to all communities. In this respect the challenge of the past may be of different magnitude but not different in kind.

22.2.2 Material

It may not be too much of an exaggeration to say that the use of **corpora** has reoriented English historical linguistics in general, and that historical sociolinguistics has been made possible by this empirical reorientation in the field. Sociolinguistic research, modern and historical alike, requires that contextual information can be connected with the data to be analyzed. The extralinguistic information supplied by the annotation schemes and databases attached to historical corpora is basically of two kinds: stylistic and social. The emphasis selected by the corpus compilers has typically decided the **sampling unit** they have used. Those primarily interested in stylistic variation focus on **texts** as indicators of genres and registers, and those studying social variation base their corpora on **individuals** coming from different walks of life.

A number of electronic corpora have become available from the early 1990s onwards, enabling diachronic research into the history of English. One of the first was the *Helsinki Corpus of English Texts*, a 1.5 million-word corpus, which covers a millennium from the eighth to the eighteenth centuries. So as to allow genre and register comparisons across time, the corpus uses text as its sampling unit, the texts selected representing a range of established genres (Rissanen et al. 1993; Kytö 1996). They form a continuum of formality from statutes and other official documents to drama, fiction, and private correspondence. Regional dialects have also been taken into account within the text-based framework. Constructed on similar principles, the ARCHER Corpus (*A Representative Corpus of Historical English Registers*) covers the period from 1650 to 1990 and includes both British and, from 1750 onwards, American materials (Biber and Finegan 1997).

The different periods of English now all have their databases, ranging from the *Dictionary of Old English Corpus* to the *Corpus of Nineteenth-century English*. There are also text-based corpora focusing on regional varieties of English, such as the *Helsinki Corpus of Older Scots* (1450–1700) and the *Corpus of Irish English* (fourteenth to twentieth centuries) or on particular genres, such as the *Corpus of Early English Medical Writing* (1350–1800) and the *Lampeter Corpus of Early Modern English Tracts* (1640–1740).[2]

The diverse social contexts for language variation and change cannot be studied without large enough corpora compiled for this specific purpose. The sampling unit of these sociolinguistic corpora is the individual: data produced by persons coming from different social backgrounds. Corpora of this kind include the *Corpus of Early English Correspondence* (CEEC; 1410–1681), and its sampler version (CEECS) first published in 1998 (Nevalainen and Raumolin-Brunberg 1996, 2003; Nurmi 1998). The CEEC consists of 2.7 million words of personal letters written by 778 people, who represent the literate social section of the period reconstructed from material available in an edited form. As there is no shortage of unedited personal letters in libraries in Britain and elsewhere, we can expect the English historical sociolinguists' database to be considerably widened in the future. This is already in evidence, for instance, in the ongoing work on early American immigrant letters (Montgomery 1996) and Scottish correspondence (Meurman-Solin 2000).

22.2.3 *Methods*

Most of the studies carried out within different historical sociolinguistic frameworks use quantitative methods. Typically, they cross-tabulate the frequencies of the (linguistic) study variable and one or more independent external variables, such as real time or genre, or often both. These cross-tabulations can be used to show the time course of a linguistic change in progress, typically an S-shaped curve, which depicts how the incoming variant starts off as a rare form, then rapidly gathers momentum, but takes some time to become categorical (if it ever does; not all majority variants rule out all others). Figures 22.1 and 22.2 in section 22.3.2, below, illustrate typical S-curves (for more discussion of S-curves, see Denison 2003; Nevalainen and Raumolin-Brunberg 2003: 53–5).

The variationist methodology presupposes the construction of **linguistic variables**, alternative ways of saying the same thing. In many instances linguistic change may be thought of as involving choices between two or more equivalent expressions, and can therefore be analyzed in terms of linguistic variables. In modern sociolinguistic practice such competing and to all intents and purposes synonymous variables have proved to be easiest to construct in phonology and morphology, but certain complex structural patterns such as multiple negation (negative concord) have also been analyzed (e.g. Labov 2001). For English historical sociolinguistics, both for reasons of the available data sources and the changes that have taken place in the language, orthographic and morphosyntactic variation have to date proved to be the major areas of interest.

22.3 The Widening Scope of Research

Romaine (1982) applied statistical tools used by modern sociolinguists (variable rule analysis and implicational scales) to register differences in the distribution of relativizers in Middle Scots. Her results indicate that relative marker use was conditioned by register, the *th*-paradigm being particularly favored in informal texts and the *wh*-paradigm, to the extent it was used at all, in more official kinds of writing in the period 1530–50. Since the early 1990s, studies of the social embedding of language variation and change have diversified considerably, although register still has a central role to play in the research tradition. The next two sections place linguistic variation within the context of real time.

22.3.1 *Real time*

Access to the process of language change in real time is probably the single most obvious advantage that English historical sociolinguists have over their colleagues working with present-day data. For various reasons, the real-time variable has, however, attracted less systematic attention in recent years than it deserves. The earliest stages of a change in progress may be inaccessible to the researcher for lack of primary data. Although there are texts available from the latter half of the first millennium to the beginning of the third, they are scarce from the earliest periods: the entire corpus of Old English consists of only 3.5 million words. On the other hand, with long-term processes the periodization of the history of English into Old, Middle, and Modern English may also act as a mental barrier discouraging research across these conventional boundaries (Lass 2000).

In some cases, traditional boundaries do correlate with empirical facts. Reflexive pronouns, for instance, display a crossing-over pattern from simple pronouns to *-self* compounds around 1500 (Peitsara 1997: 289). But traditional period divisions can also mask nonlinear developments. So the boundary between Middle and Modern English at 1500 hides the nonlinear process of diffusion of the originally northern third person singular suffix *-(e)s* to the south: it is first attested in London in the latter half of the fifteenth century, but its progress is then halted for half a century, only to pick up in the latter half of the sixteenth century (Bailey et al. 1989; Nevalainen 2000; Nevalainen and Raumolin-Brunberg 2000).

The *Helsinki Corpus* subdivides into periods of one hundred or seventy years. But even shorter time spans may prove significant when linguistic changes are followed from inception to completion. The *Corpus of Early English Correspondence* makes it possible to subdivide the data flexibly into periods of different lengths. The work done on the CEEC has mostly used periods of twenty and forty years. It reveals that historical changes can be remarkably rapid. A case in point is the replacement of the subject form *ye* by the oblique form *you* in the data, illustrated by examples (1) and (2). They come from the correspondence of the Johnson family, wool merchants active in London, Calais, and Northamptonshire in the 1540s and 1550s.

(1) I praie you yf **ye** can, write me what the remayner of fellis is in Callais and what **ye** thincke of the markettes . . . (John Johnson, 1546; CEEC Johnson, 570)

(2) Mr. Douse is nowe at London for the same mater: if **you** spake with hym, **you** shall knowe all. (Sabine Johnson, 1545; CEEC Johnson, 245)

Figure 22.1 indicates that nothing much happens in the replacement process in the fifteenth century: the change is still in its incipient stage, the incoming form having a frequency below 10 percent of the cases. What follows in the next two forty-year periods is a steep rise in the incidence of *you*. The change, which presumably originated in the spoken language, was completed in eighty years in informal records such as personal letters. Leveling also took place in regional speech, although not as rapidly and completely as among the literate sections of early modern society. Wright (1905: 273) lists some nineteenth-century dialects with a *ye/you* distinction.

Rapid processes are not only witnessed in single-genre corpora based on individual informants, but they are also found in multigenre databases. Amy Devitt (1989) studied anglicization in Middle Scots, comparing five genres of

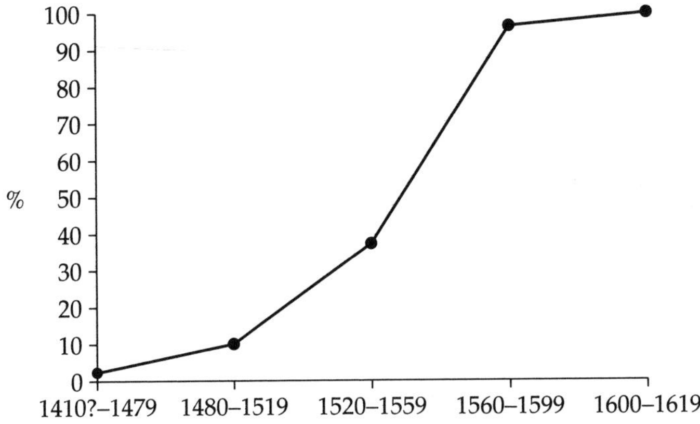

Figure 22.1 Replacement of subject *ye* by *you*: percentages of *you* (Nevalainen and Raumolin-Brunberg 2003: 60)

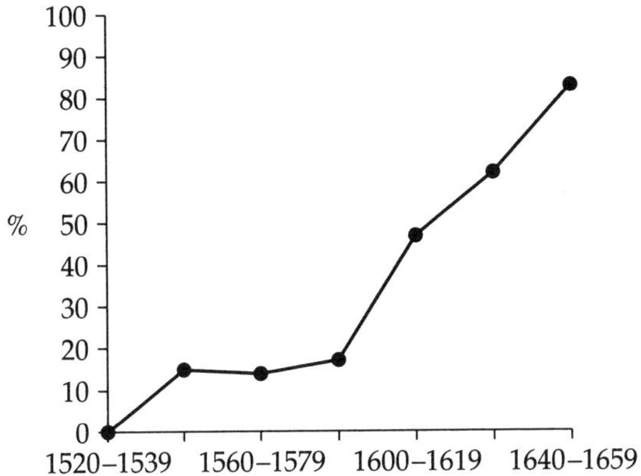

Figure 22.2 Anglicization of Scots relative markers by date: percentages of *wh*-forms (based on Devitt 1989: 18, 87)

writing. Figure 22.2 shows the spread of the southern *wh*-relatives (*which, whilk, who, where-*, and their variants), which replaced the native *quh*-forms (*quhilk, quha, quh-*, and their variants; Devitt 1989: 19).

Figures 22.1 and 22.2 both display quite regular S-shaped curves of diffusion. They do not tell us, however, whether the changes advanced steadily in all linguistic environments or whether they diffused from one linguistic context to another. Although the latter might have been a plausible manner of diffusion, especially with the relative markers in figure 22.2, this was not the

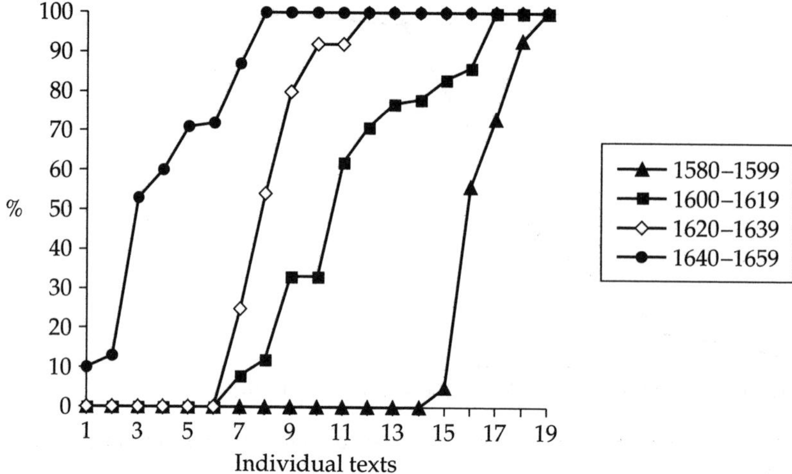

Figure 22.3 Anglicization of Scots relative markers in individual texts, 1580–1659: percentages of *wh*-forms (based on Devitt 1989: 42, 94)

case (Devitt 1989: 19–20). But as will appear in the following sections, both these S-curves do mask a good deal of extralinguistic variation.

Real-time variation in both text- and people-based corpora can also be analyzed in more detail by displaying each text or individual writer as a data point in successive periods. Figure 22.3 plots the frequency of the *wh*-forms in each text in the Middle Scots corpus in four subperiods (19 texts per period). Showing the range of variation within a given period, these four S-curves may also be viewed as **apparent-time** representations of the ongoing change (see also section 22.4.1).

Figure 22.3 indicates that except for subperiod 1600–19, when both forms were common, the majority of the texts in each subperiod displayed near-categorical usage, either *quh-* or *wh-* (Devitt 1989: 43). Similar findings were obtained by Meurman-Solin (1997: 204) for both interrogative and relative pronouns in Middle Scots. The fact that the pattern in figure 22.3 is the only one of its kind among the five processes studied by Devitt (1989) suggests that changes diffuse in various ways.

In the leveling of second person pronouns shown in figure 22.4, we find a good proportion of mixed usage in the first two subperiods but a sharp transition to categorical *you* in the last, 1560–79 (with each subperiod represented by 24 to 27 individuals). But the diffusion of *you* presents relatively fewer individuals with variable grammars (*ye* and *you* side by side) than some other changes in progress at the same time, such as the replacement of the relative pronoun *the which* by *which*, or of the third person suffix *-th* by *-s* (Nevalainen and Raumolin-Brunberg 2003: 97). The two processes will be discussed in more detail in the following sections.

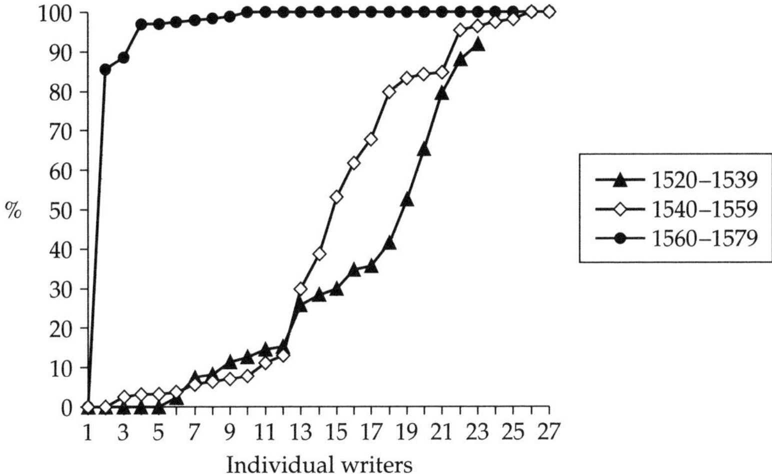

Figure 22.4 Generalization of subject *you* in individual writers, 1520–1579: percentages of *you* (based on Nevalainen and Raumolin-Brunberg 2003: 93, 101–3)

22.3.2 *Variation across genres*

With the appearance of multigenre corpora since the early 1990s, historical register variation has become one of the foci of scholarly attention. A number of studies have appeared cross-tabulating linguistic variables and register either diachronically or in a given time period. In these studies, **register** has often been used synonymously with **genre** or **text type**, all three usually defined in terms of situational rather than of linguistic criteria (Biber 1995: 9–10; Diller 2001: 24–31).

Real time and text type have both been charted in many studies using the *Helsinki Corpus of English Texts* and the ARCHER Corpus. One of the aims in this line of research is to correlate register variation with language change, distinguishing between changes that emanate from literate and learned genres as opposed to those diffusing from the colloquial, oral end of the genre continuum (see Biber 1995; Biber and Finegan 1997; Rissanen et al. 1997a, 1997b). In sociolinguistic terms the distinction often corresponds to **change from above** as opposed to **change from below** the level of conscious awareness (Labov 1994: 78).

The results obtained indicate that both kinds of change are in evidence. The replacement of the suffix *-th* by *-s* in the third person singular present indicative was an oral change: it appeared earlier in plays, private letters, and trial transcripts than in more literate texts in the south (Kytö 1993). Trial proceedings were similarly associated with the use of periphrastic *do* in affirmative declaratives in the sixteenth century (Rissanen 1991). On the other hand, many new conjunctions such as *provided (that)*, the rise of non-assertive *any*, and the

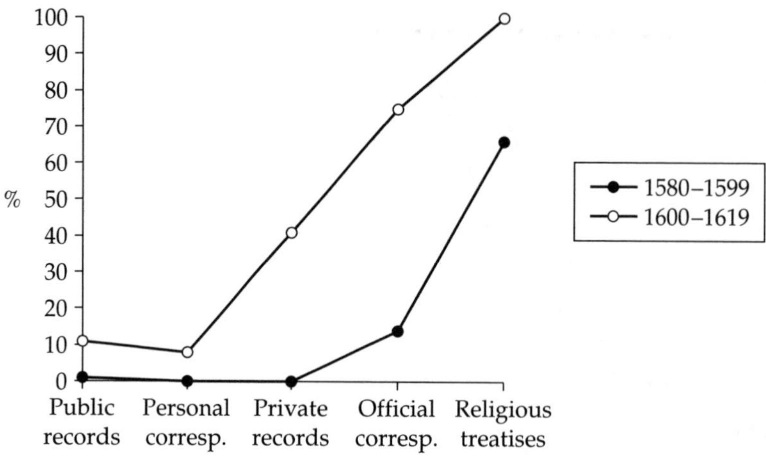

Figure 22.5 Anglicization of Scots relative markers across genres (real and apparent time): percentages of *wh*-forms (based on Devitt 1989: 61, 97)

disappearance of multiple negation (negative concord) in the fifteenth and early sixteenth centuries can be traced back to official documents (Rissanen 2000b: 125; Iyeiri 2002).

In terms of register, the anglicization processes in Middle Scots were also changes from above. Figure 22.5 shows the diffusion of the *wh*-relative markers across genres in two successive periods of time. The change is promoted by religious treatises and official correspondence. Scottish public records and private letters are the slowest to abandon local norms. The order of preference is repeated in the two periods, the five genres basically displaying the same apparent-time pattern in both.

However, it is not always possible to determine the directionality of a linguistic change in progress by means of a simple register analysis: the choice between the relative pronouns *which* and *the which*, for instance, displays more "disorderly" than "orderly" heterogeneity in this respect (Raumolin-Brunberg 2000: 221). Examples (3) and (4) come from letters exchanged by spouses.

(3) Victor hath gotten a byll of him **which** is signed by hys aunt, Joes Diricken's wyfe . . . (John Johnson, 1545; CEEC Johnson, 323)

(4) Your letter by Mr. Brudenell I have receyved, for **the which** I thancke you. (Sabine Johnson, 1545; CEEC Johnson, 266)

What looks like random variation may arise from the multidimensional nature of register variation, as the simple division of genres into oral and literate potentially oversimplifies register differences (Biber and Finegan 1997; Taavitsainen 1997; Biber 2001). Biber's statistical analyses reveal up to half a dozen interpretable dimensions of written and spoken genres (such as involved vs. informational production, narrative vs. non-narrative discourse, elaborated vs. situation-dependent reference, and abstract vs. non-abstract style), demonstrating that linguistic features can combine in varying proportions in different registers. Moreover, it is obvious that linguistic changes pattern along other parameters as well, typically the writer's domicile, education, social status, and gender (see sections 22.3.4 and 22.4.2).

Within one genre, such as personal correspondence, register variation may even have only a secondary role to play. In the case of the second person pronoun, register (defined in terms of the relationship between the writer and the addressee) did play a significant role when the change was in its early stages: the incoming form *you* was used among intimates, and the recessive form *ye* by more distant correspondents. However, in later stages the fact that *you* was favored in the capital region, and by women in particular, was more heavily weighted than its register associations (Nevalainen and Raumolin-Brunberg 2003: 194).

22.3.3 *Networks*

Sociolinguists often refer to **social network** differences when explaining why some communities maintain their linguistic norms while others more readily accept external influences (L. Milroy and Gordon 2003: 116–33). Historical sociolinguists applying a social-network approach are both privileged and disadvantaged; privileged in that they can work with real-time, macro-level comparisons, and disadvantaged because on the micro level they often lack the detailed ethnographic evidence necessary for constructing the historical networks relevant to transmitting linguistic influence (L. Milroy 2000: 219–20).

At the **macro level**, James and Lesley Milroy (1985: 377–9) contrast two Germanic languages, Icelandic and English, whose histories display vastly different rates of language change. Icelandic has largely retained its medieval morphological and phonological structures, while the faster rate of change in English has resulted in a phonologically very different, weakly inflected language.

It is suggested that these differences could be correlated with the strong network ties found in Iceland acting as a norm-enforcement mechanism, as opposed to the large-scale replacement of strong ties by weak ones in England beginning in the Old English period. A combination of external factors, such as the Scandinavian invasions and the Norman Conquest, contributed to the break-up of strong ties in Anglo-Saxon England. This, the Milroys argue, paved the way for an institutional system of social stratification, and the rise of London as the seat of government and the national center of commerce.

Rapid population growth and migration to the capital increased dialect contacts and the potential for linguistic change in the Renaissance period. When the material in the CEEC is localized, it reveals the centrality of London to **supralocal** processes of language change in Tudor and Stuart England: most

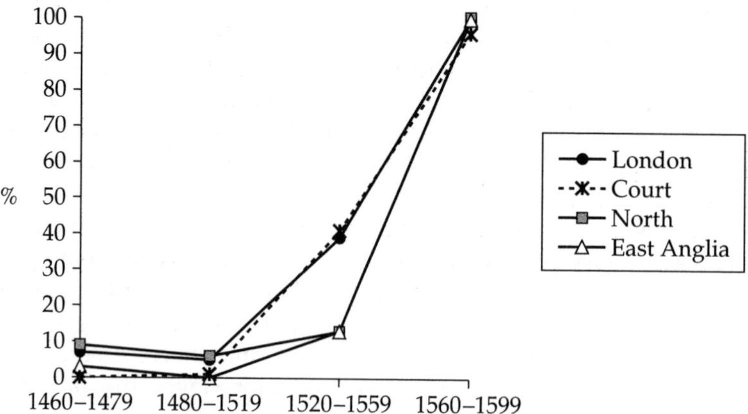

Figure 22.6 Replacement of subject *ye* by *you*: regional distribution of *you* (Nevalainen and Raumolin-Brunberg 2003: 172)

of the changes studied in the data so far were led by the capital (Nevalainen and Raumolin-Brunberg 2003: 170–83; see also section 22.3.4). Figure 22.6 shows the regional diffusion of *you* as a subject form in the fifteenth and sixteenth centuries. London (the City) and the Royal Court led the process in the first half of the sixteenth century, and East Anglia and the North only caught up with the capital in the latter half of the century.

Another application of the network theory at the macro level is the study of catastrophic events, which increase mobility and can therefore speed up ongoing processes of linguistic change. Acceleration in the diffusion of the neuter possessive pronoun *its*, for instance, may be connected with the English Civil War around the mid-seventeenth century (Raumolin-Brunberg 1998: 372–73). A number of linguistic developments have similarly been attributed to the aftermath of World War II in the American Southwest (Bailey et al. 1996).

At the **micro level**, a potential context for linguistic influence is a social network founded on multiple family, patronage and business ties. Such a network can be illustrated by the wool-merchant circle mentioned in section 22.3.1, including John and Sabine Johnson, husband and wife, who were both involved in the running of the family business and their country estate; Otwell Johnson, John's brother and business partner; Anthony Cave, the wool merchant to whom John had been apprenticed; and Richard Preston, John's servant, responsible for buying the merchandise to be sold. Table 22.1 places these five individuals on scales of linguistic change running from zero to 100 percent, depending on the extent to which each of them had accepted the four supralocal linguistic changes in progress at the time.

No single pattern emerges from the analyses. The closest we get to one is the four men agreeing on the use of *which* as opposed to *the which*, and of single negation followed by non-assertive forms as opposed to negative concord. Richard Preston deviates from the rest in his preference of *-s* in the third

Table 22.1 Frequency of occurrence (%) of *-(e)s*, *you*, single negation, and *which* in the Johnson circle 1542–53

Frequency of use (%)	You *(%) vs.* ye	-(e)s *(%) vs.*-(e)th*	*Single NEG (%) vs. Multiple NEG*	Which *(%) vs.* the which
100	Otwell Johnson	Richard Preston		Richard Preston
	Sabine Johnson			Anthony Cave
90				Otwell Johnson
				John Johnson
80			Anthony Cave	
70				
			Otwell Johnson	
60			John Johnson	
			Richard Preston	
50				
40		**Sabine Johnson**		
30				
			Sabine Johnson	
20		Anthony Cave		
10		John Johnson		
	Anthony Cave	Otwell Johnson		**Sabine Johnson**
0	John Johnson			
	Richard Preston			

* Excluding *do* and *have*.
Source: Nevalainen (1999: 517, 532).

person present-tense singular, and Otwell and Sabine Johnson in their preference of *you* as the subject pronoun. It is Sabine Johnson who deviates most from the rest: except for *-s*, where her usage approaches mid-range, she comes out either as a leader (*you*) or a late adopter (single NEG, *which*) of the changes in progress within her circle.

There are at least two possible interpretations for these results: either this network contained several early adopters of incoming forms (Otwell and Sabine Johnson and Richard Preston), or their linguistic behavior could be explained by other factors, such as differences in dialectal and social background, education, or age. This can only be guessed at if no baseline evidence of these factors and their role in the transmission of the changes in progress is available. The evidence we have will be considered below.

Some of the prospects and problems of historical network analysis are considered in the special issue of *European Journal of English Studies* devoted to the topic (Tieken-Boon van Ostade et al. 2000). One of the lines of inquiry that emerges from these contributions is the study of **coalitions**, alliances contracted for a specific purpose. Considering the eighteenth-century *Spectator* alliance, Fitzmaurice (2000: 276) concludes that the use of coalition as a descriptive social category facilitates a focused investigation of social influence, but that it is perhaps better suited to the analysis of language maintenance than of language change. Linguistic norm-enforcement mechanisms are often associated with religious and political alliances, such as the Winchester School at the end of the tenth and beginning of the eleventh centuries (Lenker 2000) and the Lollard Circle of John Wycliffe's supporters in the fourteenth century (Bergs 2000: 246–9).

22.3.4 *Social and regional embedding*

Modern sociolinguistic research has revealed the consistency of speaker variables such as gender, social status, and education as elements in the social embedding of changes in progress. Although it may be argued that the Principle of Contingency – linguistic changes are socially unique (Labov 2001: 503) – must hold for social constraints on language changes both today and in the past, broader generalizations also emerge. **Gender differentiation** in language change has been presented as one of the most robust sociolinguistic "facts" in the English-speaking world today. It will be discussed separately in section 22.4.2.

One of the variables that has been found to correlate with variation and change in Present-day English is **social status**. Thinking of the deeply entrenched social hierarchies of the medieval and early modern world, it is to be expected that similar correspondences could be detected in these earlier societies. We have ample evidence showing that in early modern England, for instance, social status hierarchies correlated with forms of address and titles to a much higher degree than at present. It might even be argued that status differences were partly created by linguistic means. But many titles were also generalized in the course of time, and therefore cannot be taken as reliable indicators of social status distinctions. The terms *master* and *mistress*, for instance, ceased to be the sole property of the gentry in the sixteenth and seventeenth centuries.[3]

Sociolinguistic studies of present-day speech communities hardly ever analyze the uppermost social groups. As Romaine (1988: 1464) points out with reference to the upper class and the working class: "Focussing at both ends of the social class continuum has operated to provide closed networks which have fostered the maintenance and development of what are to some extent autonomous varieties of speech." Such isolation cannot always be detected in earlier societies. As evidence for greater social uniformity in speech earlier on, Romaine mentions the existence in both the highest and lowest social groups of forms such as *huntin*, *fishin*, etc., which are now considered nonstandard.

This does not mean that the prestige factor attached to the uppermost groups was not recognized in the past. On the contrary, it was explicitly evoked by early commentators. In his *Arte of English Poesie* (1589: 120–1),

George Puttenham gave advice to aspiring poets, recommending that they follow the speech of "the better brought vp sort" and imitate "the vsuall speach of the Court, and that of London and the shires lying about London within lx. myles, and not much aboue."

Historical research supports the sociolinguistic idea of the middle ranks as instigators and propagators of linguistic innovations. The letter corpus shows, for instance, that the subject form *you* was initiated by the middle ranks. However, historical findings also challenge the usual notion of the interior social ranks as the decisive leading force in changes in progress. The CEEC data indicate that not only did the upper ranks participate in linguistic changes, they also led some of them (such as the generalization of the relative *which* vs. *the which*), and their participation usually played an important role in the **supralocal** diffusion of a process.

In the past, linguistic differences encoding social status could be, and often were, overridden by the person's domicile even in the higher social ranks. This is obvious in the Middle English period, when no nationwide standard language existed, and even in the Early Modern English period after the advent of printing, when supralocal usages were established in many domains of language structure (McIntosh et al. 1986: 3–7). On the other hand, the empirical evidence of supralocalizing morphosyntactic changes suggests that internal migration, say, from the north to the south provided an important source of regional input to linguistic changes in the capital region (Britton 2000; Nevalainen and Raumolin-Brunberg 2000).

The CEEC data show that regardless of where supralocalizing forms or constructions originated (typically in the south but also in the Midlands and in the north), they at some point also gained ground at the Royal Court. If a change spread from the lower social ranks but did not make it to the upper ranks and the Court, it failed to be generalized. This was the case with the northern third person singular present-tense suffix *-(e)s* in the late fifteenth century, when it was attested in the London wool-merchant community, but did not gain ground at Court (or in East Anglia, for that matter). At the time the stronger contender for a supralocal norm was the southern *-(e)th*, which also had the institutional support of the King's Chancery. The conflict was felt in the north, where the most frequent *-(e)th* users can be found in the highest social and professional ranks, and the least frequent users among low officers, tenants, and servants (Moore 2002; Nevalainen and Raumolin-Brunberg 2003: 177–80).

But *-(e)s* similarly persisted among the lower ranks in the south, with the consequence that it began to spread again, also gaining ground at Court towards the end of the sixteenth century. East Anglia was slower in adopting it than the capital region, partly, presumably, because of the presence there of a third alternative, the zero suffix (Nevalainen et al. 2001). It is clear that we are also dealing with a process of lexical diffusion here: *have* and *do*, auxiliary and main verb alike, both resisted *-s* forms much longer than other verbs; cf. examples (5) and (6). In personal letters *hath* and *doth* continued in common use until the late seventeenth century (Nevalainen 1996).

(5) This **hath** changed my resolucon, for I intend now to staie here a fortnight longer . . . (Thomas Wentworth, 1624; CEEC WENTWORTH, 215)

(6) I haue sent you a partriche pye, which **has** the two pea chikeins in it . . . (Brilliana Harley, 1627; CEEC HARLEY, 3)

The presence of a pattern at Court or in print did not, however, always guarantee its supralocal diffusion. A case in point is the Type of Subject Constraint affecting subject–verb concord in northern English dialects. According to this principle, a plural NP subject took a verb ending in *-s*, but a pronoun subject required no ending (*'NP Vs'* but *'they V'*). The constraint had spread as far south as the Chester–Wash line in the late Middle Ages (McIntosh 1989) and it was attested in the London wool-merchant community in the fifteenth century (Bailey et al. 1989). Over 10 percent of the full NP subjects in Shakespeare's First Folio (1623) have the verb ending in *-s* in the plural. But Shakespeare does not provide evidence of the other requirement of the Northern Subject Rule (NSR), the Proximity of Subject Constraint. This principle inserts *-s* into the second verb of a coordinated VP if the pronoun subject is not repeated (*'they V and Vs'*; Schendl 2000a).

The Type of Subject Constraint and the Proximity of Subject Constraint are both found in a number of printed sources in Early Modern English, including Queen Elizabeth's translation of *Boethius*, but their overall use is sporadic. The NSR remained a variable rule and never gained the same supralocal status as the northern suffix *-s* (Montgomery 1996; Schendl 1996: 150; Nevalainen and Raumolin-Brunberg 2000).

Labov (2001: 28–9) argues that we should not expect abstract structural patterns to be subject to the same kind of social conditioning as phonemes or morphemes. Although this may be true of the NSR – and even there social stratification is detected in the north (Moore 2002: 12–13) – there is evidence to the contrary. A case in point is multiple negation, discussed in section 22.4.3.2, which often functions as a social-class marker in modern speech communities (see Chambers 1995: 51).

22.4 Time-depth of Sociolinguistic Generalizations

There are a number of general issues to do with linguistic variation and change that are widely accepted by sociolinguists today. They include the apparent-time construct as an indicator of a linguistic change in progress, gender differentiation in language change, and vernacular universals. As historical sociolinguists provide the long-term real-time perspective that is missing from present-day research, these broad generalizations become empirical issues that can be tested with diachronic data from languages like English. Here the past begins to be used to explain the present.

22.4.1 *Generational vs. communal changes*

Modern sociolinguists typically operate with **apparent-time** patterns as indicators of **real-time** language changes, especially in phonology and morphology. This implies that members of each generation acquire a set of features and, as Labov (1994: 84) put it, "enter the community with a characteristic frequency for a particular variable, maintained throughout their lifetimes." According to this model, language change can be traced by analyzing the linguistic behavior of successive generations, as shown by figure 22.7(a) (**generational change**).

An alternative to this generational change is **communal change**, "where all members of the community alter their frequencies together, or acquire new forms simultaneously" (Labov 1994: 84). Figure 22.7(b) illustrates this pattern schematically. Labov expects phonological and morphological changes to follow the generational pattern, but lexical and also syntactic changes to diffuse communally (presumably because he does not expect abstract structural patterns to be socially conditioned in the same way as phonemes or morphemes are).

This issue is also raised by researchers working on grammaticalization (e.g. Janda 2001: 304–15, whose diagrams are reproduced in a modified form in figure 22.7). As far as historical processes are concerned, Labov's generalization is too categorical. A syntactic change such as the introduction of periphrastic *do* into affirmative and negative statements has been shown to follow the

(a) Generational change

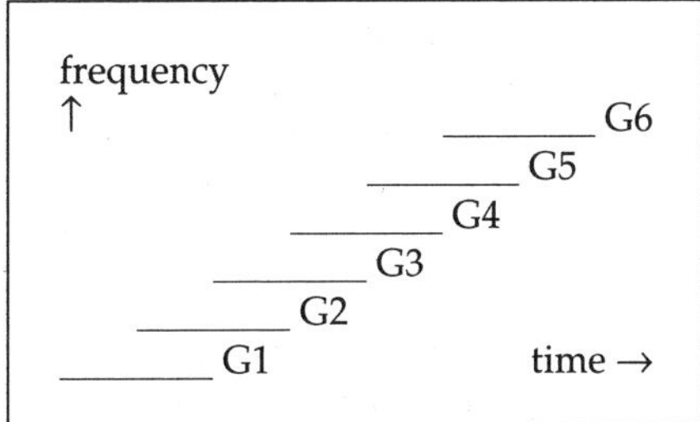

(b) Communal change

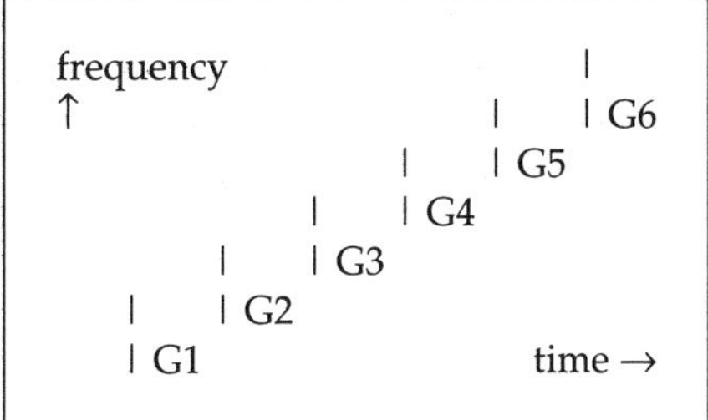

Figure 22.7 Generational and communal change (adapted from Janda 2001)

generational apparent-time pattern in the sixteenth century (Kallel 2002). The subsequent decline of affirmative *do* in the seventeenth century appears to pattern both generationally and communally (Nurmi 1999: 130–2). But, as predicted, the rise of the progressive in the nineteenth century follows the communal model (Arnaud 1998).

The CEEC data also suggest both generational and communal diffusion for morphological changes. They include morpheme substitutions such as the replacement of *-th* by *-s*, as well as changes involving reanalysis such as the generalization of the object form *you* as a subject pronoun. When cross-tabulated by individual generations in both apparent and real time, the changes analyzed were commonly found to progress on both axes (Raumolin-Brunberg 1996; Nevalainen and Raumolin-Brunberg 2003: 86–92). Even where no real-time increase was detected in a generation, its usage rarely remained fixed from one period to the next.

This real-time evidence tallies with the fact, shown in section 22.3.1, that a large proportion of the individuals participating in changes in progress displayed variable grammars, using both incoming and receding forms. These sociolinguistic findings can therefore be used to support arguments in favor of the gradual nature of syntactic change reflected in the gradual nature of grammatical competition (Pintzuk 2003: 510).

22.4.2 *The Sex/Prestige Pattern*

Some sociolinguistic "facts" – so called by Hudson (1996: 202) because they are so robust and clear – have already been related to the history of English in the preceding sections, where genre variation, social networks, and social status were discussed. In principle, they also appear robust in the historical data. It has similarly been shown that the correlations found between linguistic variables and social variables in the historical data are typically probabilistic – a matter of more or less rather than all or none – in the same way as they are today.

There is one correlation between linguistic and speaker variables that many sociolinguists regard as universal, the **Sex/Prestige Pattern**, which states that if both sexes have the same access to standard-language forms, women use them more than men (Hudson 1996: 195). Labov (2001: 293) takes the argument further by introducing a **Gender Paradox**: "women conform more closely than men to sociolinguistic norms that are overtly prescribed but conform less than men when they are not." This can also be taken to mean that women typically emerge as the leaders of linguistic change – or as formulated by Labov (1990: 213–15; 2001: 274, 292):

1 in linguistic change from above, women adopt prestige forms at a higher rate than men;
2 in linguistic change from below, women use higher frequencies of innovative forms than men do.

Table 22.2 Gender advantage in ten linguistic changes (c.1500–1680)

Gender advantage/Process of change	*Female adv.*	*Male adv.*
(a) subject *ye* → *you*	yes	no
(b) third-person *-th* → *-s*	yes	no
(c) determiner *mine/thine* → *my/thy*	yes	no
(d) rise of prop-word *one*	yes	no
(e) rise of direct object of the gerund	yes	no
(f) rise of periphrastic *do* in negative declaratives	yes	no
(g) relative *wh*+prep → prep+*wh*	yes	no
(h) relative *the which* → *which*	no	yes
(i) multiple NEG → single NEG + non-assertive forms	no	yes
(j) rise of negative inversion	no	yes

The CEEC provides evidence in support of this generalization, but it also suggests that the two sexes did not have the same access to prestige forms in the past as they have today. Table 22.2 presents ten changes discussed in Nevalainen and Raumolin-Brunberg (2003). Seven of them were led by women and three by men, and all except the last one reached the 5 percent level of statistical significance (chi-square test, $p < 0.05$).

The first two changes were illustrated above in examples (1) and (2), and (5) and (6), respectively. The determiner change from *mine* and *thine* to *my* and *thy* is exemplified below in (7) and (8). The incoming prop-word *one* is shown by (9) (cf. Rissanen 1997).

(7) At **my** departing from Callais, amongest other thinges that I desired you to take pains in **myne** absens from thens . . . (John Johnson, 1546; CEEC JOHNSON, 582)

(8) The couart shal be cepte here on Fryday next. **My** ounckell Bryand and Mr. Douse wel be here at yet; (Sabine Johnson, 1546; CEEC JOHNSON, 623)

(9) I with all your lytell **ons** be in helthe, the Lord be prasid. (Sabine Johnson, 1546; CEEC JOHNSON, 668)

As suggested by Fanego (1996), the object of the gerund had two basic variants between the fifteenth and seventeenth centuries. The *of*-phrase is shown in (10), and the incoming direct-object construction in (11), both from the correspondence of Queen Elizabeth I.

(10) bicause that she hathe bene with me a longe time, and manye years, and hathe taken great labor, and paine in **brinkinge of me up** in lerninge and honestie . . . (Elizabeth I, 1548; CEEC ROYAL 1, 154)

(11) I assure you, you ar wel worthy of suche traitors, that, whan you knewe them, and had them, you betraied your owne seurty in **fauoring ther liues**. (Elizabeth I, 1590; CEEC ROYAL 1, 58)

The use and non-use of periphrastic *do* in negative declaratives is shown in (12). Here, too, we have a case of lexical diffusion as verbs belonging to the *know*-group were much slower in acquiring the auxiliary than other verbs (Nurmi 1999: 148–52; Trudgill et al. 2002). An early instance of the use of *do* is found in example (15), below.

(12) he went awaye withowt any speakyng with me for I **knew not** of yt, **neyther dyd** I . . . **see** hym after tyll your letter came to me that I sent to hym to speake with hym. (Francis Wyndham, 1577; CEEC BACON I, 257)

Variation between a relative adverb (such as *whereof*) and a prepositional phrase (*of the which*) is illustrated by examples (13) and (14). Example (14) also contains a case of the relative pronoun *the which* (as do examples (3) and (4); see Raumolin-Brunberg 2000).

(13) I shall ryght hertely desier you that we maye mete as we have done, trusting that these holydaies ye wil be hier, **wherof** bothe my wyf and I wold be glad. (John Johnson, 1545; CEEC JOHNSON, 231)

(14) I perceve that you arrived in savety at Callais, and that the plage is well seased, the Lord be prased, **of the which** I am glad to here; (Sabine Johnson, 1545; CEEC JOHNSON, 289)

Example (15) illustrates negative concord in the CEEC, and (16) shows simple negation followed by a non-assertive form (Nevalainen 1998). The decline of multiple negation will be discussed in section 22.4.3.2, below.

(15) I answared that I **dyd not** knowe of **no** end that was maed . . . (Sabine Johnson, 1545; CEEC JOHNSON, 515)

(16) for in good faithe I promes youe I had **no** joye of **annything**. (John Johnson, 1551; CEEC JOHNSON, 1250)

The last change in table 22.2, the introduction of (Subject–Auxiliary/Verb) inversion after the clause-initial negative adverbs and conjunctions *nor, never,* and *neither* is illustrated by examples (17) and (18). In this case the material is not very plentiful, but male advantage is clearly in evidence when inversion reaches the rate of 20 percent (Nevalainen 1996, 1997).

(17) Your gold that you sent me by Ambrose is not yett exchaunged, **nor I can** gett but xlvj *s st.* for an once therof . . . (Otwell Johnson, 1544; CEEC JOHNSON, 121)

(18) I perceyve youre opinion of owre monneyes, which dissentyth not partely from others I have herd of beffore; **neither dyd I** suppose **anny** better sequele of it. (Anthony Cave, 1551; CEEC JOHNSON, 1476)

As table 22.2 indicates, there is no single linguistic pattern associated with the changes promoted by either gender, but both morpheme substitutions (*-s* for *-th* in the third person singular, and relative *which* for *the which*, for instance) and abstract structural patterns, such as object of the gerund and the disappearance of multiple negation, are involved. Some of them, such as the spread of *you*, were completed in the sixteenth century, others in the course of the seventeenth, while a few, such as the direct object of the gerund (e.g. *in favoring* ***their lives***), had not reached their completion by the end of the second millennium.

There are three changes systematically promoted by male writers in the CEEC. The generalization of plain *which*, (h) in table 22.2, and the disappearance of multiple negation (i) can both be thought of as changes from above in that they represent literate and educated usage. Direct word-order after initial negative adverbs and coordinators is typically accompanied by multiple negation, but negative inversion (j) is not (Bækken 1998: 268–75; Nevalainen 1998: 283–4). The incoming pattern, single negation with non-assertive forms, is promoted by educated and professional men such as the administrators at the Royal Court. It was also the Court circles and upper-ranking males who preferred the relative *which* to *the which* (Raumolin-Brunberg 2000). These changes can therefore be associated with linguistic practices that were only indirectly accessible to women at the time.

What the ten changes have in common is that their gender alignment is not altered in the course of the process, but a given preference persists until the change nears completion. There are only two partial exceptions here, the early stages in the introduction of *do* to negative statements (f) and in the replacement of relative adverbs by prepositional phrases (g), which both start with a male advantage. In these cases, too, a consistent female advantage appears when a change has passed its incipient stage and can be labeled, following Labov's terminology (1994: 79–83), "new and vigorous."

Other studies support these generalizations. Kytö (1993) and Stein (2002) also find that women promote the third person singular suffix *-s*. Nurmi (1999) provides more detailed evidence of the rise of periphrastic *do* in affirmative and negative statements. Romaine (1982) finds that women favor vernacular *th*-relativization strategies in Middle Scots, and they provide earlier evidence than men of Aitken's Law in Meurman-Solin's Middle Scots data (2000). In Arnaud's study (1998), women authors favor the incoming progressive form in the eighteenth and nineteenth centuries.

All these changes constitute processes of **supralocalization**, which result in **dialect leveling** or new **dialect formation**. Leveling was similarly under way when the young Norfolk women who went into service in the nineteenth and early twentieth centuries gave up their local relativizer *what* in favor of other forms (Poussa 2002). It appears that in England today localized phonological forms are preferred by males, whereas the high-frequency variants used by females typically gain a supralocal status (e.g. Milroy and Milroy 1993; Docherty et al. 1997). Studying New Zealand English, Janet Holmes (1997: 131) concludes that the success of linguistic innovations, prestige and vernacular, depends on their being adopted and endorsed by women. If this generalization holds for linguistic changes more generally, and conforming to and changing the standard language is also considered as tending towards a supralocal norm, Labov's Gender Paradox disappears. The Early Modern English findings, which date to a period before overtly prescriptive grammar, support the notion of women promoting incoming supralocal forms, to the extent that they had direct access to these forms.

22.4.3 English vernacular "universals"

Sociolinguists use the term **vernacular** in several closely related senses. It is defined as "real language in use" (Milroy 1992: 66), "the language used by ordinary people in their everyday affairs," and "the style in which the minimum of attention is given to the monitoring of speech" (Labov 1972: 62, 69, 208). There are certain linguistic features that are found in English vernaculars all over the world. Chambers (1995: 242–3) lists five of these vernacular "universals": alveolar realization of the nasal in the suffix *-ing* (ng); final stop deletion (C<u>C</u>); the use of *was* with plural subjects ("default singulars"); conjugation regularization ("leveling of irregular verb forms"); and multiple negation ("negative concord").

The general problem these vernacular features raise for the sociolinguist is their origin: as they are so widespread, as well as being attested in children's language regardless of their adult models, it is difficult to maintain that they have spread from a single ancestor dialect to all the rest. Chambers (1995: 246–50) therefore opts for a language-internal structural position, claiming that they must be somehow privileged or primitive linguistic processes, suppressed in the standard language.

What interests the historical sociolinguist here is the time-depth of these features: if they are also to count as vernacular primitives historically, they ought to be attested in earlier English or at least in those stages of the language that can be identified as English. In the following sections two of the morphosyntactic features listed by Chambers will be focused on, *was/were* variation with plural subjects, and multiple negation. As far as the alveolar realization /n/ of the (ng) variable in word-final position is concerned, its historical prevalence can be questioned. Although attested from the late fourteenth century onwards, it may not have been as ubiquitous as claimed, for instance, by Wyld (1936: 289–99).

Raumolin-Brunberg's study of the CEEC (2002) reveals that the alveolar realization *-in* appears sporadically throughout the country, and more in East Anglia than elsewhere, but that it is the velar nasal that predominates in the data in the fifteenth and sixteenth centuries. This is an important finding in that the period is generally marked by a great deal of spelling variation in personal correspondence. It supports the notion that the alveolar nasal may have started life as a dialectal feature: in East Anglia, the preferred participial suffix was *-nd*, not *-ng*, in late fourteenth-century local documents (Wright 2001: 87).

22.4.3.1 Was/were *variation*

Northern origins have been suggested for the generalized past-tense use of *was* with plural subjects in Middle English (Forsström 1948: 207). Today it is reported to be more frequent in East Anglia than elsewhere in Britain in affirmative contexts (Anderwald 2001). The CEEC confirms its high frequency of use in the north in the fifteenth and sixteenth centuries (between 40 and 55 percent), but it also shows that it was more common in London than in East Anglia at the time (13 percent vs. 7 percent). In the seventeenth century, the overall frequency of the pattern fell below 10 percent in all the regions studied.

This leveling to *was* in the plural follows a particular subject hierarchy in modern nonstandard dialects. The most common subject type triggering *was* is NP existential subjects with *there*, the next most common are the subject pronoun *you* and plural NPs, followed by the subject pronouns *we* and *they* (Tagliamonte 1998: 161). The correspondence data lend support to the notion of a subject hierarchy: existential *there* serves as the most common trigger of *was* from the fifteenth to the late seventeenth century (over 25 percent of the cases in all subperiods). Unlike today it is not, however, followed by the subject pronouns *ye* or *you*, but by plural NPs. These two frequent types are illustrated by (19) and (20). Pronoun subjects in general are rare with *was*, and *you* in particular is a relative latecomer here. In the CEEC it is first found in the seventeenth century in cases like (21).

(19) . . . the said rowle could not be found; howbeit, **theare was all the rowles** of this King reigne but onely that of that yeare. (John Doddington, 1539; CEEC Plumpton, 239)

(20) There hase bene a gret councell at Saynt Johnstone, and **all the lords of Scotland was** there with the Quene. (Thomas Dacre, 1513; CEEC Clifford, 98)

(21) You tould me **you was** become a water drinker. (John Cosin, 1661; CEEC Cosin II, 312)

A connection may exist between plural NP subjects followed by *was* and the Northern Subject Rule (*'NP Vs'*; see section 22.3.4). This is historically plausible, especially as the NP subject constraint loses ground in the seventeenth century at a time when the use of plural *was* drops among the literate social ranks in the north. The NSR could also explain the infrequency of plural personal pronoun subjects with *was* in the CEEC. The rise of *you* in the subject hierarchy takes place later. Using a variety of data sources, Tieken-Boon van Ostade (2002) shows that it only becomes generalized in the course of the eighteenth century.

22.4.3.2 *Multiple negation (negative concord)*

Multiple negation has a long history in English. In Old English *ne* was the principal sentential negator, which also co-occurred with other negative-incorporating elements. In Middle English *ne* was typically reinforced with *not* (from *nawiht*), and the two-part negator could be accompanied by other negative elements (*ne . . . not . . . ne/never*, etc.). In the fourteenth century *ne* began to lose ground, *not* progressively replacing it as the sentential negator, and non-assertive indefinites started to appear ((*ne . . .*) *not . . . any/ever*; see Jack 1978; van Kemenade 2000; Iyeiri 2001).

In the late fifteenth and sixteenth centuries the disappearance of multiple negation and rise of non-assertive indefinites was a selective process from above in terms of the speaker-writer's education and social status. As noted in section 22.4.2, the correspondence material suggests that the decline of multiple negation was promoted by male professional circles in the middle and upper social ranks. Figure 22.8 presents this process across the literate social spectrum making a distinction between male and female writers. The figures for

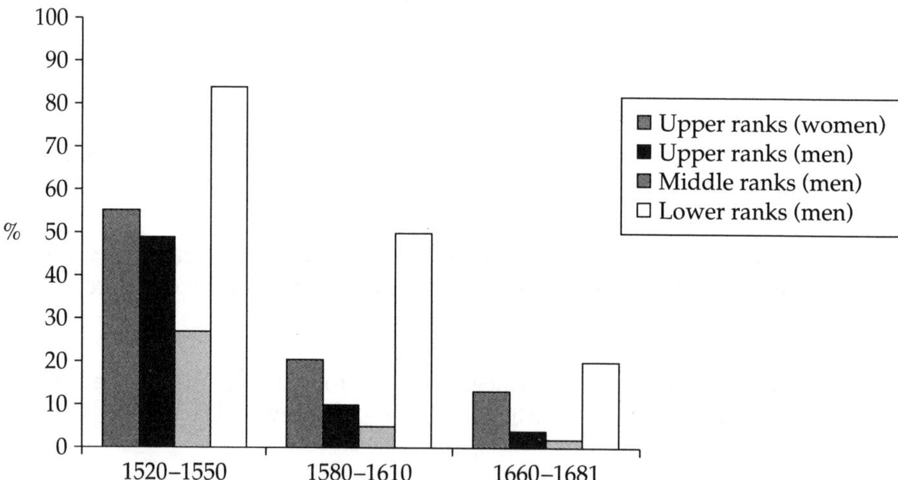

Figure 22.8 Multiple negation according to social rank: percentage of multiple negation of the total of multiple and single negation with non-assertive forms (Nevalainen 1999: 523)

Upper ranks: royalty, nobility, gentry; *middle ranks*: professionals, merchants, social aspirers; *lower ranks*: other ranks below the gentry.

the lower-ranking men are not as representative as the rest, but nonetheless indicate a systematic trend: multiple negation persisted longest in the language of women and low-ranking men (Nevalainen 1998, 1999; Nevalainen and Raumolin-Brunberg 2003: 145–52).

Multiple negation had largely disappeared among the higher ranks, male and female, before the era of prescriptive grammar. In the course of the eighteenth and nineteenth centuries the prescriptive movement stigmatized multiple negation, including the *not . . . neither* construction, which was one of the contexts in which it had persisted even in the upper social ranks (Tieken-Boon van Ostade 1998: 218–22).

The rise of non-assertive forms in negative clauses is clearly associated with educated and professional usage in Late Middle and Early Modern English, but this is not the whole story. Placing the process in a broader linguistic and typological perspective, negatives prove to be only one of the negative-polarity contexts where non-assertive forms have emerged in the history of English (cf. Haspelmath 1997). The others are earlier, and include interrogatives, conditionals, comparatives, and implied negative clauses with verbs such as *doubt* and *deny*. As shown by Iyeiri (2002) on the basis of the *Helsinki Corpus*, non-assertive *any* becomes increasingly frequent in these contexts from the fourteenth century onwards. The part played by prescriptive grammar in this long-term semantic process therefore turns out to be an epiphenomenon rather than a major guiding influence. Viewed against this background, we may have good grounds for adding **negative polarity concord** to the historically privileged processes of the English language.

In sum, modern English vernacular universals have varying time-depths. The historical evidence considered here suggests that they are also likely to have varying dialectal backgrounds.

22.5 Conclusion

Future studies will no doubt give more accurate sociolinguistic accounts of many real-time processes of change in English, and provide more definitive answers to the theoretical questions addressed in this chapter. Part of the evidence will come from successful replications of apparent-time investigations, such as those discussed by Trudgill (1988) and Labov (2001: 421–45). For earlier periods, new corpora will provide tools for exploring not only the history of the vernacular but also the impact of prescriptive grammar on language changes in progress in the eighteenth and nineteenth centuries. Work on early grammars, usage guides, and contemporary commentaries will provide the backdrop against which empirical findings can be evaluated.[4]

Historical sociolinguistics will also expand to encompass new domains of research. They include dialect contact and code-switching, which have already attracted some scholarly attention. But what will remain crucial to the English historical sociolinguistic enterprise is the need to continue to accumulate diachronic baseline evidence against which to measure the linguistic variation found in and between individuals, registers, social status groups, networks, and communities of practice.

ACKNOWLEDGMENTS

I gratefully acknowledge the financial support for writing this chapter that I received from the Research Unit for Variation and Change in English, funded by the Academy of Finland and the University of Helsinki.

NOTES

1 These findings were replicated for the nineteenth century by Arnaud (1998) and Geisler (2002), for the period from 1650 to the 1990s by Biber and Finegan (1997), and for the fifteenth and sixteenth centuries by González Álvarez and Pérez Guerra (1998).
2 More details about these and other historical corpora can be found in Rissanen (2000a), Meurman-Solin (2001), and in the back issues of the *ICAME Journal*.
3 The generalization of titles and simplification of address forms have attracted the attention of both social historians (Laslett 1983; Williams 1992; Wrightson 1991) and historical sociolinguists (Busse 2002; Nevala 2003; Nevalainen and Raumolin-Brunberg 1995).
4 For discussions of contemporary attitudes to earlier English, see Blank (1996), Mugglestone (1995), and Tieken-Boon van Ostade (chapter 21, this volume). Studies of code-switching include Wright (1994), Schendl (2000b), and Nurmi and Pahta (2004).

REFERENCES

Anderwald, L. (2001). *Was/were* variation in non-standard British English today. *English World-Wide* 22.1: 1–21.

Arnaud, R. (1998). The development of the progressive in 19th century English: a quantitative study. *Language Variation and Change* 10: 123–32.

Bækken, B. (1998). *Word Order Patterns in Early Modern English, with Special Reference to the Position of the Subject and the Finite Verb*. Oslo: Novus Press.

Bailey, G., N. Maynor, and P. Cukor-Avila (1989). Variation in subject–verb concord in Early Modern English. *Language Variation and Change* 1: 258–300.

Bailey, G., T. Wikle, J. Tillery, and L. Sand (1996). The linguistic consequences of catastrophic events: an example from the American Southwest. In J. Arnold, R. Blake, B. Davidson, S. Schwenter, and J. Solomon (eds.), *Sociolinguistic Variation: Data, Theory, and Analysis* (pp. 435–51). Stanford, CA: CSLI Publications.

Bergs, A. T. (2000). Social networks in pre-1500 Britain: problems, prospects, examples. *European Journal of English Studies* 4.3: 239–51.

Biber, D. (1995). *Dimensions of Register Variation*. Cambridge: Cambridge University Press.

Biber, D. (2001). Dimensions of variation among 18th-century speech-based and written registers. In H.-J. Diller and M. Görlach (eds.), *Towards a History of English as a History of Genres* (pp. 89–109). Heidelberg: Universitätsverlag C. Winter.

Biber, D. and Finegan, E. (1989). Drift and the evolution of English style: a history of three genres. *Language* 65: 487–517.

Biber, D. and Finegan, E. (1997). Diachronic relations among speech-based and written registers in English. In T. Nevalainen and L. Kahlas-Tarkka (eds.), *To Explain the Present* (Mémoires de la Société Néophilologique de Helsinki 52) (pp. 253–75). Helsinki: Société Néophilologique.

Blank, P. (1996). *Broken English: Dialects and the Politics of Language in Renaissance Writings*. London: Routledge.

Britton, D. (2000). Henry Machyn, Axel Wijk and the case of the wrong Riding: the south-west Yorkshire character of the language of Henry Machyn's diary. *Neuphilologische Mitteilungen* 101.4: 571–96.

Busse, U. (2002). *Linguistic Variation in the Shakespeare Corpus: Morphosyntactic Variability of Second Person Pronouns*. Amsterdam and Philadelphia: Benjamins.

Chambers, J. K. (1995). *Sociolinguistic Theory*. Oxford: Blackwell.

Denison, D. (2003). Log(ist)ic and simplistic S-curves. In R. Hickey (ed.), *Motives for Language Change* (pp. 54–70). Cambridge: Cambridge University Press.

Devitt, A. (1989). *Standardizing Written English: Diffusion in the Case of Scotland 1520–1659*. Cambridge: Cambridge University Press.

Diller, H.-J. (2001). Genre in linguistic and related discourses. In H.-J. Diller and M. Görlach (eds.), *Towards a History of English as a History of Genres* (pp. 3–43). Heidelberg: Universitätsverlag C. Winter.

Docherty, G. J., Foulkes, P., Milroy, J., Milroy, L., and Walshaw, D. (1997). Descriptive adequacy in phonology: a variationist perspective. *Journal of Linguistics* 33: 275–310.

Fanego, T. (1996). The gerund in Early Modern English: evidence from the Helsinki Corpus. *Folia Linguistica Historica* 17: 97–152.

Fitzmaurice, S. (2000). Coalitions and the investigation of social influence in linguistic history. *European Journal of English Studies* 4.3: 217–76.

Forsström, G. (1948). *The Verb 'To Be' in Middle English: A Survey of the Forms*. Lund: Gleerup.

Geisler, C. (2002). Investigating register variation in nineteenth-century English: a multi-dimensional comparison. In R. Reppen, S. M. Fitzmaurice, and D. Biber (eds.), *Using Corpora to Explore Linguistic Variation* (pp. 249–71). Amsterdam and Philadelphia: Benjamins.

González Álvarez, D. and Pérez Guerra, J. (1998). Texting the written evidence: on register analysis in Late Middle English and Early Modern English. *Text* 18.3: 321–48.

Haspelmath, M. (1997). *Indefinite Pronouns*. Oxford: Clarendon Press.

Holmes, J. (1997). Setting new standards: sound changes and gender in New Zealand English. *English World-Wide* 18.1: 107–42.

Hudson, R. A. (1996). *Sociolinguistics* (2nd edn.). Cambridge: Cambridge University Press.

Iyeiri, Y. (2001). *Negative Constructions in Middle English*. Fukuoka: Kyushu University Press.

Iyeiri, Y. (2002). Development of *any* from Middle English to Early Modern English: a study using the *Helsinki Corpus of English Texts*. In T. Saito, J. Nakamura, and S. Yamazaki (eds.), *English Corpus Linguistics in Japan* (pp. 211–23). Amsterdam and New York: Rodopi.

Jack, G. B. (1978). Negation in Later Middle English prose. *Archivum Linguisticum* 9: 58–72.

Janda, R. D. (2001). Beyond "pathways" and "unidirectionality": on the discontinuity of language transmission and the counterability of grammaticalization. *Language Sciences* 23.2–3: 265–340.

Kallel, A. (2002). The age variable in the rise of periphrastic "do" in English. *Reading Working Papers in Linguistics* 6: 161–85.

Kemenade, A. van (2000). Jespersen's cycle revisited: formal properties of grammaticalization. In S. Pintzuk, G. Tsoulas, and A. Warner (eds.), *Diachronic Syntax: Models and Mechanisms* (pp. 51–74). Oxford: Oxford University Press.

Kytö, M. (1993). Third-person present singular verb inflection in early British and American English. *Language Variation and Change* 5: 113–39.

Kytö, M. (comp.) (1996). *Manual to the Diachronic Part of the Helsinki Corpus of English Texts* (3rd edn.). Helsinki: Department of English, University of Helsinki.

Labov, W. (1972). *Sociolinguistic Patterns*. Philadelphia: University of Pennsylvania Press.

Labov, W. (1990). The intersection of sex and social class in the course of linguistic change. *Language Variation and Change* 2: 205–54.

Labov, W. (1994). *Principles of Linguistic Change*. Vol. 1: *Internal Factors*. Oxford: Blackwell.

Labov, W. (2001). *Principles of Linguistic Change*. Vol. 2: *Social Factors*. Oxford: Blackwell.

Laslett, P. (1983). *The World We Have Lost – Further Explored*. London: Routledge.

Lass, R. (2000). Language periodization and the concept of "middle." In I. Taavitsainen, T. Nevalainen, P. Pahta, and M. Rissanen (eds.), *Placing Middle English in Context* (pp. 7–41). Berlin and New York: Mouton de Gruyter.

Lenker, U. (2000). The monasteries of the Benedictine reform and the "Winchester School": model cases of social networks in Anglo-Saxon England? *European Journal of English Studies* 4.3: 225–38.

McIntosh, A. (1989). Present indicative plural forms in the later Middle English of the North Midlands. In M. Laing (ed.), *Middle English Dialectology: Essays on Some Principles and Problems* (pp. 116–22). Aberdeen: Aberdeen University Press.

McIntosh, A., Samuels, M. L., and Benskin, M. (1986). *A Linguistic Atlas of Late Mediaeval English* (vol. 1). Aberdeen: Aberdeen University Press.

Meurman-Solin, A. (1997). Text profiles in the study of language variation and change. In R. Hickey, M. Kytö, I. Lancashire, and M. Rissanen (eds.), *Tracing the Trail of Time: Proceedings of the Second Diachronic Corpora Workshop* (pp. 199–214). Amsterdam and Atlanta: Rodopi.

Meurman-Solin, A. (2000). On the conditioning of geographical and social distance in language variation and change in Renaissance Scots. In D. Kastovsky and A. Mettinger (eds.), *The History of English in a Social Context: A Contribution to Historical Socio-linguistics* (pp. 227–55). Berlin and New York: Mouton de Gruyter.

Meurman-Solin, A. (2001). Structured text corpora in the study of language variation and change. *Literary and Linguistic Computing* 16.1: 5–27.

Milroy, J. (1992). *Linguistic Variation and Change: On the Historical Sociolinguistics of English*. Oxford: Blackwell.

Milroy, J. and Milroy, L. (1985). Linguistic change, social network and speaker innovation. *Journal of Linguistics* 21: 339–84.

Milroy, J. and Milroy, L. (1993). Mechanisms of change in urban dialects: the role of class, social network and gender. *International Journal of Applied Linguistics* 3.1: 57–77.

Milroy, L. (2000). Social network analysis and language change: introduction. *European Journal of English Studies* 4.3: 217–23.

Milroy, L. and Gordon, M. (2003). *Sociolinguistics: Method and Interpretation*. Malden, MA: Blackwell.

Montgomery, M. (1996). Was colonial American English a koiné? In J. Klemola, M. Kytö, and M. Rissanen (eds.), *Speech Past and Present* (Bamberger Beiträge zur Englischen Sprachwissenschaft 38) (pp. 213–35). Frankfurt am Main: Peter Lang.

Moore, C. (2002). Writing good Southerne: local and supralocal norms in the Plumpton letter collection. *Language Variation and Change* 14: 1–17.

Mugglestone, L. (1995). *"Talking proper": The Rise of Accent as Social Symbol*. Oxford: Clarendon Press.

Nevala, M. (2003). Family first: address formulae in English family correspondence from the 15th to the 17th century. In I. Taavitsainen and A. H. Jucker (eds.), *Diachronic Perspectives in Address Term Systems* (pp. 147–76). Amsterdam: Benjamins.

Nevalainen, T. (1996). Gender difference. In T. Nevalainen and H. Raumolin-Brunberg (eds.), *Sociolinguistics and Language History: Studies Based on the Corpus of Early English Correspondence* (pp. 77–91). Amsterdam and Atlanta, GA: Rodopi.

Nevalainen, T. (1997). Recycling inversion: the case of initial adverbs and negators in Early Modern English. *Studia Anglica Posnaniensia* 31: 203–14.

Nevalainen, T. (1998). Social mobility and the decline of multiple negation in Early Modern English. In J. Fisiak and M. Krygier (eds.), *Advances in English Historical Linguistics (1996)* (pp. 263–91). Berlin and New York: Mouton de Gruyter.

Nevalainen, T. (1999). Making the best use of "bad" data: evidence for sociolinguistic variation in Early Modern English. *Neuphilologische Mitteilungen* 100.4: 499–533.

Nevalainen, T. (2000). Processes of supralocalisation and the rise of Standard English in the Early Modern period. In R. Bermúdez-Otero, D. Denison, R. M. Hogg, and C. B. McCully (eds.), *Generative Theory and Corpus Studies: A Dialogue from 10 ICEHL* (pp. 329–71). Berlin and New York: Mouton de Gruyter.

Nevalainen, T. and Raumolin-Brunberg, H. (1989). A corpus of Early Modern Standard English in a socio-historical perspective. *Neuphilologische Mittelungen* 90.1: 61–104.

Nevalainen, T. and Raumolin-Brunberg, H. (1995). Constraints on politeness: the pragmatics of address formulae in early English correspondence. In A. Jucker (ed.), *Historical Pragmatics: Pragmatic Developments in the History of English* (pp. 541–601). Amsterdam: Benjamins.

Nevalainen, T. and Raumolin-Brunberg, H. (1996). The Corpus of Early English Correspondence. In T. Nevalainen and H. Raumolin-Brunberg (eds.), *Sociolinguistics and Language History: Studies Based on the Corpus of Early English Correspondence* (pp. 39–54). Amsterdam and Atlanta, GA: Rodopi.

Nevalainen, T. and Raumolin-Brunberg, H. (2000). The changing role of London on the linguistic map of Tudor and Stuart England. In D. Kastovsky and A. Mettinger (eds.), *The History of English in a Social Context: A Contribution to Historical Sociolinguistics* (pp. 279–337). Berlin and New York: Mouton de Gruyter.

Nevalainen, T. and Raumolin-Brunberg, H. (2003). *Historical Sociolinguistics: Language Change in Tudor and Stuart England*. London: Longman.

Nevalainen, T., Raumolin-Brunberg, H., and Trudgill, P. (2001). Chapters in the social history of East Anglian English: the case of the third person singular. In J. Fisiak and P. Trudgill (eds.), *East Anglian English* (pp. 187–204). Cambridge: D. S. Brewer.

Nurmi, A. (ed.) (1998). *Manual for the Corpus of Early English Correspondence Sampler CEECS*. Department of English, University of Helsinki.

Nurmi, A. (1999). *A Social History of Periphrastic Do* (Mémoires de la Société Néophilologique de Helsinki 56). Helsinki: Société Néophilologique.

Nurmi, A. and Pahta, P. (2004). Social stratification and patterns of code-switching in early English letters. *Multilingua* 23: 417–56.

Peitsara, K. (1997). The development of reflexive strategies in English. In M. Rissanen, M. Kytö, and K. Heikkonen (eds.), *Grammaticalization at Work: Studies of Long-term Developments in English* (pp. 277–370). Berlin and New York: Mouton de Gruyter.

Pintzuk, S. (2003). Variationist approaches to syntactic change. In B. D. Joseph and R. D. Janda (eds.), *The Handbook of Historical Linguistics* (pp. 509–28). Malden, MA: Blackwell.

Poussa, P. (2002). Gendered speech in a dialect corpus from North Norfolk. In H. Raumolin-Brunberg, M. Nevala, A. Nurmi, and M. Rissanen (eds.), *Variation Past and Present* (Mémoires de la Société Néophilologique de Helsinki 61) (pp. 231–47). Helsinki: Société Néophilologique.

Puttenham, G. (1589). *The Arte of English Poesie*. London: Richard Field. (Cited from Scolar Press reprint (English Linguistics 110), Menston: Scolar Press, 1968.)

Raumolin-Brunberg, H. (1996). Apparent time. In T. Nevalainen and H. Raumolin-Brunberg (eds.), *Sociolinguistics and Language History: Studies Based on the Corpus of Early English Correspondence* (pp. 93–109). Amsterdam and Atlanta, GA: Rodopi.

Raumolin-Brunberg, H. (1998). Social factors and pronominal change in the seventeenth century: the Civil War effect? In J. Fisiak and M. Krygier (eds.), *Advances in English Historical Linguistics* (pp. 361–88). Berlin and New York: Mouton de Gruyter.

Raumolin-Brunberg, H. (2000). *Which* and *the which* in Late Middle English: free variants? In I. Taavitsainen, T. Nevalainen, P. Pahta, and M. Rissanen (eds.), *Placing Middle English in Context* (pp. 209–26). Berlin and New York: Mouton de Gruyter.

Raumolin-Brunberg, H. (2002). Stable variation and historical linguistics. In H. Raumolin-Brunberg, M. Nevala, A. Nurmi, and M. Rissanen (eds.), *Variation Past And Present* (Mémoires de la Société Néophilologique de Helsinki 61) (pp. 101–16). Helsinki: Société Néophilologique.

Rissanen, M. (1991). Spoken language and the history of *do*-periphrasis. In D. Kastovsky (ed.), *Historical English Syntax* (pp. 321–42). Berlin and New York: Mouton de Gruyter.

Rissanen, M. (1997). The pronominalization of *one*. In M. Rissanen, M. Kytö, and K. Heikkonen (eds.), *Grammaticalization at Work: Studies of Long-term Developments in English* (pp. 87–143). Berlin and New York: Mouton de Gruyter.

Rissanen, M. (2000a). The world of English historical corpora: from Cædmon to the computer age. *Journal of English Linguistics* 28: 7–20.

Rissanen, M. (2000b). Standardization and the language of early statutes. In L. Wright (ed.), *The Development of Standard English, 1300–1800: Theories,*

Descriptions, Conflicts (pp. 117–30). Cambridge: Cambridge University Press.

Rissanen, M., Kytö, M. and Palander-Collin, M. (eds.) (1993). *Early English in the Computer Age*. Berlin and New York: Mouton de Gruyter.

Rissanen, M., Kytö, M. and Heikkonen, K. (eds.) (1997a). *Grammaticalization at Work: Studies of Long-term Developments in English*. Berlin: Mouton de Gruyter.

Rissanen, M., Kytö, M. and Heikkonen, K. (eds.) (1997b). *English in Transition: Corpus-based Studies in Linguistic Variation and Genre Analysis*. Berlin: Mouton de Gruyter.

Romaine, S. (1982). *Socio-historical Linguistics: Its Status and Methodology*. Cambridge: Cambridge University Press.

Romaine, S. (1988). Historical sociolinguistics: problems and methodology. In U. Ammon, N. Dittmar, and K. J. Mattheier (eds.), *Sociolinguistics: An International Handbook of the Science of Language and Society* (pp. 1452–69). Berlin and New York: Walter de Gruyter.

Schendl, H. (1996). The 3rd plural present indicative in Early Modern English – variation and linguistic contact. In D. Britton (ed.), *English Historical Linguistics 1994* (pp. 143–60). Amsterdam and Philadelphia: Benjamins.

Schendl, H. (2000a). The third person present plural in Shakespeare's First Folio: a case of interaction of morphology and syntax? In C. Dalton-Puffer and N. Ritt (eds.), *Words: Structure, Meaning, Function* (pp. 263–76). Berlin and New York: Mouton de Gruyter.

Schendl, H. (2000b). Syntactic constraints on code-switching in medieval texts. In I. Taavitsainen, T. Nevalainen, P. Pahta, and M. Rissanen (eds.), *Placing Middle English in Context* (pp. 67–86). Berlin and New York: Mouton de Gruyter.

Stein, D. (2002). Sexist morphology: the morphological consequences of writing a letter, or having a letter written to, (as) a woman in Early Modern English. In S. Scholz, M. Klages, E. Hantson, and U. Römer (eds.), *Language: Context and Cognition* (pp. 279–87). München: Langenscheidt-Longman.

Taavitsainen, I. (1997). Genre conventions: personal affect in fiction and non-fiction in Early Modern English. In M. Rissanen, M. Kytö, and K. Heikkonen (eds.), *English in Transition: Corpus-based Studies in Linguistic Variation and Genre Analysis* (pp. 185–266). Berlin: Mouton de Gruyter.

Tagliamonte, S. (1998). *Was/were* variation across the generations: view from the city of York. *Language Variation and Change* 10: 153–91.

Tieken-Boon van Ostade, I. (1998). The origin and development of the "Neg . . . *neither*" construction: a case of grammaticalisation. In I. Tieken-Boon van Ostade, G. Tottie, and W. van der Wurff (eds.), *Negation in the History of English* (pp. 207–31). Berlin: Mouton de Gruyter.

Tieken-Boon van Ostade, I. (2002). *You was* in eighteenth-century normative grammar. In K. Lenz and R. Möhlig (eds.), *Of Dyuersitie and Chaunge of Langage* (pp. 88–102). Heidelberg: Universitätsverlag C. Winter.

Tieken-Boon van Ostade, I., Nevalainen, T., and Caon, L. (eds.) (2000). *European Journal of English Studies* 4.3. (Special issue: Social network analysis and the history of English.)

Trudgill, P. (1988). Norwich revisited: recent linguistic changes in an English urban dialect. *English Word-Wide* 9: 33–49.

Trudgill, P., Nevalainen, T., and Wischer, I. (2002). Dynamic "have" in North

American and British English. *English Language and Linguistics* 6.1: 1–15.
Williams, J. M. (1992). "O! When the degree is shak'd": sixteenth-century anticipations of some modern attitudes toward usage. In T. W. Machan and C. T. Scott (eds.), *English in its Social Contexts: Essays in Historical Sociolinguistics* (pp. 69–101). New York and Oxford: Oxford University Press.
Wright, J. (1905). *The English Dialect Grammar*. Oxford, London and Glasgow: Henry Frowde.
Wright, L. (1994). Early Modern London business English. In D. Kastovsky (ed.), *Studies in Early Modern English* (pp. 449–65). Berlin and New York: Mouton de Gruyter.
Wright, L. (2001). Some morphological features of the Norfolk guild certificates of 1388/9: an exercise in variation. In J. Fisiak and P. Trudgill (eds.), *East Anglian English* (pp. 79–162). Cambridge: D. S. Brewer.
Wrightson, K. (1991). Estates, degrees and sorts: changing perceptions of society in Tudor and Stuart England. In P. J. Corfield (ed.), *Language, History and Class* (pp. 30–52). Oxford: Blackwell.
Wyld, H. C. (1936). *A History of Modern Colloquial English* (3rd edn.). Oxford: Blackwell.

23 Global English: From Island Tongue to World Language

SUZANNE ROMAINE

23.1 Introduction

"Our story centres in an island," wrote Churchill (1956) in the preface to a four-volume work he called *A History of the English-speaking Peoples*. Although the volumes sound a confidently triumphant tone, concluded as they were in the wake of World War II, when Britain had just emerged from one of its darkest hours, Churchill still saw England as THE center of a British empire of English-speaking peoples. For roughly 1,200 years after the arrival in Britain of the invading Germanic tribes whose descendants would be known as English speakers, up to the time of the first permanent settlement of English colonists in the North American colonies, one can speak with some justification of only one national standard. Yet by the time Churchill was writing, English explorers and colonists had spread the language to the farthest reaches of the Empire on which the sun was alleged never to set. The demographic shift in the English-speaking population had already moved away from Britain, and the unity of the language whose history had once centered on an island was forever broken. The twentieth century would be declared the American century, the Empire would strike back, and the center would not hold. Although most of Churchill's so-called English-speaking peoples were white and their history was largely the history of the Anglo-Saxons and their descendants, now black Americans alone, who speak English, are equivalent to nearly half of the population of Britain, and the speakers of English in Britain itself by the end of the twentieth century included a few million black Britons.

Our story in this chapter is as much about changes in the English language itself as it is about changing perceptions of the English language as its users spread it from its origins as the tongue of a small island to become a world language spoken by millions. Over the course of its 1,500 years of use, English has undergone quite dramatic changes, as noted in other chapters of this volume. By the time the story of this chapter begins, in the seventeenth century or the Early Modern English period, the most radical changes to English grammar had already taken place, and certainly, the phonology of English underwent nothing like the series of changes called the Great Vowel Shift (see chapter 1, this volume). The main linguistic changes in the modern period would be in vocabulary as English expanded to meet the demands of an increasing number of users and uses. The seventeenth century had seen concerted efforts on the part of lexicographers, grammarians, and writers to remedy the perceived inadequacies of English to enable it to meet a continually expanding range of functions, and the eighteenth century was a time for putting the final touches on it, to fix things once and for all. It was also in the eighteenth century, however, that the unity of English was in effect broken by the establishment of new national standards, first in the United States, and later in Australia, South Africa, and New Zealand.

Who would have predicted that English would cease to be an "English" language? Before 1600 the idea that English might be a world language was not seriously considered because it was thought to have too many flaws. By comparison with classical Latin, English was in many respects stylistically limited. Furthermore, its use was confined to England and therefore its utility as the lingua franca of science and technology that it was to claim in later centuries was at this stage doubtful. Now that English is so well established as a discipline, we tend to forget that even as late as the nineteenth century it was not recognized as a legitimate subject. It would take some centuries before people were confident enough about English to deem it worthy of study.

Sir Thomas Bodley (1545–1613), founder of Oxford University's Bodleian Library, one of the oldest libraries in Europe, would not allow works of English literature in it, dismissing them as "idle bookes and riffe raffes" at a time when only books in Latin, and a few books in the vernacular languages of Europe such as Italian, were thought to be serious. Knowledge of English was virtually useless in traveling abroad in Bodley's time. As a diplomat, Bodley was well versed in many of the modern languages of his day, in addition, of course, to Greek and Latin, and also Hebrew, which he had studied in Geneva at the age of twelve. Nowadays, one can go practically anywhere in the world and hear English spoken. The language of the "global village" is indeed English.

23.2 From Island Tongue to World Language

In fact, it was in the last few years of Bodley's lifetime that English took its first significant steps toward becoming a world language, with the first permanent English settlement in North America established at Jamestown, Virginia, in 1607. Around that time, Crystal (1995: 92) estimates, the number of mother-tongue English speakers, almost all of them living within the British Isles, was between five and seven million. However, between the reigns of Queen Elizabeth I (1558) and Queen Elizabeth II (1952), the number increased by almost fifty times to about 150 million, the majority of whom (around four-fifths) lived outside the British Isles. Most of these new speakers were, and continue to be, North Americans. In the same year as the American Revolution ended in 1783, another revolution of a different type was beginning in England. James Watt's invention of the steam engine launched the Industrial Revolution. Even after its loss of the American colonies, England dominated the world during the nineteenth century in what was still an age of exploration and discovery. By this time, however, center stage had shifted to the Pacific rather than the Atlantic. James Cook's three voyages put much of the remaining New World on to European maps and opened the way for further colonial expansion and settlement. This brought the English language to the southern hemisphere, where it became established in places such as South Africa, India, Australia, and New Zealand.

Certainly, there had been other languages of empires propelled to far-flung colonial outposts. However, even at the height of the Roman Empire, Latin, with which English is often compared, did not spread this far. To be sure, it played an enormous role in the world of European learning until quite recently, but no other language has enjoyed the success or popularity of English. Other European languages such as Spanish and French also have a global reach due to colonization. What has made the difference for English? As the world's economy has shifted from an industrial base to one based on exchange of information, the globalizing new world order is founded on communications technology, which underlies the linking of national economies. Hence the role of language and communication is destined to play a more critical part than ever before.

Technological innovations of the late nineteenth and twentieth centuries such as the telegraph, telephone, film, radio, television, and computer would spread English even further without the necessity of travel and conquest. Because the technology facilitating these developments originated largely in the English-speaking world, English is at the leading edge of global scientific and economic development. In 1922 the BBC (British Broadcasting Corporation) became the first radio broadcasting service. With the launching of Intelsat III in 1967, for the first time in history no part of the globe was completely out of touch with any other part. When Princess Diana died in 1997, live satellite broadcasts of her funeral reached an estimated audience of 2.5 billion, or more than a third of the world's population. The BBC provided coverage to 187 countries, and American-owned CNN (Cable News Network) made pictures available to 210 countries. These two broadcasting companies, relying on a team of hundreds of English-speaking correspondents based all over the world, are the commercial superpowers of global English-language news in terms of resources and coverage. Their saturation of the market has increased global reliance on English-language news and ensured the flow of English around the world.

The internet has also become increasingly important in the spread of English, due to the fact that computer hardware and software was developed primarily by English speakers who tailored it to English. Until 1995 it was difficult to communicate via the internet in any language that could not be expressed in the standard English alphabet as defined by the American Standard Code for Information Exchange (ASCII), set down in 1982. As much as 80 percent of the information stored in the world's computers is in English and 90 percent of the world's computers connected to the internet are located in English-speaking countries.

Similarly, the corporations and financial institutions of the anglophone countries have dominated world trade and made English the international language of business. The official language of the European Central Bank is English, despite the facts that the bank is located in Frankfurt, the UK has not joined the European Monetary Union, and only 10 percent of the bank's employees are British. Many European companies such as Louis Vuitton, owned by the French conglomerate LVMH, and Merloni SpA in Italy have declared English their official language. Virtually all major corporations advertise their products in English. English is also the language of international popular culture for today's youth. Many rock groups whose native language is not English nevertheless record in English, and English is the most popular language for entries in the Eurovision Song Contest. MTV spreads American English language and and culture through music to its target group of young people in their teens and twenties around the world.

Crystal (1997) estimates that 85 percent of international organizations use English as one of their working languages, among them the United Nations and its subsidiary organs. French is the only real rival to English in this arena and it has been continually losing ground. English has also surpassed German, the most important international language of science until World War I, particularly in the hard sciences such as physics, chemistry, etc. Books in the English language have dominated the publishing business. English is the now the most widely used language in publication, with over 28 percent of the world's books printed in English and over 60 countries publishing books in English. English is also the language of international air traffic control and the basis for Seaspeak, used in international maritime communication. Today English is the dominant or official language in over sixty countries. It is represented on every continent and in the three major oceans, Atlantic, Pacific, and Indian (Crystal 1995: 106).

23.3 Englishes Old and New

Although English is not the largest language in the world (Chinese has more first-language speakers), the preceding statistics leave no doubt that English is one of a small handful of what may be called global languages in terms of geographic spread and number of users worldwide. Yet, it is impossible to give an exact count of the number of people in the world who speak English. Hard data directly relating to the development of global English are surprisingly scarce because there is no central information authority which collects such information.

At best, we can make some guesses based on population data, but it is not clear who counts as native or non-native, or how well those counted as users may speak and understand it. The more willing we are to accept minimal competence as sufficient for inclusion in the category of speakers of English as a second or foreign language, the more the figure can be inflated. At the extreme high end of the estimates, we find ones such as that of 1.5 billion speakers (roughly a quarter of the world's population) offered by the British Council in its specially commissioned report, *The Future of English* (Graddol 1997). The report categorizes users into three groups:

1 Speakers of English as a first (and often only), language: about 375 million (e.g. US, UK, Ireland, Canada, Australia, New Zealand).
2 Speakers of English as a second language, which may not be their indigenous language but is used within their own country to communicate with others: about 375 million (e.g. India, Singapore, and over 50 other countries where English plays a dominant role in the country's institutions).
3 Speakers of English as a foreign language who have studied it to communicate with people outside their own cultures: about 750 million (e.g. China, Europe, and most other countries where English is learned as an additional language but has no special place).

Crystal's (1995: 108) estimates are much lower for the second group (98 million) and he does not attempt to provide statistics for the third. Even within this second category we can see a huge range in the estimates of second language speakers from 98 to 375 million. Estimates of the number of foreign-language speakers of English vary even more dramatically from as low as 100 million to as high as 1,000 million. Although the latter figure appears inflated, it is hard to overestimate the demand for knowledge of English, one which was already recognized by grammarian John Wallis (1616–1703), whose *Grammatica Linguae Anglicanae* (Grammar of the English Language, 1653 [1765]) contained a preface in which he explained that he had undertaken to write his grammar of English because

> there is clearly a great demand for it from foreigners, who want to be able to understand the various important works which are written in our tongue . . . all kinds of literature are widely available in English editions, and without boasting, it can be said that there is scarcely any worthwhile body of knowledge which has not been recorded today, adequately at least, in the English language. (translated from the preface of the 6th edn. [1765]: 78, cited in Crystal 1995: 106)

The grouping of English users into three categories of native speakers, second-language users, and foreign-language learners has become conventional, even if not uncontroversial for a variety of reasons. One problem is the assumption that it is possible to distinguish native from non-native users. Now that English is one of a few languages whose non-native speakers outnumber its native speakers, the concept of "native speaker" itself has become problematic.

As more people learn English, the distinction between second-language and foreign-language users may become less meaningful too. Kachru (1980) offers a similar typology but avoids using labels such as "native" or "mother tongue" by proposing three concentric circles characterized by various functions and domains of usage as well as by modes of transmission and maintenance. In practice, however, Kachru's tripartite categories comprise more or less the same countries and groups of users as the ones recognized by the British Council.

In the so-called "inner circle" English is multifunctional, transmitted through the family and maintained by governmental or quasi-governmental agencies (e.g. media, school, etc.), and is the language of the dominant culture. The "outer" circle contains countries (usually multilingual) colonized by English-speaking powers. English is typically not the language of the home, but transmitted through the school, and has become part of the country's chief institutions. Norms come officially from the inner circle, but local norms also play a powerful role in dictating everyday usage. The term "new Englishes" is often used to refer to indigenized varieties such as Singapore English, Indian English, etc. These new Englishes have their own structural norms, their own characteristic features, communicative styles, and in some cases, their own literatures. The expanding circle contains those countries which do not have a history of colonization by the inner circle, but where English is taught as a means of communication with the rest of the world. It has few, if any, domains of use or special status within the respective countries. Its norms come exclusively from the inner circle. In the case of the inner circle one could also argue that its users created a new environment through English, whereas in the case of the outer circle, there was already another cultural environment in place which affected English. The distinctions are, however, not watertight in this model either, and there are some countries or categories of users which may fall under more than one heading. Some in the expanding circle may have higher levels of competence in English and use it more frequently than those in the outer circle. Compare, for instance, a European scientist or business person with a rural villager in India. Although it was not Kachru's intention to privilege native users, this is in fact suggested by his term "inner circle" and the location of the inner circle at the very center of the three concentric circles.

23.3.1 Declarations of independence

The challenge to the hegemony of British English came first from the inner circle, but now increasingly it comes from the outer circle too, whose speakers claim legitimacy for exogamous norms. Not long after the political separation of the American colonies, Noah Webster (1758–1843) declared linguistic independence when he announced that Great Britain would no longer determine the standard:

> As an independent nation our honour requires us to have a system of our own, in language as well as government. Great Britain, whose children we are, and whose

> language we speak, should no longer be our standard. For the taste of her writers is already corrupted, and her language is on the decline. But if it were not so, she is at too great a distance to be our model and to instruct us in the principles of our language. (Webster 1789: 20)

Although there are no signs in this text of a variety which was already on its way to becoming distinct from British English, it was Webster who adopted some of the spellings that were later to become distinctly American, e.g. <or> instead of <our> in words such as *honour*, <er> instead of <re> in words such as *center*, etc. Webster believed he was saving the language from the corruption by foreign influences (i.e. Latin, French, etc.) of ancient Saxon spelling, but more importantly, he saw a "capital advantage" in his reforms that would "make a difference between the English orthography and the American." Webster's two-volume work, *An American Dictionary of the English Language* (1828), included not only new words in what was to become American English but also words which had taken on a different sense in their new location. In the title, however, Webster sought no less than to validate linguistically the creation of a new nation and national identity in his belief that "a national language is a band of national union." By the time his dictionary appeared, he had already published a grammar and a speller, which was to sell over 70 million copies. Webster's lexicographical tradition was carried on after his death by a succession of direct literary heirs down until the present day. Until 1890 the title of his dictionary remained unchanged. Subsequent editions dropped the word *American* and were referred to as "International," a sign that American norms were legitimate and authoritative in the widest possible sense.

Over time, the American declaration of linguistic independence would make itself felt on the development of the English language as a whole. By the eighteenth century a single, unified standard for English had ceased to exist. No variety since has declared its own distinctive spellings, but has tended to follow either British or American spelling. Although Webster's linguistic declaration of independence was unparalleled for more than two hundred years, its repercussions would eventually be felt in other corners of the empire. Australia was the next to follow suit. Sidney Baker's (1945), *The Australian Language*, confidently asserted in its title the autonomy of Australian English in the same way that H. L. Mencken (1919), following in Webster's footsteps, had attempted to do for American English with his book, *The American Language*. Baker (1945: 11) wrote:

> we need some better starting point than Murray's Dictionary. We have to work out the problem from the viewpoint of Australia, not from the viewpoint of England and of the judgements she passed upon our language because she did not know it as well as we do.

Australia, too, now has its own dictionary (Ramson 1988), and a National Dictionary Centre established in 1988, as do other varieties in the inner circle (see Orsman 1997; Silva et al. 1996).

23.3.2 *Shifting centers of gravity from English to Englishes*

Each new variety has had to declare its independence against considerable opposition. Now that the time has come for New Englishes in the outer circle to assert their autonomy, the same arguments once made against American English *vis-à-vis* British English are being used to deny them their legitimacy in relation to the inner circle or native varieties. Noah Webster predicted that a language would develop in North America as different from the future language of England as Modern Dutch, Danish, and Swedish are from German, or one another. For patriotic reasons, Webster did not regard this as an undesirable development.

Although Webster's prediction has not yet come to pass, if indeed it ever will, others have voiced concerns that unless standard English is policed, the integrity of the language will be undermined by changes introduced by users beyond the inner circle, and English will disintegrate into a mass of unintelligible varieties. In 1991 Prince Charles warned that this "nightmare could possibly become a reality unless there are enduring standards, a common core of the language, and common standards of grammar." Speaking to teachers of English as a foreign language in what was then Czechoslovakia, he asked them to play their part in "maintaining standards and safeguarding the language's heritage" (*Guardian*, May 9, 1991). The unstated assumption was that Britain and British English would provide the normative basis for the so-called common standard. Similarly, Burchfield (1989: xii) assumed that British English is synonymous with Standard English when he said that "overseas varieties of English, in the United States, Australia and elsewhere, are steadily moving away, in small matters and large, from Standard English and from one another, at a somewhat accelerated rate." When the British Council's English 2000 Project was launched in 1995, Prince Charles made clear the assumption that the English of England was or should be the foundation for World English. He claimed that "American English is corrupting and should be avoided at all costs . . . Americans tend to invent all sorts of new nouns and verbs and make words that shouldn't be . . . we must act now to ensure that English – and that to my way of thinking means English English – maintains its position as the world language" (*Guardian*, April 6, 1995).

There is, of course, an economic dimension which cannot be overlooked in any discussion of norms. Countries such as the US and Britain derive a significant income from exporting the English language, related products, and professional expertise. The economic power to be derived from exporting English provides the inner circle with incentives for maintaining control over both standards and attitudes. Quirk (1990: 7), for example, continued the argument for a global norm based on the inner circle, noting that it is the "leading English-speaking countries" which know best how English should be taught. Graddol (1997: 3), too, believes that the use of English as a global lingua franca requires intelligibility and the setting and maintaining of standards, but avoids clarifying who would set these standards. Others, however, such as Phillipson (1992), see the attempt to impose the standards of native varieties along with native teachers as part of linguistic imperialism.

After the devolution of the British Empire into a number of independent nations linked by history, culture, and language, the singular term "English" is no longer adequate to describe the social, regional, and other variation in a language used by millions. Global English is best described as a "pluricentric" language, i.e. one whose norms are focused in different local centers, capitals, centers of economy, publishing, education, and political power. Most of the major languages of Western Europe such as French, German, Spanish, and Portuguese are likewise pluricentric, as are some non-Western ones such as Arabic and Chinese. Pluricentric languages can, however, be of different types. Some, such as Swedish, have one "real" center with one or more satellites of emigrant communities. Moreover, the centers of pluricentric languages can shift over time, as has happened in the history of English.

23.3.3 *Linguistic characteristics of international standard English*

Although there are many national varieties of standard English spoken around the world today (each with their own regional and social dialects), from a linguistic point of view there are only two major types: British and American. These were the first two national varieties to come into existence after the unity of English was broken in the eighteenth century. All other varieties, such as Australian English, Canadian English, Indian English, etc., can be clearly related to one of these two by virtue of either settlement history (e.g. British colonization of Australia and New Zealand vs. American colonization of Guam, Hawai'i, etc.) and/or geographical proximity (e.g. the case of Canadian English *vis-à-vis* American English). Standard British English is that variety spoken and written by educated speakers in England, and with minor differences in Wales, Scotland, Northern Ireland, Eire, Australia, New Zealand, and South Africa. The main linguistic influences on these varieties seem to come from south-eastern England. These varieties are therefore phonologically similar to RP (received pronunciation). Standard (North American) English is that variety spoken and written by educated speakers in the United States and Canada.

American and British English are also clearly the two most important varieties in terms of number of speakers, as well as their influence as a norm for foreign learners. They can also be thought of as the most fully institutionalized and most highly codified varieties of English, as can be seen in their range of uses and the number of books devoted to their description. Until recently, however, the norm adopted for teaching English as a foreign language throughout much of Europe was British Standard English. This was the result of a conscious policy motivated at least partly by fear that competing norms would confuse students. Now that many more Europeans study in the United

States and are increasingly exposed to American media, there is a greater tolerance for Standard American English. Nevertheless, there is often still an intolerance of mixing the norms. Publishing houses are generally reluctant to accept any inconsistencies in spelling and other norms. This is an increasingly unrealistic position to adopt, especially in teaching. A German student, for instance, who has studied standard British English at school in Germany and who later studies in the United States will most likely adopt some North American forms into her speech, just as native speakers of British English also do when they spend time in the United States. All that should matter is that students aim for native-like competence, even if that competence is an amalgam of different varieties. Foreign learners increasingly want dictionaries to show both American and British variants.

Grammatically speaking, the differences between these two varieties tend to be for the most part minor, and are not very likely to lead to misunderstanding (unlike some of the differences in vocabulary). Compare British English *I'll give it him* with American English: *I will give it to him*. Or, consider these differences in the use of definite articles or determiners. British English sometimes lacks a determiner where American English would have one, e.g. *to be in (the) hospital, to leave (the) university, to have (the) flu*. Compare, however, *in school*, common to both varieties, although *school* itself has wider reference in the US than in Britain, where one would not, for instance, refer to a university student as being still in/at school. Probably for speakers of each national variety the special uses of the other are obtrusive and seem to be more frequent than they are. Nevertheless, if no distinctive vocabulary items are used, it is quite often not possible to tell in certain text types (apart from spelling) what nationality the author is.

It is obvious that the history of words offers a window into the history of a language. Linguistic changes having their origin in social and cultural developments can be readily seen in vocabulary and semantics. When a language is transplanted to a new place, as English was to the new English colonies in North America, or to the southern hemisphere, new names were needed for the novel flora and fauna encountered by the early explorers and settlers. In this way many distinctive words, such as *chipmunk* and *kangaroo*, adopted into transplanted varieties of English from indigenous languages, subsequently made their way into International Standard English. Many others, however, have remained specific to national varieties.

The vocabulary of the English-speaking world is now so intertwined that it must be treated as a fundamental unity with only marginal national variation. Standard International English includes all expressions for which there are no significant national variations, e.g. *nation, computer, telephone*, etc. By comparison, *outwith* ('outside') is confined to Scotland, *dacoit* ('thief') to Indian English, *bach* ('cabin/cottage' from bachelor) to New Zealand, *handphone* ('cell/mobile phone') to Singapore English, *busy* (telephone number or line) to American English, *bioscope* ('cinema/movie theater') to South African English, etc. Each national variety of English has thousands of such words to express its local character.

An important characteristic of International Standard English is the great increase in scientific vocabulary and the ever-increasing number of new terms in common use among modern English speakers. Over time, citation sources for the OED (Oxford English Dictionary) drew more on science than humanities, reflecting the increasingly important role of science and technology in everyday modern life. A sentence such as this one would hardly have made any sense in 1985 (and perhaps will be unintelligible in another 15 years): *I have a 40-gig hard drive with 512 megs of RAM, and can burn CDs on my external CD-RW drive plugged into my USB port.* It contains not only new words and acronyms for technological innovations such as CD (compact disk), but new meanings for old words such as *burn* and *port.*

23.4 Innovation in Global English

Linguistic change tends to emanate from centers of influence and power, and then radiates outwards into the periphery. Despite a continuing reluctance in some quarters to acknowledge a shift in the balance of power from British to American English, it is clear that American English is currently the most important center of gravity for Global English due to the dominant position of the United States as a global industrial, technological, and political superpower. One of the most often-discussed aspects of globalization is so-called Coca-Colonization (alternatively, McDonaldization), i.e. the spread of American culture, products, and language. In this view the global village has become a homogenized McWorld, where everyone speaks English, drinks Coke, and eats at McDonalds.

Although this is clearly an exaggerated view of the extent of (American) English influence, there is evidence of an increased flow of new words from English into other languages such as Japanese (e.g. *aisu kurimu* 'ice cream') and French (e.g. *le weekend*). In France and other countries legislation has been proposed (and even adopted in some cases) to try to limit the use of English in printed documents, on billboards, etc.

Despite the fact that there is some evidence of speakers of non-American forms of English adopting some features of American English, there is little evidence of a wholesale shift towards American norms. In a survey of pronunciation trends in the UK, Wells (1999) found evidence of American pronunciations for words such as *schedule* (pronounced with /sk/ in American English) among young people under 26. However, most of the older respondents of the 2,000 people surveyed said they used the typical British pronunciation. Wells found no evidence of a shift towards the American variant for other words such as *niche,* which Britons still pronounce with /iː/ rather than /ɪ/.

There is mixed evidence with respect to vocabulary. Chambers (1992: 679) found that British adolescents opted for British rather than American lexical variants when tested for items such as *chips* vs. (*french*) *fries*, *jumper* vs. *sweater*, etc. Although the American variants are a feature of daily life in advertising in Britain as well as in other parts of the world, they have scarcely penetrated everyday use among the group where one might expect them to have the most prestige. Evidence from other varieties is likewise mixed. Australian usage aligns itself with the norms of American English in some cases, preferring, for instance, *movie* over *film* and *trip* over *journey*, but in other cases, with that of British English, favoring, for example, *holiday* over *vacation* (Peters 1998).

With respect to spelling, there are also divergent tendencies, with <or> on the increase in words like *color*, but persistence of <re> instead of shift to <er> in words like *theatre*. Delbridge (1990: 73) observed that by mid-1985 six of Australia's major urban newspapers used the American <or> spellings. Although most Australians have learned at school to take an anti-American stance in language, especially in spelling, it is not necessarily the case that Australian English is becoming unilaterally more Americanized, as some have suggested (or indeed complained). Peters (1998) says that, overall, Australian English still has more in common lexically with British than American English, although this is changing among younger Australians.

Similarly, in Britain departures from British spelling norms have not been welcomed in all quarters and have attracted attention. When in 2000 it was suggested that Britain should adopt "internationally standardized spellings of scientific terms," such as *fetus* and *sulfate* (instead of *foetus* and *sulphate*), the *Independent* printed this response in its reader comment section (November 25, 2000):

> Well, this really makes us mad. In fact, it makes us see a kinda red colored mist. As if Microsoft, the internet, Disney, rap, McDonald's and chads were not enough to contend with, we now find an American fifth column in our own midst. . . . Are we really going to take lessons in language from the land whose president came up with "It depends on what the meaning of 'is' is." Hell, no! When it comes to the Americanisation of the English language, it is time for the Brits to kick some ass."

In fact, when one looks at the British National Corpus, containing 100 million words of contemporary spoken and written British English from the 1990s, it is evident that the American spelling *fetus* has already made considerable inroads into written British English. Just over one-third (36 percent) of the 353 examples follow the American spelling, and 64 percent use the traditional British spelling *foetus*. The trend for *sulphate/sulfate*, however, runs in favor of the British spelling *sulphate*; only 3 percent of the 410 occurrences of the word use the American spelling *sulfate*. In the case of other words such as *globalization/globalisation*, the American spelling predominates in 63 percent of the 64 occurrences, and the British variant *globalisation* is in the minority with 37 percent.

These alterations to standard written English are all fairly minor changes, however, when seen in the light of long-term phonological evolution as a whole, where the trend is towards increasing divergence with respect to British and American English as well as with respect to other varieties of English around the world in general. Studies of sound change have found that the dialects of

Boston, Los Angeles, London, and Sydney are now more different from one another than they were 100 years ago. The limited influence of popular media on actual speech behavior suggests that what is crucial is actual social interaction rather than passive exposure through mass media such as television. Sociolinguistic research also suggests that pronunciation serves an important identity-marking function, perhaps more so than vocabulary or syntax. T. T. B. Koh, former Ambassador to the United Nations from Singapore, affirmed these sentiments when he said:

> When one is abroad, in a bus or a train or aeroplane and when one overhears someone speaking, one can immediately say this is someone from Malaysia or Singapore. And I should hope that when I'm speaking abroad my countrymen will have no problem recognizing that I am a Singaporean. (cited in McCrum et al. 1986: 337)

Likewise, former Prime Minister Lee Kwan Yew, the architect of modern Singapore, recognized the need for identity planning to go hand in hand with nation building. His "Speak Mandarin" campaign was largely a countermeasure aimed at preventing English from becoming too dominant in a context where it is the most widely used language of inter-ethnic contact. His larger aim was not to reduce the use of English, but to provide the younger generation with an identity rooted in Asian rather than Western values. Lee's pragmatic acceptance of English while rejecting the world view it offers is indicative of the clash of values inherent in the struggle between the global and the local. The language of McWorld is English: not to use it is to risk ostracism from the benefits of the global economy. It is for this reason that many developing countries such as Nigeria opted to use the language of their former colonizers rather than try to develop their own language(s). The national literatures of many African countries and Pacific Island nations are already written in English and many more will be.

Over a quarter of a century ago, George Steiner (1975: 5) had already detected a major shift in gravity beyond the inner circle as far as the literary language is concerned when he noted that the "principal energies of the English language, . . . its genius for acquisition, for innovation, for metaphoric response, had also moved away from England." As evidence, consider that in recent years the Booker Prize for fiction, arguably Britain's most prestigious literary award, has gone to a number of writers writing in English who have never lived in Britain. Some of them write in non-mainstream varieties of English, including, for instance, Keri Hulme of New Zealand, 1985 prize-winner for her novel *the bone people*. An article bemoaning "Britain's lost literary horizons" (*Times Higher Education Supplement*, February 12, 1993) suggested that "it is probably no coincidence that the Booker Prize for Fiction has in the past ten years been awarded mainly to writers from wider cultural backgrounds," among them several Africans, including Ben Okri of Nigeria who won the prize for his book *The Famished Road*. Similarly, the Nobel Prize for Literature has included among its recent winners Derek Walcott from St. Lucia (1992) and Seamus Heaney (1996) from Ireland.

Ironically, in 1994 when a British author did win the prize, critics were not pleased at his use of Glaswegian dialect in his novel's description of a week in the life of an ex-convict. One judge, Rabbi Julia Neuberger, declared the novel "completely inaccessible." In his acceptance speech, however, Scotsman James Kelman placed his novel, *How Late It Was, How Late,* in the context of a world-wide process of decolonization and self-determination. In explaining his wish to write in an authentic Scottish voice, he said, "My culture and my language have the right to exist" (*Financial Times*, October 12, 1994).

In Australia, too, authors such as Les Murray would insist that an authentic Australia would be a vernacular republic founded on an Australian consciousness which had severed its ties to England. Similarly, in New Zealand Frank Sargeson saw his task as getting out from under the shadow of the great English novelists of the eighteenth century by inventing a literary language drawn from and representing the New Zealand subject. Later, when the Empire writes back in what Jamaican poet Louise Bennett would call "colonization in reverse," a generation of indigenous writers would set out to break consciously with imported writing styles and to use the text as a site of resistance to European literate traditions, in order to write their own emerging national literatures.

23.5 Is the Future English-speaking?

Josiah Smith, a Congregationalist minister, confidently asserted just before the turn of the twentieth century that the language of Shakespeare would eventually become the language of mankind. Predicting the future is always risky, and Smith's forecast was probably uttered more from a conviction of cultural and moral superiority than from knowledge of the forces of the linguistic marketplace. Nevertheless, many interest groups watch the developing position of English, among them English-language professionals as well as national governments such as those of the US and UK, in addition to people concerned about the erosion of the status of smaller national languages. Just as no one would have entertained the notion in 1600 that English would become a global language, some today have gone to the other extreme to imagine that English will continue to spread until all other languages have virtually disappeared.

In 1999, when Chester D. Haskell was appointed President of the Monterey Institute of International Studies in Monterey, California, which teaches a number of foreign languages, several former members of the Board of Trustees asked him what the future of the school would be since everyone would soon be speaking English. Haskell (2002: 3–4) notes that there has been amazingly little discussion of the role of languages in the literature on globalization and its effects. This may reflect the fact that most of these commentators who take the continued role of English for granted are an educated English-speaking elite, many of whom are monolingual. Like Josiah Smith, they have consistently underestimated the strength and persistence of local identities. Although English is spoken as a lingua franca by an important segment of the world's elite, that population is fairly small and declining.

Just as we must look to past global trends in politics, demography, society, and the economy to understand how English has come to be the world's most important global language, we must make our predictions about its future in the light of prognostications about future trends in these areas which may affect the role of English *vis-à-vis* other languages. However, the impact and consequences of the driving forces behind the spread of English are not easily predictable and appear to lead in contradictory directions. Tendencies likely to lead to increasing use of English are counterposed by others which may decrease demand for it. Likewise, forces propelling one variety, namely American English, as standard, are opposed by the rise and strengthening of local forms of English in the outer and expanding circles, leading to fragmentation and diversity. Graddol (1997: 3) remarks that it is no longer the case, if it ever was, that English unifies all who speak it.

This is hardly surprising since language spread and use is part of a much larger process called globalization, whose complex forces must be understood. The Anglocentric vision in which everyone speaks English is founded on certain myths as well as some pragmatic realities. Similarly, one of the beliefs about globalization is that it is inexorably moving the world towards greater homogeneity, in favor of American culture. The prediction that the future will be English-speaking rests on an often-unstated assumption of the continuance of American power and hegemony.

Yet when we consider global realities, there is virtually no end to the possible eventualities that could transform the world language picture, and indeed could have transformed it earlier. It is instructive to think of what might have happened had Japan or Germany won World War II, or if the Soviet Empire had not collapsed. If the United States had not succeeded Britain as global superpower, the world position of English might have declined in favor of another language. Consider the effects of the disintegration of the Soviet Union on the use of Russian. In the absence of a central authority imposing the language on schoolchildren throughout the Soviet bloc, few countries besides Russia itself require students to learn it, with the result that the language is less and less used. Large languages like Chinese, Hindi/Urdu, Spanish, and Arabic are already close to English in terms of size. Will China or some other country be the economic superpower of the twenty-first century, and will its language have a similar impact on language patterns and communications worldwide to the one English has had in the twentieth?

The very fact that from 1950 to 2000 the United States (and the rest of the developed world) constituted an ever-declining share of the world's population, as less developed countries grew more rapidly, requires that we consider this very question. The populations of China and India are already larger than that of the US; meanwhile, Germany, the UK, and Italy are no longer among the top ten most populous countries, having been replaced by Bangladesh, Nigeria, and Pakistan. China alone contains one-fifth of the world's population and one-third of the world's population lives in either China or India (Hobbs and Stoops 2002: 19). It is therefore undeniable that English speakers now have lower birth rates than speakers of Hindi/Urdu, Arabic, and Spanish. Graddol (1997) suggests that the proportion of native English speakers in the world population can be expected to shrink over the century 1950–2050 from more than 8 to less than 5 percent. Thus, if the use of English is going to increase, the gains will have to come from people who adopt it as a second language or a foreign language. We could witness a new world order in which the size of the global market for English may increase in absolute terms, even though its market share will probably fall.

At least two consequences follow from this. The first is that it may be Europe, rather than the US, which provides the main economic backing for English in the future. As the European Union expands and more countries join the European Monetary System, the Eurobloc will provide a formidable challenge to the market dominance of the US and its currency in world financial markets. *The Future of English* suggested that Europe was evolving into a single, multilingual space having a language hierarchy with English at the top (Graddol 1997). The second is that the center of authority for English will shift from native speakers, as they become "minority stakeholders." Unlike the majority of English speakers in the UK and the US, who are monolingual, these speakers of English will be bi- and multilingual. The television and literature from the inner circle countries may no longer provide the focal point of a global English-language culture, and their teachers will no longer be the unchallenged experts in the use and teaching of the language. Most people in the northern European countries such as the Netherlands, Germany, and Scandinavia are becoming bilingual in English at an increasingly earlier age. Soon there will be few monolinguals among their school-age populations.

Meanwhile, there are further demographic shifts within the US and Europe which may have a dramatic effect on the future position of English. Immigration and migration have brought about increasing linguistic and cultural diversity in both these regions. At the beginning of the twentieth century 1 in 8 persons in the US was non-white; by the end of the century the proportion had increased to 1 in 4. The white population also grew more slowly than any other group in the latter half of the twentieth century. From 1980 to 2000 the Hispanic population in the US doubled. The US Census 2000 revealed that persons claiming Hispanic or Latino origin have replaced African Americans as the largest ethnic minority group. A third of California's population belongs to this minority and nearly 40 percent of its population claims to speak a language other than English at home (Hobbs and Stoops 2002). Cities such as Miami and Los Angeles are now predominantly Hispanophone, and Los Angeles has been Latinized by its continuing immigration from Mexico. In three states, California, New Mexico and Hawai'i, as well as the District of Columbia, minority populations constituted the majority.

In Europe similar trends prevail, with one-third of the urban population under the age of 35 composed of ethnic minorities, the result of widespread migration in the 1950s and 1960s when Europe experienced an acute labor shortage. Around 10 percent of the school-age population already has a culture and language different from that of the majority of the country in which they reside (Extra and Verhoeven 1999: 6). London has become an increasingly diverse city with as many as 200 languages spoken in its schools as a result of the influx of overseas migrants from the Caribbean and Asia. Similarly, Melbourne, once primarily a monolingual town, now has the largest concentration of Greek speakers in the world. Unprecedented mobility the world over is creating new hybridized identities. This is no less evident in the English language itself, with its multiple varieties.

The global shift in the location of young people, particularly those with disposable income in large urban areas, could also have significant linguistic consequences. The popularity of languages is largely driven by the economic marketplace as merchants cater to the language preferences of their customers. The Hispanic community consists of an estimated 31 million people in the United States alone, or about 12 percent of the total population. The expansion of Spanish-language cable TV and Spanish-language retailers such as Mexican supermarket chain Gigante into the United States are signs of the marketplace shifting to cater its products to this growing population of consumers. Meanwhile, in other parts of the world, satellite broadcasting in languages other than English is challenging the dominance of English-medium audiovisual services. Arabic-language media such as Al-Jazeera, based in Qatar, have become increasingly influential as a voice of opposition to Western (especially American) values and culture.

English may be expected to give way to a wider mix of languages in a few other key sectors of the global economy. One of these is the internet and computer-related communications and technology transfer. A few decades ago the link between English and computers and the internet might have seemed unbreakable because the United States has been in the vanguard of scientific and technological innovation. Graddol (1997: 51), however, predicts that the current dominance of English as the most important language for web content may fall to less than 40 percent with the introduction of new protocols for web browsers that facilitate the use of other languages. In the future browser software will transmit language preference to a remote site and will display information in French to a French user, in German to a German user, etc. As automatic translation improves, providers will not have to supply web pages in different languages. Today, the latest versions of Microsoft Windows, the dominant computer operating system, offer a spell-checker in four varieties of English, and can cope with other major languages using non-Roman scripts such as Chinese and Arabic, as well as with minority languages such as Hawaiian and Welsh, which contain non-English diacritics and symbols. In adapting these new technologies to their own languages, many minority language communities have established a presence on the World Wide Web capable of reaching millions of people. Here again, we see how the same forces of globalization fostering cultural and linguistic homogenization can be marshaled as tools of resistance.

Although many have regarded the internet as the flagship of Global English, internet growth is actually strongest in languages other than English. Approximately 220 million native English speakers had direct internet access in 2001, and that number grew by another 10 to 15 million in 2003 (Global Reach 2001). Yet, there are more non-English-speaking internet users (266 million), and the number was expected to increase to more than 560 million in 2003. Thus, the use of English on the internet has declined from 45 percent to less than 30 percent in the space of a couple of years. We can expect the locus of the shift to follow the demographic trends already noted above: namely, the biggest increases in internet use will occur among young people in Asia and Latin America, as the internet becomes more accessible outside the academic elite population it originally served and is used more widely for local commercial and cultural purposes.

Significantly, Graddol (1997: 51) observes that the growth of the internet is not following the usual pattern of geographic diffusion from a central point to more widely dispersed locations. Instead, we see a widely dispersed global network moving towards one with denser local hubs. Thus, a typical user may use e-mail more frequently to order a pizza or contact a local business in a local language than to contact someone on the other side of the world using English as a lingua franca. The shift of control from institutional-based users to local, home-based users is one of the democratizing trends which will lead to increasing use of languages other than English.

Because the relationship between English and science and technology is accidental, we cannot discount the possibility that world-changing technological innovations will arise out of nations where English is little spoken at present. India, for example, is an emerging center for telecommunications and computer technology. Some of its top experts started companies which have been at the forefront of the high tech boom in the 1990s in the US, and have returned to India to open businesses there. Although English plays a significant role in India, this may decrease if economic opportunities are available locally through its dominant indigenous languages. Hence, there is reason to question the continuation of the economic dominance of the US and Europe which has helped to spread English into emerging market economies, in Asia in particular.

Similarly, the rapidly shifting nature of political alliances in a world without a cold war between superpowers means that there are multiple centers of power and not just one. In a world of instantaneous communication, there is no longer a single political or financial center. Instead, we see regional trading blocs, in such places as Asia, the Arab world, and Latin America, in which English-speaking countries are not key players. Although globalization has been conceptualized as a struggle between increasing homogeneity vs. cultural and linguistic diversity, the reality is that globalized markets have created more and not fewer choices. And so it will be with languages. While the European Union pushes for uniform standards in food products and a single currency, it has also fostered regional autonomy, which has benefited many minorities and their languages, such as the Welsh, Catalans, Corsicans, and Basques.

Each world language has arisen from a particular set of historical circumstances unlikely to be repeated again. In its transition from local to global language, from being English in the singular to Englishes in the plural, the story of English presents many of the paradoxes of the process of globalization. Robert Louis Stevenson drew attention to one of many ironies in this story when he observed that

> the race that has conquered so wide an empire has not yet managed to assimilate the islands whence she sprang. Ireland, Wales, and the Scottish mountains still cling, in part, to their Gaelic speech. It was but the other day that English triumphed in Cornwall, and they still show in Mousehole, on St. Michael's Bay, the house of the last Cornish-speaking woman. (cited in Treglown 1988: 163)

REFERENCES

Baker, S. J. (1945). *The Australian Language*. Melbourne: Sun Books.

British National Corpus (1995). Oxford: Oxford University Computing Services. Available at: www.natcorp.ox.ac.uk

Burchfield, R. W. (1989). *The English Language*. Oxford: Oxford University Press.

Chambers, J. K. (1992). Dialect acquisition. *Language* 68: 673–705.

Churchill, W. S. (1956). *A History of the English-speaking Peoples*. Vol. I: *The Birth of Britain*. London: Cassell.

Crystal, D. (1995). *The Cambridge Encyclopedia of the English Language*. Cambridge: Cambridge University Press.

Crystal, D. (1997). *English as a Global Language*. Cambridge: Cambridge University Press.

Delbridge, A. (1990). Australian English now. In C. Ricks and L. Michaels (eds.), *The State of the Language* (pp. 66–76). Berkeley: University of California Press.

Extra, G. and Verhoeven, L. (1999). Immigrant minority groups and immigrant minority languages in Europe. In G. Extra and L. Verhoeven (eds.), *Bilingualism and Migration* (pp. 3–29). Berlin: Mouton de Gruyter.

Global Reach (2001). Global Internet Statistics (by language). Available at: http://www.glreach.com/globstats/index.php3 (accessed January 10, 2003).

Graddol, D. (1997). *The Future of English? A Guide to Forecasting the Popularity of the English Language in the 21st Century*. London: British Council.

Haskell, C. D. (2002). Language and globalization: why national policies matter. In S. J. Baker (ed.), *Language Policy: Lessons from Global Models* (pp. 2–7). Monterey, CA: Monterey Institute of International Studies.

Hobbs, F. and Stoops, N. (2002). *Demographic Trends in the Twentieth Century*. Washington, DC: US Government Printing Office.

Kachru, B. (ed.) (1980). *The Other Tongue*. Oxford: Pergamon.

McCrum, R., Cran, W., and MacNeil, R. (1986). *The Story of English*. New York: Viking Penguin.
Mencken, H. L. (1919). *The American Language*. New York: Alfred A. Knopf.
Orsman, H. W. (ed.) (1997). *The Dictionary of New Zealand English: A Dictionary of New Zealandisms on Historical Principles*. Auckland: Oxford University Press.
Peters, P. (1998). Australian English. In P. Bell and R. Bell (eds.), *Americanisation and Australia*. Sydney: University of New South Wales Press.
Phillipson, R. (1992). *Linguistic Imperialism*. Oxford: Oxford University Press.
Quirk, R. (1990). Language varieties and standard language. *English Today* 21: 3–10.
Ramson, W. S. (ed.) (1988). *The Australian National Dictionary: A Dictionary of Australianisms in Historical Perspective*. Melbourne: Oxford University Press.
Silva, P., Dore, W., Mantzel, D., Muller, C., and Wright, M. (eds.) (1996). *A Dictionary of South African English on Historical Principles*. Cape Town: Oxford University Press.
Steiner, G. (1975). Why English? Presidential Address delivered to the English Association. London.
Treglown, J. (ed.) (1988). *The Lantern Bearers and Other Essays by Robert Louis Stevenson*. New York: Farrar Straus Giroux.
Wallis, J. (1653 [1765]). *Grammatica Linguae Anglicanae* [Grammar of the English Language]. Oxoniae: Excudebat Leon. Lichfield. Veneunt apud Tho. Robinson. (citation by D. Crystal from 6th edn. 1765. Londini: Excudebat Guil. Bowyer; prostant apud A. Millar).
Webster, N. (1789). *Dissertations on the English language*. Boston: Thomas.
Webster, N. (1828). *An American Dictionary of the English Language*. New York: Converse.
Wells, J. C. (1999). British English pronunciation preferences: a changing scene. *Journal of the International Phonetic Association* 29.1: 33–50.
Wells, J. C. (2000). *Longman Pronunciation Dictionary* (2nd edn.). Harlow: Pearson Education.

FURTHER READING

Burchfield, R. W. (ed.) (1995). *English in Britain and Overseas*. Vol. V of *The Cambridge History of the English Language*. Cambridge: Cambridge University Press.
Cheshire, J. (ed.) (1991). *English around the World: Sociolinguistic Perspectives*. Cambridge: Cambridge University Press.
McArthur, T. (1998). *The English Languages*. Cambridge: Cambridge University Press.
McArthur, T. (2002). *Oxford Guide to World English*. Oxford: Oxford University Press.
Nettle, D. and Romaine, S. (2000). *Vanishing Voices: The Extinction of the World's Languages*. Oxford: Oxford University Press.
Romaine, S. (1998). Introduction. In S. Romaine (ed.), *1776 to 1997*. Vol. IV of *The Cambridge History of the English Language* (pp. 1–56). Cambridge: Cambridge University Press.
Trudgill, P. and Hannah, J. (2002). *International English: A Guide to Varieties of Standard English* (4th edn.). London: Edward Arnold.

Appendix: Useful Corpora for Research in English Historical Linguistics

This is a list of corpora that are useful for research in English historical linguistics. Note that this list is not exhaustive. We have restricted ourselves to corpora that are readily available. The website addresses provided were correct at the time of going to press.

Historical Corpora

The Toronto Corpus: a spinoff of The Dictionary of Old English Project. This is a text corpus which contains most of the text material written in Old English, and is available from the Oxford Text Archive (http://ota.ahds.ac.uk). The texts are listed in A. D. Healey and R. L. Venezky (1985 [1980]). *A Microfiche Concordance to Old English*. Toronto: The Pontifical Institute of Mediaeval Studies. (See also http://www.doe.utoronto.ca/)

The Helsinki Corpus of English texts. This is a text corpus created under the direction of Professor Matti Rissanen at the University of Helsinki. It spans from the earliest Old English to AD 1720, in text extracts from representative genres, and is available from the Humanities Information Technologies Research Programme in Bergen, Norway (URL: http://www.hit.uib.no/). The texts are listed in M. Kytö (ed.) (1993). *Manual to the Diachronic Part of the Helsinki Corpus of English Texts: Coding Conventions and Lists of Source Texts* (2nd edn.). Helsinki: University of Helsinki, English Department (http://www.eng.helsinki.fi/varieng/main/corpora1.htm). The corpus is also available through the Oxford Text Archive (see below).

The York-Toronto-Helsinki Parsed Corpus of Old English Prose (YCOE), a 1.5-million-word syntactically annotated corpus of Old English prose texts created at the University of York (England), based on the Helsinki Corpus (see previous entry) and on the Toronto Corpus. It uses the same form of annotation as the Penn-Helsinki Parsed Corpus of Middle English 2 (see below) and is accessed by the same search engine, CorpusSearch. The corpus itself (the annotated text files) is distributed by the Oxford Text Archive (http://ota.ahds.ac.uk). It is freely available for non-commercial use. See also http://www-users.york.ac.uk/~lang22/YcoeHome1.htm. Any mail about the corpus can be directed to Ann Taylor (at9@york.ac.uk).

The Penn-Helsinki Parsed Corpus of Middle English (second edition, PPCME2) is based on the Helsinki Corpus and was annotated by Ann Taylor under the direction of Professor Anthony Kroch (University of Pennsylvania). Search engine: CorpusSearch. For availability and text composition, see http:// www.ling.upenn.edu/hist-corpora/

The Penn-Helsinki Parsed Corpus of Early Modern English (PPCEME) is based on the Helsinki Corpus and was annotated by Beatrice Santorini under the direction of Professor Anthony Kroch (University of Pennsylvania), using the same annotation as YCOE and PPCME2. Search engine: CorpusSearch. For availability and text composition, see http://www.ling.upenn.edu/hist-corpora/

The Corpus of Early English Correspondence (CEEC) and the Corpus of Early English Correspondence Sampler (CEECS) have been compiled by the *Sociolinguistics and Language History* project team at the Department of English, University of Helsinki, under the direction of Professor Terttu Nevalainen. The source material consists of personal letters written in England between c.1410 and 1800. These letters constitute The Corpus of Early English Correspondence (CEEC), a socially representative electronic corpus, which contains more than 6,000 letters written by nearly 800 individuals. The CEECS contains 23 letter collections included in the CEEC that are no longer in copyright. It is distributed through ICAME (http://gandalf.aksis.uib.no/icame/cd/) and the Oxford Text Archive (http://ota.ahds.ac.uk). The CEECS manual has been edited by Arja Nurmi, and is available at http://khnt.hit.uib.no/icame/manuals/ceecs/INDEX.HTM. See also http://www.eng.helsinki.fi/doe/projects/ceec/

The Parsed Corpus of Early English Correspondence (PCEEC) is an annotated version of the CEEC (tagging by Arja Nurmi in Helsinki, and parsing by Ann Taylor in York).

The Oxford Text Archive: various text collections. See http://ota.ahds.ac.uk

The Middle English Compendium, University of Michigan. See http://www.asu.edu/lib/resources/db/midengl.htm, http://www.hti.umich.edu/c/cme/

The Titus Project, under the direction of Jost Gippert, makes available electronic texts of various early Germanic dialects, including Old and Middle English. See http://titus.uni-frankfurt.de/indexe.htm

Modern English Corpora

The British National Corpus, the *BNC* (texts mostly 1985–93).

The Brown Corpus: The Brown Corpus of Standard American was compiled by H. Kučera and W. Nelson Francis at Brown University, Providence, RI. It contains a selection of current American English, totaling about a million words drawn from a wide variety of sources. See W. N. Francis and H. Kučera (1979 [1967]). *Manual of Information to Accompany a Standard Corpus of Present-day Edited American English, for Use with Digital Computers.* Providence, RI: Department of Linguistics, Brown University.

The Frown Corpus: The Freiburg–Brown Corpus of American English. It contains present-day American English data from 15 genres. The texts are from 1992, and the corpus set-up mirrors that of the earlier Brown Corpus. See http://khnt.hit.uib.no/icame/manuals/frown/INDEX.HTM

The LOB Corpus (1961). The Lancaster-Oslo/Bergen Corpus of British English (LOB) was compiled at the University of Lancaster, Department of Linguistics and Modern

English Language, under the direction of Geoffrey N. Leech (1970–7) and at the University of Oslo, English Department, under the direction of Stig Johansson (1977–8). It consists of one million words of British English texts from 1961. The texts for the corpus were sampled from 15 different text categories. Each text is just over 2,000 words. See http://khnt.hit.uib.no/icame/manuals/lob/INDEX.HTM

Other Useful Data Collections

OED: The Oxford English Dictionary on CD-ROM (1989). 2nd edition. Edited by J. A. Simpson and E. S. C. Weiner. Oxford: Clarendon Press.

Visser, F. T. (1963–73). *An Historical Syntax of the English Language* (vols. 1–3). Leiden: E. J. Brill.

Books on Corpus Use, a Selection

Beal, J. C., Karen Corrigan, and Hermann Moisl (eds.). *Models and Methods in the Handling of Unconventional Digital Corpora*. Vol. 1: *Synchronic Corpora*. Vol. 2: *Diachronic Corpora*. Basingstoke: Palgrave Macmillan.

Hunston, Susan (2002). *Corpora in Applied Linguistics* (Cambridge Applied Linguistics Series). Cambridge: Cambridge University Press.

Leistyna, Pepi and Charles F. Meyer (eds.) (2003). *Corpus Analysis: Language Structure and Language Use* (Language and Computers 46). Amsterdam and New York: Rodopi.

Meyer, Charles F. (2002). *English Corpus Linguistics: An Introduction* (Studies in English Language). Cambridge: Cambridge University Press.

Nelson, Gerald, Sean Wallis, and Bas Aarts (2002). *Exploring Natural Language: Working with the British Component of the International Corpus of English* (Varieties of English around the World, General Series 29). Amsterdam/Philadelphia: Benjamins.

Reppen, Randi, Susan M. Fitzmaurice, and Douglas Biber (eds.) (2002). *Using Corpora to Explore Linguistic Variation* (Studies in Corpus Linguistics 9). Amsterdam/Philadelphia: Benjamins.

Index